NATIONAL GEOGRAPHIC

TRAVELER

Japan

NATIONAL GEOGRAPHIC

TRAVELER
Japan

Nicholas Bornoff

National Geographic
Washington, D.C.

SHIBUYA
109
渋谷に[夜]が来る
バットマン ビギンズ
6·18
30
SHIBUYA
MITSUMARU

Contents

How to use this guide 6–7 About the author 8
The regions 59–348 Travelwise 349–88
Index 389–97 Credits 398–99

History & culture 9
Japan today **10–27**
History of Japan **28–41**
The arts **42–58**

Tokyo 59
Introduction & map **60–61**
Central Tokyo 62–65
Feature: Modern architecture **66–67**
Ginza–Hibiya–Yurakucho 68–70
Tsukudajima 71–73
Feature: The water trade—Japan after dark **74–75**
Roppongi-Shiba-koen Park 76–77
Aoyama-Harajuku-Shibuya 78–85
Two walks through Shibuya-ku **80–81**
Shinjuku & Ikebukuro 86–89
Ueno 90–95
A walking tour of Ueno-Nezu-Yanaka **96–97**
Akihabara 98–99
Feature: Low City, high times **100–101**
Asakusa 102–104

Excursions from Tokyo 107
Introduction & map **108–109**
Fuji-Hakone-Izu 121–28
Feature: Climbing Fuji-san **124–25**

Hokkaido 129
Introduction & map **130–31**
A walk in Hakodate **140–41**

Northern Honshu (Tohoku) 151
Introduction & map **152–53**

Central Honshu 171
Introduction & map **172–73**

Kansai 197
Introduction & map **198–99**
Kyoto 200–33
Introduction & map **200–201**
Feature: Geisha **206–207**
Higashiyama walk **216–17**
Feature: Japanese gardens **220–21**
Feature: Buddhism **226–27**
Feature: Shinto **244–45**

Western Honshu (Chugoku) 261
Introduction & map **262–63**
San-In coast 264–76
A hike through Hagi **266–67**
Tsuwano walk **268–69**
Feature: *Obake*—ghosts & demons **270–71**
San-yo 277–90

Shikoku & the Seto-naikai 291
Introduction & map **292–93**
Shikoku 294–311
The Seto-naikai 312–14

Kyushu 315
Introduction & map **316–17**

Okinawa & the Ryukyu-shoto 341
Introduction & map **342–43**

Travelwise 349
Planning your trip 350–51
How to get to Japan 351
Getting around 351–54
Practical advice 354–56
Emergencies 356–57
Language guide 357
Hotels & restaurants by region 358–79
Shopping 380–83
Entertainment & festivals 384–88

Index 389–97
Credits 398–99

Page 1: Child dressed for a festival at Meiji-jinju Shrine
Pages 2–3: Garden font and dipper in fall, tea garden in Kyoto
Left: High-rise building in Shibuya, Tokyo

How to use this guide

See back flap for keys to text and map symbols

The *National Geographic Traveler* brings you the best of Japan in text, pictures, and maps. Divided into three main sections, the guide begins with an overview of history and culture. Following are ten regional chapters with featured sites selected by the author for their particular interest. Each chapter opens with its own contents list.

The regions and sites within the regions are arranged geographically. Some regions are further divided into smaller areas. A map introduces each region, highlighting the featured sites. Walks, plotted on their own maps, suggest routes for discovering an area. Features and sidebars give intriguing detail on history, culture, or contemporary life.

The final section, Travelwise, lists essential information for the traveler—pre-trip planning, getting around, emergencies, and a language guide—plus a selection of hotels, restaurants, shops, entertainment, and festivals.

To the best of our knowledge, all information is accurate as of the press date. However, it's always advisable to call ahead when possible.

162

Color coding

Each region is color coded for easy reference. Find the region you want on the map on the front flap, and look for the color flash at the top of the pages of the relevant chapter. Information in **Travelwise** is also color coded to each region.

Matsushima
153 B3
Visitor information
Outside Matsushima-Kaigan Station
022/354-2263

Zuigan-ji Temple
91 Aza-chonai (7 mins. walk from Matsushima-Kaigan Station
022/354-2023
$$

Visitor information

Practical information for most sites is given in the side column (see key to symbols on back flap). The map reference gives the page number of the map and grid reference. Other details are address, telephone number, days closed, entrance charge in a range from $ (under $4) to $$$$$ (over $25), and public transportation. Other sites have information in italics and parentheses in the text.

TRAVELWISE

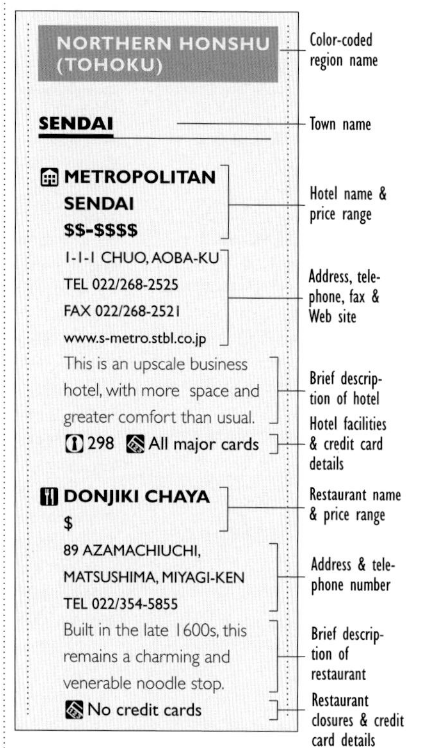

Hotel & restaurant prices

An explanation of the price bands used in entries is given in the Hotels & Restaurants section (on p. 360).

REGIONAL MAPS

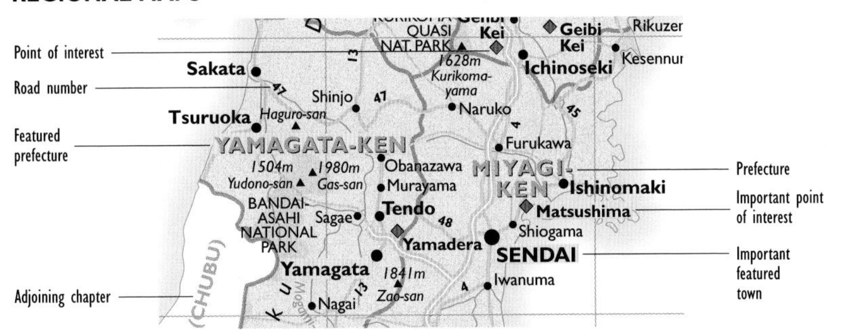

- A locator map accompanies each regional map and shows the location of that region in the country.
- Adjacent regions are shown, each with a page reference.

WALKING TOURS

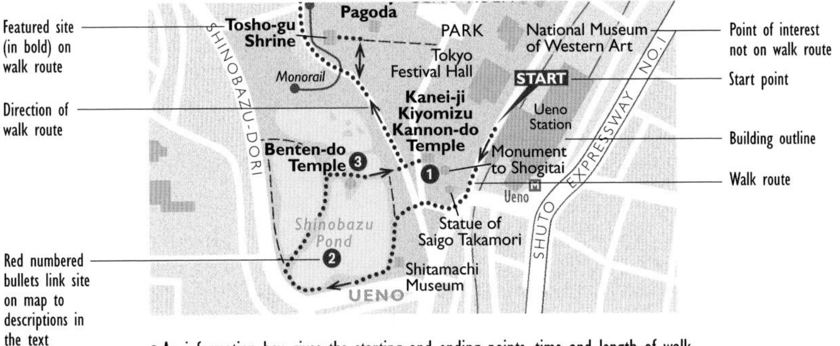

- An information box gives the starting and ending points, time and length of walk, and places not be missed along the route.
- Where two walks are marked on the map, the second route is shown in orange.

METROPOLITAN MAPS

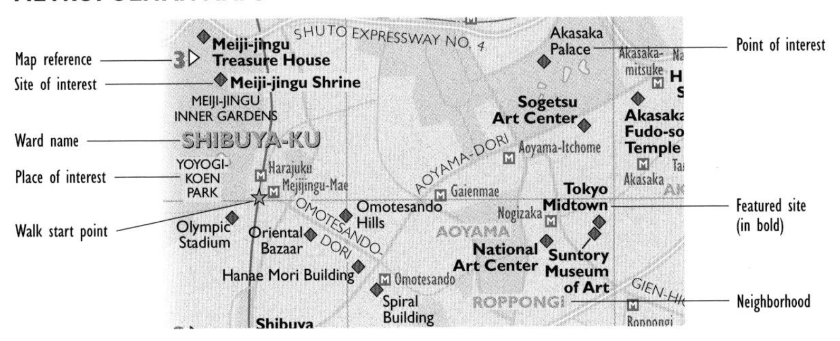

- An overview of the metropolitan area of major cities.

NATIONAL GEOGRAPHIC
TRAVELER
Japan

About the author

Born in London of Anglo-French parentage, Nicholas Bornoff was educated in both France and the United Kingdom. Fresh out of a Parisian film school in 1974, he worked as an assistant director on documentary movies for UNESCO in Indonesia, sparking his lasting fascination with the Far East. Five years later he moved to Japan and a job in a Tokyo advertising agency. Branching out into journalism, he worked as film critic for the *Japan Times* for nine years, during which he also contributed articles about contemporary Japanese arts and society to the *Far Eastern Economic Review*, *Asian Advertising & Marketing*, the *Tokyo Journal*, and other English-language magazines in the Asian region.

Bornoff's nonfiction survey, *Pink Samurai: Love, Marriage & Sex in Contemporary Japan*, was published to critical acclaim in 1991, the year he returned to Europe. Now making his home in London with his Japanese wife and young son, Bornoff still focuses mainly on Japan. He has written a book introducing Japan to schoolchildren, and his articles appear in *The Guardian* newspaper and many other publications in Europe and the United Kingdom.

History & culture

Japan today **10–27**
History of Japan **28–41**
The arts **42–58**

***Ukiyo*-e print depicting a warrior (Osaka school, 18th century)**

Japan today

FIRST THERE IS JAPAN THE ARCHIPELAGO. IT'S A NARROW CHAIN ALONG THE Asian mainland stretching some 1,860 miles (2,994 km) from eastern Siberia down almost to Taiwan. North to south, Hokkaido, Honshu, Shikoku, and Kyushu are the four largest islands; the whole is administratively divided into 47 prefectures. Then there is Japan the concept. Chances are you're already familiar with the traditional icons—Buddhist temples, flower arrangements and gardens, the kimono, and martial arts. You've probably eaten sushi, played computer games, and either used or endured karaoke; you know that many of the products and components involved in your daily communication, entertainment, and transport are made in Japan. So most visitors pose themselves the question long before they get there: Which is the real Japan?

Everyone knows the hackneyed calendar image of snowcapped Fuji-san at cherry blossom time with the sleek bullet-train streaking past—perhaps with a kimono-clad girl in the foreground. A Japanese invention, the image symbolizes how the Japanese see themselves. As they never tire of pointing out (along with the fact that they have four seasons), ancient arts, crafts, and traditions coexist in harmony with the cutting edge of modern technological civilization. As different as the composite parts may seem, they're *all* the real Japan. Quite happy with the coexistence of old, new, East, West, tradition, and change, the Japanese take for granted the contradictions and paradoxes that so often leave visitors bewildered. No country wears the old tourist brochure cliché "land of contrasts" at once quite so naturally and with so much style.

Perhaps it's not so surprising. Emerging during the 1860s from the isolation its rulers had enforced for 300 years, the Japanese made as much effort to modernize as they did to retain their cultural identity.

So the real Japan can be made a matter of personal preference; you can devise your itinerary accordingly. Multicultural Tokyo or bastions of culture and traditions like Kyoto; the older, quieter Japan off the beaten track in Northern and Western Honshu or Shikoku. Seventy-five percent of the land area is mountainous, much of it forested and volcanic; depending on the season you can hike, ski, enjoy the great outdoors, or the purely Japanese pleasure of the hot spring. Explore the rugged coast of the far north or the tropical islands of Okinawa-ken—nowhere is very far from the sea. Whichever way you go, it will always be an encounter with one of the most fascinating countries and cultures in the world.

ECONOMY

Japan's economic miracle, emerging from the advantages of cheap labor and a low yen during the postwar period, saw exports increasing rapidly from inexpensive tin toys to quality goods. Transistor radios (a Japanese first) paved the way for cameras, electrical appliances, ships, steel, color televisions, and cars. With a phenomenal growth rate of 11 percent, Japan was already the world's second largest economy outside the Iron Curtain by 1967.

By devaluing the yen, accepting wage cuts, and redoubling their effort, the Japanese softened the impact of the oil crisis of 1973. Exports soared, pushing up a trade surplus that had started five years before. In 1979 the second oil crisis was dealt with in a similar way.

During the 1980s Japan's economy surpassed even that of the United States. Its formidable wealth was sustained by booming domestic financial and consumer markets, low interest rates, and soaring real estate values. Japanese fortunes swelled in what was called the "bubble economy." A huge overseas trade imbalance, however, prompted international currency markets to force up the yen/dollar exchange rate in 1985. *Endaka*—the high value yen—slowed exports and economic

Harmony between tradition and high-tech: a Japanese ideal

performance at home, but it also doubled the value of national savings and generated a spending spree on overseas property markets. The bubble continued to inflate.

In 1990 the value of Japan's overseas holdings plummeted; its stock market had lost almost half its value by the end of the year. In 1991 beleaguered Japanese banks raised interest rates to cover the loss—only exacerbating the growing problem of bad loans. The bubble burst.

Japan's economic recovery was increasingly hampered by recession in the Asia-Pacific region because of enormous investments in the area. As bad loans accumulated, bankruptcy became rife among the largest financial institutions during the 1990s.

The country's faltering economy has brought changes. During the 1980s the complex, tiered distribution system continued to fatten middlemen, keeping the benefits of cheaper imports from consumers. The 1990s

saw direct imports becoming common practice, with the middlemen circumvented and retailers turning to discount marketing.

Japanese consumers are tightening their belts, but the country is only marginally cheaper for foreign visitors. Life insurance savings are astronomical, but no decisive measures have been taken to tap these formidable funds, suggesting that Japan's economy is likely to remain comparatively sluggish for the foreseeable future.

Japan's urban centers are some of the most densely populated in the world.

THE WORLD OF WORK

The Japanese work ethic is legendary. According to the traditional pattern, the salaryman (male office worker) commutes for an average of two hours and spends up to ten hours in the office, six days a week. O.L.s (Office Ladies—female employees) work eight hours a day. When the office closes, the salaryman

is expected to join co-workers for a drink. His children will be asleep when he gets home; he spends only Sunday with them—if he can stay awake. He is entitled to two weeks' paid holiday a year; his sense of corporate loyalty will reduce this to around four days.

Until about ten years ago, the salaryman was employed for life; he ascended the corporate hierarchy according to age rather than ability. When he reached middle management in his 40s, his added responsibilities to both his seniors and his juniors increased his workload. If he did not succumb first to *karoshi*—dropping dead from overwork—he went on to senior management and retirement at 60.

Although still typical, this scenario is currently being redefined. Recession has greatly changed working patterns in Japan. Promotion is based increasingly on ability; head-hunting and job-changing are becoming much more common. Japan's targeted 40-hour work week remains some way off, though larger

Neon lights up evenings on the busy streets of Shinjuku in Tokyo.

corporations and factories adopted the five-day week in the late 1980s, and most six-day firms concede a half-day on Saturday or work six days on alternate weeks.

The smaller the company, the greater the likelihood of a 48-hour week. The backbone of the economy, many small businesses are subcontractors manufacturing parts for larger ones. Competition remains sharp even during recession: If one firm cannot meet low prices and hard deadlines, another is ready and willing. Many such companies are sweatshops employing foreign labor, much of it illegal.

Unemployment, which still stood at 2.5 percent in 1991 as it had for decades, shot up in early 1998. Even at the start of the 21st century, the life employment system—though declining—keeps Japan's unemployment at an enviably low rate, between 3 and 4 percent.

Digital camera usage in Japan continues to increase by as much as 46% annually.

MEN & WOMEN

Brought up to prefer the company of their own sex and frequently marrying by arrangement, men and women spend little time together. Outings in mixed company are increasing among the young, but restricted social life arising from work can reduce opportunities to meet members of the opposite sex.

Japan remains preponderantly male dominated. Only about a third of university students are women, and female postgraduates are few. Half the workforce is female, but only around 8 percent reach executive levels. The Equal Employment Opportunity Law, introduced in 1979 to encourage equality in the workplace for women, provides no sanctions for violations. Irrespective of qualifications, the work of female employees tends to be menial and subservient: They often wear uniforms while men do not, answer phones, and serve tea to male colleagues. They are hired at the age of 20 on lower pay than male counterparts and are expected to quit when they marry. Some conservative companies routinely hire only young women living with their parents and fire them after the age of 26, combining prim Confucian ideals with the excuse to pay their female employees less. Women have long rejoined the workforce after raising their family, but the number marrying later in order to pursue careers is still rising.

Americans and Europeans are often shocked by the status of women in Japan. But if opposition to greater equality comes from male politicians, it also comes, paradoxically, from legions of women content to wield domestic power and unworried by the issue of image. The male TV show host's pretty female sidekick, nodding like an awed schoolgirl and agreeing with what he says, has more to do with public "face" than reality. In a country in which the toughness of women is proverbial, the fondly imagined Western icon of the meek and acquiescent Japanese woman is only a matter of manners. Japanese men, subjected to a routine placing greater pressure on them to conform, can sometimes seem more reserved and hidebound than women.

HOME & FAMILY

The old *ie* (household) system, male-dominated and based on seniority, was banned by the constitution in 1946—a factor contributing to the mass urban migration prompted by job opportunities. Traditionally, three generations lived under one roof, an extended family pattern now typical only in rural areas; more than

Couples now wed later, though fewer are marrying in traditional ceremonies.

77 percent of the population lives in towns, where the nuclear family is the norm. However, a falling birthrate poses the growing problem of a graying society. With care for the elderly woefully inadequate, extended households are slightly increasing again, but, thanks to generations living in separate apartments in the same building, with much greater privacy and independence for the occupants.

Home for the average one-child urban family is 2LDK (two bedrooms, living/dining/kitchen in one). Because of the lack of living space, the majority of Japanese—especially men—seek entertainment outside the home.

Male domination appears to survive in the modern home, where the oldest male takes his bath first and the youngest female last. When entertaining guests, a wife often serves food to them and her husband first, eating hers later.

The education challenge starts early—uniformed girls commute to school via the subway.

On the other hand, a Japanese woman's home is her castle. She manages household finances and makes decisions concerning children and their education, as well as about moving house. A husband brings his wages to her, and she gives him his pocket money: *kozukai.*

Families living under the *ie* system often lived in extended families, making it convenient for family businesses. A woman used to become the property of her husband's family upon marriage, often severing ties with her own. Yet from feudal times, if his wife's family had no male heir, a husband occasionally entered her family and took its name. Blood has never been considered the quintessence of kinship in Japan, and even today men are "adopted" by families wanting a male heir.

Upbringing & education

Westerners are often said to grow out of the strictures of childhood into the relative freedom of adulthood, while in Japan the reverse is the case. Japanese children are generally indulged to a greater degree than Western counterparts. Spanking is frowned upon; a naughty child is usually threatened with either maternal abandonment or ridicule by others.

The vise starts tightening outside the home. During six years of elementary school and three of high school, the pressures to conform to rules and group restraints tend to override individual aspirations. The high school workload before university entrance examinations is notorious; the *jiken jigoku* (examination hell) period leaves many children with about five hours' sleep a night. With at least double the homework of U.S. counterparts, children enroll in *juku* (cram schools) for up to three hours after school.

Many Westerners have misconceived awe for Japanese education, assuming that it underlies economic success. In fact, although the form changed to follow American patterns during the Occupation (1945–1952), little was done to alter the traditional content. Set out like questionnaires, Japanese exams dictate the rote learning of facts and figures, with neither essays nor anything else to encourage individual thinking. Failure to be admitted to the desired university causes great anguish in parents and pupils alike; those redoubling their efforts to succeed by studying at full-time cram schools outside the state education system are known as *ronin* (masterless samurai). The government has introduced a "relaxed education" policy to remedy this.

University—four halcyon years of comparative freedom before mounting the corporate

Though small, the average Japanese home boasts a wide array of electronic equipment.

treadmill—is widely regarded as a sinecure. Japanese companies train new recruits on the job and will often employ graduates on the strength of the prestige of the university they attended rather than their academic achievements. With mounting competition in the marketplace, however, the need for specialization is placing emphasis on university degrees.

LANGUAGE & WRITING

The origin of the Japanese language is unknown. Possibly related to the Ural-Altaic group, which includes Finnish, Mongolian, Turkish, and Korean, it is grammatically similar to Korean but shares almost no words. Despite Japan's adoption of many aspects of Chinese culture, including writing, the language is unrelated to Chinese. It may go back to the early inhabitants of Japan, such as the Ainu, but beyond a few words and place-names, the Ainu language appears unconnected to Japanese. There is some evidence of a distant relationship with Austronesian languages, such as those of Malaysia, Indonesia, and the Philippines, mainly through similarities in vowel sounds. The mystery continues to inspire theories.

A Latin-sounding A-E-I-O-U syllabary makes picking up a few words of Japanese easy, but learning to speak well is another matter. Instead of the subject-verb-object sentence order of most European languages, Japanese places the object first and the verb, which incorporates the subject, last. Speech is divided into familiar, informal, formal, and humble forms; men and women express themselves using different personal pronouns and synonyms appropriate to the context.

Japanese uses three alphabets—simultaneously. *Kanji,* or Chinese characters, were imported during the fifth century A.D.; of purely Japanese origin, the phonetic *hiragana* and *katakana* alphabets were adopted during the eighth century. Very simply, kanji characters are used for nouns, hiragana for turning them into adjectives and verbs, and katakana for rendering words of foreign origin. Widely used in contexts such as advertising, *romaji* (Roman characters) is virtually a fourth character set. There are too many homophones to make a single phonetic script viable (for instance, unless shown as a kanji character, *seki* could mean a dam, a cough, or a seat).

JAPANESE HOMES

When entering a Japanese home, the first-time visitor may be surprised at the indicators of a different lifestyle beginning in the entrance

hall with rows of shoes on the floor, which is where you must leave yours. Shoes would quickly destroy the *tatami*—thick, densely woven rush mats found on at least one floor, even in modern apartments. For hygienic and practical reasons, no one enters a Japanese home in footwear—not even on carpets. You are usually provided with slippers; including ones specially for the toilet.

If the home is traditional, it will have *fusuma,* sliding room-dividers made of thick paper stretched on a wooden frame. It will also have *shoji,* wooden grids covered in thin white paper, that slide open and shut behind the windows.

A lot of homes have Western beds, but the traditional bedroom contains nothing at all. Stored away in a cupboard during the daytime, the futon mattresses and bedding are laid out on the floor at night. Chairs are now common in the dining area, but especially in a tatami room you will be entertained at a low

table while seated on cushions on the floor. In winter you will probably sit snugly at the *kotatsu*—a low table with a heater underneath and quilting around the sides.

The bath *(ofuro)* is usually a deep cube in which you sit and soak, but only once you are squeaky clean. You soap yourself first and rinse off using a tap, a shower, or water drawn from the bath in a bucket or bowl. You must never wash in the bath; others will use the water after you.

Visiting gardens is a favorite Japanese pastime whatever the weather.

Western toilets are common, as are astonishing high-tech variants such as the "Washlet," with heated seats and a jet of warm water providing fundamental cleaning at the press of a button. Equally common is the squat-toilet. The Japanese variety has a hood at one end and that is the way you face when you use it.

Boisterous and colorful, Shinto festivals are vital events on each community calendar.

RELIGION

It is facetiously said that the Japanese are born Shintoist, marry Christian, and are buried Buddhist. Although Buddhism and Shinto have countless devotees, Japan is increasingly materialistic and, for many, observances are a matter of form. Over 90 percent of the Japanese practice both Shinto (for the rites of baptism and marriage) and Buddhism, mainly reserved for funeral ceremonies. Christianity is practiced by a minority, but a Christian wedding presents a novel alternative to the standard Shinto ceremony.

Shinto

Shinto (the Way of the Gods) is the name given to various animistic belief systems of prehistoric origin that worship *kami*, the deities in all things. According to Shinto creation myths, the Japanese and their emperor descended from the gods. Many Shinto variants are based on the belief that all people become kami after death and that ancestors should be revered as such. The most sacred Shinto shrine is Ise-jingu (see pp. 259–60).

Very few entertain truly animist beliefs today, but Shinto thrives as a matter of ceremony. Colorful *matsuri* festivals are popular events, throughout the year, and some 70 million people visit shrines during New Year's celebrations. (See also pp. 244–45.)

Confucianism

The code of ethics based on the teachings of the Chinese sage Confucius (551–479 B.C.) preaches humility, frugality, generosity, and temperance. Founded on filial piety, respect for the aged, and the observance of tradition, it was applied to governmental principles in Japan from around the seventh century, but had little direct influence until after 1333, when new Chinese forms were adopted and adapted by the samurai. Confucianism served to reinforce social hierarchy and loyalty to these feudal lords and/or the emperor, according to the swing of the pendulum of power. It also dictated the *ie* system, a patriarchal hierarchy in the household (see p. 17).

Confucianism, with its emphasis on conformity, bolstered strict government control between 1603 and 1868, and was more recently exploited by nationalists. It is still taught in a diluted form in Japanese schools. Conformity remains a virtue, corporate loyalty overrides family life, and society remains deeply hierarchical. The Japanese love of social harmony and avoidance of confrontation are also legacies of Confucianism.

***Zazen* meditation demands composure, not dozing. Awakenings come from a monk's stick.**

Buddhism

Holding that the remedy for the pain of existence lies in meditation, the elimination of desire, and awareness of the transience of life, the teachings of the Buddha (Enlightened One) made their way from India to Japan via China and Korea. Brought by Korean emissaries in the mid-sixth century A.D., Mahayana Buddhism was decreed a state religion by Prince Shotoku in 593. During ensuing centuries the Buddhist influence increased as various sects evolved.

Zen Buddhism was introduced from China during the Kamakura period (1185–1333). It discards scriptures and doctrine, believing that enlightenment is attainable only through individual effort, special meditation *(zazen)*, and abstinence. Zen was greatly favored by the samurai and, like all other forms of Buddhism, has had a profound and permanent influence on the architecture, arts, and culture of Japan.

Christianity

Christianity was brought to Japan by Portuguese and Spanish friars, notably the Jesuit St. Francis Xavier, in the mid-16th century. It made much headway, especially in Kyushu, but its spread posed a political threat to the shoguns (military governors) who, fearful of European colonial objectives, repressed it with ruthless cruelty. With the closure of the country to outsiders in 1635, Christianity went underground; sects of secret Christians emerged from hiding when the shogunate fell in 1868. Persecution resumed but was stopped due to international pressure.

Although the faith remains largely alien, missionary work in the development of hospitals, in schools, and among the poor has earned Christianity respect. Today there are approximately 6,000 Christian churches in Japan and about one million Christians.

MANNERS & BEHAVIOR

In Japan, harmony, achieved through conformity and consensus, is of utmost importance; it dictates masking private cares with public smiles, along with the individual's obligation to conform with the group. People abhor being conspicuous and are reluctant to air personal opinions. Japanese prefer the vague and understated to the forthright. Outspokenness is bad manners, and conversations find participants doing their utmost to agree with each other. Decisions are reached through consensus; in corporate contexts the process can take quite some time. This underlies the difficulties sometimes encountered by foreigners doing business in Japan, as well as why Japanese politicians may be viewed as somewhat inarticulate abroad. (See also Travelwise, pp. 354–55.)

Below: Stand-up noodle stalls proliferate near most train stations throughout Japan.

FOOD & DRINK

Visitors will marvel at the gastronomic cornucopia awaiting them in Japan. Eating out ranks highest of all leisure activities among the Japanese—there are over 80,000 restaurants in Tokyo alone.

The great food staple is rice—so sacrosanct that the words for it when cooked, *gohan* and *meshi,* have simply come to mean a meal. Buckwheat noodles—*soba* and *udon*—are very popular. Necessity has led to many delicious discoveries in Japan, notably several different kinds of seaweed and vegetables that, formerly growing wild, include roots and ferns.

Meat-eating, forbidden by Buddhist law from the 10th century, became widespread with the introduction of beef from abroad during the late 19th century. Although most people eat meat today, a marked preference for fish prevails. Ubiquitous and a great source of protein, tofu (soybean curd) is prepared in so many different ways that some restaurants have made it a specialty.

Japanese cuisine is a feast for the eyes; presentation is its quintessence. Food is beautifully served on lacquered trays and attractive ceramics. The importance attached to freshness in Japan is akin to religious ritual. The Japanese consider that between the sea and your palate there should be only the chef's expertise with a knife. Despite the marvelous texture and delicate flavor of sashimi (raw fish), some non-Japanese find it a difficult taste to acquire. Meat too is sometimes thinly sliced and eaten raw.

Thirty years ago the Japanese consumed almost no milk or cheese, but today supermarket shelves sag beneath the weight of milk products and frozen pizza. Fast-food chains, both American (McDonald's, Pizza Hut, KFC) and domestic clones, proliferate. Quality Western cuisine, especially Italian and French, has many devotees and, after training in

One of Tokyo's many thousand restaurants; of all leisure activities in Japan, eating out tops the list.

Europe, many Japanese cooks, even in rural areas, produce high-quality Western food.

Mentioned as the standard tipple among the gods in Shinto myths, *sake* (rice wine) entered Japan along with rice culture in prehistoric times. "Sake" has come to mean alcoholic beverages in general; the specific Japanese word for rice wine is *nihonshu.* Good sake is as easy to drink as wine, but beware: The higher alcohol content packs a wicked hangover. This may explain why Japan's most popular beverage is beer. Several brands started brewing in the 1870s, among them Asahi, Kirin, and Ebisu. Hokkaido's Sapporo beer followed in the 1900s, though connoisseurs prefer the island's microbreweries. Pioneered in Japan by Suntory, whiskey remains a favorite after-work drink. Several prefectures produce wine; whites from Yamanashi are the most commendable, though the price of a really good bottle is exorbitant. As a domestic content of 5 percent is sufficient for qualification as "Japanese wine," local vin ordinaires consist mainly of imported bulk wines. Selling at the same price or less than a Japanese bottle, foreign wines are a better buy.

Shochu is a cheap grain distillate akin to vodka. Once the preferred liquor of hard-drinking laborers, it has become fashionable in recent years. It can be drunk hot *(oyuwari)* but is popular cold as *chu-hai* (shochu highball), mixed with ice, water, and lemon. It is often marketed in fruit-flavored cocktails.

THE LAND

Vegetation found in North America, Europe, and all but the tropical regions of Asia grows in Japan. Japanese cedar (cryptomeria) and species of maple, beech, and magnolia are cultivated over most of the country. Forests cover nearly 60 percent of the land. Chinquapin (chestnut), oak, and beech occur mainly in the forests of Honshu, and fir and silver fir in the subarctic climate of Hokkaido.

The vegetation in Kyushu and Okinawa takes a more tropical turn, with several varieties of palm, and flowers that north of Tokyo could bloom only in a hothouse. Trees admired for their spring blossoms, especially plum and cherry, are found over most of the country. Azaleas, hydrangeas, and irises are widespread during early summer, and red maples and chrysanthemums in the fall.

Many animals found in Honshu, Shikoku, and Kyushu are of the same species found in other areas in the Northern Hemisphere. They include black bears, ferrets, wild boar, and the *tanuki* (raccoon-dog), as well as birds such as pheasants, hawks, ducks, and cranes. Unique to Japan is the giant salamander, as well as the Japanese macaque—ubiquitous except on Hokkaido. Up in snowy Tohoku (Northern Honshu), the adaptable macaque has not only acquired a taste for wallowing in hot springs but has also developed thicker fur. Animals in subarctic Hokkaido include sables and red foxes, as well as the brown bear. Standing some 6 feet (2 m) and weighing 880 pounds (400 kg), it is about twice the size of its temperate Honshu counterpart. Okinawa has, in addition to animals commonly found in East Asia, unique species of its own: the Iriomote wildcat, Amami hare, and habu viper.

Frequently hunted or forced out of their natural habitats through urbanization, Japan's animal and bird populations have been steadily declining. Conservation measures adopted by the Environment Ministry during the 1980s protect 136 endangered species, but for the rare Iriomote wildcat (regarded by zoologists as a living fossil), it may already be too late.

RESOURCES

Up to the mid-20th century Japan was mainly agricultural, but after World War II farming declined dramatically with the mass migration from the countryside. Since the war, manufacturing, mining, and construction have continuously accounted for about a third of national industry. And booming retail and service industries account for some three-fifths of the total national industry.

Today, with their livelihoods increasingly threatened by imports, farmers are major recipients of government subsidies. Rice, the national staple for centuries, is overproduced (there are paddies even in suburban Tokyo). A traditional fondness for soybean products means that Japan imports more than 15 times the soybeans it produces. Eggs, poultry, and most vegetables are domestically produced, but half the country's fruit is imported.

Dairy products are gaining ground; three-quarters are produced in Hokkaido, the rest imported. Hokkaido also produces a substantial amount of wheat, feeding a growing appetite for bread, but its crop represents only about one-seventh of the total consumed. The world's largest per capita consumer of fish and seafood supplies half of its demand with imports; Japan also imports half its meat, especially beef. Increases in imports generally may indicate change in consumer tastes but are mainly the result of economics: Many domestic products are more expensive than imported counterparts.

Japan's per capita consumption of wood is only 17 percent of the level in the United States—from its own forests, that is. Its notorious extravagance with wood and pulp products for everything ranging from houses to books—and a tendency to wrap almost everything in shops—is fueled by imports, notably from nations little concerned with the impact of deforestation on the global environment.

A major steel producer, Japan has to import iron. Having very few energy resources, its industry is highly dependent on overseas sources, especially for oil. Some headway is being made with research into greener, cleaner alternative-energy sources, but nuclear energy is a strong competitor—albeit with fairly widespread and vociferous public opposition. ■

Rice paddies form hillside terraces on the island of Shikoku.

History of Japan

STONE IMPLEMENTS FOUND IN JAPAN SHOW THAT PEOPLE WERE LIVING there before the Ice Age, when the islands were linked to the Asian mainland. However, the earliest recognizable culture is known as Jomon, after the method used for decorating pottery and figurines.

PREHISTORY

Jomon means "straw rope," and the era, which lasted from 10,000 B.C. to 300 B.C., gets its name from the use of rope to imprint wet clay. The Jomon people's origins are disputed, but it is known they were hunter-gatherers and fishermen; among them were the ancestors of the Ainu, a people of prehistoric Siberian origin now living on Hokkaido. During the millennium after 500 B.C., mainland migrants gradually pushed these tribes to the far north and came to outnumber them ten to one.

Meaning "early spring," the Yayoi period (300 B.C.–A.D. 300) is the era of the most important mass migrations, mainly of Koreans arriving in northern Kyushu. They brought iron and bronze and, most important, the cultivation of rice. The arrival of agriculture early during the Yayoi was the great determinant in shaping Japan. As farming spread, land ownership became the basis for the pecking order in the community; these changes in social structure paved the way for the feudal systems that would dominate in the future.

EARLY JAPAN

KOFUN (300–552)

During the Kofun (old tomb) period, rice cultivation was concentrated in the region that is now Kansai—probably the country described in fourth-century Chinese records as Yamato, ruled by Queen Himiko, a female shaman. The numerous burial mounds, some of enormous size, found on Honshu and Kyushu indicate that the Kofun era saw tribal headmen replaced by powerful chieftains ruling substantial areas.

Some of the larger burial mounds, typically shaped like a keyhole and surrounded by a moat, have yielded sophisticated artifacts, including *haniwa* (clay representations of animals, objects, and humans), bronze mirrors, armor, swords, and jewelry. The largest of all Kofun tombs, near Osaka, is thought to contain the remains of the fifth-century emperor Nintoku. To this day, however, the excavation of imperial tombs is forbidden.

ASUKA (552–710)

Named after Yamato's first capital, thought to be in the area of present-day Osaka and Nara, the Asuka period saw the accelerated adoption of Chinese culture. Introduced by visiting Korean statesmen during the mid-sixth century, Buddhism brought with it a cultural package including administration and bureaucracy, medicine, geomancy (like the Chinese *feng shui,* a belief in lucky and unlucky cardinal points), Confucianism, and writing.

The process intensified under the scholarly and devout Shotoku Taishi (574–622), prince regent of the ruling Soga family. His active exchanges with China prompted major political, educational, and ethical reforms—including Japan's first constitution, based on Confucian principles—and also brought more sophisticated architecture, sculpture, painting, music, and poetry. Shotoku sponsored the building of many temples in the Asuka area, including Horyu-ji (see p. 247).

Fierce rivalries followed Shotoku's death; his son was assassinated in 643, and the Soga rulers were ousted. Japan lost its foothold in Korea following a sea battle in 663, but exchanges with China continued. The new capital, Fujiwara (see p. 31), the first of three emulations of the great Chinese city of Ch'ang-an, was built south of Asuka in 694.

The Taika (Great Change) Reform, which followed the demise of the Soga, introduced the first legal and penal codes and implemented a system of regional governments. The emperor was established as the sacred figurehead he still remains.

The greatest example of a 4th-century "keyhole" tumulus—said to be the tomb of Emperor Nintoku near Mozu, Osaka-ken

The great hall of Todai-ji Temple houses a colossal statue of the Buddha.

NARA (710–794)

Heijo, a new, larger capital, was established just west of what is now Nara in 710 (see pp. 237–48). In the eighth century greater unification was achieved through a new network of main roads connecting provincial capitals, thus consolidating central government power. Buddhism made substantial headway under the pious Emperor Shomu (*R.*724–749), who built temples and monasteries—among them Nara's great Todai-ji Temple—in each province of his realm.

Centralized government came under threat from both the Buddhist clergy and clans controlling outlying districts. Prominent in the labyrinth of intrigue was the Fujiwara family, which rose through the astute marriages it arranged for its daughters. Koken, daughter of Shomu by a Fujiwara consort, succeeded him as empress in 749. Koken fostered Buddhism at the expense of temporal government, a failing that is thought to have prompted the banning of women from imperial succession for almost a thousand years. To sever the influence of the Buddhist priesthood over the state, the capital was moved again in 784 to Nagaoka, southwest of what is now Kyoto.

HEIAN (794–1185)

Conspiracies and assassinations spurred the emperor Kammu to move the capital again in 794, to a site 10 miles (16 km) northeast of Nagaoka. Heian-kyo—the capital of peace and

tranquillity (later to become Kyoto)—was the grandest of all the copies of Ch'ang-an. The era was dominated by the Fujiwara family, which reached its zenith with Michinaga (966–1028), who married four daughters into the imperial line and successively placed two nephews and three grandsons on the throne.

Buddhism made great progress with new sects, notably the Tendai, which had greater appeal to commoners and became the state religion.

Exchanges with China ceased with the collapse of the T'ang dynasty in 907. Japanese culture now developed on its own. The arts and culture reached their apogee during Heian; literature flourished with diaries and the earliest novels in the world, notably the female courtier Murasaki Shikibu's *Tale of Genji.* Splendidly dressed courtiers enlivened their languid existence with lavish ceremonies and the avid pursuit of the arts.

The ruling Fujiwara excelled more as aesthetes than politicians, and there was in fact much unrest. By the late tenth century the Buddhist monks on Mount Hiei (see p. 235) had degenerated into bandits sporadically staging devastating raids on the city. Fonder of dancing than defense, the army was notoriously ineffectual.

In the 12th century, provincial clans increasingly broke away from the Fujiwara. Threatened by the Taira (or Heike) clan during a dispute over imperial succession, the Fujiwara sought protection from the Minamoto (or Genji clan), but the latter was defeated when an army led by Taira Kiyomori (1118–1181) invaded Heian-kyo in 1156. Meting out executions for the first time in centuries, the Taira disposed of the Fujiwara courtiers and put emperors of their own on the throne.

The Minamoto took their revenge during the ensuing Heike War. The army raised by Minamoto Yoritomo (1147–1199), with his half-brother Yoshitsune (1159–1189) among its commanders (see p. 32), drove the Taira from the capital in 1180 and crushed them at the sea battle of Dan-no-ura in 1185. Many survivors leaped into the water and drowned; among them perished the seven-year-old emperor Antoku.

MEDIEVAL PERIOD

SAMURAI

In ancient Japan clan chieftains kept a tenuous hold on territories fraught with brigands, bands of warrior monks, and desperadoes of every description. Having had to raise armies to protect themselves (often from each other), some chieftains became immensely powerful—the forerunners of the great feudal lords. During the peaceful Heian era (794–1185) conflicts dwindled, but in the 12th century the fierce Heike wars broke out between the Taira and Minamoto clans. These inevitably favored the glorification of the warrior, and the protagonists have been enshrined ever since as the first manifestations of the samurai.

The great hero Minamoto Yoshitsune, who finally crushed the Taira in 1185, became a samurai paragon, but it was his brother Yoritomo who established the samurai as the ruling caste for the next 700 years.

The Kamakura period (this page) saw the establishment of *bushido* (the way of the warrior)—the samurai code of ethics, conduct, and strategy. Bushido dictated upholding the clan's honor even at the cost of individual annihilation, figuratively and literally. Glorifying self-sacrifice, it decreed absolute loyalty to the feudal lord. Atonement for any misconduct shaming the clan, which included defeat, demanded *seppuku* (or *hara-kiri*—belly slitting), a gruesome ritual involving self-disembowelment.

The ultimate goal of the warlords was national unification, achieved by the shoguns Oda Nobunaga (1534–1582), Toyotomi Hideyoshi (1536–1598), and Tokugawa Ieyasu (1542–1616). Although Nobunaga's adoption of firearms introduced by the Portuguese changed the style of warfare forever, the samurai never lost their reverence for the sword—which, like armor, displayed exquisite craftsmanship. During the 15th century, samurai attracted to Zen Buddhism for its austerity and self-discipline founded the principles of swordsmanship, archery, and martial arts on its concepts.

In the 17th century Confucian-inspired revisions of samurai codes permeated society with the introduction of a caste system headed by a military aristocracy (see p. 34). Provincial governors became the *daimyo* (great names), and to make sure they remained loyal, they were obliged to divide their time between Edo and their fiefdoms on alternate years, leaving their families behind in the capital as virtual hostages. Although there were no longer any wars to fight, the samurai held power until they were ousted in 1867 (see p. 36).

As with the Crusaders from Europe, the samurai evinced a brutality that has faded in the light of popular culture. Although they were certainly experts in martial arts, the *ninja*—mainly spies skilled at scaling castle walls during sieges—have been idealized out of all proportion. The samurai were often great knights, but unlike their medieval European counterparts, their regard for their womenfolk was nil. Confined to the inner recesses of the home, women were even forbidden to eat at the same table as men.

The samurai era saw the creation of magnificent castles and thriving castle cities, of the Noh theater (see pp. 46–47), the Zen garden (see p. 42 and 220–221), and the tea ceremony (see p. 42 and 225). Many a shogun, such as Ashikaga Yoshimitsu and Toyotomi Hideyoshi, was also a great patron of the arts. The master 17th-century swordsman Miyamoto Musashi (died 1645) was also a philosopher, writer, and master painter. Underlying some of the fanatical excesses of the Japanese army in World War II, the samurai legacy finds echoes in the national characteristics of forbearance and stoicism.

KAMAKURA (1185–1333)

Minamoto Yoshitsune, hounded by his brother Yoritomo, who had turned against him, committed suicide in 1189. Three years later Yoritomo established a new military capital in Kamakura, southwest of present-day Tokyo. The object was to keep the emperor apart from the affairs of state as a divine figurehead in Kyoto—a pattern that was to prevail for some 700 years. As self-appointed shogun (generalissimo), Yoritomo headed a military government known as the *bakufu*. Consisting of provincial governors served by *bushi* (warriors), it was a military dictatorship. When Yoritomo died in 1199, power was taken by his wife's family—the equally ruthless Hojo.

The Hojo established a branch of the bakufu in Kyoto, tightening their grip on the imperial court. Resistance from the court and its provincial allies was crushed during the Jokyu War of 1221, and the Hojo gained direct control over the imperial line.

Later in the 13th century the Mongol emperor Kublai Khan, whose empire embraced all Asia, turned his attentions to Japan. He reached Hakata, Kyushu (see p. 318), in 1274, but his fleet was repelled, thanks largely to a storm at sea. In 1281 Kublai Khan redoubled his efforts with a massive armada of over a thousand ships and 140,000 men. As he neared the Kyushu coast, nature intervened again: A raging typhoon destroyed Kublai Khan's fleet. The Japanese called these fortuitous storms *kamikaze*—the wind of the gods—the name adopted by suicide pilots during World War II.

The Hojo, bankrupted by the preparations for the Mongol Wars, lost popular support. They were driven from Kyoto in 1333 by an army raised by the exiled emperor Godaigo, who exploited growing discontent to restore his power.

Although it was intensely militaristic, the Kamakura era produced many beautiful temples and outstanding works of art. Great castles such as those of Osaka and Himeji were built; swords and armor were exquisitely fashioned and decorated. The age saw the establishment of further Buddhist sects—especially Zen, which was to become a permanent influence on culture and the arts.

MUROMACHI—ASHIKAGA SHOGUNATE (1333–1573)

A poor politician, Emperor Godaigo levied unpopular taxes to support his lavish lifestyle; his brief reign ended when the shogun Ashikaga Takauji (1305–1358) sent him back into exile. The military government moved to the Muromachi district of Kyoto. When Godaigo set up a rival government, known as the Southern Court, in the mountains of Yoshino, south of Nara, Takauji founded the Northern Court in 1336 with handpicked emperors of his own. The rival imperial courts continued for more than 50 years until reunited by the shogun Ashikaga Yoshimitsu (1358–1408) in 1392.

Probably the greatest of the Ashikaga shoguns, Yoshimitsu substantially increased both financial and cultural assets in Japan by accelerating trade with China. He is renowned for nurturing the Noh theater (see pp. 46–47), which reached its apogee under his patronage.

Culture flourished during the Muromachi period. Chinese art, especially ceramics and painting, was widely collected and influenced Japanese culture. The greatest cultural innovations emerged from Zen Buddhism, which was increasingly adopted by the samurai. For all its strife, the Muromachi was an era of great progress. Ports and castle towns thrived; farming and industry prospered.

By the reign of the decadent Yoshimasa (1436–1490), the eighth Ashikaga shogun, the country was falling apart. Provincial warlords came to the fore, and feudal clans such as the Hosokawa undermined the government; many regions became virtually autonomous. Fanned by a dispute over Yoshimasa's succession, conflict culminated in the Onin War (1467–1477), during which Kyoto was burned to the ground. The war was inconclusive and merely heralded the Sengoku Jidai—the century-long era of Warring States. The enfeebled Ashikaga shoguns remained in Kyoto despite their successive domination by other clans, a situation remedied only with the arrival of Oda Nobunaga (1534–1582), a unifying leader.

A suit of samurai armor

Nobunaga began his sudden rise to power by crushing the Inagawa clan's bid to invade Kyoto in 1560. Eight years later he invaded the city himself, temporarily restoring power to the Ashikaga shogun Yoshiaki before removing him and closing down the dynasty in 1573.

The Christian century

Three Portuguese sailors from a vessel run aground on Tanegashima, Kyushu, in 1543 were the first Europeans to land in Japan. They brought muskets, which were copied by Japanese swordsmiths within months; in 1549 Nobunaga ordered 500 for his army.

Merchants paved the way for Portuguese and Spanish missionaries, notably St. Francis Xavier, who landed in Kyushu in 1549. By the end of the century missionaries had converted 150,000 Japanese. Initially welcome as a buffer between a shaky state and militarizing Buddhist sects, Japanese Christians were soon seen as a threat. Over the next century, clampdowns on Christianity escalated, with vicious persecution culminating in a total ban and the expulsion of missionaries. During the Shimbara Rebellion (1637–1638), 37,000 people, mainly Christians, were massacred.

AZUCHI-MOMOYAMA (1573–1603)

Nobunaga incorporated 3,000 musketeers into his army to wipe out the troops of warlord Takeda Yoshiaki at Nagashino in 1575. After building a colossal castle at Azuchi, Nobunaga controlled most of the country until 1582, when, betrayed by one of his own generals and ambushed in Kyoto, he committed seppuku.

Nobunaga's avenger, Toyotomi Hideyoshi (1536–1598), conquered eastern Japan in 1590. To secure dominion over the entire country, he conducted a land survey to streamline taxation and forbade peasants to carry arms. Hideyoshi was fond of the arts. The Kano school of painting (see p. 51) burgeoned under his patronage, and the aesthetic pursuit of the tea ceremony flourished during his reign—but he was as ruthless as any military despot.

In 1592 Hideyoshi rashly staged an invasion of Korea. Undaunted by its disastrous failure, he launched a second attempt in 1598; interrupted by his death, it was abandoned. Before he died, Hideyoshi entrusted guardianship of his son, Hideyori, to Tokugawa Ieyasu (1543–1616), a trusted ally.

Territorial rivalry raged again after Hideyoshi's death. Wanting unified Japan for himself, Ieyasu crushed all his opponents, including Hideyori's followers. Raising a formidable army with four leading provincial warlords, he won the decisive Battle of Sekigahara on October 20, 1600, and founded the military dynasty that was to rule the country for 268 years.

EDO PERIOD (1603–1868)

Ieyasu considered Kyoto to be a powerless imperial realm and sought a spot for a new, unassailable military capital. He chose the old outpost of Edo, near Kamakura; it was a strategic base with access to the rest of the country and had the right topography for developing a port. Having proclaimed himself shogun of all Japan, in 1603 he founded Edo (later to be renamed Tokyo) as the new capital city.

The last of the regime's opponents, Toyotomi Hideyoshi's son Hideyori, committed seppuku after the year-long siege of Osaka castle in 1615. Ieyasu died the following year. His legacy of laws governing society and national administration secured unprecedented national stability.

A social hierarchy placed samurai at the top, followed by farmers, artisans, and merchants. Actors, artists, entertainers, and licensed prostitutes were classless. Beneath them were social outcasts and criminals.

Sparkling Himeji-jo Castle is the grandest and most beautiful of the handful of authentic samurai castles still standing.

From Edo the shogun ruled over a country of fiefdoms governed by the daimyo in his service.

In 1635 the country's doors were officially closed. No citizen was allowed out of or back into Japan—on pain of death. The only visitors were the Chinese; the only Europeans allowed to trade were the Dutch, from the tiny island of Dejima in Nagasaki Bay.

The rise of the townsman

With a population of over a million by the middle of the 18th century, Edo was the largest city on Earth. Commerce, considered beneath the dignity of the ruling caste, was the preserve of merchants, and merchant princes came to outnumber ten to one samurai with comparable wealth. As money swung the balance of power, the bakufu hit back at intervals with Confucian reforms decreeing sumptuary laws. Ostentatious trappings of wealth were forbidden or confiscated, but to little avail.

Edo's famous Yoshiwara (red light district) moved east after the great Meireki fire of 1657. By the prosperous Genroku era (1688–1704), the heyday of Edo, the pleasure quarters in major cities were flourishing as the *ukiyo*—the Floating World. The home of geisha and courtesans, it formed the hub of an entire popular culture, including fashion, literature, Kabuki theater (see pp. 47–49), and graphic art.

During the Edo period, the arts flourished, boosted by extensive patronage and the mass production of books and woodblock prints. With widespread education, some 40 percent of the population was literate.

"The black ships"

A four-year famine culminated in insurrection in Osaka in 1837. Similar rioting had once been easily quashed, but the bakufu, by now impoverished and politically diminished, barely won the day.

During the 1840s the United States had twice made vain requests for a Japanese port of call on the long trade route between Shanghai and California. In 1853 Commodore Matthew Perry steamed into Edo Bay with his three vessels, which the Japanese refer to as "the black ships." The visitors' tone was cordial but the message clear: Swords and rusty muskets would be no match for modern weapons. After the signature of the Kanagawa Treaty between the United States and Japan when Perry returned a year later, treaty ports (open to foreign trade) were established in 1859 and the doors of the country creaked open.

The balance of provincial power was shifting between the daimyo and away from the ruling bakufu. The great southwestern clans of Satsuma, Tosa, and Choshu rose to prominence; the armies sent by the enfeebled shogunate to repress them in 1866 were defeated. As civil unrest escalated all over Japan, the clans united to overthrow the old samurai regime and restore the emperor to power. Following a coup d'état with comparatively little bloodshed, the Tokugawa shogunate fell in 1867. The last shogun, Yoshinobu, staged a futile attempt to attack Kyoto, but following the defeat of his samurai troops, Edo was captured by the armies of the clan alliance.

MEIJI (1868–1912)

Enlightenment

In April 1868 the 16-year-old emperor Mutsuhito moved from Kyoto to Edo, which was renamed Tokyo—the Eastern Capital. The new era was called the Meiji (Enlightenment), and the return of imperial rule is known as the Meiji Restoration.

The new Meiji rulers, mainly Satsuma and Choshu clansmen, instituted rapid and radical changes. Abolishing the old samurai caste system and prohibiting the carrying of swords, they adopted the solar calendar and introduced compulsory education and military service. As American and European merchants, missionaries, and advisers flocked into Japan, legions of young Japanese went abroad to learn about Western civilization.

Following construction of a railroad between Tokyo and Yokohama in 1872, Tokyo and other cities began sprouting Western-style buildings. Modernization hurtled ahead with mining operations, heavy industry, and factories; mass production turned textiles into a major export. In 1873 a criminal code of French origin was adopted, along with German systems of administration. Western dress became usual working-day attire for men in corporate and government offices.

Satsuma clansman Saigo Takamori, one of the architects of the Meiji Restoration, feared that Westernization was undermining Japan. This last samurai headed 40,000 insurgents in Kyushu during the Satsuma Rebellion in 1877; when defeated, he committed suicide.

Rifts within the government led to the establishment of party politics. Government leader Okubo Toshimichi was assassinated in 1881, and Ito Hirobumi became Japan's first prime minister in 1885. The Meiji Constitution he drafted was approved by the emperor in 1889, setting up a system of government that survived until 1945.

The Emperor was revered as the paramount figure of the era, although his real power was debatable. A legacy from the Edo period, nationalist ideology was revived and became a basis for emperor-worship. The introduction of Shinto as the official national religion was designed to eliminate Buddhist political influence, and succeeded in severely curtailing Buddhism after 1870. Affirming the divine lineage of the emperor and the Japanese, seventh-century Shinto myths were taught as historical truth in schools—with dire consequences in the next century.

Expansion

Colonial expansion was one of the hallmarks of industrialized nations in the late 19th

U.S. ships escorted from Edo Bay in 1846, several years before Commodore Perry's intervention.

century; Japan turned to empire-building to join their ranks. China eyed Korea, but the Japanese invaded it first in 1894. Losing the ensuing Sino-Japanese War, China was forced to cede Taiwan and the Liaodang Peninsula on the mainland to Japan. Germany, France, and Russia, however, prevented Japan from claiming its gains on the Chinese mainland.

In 1900 Japan's key role in releasing thousands of foreign hostages in Peking (Beijing) during the Boxer Rebellion enhanced its status in the West. Wary of Germany's colonial maneuvers, the British sought a strong Pacific ally; the Anglo-Japanese Alliance was signed in 1902. In 1904 Japan astonished the world when its British-trained navy annihilated the Russian fleet. Deadlocked on land, the Russo-Japanese War ended with the intervention of Theodore Roosevelt and the signing of the Portsmouth Treaty in 1905.

The Japanese tightened their grip on Korea, forcing the king's abdication and installing Ito Hirobumi as governor. Following the latter's assassination by a Korean patriot in 1909, Japan annexed the country in 1910, triggering resentment that is only gradually abating today.

With the death of the emperor in 1912, a momentous era came to an end. During Meiji, Western culture had a deep impact on Japanese artistic and literary trends, sometimes to the detriment of traditional arts. The zeal for modernism caused many samurai buildings, notably castles, to be destroyed. Endorsed by imperial approval, the Kabuki (see pp. 47–49) became respectable and Western-style drama took root. By the end of the era Japan was producing its own movies.

TAISHO (1912–1926)

Taisho means "Great Righteousness" but, being mentally impaired, its emperor was unable to make public appearances. Crown Prince Hirohito (1901–1989) became regent in 1921.

Japan sided with the Allies in World War I and seized East Asian and Pacific territories from Germany, including Changdong in China. In 1920 Japan joined the League of Nations and in 1922 the Washington Naval Conference accorded greater power to the Japanese in the Pacific, against British objections. The Anglo-Japanese Alliance was dissolved, but friendship between the two nations was undented.

Democratic aspirations colored Japanese politics during the 1920s. It was a time of socio-political ferment, when Japan saw the introduction of a wealth of concepts and ideologies from overseas, including socialism, communism, labor unions, campaigns for women's suffrage, and student movements. Despite the woeful gap between urban rich and rural poor, the early Taisho period is still regarded as a golden age of emerging democracy—until tolerance was swamped by rising nationalism.

Emperor Hirohito (1901–1989) reigned for 63 eventful years.

World War I triggered an industrial boom, but recession and inflation followed. Cheaper rice was imported, sparking anger among farmers and leading to civil unrest, which culminated in the Rice Riots of 1918.

The Taisho governments never lived up to their liberal ideals. Those calling the tune belonged to the same oligarchy that had ruled during Meiji: a conservative aristocracy, nationalistic politicians, and big business; the huge corporations thrived on militarization.

Calamity struck in 1923: The Great Kanto Earthquake reduced Tokyo and Yokohama to rubble, killing 140,000 and destroying some three million homes. The impact on the economy was equally catastrophic.

The Taisho emperor died in 1925. The year brought good news with the right to vote for all men over 25, and bad news with the imposition by nationalists of the Peace Preservation Law. This spawned the increasingly virulent repression of communists and dissidents and a special police division to deal with "dangerous thoughts."

Taisho was at the same time an age of intense intellectual activity, producing legions of new writers and thinkers. *Moga* (modern girl) and *mobo* (modern boy) reveled in the Roaring Twenties. Western trends and fashions made deeper inroads—but not for long. Much as in Weimar Germany, the party was to end with the rise of ultranationalism.

SHOWA (1926–1989)
The dark valley

Crown Prince Hirohito became emperor in 1926. The era name was Showa, meaning "Enlightened Harmony," something that was to be a long time coming. The country was sinking rapidly into what the Japanese now call *kurai tanima*—the dark valley.

The economic afflictions of the Taisho era worsened with the Wall Street Crash of 1929. Japanese exports plummeted; unemployment soared. A growing number of nationalists advocated exerting greater control in Asia. Now that the voices of liberals had been silenced in crackdowns, the notion met with little opposition. Out in the hungry countryside, rightist societies, militaristic youth groups, and patriotic farmers' associations proliferated as ultranationalism rapidly gained ground.

During an international conference in London in 1930, Japanese government representatives signed a treaty reducing Japan's armaments, but it infuriated army chiefs of staff and was nullified in Japan. The prime minister was assassinated by a right-wing fanatic the same year.

In 1931 the Japanese army staged the sabotage of a railroad under its protection in Guangdong, China. The fabrication provided a pretext to attack Chinese troops and overrun Manchuria, which fell under Japanese rule as Manchukuo. Condemned by all world powers, the action was also opposed by Japanese Prime Minister Inukai Tsuyoshi, who was murdered in 1932.

Faced with international opprobrium, Japan withdrew from the League of Nations in 1933. Ultranationalism, resentful in its isolation, became more focused. Efforts were made to purge Japan of foreign concepts and words; regressing to nationalistic Meiji-era emperor worship, education promulgated historical disinformation (mythical emperors and warriors were presented as fact) and the glorification of the Japanese race.

By 1942 Japan had invaded almost the whole of Southeast Asia. The same year its navy was drastically battered during the Battle of Midway, which turned the tide. Fanaticism sent young men on mainly futile suicide missions as human bombs. Civilians and soldiers were soon almost starving, but the war effort pressed on relentlessly. Taken by U.S. forces in 1944, the Pacific island of Saipan became a base for bombing the whole of Japan.

In March 1945 the three-day incendiary bombing of Tokyo left over 100,000 dead and 700,000 homes destroyed; the attack was repeated on key sites around Japan. In April the Allies invaded Okinawa, where more than 200,000 died, half of them civilians. The Potsdam Declaration in July, calling for Japan's unconditional surrender, was ignored. On August 6 the U.S. dropped an atomic bomb on Hiroshima, obliterating the city and killing 150,000 people—over half of them instantaneously. Three days later another atomic bomb was dropped on Nagasaki.

A week later the emperor, apparently taking his own initiative against hard-line opposition, stunned Japan by announcing the inevitability of capitulation. In September

Schoolchildren on a visit to Hiroshima's Peace Museum

The Pacific War

In 1936 Japan signed the Anti-Comintern Pact, allying it to fascist Italy and Nazi Germany. Its aggression in China reached a climax in 1937 with the taking of Nanking, during which some 200,000 civilians were savagely massacred. The military forced the government to pass the National Mobilization Law, placing Japan on a war alert.

Prince Konoe and his cabinet were ousted in 1941. The government was taken over by the military, with Gen. Tojo Hideki as prime minister. The United States reacted to Japan's aggression in China by ceasing to supply raw materials, freezing Japanese assets in U.S. territory, and imposing an oil embargo. Retaliating with a surprise attack on Pearl Harbor on December 7, 1941, Japan plunged blindly into war. Its fierce expansionism, nobly dressed up as the foundation of a Greater East Asia Co-prosperity Sphere, wrought some of the worst atrocities in the history of world colonialism.

During the 1980s, Japanese automotive firms came to dominate the world car market.

officials signed the surrender before Gen. Douglas MacArthur, who headed the U.S. Occupation forces landing in Japan. With over 2 million dead and 13 million homeless, Japan was broken; having lost all its overseas territories, it would have to feed some 6 million extra mouths when its soldiers and expatriates returned.

The Occupation

Tokyo citizens came out of hiding when they realized that the carnage predicted by militarists was not going to happen. General MacArthur was widely respected as Supreme Commander of the Allied Powers (SCAP), even by the Japanese. In 1946 the International Military Tribunal for the Far East (IMTFE) jailed 25 former militarists for war crimes; seven were executed two years later, including Tojo Hideki. Some 4,000 war criminals were simultaneously tried by IMTFE tribunals around the Pacific. It was suggested that the emperor should have been among them, but MacArthur retained him as a figurehead vital to the peaceful restructuring of Japan.

With the exception of Okinawa (which reverted to Japan by popular vote in 1972), the U.S. Occupation forces left Japan to the Japanese. Having abolished the armed forces and purged the government of militarists, the Occupation authorities administered on the basis of mutual cooperation. In 1946 they drafted a new American-style democratic constitution that remains in force today. Emphasizing individual fulfillment and egalitarianism, it announced land reforms, the emancipation of women, and a new education system.

Special procurements for the Korean War in 1950 substantially helped to relaunch Japanese industry, but caused a shift from left to right in U.S. Occupation policy. America needed a strong anti-Communist ally in East Asia; though democracy had been firmly established, Japanese politics were pushed right of center.

In 1951 Prime Minister Yoshida Shigeru (1878–1967) signed a treaty with 48 nations at the San Francisco Peace Conference. The Occupation ended the next year. At the end of the Korean War in 1953, Japan signed the U.S. Security Treaty, allowing substantial American bases to remain on its soil. In 1955 Yoshida lost the vote to the new Liberal Democratic Party, which has remained in power ever since (except for a brief flirtation with coalitions in 1993).

Earthquake-ready Japan was shocked by the destruction of the Kobe Earthquake in 1995.

MODERN JAPAN (1989–PRESENT)

When Japan joined the United Nations in 1956, the economy was growing at twice the predicted rate. Thanks to soaring industry, exports, and good living standards, the country's recovery was declared complete by 1958.

With the renunciation of war written into the constitution, Japan is theoretically forbidden an army, but its SDF (self-defense force) ranks sixth in the world in terms of military strength. Widespread rioting erupted in 1960 with the renewal of the U.S. Security Treaty, but Japan's darkest clouds come mainly from pollution—the price paid for rapid industrialization.

1964 was a landmark year for Japan, when it hosted the Tokyo Olympic Games and launched the *shinkansen*—then the fastest train service in the world. Come 1970 and the International Exposition in Osaka, Japan had a formidable world-class economy based on a widening spectrum of quality industrial products.

Weathering oil shocks in both 1973 and 1979, Japan's spectacular growth prevailed but drew international flak in the 1980s for huge trade surpluses; fraught with tariff barriers, its markets were virtually closed to the outside world. Prizing them open had little effect on the balance of trade. Japan's wealth swelled throughout the 1980s.

In 1972 the Lockheed bribery scandal forced the resignation of Prime Minister Tanaka Kakuei and exposed the corruption endemic in the ruling Liberal Democratic Party. Scandals continued to taint the party through the 1990s and the early 21st century.

The death of the Showa emperor in 1989 marked the end of an extraordinary era. With the accession of his son Akihito in 1990, the Heisei era finds Japan facing an uncertain future. The miracle ended with the collapse of the bubble economy in 1991; the resulting recession subsided, but not the social malaise.

Prominent from the postwar, the generation gap continues to widen, the two separated by a flood tide of cell phones and cyberspace. Crime statistics remain enviably low, but juvenile offenses have soared. Many Japanese blame the erosion of traditional values on materialism, leaving a moral and spiritual vacuum. Attempts to fill that gap include a proliferation of religious cults, some as demented as Aum, which launched a deadly sarin gas attack in the Tokyo subway in 1995. That same year, the Kobe earthquake, which killed more than 5,000 people, uncomfortably reminded modern Japan of the permanent perils of nature. ■

The arts

SYMMETRY PLAYS NO PART IN JAPANESE AESTHETICS. A MILLENNIUM OR SO ago, Japanese temple complexes abandoned the regular ground plan of the Chinese model they emulated; the most highly regarded ceramic tea bowls are irregularly shaped; flower arrangements evoke the random patterns of nature; and the balance of the composition in prints and paintings is ingeniously off-center. In speech, prose, poetry, and visual arts, the implicit is frequently preferred to the explicit.

During the 13th century Zen Buddhism (see p. 227) inspired radically new forms and concepts, influencing painting, calligraphy, and poetry. Tea drinking, ritualized in China by Zen monks seeking no more than a means of staying awake during meditation, was transformed into a deeply aesthetic and philosophical ceremony in Japan. As developed by, among others, the great tea master Sen-no-Rikyu (1522–1591), *chado* or *chanoyu*—the Way of Tea—spurned ostentation and ushered in a new system of aesthetics.

The tea room is small, spotless, and plain. It contains a *kakemono* (hanging scroll) and a flower arrangement in the *tokonoma* (alcove); plain and rough in appearance, the tea bowls almost belie their master craftsmanship. The kakemono can be a calligraphy (often a poem) or an ink painting; like the flower arrangement, it should reflect the mood and hues of the season. The tea room becomes a space for the appreciation of different art forms working together.

In requiring works created specially for it, chanoyu engendered other forms, notably ikebana—the art of flower arrangement. Zen and the tea ceremony greatly influenced landscape gardening as teahouses had to have the proper surroundings. Kyoto's great Zen gardens of stone and gravel, representing water and mountains and reflecting philosophical ideals, are perhaps the world's earliest examples of conceptual and installation art.

Chanoyu and its correlative arts always reflect *wabi* (quiet taste) and *sabi* (elegant simplicity). These are the criteria for *shibui* (sober refinement), the paramount principle of Japanese taste, whereby less is more. Although not always so refined, aesthetics still preoccupy the Japanese, from the painstaking wrapping of gifts and the elaborate presentation of food to clusters of artificial flowers in toilets.

TRADITIONAL ARCHITECTURE

Japanese architecture is based on wood. The purely Chinese designs of the great Buddhist temples of Horyu-ji (see pp. 247–48), near Nara, set a precedent for religious architecture little altered today. However, some of the oldest and most sacred Shinto shrines, like those at Ise and Izumo, predate the Chinese model and replicate the prehistoric originals.

The raised structure of Ise Jingu is modeled after an ancient granary. Older shrines such as this have thatched roofs, with rafters alternating like crossed fingers placed against the ridge-piece. Others, like the shrine at Izumo, imitate ancient headmen's houses. At the gabled end of Shinto shrines, including many of those in the Chinese style, are the distinctive ornamental *chigi*—large crossed beams protruding from the roof like horns.

Beginning in the 16th century, the heads of the supporting pillars and crossbeams were sometimes carved, often with embellishments in gilded metalwork. Most shrines and all temples stand on foundations of stone and display sweeping roofs tiled in clay or bronze with eaves sloping elegantly upward.

Many temple complexes incorporate a pagoda, typically with five stories according to the Chinese geomantic principle of the five elements: earth, water, sky, wind, and fire. Most castles, regardless of the number of floors inside, also show five roof levels on the exterior. As with most Japanese wooden architecture, these intricate buildings have been constructed without using a single nail.

The traditional Japanese house is raised on low stilts, sometimes above a foundation. The single-story model is said to emulate the

Widely practiced today, ikebana—flower arranging—is an art form rooted in Zen Buddhist culture.

aristocratic dwelling of the 12th century, but between the 17th and mid-19th centuries two and sometimes three stories became common. The walls consist of a bamboo framework set between the support pillars and coated with daub. They are then plastered and often white-washed on the outside, while inside they are either plastered or coated with a smooth daub

The International Forum Building in Tokyo, designed by U.S. architect Rafael Viñoly

made from paper pulp. Such traditional houses are light, airy, and designed to open onto the outside world rather than to seal it off, as in the West. Roofs vary according to place and time. They can be steep and narrow to avert snow or wide and sweeping to provide shade. Thatch was ubiquitous until the 16th century, even on samurai dwellings, but is used today only on a few old farmhouses and some historic buildings. Shingled roofs appeared later; they can still be seen on some old mountain farmhouses, especially in Nagano. Clay tiles, first used in towns during the 17th and 18th centuries, became widespread. The roofs of modest homes now commonly display many cheaper alternatives, including metal, corrugated iron, and plastic.

The cost of building a traditional house is prohibitive today, calling upon vanishing skills and increasingly scarce wood. Many modern homes are prefabricated, incorporating concrete slabs and plastics—materials also used to build houses in the traditional style.

Originally reserved for official buildings, Western architecture first appeared during the late 19th century. It was typically massive, of red brick and Victorian in style, and was greatly influenced by the British architect Josiah Conder (1852–1920); Tokyo Station was built by one of his pupils in 1914.

Reinforced concrete multistory apartment buildings, built according to utilitarian rather than aesthetic criteria, are becoming dominant in cities. But the profile of modern architecture was heightened during the 1960s with many remarkable buildings, notably Tange Kenzo's structures for the 1964 Olympic Games. Highly regarded internationally, architects such as Tange and Ando Tadao often incorporate traditional concepts into modern buildings to striking effect.

LITERATURE

The *Kojiki (Record of Ancient Matters)* and the *Nihon Shoki (Chronicles of Japan)*, eighth-century history books that meld creation myths and fact, held sway over Shinto belief and national thinking for more than a millennium. The eighth-century *Man'yoshu*

(Collection for Ten Thousand Generations) is a compilation of 4,500 poems by emperors and aristocrats as well as ordinary people. Many are in the brief, evocative tanka style—a forerunner of the better known haiku (see below) and a poetry form still in fashion.

The great advances in literature during the Heian period (see pp. 30–31) were mainly due to female writers of *nikki* (diaries) and *monogatari* (tales)—the world's oldest true novels. Most prominent were the courtiers Sei Shonagon and Murasaki Shikibu, who created literary milestones around the year 1000. Sei Shonagon's candid *Makura Soshi (The Pillow Book)* is a compilation of vivid (and often unabashedly bitchy) observations of life at court. Murasaki's 54-chapter *Genji Monogatari (The Tale of Genji)*, tracing the rise and fall of a philandering prince, is one of the classics of world literature.

After the 13th century, literature was eclipsed for almost 400 years by war—though war itself was the source of inspiration for the great classic *Heike Monogatari (The Tales of Heike)*, an epic prose poem recounting the wars between the Taira and Minamoto clans. Often recited or sung, Heike-style epics were adapted for the theater; the melancholy and richly evocative Noh plays of Zeami Motokiyo (1363–1444) are outstanding for their poetic sensitivity.

During the Edo period (see pp. 34–36), plays were written interchangeably for the Bunraku puppet theater and Kabuki drama, notably by Chikamatsu Monzaemon (1653–1725), often regarded as a Japanese Shakespeare. His plays were mainly historical, but the most popular were contemporary tragedies about doomed lovers running afoul of the rules of caste and society. Social and dramatic realism came to color both the theater and novels—the latter revived as a genre after 600 years. Many novels, most notably those by Ihara Saikaku (1642–1692), were satires recounting the adventures of profligates and prostitutes in the Floating World (see p. 35).

In poetry the 17-syllable haiku was brought to perfection by Matsuo Basho (1644–1694). A samurai who converted to Zen, the wandering Basho produced haiku anthologies based on his journeys—masterpieces widely revered today.

The Meiji period (see pp. 36–37) brought Western realism to the Japanese novel. Among the first modern novelists were Mori Ogai (1862–1922) and Natsume Soseki (1867–1916). The novels of Nagai Kafu (1879–1959) cast a wistful glance at the vanishing Floating World in the 1900s. Women writers emerged for the first time since the Heian period,

Nobel laureate Kawabata Yasunari (1899–1973), one of Japan's finest novelists

among them the tragically short-lived novelist Higuchi Ichiyo (1872–1896) and the poet and scholar Yosano Akiko (1878–1942).

The postwar period was something of a renaissance highlighted by the best work of established writers such as Kawabata Yasunari *(Snow Country,* 1948) and Tanizaki Junichiro (1886–1965), whose masterpiece, *The Makioka Sisters,* was banned by the militarists. A wealth of emerging talent included Yukio Mishima, Abe Kobo, Endo Shusaku, and Oe Kenzaburo, winner of the Nobel Prize for Literature in 1994. Murakami Ryu's *Almost Transparent Blue* reflects youthful nihilism during the 1970s. Among the most popular current authors are Murakami Haruki *(Dance, Dance, Dance)* and the lightweight Banana Yoshimoto *(Kitchen),* deplored by some as an indicator of the growing superficiality of Japanese taste.

THEATER & DANCE

The sacred masked dance of *kagura*, taking the form of pantomime and featuring musical and vocal accompaniment, goes back to ancient times. Still performed during Shinto festivals, it is the source of inspiration for other forms of dance and drama. *Bugaku*, which survives in imperial ceremonies, and *gagaku* are of Chinese origin. They were forms of music and dance performed at the court in Heian times (see pp. 30–31). More popular types of entertainment were *dengaku* (field music, originating in peasant dances) and *sarugaku* (monkey music), both based on kagura. During the 14th century, sarugaku was refined into Noh, which means "skill." Under the patronage of the shogun Ashikaga Yoshimitsu, the art was perfected by Kan'ami Kiyotsugu (1333–1384) and his son Zeami Motokiyo (see p. 45), who turned Noh into a great classical theater form. Noh has a repertoire of five categories: Using poetic language and an

exquisitely costumed cast of three, it enacts tales of gods, ghostly warriors, madness, women, and demons. Noh performances are traditionally accompanied by a *kyogen* (comic interlude), a direct derivative of sarugaku.

Noh became the preserve of the samurai elite; during the Edo period, commoners were forbidden to see it. Early in the 17th century, however, a woman named Okuni presented a new kind of dance drama for the people of Kyoto. Called Kabuki, it went on to take Edo

Devised in the 17th century, the flamboyant Kabuki theater features gorgeous costumes and an all-male cast.

and the rest of the country by storm. It was often a front for prostitution, and the shogunate attempted to kill it by banning actresses from the stage. Kabuki quickly rebounded with an all-male cast; the female roles were portrayed by *onnagata* (woman-forms). Flamboyant and fast-moving in contrast to

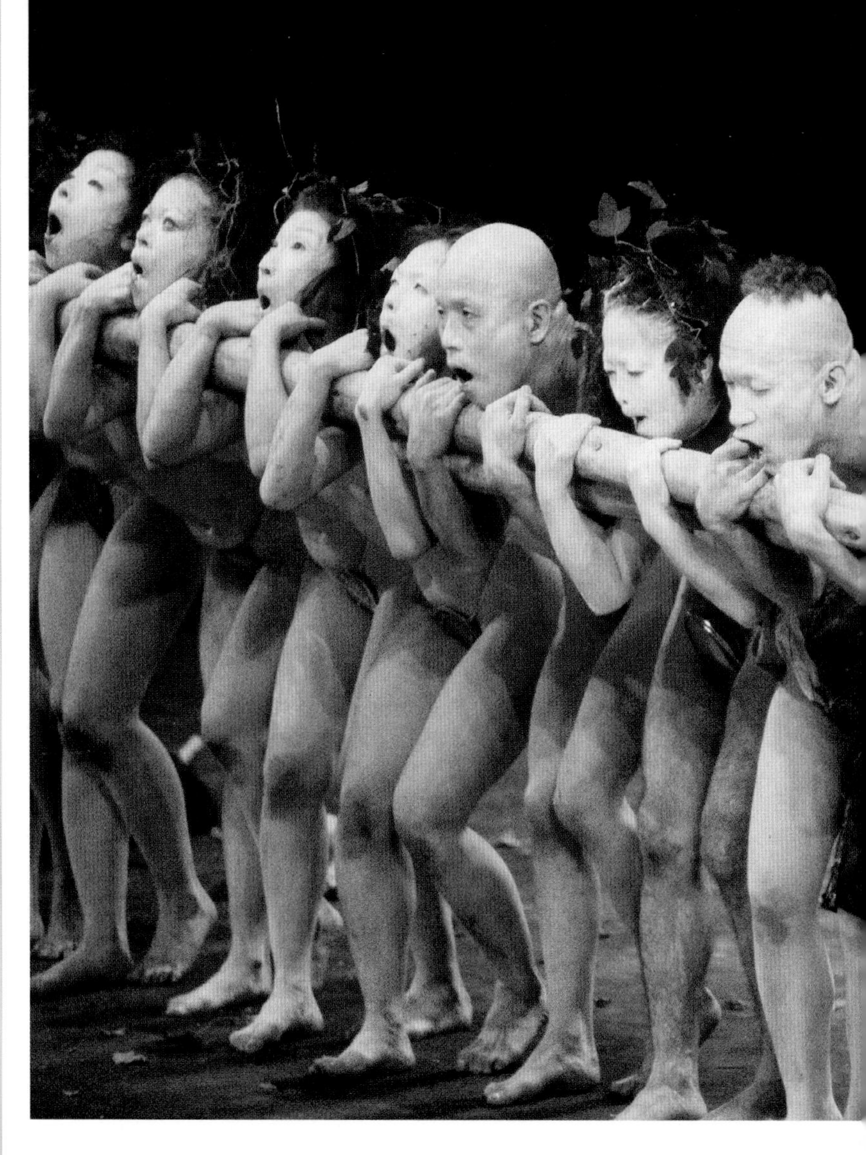

Noh, Kabuki featured gaudy costumes, spectacular sets, and special effects. The plays were enacted in contemporary language and embraced modern themes.

The same applies in miniature to the very popular contemporary Bunraku puppet theater; the works of many playwrights, including the great Chikamatsu, are staged in both forms. One-third life size, each stringless marionette is manipulated by as many as three handlers on stage (their presence is soon forgotten). Bunraku remains one of the world's most exquisite forms of puppetry.

Until Western-style alternatives gradually came to eclipse it after the mid-19th century, Kabuki remained synonymous with popular theater in Japan. It retains a wide following and, like Noh, is a revered facet of the national cultural heritage.

Apart from an enduring profile in festivals and drama, dance never evolved much as an independent form until the 19th century.

During the 18th century geisha and dancing girls in the entertainment quarters borrowed heavily from Kabuki, and it is in this form that *nihon buyo*—Japanese dancing—is widely practiced today, mostly by women and girls.

Plays have been written and performed in the Western tradition in Japan for over a century. Ballet and modern dance are gaining in popularity and command a wide following. *Angura* (underground) dance and theater made waves in the late 1960s, notably with

Plotless, grotesque, and fascinating, *butoh* dance theater is a blend of traditional Japanese fantasy and Western avant-garde.

butoh (the dance of darkness), introduced by Hijikata Tatsumi (1930–1986). Melding grotesque Western-style imagery with the traditional physicality of Noh and Kabuki, butoh has a global following. Much the same applies to Japan's avant-garde theater; led by Kara Juro and Terayama Shuji during the 1970s, the

The popular band Dreams Come True plays a fusion of jazz, rock, techno, funk, pop, and R&B.

movement has seen the emergence of several troupes admired overseas. From the dance innovations of Teshigawara Saburo to the stylish theatrical productions of Ninagawa Yukio, Japanese dance and theater come increasingly under the global spotlight.

MUSIC

The grand and sedate *gagaku* (court music) orchestra, using instruments from T'ang dynasty China, has remained in use for imperial, Shinto, and Buddhist ceremonies for more than a thousand years. Its main instruments are the *biwa* (a large teardrop-shape lute), *koto* (a 13-stringed zither), side-blown flutes, and percussion, including the *tsuzumi* shoulder drum and the enormous, vertically played *dadaiko* drum.

Shomyo, chanting of Buddhist ritual, exerted a strong influence on singing styles in Japan, where itinerant monks often gathered alms by singing epic poems to a biwa accompaniment. The epic poem singing style gave rise to *naga-uta* (long songs), influential on the Noh theater in the 15th century, which in turn engendered the *joruri* singing adopted in the 17th century by the Kabuki theater. Joruri was also practiced by geisha in the Floating World as well as by blind minstrels, who had a monopoly on singing epic poems until 1871.

During the Edo period (see pp. 34–36), the *samisen* gradually replaced the biwa. The samisen, introduced from China via Okinawa, is a three-stringed lute with a long, thin neck and a small, round sound box covered in snakeskin (Okinawa) or animal skin (mainland Japan). Adopted in the Kabuki theater, the samisen soon became the instrument of choice for geisha and blind minstrels and for folk music. The Edo period also saw the appearance of the *shakuhachi,* a bamboo flute about 18 inches (45cm) long. It gives the player much scope for expression, and its unique tone makes it a popular instrument today.

The classic singing technique, plaintive and heavily stylized, is an acquired taste for many modern Japanese used to Western harmony. Composed using the pentatonic scale, traditional Japanese music is not always easy listening to the unaccustomed ear—but it is worth the effort.

Western music accompanied the Portuguese in the 16th century but was soon forgotten with the closure of the country. Returning in the form of military bands during the 1860s (most samurai clans wanted one), Western music had a colossal and lasting

Katsushika Hokusai (1760–1849) woodblock print from his "36 Views of Mount Fuji" series

impact. Japanese symphony orchestras, such as the Saito Kinnen and Tokyo Symphony orchestras, are among the world's finest, and the country has produced many outstanding Western-style musicians, among them conductor Ozawa Seiji and pianist Mitsuko Uchida. During the 1960s, composers such as Takemitsu Toru combined gagaku with contemporary Western music to explore new horizons of sound. Japan has many fine jazz musicians, and countless city venues present a broad array of imported and domestic musicians of all types.

VISUAL ARTS

Painting

In early Japan painting was Chinese in form and exclusively Buddhist in content. Among the earliest examples are the murals in the main hall of Horyu-ji Temple near Nara, executed in the seventh century. During the Heian period (794–1185), painting took a more Japanese turn, with landscapes and scenes from court life decorating screens and sliding doors; portraiture and illustrated scrolls became popular.

In the Kamakura period (1185–1333) art of this kind came to be called *yamato-e* (Japanese painting) as distinct from *kara-e* ("outside" paintings in the Chinese tradition). The yamato-e tradition favored fine detail and vivid colors. Focusing on black-and-white, kara-e was characterized by *sumi-e (*ink paintings); the school progressed with the spread of Zen Buddhism and reached its zenith during the 15th century with the monk Sesshu (1420–1506), whose works depicted real (as opposed to the hitherto imaginary) landscapes.

From the late 16th century, wealthy warlords lavished patronage on the rival Kano school, which combined elements of kara-e and yamato-e to embellish the interiors of houses and castles with magnificent works. Motonobu (1476–1559) and Eitoku (1543–1590) were Kano's finest artists. Thanks to the growing patronage of wealthy merchant princes, the established schools flourished alongside growing demand for purely decorative art. This was met notably by the Rimpa school, of which Ogata Korin (1658–1716), famed for his composition of irises on a golden screen door, was a major exponent.

Hishikawa Moronobu (d. 1694), a prominent painter in the Kano style, was the first master—though not the inventor— of *ukiyo-e,* woodblock prints depicting the Floating World. The works of ukiyo-e masters such as Kitagawa Utamaro (1753–1806), Katsushika

Hokusai (1760–1849), and Ando Hiroshige (1797–1858) caused a sensation in Europe during the 19th century.

Sculpture

Archaeological excavations have unearthed Jomon-period statuettes, and the Kofun era's more sophisticated *haniwa* clay figures. The latter, representing humans, animals, and buildings, were put in the grave mounds of chieftains, paralleling the Chinese practice.

Circa sixth-century terra-cotta figure of a warrior

Bronze figures of the Buddha were first introduced from Korea during the sixth century. Although Buddhism continued to dictate the same formal conventions as the original Sino-Korean prototypes, the Japanese were soon making their own. Styles changed with the introduction of new sects but, although an abundance of magnificent examples reveal the sculptor's individual skill, religious sculpture never displayed the variety of secular art. During the Kamakura period (see pp. 32–33), wooden sculptured portraits became quite common to commemorate both noted priests and secular dignitaries.

Sculpture thrived in miniature. Swords and armor often displayed fine decorative metalwork; many *netsuke,* the wood or ivory toggles used for attaching small medicine cases *(inro)* to kimono sashes, were tiny sculptures of consummate skill. As demand for these declined during the 19th century, former metalworkers and netsuke carvers turned to statuettes and figurines, many destined for export.

Sculpture by Mineda Yoshihiro, Makuhari Messe Exhibition Centre, Chiba

Modern art

The resounding impact of Western art during the Meiji period (see pp. 36–37) prompted many Japanese artists to study in Paris, among them the influential Kuroda Seiki (1866–1924), founder of the first Western-style art school. Traditionalists' opposition led to the official division of *ninhonga* (Japanese painting) and *yoga* (Western painting), with the latter deprived of government sponsorship. Nevertheless, all significant Western art movements have produced major Japanese representatives from the 1900s to the present day. Although incorporating Western styles, ninhonga painters continue to thrive.

Film

Born with the flickering images of a Kabuki actor in 1896, the Japanese cinema took off during the 1910s with hundreds of one-reelers borrowing themes and actors from Kabuki theater.

Directors perfecting their craft during the 1920s absorbed Russian (Eisenstein), American (D.W. Griffiths), and German (Expressionist) film technique. Among them were Mizoguchi Kenji (1898–1956) and Ozu Yasujiro (1903–1963), whose films progressed from rickety, silent one-reelers to masterpieces of world cinema.

Akira Kurosawa's *Rashomon* (1951) put Japanese cinema on the world map.

In 1951 Kurosawa Akira's period drama *Rashomon* won the grand prize (the Golden Lion) at the Venice Film Festival. Mizoguchi's *The Life of Oharu* won the festival's international award in 1952; his exquisite medieval ghost story *Ugetsu* won the Silver Lion the next year. At its zenith, epitomized too by Ozu's *Tokyo Story* (1953), a poignant portrait of a rural family overwhelmed by social change, Japanese cinema earned international accolades and had far-reaching influence.

Meanwhile, to counter the onslaught of television, major Japanese film companies increasingly churned out formula flicks. Despite a vogue in the 1960s for the Japanese Nouvelle Vague cinema epitomized by Oshima Nagisa (*In the Realm of the Senses,* 1976, *Merry Christmas Mr. Laurence,* 1983), film audiences declined tenfold between 1958 and 1998. Fighting off bankruptcy during the 1970s, the venerable Nikkatsu Company, founded in 1912, launched soft-core *roman poruno* (porno romance), a genre in which many prominent directors and actors cut their teeth until hard-core video killed it overnight. Some directors sought finance abroad, including Kurosawa (both in Russia and the U.S.) and Oshima (in France); others, like Imamura Shohei (*Ballad of Narayama* in 1983), sought independent finance at home.

The 1980s saw the emergence of successful independent directors , especially the late Itami Juzo (*Tampopo, Taxing Woman*). The trend continues, despite small audience figures and the fact that two-thirds of films seen in Japan are foreign. Best known for hardboiled cop movies, Takeshi Kitano has won many international awards for films such as *Hanabi* (1997) and *Zatoichi* (2004). Younger talent (e.g., Tomoda Toshiaki, Hirokazu Kore-eda) scores highly on the international agenda; Japan's quality cinema audience may be small but is reliable enough to make indie film directors flourish, if not rich. Major company formula films include *manga* animated cartoons, *yakuza*

gangster movies, comedies, and period dramas—though the noteworthy remain few.

Crafts

The rapid pace of modernization in Japan led inevitably to the loss of countless aspects of its former lifestyle, but the survival of certain traditional crafts is one of the country's marvels. Efforts have been made to preserve them, not least through a system designating older practitioners of traditional arts and crafts as Intangible Cultural Properties or Living National Treasures. The fact that arts and crafts are hereditary businesses has helped to perpetuate them, as has the survival of the traditional ceremonies and pastimes in which they are used. Works by officially treasured craftspeople are rare and revered; even those by lesser masters can be dauntingly expensive. Fortunately a vast range of marvelous handicrafts are still affordable, though unlikely to be really cheap if made in Japan.

Crafts and painterly skills coalesce in an outsize festival kite in Northern Honshu.

Ceramics

Japanese pottery goes back to the ancient Jomon culture but remained rough and practical until techniques from China and Korea became established in the sixth century. Japanese potters continued to make Korean-style ware through the 18th century. Glazed ceramics arrived with the introduction of three-color glazes during the 7th century, but it was not until the 14th century that renewed contacts with China prompted the refinements and sophistication for which Japanese ceramics are renowned. The focus of the industry was Seto in central Honshu, from whence comes the Japanese word for pottery, *seto-mono* (Seto things).

The tea ceremony ushered in stylistic innovations epitomized by the deceptively rough-hewn quality of ware such as Karatsu,

Hagi, and Raku. Introduced during the 17th century, porcelain was first produced in Arita in the Tsushima Islands, especially the blue-and-white ware (and later polychrome too) commonly called Imari. Along with polychrome Satsuma ware, Imari is still seen as most representative of Japanese ceramics today. Mass production caused a decline in traditional ceramics in the late 19th century, but there are still a hundred noted kilns and many master potters active in Japan, especially in Kyushu.

Paper

The surfaces and mats used in pen-and-ink painting and calligraphy are traditionally made from *washi*—paper handmade from wood pulp, especially mulberry bark. Although manufacture dwindled with the introduction of Western paper, washi is still in demand for a variety of uses including calligraphy, origami (paper folding), fans, decorations, paper dolls, and traditional stationery. In different thicknesses, plain, dyed, printed and decorated, and sometimes incorporating flecks of gold leaf and colored fragments, washi is sold in stationery and specialty stores.

Lacquerware, such as this covered bowl, is immediately identifiable as Japanese.

Lacquerware

Common throughout East Asia, lacquer has long been associated primarily with Japan; in 18th-century England red or black lacquering for furniture was known simply as Japanning. In Japan *nuri* (lacquer) or *urushi-mono* (lacquered things) have barely gone out of fashion since their height from the late 17th to the 19th centuries. *Tansu* (chests), boxes for various uses, tea caddies, combs and hair ornaments, wooden bowls, sake cups, and ceremonial *bento-bako* (packed meal boxes) are still produced by modern craftsmen, notably in Ishikawa, the Kiso Valley, and Okinawa. Authentic urushi-mono is a painstaking process involving three coats of lacquer, and its production commands high prices; plastic imitations, especially tableware, abound today. Often featuring inclusions of gold leaf and

mother-of-pearl, beautifully painted designs are enhanced with a deep, glossy finish. Black, red, and occasionally green were once the more common colors, along with rarer *maki-e* (lacquerware with silver and gold leaf), but some of today's craftsmen create striking modern designs in a wider array of subtle (and not so subtle) hues.

Wood and bamboo

The traditional Japanese home has little furniture, low tables and chests (tansu) being the notable exception. Popular overseas, antique tansu command increasingly high prices but remain a good buy in Japan. Although made with considerable skill and still expensive, modern equivalents are often machine finished and tend to have painted gloss where there should be a patina.

Many handcrafted objects are made of wood, notably lacquerware. Trays and bowls, turned on a lathe and hand finished, are often sold polished rather than lacquered.

Bamboo is popular for tea-related utensils and flower holders. It is either sectioned and shaped into a vase or cut into thin strips and woven into a variety of attractive shapes, for displaying on a surface or for hanging.

Textiles

The beauty of Japanese textiles is legendary; the prices of even used silk kimonos and brocade *obi* (kimono sashes) have escalated sharply in recent years. Using hand-cut stencils and rice paste applied to the fabric, *yuzen* is a

Instructors and pupils warm up for a junior high school karate tournament.

skillful dyeing technique that produces patterns of great complexity, especially in Kyoto and Kanazawa. Okinawa, too, produces beautiful textiles; the hand-painted colorful *bingata* designs, often representing stylized flowers and birds, are the most famous.

Rustic *aizome* cotton textiles, mainly dyed with natural indigo, are often exquisitely printed or tie-dyed. Used for garments, bags, and hats commonly sold in gift shops, sophisticated variants of aizome find new applications among fashion designers.

Dolls

Hina-matsuri (March 3) is Girls' Day, celebrated in people's homes with a display of dolls *(ningyo)* representing members of an old imperial court. Not toys but family heirlooms, such dolls are often exquisitely dressed and crafted; fine examples, antique or modern, can be dauntingly expensive. (Boys' Festival on May 5 finds an equivalent in small suits of armor and samurai warrior dolls.) *Hagoita,* the bats used in an ancient shuttlecock game played by girls, are decorated with brocade dolls in bas-relief, mainly representing Kabuki actors. Evolving partly from the *haniwa* figurines of the Kofun period (see p. 28), dolls have long been used as ritual charms in Japan and figure prominently among the folk arts around the country. The most primitive are the cylindrical wooden *kokeshi,* but more refined types are still produced, notably in Kyoto, Hakata, and Saga prefectures.

MARTIAL ARTS

Japan's greatest native sports, apart from sumo wrestling, are its martial arts, which arrived from China along with Buddhism. The core concepts had already been developed by monks as they honed techniques to defend themselves against bandits on their travels.

The oldest Japanese fighting arts are *kenjutsu* (based on the samurai art of swordsmanship), *jujutsu* (unarmed combat of medieval origin), and *kyujutsu* (ancient archery formalized during the Kamakura period). The suffix *-jutsu* means "skill"—especially skills useful to samurai warriors; it was replaced by *-do* (the Way) during the Meiji era.

Although martial arts always involved spiritual as well as physical discipline, the emphasis shifted to the former during the 19th century. *Kendo,* the way of the sword, was introduced into the curriculum during the 19th century and is still widely practiced in schools and universities by girls as well as boys. The same applies to a lesser degree to *kyudo* (archery), which has spiritual principles preponderantly influenced by Zen. Wearing padded armor and helmets to protect the face, kendo protagonists duel with swords of split bamboo; winning is determined according to five principles and the quality of strikes against eight strategic points on the opponent's body armor.

Martial arts are taught by masters in schools known as *dojo.* Most use the *dan* ranking system, whereby proficiency is measured from first to sixth dan, designated with colored belts worn on tunics; black generally denotes the highest level.

Judo, a synthesis of jujutsu, spiritual training, and other old fighting arts, involves grappling and body throws. It was introduced in the 1900s and became a national sport in the 1930s, but like all martial arts it was banned as a feudal remnant by the Occupation authorities. Reinstated in 1950, judo had already found experts around the world before its inclusion in the Tokyo Olympic Games in 1964, when to the disappointment of the Japanese the gold medal went to a Dutchman.

Karate (empty hand), a close relative of kung-fu, was of Chinese origin. It was much practiced in the Ryuku-shoto Islands (Okinawa) following its introduction during the 14th century, but did not reach mainland Japan until the 1900s. Akin to other martial arts in its demands for dedication and spiritual concentration, karate calls upon a variety of blows with the hands, fists, and feet. It differs from other martial arts in its emphasis on attack rather than defense.

Aikido, founded by Ueshiba Morihei during the 1920s and based on ancient arts of self-defense, is the most spiritually oriented of the martial arts. The emphasis is placed entirely on defense; throws are achieved by deftly using the opponent's momentum against him. Borrowing movement from classical Japanese dance, aikido also involves Zen-style meditation to enhance the flow of *ki,* the life-force, through the practitioner's body. ■

Tokyo means "eastern capital." The name is apt. At once perfectly familiar and totally alien to the foreign visitor, the multifaceted city is so huge, colorful, frenetic, and overwhelming that it seems like a capital for East Asia.

Tokyo

Introduction & map **60–61**
Central Tokyo 62–65
Ginza-Hibiya-Yurakucho 68–70
Tsukudajima 71–73
Roppongi-Shiba-koen Park 76–77
Aoyama-Harajuku-Shibuya 78–85
Two walks through Shibuya-ku **80–81**
Shinjuku & Ikebukuro 86–89
Ueno 90–97
A walking tour of Ueno-Nezu-Yanaka **96–97**
Asakusa 102–104
More places to visit in central Tokyo **105**
Outlying districts of Tokyo **106**
Hotels & restaurants in Tokyo **361–65**

Reflection in a window of Tokyo FM Center

Tokyo

IN 1603 EDO, A FISHING HAMLET clustered around a crumbling castle, became the military capital, replacing Kyoto. By the 18th century it was already the largest city in the world; in the early 21st century Tokyo (its name since 1868) has a core population of over eight million.

Edo was built around a colossal castle (the Imperial Palace now stands on the site), with the ruling elite living within the walls; artisans, merchants, and the populace lived in the Low City *(shitamachi),* which extended eastward to the Sumida-gawa River.

Frequent fires meant that the wooden city had to be rebuilt many times. During the national closure (1637–1868), Edo was the cradle of Japanese urban culture. After 1868 it became the nucleus for Western influences and rapid modernization. It was the city of firsts—railroads, stone buildings, factories, gas, electricity, trams, and telephones.

Almost nothing of Edo remains, and most of older Tokyo was destroyed by the Great Kanto Earthquake in 1923 and incendiary bombs two decades later. Postwar reconstruction transformed Tokyo beyond recognition. As visitors approach the gray urban-industrial sprawl en route from Narita airport to downtown Tokyo, first impressions are grim. Vestiges of the wooden city sit dwarfed beneath towers of steel and glass. Tokyo suffers from a total lack of urban planning. Yet behind busy central thoroughfares and in the suburbs, quieter residential districts have their own temple, shrine, market, and main street, and many retain their old village atmosphere.

Beauty is not confined to the city's hundreds of museums and galleries but lies hidden away from the everyday bustle or comes as an adornment or detail. It is typically Japanese to conceal a hedonistic nature behind a bland, solemn exterior. Epicurean and sensual, Tokyo's amusement districts offer an exhaustive array of pleasures from sunset to dawn.

As echoes of the past resound in traditional neighborhoods such as Ueno and Asakusa, the future looms in the ambitious skyscraper developments closer to Tokyo Bay. ■

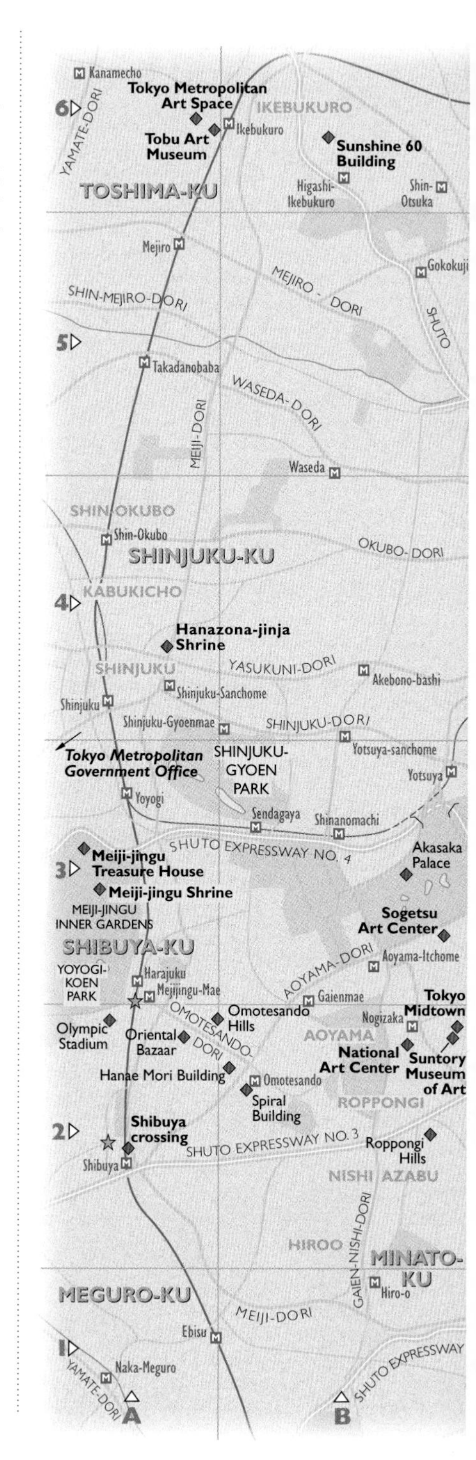

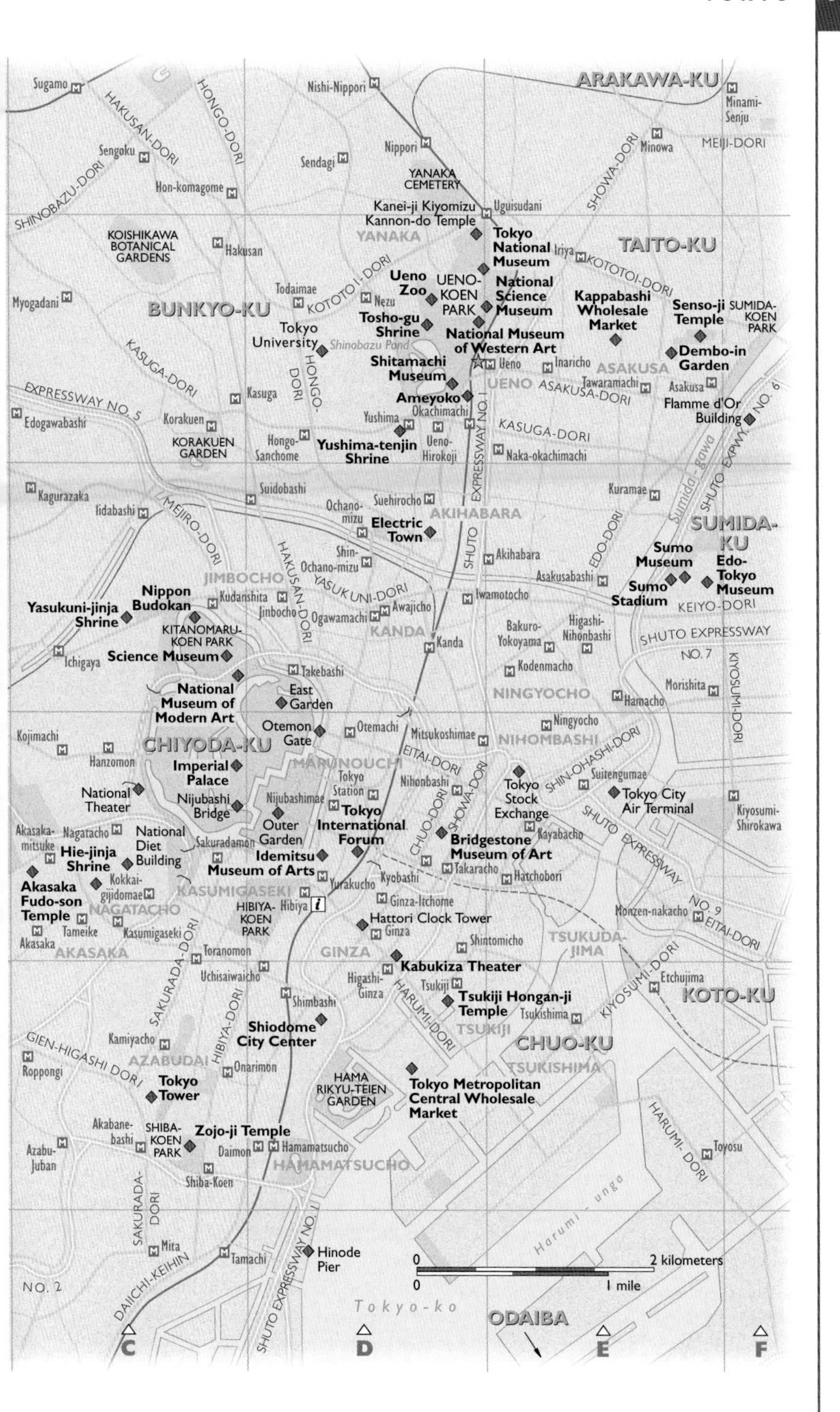
ARAKAWA-KU
TAITO-KU
BUNKYO-KU
SUMIDA-KU
CHIYODA-KU
CHUO-KU
KOTO-KU
Tokyo National Museum
National Science Museum
Ueno Zoo
Tosho-gu Shrine
National Museum of Western Art
Kappabashi Wholesale Market
Senso-ji Temple
Dembo-in Garden
Shitamachi Museum
Ameyoko
Yushima-tenjin Shrine
Flamme d'Or Building
Electric Town
Sumo Museum
Sumo Stadium
Edo-Tokyo Museum
Nippon Budokan
Yasukuni-jinja Shrine
Science Museum
National Museum of Modern Art
East Garden
Otemon Gate
Imperial Palace
National Theater
Nijubashi Bridge
Outer Garden
Tokyo International Forum
Idemitsu Museum of Arts
National Diet Building
Hie-jinja Shrine
Akasaka Fudo-son Temple
Tokyo Stock Exchange
Bridgestone Museum of Art
Tokyo City Air Terminal
Hattori Clock Tower
Kabukiza Theater
Tsukiji Hongan-ji Temple
Shiodome City Center
Tokyo Metropolitan Central Wholesale Market
Tokyo Tower
Zojo-ji Temple
Hinode Pier
ODAIBA
0 2 kilometers
0 1 mile
C D E F

Marunouchi, one of Tokyo's main business centers

Central Tokyo

Comprising Chuo-ku, Chiyoda-ku, and the north of Minato-ku, the center of Tokyo is given over mainly to administration (Kasumigaseki and Hibiya), business and finance (Marunouchi, Otemachi, and Nihombashi), and shopping at various focal points throughout. Aside from the Imperial Palace and some good museums, the tourist sights are few. The sedate streets of towering offices in Marunouchi at least afford a glimpse of the economic engine that drives Japan. At lunchtime Marunouchi business employees work off stress with a stroll in Hibiya-koen Park, near the Imperial Palace, a pleasant but unremarkable oasis of green. Despite wartime bombing and runaway modernism, some prewar Western-style buildings survive in the area, including the Bank of Japan and Tokyo Station.

The **Imperial Palace (Kokyo)** stands on the site of what was Edo-jo Castle, a crumbling 14th-century fortress magnificently restored by the shogun Tokugawa Ieyasu in the 1590s. By the mid-17th century it was the largest castle in the world, almost a walled city. The structures were burned down (notably during the Meireki Fire of 1657) and rebuilt several times. The castle was too dilapidated for Emperor Meiji to live in when he moved to Tokyo in 1868. He inhabited the Akasaka Detached Palace, pending the building of a new palace on the original castle site in 1888.

The new palace was destroyed during the bombing of 1945, and the present building was completed in 1968. The massive walls and surrounding moats are part of the original Edo-jo complex, as is the restored Otemon gate, which stands beyond the famous Nijubashi access bridge and before the East Garden, the actual site of Edo-jo. Elegantly landscaped with ponds and pines, the garden contains the ruins of Edo-jo and the 100 Guard Office, built in 1863—the last remaining original structure.

Within the garden is the Imperial Palace itself. It is open to the public only on January 2 and on

Imperial Palace Grounds

- 61 C3
- Chiyoda, Chiyoda-ku. (follow signs for correct exit)
- 03/3213-1111 ext. 485
- Garden only: closed Mon. & Fri., except during national holiday. Imperial Palace only open Dec 23 & Jan 2
- Free (plastic token handed to you on entry, returned on leaving)
- Subway: Hibiya, Nijubashimae, Tokyo; JR: Tokyo Station

Echoes of Edo

Edo lingers on in countless place-names. Marunouchi (meaning "inside the walls") was where the samurai elite lived. Ginza (seat of silver) gets its name from a long-vanished coinage mint. Akasaka (red hill) was once used for cultivating plants yielding a red dye. Edo continues too in certain neighborhood characteristics: Nihonbashi was the haunt of high finance in samurai days, and still is; and the site of the Yoshiwara licensed quarter, banned in 1957, is now the realm of "soapland" massage parlors.

Nihonbashi—the Bridge of Japan—was the starting point for measuring distances around the country. Here the main roads to the city converged, notably the old Tokaido road from Kyoto. Built in 1911, the present bridge is eclipsed by a tracery of overhead highways. Regardless of the layers of concrete, history remains almost eerily present in Tokyo. ■

Above: Birthday *banzais*—crowds greet the emperor on the Imperial Palace compound on December 23.

Kitanomaru-koen Park
- 61 C4
- Just south of Kudanshita subway station, a short walk from northern exit of Imperial Palace East Garden
- Subway: Kudanshita

National Museum of Modern Art
www.momat.go.jp
- 61 C4
- 3-1 Kitanomaru-koen, Chiyoda-ku
- 03/5777-8600
- 10 a.m–5 p.m. (open till 8 p.m. Fri.); closed Mon.
- $$
- Subway: Takebashi

the emperor's birthday (December 23), but huge crowds make this a grueling experience.

The Outer Palace Garden, within the outer moat to the south of the palace compound, is a public park. Unprepossessing except for an impressive view over Nijubashi bridge and the palace walls, it is popular with joggers, strollers from the nearby business districts, and courting couples.

Kitanomaru-koen Park, on the north side of the Imperial Palace grounds, is notable as the site of **Nippon Budokan** (*Tel 03/3216-5100),* a martial arts stadium now largely used as a venue for rock concerts, and for its museums. The **Science Museum (Kagaku Gijutsukan,** *2-1 Kitanomaru-koen, tel 03/3212-2440),* less than a quarter of a mile (300m) southeast, does not have the reputation of the national equivalent in Ueno, but hands-on exhibits make it a perennial favorite with schoolchildren.

The long-sleeve fire

Of Edo's many fires, the Great Meireki Fire of 1657 was the worst. The conflagration is also called *Furisode-no-kaji*—the long-sleeve fire. A legend attributed the cause to a *furisode*—a long-sleeve kimono—worn by a girl who pined to death because of unrequited love. According to former Buddhist custom, the kimono was given to a temple after her death. The priests sold it to another girl, who mysteriously sickened and died—a pattern that was repeated three times. The priests finally threw the furisode onto a brazier, but as it caught fire, a gust of wind sent it up to ignite the temple, causing the blaze that killed over 100,000 people and destroyed most of the city. ■

The **National Museum of Modern Art (Kokuritsu Kindai Bijutsukan),** which reopened in 2002 after extensive renovations, is to the right of the park entrance. This is one of Japan's finest modern art museums, with a substantial collection focusing on contemporary artists and tracing the major developments in Japanese art since the Meiji era in both traditional and Western styles. The museum is also Tokyo's prime venue for large retrospective exhibitions of such major Western artists as Edvard Munch, Henri Matisse, and Francis Bacon. The **Crafts Gallery (Kogeikan),** housed in the adjacent old Imperial Guard Headquarters of 1911, presents a fascinating array of exhibits showing the Japanese propensity for turning the most banal everyday objects into art. It includes ceramics, basketware, dolls, lacquerware, and metalwork.

Yasukuni-jinja Shrine, founded in 1869, honors the 2.5 million soldiers who died for their country during and since the Meiji era. The enshrinement of World War II criminals along with them has sparked bitter controversy both in Japan and abroad. However, war criminals are a minority among the soldiers honored and, as a place visited by families paying their respects to lost relatives, the shrine has great poignancy. The adjacent museum, **Yushukan,** contains military memorabilia and hardware, and is of historical interest. Despite its controversial reputation, Yasukuni is a favorite spot for viewing cherry blossoms in April. ■

A favorite Tokyo view in all seasons: Nijubashi Bridge spanning the Imperial Moat

Yasukuni-jinja Shrine

Map: 61 C4

Address: 3-1-1 Kudan-kita, Chiyoda-ku. 330 yards (300 m) due east of Ichigaya stations along Yasukuni-dori

Yushukan Museum

Tel: 03/3261-8326

Price: $$

Transport: Subway: Kudanshita

A modern look

Japan's architectural transformation from wood to reinforced concrete began in the late 19th century but really took off—and upward—with mass reconstruction during the postwar period. Much of Japan's architecture looks inspired by city-of-the-future features in sci-fi comic books of the 1950s, while the monster *danchi*—state apartment buildings—parallel Soviet architectural brutalism. With little urban planning, the astonishing heterogeneity of the urban environment, though frequently hideous, is enthralling in itself. Rickety wooden houses often stand wedged between structures of reinforced concrete; even Las Vegas could envy the palatial Chinese rococo architecture of the *onsen* (hot spring) resort, the neon-splashed *pachinko* (pinball) parlor, or the outrageous kitsch of the love hotel.

The soaring economy resulted in the *kenchiku bumu* (architecture boom), dragging a ruthless building spree in its wake through the 1980s. Most towns can boast a share of noteworthy modern buildings; Japanese contemporary architecture frequently incorporates traditional aesthetic concepts to great effect.

Foreign architects in Tokyo

The list of works by major architects in the capital reads like an international hall of fame, with Le Corbusier and Frank Lloyd Wright alongside homegrown architectural stars such as Tange Kenzo and Ando Tadao. A notable landmark is New York architect Rafael Viñoly's vast Tokyo International Forum Building in Yurakucho, completed in 1996—a kind of indoor city famous for its colossal glass atrium crossed by walkways (see p. 69). British architect Norman Foster's Century Tower was built in 1991 near Ochanomizu; U.S. architect Peter Eisenman was responsible for the Koizumi Lighting Theater and, out in Koiwa, a suburb of Tokyo, the strange Nunotani (NC) Building that looks as if it's about to fall apart; and Italian architect Renzo Piano designed the Kansai Airport Terminal (1994).

Responsible for a few of Tokyo's most surreal constructions, some foreign architects are more famous as such in Japan; at home they are designers. Britain's Nigel Coates made the Wall Building in Hiro—with a Roman facade embellished with scrap metal. In Asakusa, Frenchman Philippe Starck's quirky Flamme d'Or Building (1989) houses the Asahi Super Dry Beer Hall. Devised by premier developer Minoru Mori, the 29-acre (11.6 ha) Roppongi Hills complex (2003) in Azabu is a showcase for both domestic and international architects as well as for innovative urban green spaces.

Japanese modernism

The 1980s saw the rise of several important Japanese architects, notably Isozaki Arata (Shukosha Building, Fukuoka, Kyushu, 1974–75; Tokyo Globe Theater, 1988) and Osaka's extraordinary self-taught Ando Tadao (Rokko Housing One project, Kobe, 1983; La Collezione fashion building, Aoyama, Tokyo, 1989). The most universally famous is Tange Kenzo, noted first for his remarkable stadium buildings for the Tokyo Olympics in 1964 and, fronted with blue-tinted mirror glass, the Hanae Mori building (1977) on Tokyo's fashionable Omotesando-dori boulevard. Completed in 1991, Tange's colossal granite-and-glass Tokyo Metropolitan Government Office, a monumental blend of modernism and cathedral Gothic, is probably one of the most visited new buildings in Japan. It soars above western Shinjuku, where skyscrapers first emerged after the Tokyo Olympics. A great area for vertical architecture, Shinjuku is bleak at ground level; most people find the architecturally less remarkable eastern side of the district more colorful and congenial.

Not that all modern buildings in Tokyo are cold. Incorporating one of the city's best exhibition spaces and a restaurant-cum-auditorium, Maki Fumihiko's sweeping Spiral Building on Aoyama-dori is very much alive. With its sci-fi shapes, his extraordinary Tokyo Metropolitan Gymnasium is a 1990s answer to Tange's Olympic architecture of the 1960s. Imaginative, eclectic, and effective, Takahiko Yanagisawa's 1995 Museum of Contemporary Art, in Kiba-koen Park, was designed as an update on the old counterpart in Ueno. ■

Above: The Flamme d'Or Building, Asakusa, Tokyo. Below: Tokyo Metropolitan Government Office

Above: Fuji Television Building at Odaiba on Tokyo-wan Bay

Bright lights, big city—Ginza 4-chome crossing at night

Ginza-Hibiya-Yurakucho

During the late 19th century, Ginza became the showcase for Western-style development, with cafés and restaurants appearing in the wake of shops and department stores. Today Ginza is on a par with New York's Fifth Avenue, with many elegant shops standing on their ancestral sites. Among them is the Wako Building, a prewar landmark with a clock tower on Ginza 4-chome crossing—the heart of the district. Ginza's prosperity after World War II spread to Hibiya and Yurakucho.

New department stores and malls that appeared during the 1980s have given the district an air of mercantile futurism.

Ginza is also an entertainment district. The winking neon of small bars in Ginza backstreets may entice, but many of the exclusive hostess clubs are among the most expensive watering holes in the world. Not all of Ginza's wining and dining options are expensive; you'll find less costly options toward Hibiya and Yurakucho, even little beer-and-yakitori dives under the railroad tracks (see p.70).

The area is a nucleus for art galleries, with dozens between Ginza 1- to 4-chome and Kyobashi, and from Ginza 5- to 8-chome. The accent is on the contemporary—mainly Japanese but including some Western artists. Hibiya and Yurakucho contain scores of movie houses (many showing films in English), as well as other theaters.

A welcome cup of coffee and a relaxing break from Tokyo's fast pace of life

Sights in Ginza are varied, including museums of Japanese and Western art and a uniquely Japanese theater experience (see p. 70). **Idemitsu Museum of Arts (Idemitsu Bijutsukan),** covering 26,900 square feet (2,500 sq m), houses Tokyo's finest private collection of Japanese art and ceramics. The collection has pottery fragments from archaeological excavations all over Asia, and Chinese ceramics including Song-dynasty and T'ang-dynasty three-color ware, as well as fine antique Japanese pottery—Seto, Oribe, Kutani, Karatsu, and Kakiemon. The museum also features Zen calligraphy and ink painting, notably by the 17th-century monk Sengai.

Near Yurakucho Station is the embodiment of the indoor city of the future, **Tokyo International Forum.** It comprises a colossal atrium with interior walkways beneath a vast glass roof. Housing corporate offices, art galleries, concert and performance halls, restaurants, stores, and more, the Forum overwhelms not only for its grandeur, but for its sweeping spectrum of practical applications.

The **Sony Building** *(5-3-1 Ginza, Chuo-ku, tel 03/3573-2563)* at Sukiyabashi Crossing has all the electronics titan's latest gadgets and makes for a pleasant diversion from

A Ginza relic

The vast Sapporo Lion Ginza beer hall *(7-9-20 Ginza, Chuo-ku),* founded in 1934, retains its prewar decor down to the furnishings and art deco mosaics—but not its original home. Dismantled some 15 years ago, it was reassembled piece by piece in a modern building. Popular with the local business crowd, it's a great place to slake your thirst. ■

Idemitsu Museum of Arts

- Map: 61 D3
- Address: 9F Teigeki Building, 3-1-1 Marunouchi, Chiyoda-ku
- Phone: 03/3213-9402
- Hours: 10 a.m.–5 p.m. (open till 7 p.m. Fri.); closed Mon.
- Price: $$
- Transit: Subway: Hibiya, Yurakucho

A Tokyo landmark, the Kabuki-za is the country's foremost traditional playhouse.

Burijisuton Bijutsukan
www.bridgestone-museum.gr.jp
61 D3
2F Bridgestone Bldg., 1-10-1 Kyobashi, Chuo-ku
03/3563-0241
10 a.m–8 p.m. Tues.–Sat., 10 a.m.–6 p.m. Sun. & hols.; closed Mon.
$$
Subway: Kyobashi

sightseeing. Another good option if you want a break from walking outdoors is the **Bridgestone Museum of Art (Burijisuton Bijutsukan),** one of Tokyo's finest private art collections. Owned by Japan's foremost tire manufacturer, it specializes in major French Impressionists but also contains works by Modigliani and Picasso and some important old masters, including Rembrandt. It also focuses on *Yoga* (Japanese art in the Western tradition) and includes works by the Paris-based artist Tsuguji (or Léonard) Foujita (1886–1968).

Just outside Higashi-Ginza station, five minutes' walk along Harumi-dori from Ginza 4-chome crossing, is a Tokyo landmark that curiously blends Western and Japanese shrine architecture. The 1925 **Kabuki-za Theater** *(4-12-15 Ginza, Chuo-ku, tel 03/3541-3131)* vies with the National Theater in Nagatacho as Tokyo's premier location for Kabuki drama. The performances last about three hours. Drinks and snacks are sold in the foyer; you can also buy a ticket for a set *bento* (lunch box)—it will be served to you in the dining room downstairs during the interval. The cheapest seats are high up and farthest from the stage, so you might like to rent binoculars in the foyer, along with a taped commentary in English. ■

Hibiya under the tracks

After the war Hibiya retained some of the only stone buildings left standing in Tokyo, and it was here the Occupation authorities set up their headquarters in 1945. A legacy from black market days now popular with the office crowd, several stalls still do a thriving beer-and-yakitori (grilled chicken) business beneath a cavernous railroad archway just behind the Imperial Hotel (see Travelwise p. 361). ■

A warren of stores and eateries under the tracks

On Tokyo's periphery, working-class Tsukudajima remains much as it was in the early1900s.

Tsukudajima

On the north end of the islet of Tsukishima, off Tsukiji (now joined to the mainland by bridges), the area called Tsukudajima survived both the 1923 earthquake and World War II bombing. Despite some recent concrete redevelopments, many buildings along the main street and behind it retain an antiquarian charm and flavor. The charm comes notably from a view of the old fishing port from a humpbacked bridge, and the flavor from Tsukudajima's famous *tsukudani* (a popular condiment of fry—small fish—or seaweed preserved in sugar and soy) and its *monja-yaki.* Nevertheless, little has been done to preserve Tsukudajima. Ten'Yasu, one of the tsukudani manufacturers, has been in the same building for nearly 200 years, but much of the rest may soon be history.

Tuna aligned for early morning auction at the wholesale fish market in Tsukiji—the largest in the world

Tokyo Metropolitan Central Wholesale Market
www.tsukiji-market.or.jp
- 61 D2
- 5-2-1 Tsukiji, Chuo-ku
- 03/3541-2640
- Closed Sun. & hols., 2nd & 4th Weds.
- Subway: Tsukiji

Hamarikyu-teien Garden
- 61 D2
- 1-1 Hamarikyu Teien, Chuo-ku
- 03/3541-0200
- 9 a.m.–5 p.m.; closed Dec. 29–Jan. 3
- $

Boat trip to Asakusa
- $$
- Subway & JR: Shimbashi

One mile (2 km) southeast of the Imperial Palace, **Tokyo Metropolitan Central Wholesale Market (Chuo Oroshi-uri Ichiba)** in Tsukiji handles nearly all the meat and fish sold in the Kanto area (the whole region around Tokyo). This is a fascinating sight (though the professionals turning up for the auction at 5:20 a.m. might not agree). The auction is ostensibly closed to the public, but a discreet glimpse is usually overlooked.

It makes sense to get there early, as most of the action is over by 7 a.m. Next to the main hangar is the Tsukiji Outer Market, a dense cluster of wholesale and retail stores selling fish on ice or dried, as well as a wealth of other food products. Although none of the ramshackle wooden stalls is truly old, they suggest a market from a bygone age. The bustling activity can be a little overwhelming in narrow alleys packed with shoppers, porters, and forklift trucks, but the strong (and pungent) dose of local color is unforgettable. For workers and visitors alike, the highlight of Tsukiji is a superfresh sushi breakfast in one of the market's several small restaurants.

On your way to the Tsukiji market, you will probably pass a curious Buddhist temple. **Tsukiji Hongan-ji Temple** *(3-15-1 Tsukuji, Chuo-ku, outside Tsukiji subway station)* was built in 1935 to replace a 17th-century original destroyed in the 1923 earthquake. It was designed to evoke the classical Indian temple style by the

celebrated architect Ito Chuta. Its sheer strangeness makes it a worthy landmark.

South of Ginza, and a ten-minute stroll from the fish market, is **Hamarikyu-teien Garden.** Turned into a landscaped pleasure garden in 1709 from reclaimed land owned by the shoguns, the garden fell into disuse following damage in one of the city's great fires. It passed to the Imperial Household Agency in 1869, and became the Detached Palace Garden. Graced with a lavish Western-style pavilion, it was used for entertaining foreign dignitaries, among them Gen. Ulysses S. Grant.

Today the pavilion is gone, replaced by attractive teahouses. Although Hamarikyu's horizons are walled off by high-rise buildings, it remains a fine landscape garden and an elegant haven of green in a distinctly ungreen area of Tokyo. Hamarikyu is a stop on the boat trip on the Sumida-gawa between Hinode pier (near Hamamatsucho) and Asakusa. Boats pass roughly every half hour. ■

Hamarikyu-teien Garden is a landscaped oasis in a highly urban neighborhood.

The water trade—Japan after dark

The origin of the term *mizu shobai* (the water trade) is endlessly debated. The more prosaic interpretation is that the "water" is simply the alcohol upon which the trade floats; the more poetic is that the business reflects the impermanence of life itself. The ancestor of today's mizu shobai was the *ukiyo*—the Floating World, a name ascribed to the pleasure quarters in major towns during the 17th century.

The focus on prostitution in the ukiyo was greater than in the mizu shobai but, like today's amusement districts, the old pleasure quarters boasted a whole gamut of other entertainments—especially of a bibulous kind. The quarters declined during the 19th century with the rise of more general amusement districts elsewhere; the word "ukiyo" simply died with them.

During the postwar period, Tokyo's greatest emerging amusement district was Shinjuku. Although prostitution flourished there, Shinjuku really took off when racketeers erected rows of ramshackle drinking dives in the rubble east of the train station in 1946. Bars, already popular as "cafés" during the 1920s, were all the rage in Japan during the 1950s. The traditional *nomiya* (drinking shop), with its red paper lantern outside, now had a serious rival. The tone was ostensibly American. Sporting Western fashions, the girls enticing customers to drink were hostesses, and the owners of the establishment were *mama-san* and/or *masutaa* (master). These characters, the mainstays of the mizu shobai, signaled the demise of the teahouses and the geisha of prewar times, as their establishments increased in numbers, standing, and price.

Hostess bars are fewer since the recession, especially in Ginza, but remain for the most part exorbitantly expensive. A small minority traffic in prostitution, but not the better clubs. Hostess bars are often luxuriously appointed, but the experience generally holds little appeal for Westerners. A bevy of pretty girls (including exotic and popular Caucasians) in designer dresses cajole and flatter the tired salaryman's ego, pouring drinks and lighting cigarettes. They will also sing karaoke duets with him, often to the strains of the house combo. There may be flirtatious banter, but nothing more. Hostesses are very good at arousing a customer's desire, so that he keeps coming back—mostly in vain. There are exceptions, however, and those—like the geisha—are fishing for a wealthy *danna* (master) to keep them as a *mekake* (mistress) or rarely a wife.

All bars and many nomiya have a system called bottle-keep. On your first visit you buy a bottle of liquor (usually whisky), which is replaced on the shelf with your name on it—yours to drink from when you come back next time. If you are sharing with friends and/or planning to come back, the system can be very economical.

Things are seldom what their English name implies. A hostess bar is usually called a club *(kurabu),* which it may be, and sometimes supper club, which it is not. Be wary of piano bars, for some keep hostesses. If one sits at your table, you will be charged accordingly.

Another postwar bar legacy is the misnamed *sunakku* (snack), the hostess bar's poorer relative. Most popular in the countryside, sunakku are generally variants of the ubiquitous karaoke bar. The majority are harmless, but some are seriously sleazy; generally sunakku are best avoided unless you are taken by friends. In fact, this is the general rule for smaller bars in the mizu shobai. If a bar is inconspicuously hidden behind a thick door, the chances are that patrons have been introduced; wandering in unaccompanied feels a bit like intruding in a private living room. In a sense, it is. Home is not usually the place for socializing in Japan; the bar, presided over by a mama-san who knows all her customers by name, makes a handy substitute.

Until as recently as 15 years ago, frequenting the mizu shobai was a male preserve. However, "host clubs" for women are getting popular in areas like Shinjuku's Kabuki-cho. ■

Left: Blazing signs in Kabukicho
Above: *Mama-san:* the mainstay of the Japanese bar
Below: A drink with colleagues after work is the usual conclusion to the working day.

Life and art intersect in Rippongi Hills, where Louise Bourgeois' "Maman" looms tall.

Roppongi-Shiba-koen Park

As foreign embassies multiplied in the area during the 1950s, Roppongi developed, along with nearby Azabu and Hiro, as a residential district for expatriates. Renowned then as now for its foreign restaurants, it became a favorite with Japanese as the hub of Western-style entertainment. Today its many restaurants include some of Tokyo's best, offering a staggering array of both world and Japanese cuisine.

Roppongi rivaled Shinjuku for its proliferation of discos in the late 1970s and became one of Tokyo's most fashionable districts during the 1980s. Although still cosmopolitan and sophisticated, in recent years it has exploded as an entertainment district as raucous as any. In the process it has become more tacky here and there, but for the visitor it remains one the best and most accessible options for a fun night out in Tokyo.

Roppongi

Roppongi means "six trees," but the area is hardly renowned for its greenery today. If Roppongi seems too turbulent at night, follow the overhead expressway down to Nishi Azabu Crossing, where the backstreets on the left abound with quieter bars and restaurants. ■

During the development frenzy of the 1950s, Tokyo had to have its Eiffel Tower. Devised for radio/TV transmission, the 1,092-foot (330 m) **Tokyo Tower** *(www.tokyotower.co.jp)* was erected in 1958 on land that had belonged to **Shiba Koen Park.** Then cherished, it is now widely seen as blighting the cityscape. However, improved lighting has turned it into a surprisingly attractive feature of the nocturnal skyline. A fine Tokyo panorama is visible from the top observation platform, but the other levels, including a dusty wax museum and an aquarium, are only for lovers of things kitsch and passé.

Zozo-ji Temple was moved to what is now Shiba Koen in 1598, where it was the centerpiece of a vast temple city. Razed and rebuilt more than once, Zojo-ji has had a tumultuous history. After being torched during the Meiji Restoration, it was burned by a vagrant in 1909 before being destroyed during World War II. The *sanmon* (two-storied) gate, built in 1605, is a miraculous and magnificent survivor. One of the very few buildings of such antiquity in Tokyo, it is designated an Important Cultural Property. The main hall, built in 1974, contains several treasures, including the huge old temple bell.

Another survivor is the Nitenmon gate, which now stands on land belonging to the Tokyo Prince Hotel *(3-3-1 Shiba-koen, Minato-ku, tel 03/3432-1111);* other parts of the compound, including the old Tokugawa burial ground, now find themselves within the confines of a private golf club.

The **Roppongi Hills complex** (see p. 66), completed in 2003, finds titanic residential/office towers set in pleasant green spaces —a new, futuristic urban planning concept offering an impressive array of options for culture, entertainment, shopping, and dining.

The rooftop **Mori Art Museum** *(6-10-1 Roppongi, Minato-ku, tel. 03/5777-8600)* here showcases contemporary international art and is at the southern tip of the Art Triangle Roppongi, a trio of museums. Its other points are the relocated **Suntory Museum of Art** *(9-7-4 Akasaka, Minato-ku, tel. 03/3479-8600),* which has an outstanding collection of laquerware, painting and ceramics, in the new Tokyo Midtown complex, and the excellent, recently opened **National Art Center, Tokyo** *(7-22-2 Roppongi, Minato-ku, tel. 03/5777-8600),* which has no permanent collection but focuses on exhibitions. Information about Art Triangle Roppangi can be found online at www.mori.art.museum. ■

A monk rings the huge bell at Zojo-ji Temple.

Tokyo Tower

- Map: 61 C2
- Address: 4-2-8 Shiba-koen, Minato-ku. 550 yards (500 m) due south of Kamiya-cho subway station
- Tel: 03/3433-5111
- Hours: 9 a.m.–10 p.m.
- Price: $$
- Subway: Kamiya-cho

Zojo-ji Temple

www.zojoji.or.jp

- Map: 61 C2
- Address: 4-7-35 Shiba-koen, Minato-ku. About 550 yards (500 m) from Daimon (east), Shiba-koen (south), & Onarimon (north) subway stations
- Tel: 03/3432-1431
- Hours: Dawn to dusk
- Subway: Daimon, Shiba-koen, Onarimon

A salesperson at Beams in the Harajuku district arranges T-shirts.

Aoyama-Harajuku-Shibuya

Shibuya-ku (the ward as opposed to its central area described in the walk on pp. 82–83) as a whole covers a wide area embracing Yoyogi-koen Park, the youthful Harajuku district, the Meiji-jingu Shrine, Tokyo's most fashionable shopping precincts, and some notable museums. The Aoyama area has been the home of international chic since the mid-1970s; renowned for its expensive big-name designer boutiques, one street has been facetiously named "Killer dori." The area abounds with interesting galleries and exhibition spaces devoted mainly to modern art, and notable exhibitions are often held in some of Tokyo's finest examples of modern architecture, among them Maki Fumihiko's remarkable Spiral Building on Aoyama-dori. Kotto-dori (Antiques Street) has many outstanding antiques shops, but no bargains.

A broad, tree-lined boulevard running from Aoyama-dori to Harajuku, **Omotesando-dori** is one of Tokyo's most pleasant locales. Relax in Parisian-style cafés; explore stylish boutiques in the sleek Hanae Mori Building or the lunatic fringes of teen fashion in Harajuku and narrow Takeshita-dori. Midway along Omotesando is the Oriental Bazaar—perennial place for quality souvenirs and affordable antiques.

A controversial development project demolished some of Omotesando's older buildings, but architect Tadao Ando's Omotesando Hills complex (2005) is designed for minimal impact. On Sundays, youth flock to Jingu-bashi Bridge by Harajuku Station to flaunt their neo-gothic fashions.

The 133 acres (54 ha) of **Yoyogi-koen Park** became a park when the buildings, erected for U.S. Occupation staff, were demolished; it is now a wooded and pleasant place for strolling. It was also the main site of the 1964 Tokyo Olympics, as Tange Kenzo's amazing stadium buildings testify.

Like Tokyo's other major districts, Shibuya grew up around a major railroad terminal. Shibuya station developed rapidly after the

(continued on p. 83)

Yoyogi-koen Park
60 A3

Sundays find various youthful groups, musical and otherwise, congregating in Yoyogi-koen Park—including Rockabillies.

Two walks through Shibuya-ku

Sights tend to be scattered in Shibuya but, as a rule of thumb, the southwestern part is mainly concerned with shopping and entertainment and the northwestern sector, though it has no shortage of shops either, focuses on the Meiji-jingu Shrine and surrounding parkland.

WALK 1: SHIBUYA

Start from Hachiko Square. Standing in front of the intersection with your back to the station, you will see 109 Building (a cylinder with 109 emblazoned on the front) standing on a sharp corner to your left. Cross straight over into Koen-dori in front of you and 100 yards (90 m) up on your left is **Seibu** ❶ department store (see p. 381). The store sells everything imaginable but is particularly strong on fashion. Next turn left into the narrow street between Seibu's two buildings on Koen-dori and then take the first right behind the right-hand one.

Next turn left and left again into Koen-dori. Take a break from the stores 220 yards (200 m) up the street in the **Tobacco & Salt Museum (Tabako to Shio no Hakubutsukan)** ❷**.** Love or hate tobacco, it has a long and colorful history. Exhibiting aspects of world salt and tobacco lore from Mayan times, the museum is also notable for Edo-period woodblock prints on smoking themes.

Retracing your steps along Koen-dori will bring you to Parco 2 on your right on the next corner and the main Parco just across the road from it. Having turned right into this road (Inokashira-dori); keep walking until you reach Tokyu Hands (see p. 382). Turn left into the small street that runs down from Inokashira-dori along the side of the building and keep going straight. The array of shops and boutiques along here is a foretaste of the nucleus of Shibuya's youthful fashion and café culture. Center Gai is a narrow pedestrian street that you reach by crossing over the next intersection.

Turning left along here will bring you back to the station and crossing over it will bring you into Bunkamura-dori, level with **One-Oh-Nine** ❸**,** a "fashion building." Exit onto Bunkamura-dori and return to 109 Building, notable above all for one of Shibuya's most curious sights: a small wooden traditional restaurant sticking out of the concrete wall. The proprietor stood his ground against the developers, so they built 109 around him.

Turning sharp right here will take you to Dogen-zaka—a sloping street with bars and restaurants proliferating in the alleys on both sides. They constitute Shibuya's main entertainment district—not a bad place to wind up the day. Alternatively, if you're traveling with kids, a final destination for walks or a break between them is the **National Children's Castle (Kodomo no Shiro,** see p. 363) ❹. Easily identifiable by Okamoto Taro's weird, multicolored, totemlike sculpture outside, this is kiddie heaven: a giant activity center on several floors, including play areas and facilities for painting, handicrafts, computer games, and video, as well as a hotel for families.

WALK 2: AOYAMA-HARAJUKU

Start at JR Harajuku Station. Enter the path on your left (signposted in English) leading up to Meiji-jingu Shrine (see p. 85). After 220 yards (200 m) you will come to the entrance to the **Meiji-jingu Inner Gardens** ❶**;** always a lovely park, it's truly unmissable when the irises bloom in June. Continue along the same path to **Meiji-jingu Shrine** ❷**.** After your visit, retrace your steps to Harajuku Station. Turn left and after 160 yards (150 m) you'll find, on your right, narrow Takeshita-dori—a famed teenage shopping alley. At the end of the alley you'll reach the intersection with Meiji-dori. Turn right and walk on down the avenue toward the next intersection. The cream-colored building with the cylindrical facade on your right is Laforet Harajuku, with boutiques inside.

Just behind the Laforet building is the **Ota Memorial Museum of Art (Ota Kinen Bijutsukan)** ❸ *(1-10-10 Jingumae, tel 03/3403 0880, closed Mon. and from 27th to end of each month).* The Ota collection of 12,000 *ukiyo-e* prints is probably the largest privately

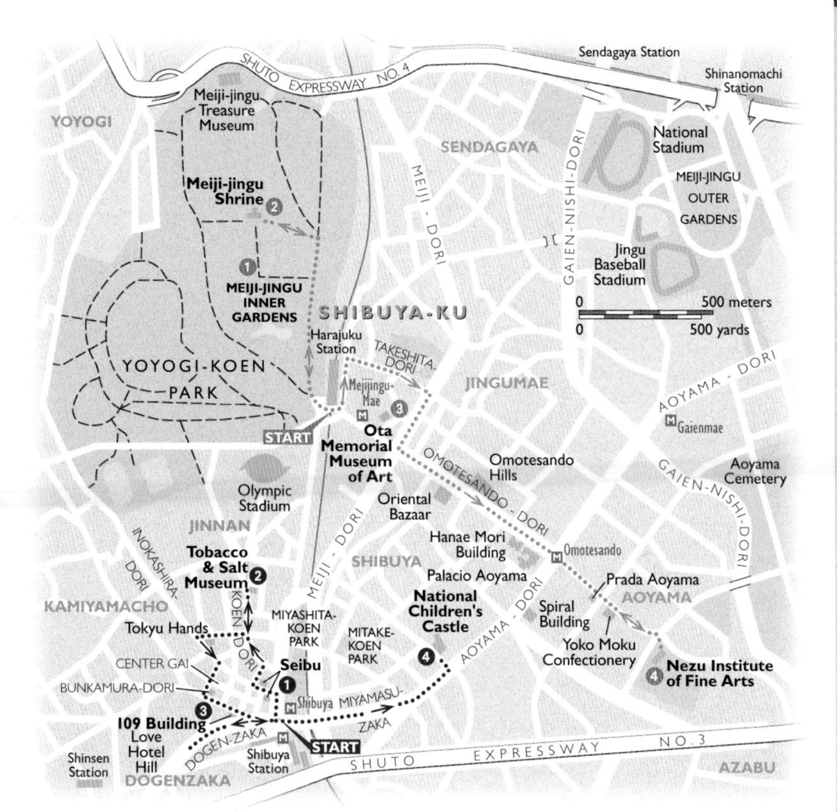

owned in Japan. The museum is beautifully laid out in Japanese style, with a small rock garden and a tea room downstairs.

Make your way down Meiji-dori again to the intersection and turn left down Omotesando-dori. After a further 160 yards (150 m), on the right-hand side of the street you will find several stores for souvenir shopping. Nearly 400 yards (350 m) farther on is architect Tange Kenzo's elegant Hanae Mori building, which contains antique stores in the basement, l'Orangerie restaurant, and fashion designer Hanae Mori's flagship store. From here, cross over the intersection with Aoyama-dori and walk some 550 yards (500 m) to the **Nezu Institute of Fine Art (Nezu Bijutsukan)** 4 *(6-5-36 Minami, tel 03/3400 2536, under renovation).* Located in a quiet residential district, this notable museum stands in a delightful Japanese garden replete with ponds and teahouses (still used for tea ceremonies). Despite its small size, the museum boasts one of the country's finest collections of Japanese (as well as Chinese and Korean) classical and Buddhist art, including the famed 17th-century screen painting of irises by Ogata Korin. Walking backward toward Aoyama-dori, you'll pass an elegant blue-and-white-tiled building on your left. It's the Yoku Moku confectionery—a premium coffee stop, and almost opposite the Issey Miyake boutique. ■

See area map pp. 60–61
Walk 1
➤ Hachiko Square
2.5 miles (4 km)
2 hours
➤ Dogen-zaka
Walk 2
➤ Harajuku Station
1.7 miles (2.8 km)
2 hours
➤ Aoyama-dori

Left: A monk receiving alms from a youthful benefactor outside Harajuku Station on New Year's Day. Right: An avant-garde kimono presentation on an Aoyama catwalk

Meiji-jingu Shrine
www.meijijingu.or.jp
- 60 A3
- 1-1 Kamizono-cho, Yoyogi, Shibuya-ku. Just west of stations
- 03/3379-5511
- Dawn to dusk; Treasure House 9 a.m.–4:30 p.m., closes at 4 p.m. Nov.–Mar.
- Grounds free; inner gardens $$; Treasure House $$
- Subway: Meiji-jingu-mae; JR: Harajuku

TEMPLES & SHRINES
All temples in Japan are Buddhist and all shrines are Shinto. Temples and shrines are usually part of a complex; the area covered by a complex can be extensive (see p. 246).

(continued from p. 79)
1923 earthquake, when many people moved to the area from devastated Asakusa, and it is the commuter gateway between the capital and the western suburbs out to Yokohama. Like other station areas, it has sprouted an amusement quarter.

From the end of the 1970s, Shibuya's Seibu and Parco department stores established themselves as the harbingers of high fashion. When nearby Harajuku became the city's prime teenage hangout, Shibuya took the overflow, especially on the narrow Center Gai street opposite the station. The trendy bars, cafés, and boutiques spread out from here over a decade; often dubbed *yangu taun* (young town) in the 1980s, Shibuya remains the ultimate mecca of fashion and culture for the under-25s.

Among the fashionable department stores is the remarkable Tokyu Hands (see p. 382); several floors are exhaustively devoted to home crafts and do-it-yourself projects. Pioneered by the Seibu conglomerate, the area abounds in theaters, movie houses, and exhibition spaces. The rival Tokyu corporation's impressive Bunkamura (culture village) presents facets of contemporary culture, including films, theater, and art exhibits, in a single building.

Straddling Shibuya and Harajuku, and just south of Shinjuku, is Tokyo's greatest shrine, **Meiji-jingu Shrine,** which commemorates Emperor Meiji, whose reign saw the momentous passage from feudal to modern Japan. Construction began in 1915, a year after the death of the emperor's wife, Empress Shoken, and was completed in 1920.

The shrine was destroyed during World War II but was rebuilt in 1958, exactly as before, standing in a broad courtyard with characteristically sweeping architecture of unadorned cypress wood beneath a splendid roof of copper tiles. With a fine cloister hung with bronze lanterns adjoining the main hall, this is Tokyo's most impressive shrine. The main approach behind Harajuku, a shaded avenue of majestic camphor trees, features at the entrance a towering *torii*

Above: Like colored streams, iris beds meander through Meiji-jingu Inner Gardens in June. Right: At New Year, thousands buy lucky *hama-ya* ("evil breaking") arrows.

gateway made of gigantic cypress trees from Taiwan.

Noh and kagura (see p. 46) performances are held in the shrine courtyard on Emperor Meiji's birthday (November 3). Meiji-jingu is Tokyo's most popular shrine for observances over the New Year holiday, when its visitors number around a million.

Mainly of interest to history buffs, the **Meiji-jingu Treasure House (Homotsuden)** displays a collection of state costumes and miscellaneous items belonging to Emperor Meiji, including the imperial carriage. *(Follow signs from the shrine's Harajuku entrance, closed 3rd Fri. each month.)*

The beautiful 150-acre (60 ha) **Meiji-jingu Inner Gardens (Meiji-jingu-gyoen,** *entrance on the left, about halfway along main approach to the shrine)* is noted for its lily pond in summer and its 126,000 trees, contributed from all over Japan when the garden was created in 1920.

Much cherished by the Meiji emperor and empress, the iris garden is particularly lovely in June, when displays of hundreds of varieties bloom along a broad serpentine bed. ■

Above right: A Shinto priest at Meiji-jingu Shrine wielding a paper wand protects the faithful from evil.

Shrine and temple merchandise

During festivals, large Shinto shrine and Buddhist temple compounds look like markets. Stalls sell delicacies such as *tako yaki* (barbecued octopus dumplings) and fried noodles, as well as toffee apples, candy, cheap toys, and souvenirs. The main buildings trade briskly in religious trinkets, notably key-ring size *mamori* (talismans) against misfortune, as well as *omikuji* (fortune papers). For around 100 yen you pull a numbered stick out of an oblong box and are given the paper with the corresponding number. Rolled up, the paper is tied to a tree (the right one is the one festooned with fortune papers) to enhance good fortune and, hopefully, avert the bad. ■

Shinjuku & Ikebukuro

Shinjuku means "new inn," after the taverns that sprouted here in the late 17th century, when the area became the post town nearest to Edo along the road out toward the Japan Alps. The township rapidly grew and soon came to include a large unlicensed red-light district—as indeed it still does. Respectability came with the building of Shinjuku Station in 1885, now one of the busiest train terminals on Earth. Less damaged than other areas after the 1923 earthquake, Shinjuku became the hub of Tokyo.

After the Olympics in 1964, Shinjuku took off—mostly upward—as the "new heart of Tokyo." Starting with the Keio Plaza Hotel, completed in 1972, the western side of Shinjuku developed a forest of skyscrapers. Tange Kenzo's new Tokyo Metropolitan Government Office became the colossal centerpiece in 1991. Combining plush hotels, official buildings, shopping areas, a lovely park, and a raucous amusement district, the marvelous eclecticism of Shinjuku is archetypically Japanese.

Ikebukuro is another station area to the north of Shinjuku, with an amusement district like the latter's Kabuki-cho (but shabbier). Devoid of sights, Ikebukuro is a notable shopping heaven and has recently gained attention for its exhibition spaces and cultural venues.

Hanazono-jinja Shrine

- 60 A4
- 5-17-3 Shinjuku, Shinjuku-ku
- 03/3200-3093
- Dawn to dusk

Below: Shinjuku's brash, Kabuki-cho amusement district

Right: Decorative rakes for sale at the Tori-no-Ichi festival at Hanazono-jinja Shrine

EAST SHINJUKU

Make sure you leave plenty of time if you catch a train at Shinjuku Station: Getting lost in the crowded station labyrinth is something that happens even to the locals. Exits from the subway lines lead straight into a gigantic underground shopping mall, and the surges of people in every direction at rush hour merely add to the general confusion above ground.

Anywhere else, **Kabuki-cho** in East Shinjuku would be sin city, but the Japanese do not believe in sin. As in other amusement districts, all the facets of pleasure exist here cheek by jowl: eating, drinking, movies, game arcades, and sex. Out of some 3,000 entertainment outlets, the 500 devoted to sleaze are signaled by tuxedoed touts in doorways or skimpily-clad *kanban gyaru*—signpost girls—enticing customers inside. The streets, a kaleidoscope of electric signs and blazing neon, are lined with speakers blaring recorded come-ons and deafening music. Full of garish *pachinko* (pinball) parlors, this is a capital of kitsch; it even has a reproduction of Rome's Trevi Fountain lit in green neon.

With so many great restaurants and thousands of bars, about 500,000 visitors flock here every night; at the long evening's end pub-crawling salarymen totter through the streets, propping each other up. The party extends beyond Kabuki-cho northward and on to Shin Okubo, a kind of little Southeast Asia renowned for both its superb ethnic restaurants and the loose ladies lurking in the alleyways. Though Kabuki-cho is perfectly safe, some caution is advisable in the backstreets when the crowds thin much later on.

Heading west, **Hanazono-jinja Shrine** provides a pleasant retreat from the sheer lunacy of nearby Kabuki-cho. Dedicated to Inari, the deity of gain and grain, the shrine was moved to its present site during the 17th century. The otherwise rather unprepossessing shrine comes into its own during Tori-no-Ichi—the chicken festival—on November 3 (see p. 38).

Shinjuku National Garden *(11 Naito-cho, Shinjuku-ku, tel 03/3350-0151, closed Mon.)* belonged to the regional governor of Naito during the Edo period, then to the imperial family, before becoming a public park after World War II. Lying to the southeast of Shinjuku, this is not only one of the city's largest parks at about 150 acres (60 ha), but it is also one of the most beautifully landscaped, with substantial sections devoted to both Japanese- and Western-style gardens. Its 1,900 cherry trees make it a highly popular location for blossom viewing in April. The view of skyscrapers over the greenery is a favorite with amateur painters.

A custom-detailed Volkswagen Bug serves as a lure at one of Shinjuku's many electronic stores.

WEST SHINJUKU

Leaving Shinjuku Station by the west exit places you in a very different world from the vibrant east side. Beneath the soaring towers lies a popular warren of cut-price camera stores (as do Shibuya and Ikebukuro). Awe-inspiring as the tall buildings are, they are utterly devoid of anything so prosaic as human warmth. That said, Tange Kenzo's impressive 797-foot (243 m) **Tokyo Metropolitan Government Office,** completed

Pachinko

Ablaze with colored neon, rural pachinko parlors can sometimes be seen for miles over the paddies; in cities their garish architecture can ruin a neighborhood. Pachinko (from *pachin*, slap, and *ko*, a ball) took off during the 1950s. In this vertical pin-ball game, hundreds of ball bearings clatter along the pins and traps on the machine's gaudy face as, immobile and mesmerized, customers spend hours twiddling a knob with one hand. The knob fires the balls: Success requires skill and luck.

There is a pachinko culture with tales of little old ladies eking out an existence playing the game. There is even a profession of "pin straighteners," whose job consists of straightening the pins on the machine face to prevent bending from ostensible overuse.

Prizes include cookies and cigarettes, often exchanged (but don't tell anyone) for cash through a backstreet pigeonhole. Pachinko profits top the entire service industry in Japan. ■

Players in a pachinko parlor

The towers of Tange Kenzo's impressive Tokyo Metropolitan Government Office dominate the Shinjuku skyline.

in 1991 and inspired by European cathedrals, is a must-see. It boasts one of the best views in Tokyo, with Mt. Fuji often visible from the twin observatories topping its towers at 202 meters.

However, for panoramic views at night, it is hard to beat the one from the nearby Keio Plaza Hotel's delightful bar, the Little Bear, where the twinkling city lights match the low lighting glinting on the bottles.

IKEBUKURO

Ikebukuro is another major terminal station area, serving commuters to the northwest. Near the station, its amusement district has long been a shabbier relative of Shinjuku's Kabuki-cho. To the east is the colossal **Sunshine 60 Building,** part of the Sunshine City complex; most of its 60 stories are devoted to offices, but several contain restaurants and shopping malls. It stands on the site of Sugamo prison, where war criminals such as Tojo Hideki were executed. Ikebukuro continues to rise as a shopping district: The Seibu and Tobu department stores on the east side are among the world's largest. Not to be outdone, the west side of Ikebukuro has recently risen to prominence with two gigantic malls, the Metropolitan Plaza and Spice 2.

Culture is Ikebukuro's rising star, enhanced recently with the multiple theaters in the **Tokyo Metropolitan Art Space,** the new headquarters of the prestigious Tokyo Metropolitan Orchestra. Despite this and its variety of shopping options, Ikebukuro remains strangely colorless, an also-ran in the race to excel as one of the great Tokyo districts. ■

Tokyo Metropolitan Government Office
www.metro.tokyo.jp
Map: 60 A3
Address: 2-8-1, Nishi-Shinjuku, Shinjuku-ku
Tel: 03/5321-1111
Observatories: 03/5320-7890
Hours: 9:30 a.m.–11 p.m., closed Mon.; North Tower deck closed 2nd & 4th Mon.; South Tower deck closed 1st & 3rd Tues.

Ikebukuro
Map: 60 B6

Sunshine 60 Building
Map: 60 B6
Address: 3-1-3 Higachi-Ikebukuro
Tel: 03/3989-3331

Tokyo Metropolitan Art Space
www.geigeki.jp
Address: 1-8-1 Nishi-Ikebukuro
Tel: 03/5391-2111

Ueno-koen Park has long been a favored location for *hanami* (flower-viewing) picnics.

Ueno

Ueno Hill (now Ueno-koen Park), scattered with shrines and temples erected by the Tokugawa shoguns and famous for its cherry trees, was the spot favored by aristocrats for *hanami*—blossom viewing. The site of the only significant (and futile) battle resisting the Meiji Restoration, the hill was a stronghold for some 2,000 Tokugawa loyalists trounced by the country's first modern army in 1867. The fleeing survivors torched the buildings of the Tokugawa's Kanei-ji Temple complex in order to deny their use to their conquerors, but they fortunately overlooked Tosho-gu Shrine, dedicated to Tokugawa Ieyasu himself (see below).

The hill area became the city's first public park in 1873 and was used for popular national exhibitions; the art gallery built for the second exhibition in 1892 was the ancestor of the Tokyo National Museum.

Ueno-koen Park contains outstanding museums, Tosho-gu Shrine, temples, Ueno Zoo, and Shinobazu Pond, which is particularly delightful in summer, but the areas of greenery seem fragmented and neglected. All this makes the park a representative centerpiece for the entire district, which presents a curious mixture of things old and venerable and others not quite so old and rather shabby.

With the development of railways, Ueno Station increased in importance after the start of the 20th century as the gateway to northern Japan. Following the devastation of World War II, the station area found many thousands of homeless Tokyoites sheltering under the elevated tracks. Since the 1950s the area has attracted a large number of poor farmers from Northern Honshu (Tohoku); they would leave their snowbound fields in winter to seek employment in Tokyo—often in vain. Although Tohoku's greater prosperity later reduced their number, the Ueno area is still haunted by the homeless.

Hanami

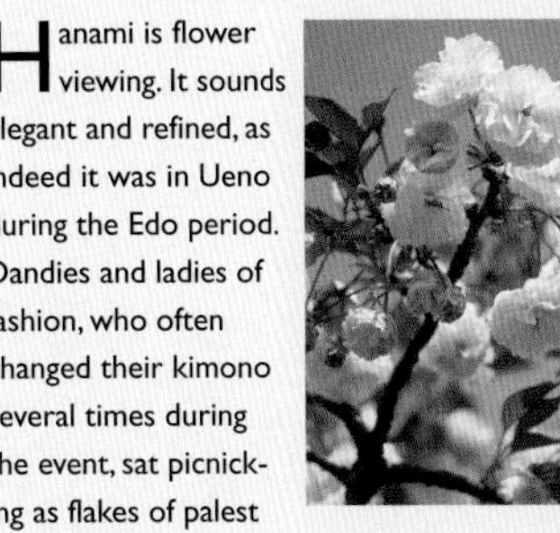

Hanami is flower viewing. It sounds elegant and refined, as indeed it was in Ueno during the Edo period. Dandies and ladies of fashion, who often changed their kimono several times during the event, sat picnicking as flakes of palest pink fell from the resplendent blossoming cherry trees above them.

Today hanami parties are enjoyed all over Japan. After spreading plastic sheeting beneath the trees, flower watchers—often in the thousands—sit down to a substantial sushi picnic washed down with copious sake and beer. Foreign observers will often be entreated to join the fray; afterwards they might feel as the parks look—littered with picnic wreckage and trampled blossoms.

People travel to some 60 prominent hanami sites around Japan from early April in southern Honshu to mid-May in Hokkaido. For springtime travelers to Japan, hanami is a must-see. Torrential rain is no deterrent: Flower-viewing parties simply sit under their umbrellas. ■

Many visitors to Ueno are northern daytrippers; the area accordingly is filled with department stores and shopping options to suit all budgets. The district includes a rather seedy if spirited entertainment area, but tucked away in the streets just below the park are some vintage restaurants and shops that make Ueno one of Tokyo's most fascinating areas. Less than 20 minutes from Ginza on the Hibiya or Ginza subway lines, Ueno could hardly present a greater contrast to that district's glitz.

Today's colorful **Ameyoko market,** alongside Ueno Station, is a legacy of the black market that thrived in the immediate postwar period. The name is short for Ameya-yokocho (Candy Store Alley), so called after the candy stalls that were often fronts for other goods—especially those made in the United States—sold by black marketeers.

This is Tokyo's liveliest market and the last with something of the flavor of an Asian bazaar. Stalls sell jeans of every known brand and configuration, aloha shirts, leather jackets, bags, and sneakers next door to dried squid and bonito flakes, groceries, and fresh fish. The prices of famous-brand clothing are the same as elsewhere, but bargains and discounts abound on everything else.

Halfway along Candy Store Alley is Tokudai-ji Temple, a little Buddhist temple located on the first floor above a collection of sundry stores.

Yushima-tenjin Shrine, near JR Okachimachi Station, was originally built in the 14th century and restored during the 19th. The shrine is dedicated to Sugawara no Michizane (845–903), a Heian-period statesman and scholar later deified as the patron of learning. Yushima-tenjin is particularly revered by students praying for success in exams, as well as for its garden of plum trees, which attract large crowds when they blossom between mid-February and mid-March.

Yushima-tenjin Shrine

www.yushimatenjin.or.jp

- Map: 61 D5
- Address: 3-30-1 Yushima, Bunkyo-ku
- Phone: 03/3836-0753
- Hours: 6 a.m.–8 p.m.
- Transport: Subway: Yushima

Dedicated to the goddess Benten, Benzaiten Temple (Benten-do) stands in the middle of Ueno's Shinobazu Pond.

Yanaka
61 D5

Ueno-koen Park
61 D5
Ueno-koen, Taito-ku
Subway: Ueno

National Science Museum
www.kahaku.go.jp
61 E5
7-20 Ueno-koen, Taito-ku
03/3822-0111
9 a.m.–5 p.m.; closed Mon.
$$
Subway: Ueno

National Museum of Western Art
www.nmwa.go.jp
61 D5
7-7 Ueno-koen, Taito-ku
03/3828-5131
9:30 a.m.–5 p.m.; open till 8 p.m. Fri.; closed Mon.
$
Subway: Ueno

Shitamachi History Museum
61 D5
2-1 Ueno-koen, Taito-ku
03/3823-7451
9:30 a.m.–4:30 p.m.; closed Mon.
$
Subway: Ueno

To the northwest of Ueno-koen, **Yanaka Hill,** maintained as a temple town during the Tokugawa era (see p. 32), still has more than 80 temples, most managing funeral rites in nearby Yanaka Cemetery. There are so many temples that the streets are scented with incense. A survivor of both the 1923 earthquake and wartime air raids, this is the last bastion of Meiji- and Taisho-era Tokyo. Yanaka is close to Tokyo University (the nation's most prestigious seat of learning) and the University of Fine Arts and has been favored by academics, artists, and intellectuals since Meiji times.

UENO-KOEN PARK

From Ueno Station, take the west gate entrance where you will find an information desk. Walk north to the **National Science Museum (Kokuritsu Kagaku Hakubutsukan).** Presenting all aspects of science and natural history, the museum is a firm favorite with schoolchildren and sometimes holds large-scale special exhibitions. About three minutes' walk south of the science museum, the **National Museum of Western Art (Kokuritsu Seiyo Bijutsukan),** opened in 1959, was designed by Le Corbusier. The museum's impressive collection includes European old master paintings such as El Greco's "Crucifixion," Rodin sculptures ("The Thinker" and "The Burghers of Calais"), French Impressionists, and works by modern artists such as Max Ernst, Fernand Léger, and Jackson Pollock.

At the south end of the park is **Shitamachi History Museum (Shitamachi Fuzoku Shiryokan),** a two-story museum founded in 1980. Upstairs are exhibits and artifacts (many locally contributed) that afford fascinating glimpses into the lives of the *edokko*—the proud but often very poor inhabitants of the "Low City" of Edo and Tokyo (see pp. 100–101). Downstairs, the reconstructed shops, workshops, and homes of the Edo and Meiji periods, brought to life with wax figures, provide a nostalgic picture of a vanished and very different way of life.

Ueno Zoo (Ueno Dobutsuen), which opened in 1882, is particularly popular for its pandas. The grounds contain a pagoda and teahouse of Edo-period vintage, as well as a section of Shinobazu Pond (see p. 96) devoted to cormorants. The animals are well cared for, but space is cramped; if the sight of animals in cages distresses you, bypass this place.

Regrettably eclipsed these days by Ueno Zoo and the monorail connecting its two halves is **Tosho-gu Shrine.** This opulent shrine, noted for its rich Chinese-style carvings and Kano-school (late 16th-century) paintings in the prayer hall, is designated an Important Cultural Property. Among Tokyo's oldest shrines, it remains as it was when completed in 1651. To the south of the shrine approach is its famous peony garden *(mid-April to mid-May)* containing some 200 varieties.

In the north of Ueno Park, Japan's largest museum, **Tokyo National Museum (Tokyo Kokuritsu Hakubutsukan),** houses the best collection of Japanese art in the world. It comprises 86,456 works of art, plus nearly 2,000 on permanent loan; the Japanese collection includes 84 National Treasures and 521 Important Cultural Properties. It is impossible to show everything simultaneously and most exhibits are shown on a rotating basis.

The 25 rooms of the **Main Building (Honkan,** built in 1937) are devoted to Japanese art. On the first floor, sculpture and metalwork are displayed to the right; ceramics, swords and armor, textiles, and applied arts are to the left. The right-hand side of the second floor consists of paintings and lacquerware; the left has mainly calligraphy, ink paintings, and drawings. Despite the splendor of the exhibits, the museum is antiquated and the lighting gloomy; it reflects a concept of art appreciation based on deference to the work rather than pleasure in it.

Left of the main hall, the nine-room 1968 **Gallery of East Asian Art and Antiquities (Toyokan)** exhibits objects from

Ornate Chinese-style decoration characterizes Tosho-gu Shrine.

Ueno Zoo
www.tokyo-zoo.net
- Map: 61 D5
- Address: 9-83 Ueno-koen, Taito-ku
- Tel: 03/3828-5171
- Hours: 9:30 a.m.–5 p.m,; closed Mon.
- Admission: adults $$, students $
- Subway: Ueno

Tosho-gu Shrine
- Map: 61 D5
- Address: 9-88 Ueno-koen, Taito-ku
- Tel: 03/3822-3455
- Hours: 9 a.m.–5:30 p.m,; closes 4:30 p.m. Dec.–Feb.
- Admission: $
- Subway: Ueno

Tokyo National Museum

www.tnm.jp

- 61 D4–D5
- 13-9 Ueno-koen, Taito-ku
- 03/3822-1111
- 9:30 a.m.–5 p.m.; open till 8 p.m. Fri.; open till 6 p.m. weekends Apr.–Dec.; closed Mon.
- $$
- Subway: Ueno

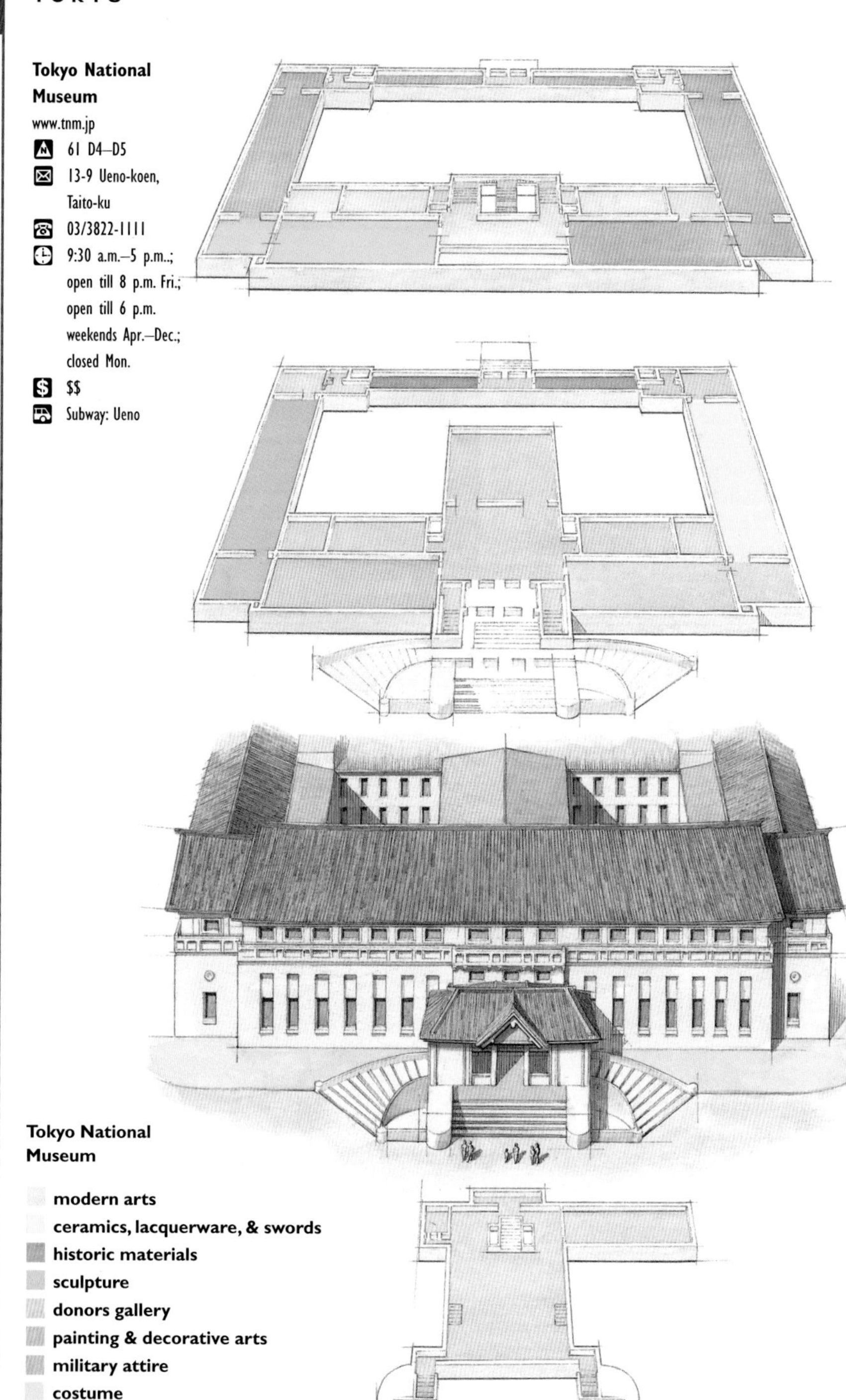

Tokyo National Museum

- modern arts
- ceramics, lacquerware, & swords
- historic materials
- sculpture
- donors gallery
- painting & decorative arts
- military attire
- costume
- other areas

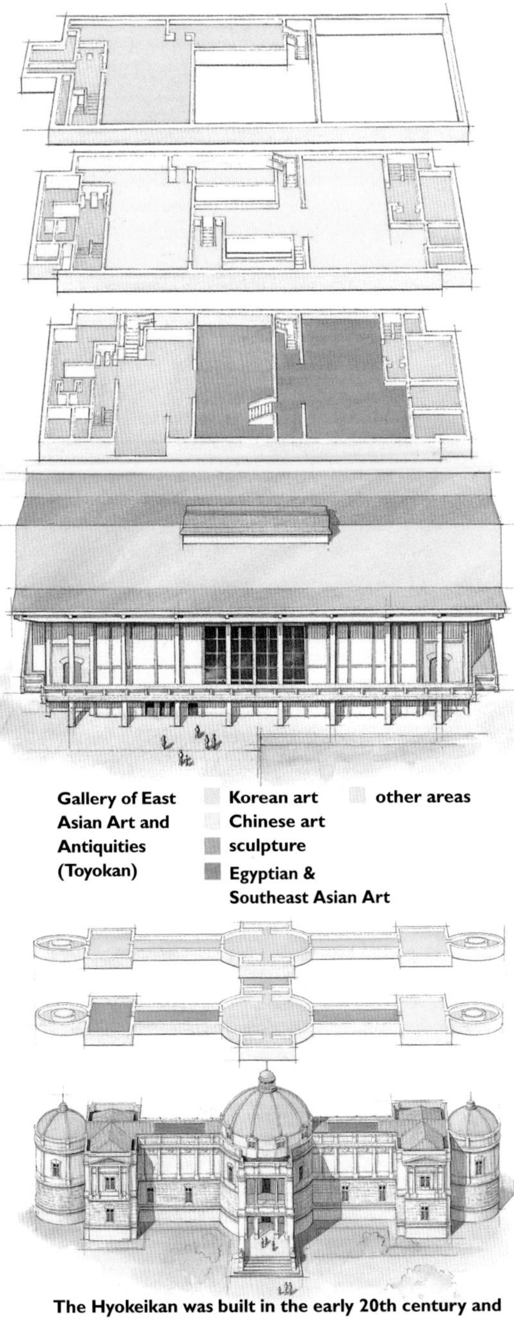

The Hyokeikan was built in the early 20th century and is a designated Important Cultural Property representing Western-style architecture of that era. The gallery space is used for education and special displays.

Clay pot created in the early sixth century

India, West Asia, and Southeast Asia on the first floor, China on the second, and Korea and the Pacific on the third. The 1909 **Heiseikan Gallery,** right of the main hall, is devoted to Japanese archaeology, notably prehistoric pottery and sculpture, and early Buddhist art.

The **Gallery of Horyu-ji Treasures (Horyu-ji Homotsukan,** built in 1964) houses a collection of 318 treasures from the great seventh-century Horyu-ji Temple near Nara, donated to the imperial family in 1878. The displays include sculptures, metalwork, furniture, painted scrolls, masks, and textiles. The building is open only on Thursdays, weather permitting. The age of these objects makes them fragile, so they are not displayed when it rains or on humid days in summer.

Several notable structures that survived the post-battle fires of 1867 (see p. 90) are almost hidden behind the museum. They include the Kanei-ji Temple (rebuilt after World War II), Edo's most important Buddhist temple, the elaborate gates of the old Tokugawa mausoleums, and the attractive Jigendo Hall, with the old Koku-mon gate in front of it. ■

A walking tour of Ueno-Nezu-Yanaka

There is more to see in the Ueno area than anywhere else in Tokyo. This walk takes three to four hours, but leave yourself a full day if you want to see the museums at the same time.

As you leave **Ueno Station** (JR or subway), turn left and walk south down the main road. Entering Ueno-koen Park on your right, you will reach the bronze statue of Saigo Takamori, commemorated (like many Japanese heroes) for his courageous espousal of a lost cause: He was defeated and died in 1877 as leader of the Satsuma Rebellion (see p. 36). Opposite, to the north, is a monument dedicated to the luckless Shogitai, the 2,000 Tokugawa loyalists who similarly opposed the imperial forces in 1867. On your right is **Kanei-ji Kyomizu Kannon-do Temple** ❶ *(1-20 Ueno-koen, Taito-ku, tel 03/3821-4749)*, one of the Kanei-ji Temple buildings to survive burning by samurai loyalists (see p. 90) and war. It was built to house a statue of the Buddhist deity Kannon presented by the abbot of the Kyomizu-dera Temple in 1631 and its design is based on Kyomizu-dera (see pp. 213–14).

From the temple, a short walk west will lead you to the path around **Shinobazu Pond** ❷. The pond was designed in the 17th century and is divided between a boating area and the famous lotus pond.

On an islet connected by a land bridge ahead of you is the **Benten-do Temple** ❸, dedicated to Benten, variously worshiped as a goddess of wealth, muse of the arts, and patron of amorous couples. There are several old teahouses nearby; some serve snacks such as *yakisoba*—fried noodles. (Ueno-koen has more substantial restaurants too; see p. 365.) During the month from mid-July, the grounds of Benten-do and the path around the pond are used for local evening fairs and festivals. Festival stalls sell plants and insects (crickets, fireflies), as well as antiques and bric-a-brac.

Continue north up the path; take a right at the first fork, then follow the signs for the **Tosho-gu Shrine** (see p. 93). The approach to the shrine, flanked with stone lanterns, is the best place to view the **Kanei-ji Pagoda (Kanei-ji Goju-no-To)** to the left, another 17th-century survivor now within the confines of Ueno Zoo. After visiting Tosho-gu, go back toward the pond, turn right, and head north along Shinobazu-dori. After passing the Ogaiso Hotel on your left, cross over the main intersection with Kototoi-dori. Some 440 yards (400 m) uphill on your left is the entrance to **Nezu-jinja Shrine** ❹ *(1-28-9 Nezu, Bunkyo-ku, tel 03/3822-0753)*, a delightful and elaborately carved shrine built in 1706. Ponds and trees adorn the shrine compound, which is renowned for azaleas. A popular azalea festival is held here between the end of May and the beginning of June.

After the shrine walk down to the southern edge of the shrine compound and turn left. Keep straight on until you reach the **Daimyo Clock Museum** ❺ *(2-1-27 Yanaka, Taito-ku, tel 03/3821-6913, closed Mon. & July 1–Sept. 30)* on your right. Housed in a very old private house, the museum exhibits a remarkable collection of rare Edo-period clocks.

From here walk northwest until you reach the Yanaka main street. To the left you will find old shops such as Isetatsu, a fancy paper shop established in 1858, and Kikumi Sembei, a rice cracker store of similar vintage. Known locally as "Yanaka Ginza," the local market street resembles a film set for 1920s Tokyo. The wealth of old temples, houses, and shops around here will tempt you to explore the side streets. Don't worry if you get lost: The Yanaka area is small, and local inhabitants are helpful.

Walk north from the main intersection on the Yanaka main street (with Yanaka cemetery on your right) toward the JR Nippori Station and Nishi Nippori (farther northeast) on the Chiyoda subway line. You will come to **Asakura Chosokan** ❻ *(7-18-10 Yanaka, Taito-ku, tel 03/3821-4549, closed Mon. & Fri.)*, the former home and studio of celebrated sculptor Asakura Fumio (1883–1964), now a museum. On your way up to Nishi Nippori there are more temples along the street, as well as the charming **Space Oguraya** ❼. Set in a restored home (once a pawnshop, where the owners lived on the premises) of the late Edo period, this gallery sells works by reputed artists and craftspeople working in traditional styles. Just before you go down toward Nishi Nippori Station you will find **Suwa-jinja Shrine** 8 on your right, a pleasant little shrine with a hilltop view over the city. For something completely different, you could indulge in coffee and homemade cakes at **Swiss Mini Chalet** (a real wooden one), set in a small garden improbably arrayed with Snow White statuary. Go downhill afterward to your right and turn right into the main street at the bottom. Nishi Nippori Station is on your right. ■

See area map pp. 60–61
Ueno station
3.3 miles (5.3 km)
3–4 hours
Nishi Nippori Station

NOT TO BE MISSED

- Kanei-ji Kyomizu Kannon-do Temple
- Shinobazu Pond
- Nezu-jinja Shrine
- Daimyo Clock Museum

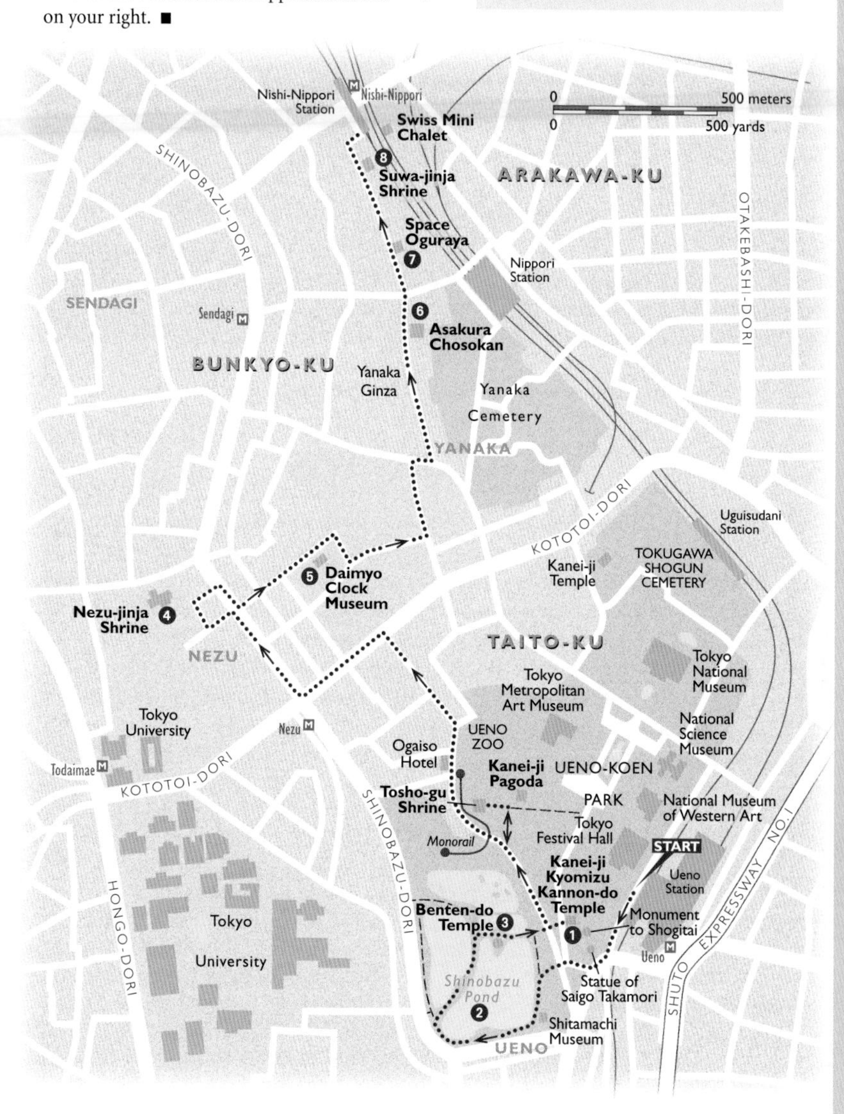

In Electric Town, bargains are hawked by a garish hubbub of loud signs.

Akihabara

One of the hottest districts in Tokyo today, Akihabara is a raucous mishmash of electronics vendors, home appliance retailers, *manga* (comics) and *anime* (animation) shops and small businesses dealing in hardware, software and everything in between. This freewheeling, 21st-century bazaar began as a postwar black market under the train tracks that specialized in vacuum tubes. It has grown to become the center of Japan's worldwide presence in the contents market—this is the homeland for *otaku*, the zealous fans who have helped make Japanese contents industries like anime a global phenomenon. Electric Town, as it's known, is now attracting new investment and redevelopment, yet this unique shopping district remains true to its humble past.

Care to Cosplay?

Take a walk down Akihabara's main drag, Chuo-dori, on the weekend and chances are you'll see Japanese in colorful, outlandish getups. This isn't dress rehearsal for a Halloween ball, but *kosupurei* (from "costume play") an increasingly popular pastime in which devotees of anime, video games, and movies dress up as their favorite character and then socialize. These "cosplayers" may even break out into song and dance—in conformist Japan, the costume is a gateway to a new self, new self-expression and, most of all, new friends. ■

You don't go to Akihabara to take in major sights, but with its endless array of shops selling high-tech gizmos as well as fantasy comics and cartoons, it's perfect for taking the frenetic pulse of post-modern Tokyo. JR Akihabara Station is right in the middle of the action. Abutting it and still tucked under the Sobu Line tracks is the venerable **Akihabara Radio Center,** a two-story warren of some fifty parts stalls that used to be a black market. This old-school bazaar deals in an eye-popping variety of gadgets, everything from the latest security systems to LEDs to vintage Bakelite receivers.

Right outside Radio Center is Akihabara's energetic main street, **Chuo-dori.** In the Edo period the area it runs through served as a firebreak to protect Edo Castle, but today its rows of high-rises, which seem to grow every year, are dedicated to high-tech commerce. Major computer and electronics retailers like LaOX Duty Free, Sofmap, and, on the eastern side of the station, Yodobashi Camera, also carry models designed for overseas markets, but prices may not be much better than back home; check before you buy. Voltage differences and Japanese-only instruction manuals are also something to consider. For specific peripherals or parts, Akihabara's fascinating backstreet stores are often cheaper, but they are less accommodating toward foreigner customers. Chuo-dori is blocked off to vehicle traffic on Sundays, which is a good time to browse the many stalls that shops set up on the sidewalk. You may also see young Japanese women dressed up as French maids to entice customers to "maid cafés," a recent area fad that has grown into its own industry. If you fancy an overpriced coffee served by a Japanese woman in maid attire, there are plenty of shops to choose from; just don't expect a geisha-like experience.

A block north and east of the overhead railway is the **Tokyo Animation Center,** which specializes in the animated fantasy worlds that have spawned Akihabara's maid cafés. Located on the fourth floor of the recently built UDX Building skyscraper, the Center is a convenient spot to pick up anime toys and limited-edition merchandise (it's also free of the raunchier material found in the backstreet stores). There's a recording studio where you can try voice-acting like an anime star, as well as a 3D theater that screens anime movie previews and popular classics. Before returning to the station, a stroll through the backstreets west of Chuo-dori always brings surprises. ■

Akihabara (Electric Town)
Map 61 D-4

Akihabara Radio Center
✉ 1-14-12 Sotokanda, Chiyoda-ku
☎ 03/3251-0614
JR Akihabara station

Tokyo Animation Center
www.animecenter.jp
✉ 4-14-1 Sotokanda, Chiyoda-ku
☎ 03/5298-1188
11 a.m.–7 p.m.; may close for special events

Low City, high times

Extending northeast across the Sumida-gawa River, *shitamachi* comprises Ningyocho and Ueno, with Asakusa as its heart. The world shitamachi (*shita* means "down" and *machi* means "town") harks back to early 17th-century urban planning.

The "down" referred to the lower castes; Edo's samurai class lived sedately behind the castle walls up on the hill. Plebeian shitamachi was the more lively home of commoners, merchants, entertainers, artists, craftsmen, and the demimonde. Then as now, anyone born and raised in shitamachi—the Low City—is an *edokko,* a child of Edo. The Yoshiwara pleasure quarter, the heart of the old Floating World, stood just beyond in Asakusa. Originally near Ginza, shitamachi sprawled as the city grew.

Rivaling the Yoshiwara it embraced, Asakusa rose from the 1880s through the 1930s as the nation's prime entertainment district and a favorite haunt for writers and poets, artists and intellectuals. It was a gaudy merry-go-round whirling millions through a kaleidoscope of fairs and markets, playhouses, movie theaters, music halls, comedy houses, and thousands of bars and restaurants.

Allied fire-bombing devastated the Low City in 1945, but then so had many earlier city conflagrations, notably in 1657, 1872, and 1923 after the earthquake. Destruction is a harbinger of rebirth; taking disaster in their stride, the hardy survivors retain edokko attributes today: nonchalance, facetiousness, pluck, and, despite a certain mistrust of authority, conservatism.

Reaching its height during the building sprees of the 1980s, modernism took care of whatever had not been accomplished by the bombs. No longer fashionable, postwar Asakusa declined with the rise of Shinjuku as the city's main amusement district. Once Asakusa's theater land, Rokku Avenue became the seedy domain of shabby movie houses and dilapidated striptease theaters. Attempts to revive the district during the 1980s failed; two art deco cinemas (Japan's oldest) were replaced with featureless concrete boxes in 1994. Refusing to concede that Asakusa is visited mainly as a bastion of tradition, developers also erected the gleaming Rox Plaza, a glaring failure in a city with too many shopping alternatives already.

In the streets behind Senso-ji Temple (see p. 103), loud clothes and florid kimono are sold in a flea market setting; small bars look unabashedly Asian, especially where Korean stores stock garishly colored fabrics and fiery *kimchee* pickles.

Asakusa retains its atmosphere. Scores of shops sell sweet *dango* rice dumplings and *sembei* biscuits; you can often watch them made on the premises. In the shopping arcades northwest of Senso-ji, behind the Nakamise, or even along the main avenue, you can still find such Japanese arcana as firemen's lanterns, *happi* coats, traditional ironmongery, combs and hair ornaments, fans, wooden footwear, high-quality kimono fabrics, festival paraphernalia, and musical instruments.

The area is still full of bars and restaurants, but the grandest, boasting geisha entertainment, are almost gone; from more than a thousand before the war, the Asakusa geisha now number about 40. You are more likely to see them in the woodblock prints on the walls of several more sophisticated *nomiya* (bars) boasting an antiquarian decor. To modern Tokyo, shitamachi is exotic.

Asakusa is the heartland, but parts of Ningyocho and Ueno are contenders. Although originally created as a Buddhist temple enclave and thus not strictly speaking shitamachi, Yanaka is architecturally the last area affording a glimpse of the Meiji and Taisho plebeian neighborhood.

Every May the edokko put heart and soul into the celebration of the Sanja Matsuri in Asakusa (see p. 386). Some 800,000 people leave technopolitan Tokyo behind and for two frantic days bring shitamachi alive with the last remnants of the frenzies of Edo. ■

Above: Female shrine bearers—a popular recent addition to the Sanja festival
Left: A fan shop in Asakusa
Below: Cycling along Yanaka Ginza

Bearers strain beneath the weight of portable shrines during Asakusa's Sanja festival.

Asakusa

The very heart of the old city, Asakusa remains Tokyo's most colorful and traditional district. Combining old-fashioned Japanese refinement with the brash and lively aspects of a working-class neighborhood, Asakusa has a wonderful atmosphere. Moreover, with some of the city's most important attractions, it is understandably a premium stop for visitors.

The Yoshiwara

The Tokugawa shogunate believed in confining social evils (including Kabuki theater) in one place. Licensed quarters opened in Japanese cities, starting with the Yoshiwara in Edo in 1617. Moved to Asakusa following the disastrous Meireki Fire in 1657, it was the most dazzling pleasure quarter on Earth. The brothel inmates were slaves, but some rose to become great courtesans; like geisha and Kabuki actors, they were the celebrities of the "Floating World." Decline started in the 1870s, due both to Western opprobrium and to the departure of Kabuki theaters for sites elsewhere. Destroyed by fires and war, the Yoshiwara always rose again until Japan outlawed prostitution in 1957. ■

The sights here are mainly in the area around **Senso-ji Temple,** probably the only Buddhist temple in Japan to constitute such a strong focus for a neighborhood—a privilege normally reserved for Shinto shrines. Senso-ji is approached from Kaminarimon, the Thunder Gate, renowned for its colossal central red paper lantern and the fierce guardian deities on either side. Beyond it is the Nakamise, an avenue of souvenir and specialty stores leading to the temple itself.

Senso-ji (also called Kannon-sama) has been standing on the same spot for more than a millennium; legend has it that the temple was built by three fishermen in the seventh century. After finding a statuette of Kannon, goddess of mercy, in their nets, each dreamed that the deity told him to build the shrine. It was restructured several times from the ninth century, and took its final form early in the 17th. This version survived the earthquake in 1923, but vanished completely during World War II. The gigantic concrete replacement, built in 1958 with a sweeping roof of 70,000 bronze tiles, is sufficiently imposing to do justice to the original; the same applies to the great five-storied pagoda to the west of the temple. Paintings on the ceiling of the main hall are originals saved from the bombing. In the temple courtyard stands a huge bronze caldron full of burning incense; it is considered auspicious to spread the smoke over your head.

West of the temple compound is the tranquil **Dembo-in Garden,**

Visitors to Senso-ji Temple congregate around a roofed caldron of incense—the smoke is thought to ward off misfortune and disease.

Senso-ji Temple

- Map: 61 E5
- Address: 2-3-1 Asakusa, Taito-ku
- Phone: 03/3842-0181
- Hours: Dawn to dusk
- Transport: Subway: Asakusa

***Sumotori* battle it out at Sumo Stadium in Tokyo, where good seats sell out a year ahead.**

Dembo-in Garden

- 61 E5
- Dembo-in-dori, Taito-ku
- 03/3842-0181
- Dawn to dusk; closed Sun.
- Subway: Asakusa

Edo-Tokyo Museum

www.edo-tokyo-museum.or.jp

- 61 E4
- 1-4-1 Yokoami, Sumida-ku
- 03/3626-9974
- 9:30 a.m.–5:30 p.m., open till 7:30 Sat.; closed Mon.
- $$
- Rail: JR Sobu line, Ryogoku Station

which is not only an original surviving from the 19th century but probably Tokyo's most beautiful garden. Although not officially open to the public, tickets for Dembo-in can be obtained from the Senso-ji office at the foot of the pagoda. As you go through from Senso-ji, turn left at the intersection on Nakamise into Demboin-dori. The garden is about 55 yards (50 m) along on the right side of the road. Look for the sign indicating it in English. Collect pieces of dried bread on the way in to feed the turtles and rapacious carp in this unmissable garden.

On the banks of the Sumida-gawa River, **Sumida-koen Park** has long been a favorite place for cherry blossom viewing despite its unattractive concrete embankment. *Yakatabune* pleasure boats are hired for private parties, especially for the Sumida fireworks display (see p. 387). A cheaper option is to take the Sumida-gawa cruise from Azumabashi Bridge to Hamarikyu-teien (see p. 73). The trip is not especially scenic but offers a welcome sit-down after sightseeing. The Azumabashi skyline is dominated by French designer Philippe Starck's eccentric Flamme d'Or building (see pp. 66–67).

You may be coveting those amazing plastic food displays you see in restaurant windows; one stop south from Asakusa (Tawaramachi Station) is **Kappabashi wholesale market (Kappabashi Dogugai).** Here you can buy such gastronomic emblems as a forkful of spaghetti suspended above a plate, plastic sushi, and all kinds of kitchen paraphernalia.

Across Sumida-gawa from Asakusabashi is an astounding building, seemingly from the realm of science fiction, that houses **Edo-Tokyo Museum (Edo-Tokyo Hakubutsukan).** With a fascinating array of exhibits evoking the Tokyo of the past, this facility has a reputation as the premier city history museum. It lies east of the main national **Sumo Stadium (Kokugikan).** While you are in the area, you could visit the **Sumo Museum (Sumo Hakubutsukan),** near the stadium entrance (www.sumo.or.jp). ■

More places to visit in central Tokyo

AKASAKA

Going southeast from the Imperial Palace, close to Kasumigaseki district and the Diet Building in Nagatacho, Akasaka is devoted to both business and upscale entertainment. Hie-jinja Shrine, also called Sanno-sama, was the favorite shrine of the Tokugawa shoguns and the focal point of the grandest festival in Edo. Accessible via a steep path straddled by rows of small red *torii* (shrine gateways), this is a very pleasant haven. In mid-August, Hie-jinja stages Takigi Noh outdoor Noh theater performances of some of the most representative plays in the repertoire—an unmissable experience. Less than 200 yards (150 m) northwest of Akasaka-mitsuke subway station on Aoyama-dori, the Suntory Museum of Art (Santori Bijutsukan) has excellent collections of ceramics, paintings, prints, and more.
61 C3 Subway: Akasake-mitsuke, Kokkai Gijidoe-mae for Hie-jinja Shrine

NINGYOCHO

Farther south, near the Tokyo City Air Terminal, is Ningyocho, one of Tokyo's oldest neighborhoods. Site of the original Yoshiwara pleasure quarter built in 1617, it remained a major theater district until Asakusa took over in the 1870s. Ningyocho (Doll Town) was named for the many workshops making and repairing puppets for the Bunraku theater. Leveled by the 1923 earthquake but unscarred by wartime bombing, the neighborhood has many buildings dating from the 1920s. The traditional shops selling *wagashi* candy, green tea, and *sembei* crackers are among Tokyo's most venerable.
61 E4 Subway: Ningyocho

JIMBOCHO

The focus for antiquarian booksellers since the 1880s, this is Tokyo's main center for books new and used. Its stores yield used books in many languages, as well as woodblock prints and delightful Edo-period illustrated paper books. The Tuttle bookstore is a gold mine for books in English about Japan. The bookstores extend from Jimbocho subway station, going left toward Kanda along Yasukuni-dori.
61 C4 Subway: Jimbocho ■

Hie-jinja Shrine in Akasaka is one of Tokyo's most important Shinto shrines.

Outlying districts of Tokyo

HORIKIRI SHOBUEN IRIS GARDEN

Every June Horikiri Shobuen provides a spectacular note of color in the drab northeastern urban-industrial sprawl. The garden, already popular in the 1800s, was celebrated by artists in woodblock prints. Uprooted during World War II to make paddies, it was restored in 1960 and contains more than 6,000 iris plants of 130 varieties.

109 C3 03/3697-5237 Rail: Horikiri Shobuen stop on Keisei main line from Ueno, then 15 minutes' walk southwest

KAWAGOE

A castle town important to the shoguns because of its proximity to Edo, it is now home to 300,000 living an hour from Tokyo on the northwestern commuter belt. After a fire in 1893, local merchants used clay to build *dozozukuri*—picturesque structures combining home and business and which still stand, some as museums. The local Kita-In temple includes a pagoda and dates from the 17th century.

109 B3 Train: Hon-Kawagoe (Seibu Shinjuku line) from Tokyo's Seibu Shinjuku station. Journey time 60 minutes

Buddhist pilgrims walk over burning coals on Mount Takao-san.

MOUNT TAKAO-SAN

Tokyo's western urban sprawl fades into the hills and forests around 1,968-foot (600 m) Takao-san, a perfect day trip—but crowded on weekends. Hiking trails to and from the summit are signposted; there is a cable car. Near the summit is Yakuo-in temple, famous for its Hiwatari festival (second Sunday in March), when devotees walk unharmed beds of hot coals . In the valley are the delightful **Ukai Tori-Yama** *(3426 Minami, Asakawa-machi, Hachioji-shicho, tel 0426/61-0739)* and **Chikutei** *(2850 Minami Asakawa-machi, Hachioji-shi, tel 0426/61-8419)* restaurants, featuring authentic traditional buildings in garden settings.

109 B2 Train: Takaosan-guchi Station from Shinjuku (Keio line or Chuo line, changing for the Keio line at Takao Station). Journey time 50 minutes

ODAIBA

Built as a fort on reclaimed land for defending Edo Bay from foreign invasion in the 1850s, Odaiba underwent massive development from the late 1980s. Featuring Kenzo Tange's futuristic Fuji Television Building, it boasts offbeat theme parks and museums, unique shopping malls, food plazas, and the world's largest Ferris wheel. Now a premier Japanese tourist attraction, it offers foreign visitors a blend of kitsch, high tech, and hedonism.

109 B2 Train: Yurikamome train from JR Shimbashi station to Daiba, 15 minutes. Tokyo Water Cruise (aka Suijo Bus) from Hinode Pier to Odaiba Seaside Park, 20 minutes.

OGASAWARA-SHOTO ISLANDS

Official administration places Ogasawara-shoto in Tokyo, but at some 1,200 miles (1,930 km) away, it's about as "outlying" as a district can get. Most of the 2,000-odd inhabitants live on Chichi-Jima (Father Island), with the remainder on Haha-Jima (Mother Island) and minute Ani-Jima (Brother Island). The other is Iwo-Jima. Hosting one of the fiercest battles of World War II, it is still strewn with live ammunition and off-limits to visitors.

The climate is subtropical; there is excellent scuba diving but few beaches. Though ferries run from Tokyo only once weekly, there are 30 small inns catering to vacationers.

See map on inside front cover Journey time 28–30 hours ■

Soaring above the Kanto plain is Fuji-san, probably the world's most beautiful conical volcano. Tokyo is a base for visiting Fuji-san, as well as Yokohama and Kamakura. Slightly farther afield is historic Nikko.

Excursions from Tokyo

Introduction & map **108–109**
Yokohama **110**
Kamakura **111–113**
Nikko **114–120**
Fuji-Hakone-Izu 121–128
Hotels & restaurants **365–66**

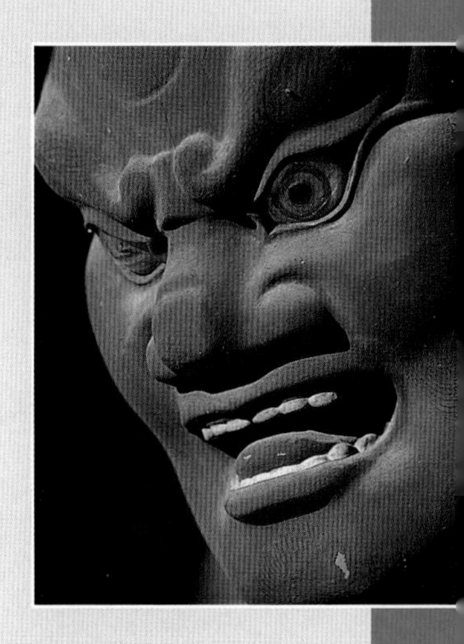

Nio guardian deity, main gate Sugimoto-dera Temple, Kamakura

A picturesque image of Lake Chuzenji-ko and Kyusu Falls, Nikko

Excursions from Tokyo

TOKYO MAKES AN EXCELLENT BASE FOR A NUMBER OF EXCURSIONS INTO the surrounding areas. The most popular day trips are to Yokohama, Kamakura, Fuji-Hakone, and farther afield to Nikko. Yokohama is the closest to Tokyo, but a trip to Nikko will introduce you to some of the region's best-known historic sights.

From Tokyo, there are several ways to get to Yokohama, Japan's most important 19th-century doorway to the outside world. From Shibuya Station, take the Toyoko line to Sakuragicho and Yokohama Stations. The trip takes around 45 minutes by ordinary train *(kakueki teisha)* or 35 minutes by limited express *(kyuko)*. From Shinagawa, Shimbashi, or Tokyo Stations, either the JR Keihin Tohoku or JR Yokosuka lines stop at Yokohama (35-minute journey). The shinkansen stops at Shin-Yokohama Station; you need to change to the Yokohama line.

Kamakura, capital of medieval Japan, is slightly farther on the JR Yokosuka line from Shimbashi or Shinagawa Stations in central Tokyo. The journey to Kita Kamakura takes 60 minutes, and to Kamakura it takes 63 minutes.

The fastest way to reach the Fuji-Hakone area is to take the JR Tokaido Shinkansen from JR Tokyo Station to Odawara, which takes just over 40 minutes. Note that whether you are

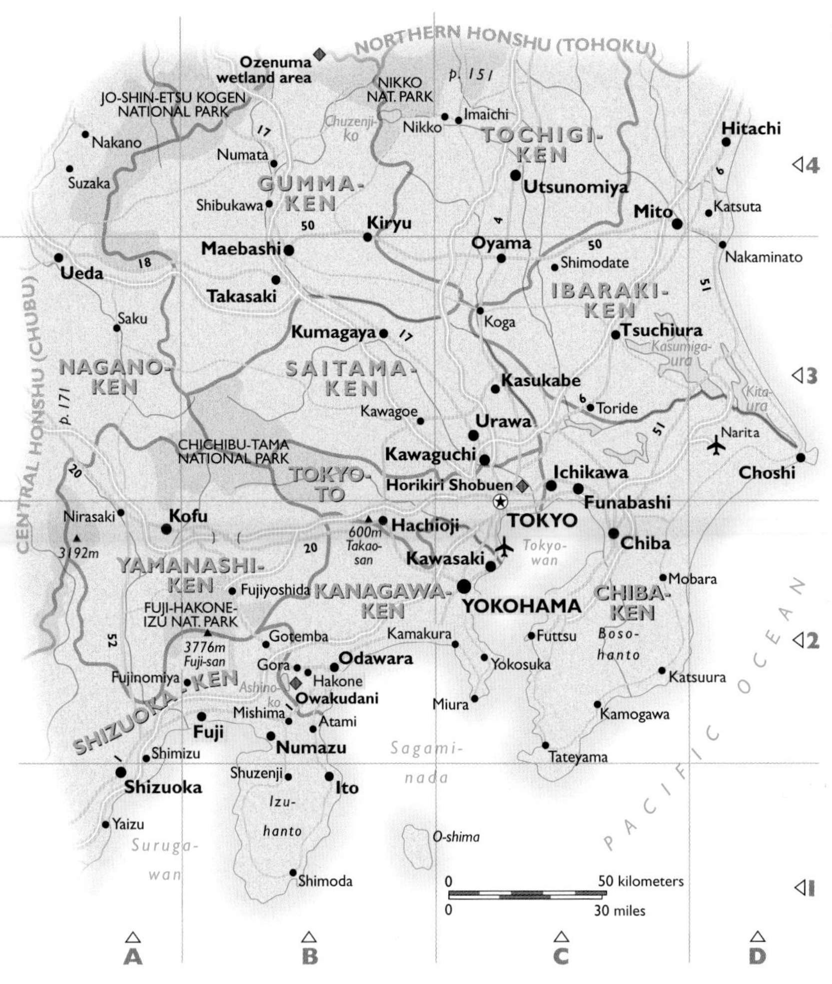

coming from Kansai or Tokyo you must take the Kodama Shinkansen and not the super expresses (*hikari* or *nozomi*). If you have no JR pass, you can take the Odakyu line from Shinjuku Station either to Odawara or to Hakone Yumoto. The best of the Odakyu trains is the luxury Romance Car; it costs about the same as the shinkansen. Whatever line you take, change at Odawara or Hakone Yumoto for the local Hakone-Tozan line to Gora.

The fastest and cheapest way to get to Nikko, site of a magnificent 17th-century shrine honoring the shogun Tokugawa Ieyasu, is to take the Tobu Nikko line from Tobu Asakusa Station. The journey time by limited express is just under two hours. Rapid train (*kaisoku*) takes only 15 minutes longer than the express, but costs almost half. If (and only if) you have a JR rail pass, you might consider using it to go to Nikko, but it is much slower and less convenient: You take the Tohuku Shinkansen from Ueno Station and change at Utsumomiya for an hourly train to Nikko. ■

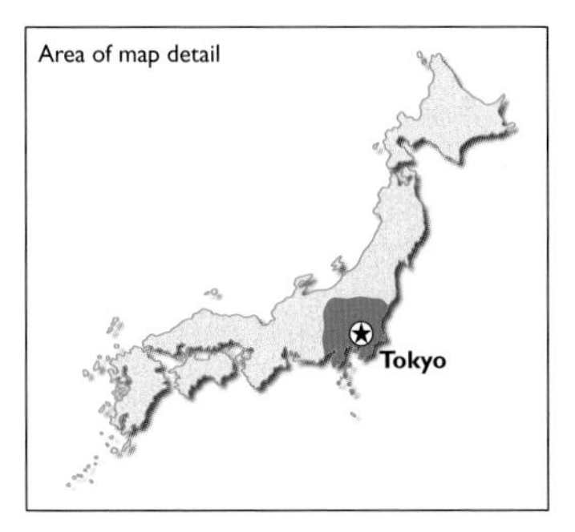

Often hungering for exotica, the Japanese find it in the gaudy decors and culinary delights of Yokohama's famous Chukagai (Chinatown).

Yokohama

IT SEEMS JUST A CONTINUATION OF TOKYO'S GIGANTIC urban sprawl, but Yokohama is Japan's second largest city and its largest port. Yokohama has a fascinating history as one of the first ports opened to foreigners in 1858, but the 1923 earthquake and wartime destruction have left little of the old city behind.

The central Kannai district is being transformed with architecturally striking new developments. This applies even more spectacularly to the Minato Mirai 21 development to the west, dominated by the **Landmark Tower,** at 971 feet (296 m) one of the tallest buildings in Japan. While you are there, take in the **Yokohama Maritime Museum** *(Nippon Maru Memorial Park, 2-1-1 Minato Mirai, Nishi-ku tel 045/221-0280),* which has displays about Japanese and world shipping, as well as *Nippon Maru,* a beautiful tall ship (built 1930). The port was the point of departure for Japan's once-colossal silk trade, detailed in the **Silk Museum (Shiruku Hakubutsukan),** whose fascinating exhibits focus on silk processing, textiles, and trade.

On the promontory to the south is the **Sankei-en Garden** *(58-1 Honmoku San-no-tani, Naka-ku, tel 045/621-0634).* Laid out in 1906, it incorporates a 15th-century pagoda and other buildings moved from different parts of Japan.

For many, however, Yokohama's star attraction lies in Japan's largest **Chinatown** and its wealth of restaurants, sundry goods stores, and pharmacies. ■

Yokohama

Map 109 C2

Visitor information

Address: Yokohama Station, 2-16-1 Takashima-cho

Tel: 045/441-7300

Silk Museum

www.silkmuseum.or.jp

Address: 1 Yamashita-cho, Naka-ku

Tel: 045/641-0841

Hours: 9 a.m.–4:30 p.m.; closed Mon.

Admission: $$

Cast in 1252, the colossal Daibutsu (Great Buddha) sits serenely, unmoved by wars and natural disasters over the centuries.

Kamakura

OVERLOOKING SAGAMI-WAN BAY, KAMAKURA, FOUNDED in 1192, was perfect as both a samurai stronghold and a temple city; it was the capital of Japan until 1333. Badly damaged during the Kanto Earthquake of 1923, it was spared Allied bombing in World War II. Now a plush residential town on Tokyo's outer commuter belt, hilly Kamakura has enough historic buildings intact or restored to justify its reputation as one of the must-sees in Japan.

Kamakura

109 C2

Visitor information

Outside Kamakura station east exit

0467/22-3350

Kokuhokan National Treasure Museum

2-1-1 Yukinoshita

0467/22-0753

9 a.m.–4:30 p.m.; closed Mon.

$

Kamakura's sights (65 temples and 19 shrines) are far too many to be visited in a single day. They are largely distributed on a loop around Kamakura Station, with most of the major ones to the north. The five most important Zen temples of the Rinzai sect, collectively known as the Kamakura Gozan, still stand, but only Engaku-ji and Kencho-ji Temples—the most popular with sightseers—retain period buildings. Both of these are closer to Kita-Kamakura, the station to the north. The famous Great Buddha, however, sits farther southwest and is reached more comfortably by bus or local train from Kamakura Station.

One way to cover the area is to arrive at Kita-Kamakura and zig-zag your way through the temples and sights. Or begin with a round-trip to the Great Buddha in the south and return to Kamakura Station. From there, go northeast along Wakamiya-oji, the wide main boulevard, to the National Treasure Museum and Tsurugaoka Hachimangu Shrine, then continue northwest to Kita-Kamakura Station. There are recommended hiking routes on a bilingual map posted outside Kamakura Station. Copies are available from the visitor center.

Kamakura's colossal **Daibutsu (Great Buddha)** sits in the precincts of Kotoku-in Temple *(Tel 0467/22-0703)* and is one of the two largest pre-modern bronze Buddhas in Japan, (the other is in Todai-ji in Nara; see pp. 241–43). Cast in 1252 and 37 feet (11m) high, this seated Buddha was once housed in a vast wooden hall that was swept away by a tidal wave in 1495. With its serene countenance enhanced by the elegant flow of drapery, this is a great work of art. The statue is hollow—a ladder inside provides access to shoulder level.

Less than a quarter of a mile south is **Hase-dera Temple** *(Tel 0467/22-6300)* with a breathtaking view over Sagami Bay. Founded during the early eighth century, this temple was rebuilt by the shogun Ashikaga Yoshimasa (who also built Kyoto's Ginkaku-ji) in 1459. The temple stands beyond a beautiful garden in the precinct. Close to the steps to the buildings, as well as to the west of the compound, are serried ranks of hundreds of statues of Jizo, typically festooned with bibs and children's toys. The patron deity of travelers and children, Jizo is venerated especially by women as the guardian of the souls lost in terminated pregnancies. The main Amida Hall and Kannon Hall are open to the public (unlike in most temples). They contain fine Buddha figures, but Kannon Hall is renowned for its great *juichimen* (11-faced) statue of Kannon. Carved in 721 from a giant camphor log, the splendidly gilded figure stands 30 feet (9 m) high—the tallest wooden statue in Japan. The Buddhist deity of compassion, Kannon is represented here with one main face and ten subsidiary ones; sometimes the figure is depicted with a thousand arms. Kannon was later mainly represented as female, but this statue predates the trend.

Presenting a wealth of exhibits revealing facets of Kamakura's rich history, the **National Treasure Museum (Kokuhokan)** is noted for its collection of temple treasures and fine Buddhist works of art.

Tsurugaoka Hachiman-gu Shrine is dedicated to Hachiman, god of war. The original 11th-century shrine burned down in 1191, but was rebuilt on nearby Tsurugaoka—the hill of cranes—the same year. Fire struck again six centuries later; most of the current structures date from 1828. Noted for its panorama over the town and the bay, the shrine is cherished for the beauty of its fine vermilion buildings in a leafy setting—but most of all for historical associations dear to the Japanese. On the square at the foot of the steps leading to the shrine is the Mai-den (dance stage), revered as a replica of the one on which Shizuka, beloved of the ill-fated hero Minamoto Yoshitsune (1159–1189), performed centuries ago. Nearby stands a huge *ginkgo* tree—the very one beneath which the son of Yoritomo (see p. 31) was assassinated in 1219.

Engaku-ji Temple *(Tel 0467/22-0478)* is the first temple you come to, about 110 yards (100 m) southeast of Kita-Kamakura Station. It was founded in 1282 to commemorate those who fell during the Mongol Wars (see p. 32). Destroyed and rebuilt several times, most of the buildings finally succumbed to the earthquake of 1923. Current structures are mainly concrete reproductions, but the beautifully carved two-story sanmon gate of 1780 survives, as does the great

Tsurugaoka Hachiman-gu Shrine

- 2-1-31 Yokinoshita
- 0467/22-0315
- 7 a.m.–9 p.m.
- $
- JR Yokosuka Line: Kita-Kamakura

A display of *yabusame*—archery on horseback—at Tsurugaoka Hachimangu Shrine during the Kamakura Festival

bell, cast in 1301. Closed to the public, the oldest extant building is the Shariden Hall, which contains a reliquary said to hold one of the Buddha's teeth. The compound has two small gardens: Obai-in, a mausoleum for the 13th-century Hojo family rulers, and Butsunichian, where green tea is served.

About 280 yards (250 m) southwest of Engaku-ji and across the train tracks, **Toke-ji Temple** *(Tel 0467/22-1663)* is set in a leafy valley. A former nunnery, this temple is also known as Enkiri-dera (Divorce Temple). In the 1600s, divorce—exclusively a male privilege—came to be recognized as the only refuge for battered wives. A year spent here made a woman's divorce official. The temple's directives inspired the first national divorce law in 1873. The complex embraces **Matsugaoka Treasure House,** a small museum exhibiting items relating to the temple's history.

Kencho-ji Temple *(Tel 0467/22-0981),* about half a mile (600 m) southwest of Kita-Kamakura, stands among majestic cedars. It is the most important of Kamakura's five main Zen temples. Founded by a Chinese Zen master in 1253, it was formerly a seminary and is now the headquarters of the Rinzai sect. The current buildings date from the mid-17th century; cast in 1255, the great bronze bell near the sanmon gate is a National Treasure. Behind the main Ryuoden (Dragon King Hall) is a fine garden laid out by the Zen master Muso Kokushi. ■

Shin-kyo Bridge is one of the most famous sights on the way to Nikko's renowned Tosho-gu Shrine.

Nikko

EVEN IF YOU PLAN TO STAY ONLY IN TOKYO, YOU SHOULD consider taking one day to visit Nikko, just 80 miles (128 km) north. Some of Japan's greatest historic sites are here. Nikko lies on the southeastern edge of Nikko National Park, an alpine wonderland for hikers in summer and skiers in winter, abounding with lakes, waterfalls, and *onsen* (hot springs).

Nikko
109 C4
Visitor information
www.nikko-jp.org
Tobu Nikko Station, 4-3 Matsubara-cho
0288/53-4511
8 a.m.–5 p.m.; open till 4 p.m. Nov.–March
$$$ Multiple entry ticket for Rinno-ji, Tosho-gu, & Futara-san-jinja

The elegantly curved vermilion **Shin-kyo (Sacred Bridge)** spans the Daiya-gawa River, taking you from the east section of the city to the main temple and shrine area. Two *torii* (gateways) mark the ends of Shin-kyo, which was formerly used only for ceremonial purposes. Built in 1636, it commemorates an old legend about the eighth-century priest Shodo Shonin, said to have crossed the river on this spot on the backs of two gigantic serpents. The bridge was reconstructed in 1907, shortly after being washed away in a flood.

Rinno-ji Temple is on the right along the main Omotesando Avenue to the Tosho-gu Shrine, which is less than a quarter of a mile farther north. Founded by the priest Shodo Shonin during the eighth century and maintained by the Buddhist Tendai sect, the

temple is renowned for its Sanbutsudo (Hall of the Three Buddhas), erected in 1648. The three large gilded and lacquered statues inside represent the thousand-armed Kannon on the left, the Amida-Nyorai Buddha in the center, and the unusual Bato (horse-headed) Kannon on the right. Featuring a horse's head jutting from the forehead, this incarnation of the deity of compassion is devoted to animal welfare. The nearby Gohotendo, containing other statues, is notable for the Sorinto, a large bronze pillar inscribed with 10,000 sutras (Buddhist texts) and bearing 24 bells. Exhibiting various items connected with the temple's history, the Treasure Hall (Homutsuden) has a beautiful garden behind it.

When the great shogun Tokugawa Ieyasu died in 1616, Nikko was selected as the site for his mausoleum. At Ieyasu's request, this was a modest affair, but in 1634 Ieyasu's grandson, Iemitsu, began building **Tosho-gu Shrine** on a scale commensurate with his grandfather's stature. Some 15,000 craftsmen, among them the finest carpenters, carvers, and painters in the land, worked on the project, the cost of which today would translate into hundreds of millions of U.S. dollars. Incorporating some 2.5 million sheets of gold leaf, the shrine's lavish buildings remain paradigms of the ornate style of the late 16th-century Momoyama period. They have both admirers and detractors: The Tosho-gu structures are a far cry from the simple elegance of classic Japanese taste, reflecting the rococo excess of Ming dynasty China and the parvenu taste of military dictators. Still, if they tend to be massive and overdecorated as a whole, charm and subtleties lie in a wealth of detail, particularly in the hundreds of intricate polychrome carvings, many based upon designs supplied by major exponents of the Kano school of painting. Several of the buildings are designated Important Cultural Properties and National Treasures.

As you proceed through a giant stone torii gateway along Omotesando Avenue leading to the shrine, on your left is a five-story pagoda built in 1818 to replace a 1650 original destroyed by fire. Flanked by two fierce protective kings and featuring ornate carvings, the great vermilion Omotemon is the true gate to the Tosho-gu Shrine. Beyond this are the Sanjinko, three storehouses containing sacred trappings for the shrine's great festivals (Warrior Processions, May 18 and October 18). The last of these

A stone *torii* gateway along the approach to the Tosho-gu Shrine. The font in the foreground is for orthodox Shintoists to rinse hands and mouths before entering the sacred precinct.

Rinno-ji Temple
✉ 2300 Sannai
☎ 0288/54-0531

Tosho-gu Shrine
✉ 2301 Sannai
☎ 0288/54-0560

The riot of carvings that adorn the structures of Tosho-gu Shrine goes way over the top, but the beauty of the experience lies in the charm of the details (right).

structures displays fanciful carvings of elephants. The unpainted Shinkyusha (sacred stable), containing a single effigy of a white horse, bears a delightful bas-relief sequence of monkeys, including a famous "Hear No Evil, Speak No Evil, See No Evil" trio. Monkey spirits were once believed to protect horses. Beyond this is a granite water cistern; Shinto worshippers pause here to wash hands and rinse mouths before proceeding into the sacred precinct.

Beyond the next torii gateway and up more stairs, you will find a drum tower on the left and belfry to the right, beyond which lies the Yakushi-do (extra fee for access), a Buddhist structure featuring a huge ink drawing on the ceiling of the "Naki-ryu" (roaring dragon). The

Carving of a mythical temple guardian at Tosho-gu Shrine

17th-century original was lost with the building in a fire in 1961. The current reproduction offers the same novelty: As visitors clap their hands, the reverberations are said to sound like a dragon's roar.

Back along the main path and up more steps is the amazing 36-foot (11 m) **Yomeimon** (Gate of Sunlight). The ornamentation seen so far reaches a florid climax here: The structure is alive with 400 gilt polychrome carvings of Kano-school design depicting giraffes, lions, dragons, birds, flowers, and phoenixes, along with Chinese children, sages, and immortals. One of the columns has been deliberately carved upside down to appease evil spirits; it was believed that the lavish artistic overkill might otherwise have aroused their ire. Beyond the gate to the left is the **Mikoshigura**—a building housing *mikoshi,* sacred palanquins carried in festivals. Straight ahead are the gorgeously decorated Haiden (Oratory) and Honden (Main Hall).

To the right of the Yomeimon is a corridor leading to the Sakashita-mon Gate. Just before the gate is another small portal, whose lintel features a much cherished carving of a sleeping cat—the "Nemuri-neko"—by 17th-century sculptor Jingoro. Beyond the gates, a long stone stairway through a cedar grove leads to Ieyasu's tomb, whose austere design by now comes as something of a relief. Southwest of the shrine itself, just below the pagoda is the **Tosho-gu Homotsukan Treasure**

The five-story pagoda near the entrance to Tosho-gu Shrine

House. The museum exhibits historical items pertaining to the Tokugawa shoguns, including armor, swords, and paintings.

FUTARASAN-JINJA SHRINE & TAIYUIN

There are three Futarasan shrines, dedicated to the deities of Mount Nantai-san (formerly Futara-san), in the Nikko area. The Okumiya (Inner Shrine), near the peak of the mountain itself, is the most sacred; the Chugushi (Middle Shrine) stands by Lake Chuzenji-ko; the third, beside the Daiya-gawa River, was called Honsha (Head Shrine). Founded by the priest Shodo in the eighth century, these shrines had Buddhist connotations originally but were given exclusive Shinto status in 1868. To reach the riverside **Futarasan-jinja Shrine,** from Omotesando Avenue turn left along the Ue-Shinmichi path at the crossing before the Omotemon Gate. The buildings date back to 1619. The ornate lacquered *karamon* (Chinese gate) stands before the main hall; both the hall and oratory are designated Important Cultural Properties. The shrine stands amid magnificent cedar trees; from here you can take a fine stroll toward the Nantai-san foothills.

West of Futarasan is **Taiyuin** (also called Taiyuin-byo), the mausoleum (1653) of the builder of the Tosho-gu Shrine, shogun Tokugawa Iemitsu. To find it, as you go north toward Tosho-gu along Omotesando Avenue, turn left into the Shita-Shinmichi path just before the stone torii gateway.

Futarasan-jinja Shrine
✉ 2307 Sannai
☎ 0288/54-0535

Yumoto Onsen

Bus from JR Nikko Station (stop No. 3) Approx. 80 mins.

Lake Chuzenji-ko

Bus from JR Nikko Station (stop No. 2) to Chuzenji Onsen. Approx. 50 mins.

Nikko Edo Mura

470-2, Garakura, Nikko, Tochigi Prefecture

0288/77-1777

9 a.m.–7 p.m., March 20–Nov. 30; 9:30 a.m.–4 p.m., Dec. 1–March 19; closed Weds. except hols.; closed Jan. 25–Feb. 7

$$$$$

The Kegon-no-Taki Waterfall is a highlight of Nikko National Park.

Woman dressed in Sumarai-era costume at Nikko Edo Village, a historical theme park

The precinct embraces several Important Cultural Properties. Taiyuin is beautifully ornamented but less bombastic than Tosho-gu.

OUTLYING NIKKO

If you have an extra day or more to spare, the 540-square mile (1,400-sq km) area of Nikko National Park offers scenic wonders and outstanding hiking trails. With its dramatic mountain backdrop, **Lake Chuzenji-ko** can be admired on foot or by taking a cruise or hiring a rowboat. You'll enjoy fine views of the lake from Chanokidaira, where the viewing platform is accessible by cable car from Chuzenji Onsen.

Nearby is the spectacular 318-foot (97 m) **Kegon-no-Taki Waterfall,** renowned for the display of rainbows in the spray on sunny days. **Yumoto Onsen** resort has a reputation for its traditional hot spring experience; you can reach it by bus or on foot from Chuzenji-ko. Its onsen hotels are perfect for relaxing after an afternoon of exhilarating mountain hiking from Ryuzu Waterfall to the north of Chuzenji-ko. Southeast, on the Kinugawa line from Nikko, Kinugawa Onsen is a gaudier, more conventional onsen resort than Yumoto, but for those traveling with children it has the advantage of being close to **Nikko Edo Village (Nikko Edo Mura),** a theme park with reconstructed period buildings and inspired samurai-oriented attractions. Adults might find this tacky, but kids often love it. ■

Fuji-san with the shinkansen: a cherished contemporary icon

Fuji-Hakone-Izu

The image of Japan's premier natural wonder is everywhere—on postcards, calendars, travel brochures, and old woodblock prints. Split between Yamanashi and Shizuoka Prefectures, Fuji-san is the centerpiece of Fuji-Hakone-Izu National Park. The whole area is scenically magnificent. The train lines and highways run parallel to the former Tokaido (Eastern Sea Road), which in feudal times connected Edo (Tokyo) with Kyoto and Osaka.

Hakone is renowned for its views of Fuji-san, particularly as mirrored in beautiful Lake Ashino-ko. With the region's many onsen resorts, its fuming volcanic valleys, the scenic Fuji Five Lakes area nearby, and the presence of Fuji-san itself, this is not surprisingly one of the most cherished areas for recreation and relaxation in Japan. Hakone makes a perfect day trip from Tokyo, but with so much to see and some outstanding hotels (especially the landmark Fujiya, one of Japan's first Western-style hotels), treating yourself to a stopover will make this a more leisurely experience.

One proviso is the weather: If it is cloudy or wet, Fuji-san often totally vanishes. Also, you should be aware that it is very crowded on weekends.

The giant waterside *torii* gateway of Hakone Gongen shrine and the Fuji-san backdrop both contribute to the legendary beauty of Lake Ashi-ko.

Hakone
109 B2
Visitor information
Hakone Yumoto
0460/85-8911

HAKONE

From Tokyo, the JR Tokaido Shinkansen (the Kodama train) stops at Odawara. From here change to the Hakone Tozan line to Gora. On the way to Hakone you could stop off at Chokoku-no-mori to see the **Hakone Open-Air Museum (Chokoku-no-Mori Bijutsukan),** a highly regarded repository of 19th-century and contemporary Japanese and Western sculpture; there is a pavilion devoted to Picasso, and 26 sculptures by Henry Moore are displayed outdoors.

From Gora take the funicular railway for a ten-minute trip to the summit of Mount Soun-zan. You can alight at any or all of the four stops on the way. Koen Kami is the stop for the **Hakone Art Museum (Hakone Bijutsukan,** *one minute's walk from the station, tel 0462/82-2623, closed Thurs.*), noted for its collection of fine Chinese and Japanese ceramics.

From Soun-zan you take a cable car (*ropu-ue,* or "ropeway") to Togendai. Within ten minutes, the car passes over a valley of jagged rocks, craters, and bubbling mud, where steam jets from the crevices and fumaroles belch sulfurous vapors. This is **Owakudani** (Valley of Greater Boiling), where you should alight. Weather permitting, there is a fine view of Fuji-san to the northwest. You can take a closer look at the inferno from the Owakudani Exploration Path circumventing it, and perhaps allow yourself to be tempted into sampling an egg cooked (if that is the word) in the volcanic mud by a vendor on the way. Black-shelled and distinctly sulfurous, the eggs are supposed to be good for you. Before setting out, be sure to check ahead with the tourist information staff regarding conditions, since area trails are sometimes closed due to the toxic gases emitted by the mountain. The building alongside the cable car station houses a panoramic restaurant, though the food is pretty unexciting.

Board the cable car again to make the spectacularly scenic descent toward **Lake Ashino-ko.** The cable car will stop en route only if someone wants to alight. On a fine day Fuji-san will be perfectly mirrored in the lake's calm surface; you can take a closer look by taking a ferry from Togendai, where the cable car terminates, to Hakone-machi or Moto-Hakone. The trip takes about 40 minutes; tickets should be purchased from the cable car terminal before boarding. If you are on a day trip with a train to catch back to Tokyo, you can catch the bus back to Odawara from Hakone-machi (outside the pier building) or Moto-Hakone (from Hakone Barrier) every 10 or 20 minutes.

The two stops, about half a mile (1 km) apart, have worthwhile sights nearby. Almost 220 yards (200 m) to the north of Hakone-machi is **Hakone Barrier (Hakone Sekishoato).** The original structure vanished long ago, but the replacement on the same spot reproduces the checkpoint set up for intercepting travelers along the old Tokaido Road between Kyoto and Edo. From here the Sugi-namiki, a splendid avenue of cryptomeria trees planted over 350 years ago, parallels the main road for about three-quarters of a mile (1.2 km) to Moto-Hakone.

Walkways wind past sulfurous fumaroles and boiling pools in Hakone's volcanic Owakudani—the Valley of Greater Boiling.

Hakone Gongen Shrine stands among dense woods in the foothills of Mount Koma. Marked by a huge red torii gateway emerging from the lake north of the Moto-Hakone bus stop, it is one of central Japan's largest shrines, founded some 1,200 years ago. Minamoto Yoritomo hid here in 1180 after a defeat during his ultimately successful campaign against the Taira clan. The shrine features a soaring cedar grove along the approach and a treasure hall with important historical relics.

If you have plenty of time, there is a popular hiking route along a preserved section of the old Tokaido Road from Moto-Hakone to Hakone-Yumoto. Paved as far as the Amazake-Jaya teahouse, the walk takes 3 hours 30 minutes and passes Saun-ji, Shogen-ji, and Soun-ji temples. As the area's most popular onsen resort, Hakone-Yumoto is predictably garish, but it's a good choice for the onsen experience. Moreover, a stopover with a long soak in hot water might be just what you need after a good hike.

(continued on p. 127)

Hakone Open-Air Museum

www.hakone-oam.or.jp

✉ 1121 Ni-no-Taira

☎ 0460/82-1161

🕒 9 a.m.–5 p.m., March–Nov., closes at 4 in winter

$ $$$$

Climbing Fuji-san

The paths zigzagging up the slopes of Fuji-san are fairly regular; the ascent is less a climb than a hike. There are four main routes. If you reached the area from Tokyo via Odawara, opt for the northern Kawaguchi-ko route. Buses to Kawaguchi-ko 5th Station leave from Kawaguchi-ko town until late in the evening. Since this service is suspended only from mid-November through February, you *could* make an out-of-season ascent, but the weather on Fuji is extremely unpredictable even at the best of times. In winter, when the mountain is covered in snow, the ascent can be very dangerous. There is also a direct bus service all the way from Shinjuku Station in Tokyo to the Kawaguchi-ko 5th Station.

Before you start out, check ahead for the weather conditions. Call the English-language information line at the Fuji-Yoshida visitor information service *(tel 0555/24-1236)*. Either way, bear in mind that the weather at the summit is notoriously unpredictable, changing between rain, sunshine, wind, and snow without warning.

Climbers approaching the region from the southwest make their ascent from the Fujinomiya-Mishima 5th Station; buses to the latter run from both the Shin Fuji and Mishima Stations on the JR Shinkansen line. The other options are the Gotemba and Subashiri 5th Stations to the east, but the distance from these to the summit is greater.

Like a river of light, climbers bearing flashlights ascend Fuji-san in time to reach the summit for the *goraiko*—the greeting for the first rays of the rising sun.

The ascent

The five- to seven-hour ascent (4 miles/6 km from Kawaguchi-ko) can be made either during the afternoon with an overnight stop at one of the stations, or in darkness to reach the top in time for sunrise. To a small number of Shinto pilgrims in white tunics, this is a ritual celebrating the sun goddess Amaterasu, mother of Japan. To millions of others, it is a secular must on the lifetime calendar.

Most climbers ascend from Kawaguchi-ko 5th Station. Along with inane Fuji-san trinkets, the souvenir stores here sell useful equipment. You will need a water bottle, perhaps a sunhat, and a staff, optionally sporting a flag and/or, pilgrim-fashion, a tinkling bell. The staffs are branded with commemorative logos at each station, and climbers hammer the bells as well as coins—just for luck—into a *torii* gateway near the shrine at the summit. No mountaineering experience is necessary: Solid iron chains serve as handrails on the rockier passages lower down. A trip from high summer into bleak midwinter, the climb makes a warm waterproof jacket, gloves, strong shoes or hiking boots (they will get scuffed), and woolen clothing essential. If you're climbing at night, don't forget to take a flashlight.

The summit

Hikers, Boy Scouts, families, pilgrims, and pensioners arrive panting through the stone torii gateway spanning the last few steps of the pathway to the 10th Station at the summit. A featureless expanse of chocolate brown chunks of stone, the summit is Martian in its desolation. There is a meteorological station on the crater rim, itself a rigorous walk. The 10th Station, 30 years ago a single hut, is now more like a small shantytown.

With the frequent arrival of fog, rain, or flurries of snow, everyone retreats indoors to huddle around an oil stove in the center of a room reminiscent of Klondike during the gold rush. Consisting of noodle soup or curry rice at twice the prices five miles down, the food (not included in the price) is legendary for its poor quality. You can carry your own provisions if you don't mind the weight. The cold prompts a roaring trade in alcoholic beverages from vending machines—even bottled water is expensive up here, and there is no other kind. Handed a soiled, clammy sleeping bag, you retire to a rough wooden bunk or a mattress on the floor. Keep your outer garments on: The night is short but bitterly cold. At 4 a.m. everyone runs outside with flashlights to take up position to watch the sunrise.

As the sun rises through the mist in an amazing array of picture-postcard hues, all arms are raised to the hearty cheer of "Banzai! Banzai!" If the skies are clear, with clouds drifting far below mirrored in the still waters of the lakes, the view is utterly spectacular.

After a breakfast of *o-nigiri* rice patties and thin *miso* soup, it is time to descend. Despite the views over the lakes and the conical shadow of the mountain on the plain when the sun is behind you, it is a great relief to come into greenery again. You may find yourself pondering the old Japanese adage: Everyone should climb Fuji-san once, but only a fool would climb it twice. ■

A tranquil view of Fuji-san at sunset

(continued from p. 123)

FUJI-SAN

The world's most beautiful volcano, its image immediately recognizable, Fuji-san is the highest mountain in Japan at 12,388 feet (3,776 m). Fuji-san last blew its top in 1707. The spectacular three-week eruption terrified the citizens of Edo 75 miles (120 km) away, turning skies dark during the daytime and coating the city with ash. The volcano is now dormant, but another eruption cannot be ruled out.

Of all the mountains worshiped in Shinto mountain cults, Fuji-san is the almighty; it has been revered as sacred since prehistoric times. Its sanctity is official: Following five years' wrangling over the legal ownership of the peak between the local government and Fuji's own Sengen-jinja Shrine, a hearing ruled in the latter's favor in 1962. Forbidden to women until 1868, it is now ascended annually by over 250,000 people of both sexes and all ages during the July–August climbing season. As many as one-third of the climbers hail from abroad. If you want to climb Fuji-san, note that the season extends through July and August. You may be tempted to avoid the crowds by ascending outside these months, but the visitor stations on the mountain open only shortly before the season and close soon after (see pp. 124–26).

With its outstanding scenery, including densely forested mountains and idyllic views of Fuji-san, the nearby **Fuji Five Lakes (Fuji-go-ko)** area has not gone unnoticed; the banks of the larger

Mount Fuji-san

109 B2

Visitor information

Fuji Yoshida, outside the station

0555/22-7000

lakes, **Lake Yamanaka-ko** and **Lake Kawaguchi-ko,** have been substantially developed, particularly the latter. Kawaguchi-ko is the preferred starting place for ascending Fuji-san on the north side; buses from here will take you up to the 5th Station. (The routes up the mountain are interspersed with stopping points known as stations; they culminate in Station 10 at the summit.) Up from the lakeside are some of Japan's choicest property developments for corporate and individual holiday homes, as well as vacation lodges for schools and colleges; the area abounds with facilities for sports, including tennis and golf, as well as fine hotels. The areas around Lakes Sai-ko, Shoji-ko, and Motosu-ko are a good deal more pristine, but the only really leisurely way to explore them is by car.

IZU-HANTO

The southern end of Fuji-Hakone-Izu National Park flanks the Izu-Hanto Peninsula, famous for its hot spring resorts and fine coastal scenery. Being so close to Tokyo, this is the country's most popular coastal resort area and can often be overcrowded. Where the famous scenic assets have been undermined by indiscriminate hotel development, resorts such as **Atami** have become tawdry and overpriced. This said, Atami possesses the **MOA Museum of Art (MOA Bijutsukan,** *tel 0557/84-2511, closed Thurs.);* its famous collection of Chinese and Japanese art includes several National Treasures and Important Cultural Properties. The area as a whole, which includes the Izu Seven Isles offshore, has a reputation for wonderful fresh seafood. The less ostentatious hot spring *ryokan* (traditional inns) around Shimoda, where Commodore Perry landed with his Black Ships in 1853 (see p. 36), can offer a very pleasant and peaceful off-peak getaway. But unless you are in Japan for some time, Izu-Hanto, unlike Fuji-Hakone, should not be a high priority. ■

Volcanoes & earthquakes

The most active volcanoes are those in Kyushu (notably Aso, Unzen, and Sakurajima). However, the presence of hot springs, geysers, pools of boiling mud, and emanations of sulfurous fumes in the land around the foothills of many others, including Fuji-san, belies their dormancy. Volcanic activity and the movement of tectonic plates deep underground make Japan particularly earthquake prone. Japan experiences as many as 2,000 earthquakes annually, many too small to be recorded except on sensitive seismographic equipment. Registering over 8 on the Richter scale, temblors such as the Great Kanto Earthquake of 1923 and the one that struck Kobe in 1995 have caused devastating damage and loss of life. The Kanto plain is considered especially vulnerable. For centuries, major earthquakes have hit the Tokyo-Yokohama region roughly once every 70 years, so the next one is widely regarded as overdue.

Strong earthquakes offshore trigger tsunami—colossal seismic waves that can have calamitous effects when they come crashing inland. Much of Kamakura was destroyed by a tsunami in 1495, and one wrecked the island of Okushiri-to off Hokkaido in 1993.

(See also Earthquakes on p. 357 of Travelwise.) ■

Japan's second largest island, Hokkaido is home to only five percent of the population. It is still seen as the nation's last frontier—an area of wilderness with breathtakingly beautiful landscapes comprising lakes, mountains, and volcanoes.

Hokkaido

Introduction & map **130–31**
Sapporo & beyond **132–34**
Shikotsu-Toya National Park **135–37**
Hakodate & beyond **138–39**
A walk in Hakodate **140–41**
Onuma Quasi-National Park & the south **142**
Daisetsuzan National Park & central Hokkaido **143**
Rishiri-Rebun-Sarobetsu National Park & the far north **144–45**
The northeast: Abashiri & Shiretoko National Park **146–47**
The east: Akan & Kushiro-Shitsugen National Parks **148–50**
Hotels & restaurants on Hokkaido **366–68**

Colossal ice sculpture at the Snow Festival in Sapporo

Hokkaido

THE JAPANESE HAVE ALWAYS REGARDED HOKKAIDO, their second largest island, as a wilderness. During the feudal era it was seen as a wasteland, called Ezo, inhabited only by the indigenous Ainu peoples(see p. 136). Today its wide open spaces attract growing legions who enjoy unspoiled nature and the great outdoors. With the Japan Sea on its west coast, the Pacific Ocean to the southeast, and the Sea of Okhotsk to the northeast, the prefecture of Hokkaido represents 22 percent of the national landmass but holds only 5 percent of the population.

Although there were lonely outposts in southern Hokkaido during the feudal era, exploitation of the island began only in 1859, when Hakodate was opened as one of Japan's first five treaty ports (those opened to foreign trade by treaty). Development started in earnest after the Meiji Restoration in 1868, but demographic and economic growth really took off after World War II, when millions of Japanese who had colonized Manchuria after its occupation in 1931 were repatriated. Most settled in the south of Hokkaido, particularly in the capital, Sapporo.

Hokkaido's wilderness, some of it still wild enough to be roamed by brown bears, is pristine; it possesses breathtakingly beautiful landscapes comprising dense forests, mountains, and lakes—the latter often in the calderas of extinct or dormant volcanoes. Many other volcanoes here are among Japan's most active, and the abundant hot springs dotted about the island include some of the country's favorite *onsen* resorts. The best known is Noboribetsu Onsen, 72 miles (116 km) southeast of Sapporo. It is within Shikotsu-Toya National Park, the most easily accessible of Hokkaido's several national parks.

The island's climate is Siberian, with long, cold winters and short, cool summers, but the adversity of a harsh winter has been turned into an asset. Two of Japan's finest ski resorts, Furano and Niseko, offer just some of Hokkaido's winter sports options. Many Japanese travel to Sapporo especially to see the huge, elaborate ice sculptures in Odori Park during the Snow Festival in February, and it is becoming increasingly popular to travel all the way up to the remote port of Abashiri in

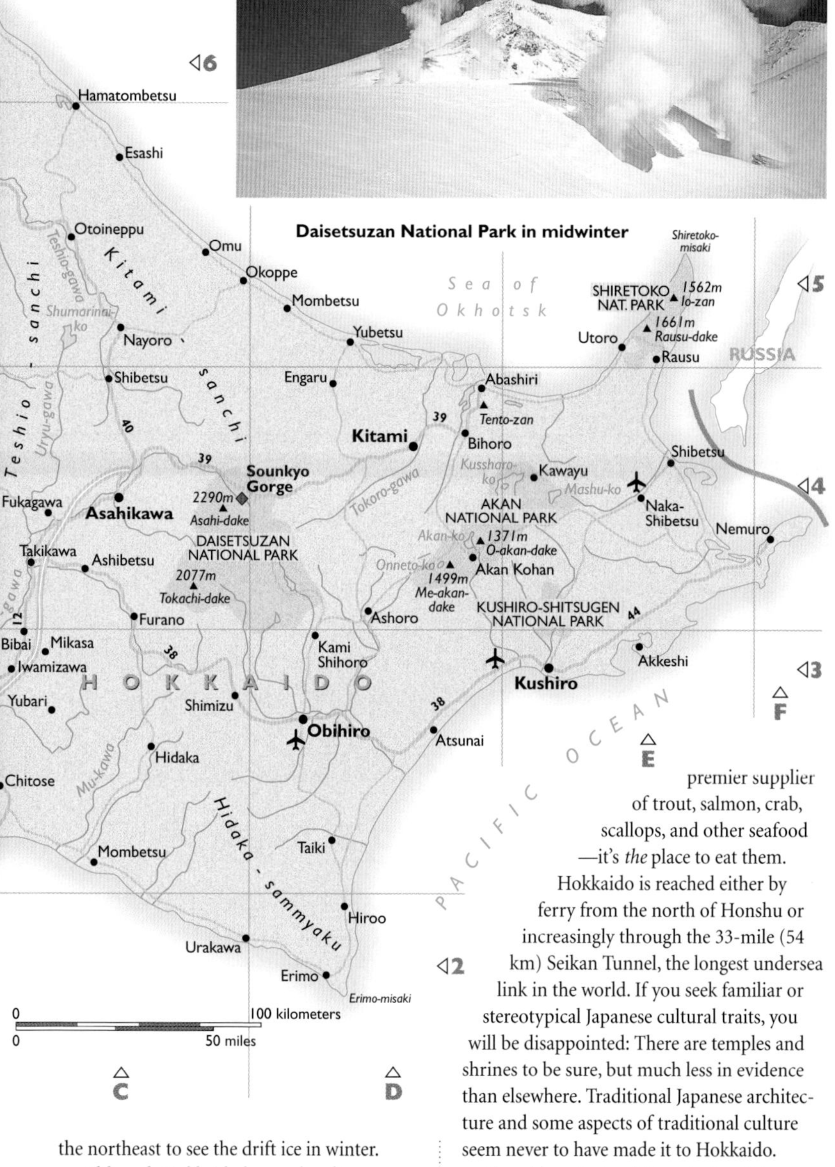

Daisetsuzan National Park in midwinter

the northeast to see the drift ice in winter.

Although Hokkaido has coal and iron ore and automobiles and electronics industries, it thrives for the most part on forestry products and agriculture. This is the one place in Japan where you're likely to see wheat fields. It is also ideal for fruit growing and dairy farming; Hokkaido supplies 90 percent of Japan's milk products. With rich fishing grounds offshore and plentiful rivers, the island is the country's premier supplier of trout, salmon, crab, scallops, and other seafood —it's *the* place to eat them.

Hokkaido is reached either by ferry from the north of Honshu or increasingly through the 33-mile (54 km) Seikan Tunnel, the longest undersea link in the world. If you seek familiar or stereotypical Japanese cultural traits, you will be disappointed: There are temples and shrines to be sure, but much less in evidence than elsewhere. Traditional Japanese architecture and some aspects of traditional culture seem never to have made it to Hokkaido.

Travel here is also different. The distances between population centers can be considerable and journeys much longer. You can fly, but if you plan to explore the island by train, you will need a rail pass. Transport between remote points in some of the national park areas can be sparse; many people find a car or a motorcycle by far the most convenient way to travel in Japan's only wild frontier. ■

Illuminated ice sculptures glow in Odori-koen Park.

Sapporo & beyond

THE FIFTH LARGEST CITY IN JAPAN, SAPPORO IS DYNAMIC and modern but has little to offer in the way of traditional sights. American urban planners helped lay out the city in 1871, and even today it feels as though its citizens have only just arrived; perhaps this is why they seem to welcome foreign visitors almost as traveling companions. Friendly and cosmopolitan, Sapporo is certainly worth an overnight stop, at the very least as the main transport hub to other parts of the island.

Sapporo
130 B3
Visitor information
Sapporo Tourist Information Center, Sapporo Station
011/213-5088

Hokudai Shokubutsu-en Botanical Gardens
N3 W8, Chuo-ku
011/221-0066
Closed Mon. (except greenhouse); closed Nov. 4–April 28
$$; Greenhouse $

Crossed east to west by **Odori-koen Park,** which cuts a swath of lawns, trees, monuments, and fountains through the center of the city, Sapporo is surprisingly green. Odori is unfortunately crowned at its eastern end by the 482-foot (147 m) TV Tower, which is every bit as hideous as its Tokyo equivalent.

The legacy of the American urban planners is a city that is uncommonly easy to get around in. Unlike elsewhere in Japan, addresses follow a simple numbered grid system: The Sapporo railroad station, for instance, is at North 5, West 3.

Sapporo's sights are mainly concentrated in the center. Among

them, about 550 yards (500 m) southwest of the station, are the **Shokubutsu-en Botanical Gardens,** a lovely oasis of green established in 1886. In addition to thousands of varieties of (mainly alpine) plants and trees, both local and from around the world, the gardens include the **Ainu Museum (Hoppo Minzoku Shiryoshitsu)** displaying historical Ainu crafts and artifacts. Also on the grounds is the first museum devoted to local wildlife—alas, of the stuffed variety.

Other buildings surviving from early days are the **Old Hokkaido Government Building** (1888, *no admission);* when Hokkaido was just beginning to attract mainland settlers, the building was called the Colonization Commission. Built of red brick in the 19th-century neo-baroque style popular in Meiji Japan, it looks attractive in its setting of lawns and greenery but is less likely to impress visitors used to similar buildings in the West.

Architectural pride is reserved for the **Clock Tower (Tokei Dai),** the symbol of Sapporo and the single most photographed sight in the city. Built of wood in 1878 for Sapporo Agricultural College, it resembles a charming old New England schoolhouse and stands incongruously dwarfed between adjacent towers of concrete, some 440 yards (400 m) south of Sapporo Station.

Sapporo has a reputation as an indoor city; if the crowds appear to thin in winter, you can be sure they're down in the huge underground shopping mall in Susukino or the 0.75-mile (1 km) Tanuki-koji shopping arcade, with shops that have been operating there for a hundred years. These areas lie to the south of Odori. The latest addition is the futuristic **Sapporo Factory** *(N2 E4, tel 011/207-5000),* just south of Sapporo Station, a shopping and leisure complex featuring trees, streams, an old redbrick brewery, and other buildings, all within an atrium spanned by the largest glass roof in Japan.

Sapporo Beer Garden (Sapporo Biiru-en) and **Sapporo Beer Museum (Biiru Hakubutsukan),** located east of the station, is owned by Hokkaido's most famous brand name and focuses on the brewery built by the company in 1891. Free guided tours of the brewery and museum are followed by free samples of the brews. The adjacent beer garden is a vast beer hall and restaurant and one of the most popular spots in town.

Not to be outdone, the

Diners at the Sapporo Beer Hall indulge en masse in "Ghengis Khan" style barbecued lamb—a Hokkaido specialty.

Sapporo Beer Garden and Beer Museum

- N7 E9, Higahishi-ku
- 011/742-1531 (beer garden); 011/731-4368 (museum)
- 9 a.m.–5:30 p.m.
- Shuttle buses about every 20–30 min. outside Sapporo Station South Gate

The entrance to Ramen Alley: The noodle stores along here are revered for serving the best of their kind.

Susukino amusement quarter to the south of the town center counts some 6,000 bars, restaurants, and places of entertainment —from swanky crab restaurants to cabarets very much in the red light category. Located due south of Sapporo Station, Susukino's **Ramen Alley (Ramen Yokocho)** is the main rival to Fukuoka's *yatai* (see p. 320) for the best ramen noodles in Japan. This narrow alley of about a dozen tiny noodle restaurants is so popular that you will probably have to wait your turn. The noodles with crab are more than worth the wait.

If you wonder about the Hokkaido of the past, you can visit the **Historical Village of Hokkaido (Hokkaido Kaitaku-no-mura),** just beyond the eastern boundary of the city. This impressive open-air museum combines some 60 buildings dismantled in Sapporo and other parts of Hokkaido and erected here. They include Sapporo's old main train station, homes, stores, and businesses, as well as structures from farming and fishing villages. Transport around the 133-acre (54 ha) site is provided by sleigh in winter and horse-drawn trolley the rest of the year.

On the coast west of Sapporo is **Otaru,** once one of the most important commercial and fishing ports on Hokkaido and still a ferry terminal. Just 40 minutes from Sapporo by local train, this attractive city is now virtually a suburb of the metropolis. Many people who can't find a room in Sapporo (or prefer something homier or more picturesque) opt to stay here instead. There are several Western-style buildings dating back to Otaru's Meiji-era heyday, among them the recently restored Offices of the Nippon Yusen Co. Ltd., built in 1906 by Shijiro Satate, a pupil of British architect Josiah Conder.

Otaru's most interesting buildings are concentrated east of the city around the port; almost all are **warehouses** dating to the 1890s that have been restored and converted into, among other things, attractive shopping areas, cafés, and microbreweries. One of them, built in the Chinese style in 1893, is the **Otaru Museum (Otaru-shi Hakubutsukan),** which evokes interesting facets of local history. Endlessly described as "romantic" in local tourist brochures, the 0.8-mile (1.3 km) **Otaru Canal Walk** takes you past streetlamps and warehouses. About three hours west of Sapporo by bus is **Niseko,** rapidly gaining renown as Japan's best ski resort. Thanks to frosty winds from Siberia, Niseko's three ski and snowboarding resorts on Mt. Annupuri (4,291 feet/1,308 m) have some of the finest, deepest powder in this part of the world, as well as excellent hot springs year-round and hiking and river rafting in summer. The view of the Fuji-like Mt. Yotei-zan from Annupuri's slopes is thrilling. ■

Historical Village of Hokkaido

- Konopporo, 50-1 Atsubetsu-cho, Atsubetsu-ku
- 011/898-2692
- 9 a.m.–4:30 p.m. June–Sept., 9:30 a.m.—4 p.m. Oct.–May; closed Mon.
- $$
- JR bus from Shin Sapporo subway

Otaru Municipal Museum

- 2-1-20 Ironai, Otaru-shi 8-min. walk due NE from Otaru Station
- 0134/33-2439
- 9:30 a.m.–5 p.m.
- $$

Shikotsu-Toya National Park

A view of Hokkaido's lush scenery over Lake Toya-ko in summer

CLOSE TO SAPPORO, THIS PARK OF NEARLY 230 SQUARE miles (600 sq km) combines some of Hokkaido's most beautiful scenery with an abundance of hot springs, making it the island's most popular destination. It gets its name from Lake Toya-ko to the southwest and Lake Shikotsu-ko in the east, which are the highlights of the two areas that constitute the park's main sections. A third area, north of Toya-ko, centers on the perfectly conical Mount Yotei-san, often called Ezo-no-Fuji for its resemblance to its more famous counterpart on Honshu.

The northernmost ice-free lake on Hokkaido, scenic **Shikotsu-ko** is surrounded by volcanic mountains; a paradise for walkers, climbers, and nature lovers in summer, it remains popular all year round with fishermen. Despite being only about an hour from Sapporo, the 30-square mile (77 sq km) caldera lake is remarkably unspoiled. The gateway is **Shikotsu Kohan,** a village lying in the woods on the lake's eastern shore. Even the *onsen* have remained rustic, with the emphasis on *rotenburo* (outdoor baths). A long soak is the perfect way to finish a good day's hike around the local peaks. Among the hiking options, **Monbetsu-dake** (2,841 feet/866 m) is closest to the village and easiest to summit (less than two hours). **Eniwa-dake** (4,331 feet/1,320 m) is the hardest: A round-trip hike takes five to six hours and should be abandoned if it rains. **Tarumae-zan** (3,405 feet/1,038 m) to the south is the most popular walk—and the most volcanic. It takes about half an hour to reach the summit from Station 7, itself accessible in three hours from Shikotsu Kohan on foot. The alternative is to take a taxi, as there is no bus. Transport round the Shikotsu

Shikotsu-Toya National Park

130 B3

Visitor information

144 Toya-ko Onsen-machi

0142/75-2446

Ainu elder at Poroto Kohan conducts a salmon-welcoming ceremony.

The Ainu

The Ainu were the original inhabitants of Honshu. Light-skinned and often wavy-haired, they are unrelated to the Japanese; anthropologists believe they are descendants of Caucasians from prehistoric Siberia. The forebears of the Japanese drove Ainu settlers in Honshu northward, and by the ninth century the Ainu inhabited Ezo (today's Hokkaido). Their culture, which embraces carving and wood-craft, vividly patterned textiles, and epic songs, has no close relatives.

Today the Ainu are thought to number about 24,000. Inter-marriage between Ainu and Japanese has been established for so long that recent surveys show there are only about 200 people left with all four grandparents of pure Ainu descent. ■

Noboribetsu Onsen
Map 130 B3
Visitor information
✉ 60 Noboribetsu onsen machi
☎ 0143/84-3311

lake area is at best highly sporadic, so a car comes in handy, though most hotels and youth hostels rent bicycles on a daily basis.

Toya-ko, the smaller of the park's two lakes, has an island right in the center, with an animal population that includes Ezo deer (Hokkaido was formerly called Ezo). The more popular of the two lakes, with an abundance of hot springs all around the shore, Toya-ko draws onsen enthusiasts throughout the year. Just to the

south is the highly active **Mount Usu-zan,** which shouldn't be missed by anyone interested in volcanoes. The latest eruption in spring 2000 caused widespread evacuations of the area. Check with the local authorities if you plan to visit this area. Usu-zan is the parent of the volcano known as **Showa Shin-zan** (New Mountain), which first appeared in a farmer's field at the eastern foot of Usu-zan in 1943; it is now more than 1,320 feet (400 m) high, and growing. Unless informed otherwise, you can safely take a cable car up to an impressive view of the infernal landscape inside the crater rim and beyond the lake to Yotei-san in the distance.

Near the park's southern coast is **Noboribetsu Onsen,** which boasts the greatest volume of hot spa water in Japan. Whatever scenic attractions may have been here are now undermined by a glut of monster resort hotels. Noboribetsu does have the advantage of an awe-inspiring **Hell Valley (Jigokudani),** with viewing platforms and wooden walkways spanning a desolate, evil-smelling landscape belching sulfurous fumes and steam from fissures in discolored rocks, not to mention the poisonous-looking, violently bubbling Oyunuma Pond.

Farther southeast is the coastal town of **Shiraoi,** noted for the reconstructed Ainu village at **Poroto Kotan.** Although the town features performances for tourists, it was set up by the Ainu themselves and boasts a particularly good Ainu museum. ■

Showa Shin-zan, a volcano that first appeared only about 60 years ago, is still on the rise.

Poroto Kotan Ainu Museum

www.ainu-museum.or.jp

- 2-3-4 Wakakusa-cho, Shiraoi-cho
- 0144/82-3914
- $$
- Train: JR from Noboribetsu Station to Shiraoi Station

From Mount Hakodate, the view over the city after dark presents a galaxy of lights.

Hakodate & beyond

HAKODATE, ON THE OSHIMA-HANTO PENINSULA IN THE FAR southwest of Hokkaido, is one of the main terminals for ferries from Honshu—and also one of the most rewarding cities to visit in the prefecture. No other city has quite so many buildings and reminders evoking Meiji- and Taisho-period Japan.

Hakodate

130 B2

Visitor information

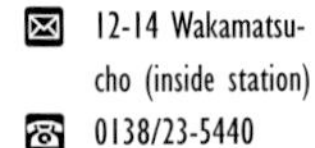

12-14 Wakamatsu-cho (inside station)

0138/23-5440

JR services from Aomori (2 hrs.). From Sapporo (3 hrs. 30 min.)

Though Hakodate is a popular gateway to Hokkaido, many Japanese visitors confine their trips to the Hakodate area alone, which has most of the attractions found elsewhere on the island.

In 1864 the shogunate built **Goryokaku** (Five Corner Fort) to defend this important outpost from foreign aggression. Ironically, it was besieged by Japanese soldiers during the Hakodate War of 1869, when the shogun's troops made a futile last stand against the imperial forces during the Meiji Restoration. The citadel itself, an early attempt at a Western-style fortification, has disappeared, but the curious star shape of the walls is still much in evidence on a hilltop east of the city as the highlight of popular **Goryokaku-koen Park.** The moat serves as a boating pond, and the whole star shape becomes a vast floral centerpiece during the cherry blossom

brewing their own beer. Streetcars are still the city's main form of public transportation; one dating from 1913 is still in service for tourists.

Painted signs and mountains of bright orange king crabs and hairy crabs characterize Hakodate's colorful Morning Market *(asa ichi)*, just south of the railroad station. It comprises some 400 stalls selling fish, seafood, fruit, and other local

Hakodate is filled with fine historic buildings.

season. Adjacent **Goryokaku Tower,** though hideous, is worth ascending to appreciate the shape of the citadel.

The city lies on a narrow spit of land, with the sea to the north and south. Beside the town is the 1,100-foot (335 m) **Mount Hakodate,** accessible either on foot or by cable car. The view from the top is spectacular. **Motomachi,** the western side of town, occupies part of the slope; it is renowned for buildings from the city's late 19th- and early 20th-century heyday. Most of these structures are open as museums (see pp. 140–41). Old buildings also pepper the area near the waterfront; warehouses have been preserved and transformed into attractive shopping areas, exhibition spaces, and café-restaurants

produce, both wholesale and retail. Open for breakfast, the local noodle restaurants are famed for their seafood soup dishes. The market opens at 4 a.m. with the sale of fresh catches and closes in the early afternoon, though some stalls remain open for tourists. Some of the wooden buildings in the picturesque alleyways out back look as if they have been around as long as Hakodate itself.

On the eastern side of the city is Yunokawa Onsen spa area; just over half an hour to the north is scenic Onuma Quasi-National Park (see p. 142). Beautiful **Cape Esan-misaki,** about 37 miles (60 km) east of the city, is cherished for two volcanic peaks carpeted with azaleas and alpine plants in late spring and summer. ■

Goryokaku Tower

- ✉ 43-9 Goryokaku-cho, Hakodate
- ☎ 0138/51-4785
- 🕒 8 a.m.–7 p.m., April 21–Oct. 20; 9 a.m.–6 p.m., Oct. 21–April 20
- $ $$
- 🚌 Streetcar: Goryokaku Koen Mae, walk 15 min.

The Old Public Hall in Hakodate is the star attraction among many historic buildings.

A walk in Hakodate

Hakodate is a small city. If you have seen Goryokaku-koen Park and the Morning Market, you can take this walk around Motomachi and the waterfront area after lunch.

Take the streetcar or bus to **Hakodate Dokku-mae** or a taxi to the **Foreigners' Cemetery (Gaikoujin Bochi)** ❶ *(Tel 0138/21-3323)*. If you're coming from the streetcar/bus stop, head southwest up Uomi-zaka, take the first right, and stay on the same road. The cemetery is on the right, overlooking the bay. A poignant reminder of Hakodate's cosmopolitan history, it contains the graves of Americans (including two of Commodore Perry's sailors, who died on the trip in 1854), British, Chinese, and Russians. From the cemetery, head southeast for about 220 yards (200 m), until you come to the **Old Russian Consulate (Kyu Roshia Ryoji-kan),** built in 1908 to replace the original of 1858. The redbrick exterior is not imposing, but the interior conveys the atmosphere of the czarist era.

After leaving here, walk downhill and take the fifth street on the right, walking four blocks to reach the **Chinese Memorial Hall (Chuka Kai-kan)** ❷ *(Tel 0138/22-1211)*. Rebuilt after a fire in 1907, it looks as though it belongs in old Shanghai—which, in a sense, it does. Completed in 1912, it was constructed by builders, carpenters, and sculptors especially imported from Shanghai. As you exit, turn right, then take the second right, and you will find yourself before the green **Soma Company building ❸,** a neoclassical wooden office building of the early Taisho period (1912–1926) that still functions as such. Located right on the main street, it's one of the most photographed buildings in Hakodate—especially with a tram passing by, when the pairing looks exactly as it did some 90 years ago. The broad avenue going uphill in front of the building leads to the main sights of **Motomachi.** As you walk up, the white building with the blue-trimmed arched windows on your left is the **Old British Consulate (Kyu Igirisu Ryoji-kan)** ❹ *(Tel 0138/27-8159)*. In service from 1859 to 1934 and now a popular setting for weddings, the consulate contains a museum and a cozy tearoom (with wax Buckingham Palace guard) construed in Japan as "English-style."

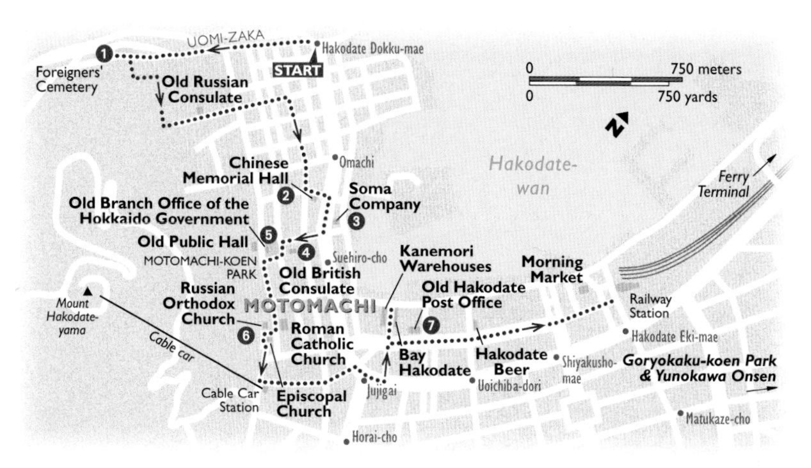

At the top of the avenue is **Motomachi-koen Park,** dominated by an imposing gray wooden building with an elegant Grecian portico: the **Old Branch Office of the Hokkaido Government (Kyu-Hokkaido-cho Hakodate-shicho chosha)** ❺ *(Tel 0138/27-3333).* Built in 1909, it contains a museum of early photography, including what is allegedly the first snapshot ever taken in Japan: Commodore Perry during his trip to Hakodate in 1854. Just behind here is the **Old Public Hall.** Built of wood in the colonial style by a Japanese architect in 1910, this delightful building has been repainted in grayish mauve with yellow highlights around the windows and friezes.

From Motomachi-koen Park, take the cobbled lane on the right. About 380 yards (350 m) farther on your left, you'll see the candy-box charm of the **Russian Orthodox Church (Hakodate Harisutosu-sei Kyokai)** ❻ *(Tel 0138/23-7387),* built in 1916. Almost alongside, on the other side of the lane, is the 1924 Gothic-style **Roman Catholic Church (Katorikku Motomachi Kyokai).** On the same street lies the **Episcopal Church (Sei Yohane Kyokai),** built by missionaries in 1874 and demolished to make way for some futurist renovations in 1979. Just east of it is the **Mount Hakodate Cable Car Station,** which takes you to the summit for a spectacular view over the city and harbor.

Down again after enjoying the view of the town and port, walk northwesterly for about 15 minutes toward the **waterfront.** As you reach the road running parallel to the seafront, you'll see to your right a large red brick building with high rounded arches—the **Old Hakodate Post Office (Kyu-Hakodate Yubinkyoku)** ❼ *(Tel 0138/27-7070).* A post office until 1955, it has been converted into a glass studio and shopping precinct. Around back are a number of 19th-century warehouses made into attractive stores, exhibition and event spaces, and café-restaurants, including **Bay Hakodate** and **Hakodate History Plaza**. Farther north along the waterfront, you'll find the **Hakodate Beer** microbrewery-restaurant; the **Kanemori warehouses** are to the southwest. Continue past the Morning Market to the train station if you intend to travel on, but dinner on the waterfront is a perfect way to wind up a walk in Hakodate. ■

See area map page 130–31
➤ Foreign Cemetery
3.5 miles (5.6 km)
4 hours
➤ Railway Station

NOT TO BE MISSED

- Chinese Memorial Hall
- Soma Company office building
- Old British Consulate
- Old Branch Office of the Hokkaido Government

Onuma Quasi-National Park

130 B2

Visitor information

Beside JR Onuma Koen Station

0138/67-2170

Train from Hakodate (50 min.), Super Hokuto Express (20 min.)

Onuma Quasi-National Park & the south

LOCATED TOWARD THE EAST OF THE OSHIMA HANTO Peninsula in western Hokkaido, Onuma Quasi-National Park is just north of Hakodate. At the center is 3,717-foot-high (1,133 m) Mount Komaga-take, an active volcano famed for the beauty of its craggy peaks and gentle slopes, which in summer are carpeted with spectacular displays of alpine flowers.

Walkers and climbers are rewarded with views south of the mountain over the twin lakes **Onuma,** which gives the park its name, and **Konuma.** Both are outstanding beauty spots. Onuma, whose waters reflect Komaga-take, is dotted with scores of tree-covered islets famed for their display of autumnal color. **Lake Konuma-ko** is no less scenic; Ezo deer roam its perimeter, and the lake's three islands are the winter habitat of wild swans.

Southwest of the park, near the point of the peninsula joined to Honshu by the Seikan Tunnel, lies **Matsumae,** virtually the only place on Hokkaido that retains vestiges of its feudal past. Its castle is a reproduction of the original built in 1854 and destroyed after the feudal era ended in 1868, though the main gate is original. ■

Wild swans winter on islands in Lake Konuma-ko.

Daisetsuzan National Park & central Hokkaido

RIGHT IN THE CENTER OF HOKKAIDO AND IN EVERY WAY the island's heart—at least to the nature lover—Daisetzusan National Park covers some 890 square miles (2,300 sq km), making it Japan's largest national park. Its backbone is a mountain range known as the "roof of Hokkaido," culminating in the 7,513-foot-high (2,290 m) Mount Asahi-dake, the island's highest peak. The park and its mountains are famed for beautiful valleys, steep cliffs, and spectacular waterfalls, in addition to the hot springs sprinkled about the foothills. Most notable is Sounkyo spa in the north of the park, which is also the main staging point for a variety of mountain walks in the region.

Above: Sounkyo Gorge

Below: Lavender fields near Furano in central Hokkaido

One excellent area for hiking is the 15-mile (24 km) **Sounkyo Gorge,** with its rich tapestry of color in the fall and lovely waterfalls, some of which cascade 500 feet (150 m) down a sheer drop, in particular over the Obako and Kobako cliffs. South of Asahi-dake is the park's other great gorge, **Tennin-kyo,** again with waterfalls in beautiful sylvan settings, as well as a number of hot springs.

Twenty five miles (40 km) northwest of Daisetsuzan National Park is **Asahikawa,** Hokkaido's second largest city. Though of little interest to travelers, it is an important transportation hub; many people therefore opt to stay here out of sheer convenience. Some use it as a gateway to the park if they plan to visit on a day trip, but this is not a truly satisfactory option: You would be better off staying in the park itself, especially in a scenic area such as that around Sounkyo Gorge.

About 30 miles (50 km) southwest of Asahikawa is **Furano—**an area important for its winter sports, scenery, and agriculture. Furano resort has some of the best snow conditions in Japan, and it often hosts international ski events. A major producer of grapes, potatoes, beans, asparagus, and other vegetables, the area around the Tokaichi foothills has become popular among Japanese tourists for its vast fields of lavender. ■

Daisetsuzan National Park
Map 131 C4
Tel 0165/82-2574
Bus from JR Asahikawa Station

Sounkyo Gorge
Tel 01658/5-3350

Asahikawa
Map 131 C4
Visitor information
Asahikawa Station
Tel 0166/22-6704

Furano
Map 131 C4
Visitor information
Tel 0167/23-3388
Train: JR Furano line from Asahikawa.

Rishiri-Rebun-Sarobetsu National Park & the far north

UP IN THE FAR NORTHWEST OF JAPAN, THIS NATIONAL park comprises the beautiful and hiker-friendly islands of Rishiri and Rebun; on the mainland opposite is the Sarobetsu Plain, a strip of coastal swampland some 21 miles (34 km) long.

Just to the north of the Sarobetsu Plain, the remote coastal town of **Wakkanai** has a reputation for bleakness. Many Japanese come here just to see the view over the disputed island of Sakhalin (presently in Russian possession) to the north, then go on to nearby **Cape Soya-misaki—**the northernmost point in Japan—just to say they've been there. As far as the average traveler is concerned, Wakkanai is primarily a jumping off point for the two breathtakingly lovely islands a short distance from the western coast.

The rounded island of **Rishiri-to** is crowned by a conical volcano often compared to Fuji-san, the magnificent 5,646-foot (1,721 m) **Rishiri-zan.** This is the island's main draw; there are several trails to the summit, including one for serious climbers. None of the routes is especially easy. To ascend and descend Rishiri-zan takes about ten hours, but there are less strenuous walks through lower, greener hills dotted with alpine flowers, notably to the scenic **Hime-numa Pond.** The visitor information center at the island ferry terminal in Oshidomari has maps and guides describing the various trails in English, although the staff does not speak English. If you're planning to climb, bring proper clothing, as it can be bitterly cold, with plenty of ice and snow even in high summer. You will also need to carry water; there is none on the mountain.

If you are not of the mountaineering persuasion, the visitor center rents out bicycles. The single road around the island links various picturesque fishing hamlets with the ports of **Oshidomari** in

Rishiri-Rebun-Sarobetsu National Park

130 B6

Visitor information

Wakkanai

0163/82-2201 (Oshidomari ferry)

the north and **Kutsugata** in the west, where there are the largest number of places to stay.

Rebun-to, a narrow, wedge-shape isle some 9 miles (15 km) long, is smaller than Rishiri but more interesting—at the very least for the sheer variety of its scenery. Famous for carpets of hundreds of varieties of alpine flowers in summer, its rolling hills culminate in the 1,607-foot (490 m) **Rebun-dake.** The most popular hiking routes on Rebun run along the west coast, taking in cliffs, remote fishing hamlets, and a striking array of both wooded and marine scenery. Details of the trails are available at the hotels and youth hostels on the island, many of which organize hiking parties. Because the trails pass through remote areas, it is better to avoid hiking on your own.

There are two main ports, Kafuka in the south and smaller Funodomari in the north; both offer a range of accommodations, as do the villages of Motochi in the southwest and Shiretoko on the southern tip. Bicycle rental is available from most hotels and *minshuku* (see p. 359), and all communities are linked by a bus service. Rebun and Rishiri are at their best from June to September.

The **Sarobetsu Genya Plain,** the remaining area of the park, is famous for its colorful summer flowers, especially irises, lilies, and rhododendrons. ■

Mount Rishiri-zan famously graces remote Rishiri-to.

The northeast: Abashiri & Shiretoko National Park

AT THE MOUTH OF THE ABASHIRI-GAWA RIVER ON THE SEA of Okhotsk is Abashiri, a port for the trout and salmon fishing industry. From December to March, when the port closes down as the bay fills with ice floes, it's a lonely place.

Say "Abashiri" to most Japanese of the baby-boomer generation, and they fondly think back to a prison rather than to the town. It's all due to an early-1970s gangster-movie series that featured tattooed antiheroes in a snowbound maximum-security lockup. Built on **Mount Tento-zan** near the city in 1890, the prison has been moved to new premises, and the old one has been turned into **Abashiri Prison Museum (Hakubutsukan Abashiri Kangoku,** *1-1 Yobito, Abashiri-shi, tel 0152/45-2411, www.kangoku.jp/world).* Now populated with wax figures, Japan's Alcatraz is a grim if fascinating reminder of the harsh, chilly conditions endured by jailbirds in prewar Japan. Also on Tento-zan is the interesting **Hokkaido Museum of Northern Peoples (Hoppo Minzoku Hakubutsukan);** it provides insights into the Ainu, Siberians, Eskimos, and Amerindians—and the connections among them. Abashiri is also home to the **Okhotsk Ryuhyo Museum (Okhotsk Ryuhyo-kan,** *245-1 Tento-zan, Abashiri, tel 0152/43-5951).* With its subzero temperatures and great blocks of ice, it seems designed to show summer visitors what they missed from the pack ice in winter. Hardier visitors can try Mombetsu, 56 miles (90 km) northwest of Abashiri, to see the ice floes on the Sea of Okhotsk in midwinter; come February, the sea is frozen to the horizon, and sightseeing excursions are provided aboard an icebreaker.

Above all, Abashiri is the gateway to **Shiretoko National Park,** Japan's only true wilderness, which was granted UNESCO World Heritage Site status in 2005. Occupying the last 30 miles (50 km) of a rugged peninsula extending some 45 miles (70 km) into the Sea of Okhotsk, Shiretoko includes peaks and dense forests. The road runs along the coast to the town of **Utoro** in the west and connects with the small town of **Rausu** in the east. Beyond it there are no more roads: *Shiretoko* is the Ainu word for "world's end." Fox, deer, and bear roam the last 25 miles (40 km) of the peninsula. The area can be explored on foot or by sightseeing boat from Utoro (a 3-to 4-hour trip around the cape).

Abashiri

131 D4

Visitor information

Outside Abashiri Station

0152/44-5849

Train: JR Abashiri from Sapporo (5 hrs. 19 min.)

Hokkaido Museum of Northern Peoples

0152/45-3888

Closed Mon.

$$

These Hokkaido brown bear cubs may grow up to weigh some 880 pounds (400 kg).

Some 6 miles (10 km) northeast of Utoro is one of the park's highlights, the beautiful **Shiretoko Five Lakes (Shiretoko-go-ko),** where wooden walkways encircle bodies of water in virgin forest crisscrossed by hiking paths. Another 6 miles (10 km) farther on is **Kamuiwakka-no-taki,** an *onsen* area characterized by a warm-water river offering the novel experience of bathing in cascades and waterfalls of hot water. Bring swimwear and shoes with soles capable of gripping slippery rock; otherwise you will fall prey to vendors waiting to rent out straw sandals at inflated prices.

Of the many walks within Shiretoko park, the most popular is the ascent of **Rausu-dake** (5,450 feet/1,661 m), the highest peak in the volcanic range at the park's center. Allow up to five hours for the climb. From the peak you can walk north to **Io-zan** (5,125 feet/1,562 m), the volcano that heats the water at Kamuiwakka-no-taki; the trek to the peak and back takes around eight hours.

Many people planning serious hikes in the area swear by the **Shiretoko Iwaobetsu Youth Hostel** some 3 miles (5 km) north of Utoro, which organizes them. Remember, if you're planning to explore the remote tip of the peninsula, traveling in a group is essential. With an estimated 600 bears on the loose out there, you would not want to take a chance—especially not in the fall, when they're out to fatten themselves before hibernating through the winter. ■

The Sea of Okhotsk freezes over in winter, leaving ice-breakers to push through the floes.

Shiretoko National Park

131 E5

Visitor information

Shari Station

0152/23-2424

Train: JR Senmo line to Shari from Abashiri, then bus to Utoro Onsen (1 hr.) or Iwaobetsu (70 min.)

Often shrouded in mist, mysterious Lake Mashu-ko was held in awe by the Ainu, to whom it was a specially sacred place.

The east: Akan & Kushiro-Shitsugen National Parks

SOUTHWEST OF THE SHIRETOKO PENINSULA, TOWARD THE center of the eastern wing of the island of Hokkaido, lies Akan National Park, an idyllic preserve of dense virgin forest, clear lakes, and volcanic mountains. The town of Abashiri (see p. 146) to the north is the most convenient access point for the park.

Akan National Park
131 D4
Visitor information
Akan Kohan Bus Center
0154/67-2254
Bus: Akan bus from JR Kushiro Station to Akan Kohan

Often regarded as the eastern equivalent of Shikotsu-Toya (see p. 135) and likewise endowed with hot springs, Akan is less accessible and therefore less crowded. The park encompasses three main lakes: Akan in the southwest, Mashu to the east, and Kussharo just north of center. Dotted with small islands and surrounded by forests, **Lake Akan-ko,** with its alpine scenery, is famous for the curious plant balls called *marimo (Aegagropila sauteri)* that form in its water. A species of pondweed growing in a perfectly spherical shape, the marimo are not much larger than a baseball but can take 200 years to form.

Akan-ko offers a multitude of hot springs, especially in the resort of **Akan Kohan** on the southern shore. Although the area is very

Hokkaido's national parks are home to a variety of wildlife.

touristy and marred by the usual monster *onsen* hotels, it is a convenient base for climbing 4,498-foot (1,371 m) **O-akan-dake.** With its trailhead some 3 miles (5 km) northeast of Akan Kohan, it can be ascended and descended in about six hours. However, the most interesting local hike is up **Me-akan-dake** (4,918 feet/1,499 m), which is not only the highest mountain in the park but also one of the most active volcanoes in Japan. Me-akan has erupted 15 times since 1800, most recently in 1988. There are a number of ways to reach the summit; the most common is via a trailhead at lovely **Lake Onneto-ko,** nestled in the depths of a thick forest. The lake is accessible from Akan Kohan by bus. If you are going to climb Me-Akan, take warm, waterproof clothing, as the

Bears on Hokkaido

Hokkaido is home to the brown bear *(ursus arctos)*. Bears are shy of humans and make themselves scarce, but can be very dangerous if frightened or hungry. In bear areas, always travel in a group. Avoid hiking just after sunrise and at dusk. Carry a bell or something to warn any bears of your approach. If you do encounter a bear, don't shout or turn your back. Instead, move slowly backward; unless you really have to, don't run. If you spy a cub, don't approach it—the mother is usually close by.

Bears have always been sacred to the Ainu, an honor lost on the animals, who were sacrificed and eaten. Raised in captivity, some bears are now confined in hideous concrete reserves. ■

Japanese cranes make their winter home in the bird sanctuary in Kushiro Marsh.

Kawayu Onsen
☎ 015/483-2255
Train: JR Senmo line to Kawayu Onsen Station (55 min. from Shari, 65 min. from Kushiro), then bus to town center (10 min., but these travel infrequently)

Kushiro-Shitsugen National Park
131 E4
Visitor information
Information counter inside JR Kushiro Station
☎ 0154/22-8294
Bus: Akan bus from JR Kushiro Station (40 min.)

weather is notoriously unpredictable. Once you reach the unearthly landscape near the summit, with its discolored ponds and steaming vents, you might find the air a little too sulfurous for comfort.

Lake Mashu-ko is a caldera lake surrounded by sheer cliffs. More than just an intense shade of blue on a clear day, the exceptionally pure lake water happens to have one of the world's highest transparency ratings, with visibility to a depth of 115 feet (35 m). A good base in the area is the wooded resort of **Kawayu Onsen** to the west of the lake, which is much more pleasant and unspoiled than Akan Kohan. Just south of Kawayu Onsen, another great volcanic hiking opportunity looms in the form of **Io-zan** (Sulphur Mountain). At only 1,680 feet (512 m) it's a less arduous trek than Me-Akan, taking under an hour. In geothermal terms, however, Io-zan pulls out all the stops: Its fascinating, extraterrestrial-looking landscape is alive with bubbling pools and vents belching sulfurous steam.

Kawayu is roughly midway between Mashu-ko and **Lake Kussharo-ko.** The largest lake on Hokkaido, Kussharo has a circumference of 35 miles (57 km) and is very popular for swimming in summer. At **Sunayu Onsen** on a beach on its eastern shore, the heat of the underground water rises to warm the sand.

South of Akan National Park is the newer **Kushiro-Shitsugen National Park.** The main attraction here is **Kushiro Marsh,** Japan's largest wetland (75 square miles/200 sq. km) and a bird sanctuary *(Kushiro Marshland Observatory, 6-11 Hokuto, Kushiro-shi, tel 0154/56-2424).* The main draw is the endangered Japanese red-crested crane; some 400 survive in the park, which is their winter habitat. Opened in 1958, the Japanese Crane Reserve continues its research into breeding and artificial incubation (not open to the public). The park is reached from the city of Kushiro, the industrial hub of eastern Hokkaido; the city is also the main southern gateway to Akan National Park. ■

Tohoku is renowned for its mountain scenery and fertile countryside, seascapes, cold winters, and the historical assets of its old towns. The people are especially welcoming and their festivals rousing. This is Japan for connoisseurs.

Northern Honshu (Tohoku)

Introduction & map **152–53**
Aomori-ken **154–56**
Akita-ken **157–60**
Sendai & Matsushima **161–63**
Iwate-ken **164–67**
Yamagata-ken **168–70**
Hotels & restaurants in Tohoku **368–69**

A Japanese macaque gets in hot water in winter.

Snug in their snowhouses, children hold parties during the Kamakura festival in February.

Northern Honshu (Tohoku)

TOHOKU MEANS "NORTH EAST," BUT WHEN THE POET BASHO (1655–1694) made his famous journey to the eponymous region at the top of Honshu in 1689, it was just the "deep north." Mountainous, wild, and often bitterly cold in winter, Tohoku was extremely remote in those days. Some of it still is.

Like much of the Sea of Japan side of Honshu, western Tohoku is known as *yuki guni* (snow country). Tohoku was the last dwelling place of the Ainu people on Honshu before they were driven to Hokkaido about a thousand years ago; until recently, much of it was backward and desperately poor.

In this happily affluent era, the area's remoteness is an asset; in a word, Tohoku is beautiful. Topped by the additional attraction of plentiful *onsen* resorts, it boasts outstanding alpine scenery in Yamagata-ken and Akita-ken. Tohoku's days of remoteness are definitely numbered. Indeed, some sites—notably Sendai, the most important regional capital—have been anything but remote for centuries. Just outside the city on the Pacific coast is lovely Matsushima Bay, long regarded by the Japanese as one of the nation's Three Great Sights. Famous too is the old castle town of Hirosaki in Aomori, especially in springtime, when millions travel there to contemplate the castle standing over a sea of cherry blossoms. Meanwhile, in Iwate-ken, the little town of Hiraizumi still contains vestiges of a glorious past fading some 900 years ago, including Chuson-ji Temple, in which the fabulously sculpted golden altarpiece is one of the country's greatest designated National Treasures. ■

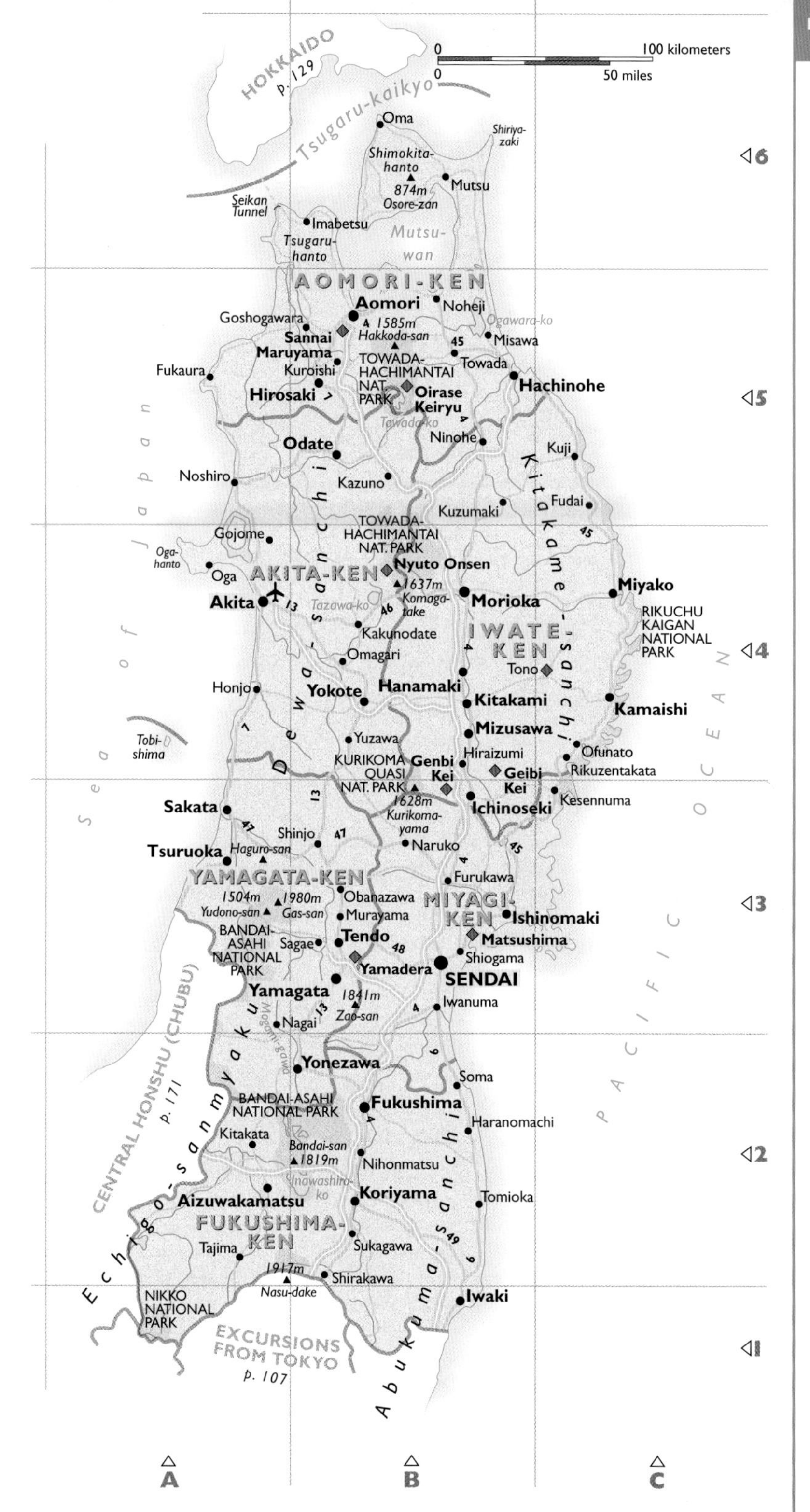
0 100 kilometers
0 50 miles
HOKKAIDO p. 129
Tsugaru-kaikyo
Oma
Shiriya-zaki
Shimokita-hanto
874m Osore-zan
Mutsu
Seikan Tunnel
Imabetsu
Tsugaru-hanto
Mutsu-wan
AOMORI-KEN
Aomori
Noheji
Goshogawara
1585m Hakkoda-san
Ogawara-ko
Sannai Maruyama
Misawa
Kuroishi
TOWADA-HACHIMANTAI NAT. PARK
Towada
Fukaura
Hirosaki
Oirase Keiryu
Hachinohe
Towada-ko
Ninohe
Odate
Kuji
Noshiro
Kazuno
Kitakami-sanchi
Fudai
Kuzumaki
TOWADA-HACHIMANTAI NAT. PARK
Gojome
Oga-hanto
Oga
AKITA-KEN
Nyuto Onsen
1637m Komaga-take
Miyako
Akita
Tazawa-ko
Morioka
Dewa-sanchi
Kakunodate
IWATE-KEN
RIKUCHU KAIGAN NATIONAL PARK
Omagari
Tono
Honjo
Yokote
Hanamaki
Kitakami
Kamaishi
Tobi-shima
Yuzawa
Mizusawa
Ofunato
Hiraizumi
KURIKOMA QUASI NAT. PARK
Genbi Kei
Geibi Kei
Rikuzentakata
1628m Kurikoma-yama
Ichinoseki
Kesennuma
Sakata
Shinjo
Naruko
Tsuruoka
Haguro-san
Sea of Japan
PACIFIC OCEAN
YAMAGATA-KEN
Furukawa
1504m Yudono-san
1980m Gas-san
Obanazawa
MIYAGI-KEN
Murayama
Ishinomaki
BANDAI-ASAHI NATIONAL PARK
Sagae
Tendo
Matsushima
Shiogama
Yamadera
SENDAI
Yamagata
1841m Zao-san
Iwanuma
Nagai
Mogami-gawa
Yonezawa
Soma
CENTRAL HONSHU (CHUBU) p. 171
BANDAI-ASAHI NATIONAL PARK
Fukushima
Haranomachi
Kitakata
Bandai-san 1819m
Nihonmatsu
Inawashiro-ko
Echigo-sanmyaku
Aizuwakamatsu
Koriyama
Tomioka
FUKUSHIMA-KEN
Tajima
Sukagawa
Abukuma-sanchi
1917m Nasu-dake
Shirakawa
NIKKO NATIONAL PARK
Iwaki
EXCURSIONS FROM TOKYO p. 107
6
5
4
3
2
1
A
B
C

Aomori-ken

Sannai Maruyama Iseki
- 153 B5
- Sannai Maruyama, Aomori-shi
- 017/766-8282
- 9 a.m.–4 p.m., April–Oct.; closes at 3:30 in winter
- Free guided tours
- Bus: from JR Aomori Station (30 min.)

Aomori City
- 153 B5

Visitor information
- By Aomori Station Central Exit
- 017/723-4670
- Train: Tohoku Shinkansen from Tokyo via Morioka (4 hrs. 50 min.)
- Tokyo (Haneda) to Aomori airport (1 hr. 10 min.)

Munakata Memorial Museum
- 2-1-2 Matsubara
- 017/777-4567
- Closed Mon.
- $$
- Bus: from Aomori Station (15 min.)

AT THE VERY NORTHERN TIP OF HONSHU, AOMORI IS Japan's world's end. The winters are harsh and Siberian; up on the far northeastern Shimokita-hanto, even the monkeys—the world's northernmost—have adapted to the conditions by growing longer coats than their relatives elsewhere in Japan. It may sound bleak, but Aomori's numerous archaeological sites prove that the region is sufficiently rich in natural resources to have attracted human beings since Neolithic times.

Featuring reconstructed Jomon-period (see p. 28) dwellings and open to the public, the most famous sites are in Korekawa, near the town of Hachinohe on the east coast, and especially at **Sannai Maruyama Iseki,** the impressive site of a village 5,000 years old just south of Aomori city. Until the 1970s Aomori was regarded as a cultural backwater; today it is revered as a nostalgic repository of customs, festivals, and folklore.

Aomori is famous for horses, although much less so than in premodern times; always an agricultural region, it now prospers as a leading national provider of rice, vegetables, and fruit and is a major producer of processed foods. With coastlines on both the Pacific and the Japan Sea, Aomori is renowned for its fish and seafood.

The capital, **Aomori,** lies in the north of the prefecture between Tsugaru-hanto and Shimokita-hanto. Blitzed during World War II, the city is now entirely modern. Nevertheless, this is another of those cities that prove indispensable to travelers exploring a region—in this case, especially those going on to Hokkaido.

If you do stop over, take a look at the **Munakata Memorial Museum (Munakata Shiko Kinenkan),** devoted to the eponymous modern woodblock print master (1903–1975), a native son. Despite Aomori's plentiful hotels and *ryokan,* be warned: The city's accommodations are often fully reserved during holiday periods, especially for the Nebuta festival. If you miss the event itself, there's the **Nebuta-no-Sato Museum,** which has floats on display and daily float demonstrations.

Aomori-ken is divided into three peninsular districts: the Shimokita in the northeast, Nambu to the southeast, and

Aomori arts & crafts

A woodblock master of international renown, Munakata Shiko (1903–1975) was a leading member of the *mingei* (folk art) movement. Evidencing his Aomori roots, his works reflected the dynamic designs of the Nebuta festival's illuminated floats (see p. 156), which are in turn inspired by *Tsugaru tako-e*—the colorful paintings on paper kites produced in the Tsugaro region. Woodcraft is another regional specialty, notably the dappled, polychrome *Tsugaru-nuri* lacquerware and a variety of charming lathe-turned toys. *Kogin* embroidery, used on clothing and souvenirs, dates to feudal times. ■

Tsugaru in the west. **Shimokita-hanto** is known for the weird, strangely twisted cliff formations along the rocky **Hotoke-ga-ura** coast on its western side, but "weird" is even more fitting to describe **Mount Osore-zan** (Mount Dread), a sacred mountain revered as a gateway to the world of the dead. Some say it is one of the most haunted places on Earth. Ravens caw across a desolate volcanic landscape with sulfurous fumes drifting from rocky fissures, and little piles of stones decorated with toys commemorate the souls of departed children. During the Bon festival for the dead at the end of July, thousands come up here to pray at **Entsu–ji Temple.** Many consult with *itako* (elderly, often blind female mediums) to talk to departed relatives.

Scenic areas in the Nambu

Rustic, old-style onsen abound in Aomori-ken.

Nebuta-no-Sato Museum

- 1 Yaegiku, Yokouchi
- 017/738-1230
- 9 a.m.–5 p.m.
- $$
- Bus from Aomori Station (30 min.)

Hirosaki
153 B5
Visitor information
outside Hirosaki Station
0172/37-5501
Train: JR limited express from Aomori (30 min.)

Hirosaki-jo Castle
Hirosaki-koen
0172/33-8733
9 a.m.–5 p.m., April 1–Nov. 23
$

Chosho-ji Temple
1-23-8 Nishi-shigemori
0172/32-0813
see right
$

district include the **Oirase Keiryu Gorge,** where torrents wind through 9 miles (14 km) of woodland, and—the source of the Oirase-gawa River—**Lake Towada-ko,** in a crater with a 25-mile (40 km) perimeter; with its clear blue waters, this is one of Japan's most beautiful lakes.

Tsugaru-hanto is of interest mainly for its scenery, from rugged Cape Gongen to the central mountain of Hakkoda-san (5,200 feet/1,585 m). West of Tsugaru are the Shirakami Mountains, declared a UNESCO World Heritage Site for possessing one of the largest virgin beech forests in the world.

Tsugaru also harbors one of Tohoku's few historical places: the old castle town of **Hirosaki.** The feudal domain of the Tsugaru clans, Hirosaki flourished during the Edo period as one of the area's most important towns. Today its reputation resides in the charm of the preservation area and castle, probably most of all for the 5,000 or so cherry trees blossoming on the castle grounds. These make Hirosaki a premier destination for *hanami* (flower-viewing) parties and, during the Hirosaki Cherry Blossom Festival (April 23–May 5), the town receives some two million tourists.

Built in 1611 and still surrounded by three moats, **Hirosaki-jo Castle** retains several original gates and towers. Lightning destroyed the five-story main keep in the 18th century; the current three-story replacement dates from 1810 and has a museum devoted to samurai armor and artifacts. Like the castle, the town's other sights, such as the Historical House Preservation Area and **Zenrin-gai,** the Zen temple district with its impressive 17th-century **Chosho-ji Temple** (*8 a.m.–5 p.m. April–Oct, 9 a.m.–4 p.m. Nov.–mid-December; closed to individuals mid-December–April),* are concentrated on the west side of town. Several charming Western-style buildings where 19th-century missionaries lived also survive. ■

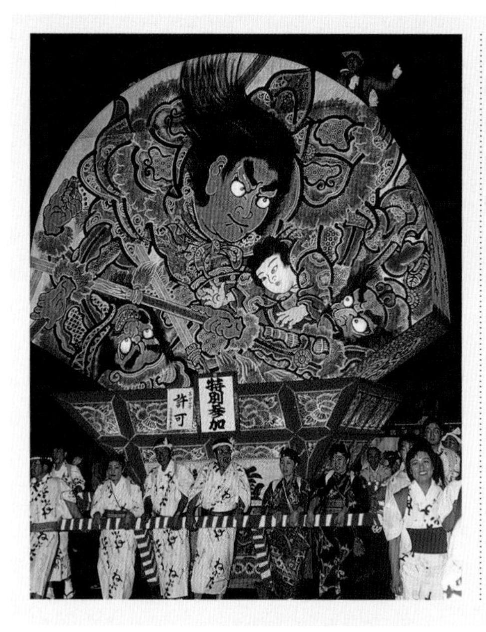

Aomori's Nebuta Matsuri festival floats epitomize Japanese folk art.

Nebuta

Spectators from all over Japan come to Nebuta Matsuri, when thousands of revelers dance in a parade (whose origins are forgotten) featuring colossal illuminated floats. One theory is that the festival commemorates a legend about the ninth-century warrior Sakanoue-no-Tamuramaro, who led imperial forces to the far north to conquer local tribes. Tamuramaro's successful strategy consisted of placing huge lanterns around the hills at night; when the hapless tribesmen came out to investigate the lanterns, they were captured. The *nebuta,* which represent the lanterns, are gigantic illuminated paper structures colorfully painted with mythical figures. ■

Akita-ken

Lake Tazawa-ko is immensely popular with Japanese holidaymakers.

IN THE NORTHWEST OF TOHOKU, AKITA-KEN ENCOMPASSes high mountain ranges in the north, east, and south; 70 percent of the land is forested. The mountains of Akita are renowned for Lakes Towada-ko and Tazawa-ko (see p. 158), for the sylvan Hachimantai Plateau, and for their sheer scenic beauty. Ski resorts abound, and being volcanic, the mountains have plenty of hot springs, notably those in the remote resort of Nyuto Onsen (see p. 158). Jutting 12.5 miles (20 km) into the Sea of Japan, the Oga-hanto Peninsula, with its green hills and craggy coastline, is a favored destination in summer, but transportation dwindles to a bare minimum in winter. The region's most interesting town by far is Kakunodate (see pp. 158–60), famed for one of the largest and best-preserved samurai districts in the country.

Winters are cold and snowbound on Akita's higher ground, but the plain on the milder seaward side is subject to the high rainfall common to much of the west coast of Japan. There can be seasonal extremes of temperature; situated halfway down on the coastal side, the prefectural capital of Akita City records temperatures dropping to 14° F (-10° C) in winter and soaring to 93° F (34° C) in summer. Particularly lush, the agricultural lowlands take in productive rice-growing districts, some yielding the highest quality crop in the country.

Archaeological finds have shown that the region was inhabited at least 20,000 years ago, probably by tribes related to the Ainu (see p. 136). The army of the Yamato court took Akita in 658 and drove the Ainu ever farther north; Akita city grew out of a permanent garrison established in the eighth century. In 1602, the year before he founded

Tazawa-ko
153 A4
Visitor information
JR Tazawa-ko Station
0187/43-2111
Train: Akita Shinkansen from Tokyo Station to JR Tazawa-ko Station (3 hrs.)

Nyuto Onsen
153 A4
Visitor information
Bus from JR Tazawa-ko Station (40 min.)

Kakunodate
153 A4
Visitor information
Kakunodate Station (just outside)
0187/54-2700
Train: Akita Shinkansen from Tokyo Station to Kakunodate Station (3 hrs. 11 min.)

Masakichi Hirano Museum of Fine Art
3-7 Meitoku-cho, Senshu
018/833-5809
10 a.m.–5 p.m.; closed Mon.
Walk from Akita Station (7 min.)
10 a.m.–5 p.m.; closed Mon.
$$

Revelers balance weighty tiers of lanterns at the Kanto festival held in Akita city in August.

the national government that would last for centuries, the shogun Tokugawa Ieyasu appointed the Satake clan as the first lords of Akita. The Satake later moved to Kakunodate, and until the fall of the shogunate in 1867, rule of the province was shared by families collectively constituting the Akita clan.

The city of **Akita** *(Tel 018/832-7941)* is a good base for regional touring. Except for the ruins of the foundations and a recent reconstruction of a lookout tower—both in **Senshu-koen Park—** nothing remains of Satake-jo Castle or the old town. But in August the city comes into its own with the colorful **Akita Kanto Festival** (August 3–6, www.kantou.gr.jp), when crowds arrive for the spectacle. The parade features some 200 men using their foreheads, hips, shoulders, and palms to balance clusters of lighted paper lanterns atop tall, thick bamboo poles. The poles, each bearing 20 lanterns, weigh about 110 pounds (50 kg) apiece. The **Masakichi Hirano Museum of Fine Art,** meanwhile, has *Events of Akita,* said to be the world's largest painting.

At 1,394 feet (425 m), **Lake Tazawa-ko** is the deepest lake in Japan. It is renowned for the views of the surrounding peaks, notably Mount Komaga-take, and their reflections in the intense blue of its crystal-clear water. The Tazawa-ko area has several nearby ski resorts but lures visitors year-round. A favorite with Japanese vacationers, the lake can be chockablock with swimmers, rented rowboats, and pleasure boats in high summer; choose off-peak periods to make the most of its great scenery. You can tour its 12-mile (20 km) circumference by bus, but the most pleasant way is to rent a bicycle from one of the outlets on either side of the Tazawa-kohan bus terminal. The area has plenty of accommodations in all categories, including campgrounds.

If you like walking, buses from Tazawa-kohan take 50 minutes to reach Komagatake-Hachigome. From there it is just over an hour's walk to the summit of **Mount Komaga-take** (5,369 feet/1637 m), the starting point for several hiking trails through fine alpine scenery. If you have the stamina, one option is to make a day's trek north over Mount Eboshi-dake and then down to the group of remote spas at Nyuto Onsen.

Reachable by bus from Tazawa-kohan, **Nyuto Onsen** comprises six spa resort hotels (all Japanese-style *ryokan)* in a beautiful mountain setting crisscrossed with hiking trails. Several of the baths, if not all the ryokan owning them, have reputations going back to the Edo period (1603–1868). Featuring both indoor baths and *rotenburo* (rustic baths in the open air), they could be the perfect place for an onsen experience. Even in the snow you will not feel the cold; there is nothing like contemplating the scenery as you luxuriate in hot water. Nyuto's remoteness has boosted its fame, so be sure to make your accommodation reservations in advance.

Around 15 minutes west of Tazawa-ko is **Kakunodate,** the prefecture's most famous town. Between late April and early May, thousands go there to see the fantastic tunnels of blossoming cherry trees planted along a 1-mile (1.5 km) stretch of the **Hinokinai-gawa River.** But the trees, planted as recently as 1934, are a recent complement to some substantial historical attractions. Founded as a castle town in 1620 by Akita clan lord Yoshikatsu Ashina, Kakunodate succumbed to fires over the years. However, it was

Aoyagi-ke
www.samuraiworld.com
26 Higashi-Katsuraku-cho
0187/54-3257
9 a.m.–5 p.m; 9 a.m.–4 p.m, Nov.–April
$$

Denshokan Museum
10-1 Omotemachi-shimocho, Kakunodate-machi
0187/54-1700
9 a.m.–5 p.m
$

flooding that determined its relocation farther south along the river. All that remains of the castle is the hill upon which it stood; the original town center, which lay to the north of it, has vanished. The new town, still divided into a northern samurai quarter and a southern quarter for merchants, contains a substantial number of old wooden houses. The most impressive are concentrated in **Buke-yashiki,** the unmissable old samurai quarter.

The houses stand behind wooden walls and stately gateways on a long avenue flanked by weeping cherries, many of them planted 300 years ago. Although most of the houses are privately owned, six of them—Kawarada, Aoyagi, Odano, Iwahashi, Ishiguro, and Matsumoto—are open to the public. The houses date from the twilight of the samurai from early to mid-19th century. Mainly modest rather than grand and featuring charming gardens, some display collections of heirlooms and memorabilia ranging from samurai relics to Western appliances.

The **Kawarada** house, for instance, has a tiny museum of swords and armor. The houses and their contents wistfully reflect a period midway between feudal power and rural middle-class gentility. **Aoyagi-ke** is the favorite with the public. Its compound, more opulent than the others', embraces several houses, five of which are museums. One is devoted to swords and armor, another to painting and calligraphy, and the rest present a fascinating miscellany of crafts, ceramics, household appliances, implements, and possessions. Concentrating on technical appliances from the 1870s through the 1920s, the collection in the **Haikara-kan** building includes clocks, phonographs,

cameras, and even a 1917 American "Indian" motorbike. *Haikara* means "high collar," the term used for Western shirts; it is now virtually synonymous with Meiji Japan.

With cherry blossom viewing a prime attraction, it is perhaps not surprising that the wood and bark of the cherry are the materials of choice for Kakunodate's attractive local handicrafts. The place to see the historical development and finest examples of *kabazaiku* (cherry bark craft) is **Denshokan Museum.** Working in one of the museum rooms, an in-house artisan is always happy to demonstrate his craft.

The museum is otherwise devoted to antiques, including armor, clothing, laquerware, and old and new examples of Kakunodate's recently revived Shiraiwa pottery. This is distinguished by its earthen hues, with subtle, semitransparent overglazes in lighter colors. There is a sales area offering quality local crafts at prices comparing favorably with the town's specialty stores. ■

Sendai & Matsushima

Piney islets dot Matsushima-wan's calm waters.

TOHOKU'S LARGEST CITY, SENDAI, IS THE CAPITAL OF Miyagi-ken. An important business center, it has a good number of hotels, making it a convenient base for exploring the region. Most of all, visitors use Sendai as a base for visiting nearby Matsushima-wan—which, along with Miyajima (see pp. 288–90) and Amanohashidate (Kyoto-ken), is one of the Three Great Sights of Japan.

The warlord Date Masumune built **Aoba-jo Castle** in 1602. The castle was ruined long ago, but its foundations still lie in the city park *(Bus from Sendai Station, 20 min., museum $$$)*. Other vestiges of the Date legacy were obliterated with most of Sendai during the air raids of World War II. Unlike most resurrected Japanese cities, Sendai breaks the monotony of concrete by lining its boulevards with trees. Along with the usual covered shopping arcades and an exuberant street market, Sendai is home to Kokubuncho, Tohoku's largest amusement district.

The Date family mausoleum, the 16th-century **Memorial Hall (Zuihoden),** and ornate **Osaki Hachiman-jinja Shrine,** built in 1607, miraculously survived the war. Otherwise, despite having a few attractive temples and gardens, Sendai is not known for historical sights. The surrounding hills boast hiking trails and hot springs, as well as beautiful scenery in the gorges of Futakuchi and Raira-kyo and especially near the town of **Naruko,** renowned for the curative properties of its spas. Near Sendai too is the 180-foot (55 m) **Akiu Otaki Waterfall,** among the country's most spectacular cascades.

"Matsushima, ah, matsushima, matsushima, matsushima!" This was not one of Basho's best haiku; the view over **Matsushima-wan** obviously left the 17th-century poet at a loss for words.

Sendai

Map 153 B3

Visitor information

Address: Sendai Station

Phone: 022/222-4069

Transport: Train: JR Tohoku Shinkansen from Tokyo (2 hrs.)

Memorial Hall (Zuihoden)

Address: 23-2 Otamayashita, Aoba-ku

Phone: 022/262-6250

Hours: 9 a.m.–4:30 p.m., closes at 4 Dec.–Jan.

Osaki Hachiman-jinja Shrine

Address: 4-6-1 Hachiman, Aoba-ku

Phone: 022/234-3606

Hours: 8 a.m.–5 p.m.

Transport: Bus from Sendai Station (20 min.)

The curiously shaped Godai-do temple (right of center) has stood on the same spot for a thousand years.

The panorama inspired the very place-name: *matsushima* means "pine island." With some 200 pine-covered islets sprinkled about a sweeping bay, the view is lovely. But what would Basho say today? Much blighted by cheap souvenir outlets, Matsushima sees hordes disgorged from a seemingly endless succession of tour buses. The bay is plied by vessels ranging from hired rowboats to luridly colored sightseeing junks with ornate sculpted dragons at the prow—ugly but fun; you can dine aboard while cruising the bay. The larger islands are connected by low red bridges, notably one 270 yards long (250 m) to **Fukuura-jima,** which has a botanical garden and pleasant paths to stroll.

By late afternoon, except during the peak season, the armies of day-trippers vanish and the promenade on the seafront becomes all the more pleasant for strolling. So does Matsushima itself, a relaxing little coastal town where kitsch emulations of the Japanese castle replace the usual monster concrete resort hotels.

Standing on an islet connected to the promenade by a short bridge is the **Godai-do.** This small, curiously shaped temple was erected in the ninth century and rebuilt in 1600 by Date Masamune. The interior is opened only three times a century, but you can look at the fine carvings of zodiac animals at the top of the pillars. Flanked by pines, the Godai-do charmingly complements the view over the sea.

As you leave the Godai-do, some 270 yards (250 m) to your left is the **Kanran-tei,** the "water-viewing" pavilion. Once a teahouse in Fushimi, a castle near Kyoto built by 16th-century warlord Toyotomi Hideyoshi, it was presented to Date Masumune and moved here, to a clifftop site overlooking the sea, in the late 16th century. Used as a moon-viewing pavilion by generations of Date lords, it contains a small museum exhibiting Date memorabilia.

The beauty of **Zuigan-ji Temple,** one of the great Zen temples of Japan, is a fitting human counterpart to the panorama on

Matsushima

Map 153 B3

Visitor information

Address: Outside Matsushima-Kaigan Station

Phone: 022/354-2263

Kanran-tei

Address: 56 Aza-machi

Phone: 022/353-3355

Hours: 8:30 a.m.–5 p.m.; closes at 4:30 p.m. Nov.–end March

Admission: $

the bay, from which it lies back, approached along an avenue of cedars. Founded in 828 by the Tendai sect, Zuigan-ji became a Zen temple during the 13th century. It declined during the long era of civil wars (15th–16th centuries) and was in a sorry state of disrepair by 1604, when Date Masamune began rebuilding it.

Surrounded by split-level corridors, three sides of the imposing **Main Hall (Hon-do)** feature doors lavishly carved in the Chinese style. The sliding screen doors in the chambers inside, completed in 1622, were covered in gold leaf and decorated with exquisite paintings. The current ones are copies. Beautifully restored between 1985 and 1995, the originals are now displayed in the adjacent **Seiryuden Treasure Museum,** along with fine Buddhist relics and paintings and statues of the Date family and the erstwhile temple abbots.

To the right of the temple approach, rows of **hermitages** have been carved into a solid wall of rock. Many contain images of the Buddha, hewn from the stone within. It is said that acolytes had to carve their way in and spend time meditating inside—the path to enlightenment seems arduous indeed!

The temple precinct of **Entsu-in** (also called Rose Temple), just next door to Zuigan-ji, contains the mausoleum of Date Masamune's grandson Mitsumune, set in a quiet glade of cedars. It is also notable for a lovely garden. Much of it is devoted to flowers not usually found in Japanese gardens—roses. ■

Zuigan-ji Temple
- ✉ 91 Aza-chonai (7 min. walk from Matsushima-Kaigan Station
- ☎ 022/354-2023
- ⌚ 8:00 a.m.–5 p.m., April–Sept.; closes at 4:30 March & Oct.; 4:00 Feb. & Nov.; 3:30 Dec. & Jan.
- $ $$

Entsuin
- ✉ 67 Aza-chonai
- ☎ 022/354-3206
- ⌚ 8:30 a.m.–5 p.m.
- $ $

Matsuo Basho (1644–1694)

Japanese poetry packs rich imagery and emotional power into few words. As the Zen influence gained ground from the 14th century on, the concept of "less is more" pervaded the cultural spectrum. Epitomizing it is haiku—a profoundly evocative, often elegiac verse form in which the 31 syllables of classical *tanka* poetry (the main poetic form from the 9th to 13th centuries) were slashed to 17. Of all haiku exponents, none is so revered as Basho.

Born a samurai, Basho studied at a Zen monastery before distinguishing himself as a poet. He habitually roamed the country for months on end, interspersing his travel diaries with haiku masterpieces. *The Narrow Road to the Far North,* recording a journey through Tohuku in 1689, is considered his greatest work. Frail and prematurely aged, Basho died on the road, succumbing to food poisoning at an inn on his way to Kyushu. ■

Snow-covered Kitayamazaki Cliffs on Honshu Island

Iwate-ken

LONG KNOWN AS THE "DEEP EAST" FOR ITS REMOTENESS, Iwate is the largest prefecture outside Hokkaido—and the least populated. Its main historic claim to fame is the old town of Hiraizumi, where the hero Minamoto Yoshitsune met his death. Today Hiraizumi is just a small town, but some of the relics from its glorious past are among the most impressive in Japan.

Morioka

 153 B4

Visitor information

Morioka Station

019/625-2090

Train: JR Tohoku Shinkansen from Tokyo (2 hrs. 20 min.–3 hrs. 20 min.). For Hachimantai take bus from station

Morioka, Iwate's prefectural capital, is publicized as a "castle town" (the castle was destroyed during the 1870s) and even as "little Kyoto." But short of a pleasant river bank, green spaces, and the occasional district with a few mid-19th- to early 20th-century vestiges, there is nothing much to see. It is a congenial place nevertheless, and as a station on the Tohoku Shinkansen from Tokyo it makes a handy stopover for visiting the prefecture. Taking in all the sights would require an overnight stay, but visiting Chuson-ji and Motsu-ji Temples takes about four hours.

Iwate-ken has a lot of unspoiled space with plenty of fine scenery, especially in the national parks. There is **Rikuchu Kaigan National Park** to the east, with

its stark seascapes of rocky coves and 650-foot (200 m) cliffs, and **Towada Hachimantai National Park** *(Bus from Morioka Station to Hachimantai Chojo, 2 hours)* to the west. In addition to being another nucleus of *onsen* spas, Hachimantai is renowned for its scenery, as well as for the option of skiing until June, notably cross-country through forests. To the south is **Kurikoma Quasi-National Park,** where the alpine scenery is spectacular when aflame with colors in the fall. Kurikoma lies near Ichinoseki, the transfer point for the town of Hiraizumi.

West of coastal Kamaishi is the quiet town of **Tono,** famed as Japan's superstition capital due to folklorist Kunio Yanagita's *The Legends of Tono* (1912). Based on interviews with a Tono man who had memorized a hundred local folk tales, the still-popular book features creatures such as *kappa* water imps and shape-shifting foxes. Tono's unique L-shaped *magariya* farmhouses are redolent with this rural tradition, and folk village **Tono Furusato Mura** features several of them. Tono is also a good choice for countryside bicycling or hiking amid its outlying rice paddies and hills.

The main avenues of modern **Hiraizumi,** unusually broad for a small rural town, faintly echo the layout of an ancient Sino-Japanese city. Hiraizumi has a strangely melancholy atmosphere; you become eerily aware of a lost city beneath your feet—underlined by such discoveries as the foundations of a 12th-century settlement when a private house was redeveloped in 1998.

Once consisting of no more than a remote garrison and two temples, Hiraizumi grew into a city of 100,000 people—the jewel of the northeast—when Fujiwara Kiyohira turned it into a regional capital in the early 12th century. Mining gold, producing silk, and breeding horses, Hiraizumi rivaled even Kyoto in opulence for over a century. The northeastern Fujiwara dynasty held the city until, greedy for gold and horses, Minamoto Yoritomo's troops invaded the city in 1189.

Hiraizumi declined rapidly and suffered a number of fires over the centuries, becoming no more than a backwater with an illustrious past.

Tono

154 C4

Visitor information

- Outside JR Tono Station
- 0198/62-2830
- Train from Shin-Hanamaki on JR Kamaishi Line (45 min.) or Hanamaki (65 min.)

Tono Furusato Mura

- 5-89-1 Kamitsukimoshi
- 0198/64-2300
- 9 a.m.–5 p.m.
- Bus from Tono station (25 min)

Yoshitsune's demise

The Fujiwara clan's last power base was Hiraizumi, which they still held when their Minamoto allies ousted the Taira at the culmination of the Heike War in 1185. Minamoto Yoritomo was the leader, but the victorious star was Yoshitsune, his younger half-brother and Japan's most revered pre-medieval hero.

Yoritomo hated his half-brother enough to conspire to murder him, whereupon Yoshitsune fled to Hiraizumi. But Yoritomo intended to turn against the Fujiwara and invade the city anyway. Faced with Yoritomo's troops, legend has it that Yoshisune committed suicide as his formidable steward, the warrior monk Benkei, died standing up in a hail of arrows.

Whatever the true circumstances, Yoshitsune died here; the Takadachi Gikeido Hall on the east side of Hiraizumi marks the spot. When the wandering poet Basho saw it in 1689, it inspired one of his most famous haiku: "The summer grass—all that remains of ancient warriors' dreams." ■

The Golden Hall at Chuson-ji is one of Japan's greatest National Treasures.

Hiraizumi
- 153 B4

Visitor information
- Outside Hiraizumi Station
- 0191/46-2110
- Train: JR Tohoku Shinkansen from Tokyo. Change at Ichinoseki for JR Tohoku Honsen line to Hiraizumi

Chuson-ji Temple
- 202 Koromoseki, Hiraizumi-cho
- 0191/46-2211
- 8 a.m.–5 p.m., April–Nov.; 8:30–4:30 in winter
- $$
- Train: Access 25 min. walk from Hiraizumi Station

Hiraizumi's finest attraction is the splendid hilltop precinct of **Chuson-ji Temple.** Founded in 850, Chuson-ji was greatly enlarged by Fujiwara Kiyohira, who built 40 halls during the 1120s. Including monks' quarters, the precinct counted 300 structures, but nearly all were destroyed during a fire in 1337. Current buildings date mostly from the late Edo period, including a fine **Noh stage** built in 1853. All that remains of the original temple is the **Sutra Hall (Kyozo)** and the breathtaking **Golden Hall (Konjiki-do),** commissioned in 1124. Housed within a large protective concrete building, this tiny hall is one of the greatest National Treasures. Intricately carved, inlaid with mother-of-pearl, lacquered, and gilded, it enshrines altars graced with outstanding golden Buddhist carvings. Beneath them lie the mummified bodies of Fujiwara Kiyohira and three of his descendants. Painted in gold on indigo paper, some of the 5,300 illustrated sutras formerly in the Kyozo are now in the nearby **Treasure Hall (Sankozo).** Also containing several sculptures designated National Treasures, the Sankozo holds such a wealth of temple relics and Heian-period artifacts that a new annex was built to accommodate them in 1999.

Chuson-ji precinct stands atop a hill with splendid views over the surrounding plain. The approach is through a magnificent grove of tall cedars, but the slope is pretty steep. You can stop at the tiny Edo-period shrine dedicated to Yoshitsune on the way up and refresh yourself in an old thatched farmhouse charmingly converted into a café.

Motsu-ji Temple, founded in the mid-ninth century, was the largest temple in northern Japan during the 12th century. Declining along with the rest of Hiraizumi, its

Memorial plaques such as these are a familiar sight in Japan.

several pagodas, 40 halls, and 500 monastic dwellings all burned down in several fires. Built in 1989, the present **main hall** is an uninspiring emulation of the Heian-period style; the precinct's only really old building is the 17th- century **Jogyo-do** hall. Archaeologists uncovered the foundation stones of several original buildings in the late 1960s, and later excavation revealed the rocks constituting the artificial watercourses and pond of a lost **garden.** Now beautifully restored, it is the only complete extant example of a Heian-period Jodo (Pure Land) garden, landscaped on a grand scale in emulation of Buddhist paradise.

The precinct also includes an iris garden containing 300 varieties; visitors come from all over Japan to admire the flowers between mid-June and mid-July. On the fourth Sunday in May the **Gokusui-no-en** (Floating Poetry Festival) finds contestants in Heian-period garb floating cups of sake down the garden's stream. The objective is to compose a poem before your cup reaches the end—very much a garden-party game enjoyed 900 years ago.

Lush and green in spring and summer, the surrounding countryside presents fine rural scenery, as well as one or two sights: the gorges of **Geibikei** (to the east) and **Genbikei** (to the west) and, en route to Genbikei gorge, **Takkoku-no-Iwaya,** a curious rock temple with a Buddhist effigy carved in the cliff face. ■

Motsu-ji Temple

- ✉ 58 Osawa, Hiraizumi-cho (7-min. walk from Hiraizumi Station)
- ☎ 0191/46-2331
- 🕒 8:30 a.m.–5 p.m., April–Oct.; closes at 4:30 p.m., Nov.–March
- $ $$

Halls and pavilions of the famous Yamadera Temple perch precariously on vertiginous outcrops of rock.

Yamagata-ken

YAMAGATA-KEN EMBRACES THE SOUTHWESTERN BOUNDARY of Tohoku. It is a prime agricultural region—in the 30 percent of it that is not mountain and forest (Yamagata means "mountain shape"). Yamagata's climate varies as much as its topography; ski resorts remain open on Gas-san in high summer, when temperatures on the plain can reach the highest recorded in Japan. Out of the four million annual tourists here, most come to ski resorts, leaving much of the prefecture refreshingly unspoiled.

Yamagata city
153 B3
Visitor information
JR Yamagata Station
023/647-2266
Train: JR Yamagata Shinkansen From Tokyo to Yamagate Station (2 hrs. 30 min.)

A boon for both farming and tourism, the Mogami-gawa River and its tributaries flow from the southwest to the northwest. Near the town of Sakata (see opposite), tour boats ply the spectacular **Mogami Gorge—**the appeal lying as much in the folk-singing skills of the boatmen as in the scenic beauty of the steep cliffs flanking the river. Yamagata thrives in winter with winter sports facilities in nearly all its mountains and at least one *onsen* (hot spring) in every village. Well known for both, **Mount Zao-san** in the southeast also attracts walkers and nature lovers year-round with its fine alpine scenery. Undamaged in World War II, Yamagata's towns suffered from Japan's ubiquitous postwar architectural brutalism; though convenient as bases for regional exploration, they retain precious few sights.

1,100 stone steps lead up through the woods to Yama-dera Temple's inner sanctum.

The prefectural capital city, **Yamagata,** is a convenient base, especially for winter sports on Zao-san and for visiting **Yama-dera Temple** (also called Risshaku-ji), the Mountain Temple, one of Tohoku's most celebrated historical and religious sites. Yama-dera dates from 860, when Ennin, its founding priest, is said to have chipped away at the rocks to build the **Main Hall (Konponchu-do).** Although the structure was rebuilt in 1356, the Buddhist figure enshrined here dates to the ninth century; the flame before it has burned for over a thousand years. The temple comprises some 40 buildings perched on peaks and cliffsides; a trek for the hardy, the route from the bottom of the path to the temple winds up 1,100 stone steps through the woods, past spectacular views of the valley below, to the uppermost **Inner Sanctum (Oku-no-in).** The poet Basho wrote a haiku about Yama-dera during his Tohoku journey of 1689:

The quiet—
shrilling into the rocks
the cicada's cry.

The northwestern town of **Sakata,** on the Mogami-gawa estuary, was the main trade link with Kyoto in feudal times; sadly, it lost many historical buildings in a 1976 fire. It still has one old samurai residence, Honma-ke Kyu-hontei (Former Honma Family Residence), which harks back to the ruling Honma clan, and Sankyo Soko, a district preserving 12 warehouses built in 1893. Sakata is the ferry port for **Tobi-shima,** a tiny island off the west coast popular both as a bird sanctuary and as a resort for fishing and diving.

Yama-dera Temple
- 023/695-2816
- 8 a.m.–5 p.m.
- $
- Train: Senzan line from Yamagata Station to Yamadera (15 min.)

Sakata and Tobi-Shima
- 153 A3

Visitor information
- 0234/24-2233

Honma-ke Kyu-hontei
- 12-13 Niban-cho, Sakata
- 0234/22-3562
- 9:30 a.m.–4:30 p.m.; closes at 4 Nov.–Feb.
- $$
- Bus from Sakata Station (6 min), then walk (4 min)

Tsuruoka
153 A3
Visitor information
Outside Tsuruoka Station
0235/25-7678

Chido Museum
10-18 Kachushin-machi, Tsuruoka-shi
0235/22-1199
9 a.m.–4:30 p.m.
$$

Dewa Sanzan
153 A3
Bus: Tusruoka Station to Haguro (35 min.)

Just south of Sakata, the city of **Tsuruoka** was the feudal domain of the Sakai family, but the only reminders today are the castle moats and the interesting open-air **Chido Museum (Chido Hakubutsukan).** Several buildings of the Sakai family in the vicinity were taken down and reerected here in a park.

Tsuruoka is convenient as a gateway to the **Three Dewa Mountains (Dewa Sanzan),** a trio of peaks ranking among the most sacred in Japan. Along with Fuji-san and On-take in Nagano prefecture, the Dewa Sanzan are the holiest of all the objects of worship of Shinto mountain cults. Because the Dewa trio—Haguro-san (1,358 feet/414 m), Gas-san (6,494 feet/1,980 m), and Yudono-san (4,933 feet/1,504 m)—respectively symbolize birth, death, and rebirth, they are supposed to be visited in that order. Of the thousands going on Dewa pilgrimages, a few belong to the *yamabushi* sects (see below) that wandered and worshiped these mountains centuries ago. Although athletic sightseers claim otherwise, visiting all three requires an overnight stopover. There are several *shukubo* (shrine or temple lodgings, see p. 359) in the Toge district at the foot of Haguro-san.

Haguro-san—the lowest and easiest to climb—is the most visited of the holy trio. Dedicated to the three deities, the **Sanshin Gosaiden Shrine** stands at the summit, along with a museum of temple memorabilia. If you are unfit you should probably stay at the bottom, but the good news is that the way up includes a waterfall and a fine 14th-century pagoda; the bad news is that from the latter there are still 2,446 stone steps to climb to the summit! You can also take a bus to the top and walk down.

Gas-san has a shrine at the top, but getting there can be quite a trial except in late summer. The mountain is best known for skiing. Snowfalls of up to 26 feet (8 m) close even the ski slopes until mid-April, which remain open until the end of July. Ideal for hiking in late summer, Gas-san is justifiably famous for its spectacular scenery.

The last of the trio, **Yudono-san** is also the holiest. The walk from the road to the shrine at the top takes only about 15 minutes. The object of worship is a rock stained bright brick red by the iron in the spring welling up around it. So sacred is it that visitors are asked to remove footwear and refrain from taking photographs. ■

Yamabushi—monks of the mountains

Kaiko-ji Temple in Sakata is famous for the remains of two monks said to have attained Buddhahood through meditating and fasting until they succumbed to deliberate self-mummification. This example is much admired by the *yamabushi*—the "monks who lie in the mountains" and follow of Shugendo, a religion embracing both Shinto and Buddhism. Believers practice austerities such as immersion in ice-cold water in midwinter or being suspended by the heels over cliff edges with a drop of hundreds of feet. Yamabushi still exist, though they practice only on an occasional basis. These days the Ideha Culture Museum *(Toge, Haguro, tel 0235/62-4727)* runs three-day Yamabushi courses, complete with a generous ration of dire hardships. For details contact the museum. ■

The regional capital of Nagoya is Japan's fourth largest city; the beaches often vie with heavy industry for space on the coast, but with densely forested mountains and historic old towns, Chubu is the ultimate Japan sampler.

Central Honshu

Introduction & map **172–73**
Aichi-ken **174–77**
Kanazawa & beyond **178–81**
Takayama **182–85**
Nagano-ken **186–87**
Matsumoto **188**
Kamikochi Valley **189**
Kiso Valley (Kisoji) **190–92**
Sado-ga-shima **193–96**
Hotels & restaurants in Chubu **369–71**

Gardeners tend Kanazawa's Kenroku-en landscape garden.

Central Honshu

CHUBU, WHICH MEANS "CENTRAL SECTION," IS THE MIDDLE PART OF THE island of Honshu—the very center of Japan. Its nine prefectures have a wealth of different topographical, climatic, and cultural features. Chubu is divided into two main regions: Tokai on the Pacific side and Hokuriku on the Japan Sea.

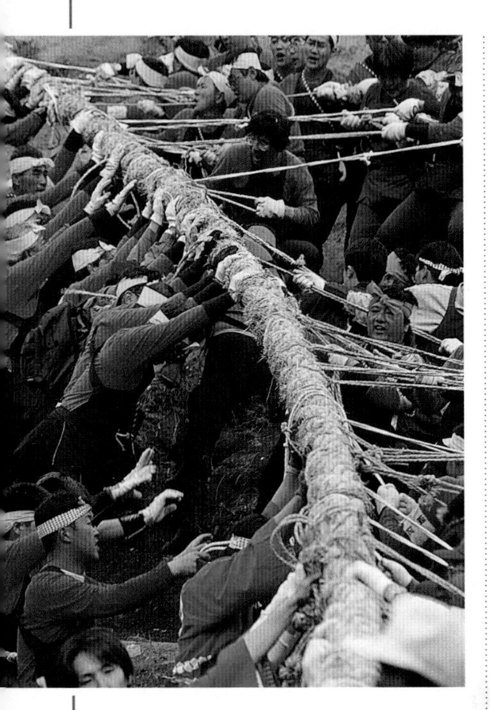

The Onbashira-sai log-pulling festival in Nagano-ken occurs once every seven years.

The great Tokaido road between Edo and Kyoto in feudal times got its name from Tokai—the eastern sea. Today's Tokai region has more transport arteries between Tokyo and southwestern Japan than ever, including the CENTRAIR on Ise Bay. Heavily industrialized and densely populated along the coast, the area has few major tourist sites, so foreign travelers stopping here en route to the district of Kansai (see pp. 197–260) are comparatively few. For those on their way to Hokuriku and the Japan Alps, the Nagoya region is a convenient gateway. Although it is one of the most industrialized areas of all, it still has some seeworthy scenic and historical sights.

Hokuriku has a great deal to recommend it. From Nagoya you can move up toward Nagano via the delightful Kiso Valley, or through Gifu to Kanazawa in the west, or north to Takayama. Historical and cultural destinations of major importance, Kanazawa and Takayama also have the advantage of being less touristic than towns in Kansai. Off the coast of Niigata-ken is lovely Sado-ga-shima; once reserved for political exiles, it is now a peaceful, scenic vacationland for those fleeing the crowds and pressure of urban Japan. ■

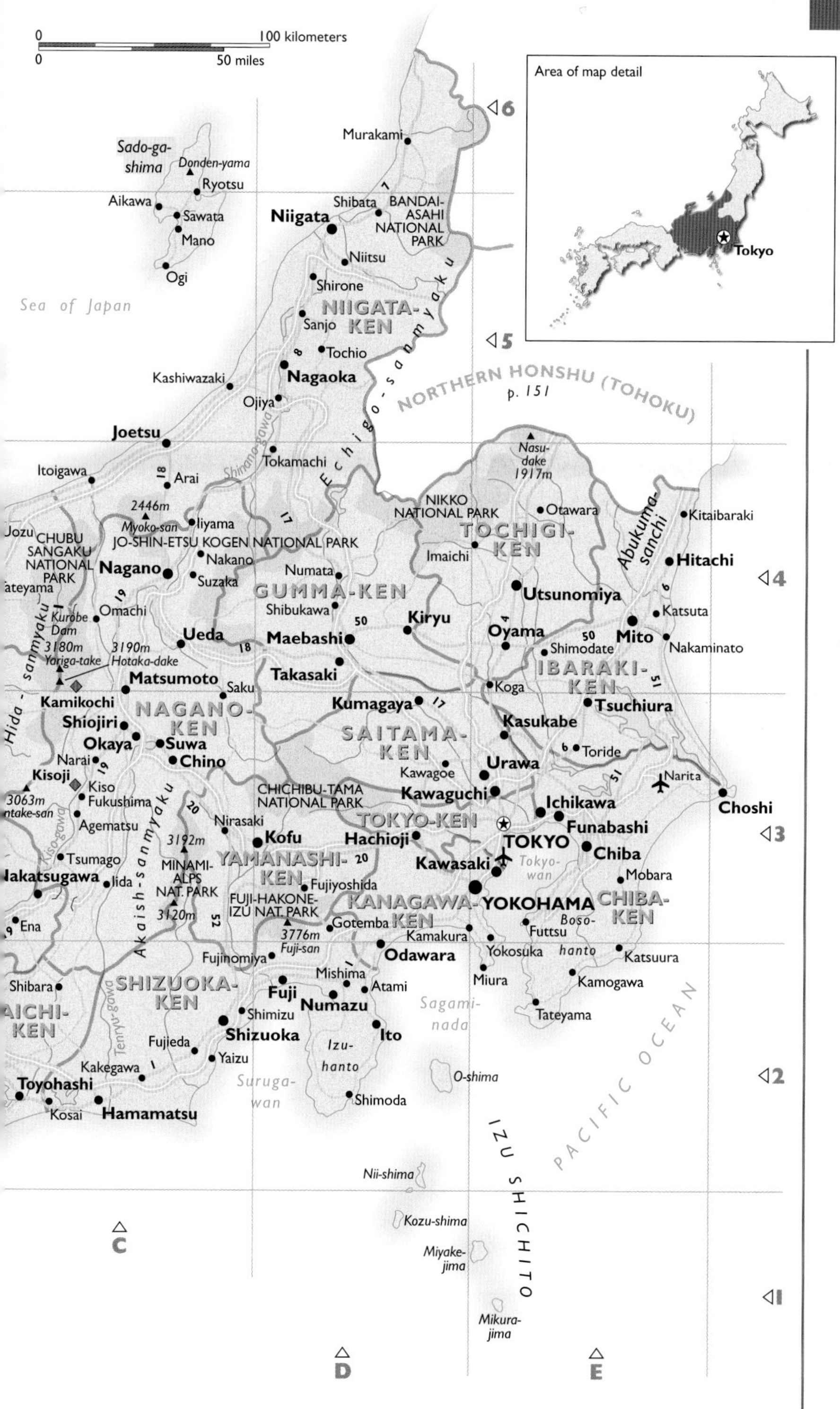
0
100 kilometers
0
50 miles
Area of map detail
Tokyo
Sado-ga-shima
Donden-yama
Ryotsu
Aikawa
Sawata
Mano
Ogi
Sea of Japan
Murakami
Shibata
BANDAI-ASAHI NATIONAL PARK
Niigata
Niitsu
Shirone
NIIGATA-KEN
Sanjo
Tochio
Nagaoka
Kashiwazaki
Ojiya
Echigo-sanmyaku
NORTHERN HONSHU (TOHOKU) p. 151
Joetsu
Tokamachi
Shinano-gawa
Itoigawa
Arai
Nasu-dake 1917m
NIKKO NATIONAL PARK
Otawara
Abukuma-sanchi
Kitaibaraki
2446m Myoko-san
Iiyama
TOCHIGI-KEN
Jozu
CHUBU SANGAKU NATIONAL PARK
JO-SHIN-ETSU KOGEN NATIONAL PARK
Nakano
Imaichi
Hitachi
Nagano
Suzaka
Numata
Tateyama
GUMMA-KEN
Utsunomiya
Omachi
Shibukawa
Katsuta
Kurobe Dam
Kiryu
Oyama
Mito
Ueda
Maebashi
Shimodate
Nakaminato
3180m Yariga-take
3190m Hotaka-dake
Hida-sanmyaku
Matsumoto
Takasaki
IBARAKI-KEN
Koga
Saku
Kamikochi
NAGANO-KEN
Kumagaya
Tsuchiura
Shiojiri
Kasukabe
SAITAMA-KEN
Okaya
Suwa
Toride
Chino
Narai
Urawa
Kawagoe
Kisoji
Narita
Kiso Fukushima
CHICHIBU-TAMA NATIONAL PARK
Kawaguchi
Choshi
3063m
Ichikawa
Agematsu
Nirasaki
TOKYO-KEN
Funabashi
Kofu
Hachioji
TOKYO
3192m
Chiba
Tsumago
MINAMI-ALPS NAT. PARK
YAMANASHI-KEN
Kawasaki
Tokyo-wan
Nakatsugawa
Iida
Fujiyoshida
Mobara
Akaishi-sanmyaku
Kiso-gawa
FUJI-HAKONE-IZU NAT. PARK
KANAGAWA-KEN
YOKOHAMA
CHIBA-KEN
3120m
Gotemba
Boso-hanto
Ena
3776m Fuji-san
Kamakura
Futtsu
Odawara
Fujinomiya
Yokosuka
Katsuura
Shibara
Mishima
Atami
Miura
Kamogawa
SHIZUOKA-KEN
Fuji
Numazu
Sagami-nada
Tateyama
AICHI-KEN
Tenryu-gawa
Shimizu
Shizuoka
Ito
Fujieda
Yaizu
Izu-hanto
Kakegawa
O-shima
Toyohashi
Suruga-wan
Shimoda
Kosai
Hamamatsu
PACIFIC OCEAN
IZU SHICHITO
Nii-shima
Kozu-shima
Miyake-jima
Mikura-jima
C
D
E
6
5
4
3
2
1

Nagoya-jo Castle, destroyed in World War II, was impressively replicated in concrete in 1959.

Aichi-ken

ALTHOUGH IMPORTANT AGRICULTURALLY, AICHI-KEN IS better known for its industrial output: electronics, chemicals, food products, ceramics, textiles, and 40 percent of the nation's cars. Because of this and the drab highway scenery on the flatlands, most travelers to Japan give Aichi a miss. For those with time to spare, however, it has its rewards. The regional capital, Nagoya, may have few sights to recommend it, but as a major transportation hub with an abundance of good hotels it makes a convenient base for exploring the Tokai region and the southern Japan Alps.

Nagoya
- 172 B2

Visitor information
- Nagoya Station
- 052/541-4301
- 2 hrs. from Tokyo, 1 hr. from Osaka (Shin Osaka Station) on the JR Tokai Shinkansen line

Nagoya-jo Castle
- 1, 1 Honmaru, Naka-ku
- 052/231-1700
- 9 a.m.–4:30 p.m.
- $$
- Shiyakusho subway station on the Meijô line, then 5 min. walk north

Coastal Aichi-ken is dotted with beach resorts and *onsen* spas, but there is little of cultural or historical interest. Also, the resorts and spas are scattered; to make the most of them, you will need plenty of time or a car. North of the coast, Aichi-ken shares mountains with Nagano-ken and Gifu-ken; if you have your own transportation, you can cover miles of idyllic sylvan scenery crossed by torrents and rivers, many offering fishing and swimming. The jewel in Aichi's crown is the delightful historic hill town of Inuyama (see p. 176), with the oldest original castle in Japan.

Nagoya is Japan's fourth largest city and has an airport served by both domestic and international flights. The city has an efficient subway network (English-language maps are available at subway stations and the visitor information center) and is easy to get around.

Inhabited since prehistoric times, Nagoya rose to prominence in the 16th century as Japan's three greatest shoguns completed the process of unifying the country (see p. 33). While Oda Nobunaga and Toyotomi Hideyoshi were from Nagoya, Tokugawa Ieyasu, founder of the military dynasty that ruled Japan until 1867, was born in Okazaki, 38 miles (60 km) southeast. (Retaining several old temples connected with Ieyasu, Okazaki may interest Ieyasu enthusiasts, but its castle was destroyed a century ago, and what you see today is a concrete reproduction.) Nagoya was virtually obliterated by World War II air raids, and the vestiges associated with its great warrior sons went with it.

Nagoya-jo Castle, built in 1612 by Tokugawa Ieyasu for his son Yoshinao, was famous for the *shachi-hoko*—golden dolphins topping the keep's gables. The pride of the city, it was destroyed in 1945 and rebuilt in 1959. The castle is set in **Ninomaru-teien Garden,** which has an attractive teahouse.

Established in the third century, **Atsuta-jingu Shrine** houses the ancient Kusanagi Sword—one of the three treasures used in the imperial enthronement ceremony (the others are the Mirror at Ise Grand Shrine and the Jewel at the Imperial Palace in Tokyo). Atsuta is of similar vintage to Ise (see p. 259) and is likewise built of unadorned cedarwood. Set in a grove of camphor trees, the precinct includes a Noh stage hosting occasional performances and a **treasure hall** displaying Shinto relics, including swords and bronze mirrors. The Kusanagi Sword is not on display; no one except high priests and emperors has ever seen it. As one of Japan's most sacred shrines, Atsuta receives millions of devotees, especially during the New Year.

From Nagoya Station take the subway to Ozone, where a short walk south leads to the **Tokugawa Museum of Art (Tokugawa Bijutsukan).** The 10,000 items that make up the Tokugawa family treasures include calligraphy, paintings, ceramics, armor, and swords. The star attraction is the celebrated 12th-century *Genji Scroll,* the oldest surviving set of text and illustrations of Lady Murasaki's great 10th-century novel, *The Tale of Genji* (see p. 45). Because of its extreme fragility, the original is exhibited only once a year; what you normally see is a reproduction.

Aichi's grand tradition of craftsmanship is displayed at the **Toyota Commemorative Museum of Industry and Technology,** which relates the company's growth from an upstart weaving machinery maker to global auto titan. Exhibits also show *karakuri* clockwork dolls, modern humanoid robots, technological gadgets and games, and even a working steam engine.

Atsuta-jingu Shrine
www.atsutajingu.or.jp
✉ 1-1-1 Jinju, Atsuta-ku
☎ 052/671-4151
🕒 9:00 a.m.–4:30 p.m.; Treasure hall closed last Wed. & Thurs. of month
$ Treasure Hall $
🚉 Train: Jingu-mae on the Meitetsu line

The Tokugawa Museum of Art
www.tokugawa-art-museum.jp
✉ 1017 Tokugawa-cho, Higashi-ku
☎ 052/935-6262
🕒 10 a.m.–5 p.m.; closed Mon.
$ $$$
🚉 Subway: Ozone on the Meijo line

Toyota Commemorative Museum of Industry and Technology
www.tcmit.org
✉ 4-1-35 Noritake Shinmachi
☎ 052/551-6115
🕒 9:30 a.m.–5 p.m.; closed Mon.
$ $$
🚉 Sako on the Meitetsu Nagoya line

Hand-enameling at Noritake china works in Aichi-ken, where traditional craftsmanship and heavy industry coexist

Osu Kannon Temple is the focus of Nagoya's most colorful neighborhood.

Inuyama
172 B3
Visitor information
Inuyama Station
0568/61-6000
Train: Inuyama is 30 min. from Shin-Nagoya Station (near the JR Nagoya Station) via the Meitetsu-Inuyama line express (or 45 min. by ordinary train). Note that the stop for the area's sights is not Inuyama, but Inuyama-Yuen

About one mile (1.5 km) east of the station, the focal **Sakae** district comprises restaurants, bars, shopping centers, and a colossal underground mall. **Osu,** to the south, is a more animated downtown neighborhood with a colorful arcade leading to the popular **Osu Kannon Temple,** which holds a good flea market on weekends. Nagoya Port, on Ise-wan Bay, is the country's third largest port.

On the south bank of the Kiso-gawa River on the boundary between Aichi-ken and Gifu-ken, the pleasant town of **Inuyama** and its surroundings are a favorite Nagoyite weekend excursion. Along with fine scenery and a historic castle, it has some unusual sights, including the remarkable Meiji Village architectural museum and Japan Monkey Park, which may be of interest to children. If you don't like zoos, be aware that some of the primates are confined to cages.

Set on a cliff overlooking Kiso-gawa, the small four-story **Inuyama-jo Castle** is one of Japan's finest castles. In fact, built in 1537, it is the oldest still in its original state. It is also the only one that is privately owned, having remained the property of the Naruse family since 1618.

The castle's survival is miraculous: When it was seized from its owners in 1871, the buildings surrounding the keep were destroyed. Damaged in an earthquake in 1891, the castle was returned to the Naruse family in 1895 on condition they restore it—and they did. The viewing platform on the top offers a wonderful panorama over the river and valley. A three-minute walk east of the castle, on the grounds of the Meitetsu Inuyama Hotel, is the **Uraku-en Garden.** In the garden is the **Jo-an,** a celebrated 17th-century teahouse (moved here from Kyoto) where visitors can drink green tea.

Tea utensils in a reconstructed interior at the Tokugawa Museum of Art

Inuyama-jo Castle
- 65-2 Kitakoken
- 0568/61-1711
- 9 a.m.–5 p.m.; closed Mon.
- $$
- Short walk from Inuyama-Yuen Station

Tagata-jinja Shrine, a short distance south of Inuyama,across from Tagata-jinja-mae Station, is one of Japan's 40 or so remaining phallic shrines. Tagata is renowned for its rousing Bumper Harvest Festival (Tagata Honen Sai, March 15). The English-language shrine leaflet explains that the festival's purpose "is to offer the huge penis to the shrine, praying for world peace, the growth of all things and a pumper [sic] crop." The monster wooden phallus leading the parade is enshrined in the main hall, and many more in an array of improbable sizes are displayed in the adjacent building. Exhibiting rocks and stones suggesting male and female genitalia, parts of the precinct are also festooned with small *ema*—votive plaques left by those entreating the gods to find them partners or grant offspring. Stronger on content than form, the shrine buildings are disappointingly utilitarian.

Tagata's female counterpart is the more demure **Oagata-jinja Shrine.** Set in wooded hills and attractively constructed, it provides insights into feminine Shinto practices: Girls leave their dolls here to be burned as a rite of passage to womanhood. Some women believe crawling through the miniature *torii* gateway in the open-sided pavilion will increase their fertility.

Inuyama's most curious attraction is **Meiji-mura Village** *(1, Uchiyama, Inuyama-shi, tel 0568/67-0314, 9:30 a.m.–5 p.m., Mar.–Oct., 9:30 a.m.–4 p.m., Nov.–Feb., www.meijimura.com, $$$)*. Set beside man-made Lake Iruka-ko in a park, this open-air museum, created in 1965, is where lucky buildings go when they die. More than 60 important early Western-style structures have been moved here from other locations in Japan and rebuilt. Highlights include the facade and lobby of Frank Lloyd Wright's Tokyo Imperial Hotel, Kyoto's St. John's Church, and the old Sapporo telephone exchange. You can ride around the village on antique streetcars and a steam railroad, making Meiji-mura a perfect outing for children. Including shops and restaurants, it covers a substantial area, so set aside half a day. ■

Tagata-jinja Shrine
- 152 Tagata-cho, Komaki-shi
- 0568/76-2906
- Train: Tagata Jinja-mae Station (10 min. from Inuyama on the Komaki line)

Oagata-jinja Shrine
- 15 min. walk east of Gakuden Station
- 0568/67-1017
- Train: Gakuden Station (8 min. from Inuyama on the Komaki line)

Kanazawa & beyond

CALLED HOKURIKU, THE NORTHERN REGION OF CHUBU encompasses four prefectures: Ishikawa-ken, northern Gifu-ken, Nagano-ken, and Niigata-ken. Mainly mountainous, the region offers aspects to please most travelers, but the old towns of Kanazawa (Ishikawa) and Takayama (Gifu) offer an array of additional historical and cultural assets to make them the firm favorites in the Hokuriku region.

Ishikawa-ken lies on the northwestern side of Honshu, extending north to the **Noto-hanto Peninsula** on the Sea of Japan. Tourism and resorts flourish on the east of the peninsula, but a beautiful coastline and peaceful fishing villages to the west demand exploration if you have time and—preferably—a car. In Ishikawa's southeast is the sacred mountain of Haku-san—revered for its spectacular alpine scenery, camping and hiking in summer, and *onsen* bathing and skiing in winter. The most famous destination is the prefectural capital of Kanazawa, a former castle town retaining many facets of its illustrious past as a center of culture and craft.

Gifu-ken includes the old province of Hida, of which the capital was **Takayama** on the western slopes of the Japan Alps. This delightful town is the region's main destination for visitors.

Lovers of mountain scenery should head for **Nagano-ken.** The capital city of Nagano in the north and Matsumoto in the center are the main bases for mountain activities. The **Kamikochi Valley,** west of Matsumoto, can claim to have the finest mountain scenery in all Japan, while the beautiful **Kiso Valley,** carved by Kiso-gawa

Kanazawa
172 B4
Visitor information
Kanazawa Station
076/232-3933
Train: JR Joetsu Shinkansen from Tokyo to Nagaoka, change for limited express (4 hrs. 30 min.–5 hrs.)

Washing silk kimono textiles in the river is part of the *yuzen* dyeing process for which Kanazawa is famous.

through the central range of the Japan Alps, is an area steeped in legend.

Niigata-ken's capital, **Niigata,** is the most important coastal city on the Sea of Japan. For most visitors, however, it serves only as the gateway to the prefecture's star attraction: Sado-ga-shima Island (see pp. 193–96).

Kanazawa was the capital of the old fiefdom of Kaga, which came to be governed by the Buddhist Jodo Shinshu sect as an autonomous republic from 1488. Conquered by shogun Oda Nobunaga in 1583, it thrived as a prominent center for arts and crafts, including ceramics, textiles, and paperware, as well as traditional *Kaga ryori* cuisine (see p. 370) and *wagashi* (Japanese confectionery). These all still continue today. The Noh theater also flourished in Kanazawa, and the Ishikawa Prefectural Noh Theater (see p. 385) is now one of Japan's most important centers for Noh. The city sprawls and its sights are scattered, which can be frustrating if you have limited time. However, main bus lines run between the station and major sights. With fine food and many a good *ryokan,* a stopover in Kanazawa is always a good idea. Be sure to stop at the **visitor information center** when you arrive at Kanazawa station, to pick up the excellent illustrated pamphlet mapping the city and its bus routes in English.

Katamachi, the town center, is nondescript, with department stores and the usual amenities;

The Kenroku-en Garden, one of Japan's most famous, blazes with early summer azaleas.

Kenroku-en Garden

www.pref.ishikawa.jp/siro-niwa/kenrokuen

✉ 1-1 Marunouchi

☎ 076/234-3800

$ $

🚌 Buses 11 and 12 run from Kanazawa Station to Kenrokuen-shita (or the Dewacho stop for Seisonkaku)

Graced with a two-story tower, the Ishikawamon Gate is all that remains of Kanazawa-jo Castle.

Nagamachi Yuzen-kan
- 2-6-16 Naga-machi
- 076/264-2811
- 9 a.m.–5 p.m.
- $

Kanazawa-shi Shinise Kinenkan
- 2-2-45 Naga-machi
- 076/220-2524
- 9:30 a.m.–5 p.m.
- $

Nomura house
- 1-3-32 Naga-machi
- 076/221-3553
- 8:30 a.m.–5:30 p.m., Apr.–Sept.; closes at 4:30 Oct.–Mar.
- $$

north of the center is lively Yoko-Yasuecho shopping arcade, and just south of this is Omicho market, which sells produce for Kanazawa's fine cuisine and some of the best seafood in Japan.

Having survived World War II unscathed, Kanazawa abounds in historical sights. Several are in or near the **Kenroku-en Garden.** Designated one of the three great gardens of Japan, Kenroku-en is named after the *kenroku* (six combinations) considered ideal for gardens: spaciousness, serenity, venerability, scenic views, subtle design, and coolness provided by watercourses. Originally the stroll garden of Kanazawa-jo Castle, it was enlarged and completed in 1819 and opened to the public in 1871. There are 12,000 trees of 150 varieties in this masterpiece of landscaping, which includes artificial hills, ponds, and waterways flanked by irises in season. Yet Kenroku-en's scale, impressive as it is, precludes the intimacy of a true garden—it is better described as a park. It can get very crowded between 11 a.m. and 3 p.m.

Just to the north outside Kenroku-en is the impressive **Ishikawamon Gate,** the last surviving structure of Kanazawa-jo, which burned down in 1881. At the southern end of the garden the refined **Seisonkaku Villa,** built in 1863, is noted for the delicacy of its interiors. The grounds include a teahouse and a garden with gnarled pines and streams meandering beneath the veranda.

About half a mile west of the villa, the old earthen walls that flank the lanes of the Nagamachi samurai quarter make the area picturesque. Most of the buildings are private, though, and few are original structures. In the 1910s the remains of **Nomura house (Nomura-ke)** were restored by a shipping magnate, who added part of a samurai house he owned in his hometown. Although not quite authentic, the building is highly evocative. Viewed from the veranda or from upstairs while sipping green tea, the exquisite little garden of rocks and watercourses is a masterpiece of miniature landscaping. Nearby stands the **Nagamachi**

Yuzen-kan, a silk-dyeing center that was once an old teahouse. Here you can watch *kaga yuzen* artisans intricately hand painting silk textiles (children are not admitted). The **Kanazawa Shinise Memorial Hall (Kanazawa-shi Shinise Kinekan),** once a wooden pharmacy in the center of town, has been dismantled and reerected here as a museum exhibiting local crafts and showing shop interiors of the late 1800s.

Three old geisha districts remain in Kanazawa. Kazue-machi along Asano-gawa River is picturesque, as is the Nishi-Chaya-gai quarter in the southwest. The finest is **Higashi-chaya-gai** to the northeast. The streetlights and buildings here remain unchanged since the 19th century, although the geisha who once frequented it are now reduced to a mere 20 or so. The 180-year-old **Kaikaro** is a teahouse, its decor an inspired blend of the traditional and the contemporary, featuring an inner garden of shards of glass. A few doors away is **Shima** *(1-13-21 Higashiyama, tel 076/252-5675),* a delightful old geisha house with original fixtures and furnishings, now a museum.

On the slopes of tranquil **Teramachi,** the temple district in the south of town, are some 70 temples and shrines. None is major but several are interesting, among them Gannen-ji, visited by the 17th-century poet Basho, Akan-ji (also called Neko-dera—Cat Temple—a former feline cemetery), and Daien-ji Temple, which has a fine Zen garden. West of Teramachi is the famous **Myoryu-ji,** also known as Ninja-dera, the Ninja Temple. The first impression on entering is of nothing special, but appearances are deceptive—intentionally. Built in the 1640s, it presents an ingenious labyrinth of 21 secret chambers, hidden stairways, and trapdoors designed as escape routes, particularly for ninja—secret agents practicing the martial art of *ninjutsu* (the art of stealth). The effect is odd and unsettling. Conducted in Japanese, tours include demonstrations of trick devices and ninja techniques. ■

The music behind these facades in the old Higashi geisha quarter fell silent long ago, but they retain their charm.

Myoryu-ji Temple

✉ 1-2-12 No-machi

☎ 076/241-0888

🕒 9 a.m.–4:30 p.m., Mar.–Nov.; closes at 4 p.m. Dec.–Feb.

$ $$

Kanazawa ceramics

A great center for ceramics since feudal times, Kanazawa is renowned both for Ohi and Kutani pottery. Craft shops selling ceramics dot the town, and the cream of antique ware is displayed in museums such as the **Ishikawa Prefectural Museum of Traditional Products and Crafts** and the **Ishikawa Prefectural Museum of Art,** both near the Kenroku-en Garden. In the southwest of town the **Kutani Pottery Kosen Kiln** welcomes visitors. You can arrange to visit workshops through the visitor information center. Just north of Kenrokuen gardens, the **Ishikawa Local Products Shop** features local art, crafts, and food; it also has a restaurant. ■

Takayama

DELIGHTFUL TAKAYAMA, ON THE WESTERN SLOPES OF THE Japan Alps in Gifu-ken, was the capital of the old province of Hida. The very name Takayama, meaning "high mountain," conveys uncommon remoteness for what was once an important town. Its carpenters reputedly played a large part in the building of ancient Kyoto and Nara. As its reputation for woodcrafts spread around Japan, Takayama continued to prosper. It suffered a decline during the modern era, but its very remoteness has helped preserve it.

Above: Floats and crowds flow over the bridges during Takayama Festival. Right: Kusakabe-ke, an old merchant house, is now a museum.

Takayama
172 B3
Visitor information
Outside station
0577/32-5328
Train: Express Hida from Kyoto (3 hrs. 40 min.)

Shiroyama-koen Park
About 200 m (220 yards) over the Miya-gawa River
Shoren-ji Main Hall
$

Today the town retains sufficient historical sights to justify the hackneyed designation "Little Kyoto"—mainly for its Teramachi temple district. Yet Takayama is nothing like Kyoto; no realm of samurai, priests, and literati, it grew up as a town of farmers, artisans, and merchants. Its charm lies in the remarkably well-preserved streets of merchant houses and venerable sake breweries concentrated in the **Sanmachi Suji** district, which also contains shops, taverns, and inns of similar vintage. Takayama's role as the hub of a rich folk culture is evidenced in its museums.

Although Takayama is small, it takes a good day to do justice to the sights on the east side of the Miya-gawa River alone; a stopover is highly recommended. Friendly and laid-back, this is not a place to rush around. You might be tempted to sample the excellent local sake; Takayama has a reputation for the quality and conviviality of its traditional inns. Expect *sansai* (mountain vegetables) with your meals, and in restaurants make a point of sampling Hida beef, which rivals that of Kobe for quality.

If you visit in spring or autumn, don't miss the **Takayama Festival** on April 14–15 and October 9–10. Famous throughout Japan, the procession features ornate floats (*yatai*) with antique *karakuri* automatons performing mechanical feats. If you cannot make the show, you can see the floats at the **Festival Floats Exhibition Hall (Takayama Yatai Kaikan,** *53-1 Sakuramachi, tel 0577/32-0881)* in Sakurayama Hachimangu shrine at the north end of town.

Hida Kokubun-ji Temple, northeast of the station on the west river bank, was founded by Nara's pious emperor Shomu in 746. It has been burned down and rebuilt

Hida Folk Village, where local antique houses go when they die.

Kusakabe Folk Museum
1-52 Ojin-machi
0577/32-0072
9:00a.m.–4:30 p.m, Mar.–Nov.; 8:30 a.m.–4:00 p.m. Wed.–Mon., Dec.–Feb.
$$

since, so all that remains of the original is a ginkgo tree thought to be 1,200 years old; next to it stands a three-story **pagoda** from 1821. The oldest current structure is the 16th-century **Main Hall.** Among the temple's treasures are two fine Buddhist statues carved in the Heian period (794–1185) and a 12th-century sword thought to have belonged to a warrior of the Heike clan—the last rulers of Kyoto during the Heian period.

Kusakabe Folk Museum (Kusakabe Mingeikan) is located on the eastern bank of Miyagawa. The building, built in 1879 as a merchant's home and warehouse, is a fine example of Takayama carpentry. Now a museum, it displays all the fixtures it contained when open for business during the 19th century. Next door, the interior of **Yoshijima-ke House** *(1-51 Oshin-machi, tel 0577/32-0038, 9 a.m.–5 p.m., Mar.–Nov., 9 a.m.–4:30 p.m.Wed.–Sun., Dec.–Feb.)* is not to be missed. A masterpiece of traditional Japanese domestic architecture, its soaring framework of huge crossbeams and posts stretches high up under the roof.

Also on the eastern side of town is **Shiroyama-koen Park,** renowned for its alpine views and spring displays of cherry blossoms; look for the feudal castle ruins.

Shoren-ji Temple in the northwestern part of the park originally stood in Shirakawa-go, some 20 miles (32 km) northwest of Takayama. It was moved and reassembled here in 1960, when the lake formed by a new dam drowned its site. The 1504 **Main Hall** is much admired as an example of Muromachi (1338–1573) temple architecture. There is a pleasant landscape garden adjacent.

A sake brewery

If you follow the paths through Shiroyama-koen, you will come to **Teramachi,** the temple district. The Higashiyama Walking Route (2 miles/3.5 km) is well signposted in English throughout. If you have visited Shoren-ji, you can take the path due south, following the loop around **Dairyu-ji Temple** and then bearing right up to **Ena-jinja Shrine.** The path from here follows the Teramachi route, which runs straight along the northeastern side of town. Though not of major importance, the 13 temples and five shrines you pass are highlights on an enchanting walk. The path winds west to Yasugawa-dori, the street crossing the rivers into the center of town. Alternatively, you can approach Teramachi by starting from Yasugawa-dori and following the path due southeast.

Sights on the town's western side include the **Historical Government House (Takayama Jinya),** reached by walking east to the end of Hachikenmachi-dori. The palatial structure on the left is one of the only government buildings surviving in Japan from the Edo period. Originally erected by the Kanemori rulers in 1615, it was rebuilt 200 years later and remained the seat of Takayama's government even after the abolition of the shogunate in the 19th century. Entered via an imposing gate through massive surrounding walls, it includes administrative and court rooms, a torture chamber, and a granary harking back to the days when fortunes were counted in rice.

Hida Folk Village (Hida Minzoku Mura) should be a high priority when visiting Takayama. More than 30 fine old farmhouses and rustic buildings from around Takayama and the Hida area have been dismantled and rebuilt in a landscape designed to evoke their original settings. The spacious village complex is on hilly ground overlooking the town. Featuring high thatched roofs and interiors with beams blackened by the smoke of cooking fires, the buildings provide fascinating insights into the simple, often harsh lifestyle of rural Japan until less than a century ago. Original fixtures and farming tools include a water mill and workshops where artisans (weavers, basketmakers, dyers, woodcarvers and others) demonstrate local crafts. It takes two to four hours to stroll around the village, which includes restaurants and craft shops.

UNESCO World Heritage Site **Shirakawa-go** *(Visitor information 05769-6-1013)* has many fine examples of these thatched-roofed, majestic farmhouses, some of which also serve as inns, in an unspoilt riverside farming village; it's only a 100-minute bus ride from Takayama and makes for an excellent side trip. ■

An interior in Takayama reveals its massive crossbeam roof structure.

Historical Government House

- 1-5 Hachiken-machi
- 0577/32-0643
- 8:45 a.m.–5 p.m, Mar.–Oct.; 8:45 a.m.–4:30 p.m. Nov.–Feb.
- $$

Hida Folk Village

- 1-590 Kamiokamoto-cho
- 0577/34-4711
- 8:30 a.m.–5 p.m.
- $$$
- Bus: from number 6 gate at station to Hida-no-Sato (fast bus takes 10 min., slow bus 30 min.); 20-min. walk southwest of station

Takayama markets

There is plenty of local color in Takayama's morning street markets *(asa-ichi),* which trade daily in produce and flowers grown by local farmers as well as in handicrafts. Both are open from 7 a.m. to noon, one at Jinya-mae near the Historical Government House and the other on the eastern bank of the Miya-gawa River, across from Kajibashi bridge.

The old town center of Sanmachi Suji holds an antique market on the 7th of each month from May through October. Good pieces won't come cheap, but they are still priced substantially lower than in Kyoto or Tokyo. ■

The winter snow enhances the beauty of the Zenko-ji Temple in Nagano.

Nagano-ken

WITH NO SHORTAGE OF MOUNTAINS, OTHER PLACES IN Japan could qualify, but to the Japanese Nagano-ken is *the* alpine prefecture. Western-style mountaineering was first introduced more than a century ago; in 1998, Nagano city was host to the Winter Olympic Games. Apart from winter sports, visitors can enjoy mountain hiking in summer, especially around Kamikochi. Picturesque Matsumoto boasts one of Japan's most magnificent examples of an old castle town; the surrounding mountains present great natural beauty and a wealth of hot springs. South of Matsumoto, an inspiring blend of mountain scenery and history pervades the Kiso Valley.

Nagano

173 C4

Visitor information

JR Nagano Station

026/226-5626

JR Shinkansen from Tokyo (1 hr. 35 min.) or JR Chuô Honsen line from Nagoya (2 hrs. 50 min.)

After coming under the spotlight in 1998, Nagano reverted to its mundane routine as prefectural capital. A small modern city, it has few sights, but it is friendly and cosmopolitan, and it makes a comfortable base for trips into the surrounding mountains. The town's one truly outstanding historic and religious asset is **Zenko-ji Temple.** So important is it that Chuo-dori, the main street, runs northward up to it in a dead straight line, a distance of one mile

Above right: Dedicated to travelers, children, and the unborn, *jizo* statues flank the approach to Zenko-ji Temple.

Zenko-ji Temple

- ✉ 491 Motoyoshi-cho
- ☎ 026/234-3591
- 🕓 4:30 a.m.–4:30 p.m. summer; 6 a.m–4 p.m. winter
- $ Main Hall free; Inner Sanctum & walk in the dark (okaidan meguri) $$
- 🚌 Bus from the station to Daimon (10 min.)

(1.5 km) from Nagano Station. Founded around 660, Zenko-ji's all-embracing tradition of worship reflects the dawn of Buddhism in Japan, but it belongs to no specific sect and is revered by all. Zenko-ji has admitted women both as worshippers and priests for centuries, even when most sacred precincts were male preserves. Of paramount importance to pilgrims, it receives up to eight million visitors annually. Those numbers swell every six or seven years for the Gokaicho ceremony honoring the Ikko Sanzon Amida Nyorai statue. Too sacred for mortal eyes, the statue traditionally remains hidden. The next Gokaicho takes place in 2009.

The temple's destruction in 1700 prompted a reorientation of the compound; built in 1707, the colossal **Main Hall (Hondo)** stands on a site northeast of its original counterpart. The **Nio-mon,** first of the two massive gates along the approach, was rebuilt in 1918.

The imposing facade of the Main Hall does justice to the magnificence of the lofty interior. Incense wafts high up into the gilded shadows of an ornate coffered ceiling hung with gigantic gold lamps; the atmosphere is awe-inspiring. Scribes are on hand to commemorate pilgrims' visits with a temple seal; for a small fee they will stamp your notebook (visitors can collect stamps from temples and shrines throughout Japan) and embellish it with votive calligraphy.

One of the main attractions—a ticket to heaven—is to touch the **key of paradise** (an icon set in wood) beneath the main altar. Claustrophobes, be warned: to touch the key you need to grope along the wall through a long, narrow tunnel in pitch darkness. If you fail to touch the key, take heart: The relief at seeing a glimmer of light at the end is symbolically equated with enlightenment.

The precinct is frequently crowded and the atmosphere festive; outside the gate, craft shops, cafés, and restaurants line a pleasant avenue leading to the town center. ■

Matsumoto

Matsumoto
173 C4
Visitor information
Outside JR Matsumoto Station
0263/32-2814
JR Shinonoi line from Nagano (55 min.). JR Chuo Honsen Line's "Azusa" limited express from Shinjuku Station, Tokyo (2 hrs. 45 min.). JR Chuo Honsen line from Nagoya (2 hrs. 30 min.)

MATSUMOTO, IN THE CENTRAL HIGHLANDS, IS THE southwestern equivalent of Nagano (see p. 186) and is similarly used as a base for mountain excursions and activities. The city is bland in the center but retains some venerable back streets. The Metoba-gawa River flows through Matsumoto east to west, and the townscapes along the banks present an engaging jumble of old and new.

Ruled by the Ogasawara clan in the 14th and 15th centuries and taken over by the Ishikawa in the 16th, Matsumoto was a castle town. **Matsumoto-jo Castle** *(4-1 Marunouchi, tel 0263/32-2902)* ranks as one of Japan's most magnificent. Only a hint of white accentuates the black wooden walls and dark-tiled roofs of this National Treasure, nicknamed Karasu-jo (Crow Castle). The name is said to derive from its shape, but more probably it shares the sobriquet with other black castles in contrast to the "White Egret" castle of Himeji (see pp. 256–57). First constructed in 1504, the castle reached its final form in the 1590s. Up steep wooden staircases, there is a spectacular alpine panorama from the viewing platform on the five-story **main keep.** The interior—actually six floors (Japanese castles have five stories outside and six inside)—displays an arsenal comprising guns, swords, and armor. The castle never saw any action—hence its excellent state of preservation. Among its turrets, the most famous is the moon-viewing turret.

Matsumoto-jo Castle is one of the finest and most authentic surviving samurai castles in the country.

Nihon Minzoku Shiryokan Museum, attached to the castle, showcases many exhibits, including the Honda Clock Collection of fine antique pieces. **Nihon Ukiyo-e Hakubutsu-kan Museum** *(2206-1 Koshiba, Shimadachi, tel 0263/47-4440, closed Mon.)* has the country's largest collection of *ukiyo-e,* or woodblock prints. The Nihon Museum is just a seven-minute taxi ride from the station; most of the town can be comfortably covered on foot.

Matsumoto is noted for scenic spots less than 30 minutes away by bus, notably the 6,500-foot (2,000 m) **Utsukushigahara Plateau (Utsukushigahara-kogen),** famed for breathtaking mountain views and carpets of alpine flowers. The plateau also boasts popular spas, **Utsukushigahara Onsen** and adjacent **Asama Onsen** at the foot. Matsumoto is a stepping-stone to Kamikochi Valley, the gateway to the Japan Alps. Hikers and cyclists crowd into the city in summer, when hotel reservations should be made well in advance. ■

Kappa-bashi suspension bridge spans Azusa-gawa River in the Kamikochi Valley.

Kamikochi Valley

THE KAMIKOCHI VALLEY, CUTTING THROUGH THE Japan Alps west of Matsumoto, is a narrow glen in Chubu Sangaku National Park. Kamikochi lies at 5,000 feet (1,525 m) above sea level between Mount Yake-dake to the southwest, Mount Kasumizawa-dake to the east, and the Hotaka range to the north. Averaging 10,000 feet (3,050 m), these peaks are among the nation's highest—a challenge to serious climbers. Hikers, campers, and nature lovers all cherish the area, too. After kaleidoscopic displays of alpine flowers in summer and blazing colors in the fall, Kamikochi is closed from November through May.

Following the Azusa-gawa River east to west, the main attractions of the area are **Taisho-ike,** a pond formed after the eruption of Yake-san in 1915, and—an hour's hike away—**Kappa-bashi,** a suspension bridge over Azusa-gawa with a spectacular view of Mount Oku-Hotaka-dake. Another good hour farther east is **Myojin-ike** pond. Kamikochi Valley extends to Yoko'o, about 4 miles (6 km) farther on. You should have mountain trekking experience and proper equipment to venture beyond here; the area is more remote and the ground steeper, while temperatures are known to dip below freezing even in summer. Kamikochi offers a wealth of hiking routes. There is an information office at the bus terminal, but you would do better seeking advice about trails and accommodations in English at visitor information centers in Matsumoto or Takayama. From mid-July to mid-August and again in October, the region is so crowded that advance booking (not to say avoidance) is essential. Note that during the rainy season in June, Kamikochi's scenic marvels tend to vanish in the drizzle. ■

Kamikochi

173 C4

Visitor information

Kamikochi bus terminal

0263/95-2405

Matsumoto Dentetsu Line to Shin-Shimashima from Matsumoto station (30 min.), then 1 hr. 20 min. by bus to Kamikochi (bus service runs from late Apr. to mid-Nov. only)

One of the gems of the Kiso Valley, Tsumago has been restored to look just as it did a century ago.

Kiso Valley (Kisoji)

KISOJI, EMBRACED BY THE MOUNTAINS OF NAGANO-KEN, is celebrated in a song known to every Japanese schoolchild. Many legends haunt Kisoji, its 230 square miles (600 sq km) of soaring cedar forests having yielded the trees used to build the most sacred Shinto shrines. To the west (weather permitting) the skyline is dominated by 10,049-foot (3,063 m) Mount Ontake-san, an active volcano held sacred to Shinto.

Kisoji
173 C3
Visitor information
Train: JR Chuo Honsen line Matsumoto–Nagoya

Narai
173 C3
Visitor information
Tourism section, Town Hall
0264/34-2001

Agematsu
173 C3
Visitor information
Outside the station
0264/52-4820

Kisoji lies along the Nakasendo (the old "through the mountains" road), the alternative to the Tokaido trunk road from Edo to Kyoto in feudal times. The road's historical post towns of Narai, Tsumago, and Magome became increasingly remote after the decline of the Nakasendo and the increase in rail travel, but gained architectural recognition during the late 1960s. Since then they have been strictly preserved and painstakingly restored. Although Kisoji's townships are linked by rail, many beauty spots, historical sites, secluded shrines, and temples are a good bus ride away from the stations; to do justice to this wonderful region, you need a minimum of three days.

Kisoji's once-flourishing forestry industry declined from the 1950s as a result of poor management, bringing down the regional economy. Recent years, however, have seen a modest revival. Village workshops, craft centers, and folk museums provide ubiquitous evidence that Kisoji maintains its centuries-old reputation for woodcraft and lacquerware. Today it depends heavily on the five million tourists it receives annually. The majority are daytrippers, so the region is enchantingly tranquil and unspoiled once the hordes go home. The deeply forested hills of larch and cedar present spectacular hiking possibilities, and their many torrents make them a fishing

Mountain paradise

Venerated since prehistoric times, Mount Ontake-san is the object of a Shinto cult. The first Ontake shrine is said to have been erected in 928, but Ontake-kyo (Ontake religion) was developed during the 18th century as an animistic composite of shamanism and *ryobushinto*—a meld of Shinto and Buddhism outlawed during the "purification" of Shinto in the 1870s. Ontake-kyo counts around two million followers. Every year some 150,000 pilgrims ascend the slopes of Ontake to a shrine near the summit (the volcano is active, so access to the crater is prohibited). Many start with ritual purification by standing under the Kiyo-taki Waterfall, in the forest near Otaki-mura. Believers erect commemorative stones called *reijin-no-hi,* believing them to be their ticket to a mountain paradise when they die. Shrouded in mist and mystery, the stones stand in their hundreds of thousands on wooded slopes and dells in the vicinity of Ontake-jinja Shrine. ■

Ontake-kyo: melding Shinto with Buddhism

paradise. Spring and summer come quite late to Kiso, where the winters can be bitterly cold. But you can always warm yourself beside a square, sunken *irori* fireplace and enjoy good mountain fare, including *sansai* (mountain vegetables), river fish, and (seasonally) stews of wild boar.

Narai, once dubbed "Narai of the 1,000 houses," was the most important post town on the Nakasendo. There are far fewer than 1,000 today, but venerable houses still flank the 0.75-mile (1.2 km) main street, which looks much as it did 200 years ago, down to the old wells for slaking travelers' thirsts. Just behind it are charming rustic shrines and temples. Some houses are now museums and craft shops; others, such as the sake brewery, an old lacquerware workshop, and the famous Echigoya Inn, maintain their ancestral function.

You can visit a large lacquerware store and museum in **Hirasawa,** about half a mile (1 km) north. About the same distance north of this is **Niekawa,** which maintains a replica of its old *sekisho* (barrier station), where the identities of travelers were checked.

Kiso Fukushima is Kisoji's largest town. Part of it was badly damaged by fire in 1947 and subsequently rebuilt. The old section on the hill, overlooking the Kiso-gawa River, was largely spared and retains an antiquarian charm. As at Niekawa, there is a handsome replica of the old barrier station. Above all, Fukushima is the gateway for those climbing Ontake-san. Taking about 70 minutes, buses from Kiso-Fukushima Station go to

Kiso Fukushima

173 C3

Visitor information

Outside the station

0264/22-4000

Train: JR Chuo Honsen line from Matsumoto (40 min.)

A Narai craftsman shapes bentwood bowls.

Nakanoyu Onsen, the starting point of the main trail up the mountain. From the trailhead it takes almost four hours to hike through the cedar forests to the summit.

Perched riverside, the otherwise unremarkable town of **Agematsu** offers a breathtaking view over the Kiso-gawa gorges. Known as a center for woodcraft, the town's factories and workshops are open to the public. The scale of these operations is somewhat industrial, but the scent of cedar is heavenly.

Tsumago is the jewel in Kisoji's crown. Another important post town and 15 miles (25 km) southwest of Agematsu, it has been officially protected since 1968; the town's buildings have been beautifully restored, with communication lines buried underground and TV aerials hidden. Highlights include a palatial wooden official residence (now the local museum) and a post office, both dating from the 1860s.

Tsumago's only drawback is that it feels rather like a museum, particularly as the often daunting crowds of visitors vastly outnumber the residents. Best appreciated in the evening and early morning, Tsumago is a delightful place to stay. The 18th-century house on the main street, famous for the tree growing right against its facade and featured on local postcards, is still a *ryokan* (inn).

The picturesque town of **Magome** was the birthplace of poet and novelist Shimazaki Toson (1872–1943), one of the first writers to combine Japanese sensitivities with Western forms of expression; a modern museum building is devoted to his life and art. However, too many of the old houses—damaged by fire and restored—have been turned into tourist cafés and kitschy souvenir shops. Compared with Narai or Tsumago, Magome feels disappointingly like a theme park. ■

A postman sports Edo-period garb in Tsumago.

Tsumago
173 C3
Visitor information
2152 Azuma, Tsumago main street
0264/57-3123
Train: JR Chuo Honsen line from Matsumoto to Nagiso (1 hr.), bus to Tsumago (10 min.)

Magome
173 C3
Visitor information
Opposite Toson Kinekan
0264/59-2336
Train: JR Chuo Honsen line from Matsumoto to Makatsugawa (1 hr. 30 min.), bus to Magome (30 min.)

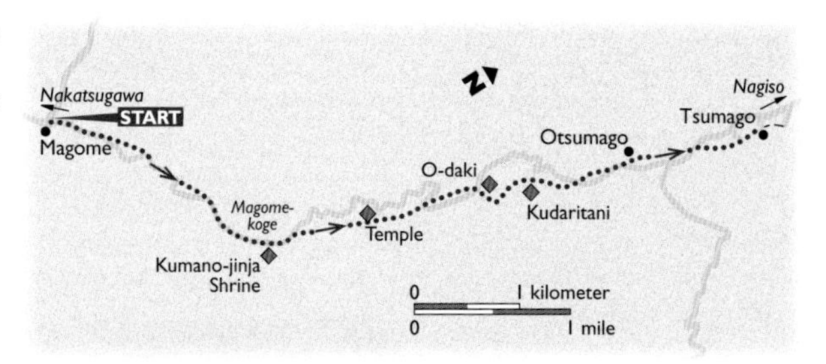

Magome to Tsumago Walk

Some 6 miles (9.5 km) long, this three-hour hike follows the old Nakasendo route. But for the first 2 miles (3 km), so does the modern road. If you feel traffic would mar your appreciation of the scenery, take the bus from Magome to Magome-toge Pass (listen for the name), and then start walking to the hamlets of O-daki, Kudaritani, Otsumago, and Tsumago. Depending on the season, you will see mountains reflected in the flooded rice fields, lush shades of green, or vivid autumn hues—a perfect prelude to the old houses of Tsumago, where time seems to have stood still. The visitor information center can arrange for luggage to be forwarded between Magome and Tsumago. ■

Sado-ga-shima

Alpine flowers enliven the seascape at Onogame in early summer.

COVERING 330 SQUARE MILES (855 SQ KM), SADO-GA-shima is one of Japan's largest islands. Its verdant northern and southern mountain ranges are separated by a lush agricultural plain; carpeted with alpine flowers, Mount Donden-yama offers spectacular views.

Medieval warlords, wary of creating martyrs, sent their more noble, pious, or learned enemies into exile. The banishment of choice was remote Sado-ga-shima, separated from the mainland by a 22-mile (35 km) strait notorious for its treacherous winter seas. Sado Kinzan Gold Mine was founded in 1601 to dig gold discovered in the hills near Aikawa and flourished under the shogunate's control during the Edo period. The gold made little difference to the islanders, whose existence depended (as it does today) on rice farming and fishing. Having closed as a mine in 1867, Sado Kinzan is now one of the main attractions in a region that relies heavily on tourism for revenue.

Sado's scenic assets belie its gloomy past. The island lures legions of modern exiles in spring and summer with endless opportunities for hiking, cycling, camping, swimming, wallowing in hot springs, and feasting on superlative seafood. Sado has accommodations to suit all budgets. Many of its quiet Japanese-style inns lie in charming country surroundings.

The island's secluded temples and shrines, often historically associated with illustrious exiles, cluster in peaceful little towns such as **Mano** and **Sawata** on the west coast and the central plain. Emperor Juntoko, who died in exile in 1242, is buried in the **Mano Goryo** mausoleum near Mano.

The coast is dotted with fishing villages, notably attractively restored Shukunegi in the south (see p. 196) The rugged coastline

Sado-ga-shima

173 C6

Visitor information

Near ferry terminal at Ryotsu

0259/23-3300

Ferry: from Niigata to Ryotsu, (2 hrs. 20 min.). Jetfoil: from Niigata (1 hr.)

features striking volcanic rock formations, especially along **Senkaku-wan,** a bay on the north coast. Although predictably crowded in high summer, Sado remains unhurried and refreshingly unspoiled, attracting young people fond of outdoor activities and fugitives from the pressures of modern Japan. For all that, it does not exert much of a hold on its constantly declining population. Job opportunities are too few to attract the young, and the relatively advanced age of many locals may seem surprising. From November through April, bus services are halved and accommodations close as islanders batten down to face harsh winters.

You could spend one night on Sado and take tours, but a stay of three or four days would be much more worthwhile. The towns are all connected by bus, and services run about once an hour. Cycle rentals abound, or you can rent a car.

Most people reach Sado by ferry from Niigata on the Honshu mainland, a journey of some two and a half hours, docking at Ryotsu, on a bay in the center of the east coast. The island capital, **Ryotsu,** lies on a strip of land separating Lake Kamo-ko from the sea. Catering mainly to Japanese package tours, this is Sado at its most developed and least attractive, but it is convenient as a base for transportation all over the island. The famous Sado Okesa dance (see p. 196) originated here, so this is the place to see it. If you miss it at a festival, there are sometimes professional performances, along with Ondeko drumming and dancing (see p. 195), at the **Ryotsu Kai-kan Hall** north of town.

A more pleasant but less convenient way to visit the island is to take the ferry from Naoetsu (south along the coast from Niigata) to Ogi, then make your way west and north. **Ogi** is the gateway to one of the island's most attractive regions. The modern ferry terminal building is deceptive: This is a sleepy fishing town small enough to cover on foot, consisting of a single main street lined with weather-beaten shops and houses—as perfectly unremarkable as it is charming.

Above left: Fisherwomen still use rotund *taraibune* near Ogi, though the boats are now mainly tourist attractions.

Ogi

173 C5

Visitor information

1935-26 Ogi, west of the post office

0259/86-3200

Bus: From Sawata (65 min.)

Ferry: from Naoetsu, Honshu (2 hrs. 30 min.)

Volcanism forged the craggy coastline of Senkaku-wan Bay.

The only notable attraction is the ***taraibune* fishing boat pier** just west of the port. The tub-shaped vessels called taraibune were used by fisherwomen for gathering squid and seaweed; they hold about four adults and are now reserved mainly for tourists. You can either rent one yourself or be paddled around the bay by a woman in colorful traditional garb.

The area west of Ogi is rural, and there are delightful scenic walks along the coast and just inland. The only road leads to Shukunegi, 2.5 miles (4 km) farther on. Along the way two temples lie across the rice fields in wooded

Kodo drummers

Accompanying dancing and parades, traditional Japanese festival combos incorporate flutes with a gamut of percussion instruments including giant upright *taiko,* hand-drums and wooden clappers —all orchestrated with dexterous precision. Among them, Sado's *ondeko* drumming is paramount; founded in 1981, its Kodo troupe stands at the pinnacle of the art. Kodo drummers (www.kodo.or.jp) train long and hard, living according to a monastic regime near Ogi in the south. The Kodo organization created Sado's international Earth Celebration festival of music and dance (third week of August). ■

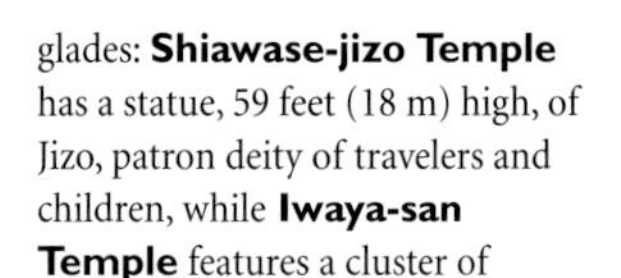

Sadokoku Folk Museum
- 270–2 Shukunegi, Ogi-machi
- 0259/86-2604
- 8:30 a.m.–5 p.m.
- $$

Sado Gold Mine
- 1305 Shimoaikawa
- 0259/74-2389
- 8 a.m.–5:30 p.m., April–Oct.; 8:30 a.m.–4:30 p.m. Nov.–Mar.
- $$

Aikawa Folk Museum
- 20 Sakashita-machi
- 0259/74-4312
- 8:30 a.m.–5 p.m.
- $

glades: **Shiawase-jizo Temple** has a statue, 59 feet (18 m) high, of Jizo, patron deity of travelers and children, while **Iwaya-san Temple** features a cluster of ancient statues in a cave.

On the way to Shukunegi, don't miss the extraordinary **Sadokoku Folk Museum (Sadokoku Ogi Minzoku Hakubutsukan).** Housed in a wooden former school complex, it is devoted to some 200 years of local history. The eclectic exhibits include farming and fishing implements, clothing, dolls, lamps, home altars, shop signs, kitchenware, clocks, radios, phonographs, and telephones. One shed contains a full-size reconstruction of a treasure ship used for carrying Sado's gold to the mainland.

Shukunegi village, a conservation area, is wedged snugly between the rocks on the bay. Separated by an arm's length along narrow alleys, the houses look much as they did a century ago; the official residences have been beautifully restored and are open as museums.

During the Edo period, when gold mining reached its peak, the northwestern coastal town of **Aikawa** had a population of 100,000—greater than modern Sado's. Declining since the mine's closure, Aikawa's population currently stands at 6,600. The town itself is rather congenial, though it offers little to detain a visitor beyond the **Aikawa Folk Museum (Aikawa Kyodo Hakubutsukan),** which displays relics from the gold-mining days and modern woodblock prints by noted local artists. There is a pleasant scenic walk among the leafy (if mainly funereal) temples up the steep slope east of town.

The major draw is the **Sado Gold Mine (Sado Kinzan),** a 10-minute bus ride (or 40-minute walk) east of town. Opened in 1601, it was exploited by the shogunate for more than 250 years and was then worked sporadically until the mid-1990s. Although skilled miners were voluntary recruits, those carrying water down the shafts were vagrants forcibly sent from the mainland. An unusual museum, the old Sodayu-Ko section of the mine retains the wooden pumping gadgetry in the narrow tunnels in which Edo-period miners toiled. The tunnels are now populated with animatronic wax figures representing miners at work, complete with sound effects. The museum's exhibition hall has an outstanding model of the town and its mining operations in feudal times. On a hilltop near Sado Kinzan is Doyu-no-wareto, the original open-pit mine that split the peak of the mountain in two. ■

An *oni-daiko* dancer on Sado-ga-shima

Sado dancing

Sado's folk culture, on display during local festivals and often performed for tourists, is very much alive. The most famous form is *Sado okesa, a* combination of melancholy ballads and graceful dancing by women. Festivals also feature *tsuburosashi*, a ribald old comic dance with phallic overtones, as well as the furious *ondeko* drumming that traditionally accompanies such dances and *oni-daiko*, a masked demon dance. The best place to appreciate Sado dancing is during a *matsuri* (festival), but the larger towns, including Ryotsu, Aikawa, Ogi, and Sawata, often stage performances nightly during the high season. Check with the local visitor information center for programs. ■

With more than a thousand years of history, Kyoto constitutes Japan's heartland for traditional culture. Nara is even older. And there is much more to discover, for this is Kansai—the region wherein resides the very spirit of Japan.

Kansai

Introduction & map **198–99**
Kyoto
Introduction & map **200–201**
Central Kyoto **202–208**
Eastern Kyoto **209–19**
Higashiyama walk **216–17**
Western Kyoto **222–25**
Outlying Kyoto **228–33**
Uji **234**
Mount Hiei-zan **235**
Biwa-ko & Hikone **236**
Nara & beyond **237–49**
Wakayama-ken **250–51**
Osaka **252–54**
Kobe **255**
Himeji **256–57**
Shima-hanto **258–60**
Hotels & restaurants in Kansai **371–75**

Statue at Fushimi Inari Taisha Shrine

At Ninnai-ji Temple, the oldest buildings date from the 17th century.

Kansai

KANSAI MEANS "WEST OF THE BARRIER." NEVER MIND THAT MID-20TH-century administrators changed the area name to "Kinki"; the Japanese still prefer to call the province by its feudal name of Kansai. It's easy to see why: Among the seven prefectures it covers are Kyoto and Nara—the very cradles of Japanese civilization. Founded more than 1,200 years ago, Kyoto is still the nation's prime temple town and its greatest repository of traditional culture. Among the temples in slightly older Nara are some of the oldest wooden buildings still standing on Earth. Small wonder, then, that Kansai boasts the most popular tourist destinations in Japan.

In Mie-ken on Kansai's eastern confines is Ise-jingu, the main shrine of Shinto for nearly 1,800 years. Founded in 552, Asuka was Yamato's first capital; Nara became the new capital in 710. The grandest old city was Kyoto. Founded in 794, it remained the imperial capital for over a millennium; its wealth of historical and cultural assets make it the single greatest tourist destination in Japan.

Hanshin, Kansai's heavily industrialized coastal area, embraces the cities of Kobe and Osaka. Kobe, capital of Hyogo-ken, still reflects the cosmopolitanism it acquired as a 19th-century treaty port. Osaka, rising to prominence during the Edo period as a mercantile and industrial hub, is now the nation's third largest city. Pleasantly situated on a hill overlooking the bay of Osaka-wan, Kobe has recovered from the devastating earthquake of 1995, but like Osaka it has little to offer visitors in search of historical sights. Just west of Kobe, however, is magnificent Himeji-jo Castle—the finest of all surviving Japanese castles.

The west of Kansai is the gateway to Shikoku and Seto-naikai Inland Sea via Awaji-shima Island and the giant Akashi-kaikyo Ohashi Bridge. The peaceful Buddhist sanctum of Koya-san, a mountain retreat offering the public firsthand experience of temple life, lies to the south in hilly, remote Wakayama-ken, famous for its rugged coast. In Shiga-ken, in Kansai's northeastern area, is Biwa-ko,

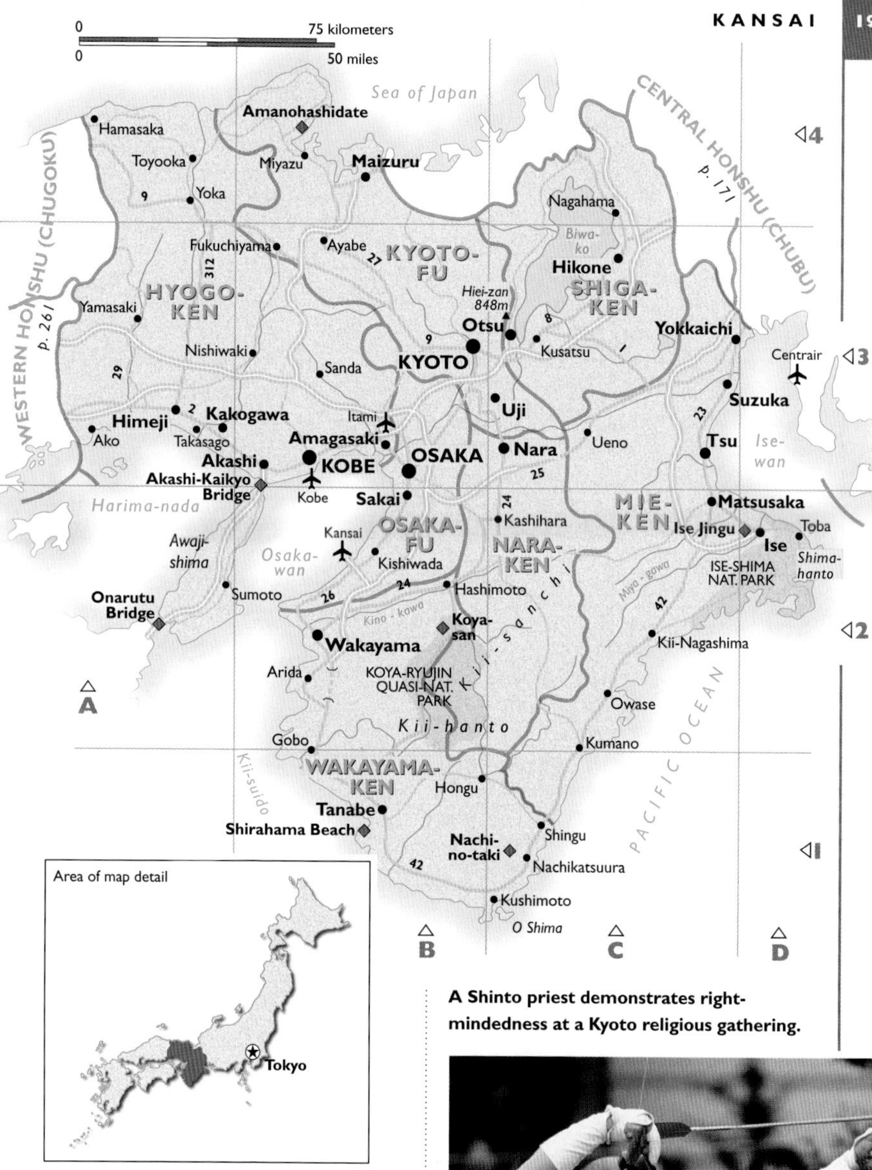

Japan's largest lake—probably best appreciated from Hikone, where there is a fine castle.

There is much to see in Kansai. Although Tokyo is less than three hours from Kyoto by train, overseas visitors often choose to confine their stay in Japan to this, Japan's historical heart. Following the opening of Kansai International Airport in 1994, the number of direct overseas flights is growing sufficiently to make this option worth considering. ■

A Shinto priest demonstrates right-mindedness at a Kyoto religious gathering.

Kyoto

Kyoto has everything visitors could wish for, with more than 1,800 temples, hundreds of shrines, historical buildings and neighborhoods, famous gardens, and beauty spots among wooded hills. As Japan's seventh largest city, however, Kyoto has not escaped some redevelopment, especially to the south. The Kyoto Station building, completed in 1997 with a colossal central concourse and shopping mall is architecturally impressive, but you emerge from it into a modern city as nondescript as any. You need not go very far, however, to find traditional beauty.

There is more in Kyoto than anyone could see in months, let alone a few days. This makes it vital to plan your sightseeing schedule. It is easy to go overboard visiting temples. Like most Asian art and architecture, Japanese examples tend toward a certain uniformity; what constitutes the best lies in age, subtleties, details, and settings. Random sightseeing can induce you to dismiss the temples on a "seen one, seen 'em all" basis long before you reach the best. Begin by visiting the city information office (see p. 202), even if only to pick up a map to the Kyoto bus and subway system. The helpful staff speaks English.

The center of Kyoto is a modern city with main shops and amusements. It includes a few sights, notably Nishi Hongan-ji Temple and Nijo-jo Castle. Crossing over the Kamo-gawa River to the east, you discover traditional Kyoto. Eastward from the old geisha district of Gion you can stroll uphill through venerable streets to Kiyomizu-dera Temple, walking along the canal on the Path of Philosophy up to Ginkaku-ji (the Silver Pavilion). To the north lie such sights as Kinkaku-ji (the Golden Pavilion) and nearby Ryoan-ji, with its world-famous Zen rock garden. Westward and north of the Katsura-gawa River is hilly Arashiyama, where many more temples nestle in sylvan settings of bamboo, cherries, and maple trees.

Kyoto is also renowned for the quality of its handicrafts and its cuisine. ■

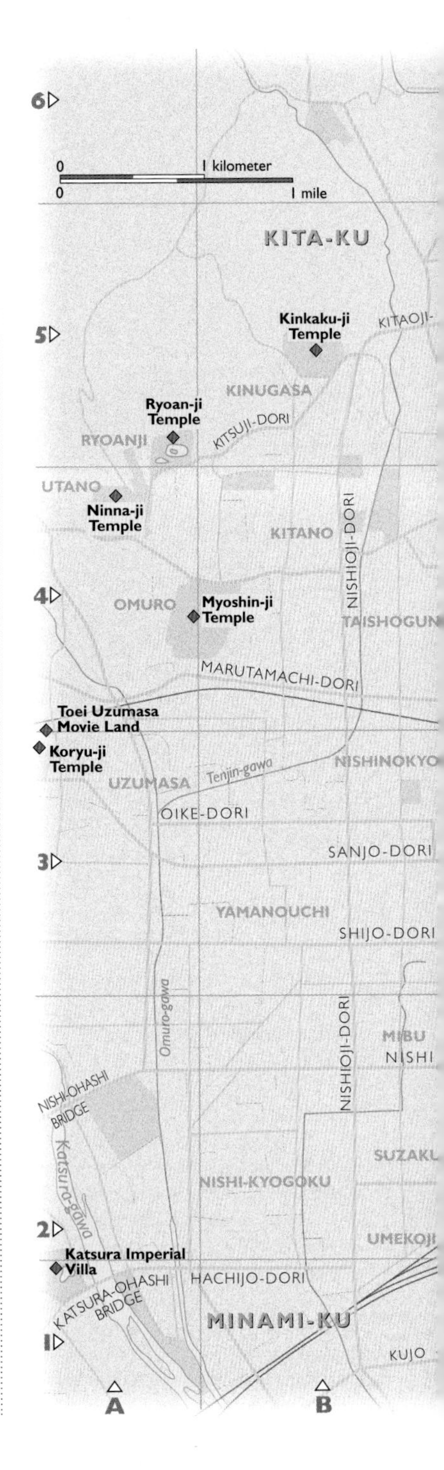

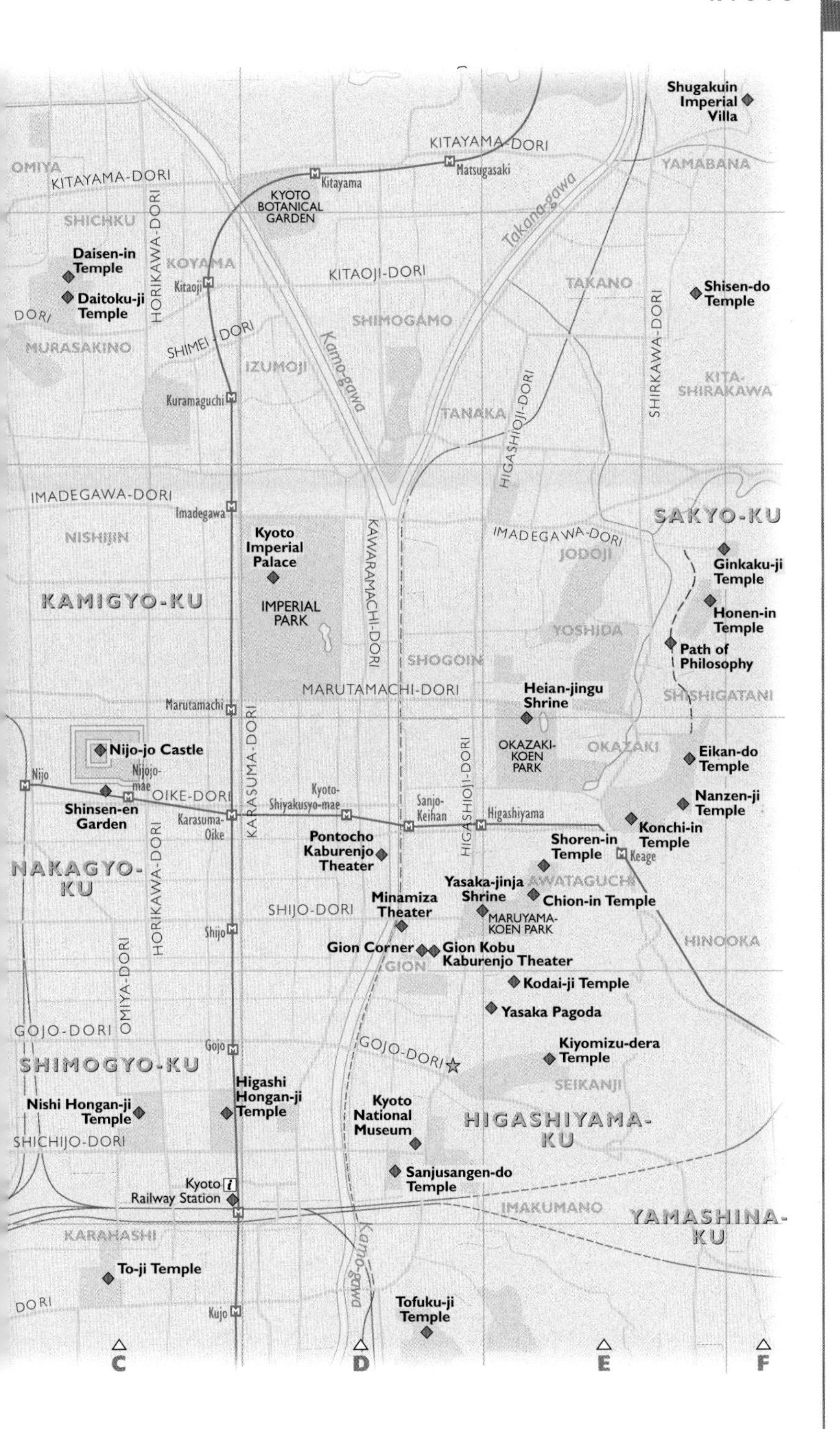
Shugakuin Imperial Villa
KITAYAMA-DORI
Matsugasaki
YAMABANA
OMIYA
KITAYAMA-DORI
Kitayama
KYOTO BOTANICAL GARDEN
Takano-gawa
SHICHKU
HORIKAWA-DORI
Daisen-in Temple
KOYAMA
KITAOJI-DORI
TAKANO
Shisen-do Temple
Kitaoji
Daitoku-ji Temple
DORI
SHIMOGAMO
SHIMEI-DORI
Kamo-gawa
MURASAKINO
IZUMOJI
HIGASHIOJI-DORI
KITA-SHIRAKAWA
SHIRKAWA-DORI
Kuramaguchi
TANAKA
IMADEGAWA-DORI
Imadegawa
SAKYO-KU
NISHIJIN
Kyoto Imperial Palace
KAWARAMACHI-DORI
IMADEGAWA-DORI
JODOJI
Ginkaku-ji Temple
KAMIGYO-KU
IMPERIAL PARK
Honen-in Temple
YOSHIDA
Path of Philosophy
SHOGOIN
MARUTAMACHI-DORI
Heian-jingu Shrine
SHISHIGATANI
Marutamachi
Nijo-jo Castle
KARASUMA-DORI
HIGASHIOJI-DORI
OKAZAKI-KOEN PARK
OKAZAKI
Eikan-do Temple
Nijo
Nijojo-mae
OIKE-DORI
Kyoto-Shiyakusyo-mae
Sanjo-Keihan
Nanzen-ji Temple
Shinsen-en Garden
Karasuma-Oike
Higashiyama
Konchi-in Temple
Pontocho Kaburenjo Theater
Shoren-in Temple
Keage
NAKAGYO-KU
HORIKAWA-DORI
Yasaka-jinja Shrine
AWATAGUCHI
Minamiza Theater
Chion-in Temple
SHIJO-DORI
MARUYAMA-KOEN PARK
Shijo
OMIYA-DORI
Gion Corner
Gion Kobu Kaburenjo Theater
HINOOKA
GION
Kodai-ji Temple
Yasaka Pagoda
GOJO-DORI
Kiyomizu-dera Temple
Gojo
GOJO-DORI
SHIMOGYO-KU
SEIKANJI
Higashi Hongan-ji Temple
Kyoto National Museum
Nishi Hongan-ji Temple
HIGASHIYAMA-KU
SHICHIJO-DORI
Sanjusangen-do Temple
Kyoto
Railway Station
IMAKUMANO
YAMASHINA-KU
KARAHASHI
To-ji Temple
Kamo-gawa
DORI
Tofuku-ji Temple
Kujo
C
D
E
F

To-ji Temple pagoda at twilight: Spared during World War II, Kyoto remains Japan's greatest repository of culture.

Central Kyoto

START YOUR VISIT TO KYOTO BY EXPLORING THE CENTER of the city. You will probably arrive at Kyoto Station at the end of a three-hour train ride from Tokyo. Do not be alarmed by the modern buildings and busy streets; Kyoto has treasures aplenty for visitors. North of the station you will find two temples. The city center has a palace, a castle, and gardens as well as busy shopping arcades.

Kyoto visitor information
www.pref.kyoto.jp/visitkyoto/en/
- ✉ 9th fl. Kyoto Station (elevator in Isetan Department Store)
- 🕒 10 a.m.–6 p.m.; closed 2nd & 4th Tues.
- ☎ 075/344-3300

Built by the shogun Toyotomi Hideyoshi in 1591, **Nishi Hongan-ji Temple,** headquarters of the Jodo Shinshu sect of Buddhism, is one of Japan's most important temples. The current buildings, erected in the 17th century, are among the finest examples of Japanese Buddhist architecture.

Behind the imposing main gate, the **Founder's Hall (Goeido)** was rebuilt in 1636 and contains a wooden sculpture of the sect's founder, Shinran, which he is said to have carved himself in the 1250s. Moved from Hideyoshi's Fushimi Castle in 1632 along with the great **Chinese gate (karamon)** in front of it, the ornate **Daisho-in Hall,** a National Treasure, is graced inside with screen doors exquisitely painted by masters of the Kano

An ornate gateway at Nijo-jo Castle

school (see p. 51). Of the two **Noh stages** north and south of the structure, the former was also brought from Fushimi Castle and is treasured as one of the oldest and finest in Japan. The three-story **Hiunkaku** pavilion, once Hideyoshi's private mansion, was moved here in 1615. Panels of birds and flowers by the Kano school decorate the interior; the shogun even had his bathroom adorned with work by the great Kano artist Eitoku (see p. 51).

Formerly plain Hongan-ji, the temple became known as Nishi (West) Hongan-ji when **Higashi Hongan-ji Temple,** its eastern counterpart, went up nearby. A renegade abbot left the Jodo Shinshu sect to found a rival school, and Higashi Hongan-ji was built in 1602 to house it. Burned in a fire and reconstructed in 1895, the temple rivals its predecessor in sheer size; the colossal main hall is the largest wooden structure in Kyoto.

From Kyoto Station, Nishi Hongan-ji is a ten-minute walk northwest; Higashi Hongan-ji is

Nishi Hongan-ji Temple

- Map: 201 C2
- Monzen-cho, Shimogyo-ku
- 075/371-5181
- City Bus: 9 to Nishi Honganji-mae
- $ Grounds of Nishi Hongan-ji freely accessible; entrance to buildings (and Japanese-language tours) subject to permission, which must be applied for at least 7 working days prior to your visit. Apply through a visitor information center or JNTO office overseas, or write to the above address with details of your proposed visit and party size using SAV and international postage coupons.

Jodo Shinshu sect

Founded by the priest Shinran (1173–1262) in 1224, the Jodo Shinshu (Pure Land New Faith) sect of Buddhism rejects the need for vegetarianism, asceticism, and celibacy for the priesthood. Instead, it teaches that enlightenment may be achieved simply through repeatedly chanting a sutra exalting the Amida Buddha: *"Namu Amida Butsu."* Seen as a political threat, the sect was persecuted. But so great was its following that Toyotomi Hideyoshi realized that his campaign to unify Japan would fail without it; he built Nishi Hongan-ji in Kyoto in 1591. Jodo Shinshu now counts 12 million followers worldwide. ■

Ornate gate at Nijo-jo Castle, with detail at right

Nijo-jo Castle
- 201 C3
- Nijojo-cho, Nijo-dori, Horikawa Nishi-iru, Nakagyo-ku
- 075/841-0096
- 8:45 a.m.–5 p.m.
- $$ (including garden)
- Subway: Nijojo-mae City Bus: 9, 12, 50, 101 stop at Nijojo-mae

five minutes north of the station.

After founding Kyoto's ancestral capital in 794, the emperor Kammu had **To-ji Temple** constructed two years later. Repeatedly burned down and rebuilt over the centuries, the temple buildings were destroyed during 15th-century civil wars. The **Main Hall (Kondo,** 1606) is a National Treasure, as are some of the eighth- and ninth-century works of religious art in the **Lecture Hall (Kodo,** 1491), which contains 21 renowned statues of Buddhas and deities. To-ji possesses a substantial garden elegantly decked out with ponds, at the southern end of which is the **pagoda** built by shogun Tokugawa Iemitsu in 1644; standing 180 feet (55 m), it is the tallest in Japan. To-ji's other attraction lies in the popular antique and flea markets held on the grounds monthly; a larger one is held on the first Sunday of every month and a smaller on the 21st. The temple is a 15-minute walk southwest of Kyoto Station.

Built in 1603, **Nijo-jo Castle** was not so much a fortress as a palatial residence for the shogun Tokugawa Ieyasu (1542–1616) during his visits to Kyoto. A fire destroyed the keep and many buildings in the 18th century; following the Meiji Restoration, the remainder—proud symbols of former samurai power—became the home of the Kyoto prefectural government in the 1870s. Modernizing zeal dictated contempt for feudal remnants; the willful damage wrought on Nijo-jo by erstwhile bureaucrats still causes culturally sensitive souls to shudder. Happily, what is left is more than impressive.

The castle passed to the imperial family in 1893, when the **Main Palace (Honmaru)** was moved here from the Imperial Palace precinct as a home for Prince Katsura. The Honmaru is open to the public only on special days.

Reached through the ornate carved **Chinese gate** (karamon), the **Second Palace (Nino-**

maru) is really the first; its five buildings are all 17th-century originals. The first and largest, the **Tozamurai,** complete with "nightingale" flooring (specially constructed so that the boards squeaked underfoot—Ieyasu took no chances with unexpected visitors), has fine carvings, coffered ceilings, and screens painted by the Kano school, notably by the master Tanyu (1602–1674). Tanyu's paintings also grace three rooms in the **second building (Shikidai).**

Exquisite paintings and carvings adorn the **third building (Ohiroma),** which was the shogun's audience chamber. Smaller but lavishly decorated, the **fourth building (Kuroshoin)** is highly regarded for its Kano-school pictures of birds. The style of the shogun's private residence, the **fifth building (Shiroshoin),** is often considered all the more beautiful for its comparative restraint. Particularly charming is a snowscape mural depicting sparrows sleeping in a bamboo grove.

South of the Ninomaru and outside the walls is the **Shinsen-en Garden,** designed by the great landscape architect Kobori Enshu (1579–1647). It was originally treeless (falling leaves were felt to emphasize the transitory nature of life), but the later inclusion of trees did not endow it with much cheer; the garden's rather gloomy atmosphere is often attributed to the fact that it is now all that remains of the precinct of the great imperial palace from Heian times. Built by the emperor Kammu in 794, the original **Kyoto Imperial Palace (Kyoto Gosho)** stood northwest of its present site for more than a thousand years before being consumed by fire in 1788. Completed in 1790, the last palace burned down in 1854. The current, smaller one was built the following year on a new site.

Still used for the imperial enthronement ceremony, the Gosho is notable for the stark simplicity of its grand-scale architecture. Containing majestic but simple silk hangings and fine painted screens, the interiors somehow lack atmosphere. This is not to say the Gosho is devoid of interest; its sheer grandeur conveys a sense of its great ceremonial importance.

The grounds embrace the elegantly landscaped **pond garden (Oike-niwa)** and lie on one of Kyoto's most beautiful public parks, particularly popular when the cherry trees blossom in April.

(continued on page 208)

Imperial Palace

- 201 D4
- Kyoto Gyoen-nai, Kamigyo-ku
- 075/211-1215
- English-language tours (50 min.) at 10 a.m. & 2 p.m. Mon.–Fri. Tour at 10 a.m. every Sat. in April, May, Oct., Nov. and every 3rd Sat. during other months; check first for availability—the Imperial Palace is often used for official functions.
- Subway: Imadegawa

Imperial Household Agency

- Kunaicho Kyoto Jimushu, 3 Kyoto Gyoen, Kamigyo-ku,
- 075/211-1215

Permission to visit

There are restrictions on visiting the Imperial Palace and Katsura Villas (see p. 231). Non-Japanese visitors are generally permitted to visit the same day if they apply before 9:40 a.m. at the Imperial Household Agency in Kyoto (north of the palace precinct). You can obtain permission by using the forms provided at the visitor information office in either Kyoto or Tokyo or in JNTO offices overseas. Your application should include a stamped addressed envelope if made in Japan, or a postage coupon if from abroad. In all cases, you must bring your passport. Permission must similarly be obtained from the Imperial Household Agency for the Katsura Villas; you can apply for them all at the same time, but note that admission is restricted to people over 20 years old. ■

Geisha

Most Japanese have seen true geisha only on television or in festival parades; the *onsen* geisha in spa resorts may well be only hookers in fancy dress. Genuine geisha entertain the political and industrial elite in exclusive traditional *ryotei* restaurants, *cha-ya* (teahouses), and *machi-ai* (assignation houses)—all antiquarian establishments boasting inner gardens graced with flickering stone lanterns. Numbering about 100,000 before World War II, the geisha declined with the rise of the bar hostess after the war; they now number around 1,500.

The geisha have their origins in the pleasure quarters—the Floating World—of 300 years ago. More than mere bordellos, the great Green Houses of the 17th-century pleasure quarters offered banquets enhanced by courtesans adept at singing and dancing. Itinerant entertainers and musicians often accompanied them, the most skilled being dubbed *otoko geisha* (male arts people). By the 1700s the best female entertainers became known as *geiko* (arts girls), a name still used in some regions. To call them by any other name in Kyoto would ruffle their fine plumage but, elsewhere, the generic "geisha" stuck.

The geisha, her face whitened and her mouth reduced to little petals of brilliant red, became a living work of art, an icon of womanhood. Spirited, garrulous, talented, and sexy, she had all the dazzle that Confucian strictures forbade in a virtuous wife. Geisha are also table entertainers, sought for their wit and powers of conversation. Even in advanced years, some geisha continue to be revered as exponents of traditional performing arts.

At first, many geisha doubled as prostitutes. Infuriated by the rivalry, the courtesans successfully petitioned the government to pass a law forbidding geisha to sleep with customers in the pleasure quarters. As a result, the profession went upscale.

Today's geisha earns a lot of money. She has to, for her wardrobe includes a collection colored according to each season. She shuns wearing the same kimono in front of the same customers twice. The goal of most geisha is to find a *danna*—a wealthy patron to support her as a mistress. Some have been brides for prime ministers—Katsura during the Meiji era and Yoshida in the 1950s. A scandalous affair with a geisha in 1989 felled Prime Minister Uno after just two months in office.

In the old days, girls trained as geisha from childhood; nowadays they start in their late teens. Hundreds of girls still aspire to become geisha, but only three out of ten weather the harsh training as *maiko* (apprentices) at the *okiya* (geisha house), where they are strictly schooled in singing, dancing, playing the *samisen* (Japanese three-string lute), and deportment.

You might see geisha in Kyoto's Gion (see p. 218), where the *maiko*—gaudy little dolls with whitened faces—bustle along, pigeon-toed on high sandals, while the geisha glide past in their silken finery with regal nonchalance. Appearances are deceptive, however. In Tokyo, where they are rarely glimpsed, there are less than a thousand geisha. In Kyoto, despite their higher profile, there are slightly more than 300 left.

Geisha are not as old-fashioned as they seem. Their conversational skills are utterly contemporary, and many attend corporate functions in modern dress. If geisha disappear altogether, it will not be because they are out of tune with the times, but a matter of simple economics. Catering to a dwindling elite, they have priced themselves out of the market. ■

Once generalized, the elaborate makeup and unnatural whiteness characterizing the traditional geisha are now confined mainly to appearances on stage and in festival parades. Some brides have adopted the look for mainstream weddings.

Pontocho Kaburenjo Theater
- 201 D3
- Pontocho, Sanjo-sagaru, Nakagyo-ku
- 075/221-2025
- Maiko dances May 1–24
- Subway: Sanjo
- $$$$

(continued from page 205)

Kawaramachi, Kyoto's prime shopping district, extends eastward along Shijo-dori to the Kamo-gawa River. Here are major department stores such as Hankyu and Takashimaya, as well as fashion stores and boutiques. If you're interested in traditional handicrafts, Kawaramachi is full of specialists in local products, such as ceramics, kimono and textiles, dolls, fans, and paper umbrellas.

Traditional goods and crafts are plentiful, too, in two shopping arcades: Shinkyogoku-dori and the more upscale Teramachi-dori, off the left-hand side of Shijo-dori as you walk east. The two alleys intersect with Nishikoji-dori, a lively and colorful covered arcade that serves as Kyoto's main food and vegetable market.

To the left of Shijo-dori and flanking the western bank of Kamo-gawa, **Pontocho** is one of the two great centers for traditional, geisha-oriented Kyoto nightlife; the other is Gion (see p. 218). A long alley of low wooden buildings festooned with red paper lanterns and housing hundreds of bars and restaurants, Pontocho makes for some enchanting nighttime strolls. Many restaurants have riverside verandas, where wealthy patriarchs are entertained by fluttering bevies of geisha in summer. Like geisha entertainment, however, these restaurants tend to be accessible only with an introduction and are astronomically expensive.

More affordable dining options lie closer to the Kawaramachi end of the alley. Bars, too, in this area tend to be exclusive and expensive; whatever the establishment, as a rule of thumb venture only into those displaying prices, menus, or food exhibits in the window. More contemporary and cheaper restaurants and entertainment (the latter becoming raunchier the farther south you walk across Shijo-dori) abound around Kiyamachi-dori, which runs parallel to Pontocho along a canal. Like its equivalent in Gion, **Pontocho Kaburenjo Theater** at the northern end of Pontocho stages dances by *maiko*—apprentice geisha—twice annually as it has since the 1870s. ■

Women in traditional dress shop at a souvenir store near Kiyomizu-dera Temple.

Eastern Kyoto

The attractive garden at the Heian-jingu Shrine

WHEN YOU CROSS OVER THE KAMO-GAWA RIVER, YOU discover a city that comes closest to everyone's ideal of an older Japan. The one caveat here applies to all of Japan's famous sites: Unless you visit early in the morning or on weekdays out of season, you will have to contend with formidable crowds. Bordering lush Mount Higashiyama, the area possesses some of Kyoto's greatest sights.

As was once the case in all Japanese cities, the realms of religion and the senses exist cheek by jowl in eastern Kyoto: The world of temples extends east toward Higashiyama, which sits next to Gion, the oldest extant geisha district in Japan.

Eastern Kyoto begs exploration on foot. Between Ginkaku-ji Temple to the north and Nanzen-ji Temple to the south is the 0.75-mile (1 km) **Path of Philosophy (Tetsugaku-no-michi),** a pleasant stroll alongside a canal, past old wooden houses with gardens and several temples. From **Maruyama-koen Park** southward toward Kiyomizu and westward toward Gion, you discover steep cobbled lanes lined with traditional buildings; they may house a glut of souvenir shops that are architecturally the genuine article. Traditional buildings in such profusion are unique in modern Japan.

Walk north from Higashiyama subway station for about half a mile (1 km) to the **Heian-jingu Shrine** in Okazaki-koen Park. Built in 1895 to commemorate the 1,100th anniversary of the founding of the city, the shrine is a two-thirds-scale reproduction of the Heian-period (794–1185) imperial palace. As the colossal red *torii* gateway (made of steel) towering over the approach portends, the shrine is nothing if not bombastic. Incorporating two pagodas and a complex of ornate buildings in regulation Shinto scarlet with intricate Chinese-style roofs in blue-green

Heian-jingu Shrine
www.heianjingu.or.jp
- Map: 201 E4
- Address: 97 Nishi Tenno-cho, Okazaki, Sakyo-ku
- Phone: 075/761-0221
- Hours: 6 a.m.–5:30 p.m. March–Aug., closes at 5 p.m. Sept.–Feb.
- Price: $$
- Bus: City Bus: 5, 4, or 6 to Kyoto Kaikan Bijutsukan

Heian-jingu Shrine faithfully reproduces 10th-century Japanese architectural taste—down to the vivid colors.

Nanzen-ji Temple

- 201 E3
- Fukuchi-cho, Sakyo-ku
- 075/771-0365
- 8:30 a.m.–5 p.m. March–Nov., closes at 4:30 p.m. Dec.–Feb.
- $$
- Subway: Keage City Bus: Hoshojicho or Eikandomichi

tiles, the Heian shrine is certainly colorful—too new and over the top for those with antiquarian leanings. Ironically, bright colors were very much part of the picture in Heian times, though the gaudy paint has vanished from the few authentic remnants over the centuries.

With a profusion of weeping cherry trees, maples, azaleas, and lily ponds, the garden behind the shrine is attractive most of the year. Heian-jingu stages Takigi Noh theater performances at intervals and is also host to (and starting point of) one of Kyoto's great festivals, the Jidai Matsuri. Held on October 22, it features parades by celebrants attired in the lavish costumes of Heian times.

Built originally as a villa for Emperor Kameyama in 1264 and dedicated as a temple in 1293, **Nanzen-ji Temple** is one of the most important temples in Kyoto as well as the headquarters of the Rinzai sect of Zen. It is about half a mile (1 km) southeast of Heian-jingu. Standing in a spacious grove of pines that stretch back into forested hills, the subsidiary temples, some with lovely gardens, are so numerous that Nanzen-ji amounts almost to a temple city. The most notable current buildings (the original structures were destroyed) were erected in the early 17th century.

The imposing **sanmon gate,** a massive structure of dark wood in front of the entrance, was built in 1628; the climb up a steep flight of stairs inside is rewarded with a fine view over the city from the upper

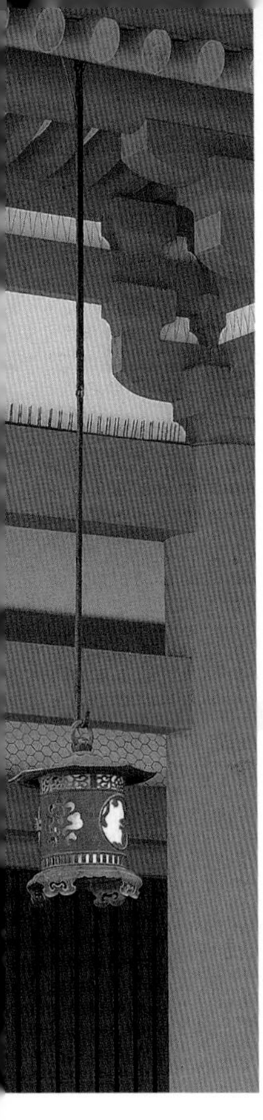

floor. Moved from the former Kyoto Imperial Palace, the **Hojo Hall** beyond the gate contains screen doors decorated with masterpieces by the Kano school, most notably a celebrated composition by Kano Tanyu (1602–1674) of tigers drinking in a bamboo grove. Attached to the Hojo is a fine Zen garden landscaped with shaped trees, rocks, and raked sand; you can contemplate it while sipping *macha,* the brew consumed during tea ceremonies.

About 220 yards (200 m) south of the main precinct and reached by passing under an old brick aqueduct is **Nanzen-in,** a subtemple of Nanzen-ji and once Emperor Kameyama's private villa. A beautiful garden features pines, mosses, and a pond full of variegated carp. Carrying water from Lake Biwa-ko, the raised aqueduct just south of Nanzen-in is an unusual structure in Japan, incorporating Roman-style redbrick arches. Follow the aqueduct uphill to a pine forest. The path passes under some red torii gates before reaching a lovely clearing with a small Shinto shrine honoring a sacred waterfall, beneath which hardy pilgrims undergo ritual cleansing—considered especially efficacious in winter. From here hiking trails lead up into the eastern hills.

Tenju-an, a subtemple constructed in 1337 near the sanmon gate, has another fine garden, but the star attraction among the gardens is at **Konchi-in,** just outside the temple compound. Using rocks, raked sand, and dwarf trees to depict a scene of mountains and islands in the sea, the garden was laid out in 1627 by Kobori Enshu and is regarded as a masterpiece.

The roads leading away from the approach to Nanzen-ji have several good restaurants (often in lovely garden settings) that specialize in *yudofu* (boiled tofu) cuisine, among them some with nationwide reputations (see p. 373).

Founded in 856, the Buddhist **Eikan-do Temple,** also called Zenrin-ji, was dedicated in the 11th century to the priest Eikan, greatly revered for his benevolence. Most of the current structures were built after the wars of the 15th century. The temple lies 440 yards (400 m) north of Nanzen-ji, on the southern end of the Path of Philosophy to the right.

To the south of the precinct, the main **Amida-do Hall** is reached via a staircase on the right. It contains the Mikaeri-no-Amida, an unusual statue showing the Amida Buddha glancing over his shoulder. Connected by cloisters and giving

The garden of Tenju-an, a subtemple of Nanzen-ji

Eikan-do Temple
www.eikando.or.jp
- Map: 201 E3
- Address: 48 Eikando-cho, Sakyo-ku
- Phone: 075/761-0007
- Hours: 9 a.m.–5 p.m.
- Admission: $$
- Transport: Subway: Keage City Bus: Eikando-mae

Honen-in
- Map: 201 E4
- Address: Goshonodan-cho, Shishigatani, Sakyo-ku
- Phone: 075/771-2420
- Hours: Main hall only open spring & autumn
- Admission: $ in spring; $$ in autumn. Free entrance to grounds
- Transport: City Bus: Jodoji

Ginkaku-ji Temple
www.shokoku-ji.or.jp
- Map: 201 E4
- Address: 2 Ginkakuji-cho, Sakyo-ku
- Phone: 075/771-5725
- Hours: 8:30 a.m.–5 p.m. Mar.–Nov., 9 a.m.–4:30 p.m. Dec.–Feb.
- Admission: $$
- Transport: City Bus: 5 from Kyoto or Sanjo Stations, or 203 from Shijo or Demachiyanagi to Ginkakuji-michi bus stop (5 min. walk)

onto gardens noted for their maple trees, the other buildings display fine painted screens. South of the compound, the stone staircase on the right leads to the Taho-to Pagoda, with views over the city.

Walking north on the Path of Philosophy, you come to **Honen-in Temple.** Built in 1680 to honor the priest Honen, founder of the Jodo sect, this unassuming thatched temple appears rustic and peaceful. The narrow approach, passing through an imposing grove of trees, is flanked by areas of gravel subtly raked and shaped to complement the wooded setting. There is also a landscaped garden.

About 550 yards (500 m) north of Honen-in is the **Ginkaku-ji Temple** (Silver Pavilion). A sybarite and aesthete, the shogun Ashikaga Yoshimasa built Ginkaku-ji in 1482 as a luxurious country retreat. He intended to cover it with silver leaf to create something similar to the Golden Pavilion built by his grandfather Yoshimitsu (see p. 32), but money ran out, and Ginkaku-ji was never given its silver coating. It was turned into a temple after Yoshimasa's death.

A magnificent structure nonetheless, this is one of Kyoto's greatest sights. The surrounding garden, with its tall pines, raked sand, and pond of gorgeous carp,

was designed by the great landscape architect Soami with Yoshimasa's autumn moon-viewing parties in mind. The little tea room in the Togudo Hall (1482), the oldest in Japan, is believed to be the prototype for all others. The adjacent

Honen-in Temple seen through its forest shroud

From the foothills of Higashi-yama, visitors to Kiyomizu-dera Temple can take in the view across Kyoto.

rooms are reproductions of the ones used for incense parties.

A tree-lined path winding up the hill affords a splendid view of the grounds and the city. Early and out-of-season visits are particularly recommended for Ginkaku-ji, which can attract the biggest crowds in all Kyoto.

Located in the wooded foothills of Higashiyama is the temple of **Kiyomizu-dera,** a ten-minute walk from Gojozaka bus stop.

The temple, established in 798, is dedicated to the 11-faced Buddhist deity Kannon. The current buildings were erected by the shogun Tokugawa Iemitsu in 1633. The **main hall,** a National Treasure, is perched ingeniously atop a cliff on a massive framework incorporating 139 colossal wooden pillars. From the veranda jutting out over a steep valley, there is a famous view (see above) over the roofs of Kyoto and Yasaka pagoda. The **Otowa Waterfall (Otowa-no-Taki),** known for its purifying properties, drops down from below adjacent buildings on a second cliff; the faithful gather here to cleanse themselves, sometimes by immersion under the fall. (The not-so-faithful line up to pass their hands beneath the cataract.) As Kyoto's most celebrated site, Kiyomizu is also the most crowded. Visiting in the early morning or on weekdays during off-peak periods (autumn and winter, excluding New Year's) is highly recommended; in winter, the temple setting is particularly lovely—and empty—in the late afternoon. Despite its

Kiyomizu-dera Temple

- Map: 201 E2
- Address: 1–294 Kiyomizu, Higashiyama-ku
- Phone: 075/551-1234
- Hours: 6 a.m.–6 p.m.
- $
- City Bus: 206 to Kiyomizu-michi or Gojozaka

overwhelming array of souvenir stores, the charm of the approach to the temple (Kiyomizu-zaka), a steep cobbled lane lined with old wooden buildings, is irresistible.

Kodai-ji Temple lies 660 yards (600 m) northwest of Kiyomizu-dera. Built in 1605 in memory of the shogun Toyotomi Hideyoshi by his widow, it boasts five ornate original buildings in a superb state of preservation. The **Main Gate (Omotemon)** was brought from Hideyoshi's Fushimi Castle, as were the two teahouses standing in the garden in the compound, designed by 17th-century landscape architect Kobori Enshu. The elaborate **Founder's Hall (Kaisando)** is noted for its ceilings and panels, painted by masters of the Kano and Tosa schools. The **Otama-ya,** Hideyoshi's mortuary chapel, is beautifully enhanced with raised lacquerwork inlaid with gold.

Left: Visitors at Kiyomizu-dera Temple catch water from the sacred fall for luck, longevity, and simply because it is the thing to do.

Kodo—the way of incense

Incense, which supposedly displeases evil spirits, permeates the air wherever Buddhism prevails—the temple, home altar, or cemetery. Incense came to Japan with Buddhism via China and Korea in the sixth century. During the Heian era (794–1185), its religious and funereal connotations were complemented by its pleasures as a perfume. Presented to emperors and clerics, chunks of priceless incense wood feature among exhibits in temple treasure halls. Collecting varieties far too precious for the common nose, Heian aristocrats entertained themselves with *kokai* (incense parties). The object was to guess the provenance of an incense as it burned—a refined game played according to strict etiquette. The shogun Ashikaga Yoshimasa collected and named 130 different varieties of incense during the 13th century. Although the practice largely died out with the shoguns, there are still devotees of Kodo—the way of incense—today. ■

Kodai-ji Temple

- 201 E2
- 526 Shimokawara-cho, Kodaijishita, Higashiyama-ku
- 075/561-9966
- 9 a.m.–5 p.m.
- $$
- City Bus: 206 to Higashiyama-Yasui

Statues of the Boddhisatva Kannon at Sanjusangen-do

Sanjusangen-do Temple *(657 Mawari-cho, Sanjusangendo, Higashiyama-ku, tel 075/525-0033, 8 a.m.–4:30 p.m.)* was founded in 1132 and rebuilt in 1266 following a fire. Named for the number of spaces between the pillars of the hall (sanju-san means 33), it is renowned for sheltering more than a thousand statues of the Buddhist deity Kannon. These flank the most famous of all, a thousand-armed Kannon carved in 1254 by master sculptor Tankei. At the hall's far end stand 28 statues of guardian deities; along with the centerpiece by Tankei, these are designated National Treasures.

Sanjusangen-do is 220 yards (200 m) southwest of the Higashiyama-shichijo bus stop. Opposite it is the **Kyoto National Museum (Kyoto Kokuritsu Hakubutsukan),** which occupies two buildings. Kyoto's finest museum was built by the Imperial Household Agency in 1879 as a repository for the emperor's own collection of artworks and historical relics, and was later passed on to the city. There are about 2,000 exhibits in 17 rooms divided into sections: historical, fine arts, and handicrafts.

The fine arts section contains more than 230 items designated Important Cultural Properties or National Treasures. The exhibits from the permanent collection are changed regularly and displayed in one building, and special exhibitions are staged throughout the year in the original hall. ■

Kyoto National Museum

www.kyohaku.go.jp

- 201 D2
- 527 Chaya-machi, Higashiyama-ku
- 075/541-1151
- 9:30 a.m.–5 p.m.; closed Mon.
- $$, more for special exhibits
- Subway: Keihan Shichijo
  City Bus: 206, 208 to Hakabutsukan-Sanjusangendo-mae

Higashiyama walk

This walk takes in several of Kyoto's best-known sights; allow extra time if you plan to visit any of the places on the way. It will probably take a full day to follow the route and stop off for sightseeing and refreshments. If you are in a hurry, be sure not to miss Kiyomizu-dera and Chion-in Temples.

From Gojozaka bus stop, walk up Gojo-zaka slope, veering right for 550 yards (500 m) up to **Kiyomizu-dera Temple ❶,** Kyoto's most famous landmark (see p. 213). The temple buildings were erected in 1633; perched on pillars on top of a cliff, the main hall is designated a National Treasure. Having admired the view from up here, particularly beautiful in the cherry blossom season, wander down the narrow lane called **Kiyomizu-zaka.** The number of craft and souvenir stores here is overwhelming; 19th-century Western visitors did not dub the street "Tea-pot Alley" for nothing. At the bottom turn to your right down Sannen-zaka and on to Ninnen-zaka slope.

To your left is the five-story, 128-foot-high (39 m) **Yasaka-jinja Pagoda ❷,** built by the shogun Yoshinori Ashikaga in 1440. Follow the street on your right (passing Ryozen Kannon Temple, notable for a colossal statue of the Buddhist deity, Kannon, 80 feet/24 m high) to **Kodai-ji Temple ❸** (see p. 214), which dates from 1606. The grounds include an elegant garden, and the screens inside the buildings are decorated with fine paintings. Proceed north 650 yards (600 m), then cross through **Maruyama-koen Park,** a Kyoto favorite containing several landscaped gardens. At the northern end visit magnificent **Chion-in Temple ❹** (see p. 218), with its fine 17th-century buildings on a colossal scale.

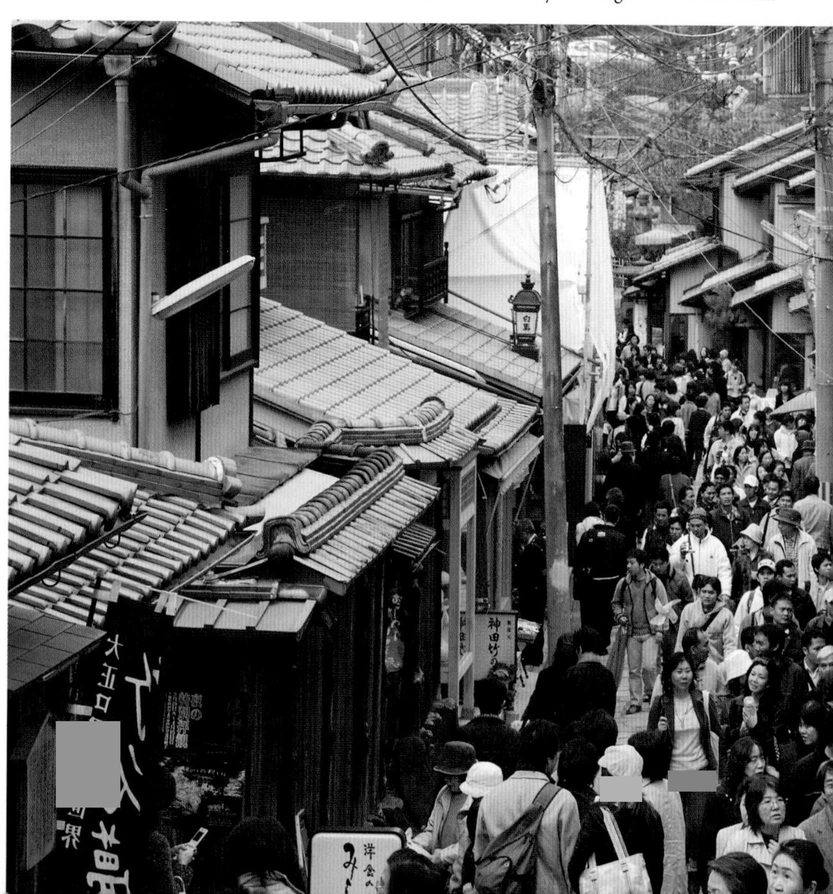

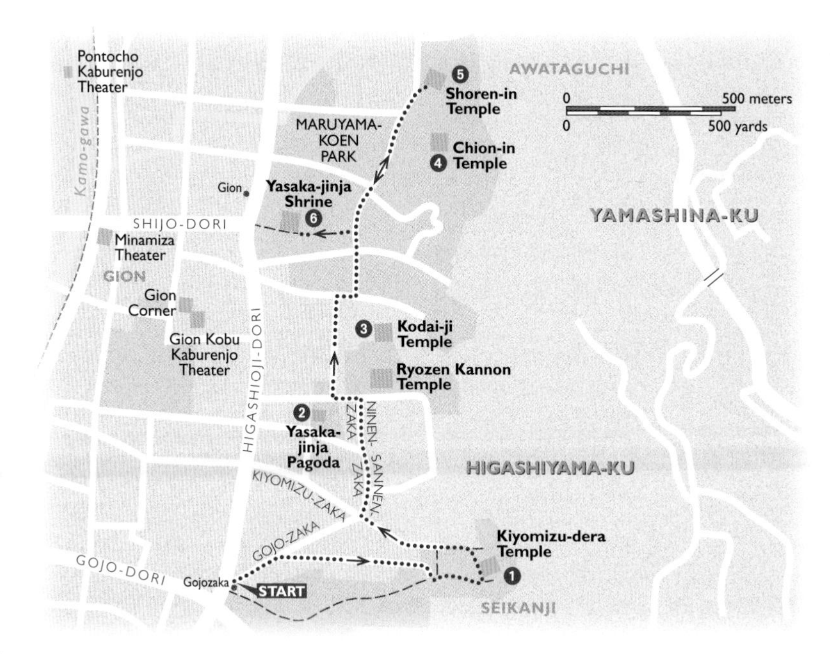

From here walk 220 yards (200 m) north to **Shoren-in Temple** ❺ (see p. 219), noted for its excellent 17th-century paintings inside and for its landscape garden, one of Kyoto's most famous. Retrace your steps as you leave, and walk 550 yards (500 m) down to **Yasaka-jinja Shrine** ❻, the shrine favored by the residents of Gion and known locally as Gion-san. From here you can go on to explore Gion (see p. 218) itself, or call it a day at the Gion bus stop, which is opposite the *torii* gateway in front of the main entrance to Yasaka. ■

Active Sannenzaka Street in Kyoto

- See area map page 200–201
- ➤ Gojozaka bus stop
- ⟺ 1 mile (1.5 km)
- 3–4 hours
- ➤ Gion bus stop

NOT TO BE MISSED

- Kiyomizu-dera Temple
- Kodai-ji Temple
- Maruyama-koen Park
- Chion-in Temple
- Shoren-in Temple

Chion-in Temple
- 201 E3
- 400 Rinka-cho, Higashiyama-ku
- 075/531-2111
- 9 a.m.–4 p.m. Nov.–Mar.; closes at 3:40 p.m. Dec.–Feb.
- $
- City Bus: 12, 46, 203, or 206 to Chionin-mae

GION

Crossing the bridge eastward over the Kamo-gawa River toward Higashiyama will find you in Gion, Kyoto's old entertainment and geisha district. Although the onslaught of concrete and neon, discos, cabarets, pachinko parlors, and traffic has changed its face irrevocably, particularly during the past 20 years, old *cha-ya* (teahouses), *machi-ai* (assignation houses), and venerable *ryokan* (inns) and restaurants still exist here and there, concentrated mainly along Hanami-koji.

Hanami means "flower watching," the blossoms in question being the geisha, the central characters in the realm popularly known as *kairyukai*—the "world of flowers and willows." With its ancient wooden facades and flickering lanterns, Gion—to an even greater degree than Pontocho (see p. 208)—is one of the last places to glimpse *maiko* apprentices and full-fledged geisha on their way to assignments in the evening. Since entry into the kairyukai depends upon both substantial wealth and introduction, the streets of Gion are about as close as most people come to encountering geisha. You'll get a general idea of geisha dancing skills at **Gion Corner,** a small theater offering an eclectic, touristy digest of Japanalia from *bunraku* puppet drama excerpts to the tea ceremony. A more authentic alternative is in the adjoining **Gion Kobu Kaburenjo Theater,** where maiko have traditionally presented glittering Miayko Odori (cherry dance) spectaculars each April for almost 150 years. Standing to the left of Shijo Bridge and on the western edge of Gion, the **Minamiza Theater** is Japan's oldest Kabuki theater; check the city information office for schedules. In particular, the performances staged during December feature some of the country's most famous Kabuki actors.

To the east of Gion is **Yasaka-jinja Shrine,** the main shrine of the Gion Matsuri held in July—Kyoto's greatest Shinto festival. Beyond it lies **Maruyama-koen Park,** a popular public park with a number of landscaped gardens and ponds, as well as food stalls and restaurants.

At the northeastern end of Maruyama-koen is **Chion-in Temple,** one of the largest temples in the country. It is the headquarters of the Jodo school. Founded by the priest Honen in the 1170s, it remains one of Japan's most important Buddhist sects. The original structures, erected in 1234, were lost through fires and war; the current buildings, dating from the 1630s, are rarely rivaled for size and opulence.

The temple compound comprises Japan's largest temple gate, the giant two-story **sanmon** in front

Girls don traditional summer finery during the Gion Matsuri—one of Japan's greatest festivals, held each July.

of the main entrance, standing 79 feet (24 m) tall, and its largest **temple bell.** Devoid of clappers, Japanese temple bells are rung by pushing a suspended beam that strikes the outside. Cast in 1633 and weighing 81.5 tons (74 tonnes), Chion-in's bell traditionally requires 17 monks to handle the beam during Honen's annual memorial service (April 17) and to ring in the New Year. The **Main Hall (Hondo)** accommodates a resplendent golden altar; a statue of Honen, reputedly self-carved, is enshrined in an impressive annex behind the hall. Connected to the main hall via a corridor with a "nightingale" floor—the boards squeak when walked upon—the **Abbot's Residence (Daihojo)** contains fine screen paintings by major exponents of the Kano school. The garden outside was designed by the master 17th-century landscape architect Kobori Enshu. Southeast of the Hondo the **Scripture House (Kyozo),** built in 1616, is noted for a collection of sutras written in China during the Sung dynasty. On a hill to the northeast of the Hondo is Honen's tomb and the ornate **Chinese gate (karamon)** built in 1633. The temple complex is near the Shionin-mae bus stop,or a ten-minute walk southeast of the Higashiyama-sanjo subway station.

Five minutes' walk north of Chion-in is **Shoren-in.** Until the Meiji Restoration of 1868, the abbot here was customarily the high priest of the Tendai sect, a post held by imperial princes. Set in a grove of large camphor trees, the current buildings date from 1895, but the main hall contains superb sliding screens painted by, among others, Kano Motonobu (1476–1559) and Tosa Mitsunobu (1480–1522). The temple compound possesses one of the finest gardens in Kyoto; it was designed by the great landscape architect Soami (d. 1525) and completed by Kobori Enshu in the 17th century. ■

Each December, some of Japan's most revered Kabuki actors appear at Kyoto's Minamiza Theater.

Gion Corner

www.kyoto-gion-corner.info

Gion Hanamikoji-dori

075/561-1119

Performances daily Mar. 1–Nov. 30 at 7 p.m. & 8 p.m.

$$$$

Shoren-in

201 E3

69–1 Sanjobo-cho, Awataguchi, Higashiyama-ku

075/561-2345

9 a.m.–5 p.m.

Subway: Higashiyama City Bus: Jingumichi

Japanese gardens

Gardening, according to a recent government poll, is the seventh most popular leisure activity in Japan; there are 36 million keen gardeners in this densely populated country with little space. Lack of a backyard is no deterrent: The sills and facades of small suburban homes are festooned with pots, while bonsai cultivators tend dwarf trees high on the balconies of urban apartment buildings.

The average garden is small; neither crammed with variegated blooms nor geometrically arranged in lawns and beds, its function is contemplative. Rather than transforming nature, it strives to imitate it and shuns symmetry. The garden path uses stones of irregular shape instead of aligned bricks or flagstones; paths may consist of stepping stones, even over dry land. Fine rocks are considered as important as plants and command high prices. The most important criteria are color and shape. Rocks may be chosen to suggest, for instance, mountains, boats, or animals, especially turtles.

Early gardens

Gardening came to Japan in the sixth century with Chinese culture and Buddhism. Long lost in China, a few early prototypes survive in Japan, where the Japanese used them to develop gardening concepts of their own. Gardens are described in the tenth-century *Tale of Genji* and had become common by then among the clergy and aristocracy—the biggest being stroll gardens laid out around large ponds. A garden abandoned during the 12th century was recently unearthed during archaeological excavations at Motsu-ji Temple in Hiraizumi, Tohoku, and has now been restored; it included an artificial lake, man-made rock formations, and an artificial watercourse. Typically landscaped to represent the Buddhist universe, the ponds and rocks were arranged to evoke oceans and islands.

The garden in Kyoto's Daikaku-ji Temple retains the 215,000-square-foot (20,000 sq m) pond called Osawa-no-Ike, originally designed by the ninth-century emperor Saga. It also once had a dry waterfall, perhaps pioneering the common use of smaller stones that, often striated, are placed in rows to subtly mimic the flow of bodies of water.

Gardening manuals appeared during the 13th century but became more common in the 15th, when gardening trends diversified and spread through the influences of Zen Buddhism and the tea ceremony. Zen introduced a minimalist approach to temple gardens, sometimes landscaping them with expanses of raked sand and rocks alone (as in Ryoan-ji Temple in Kyoto). Exalting naturalism, tea masters favored lush, wooded glades floored with moss and stepping stones to harmonize with the teahouse, as well as the sight and sound of flowing water.

Gardening for all

During the Edo period (1603–1868) commoners took up gardening; most current concepts emerged from practices and manuals proliferating at the time. There are three main styles: *tsukiyama* (artificial mountain or landscape garden), *karesansui* (dry landscape in which watercourses are suggested by using stones), and *chaniwa* (a garden surrounding a teahouse). Gardens may combine them, but strict conventions dictate the positioning of the different kinds of appropriate stone lanterns *(toro)*, bamboo fences, and bridges of wood or stone. Sometimes incorporating all three styles in miniature, *tsuboniwa*—gardens in domestic courtyards—can be exquisite gems showcasing gardening as a master craft. Gardens require careful planning: How will the shadows of the rocks fall? How striking will the elements look from different angles? Consider the climate: With their rocks shining

Left: A dry stone garden with raked gravel and rocks suggesting islands and the sea
Above: Pines are covered in fall to protect them from winter snow at Kenroku-en Garden in Kanazawa.
Below: The grounds of Saiho-ji are revered as Kyoto's most beautiful landscape garden.

against the intense greens of damp moss and foliage, some gardens look best in the rain.

Although the Japanese appreciate thousands of varieties of flower, some are reserved for ikebana arrangements, while others—potted plants such as chrysanthemums and morning glories—are used exclusively for seasonal displays. The traditional garden excludes all but a few indigenous species: iris, lotus, and flowering shrubs such as camellia, azalea, hydrandgea, and tree peony—an early arrival from China in the sixth century. Large gardens are often wooded, with trees such as cherry and plum, and even tiny ones display pines, maples, and bamboo. Trees and shrubs may be cut, trimmed, twisted, and dwarfed into any traditionally accepted shape—but forget about roses and lawns. ■

Western Kyoto

THOUGH WESTERN KYOTO IS MAINLY RESIDENTIAL, WITH fewer sights than in the east, some are worth a visit. There are not always convenient subway stations for the sights, but the visitor information center can supply details of bus routes.

Lying in 27 acres (11 hectares) of grounds, **Daitoku-ji Temple** is 440 yards (400 m) northwest of Daitokuji-mae bus stop, or the same distance northeast of Funaoka-koen-mae bus stop. Daitoku-ji is important to the Rinzai sect of Zen. It was founded in 1324, but the original buildings were destroyed during the Onin War (1467–1477). They were replaced in 1479, with further additions during the 16th and 17th centuries in accordance with the practice of moving buildings from one location to another.

Presented to the temple by the empress Meisho, the **Imperial Messengers' Gate (Chokushi-mon)** was moved here from the Imperial Palace in 1640; the **Chinese gate (karamon),** featuring carvings by the great sculptor Hidari Jingoro, came from the shogun Toyotomi Hideyoshi's Fushimi castle. The building of the **sanmon gate** was undertaken by the great tea master Sen-no-Rikyu (see p. 225) in 1589; the inclusion of a statue of himself atop it is often seen as the act of *lèse-majesté* that prompted Hideyoshi to condemn him to death. The interior of the gate has a ceiling and panels painted by Hasegawa Tohaku (1539–1610). The paintings on the sliding screens in the **Abbot's Residence (Hojo)** are by Kano Tan'yu (1602–1674), grandson of the founder of the Kano school. The garden outside the Hojo is by the celebrated landscape architect Kobori Enshu. The Juko-in holding Sen-no-Rikyu's tomb lies to the west of the garden. Once the hermitage of the abbot Ikkyu Soun, the **Shinju-an** contains fine screens painted in the 15th century.

Daitoku-ji's main complex is surrounded by 23 subtemples,

Daitoku-ji Temple
- 201 C5
- Daitokuji-cho, Murasakino, Kita-ku
- 075/491-0019
- 9 a.m.–4:30 p.m.
- City Bus: 205 & 206 to Daitokuji-mae

Kinkaku-ji Temple
www.shokoku-ji.or.jp
- 200 B5
- 1 Kinkakuji-cho, Kita-ku
- 075/461-0013
- 9 a.m.–5 p.m.
- $
- City Bus: Kinkakujimae or Kinkakujimichi

Painted screen doors by Kano school master Motonobu at Daisen-in subtemple

among them **Daisen-in** (northwest of the main hall), featuring screen doors painted by the master Kano Motonobu (1476–1559). The garden is considered a masterpiece of the landscape architect Soami. Comprising a teahouse, the garden at **Koto-in** (on the southwestern edge of the complex) is particularly popular when the maples turn red in autumn. Other subtemples with fine gardens are **Hoshun-in** (north of the compound) and **Ryugen-in,** a National Treasure south of the main compound that has five. To the west of the precinct, the **Koho-an** contains seven tea rooms designed by Kobori Enshu, who also designed the garden.

About 1.5 mile (2 km) west of Daitoku-ji, along Kitaoji-dori, is **Kinkaku-ji Temple** (Golden Pavilion). Few sights are more beautiful than Kinkaku-ji mirrored in the pond in front of it, especially when the surrounding trees don their autumn colors. As one of the most famous locations in Japan, it receives crowds by the busload on holiday weekends.

The shogun Ashikaga Yoshimitsu (1358–1408) acquired a nobleman's house and transformed it magnificently into the crowning glory, his retirement villa, the Golden Pavilion (1397). According to his wishes, the villa was converted into a temple after his death. The Golden Pavilion survived the Onin War, but was burned down in an arson attack by a deranged monk in 1950, an incident fictionalized by Yukio Mishima in his famous novel *Kinkakuji.* Erected in 1955, the current structure is said to be an exact copy, although detractors (not without reason) claim that the gold-leaf coating is brighter and more extensive than it was in the original, especially since further restoration during the 1990s.

Ryoan-ji Temple (Peaceful Dragon Temple), 0.5 mile (1 km) southwest of the Golden Pavilion, is an important temple of the Rinzai sect of Zen. Founded in 1473, it is world famous for the stone garden popularly attributed to Soami. The garden, a walled rectangle about the size of a tennis court, is viewed

Though sadly only a copy, the Golden Pavilion at Kinkaku-ji Temple is revered as one of Japan's most famous landmarks.

Ryoan-ji Temple
www.ryoanji.jp
- 201 A5
- 13 Goryonoshita-cho, Ryoanji, Ukyo-ku
- 075/463-2216
- 8 a.m.–5 p.m. Mar.–Nov.; 8:30 a.m.–4:30 p.m. Dec.–Feb.
- $$
- City Bus: 59 from Sanjo-Keihan-mae to Ryoanji-mae

The font at the back of Ryoan-ji Temple provides water for tea ceremonies.

from the veranda of the temple building. It consists of 15 rocks of various sizes standing in a sea of raked white gravel. Minimalism was never as refined as in Japan 500 years ago; thought to represent islands standing in an ocean, the work portends the dawn of modern conceptual art and was devised to induce contemplation. Your meditations can be seriously jeopardized by the volume of both loudspeakers and visiting hordes; this is a temple best approached on weekday mornings during the off-season. The rock garden's fame often eclipses the beauty of the building itself, not to mention the spacious surrounding garden with a lovely pond and leafy arbors resplendent in autumn. In the precinct there is also a fine restaurant (itself like an old teahouse in a beautiful garden of its own) specializing in tofu cuisine.

Ninna-ji Temple is ten minutes' walk southwest from Ryoan-ji. Buses stop just outside. Two years after Ninna-ji was founded by his predecessor, the emperor Uda completed it in 888. Initially a residence for retired emperors and known as the Omuro Palace, it now serves as the headquarters of the Omuro chapter of the Shingon sect of Buddhism, as well as of the internationally renowned Omuro

School of Flower Arrangement.

Along with the imposing main gate, the oldest buildings go back to the early 17th century. Among them are two halls, the **Miei-do** and the magnificent main **Kondo,** both brought from the old Kyoto Imperial Palace. The Kondo and the statue of the Buddha Amida Nyorai it contains are National Treasures. North of the precinct is a fine **pagoda** 108 feet (33 m) high, erected by the shogun Tokugawa Iemitsu in 1637. A UNESCO World Cultural Heritage site, Ninna-ji is unusual for possessing a **palace (Goten)** in the precinct (to the west), with a lovely garden. Several of the buildings are exquisitely decorated inside. Lost in a fire in 1887, some were replaced during the 1900s, notably the **Shinden, Kuroshoin,** and **Shiroshoin,** connected by open-sided wooden cloisters framing gardens of rocks, pines, gravel, and meandering watercourses. Open twice a year *(Apr.–May; Oct.–Nov.),* the **Reiho-kan Treasure House** has a wonderful collection of sculptures, paintings, and ceramics. Toward the center of the elegantly landscaped precinct is a celebrated grove of dwarf cherries—a species unique to the region. Splendid in blossom, they attract large crowds in spring.

Myoshin-ji Temple is 15 minutes' walk southeast of Ninna-ji, or you can catch a bus from Ninna-ji's southern gate. Founded in 1337, this Rinzai Zen temple precinct contains many original buildings. Of the 40 subtemples, only four are open to the public. Among the subordinate temples, **Reiun-in** contains so many screens painted by Kano Motonobu that it is sometimes called the Motonobu temple. **Tenkyu-in** has paintings by Sanraku (1559–1635), a pupil of Eitoku, and **Kaifuku-in** showcases screen doors decorated with Tanyu's caricatures. **Taizo-in** has a renowned 15th-century Zen garden.

If you're tired of temples, visit the **Sumiya Motenashi Art Museum** northwest of Kyoto Station to learn what Kyoto's floating world was like. The city's only remaining *ageya,* an elegant banquet hall where geisha (see p. 206) would entertain notables, the rare 17th-century building has some 20 rooms and has been owned by the same family for 13 generations. ■

Ninna-ji Temple
- Map: 200 A4
- 33 Ouchi, Omura, Ukyo-ku
- 075/461-1155
- 9 a.m.–4:30 p.m.
- $$
- City Bus: 10 & 26 to Omura-Ninnaji Train: Keifuku Railway, Omura Station

Myoshin-ji Temple
www.myoshin.com
- Map: 200 A4
- 1 Miyoshinji-cho, Hanazono, Ukyo-ku
- 075/461-5226
- 9:10 a.m.–3:40 p.m.; closed for lunch
- $$
- City Bus & Kyoto Bus: Myoshinji-mae Train: Keifuku Railway, Myoshinji Station

Sumiya Motenashi Art Museum
- 32 Nishishinyas-hikiageya-cho, Shimogyo-ku
- 075/351-0024
- 10 a.m.–4 p.m.; closed Mon. & July 19–Sep. 14, Dec. 16–Mar. 14; tours available in Japanese
- $$
- 7 min. walk from Tambaguchi Station

Sen-no-Rikyu (1522–1591)

The tea ceremony was developed during the 16th century as an arcane art form by tea masters, notably Sen-no-Rikyu. Spurning ostentatiousness to seek refinement in simplicity, Rikyu became the highest arbiter of Japanese aesthetics.

Courted as such by the shogun Toyotomi Hideyoshi, whose tastes were nothing if not ostentatious, Rikyu walked on thin ice. Inevitably he fell from the jealous shogun's favor, and in 1591 Hideyoshi forced Rikyu to commit *seppuku* (suicide). The reasons remain unknown. Some conjecture that he was accused of plotting to poison Hideyoshi during a tea ceremony; others have it that Rikyu had slighted the ruler by placing a statue of himself on top of the sanmon gate at Daitoku-ji Temple—it was unthinkable for a shogun to pass beneath the effigy of a vassal. A more plausible explanation is that Hideyoshi had taken a fancy to Rikyu's daughter; when the tyrant demanded her for his harem, the tea master refused. ■

Buddhism

Of the 300 million Buddhists worldwide today, about a third are Japanese. That the function of Buddhism in modern Japan is mainly funereal may seem grim, but death is only the gateway to rebirth; the midsummer Buddhist O-bon festival of the dead involves much merrymaking. At other times many thousands of Japanese join in prayers, ceremonies, and retreats from the stress of day-to-day living in peaceful Buddhist temples.

Buddhism has been vital in shaping Japan. As in Europe at the end of the Dark Ages, monks held the keys to knowledge. Initially Korean and Chinese, they imparted numeracy and literacy, built temples, roads, and cities, and were responsible for laying the foundations of culture, the arts, government, and law.

The philosophy

Buddhism is based upon the discourses of the philosopher Siddhartha Gautama (circa 563–483 B.C.), also known as Sakyamuni, born in what is now southern Nepal. Posthumously known as the Buddha (Enlightened One), his verbal teachings were written down later by his disciples. According to Buddhism, all life is suffering. The cause resides in attachment, desire, and ignorance; the remedy lies in abstinence, righteousness, learning, and meditation—steps along the path to the goal of enlightenment. Then there is karma, the concept whereby your conduct in this life determines the quality of your reincarnation in the next. After death, those who have attained enlightenment break the karmic cycle of suffering and rebirth by entering nirvana, a blissful state of higher consciousness.

There are two main Buddhist doctrines: the original Theravada, practiced today mainly in Sri Lanka and Southeast Asia, and the later Mahayana, or the Great Vehicle, which, after spreading to Tibet and China, was adopted in Mongolia, Korea, and Japan. Mahayana Buddhism teaches that exceptionally enlightened saints become bodhisattvas (*bosatsu* in Japanese)—deified incarnations of aspects of the Buddha-nature. The next step up is Buddhahood, or *Nyorai* in Japanese.

Buddhism in Japan

Mahayana Buddhism, brought by Korean emissaries in either 538 or 552, was decreed the state religion in Japan by Prince Shotoku in 593. The religion progressed substantially during the mid-eighth century under Emperor Shomu, who established temples and monasteries throughout his realm. At first Buddhism appealed only to the ruling class, until the monk Saicho (767–822) founded the Tendai sect. By incorporating Shinto deities into its doctrine, it gained such a popular following that it became the state religion. The monk Kukai (774–835) studied Buddhism in China at about the same time as Saicho and returned to Japan to found the Shingon sect, which advocated esoteric (that is, with complex underlying philosophy) Buddhism. Shingon's influence had overtaken that of Tendai by the end of the Heian era. Today it counts some 12 million followers.

The Jodo and Jodo Shinshu schools, created by Honen (1133–1212) and his disciple

Shinran (1173–1262) respectively, worship the Amida (Pure Land) Buddha and believe that salvation resides in repeatedly chanting *"Namu Amida Butsu"* ("Glory to Amida Buddha"). Both sects have a membership of millions; the Shinshu branch has the largest following of all Japanese sects. The priest Nichiren (1222–1282) based the sect he founded (Nichiren-shu) upon chanting *"Namu-myoho-renge-kyo,"* believed to be the quintessence of the Lotus Sutra. Although his aggressive zeal earned him the displeasure of the shogun and a four-year exile to Sado-ga-shima (see p. 193), his Nichiren-shu school has a colossal following today. Its many sub-sects include the modern Soka Gakkai. With millions of devotees worldwide, it exerts considerable influence on Japanese politics through Komeito—the "clean government party."

Zen (*Ch'an* in Chinese, from the Sanskrit *dhyana*, or meditation), founded in China by the Indian monk Boddhidarma in the sixth century, was introduced in Japan by the Japanese monks Eisai (1141–1215) and Dogen (1200–1253), respectively the founders of the Rinzai and Soto sects, which both have a wide following. Devoid of doctrine or scriptures, Zen is imparted verbally from master to disciple and holds that enlightenment is attainable only through meditation *(zazen)*. Focusing on austere self-discipline, frugality, and hard work, Zen also bestowed spiritual concepts upon the martial arts, making it especially appealing to the samurai. Through samurai adherence and patronage, Zen reached its apogee from the 15th through 17th centuries. It brought innovations to calligraphy, poetry, and painting, introduced the tea ceremony, and virtually reinvented flower arrangement as an art in itself. Zen's influence is still much in evidence in Japan today. ■

First introduced 14 centuries ago, Buddhism has played a decisive role in defining the culture, aesthetics, and general outlook of Japan.

***Torii* gates at Fushimi Inari Shrine**

Outlying Kyoto

ALTHOUGH EASTERN KYOTO PRESERVES MORE OF THE worldly aspects of the former city, the peaceful west is felt to reflect Kyoto's aesthetic and spiritual heart. Even the emperors and aristocrats in ancient times liked to get away from the urban bustle, and when they did, their favorite escape lay in Arashiyama (Storm Mountain). Today this hilly western edge of the city is both a popular area for strolling and a choice site for luxurious suburban homes.

Koryu-ji Temple

- 200 A3
- 32 Hachigaoka-cho, Uzumasa, Ukyo-ku
- 075/861-1461
- 9 a.m.–5 p.m. Mar.–Nov.; closes at 4:30 p.m. Dec.–Feb.
- $$
- City Bus: 11 to Uzumasa-Koryuji-mae
  Kyoto Bus: 72, 73, or 74 to Uzumasa-Koryuji-mae

Before you reach Arashiyama itself, stop at Uzumasa Station on the Keifuku Arashiyama line. Across the road is **Koryu-ji Temple** (also called Uzumasa-dera). Founded to commemorate Prince Shotoku's death in 622 and belonging to the Shingon sect, this is one of Japan's oldest temples. Though none of the seminal structures remain, the **lecture hall,** built in 1165 and housing a noted statue of the Buddha Nyorai (an incarnation of the Buddha), is Kyoto's second oldest building. Erected in 1720, the **Taishi-den** behind contains a statue of Prince Shotoku, believed to have been carved by the prince himself; another statue of him is in the **Keigu-in** (or Hakkakudo—Eight-Sided Hall) to the northwest of the precinct—built in 1251 and designated a National Treasure. Behind the Taishi-den is the **treasure hall** (Reiho-kan) containing more priceless examples of early Buddhist art, among them the celebrated **Miroku-Bosatsu,** attributed to Shotoku. Carved during the Asuka period, this serene and magnificent statue of the Buddhist Messiah, due to appear 5,000 years after Buddha's attainment of nirvana, is not only the oldest in Kyoto but officially listed as No. 1 among all the National Treasures in Japan.

Just ten minutes' walk northeast of Koryu-ji is **Toei Uzumasa**

Movie Village (Toei Uzumasa Eigamura), the samurai answer to a tour around Hollywood's Universal Studios. If you need a break from temples, this could be fun, especially if you are traveling with children.

As well as a theme park, this is the Toei movie company's main studio for shooting period dramas. To avoid getting in the way of film crews, tours are guided during shoots. Permanent sets include reconstructions of Edo's Yoshiwara pleasure quarter, old shops, inns, houses, samurai mansions, and a jail. With extras wandering the sets in period garb, the theme park aspect was enhanced with new attractions in 1997; you can even don period costume for pictures or videos to take home.

From Kyoto, the usual way to get to Arashiyama is by train to Saga Station on the JR San-in Honsen line, or you can take the Keifuku Arashiyama line to Arashiyama Station from Shijo-Omiya Station in central Kyoto. A scenic alternative is to take a train 13.5 miles (22 km) west from Kyoto to Kameoka, then return to Arashiyama by river through breathtaking gorges.

Arashiyama abounds in places renowned for springtime cherry blossoms and autumn displays of maple trees, especially northward to the renowned beauty spots Takao, Makino-o, and Togano-o. Although the region's popularity and its proximity to Osaka (only 20 minutes away) draw big crowds in peak periods, it is large enough to offer the weary traveler havens of solitude and quiet. A pleasant way to explore the area is to hire a bicycle from the center *(jitensha sentaa)* just northeast of Togetsukyo Bridge near Arashiyama station, but some paths are too steep and rocky to be navigated on wheels.

When you arrive at Arashiyama Station, walk 550 yards (500 m) northwest and you come to **Tenryu-ji Temple** (Heavenly Dragon Temple). The temple, belonging to the Rinzai Zen sect, was built in 1339 by the first Ashikaga shogun, Takauji, to commemorate the emperor Godaigo. Exiled by Takauji, Godaigo subsequently died. Hearing that his vengeful spirit had appeared to an important priest in the guise of a dragon, Takauji hastily built Tenryu-ji to appease it. All that remains of the original compound

Prince Shotoku Taishi (574–622)

When Empress Suiko acceded to the throne in 593 in Asuka, Japan's first capital, power was assumed by Shotoku, the prince regent. One of Japanese history's most remarkable figures, Shotoku spurred great cultural and architectural advances through the constant ties he fostered with China. Based on Chinese concepts, the Seventeen Articles he devised amounted to Japan's earliest constitution. Government was centralized for the first time, and all people became imperial subjects—making their incomes taxable by local rulers only with the emperor's approval. A great scholar and devout Buddhist, Shotoku sponsored the building of temples in the Asuka area, including Horyu-ji near Nara. Posthumously deified, Shotoku has since been shrouded in legends about an immaculate birth and a life abounding with miracles. In a more secular vein, the saint's portrait once adorned the 10,000-yen note. ■

Toei Uzumasa Movie Village

200 A4

10 Higashi-hachigaoka-cho, Uzumasa, Ukyo-ku

075/864-7716

9 a.m.–5 p.m. Mar.–Nov.; 9:30 a.m.–4 p.m. Dec.–Feb.; closed Dec. 21–Jan. 1

$$$$ adult, $$$ child

Train: JR Sagano line to Hanazono or Uzumasa Stations. Bus: 71, 72, 73 from Kyoto station to Uzumasa-Koryuji; 61, 62, 63 from Sanjo-Keihan to Hachigaokacho-Toei Uzumasa Eigamura

Tenryu-ji Temple

68 Susukinobaba-cho, Tenryuji, Saga, Ukyo-ku

075/881-1235

8:30 a.m.–5:30 p.m. Apr.–Oct.; closes at 5 p.m. Nov.–Mar.

$$

Train: Keifuku Railway to Arashiyama Station

Daikaku-ji Temple
www.daikakuji.or.jp
4 Osawa-cho, Saga, Ukyo-ku
075/871-0071
9 a.m.–4:30 p.m.
$$
City Bus: 28, 92 to Daikaku-ji
Kyoto Bus: 61 (from Sanjo-Keihan-mae) or 71 (from Kyoto Station)

Saiho-ji Temple
231 A2
56 Kamigatani-cho, Matsuo, Nishikyo-ku,
075/391-3631
Apply for tours at least six weeks prior to visit. Send name, address, nationality, and occupation, and enclose international postal coupon. From Japan, apply at least one week prior to visit.
$$$$$ (tour only, reservation required)
City Bus: 63 & 73 to Kokedera
Kyoto Bus: 29 to Kokedera-michi

is its splendid garden, designed by Muso Kokushi in 1340.

More Buddhist temples cluster on the west side of Arashiyama above Tenryu-ji, where the sylvan scenery is particularly pretty. From the north exit of Tenryu-ji, proceed along a narrow lane through a bamboo forest—it's considered Arashiyama's most beautiful. This takes you to **Okochi Sanso Villa.** Once the property of samurai movie star Okochi Denjiro, the villa itself is not the main attraction, but the views over Kyoto and Arashiyama from its lovely grounds and gardens are especially noteworthy.

Past a fishing pond due north from here is **Jojakko-ji Temple** at the top of a flight of weathered stone steps, with a fine view over the thatched gates. North of the precinct, a paved path slopes up through groves of maple and cherry trees to **Nison-in.** With buildings erected in 1521, the temple is most attractive when the trees are at their seasonal best. Temples farther northwest include **Gio-ji** and **Takiguchi-dera,** notable mainly for their setting in a thick bamboo grove, and forlorn **Adashino Nembutsu-ji,** erected in the 1870s. On the grounds of the latter temple are thousands of statuettes of the Buddha, commemorating the unknown dead who for centuries were flung into paupers' graves on this spot.

Between Gio-ji and Nison-in a road leads eastward (past Seiryo-ji) to **Daikaku-ji Temple,** built in the ninth century as a palace by Emperor Saga and later converted into a temple. The complex includes magnificent structures from the 16th century. The buildings and the cloisters connecting them display outstanding paintings by major exponents of the Kano school, including Motonobu, Eikoku, Sankaku, and Tanyu, as well as by Ogata Korin of the 18th-century Rimpa school. East of the precinct and designed by Emperor Saga as a boating pond, **Osawa-no-ike Pond** is surrounded by a beautiful tree-lined path, particularly popular when the cherry trees blossom and the maples turn red.

On the southern foothills of Arashiyama is **Saiho-ji Temple,** of the Rinzai sect of Zen, boasting one of Kyoto's oldest, loveliest, and greenest landscape gardens. Designed by the priest Muso Kokushi (1275–1331), the garden features islets of moss set in a pond surrounded by more moss—small

wonder that the temple is better known as Koke-dera (Moss Temple). Unfortunately the volume of visitors proved such a strain on the small precinct that monks were forced into drastic measures to curtail them. Permission to visit must be obtained in advance. Whether as a further deterrent or not, visitors are first treated to a compulsory hour-long lecture about the temple in Japanese, then prevailed upon for a hefty "donation" before leaving.

Generally considered to be a model combination of classical Japanese architecture and landscaping, **Katsura Imperial Villa (Katsura Rikyu)** complex was designed by Kobori Enshu and is widely regarded as the great landscape architect's masterpiece. The villa was commissioned by Toyotomi Hideyoshi for an imperial prince, with work starting in 1590; dying in 1598, Hideyoshi never saw it completed (1624). The screen doors in the main buildings are decorated with fine works of the Kano school of painting, but the overall design concept echoes the stark elegance applied to the teahouses on the grounds. The simplicity is deceptive, however. In the **Imperial Reception Hall (Miyukiden),** the framework and fittings often employ rare and precious woods; even the *kugi-kakushi* (metal coverings concealing bolts in the structural beams) are decorated with flowers of silver and gold.

On the southeastern edge of Higashiyama, about a mile (2 km) south of Kyomizu-ji, is one of Kyoto's five foremost Zen temples, **Tofuku-ji Temple,** founded in 1236 and belonging to the Rinzai sect. Several of the 24 subtemples have gardens, the finest of which is at the Reiun-in. Built in the 1350s, the **sanmon gate** is notable not only for its imposing size, but also for the 11th-century Buddhist sculptures and early 15th-century paintings on the upper floor. Many of the temple's structures were lost in a fire in 1881 and rebuilt early in the 20th century. Surrounded by maple trees, the spacious grounds between the main hall and the founders' hall feature a stream crossed by an unusual bridge crowned with a tower. The garden behind the founders' hall is renowned for the checkerboard layout of moss and flagstones.

Fushimi Inari Taisha Shrine lies half a mile (1 km) due south of Tofuku-ji. There are about 40,000 Shinto shrines dedicated to

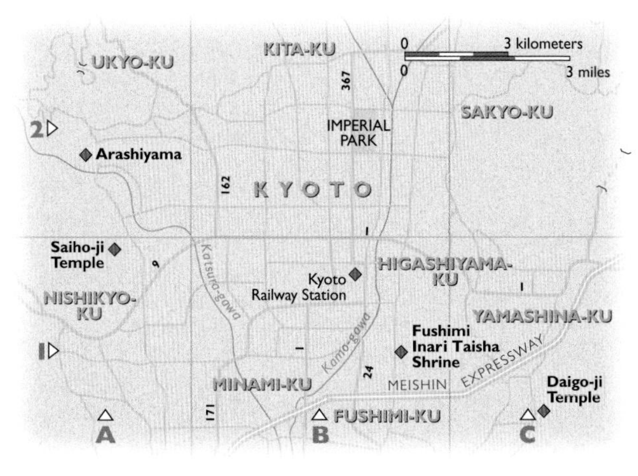

Katsura Imperial Villa
- Map 200 A1
- Misono, Katsura, Nishikyo-ku
- 075/211-1215
- Visits are subject to prior permission from the Imperial Household Agency (see p. 205).
- City Bus: 33 from Kyoto Station to Katsura Rikyu-mae, 5 min. from villa

Tofuku-ji Temple
- Map 201 D1
- 778 Hon-machi, 15-chome. Higashiyama-ku
- 075/561-0087
- 9:30 a.m.–3:30 p.m. Dec.–Oct.; 8:30 a.m.–4:30 p.m. Nov.
- $
- Train: JR & Keihan Railways, Tofukuji Station
  City Bus: 202 & 208

Fushimi Inari Taisha Shrine
- Map 231 B1
- 68 Yabunouchi-cho, Fukakusa, Fushimi-ku
- 075/641-7331
- Dawn to dusk
- Train: JR Nara line Kyoto Station to Inari on the Keihan line from Keihan-sanjo to Fushimi-Inari Station

Left: Checkerboard design at Tofuku-ji Temple garden

The 11th-century Amithaba trinity at the Sanzen-in Temple in Ohara, which also boasts a fine painted ceiling and particularly beautiful gardens

Daigo-ji Temple

- 231 C1
- Garan-cho, Daigo, Fushimi-ku
- 075/571-0002
- 9 a.m.–5 p.m.
- free, except during cherry blossom & autumn foliage seasons ($$); Sanpo-in $$ year-round
- Subway: Tozai line to Daigo Station Bus: City Bus "Higashi-9" from Keihan-Sanjo station terminal stops at Daigo-Sanpoin-mae.

the deity Inari around the country, and this one, said to have been founded early in the eighth century, is the most important of all. Standing on Mount Inari, the precinct covers a substantial area and incorporates several other shrines dedicated to other deities.

As you walk through the wooded hills on the upper reaches, you will pass under thousands of red *torii* gateways straddling the path, all presented to the shrine by devotees; the same applies to the hundreds of stone statues of seated foxes scattered over the landscape. The fox is believed to be the messenger of Inari, a deity concerned with wealth and plentiful harvests. Over New Year hundreds of thousands of people pray here for success in their business enterprises. The shrine's own Sangyo-sai festival on April 8 is a grand affair when prayers are offered for industrial enterprises. The fox also has a reputation for bewitching people, so the superstitious avoid strolling around Inari shrines after sundown.

About 3 miles (5 km) southeast of Fushimi Inari Shrine is **Daigo-ji Temple** (Temple of Heavenly Milk). Approached via an avenue of cherry trees, this vast temple compound covers much of Mount Daigo. Founded during the mid-ninth century and belonging to the Shingon sect, Daigo-ji is favored by followers of Shugendo, a stringent form of Buddhist asceticism. Comprising more than 70 buildings and subtemples, the precinct is divided into Shimo (Lower) Daigo and Kami (Upper) Daigo, with a steep path some 2 miles (3 km) long dividing them. Visiting both constitutes a pleasant (if substantial) hike taking up a whole afternoon. The structures of Kami Daigo, former Buddhist seminaries, were built between the 12th and 16th centuries. Most of the Shimo Daigo buildings were destroyed during the 15th-century Onin Wars; they were extensively restored and rebuilt by order of the shogun Toyotomi Hideyoshi in the 16th century. The notable exception is the five-story **pagoda,** erected in 951. It is not only the oldest building in Kyoto but the oldest of its kind in Japan. Rebuilt by Hideyoshi, the ornate **Sanpo-in** subtemple is noted for the Kano school paintings gracing its interior and the outstanding landscape garden outside. Nearby is the **Hoju-in treasure hall** *(open Apr. 1–May 25 and Oct. 1–Nov. 25).* It is renowned for its fabulous collection of scrolls, paintings, sculptures, and miniature shrines.

If you are on your way to Uji (see p. 234), stop off at **Manpuku-ji Temple.** Belonging to the esoteric Obaku branch of the Rinzai sect of Zen, the temple was founded by the priest Ingen in 1659. Ingen, being Chinese, had the entire temple built in the style of the Ming dynasty, which is unique in Japan.

In the far northeast of Kyoto, in the western foothills of Mount Hiei-zan, is **Shugaku-in Imperial Villa (Shugaku-in Rikyu),** built by the Tokugawa

Manpuku-ji Temple
Gokasho, Uji-shi
0774/32-3900
9 a.m.–4:30 p.m.
$$
Rail: from Kyoto on either JR Nara line or Keihan Uji line, stopping at Obaku Station (about 30 min.), then 5-min. walk

Shugakuin Imperial Villa
201 F6
Yabuzoe, Shugakuin, Sakyo-ku
075/211-1215
Reservations should be made to the Imperial Household Agency (see p. 205). Tours (in Japanese) at 9, 10, & 11 a.m., 1:30 & 3 p.m.
Bus: City Bus No. 5 to Shugakuin-rikyu-michi (about 1 hour), then 15-min. walk

Poets Hermitage
201 E5
Monguchi-cho, Ichioji, Sakyo-ku
075/781-2954
9 a.m.–5 p.m.
$$
Bus: City Bus No. 5 from Kyoto station to Ichijoji-Sagarimatsu-cho, then 5-min. walk

shogunate for former emperor Gomizuno-o in the early 17th century. The grounds are divided into three large gardens with *chaya* (teahouses) in each. Like its southwestern counterpart, the Katsura Imperial Villa (see p. 231), this palace is a fine example of landscape architecture, with buildings beautifully complementing their surrounding ponds, pathways, and trees. The uppermost Kami-no-chaya garden contains the celebrated **Rin'un-tei teahouse,** with a fine view over the city and mountains beyond.

Poets Hermitage (Shisendo) is a ten-minute walk south of Shugakuin Rikyu. Ishikawa Jozan, a samurai turned scholar of Chinese classics, had this peaceful retreat built in 1641. The garden is one of Kyoto's most celebrated.

Unspoiled rural areas lie to the north of Kyoto. The valleys of Kurama and Kibune, for example, are favored mountain getaways for Kyotoites; **Kibune** is known for its quiet and scenic riverside *ryokan* (inn).

Surrounded by wooded hills at the foot of Hiei-zan, **Ohara** is a small town renowned for its scenery—especially for its autumnal landscapes and maple trees. The 16th-century **Sanzen-in Temple** here has an exceptionally beautiful garden, tenth-century main hall, and 16th-century buildings. Nearby **Shoren-in Temple,** set in an extensive precinct, is noted for its thatched main building dating to 1013. Between the two is the garden temple of **Jikko-in,** reached by a steep flight of stone steps, where one can contemplate the delights of the setting while sipping green tea. The **Jakko-in** nunnery (see below) lies northwest of Ohara. ■

Daigo-ji Temple's five-story pagoda is the oldest building in Kyoto.

Jakko-in Temple

Jakko-in holds a special place in the hearts of the Japanese as the final haven of one of the country's greatest tragic heroines.

When the Minamoto clan finally defeated the Taira in 1185, the Taira survivors hurled themselves into the water to drown. Among them were the lady Kenreimon-in and her son, seven-year-old Emperor Antoku. To her chagrin, Kenreimon-in was saved. After renouncing the world, she retired as a nun to Jakko-in, where she spent the last 27 years of her life in melancholy contemplation. ■

Originally the villa of an 11th-century nobleman, the magnificent Byodo-in was converted to a temple by his son.

Uji

THE TOWNSHIP OF UJI, ABOUT 9 MILES (15 KM) SOUTHEAST of the city center, was one of the first places in Japan to boast a tea plantation. It still enjoys a national reputation for the premium quality of its green tea. It is also known for its historical stone bridge and for cormorant fishing in the Uji-gawa River, which can be viewed by boat from mid-June through August. Above all, Uji is famous for the lovely Byodo-in Temple, one of the most celebrated sights in Japan.

Byodo-in Temple
- 116 Uji Renge, Uji-shi
- 0774/21-2861
- 8:30 a.m.–5:30 p.m.
- $$
- Rail: Uji Station on JR Nara line or Uji Station on Keihan line; the Byodo-in is a 10-min. walk from both stations

Built as a villa by Fujiwara-no-Michinaga (966–1024), the most powerful prime minister of Heian times, the **Byodo-in Temple** (Phoenix Temple) was converted into a temple in 1052. The other palatial buildings were all lost to fire in 1336, but the **Phoenix Hall (Hoo-do),** built in 1053, still stands. It is fortunate that one of the only remaining buildings of the period should be this, which represents Heian's architectural zenith. Mirrored in the pond around it, the hall evokes a phoenix *(ho-o)* alighting; the buildings flanking the central body represent extended wings.

Inside, beneath an ornate, intricately carved canopy inlaid with mother-of-pearl, is a beautiful seated statue of the Amithaba Buddha. The surrounding walls are adorned with the 52 charming Cloud Bosatsu, delicate statuettes of Buddhist deities dancing, playing musical instruments, or holding ritual objects. Other walls are decorated with period murals, but the paintings on the doors are reproductions. The originals can be seen in the **Treasure Hall (Homutsukan),** as can the original statues of the male and female phoenixes on the roof, and the old temple bell.

Along the temple approach are several venerable tea merchants' shops that offer a chance to taste the subtleties of different grades of green tea. ■

Hiei-zan

HIEI-ZAN, ABOUT 5 MILES (8 KM) NORTHEAST OF KYOTO city center, has the area's most accessible skiing facilities, but it is special for the place it holds in the city's history. In the ninth century the priest Saicho founded the Tendai sect, an eclectic school of Buddhism that incorporated Shinto deities. Appealing to aristocrats and commoners alike, it became the state religion. According to ancient Chinese geomancy (divination based on geographical directions), the northeast is the most unlucky direction, so Hiei-zan was considered the ideal place for Saicho to build a temple complex to protect the city from evil influences.

Enryaku-ji Temple

- Sakamoto-hon-machi, Otsu-shi, Shiga-ken
- 0775/78-0001
- 8:30 a.m.–4 p.m.; closes earlier in winter
- $$
- Kyoto Bus: 51 or 57 from Kyoto Station Keihan Bus: 56 from Keihan-sanjo

Enryaku-ji Temple, Saicho's focal temple, spread across the mountain into a temple city of more than 3,000 buildings. During Saicho's lifetime, even emperors studied Buddhism at Enryaku-ji. The monks were so many that they amounted to an army, which is literally what they became. By the 11th century some of these warrior monks were bandits, terrorizing citizens with sporadic raids on Kyoto. Remaining politically and militarily powerful for centuries, the monks were eventually deemed a threat by the shogun Oda Nobunaga, who routed them in 1581 and burned the buildings around Enryaku-ji to the ground. Partially restored by Toyotomi Hideyoshi, the great monastery was also substantially enlarged during the 17th century.

Among notable buildings of the temple are the central Kompon-chu-do and Daiko-do (Great Lecture Hall) in the Toto (eastern precinct) and the Shaka-do (Shakyamuni Hall) and Sorinto pagoda in the Saito (western precinct). With its temples set in a forest of soaring cedars, the quieter western side seems the more deeply steeped in peace, piety, and the mystic ambience of Buddhism.

A scenic route to Hiei-zan is to go by Kyoto bus from Kyoto Station to Yase-Yuen. From here it is a short walk east to the station for the **Yase-Yuen cable car** up Mount Hiei-zan (10 minutes). ■

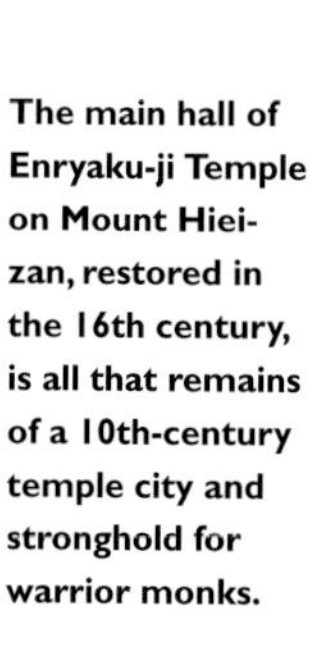

The main hall of Enryaku-ji Temple on Mount Hiei-zan, restored in the 16th century, is all that remains of a 10th-century temple city and stronghold for warrior monks.

Hikone-jo Castle overlooks delightful gardens.

Biwa-ko & Hikone

BIWA-KO LAKE, IN SHIGA-KEN EAST OF KYOTO, IS NAMED for an ancient Japanese lute whose shape it resembles. At 260 square miles (674 sq km), it is Japan's largest and best known lake. Sadly, the scenery is no longer as picturesque as it was when celebrated in 19th-century woodblock prints; many places around the shore have been overdeveloped in terms of both urbanism and tourism.

Nevertheless, the town of **Otsu** on Biwa-ko's southwestern tip offers sightseeing boat trips around the lake. The area is also home to the notable Onjo-ji and Enman-in temples. The impressive eighth-century Ishiyama-dera preserves the small hall in which Murasaki Shikibu wrote her monumental *Tale of Genji* more than a thousand years ago.

The other great attraction is **Hikone,** on the lake's eastern shore, famed for its 17th-century castle. The keep's beautiful white main tower still stands intact. ■

Hikone

199 C3

Visitor information

JR Hikone Station, outside exit for Hikone-jo Castle

0749/22-2954

Hikone-jo Castle

1-1 Konki-cho

0749/22-2742

8:30 a.m.–5 p.m.

$$

Nara & beyond

Picturesque old shops and houses in Nara's southwest

NARA IS A SMALL TOWN; ITS UNHURRIED AMBIENCE SEEMS designed to avoid disturbing the long sleep of its illustrious ancestors. While Kyoto's grandeur emerges from a comparatively recent past, Nara and its environs contain buildings of such antiquity that their very survival is astonishing. Japanese civilization first appeared in the Nara Basin; ancient burial mounds of the Kofun period (see p. 28) are on view within the modern city confines.

In 710 Empress Gemmei founded the city of Heijo, intended as a permanent capital. About 1 mile (2 km) west of modern Nara, the city was modeled on China's mighty T'ang dynasty city of Chang'an, the cosmopolitan hub of the Silk Road and the most sophisticated metropolis of the ancient world. Profoundly affected by Chang'an, Nara was Japan's window on the world. Its temple treasures include ancient Chinese, Korean, Indian, and even Persian artworks, and experts still wrangle over the influences displayed by its art and architecture.

Though Nara gave its name to an era of great progress, it never realized the permanence to which it aspired. Emperor Kammu built Heian-kyo (Kyoto) in 794, after which Nara slumbered, despite remaining an important center for Buddhism. Natural disasters, fires, and redevelopment obliterated ancient Nara over the centuries, but some of its seventh- and eighth-century temples still stand.

Occupying the northeastern quarter of the city are the 1,235 acres (500 ha) of **Nara-koen Park,** roamed by approximately 1,500 tame deer. Japan's largest city park, it embraces some of Nara's greatest treasures, including the world's largest bronze sculpture (see p. 241).

Nara

Map 199 C3

Visitor information

23-4 Kamisanjo-cho

0742/22-3900

9 a.m.–9 p.m.

Struck with a stick, this fiercely fishy wooden clapper was once used to assemble the monks at Kofuku-ji Temple.

Kofuku-ji Temple
- 48 Noborioji-cho
- 0742/22-7755
- 9 a.m.–5 p.m.
- $$
- Train: Kintetsu Nara station, then 5-min. walk east

The rest of the city is unremarkable; there are picturesque older neighborhoods in Nara-machi to the southwest, but preservation outside religious contexts is not much of a priority. Though Nara is a small city, the volume of tourists is phenomenal. The major sights can be covered on a day trip from Kyoto. Nara has a good but limited array of accommodations. If you plan to stay, book ahead.

One of the main temples of the Hosso sect of esoteric Buddhism, **Kofuku-ji Temple** was founded in 669 by the wife of Fujiwara Kamatari, an ancestor of the family that ruled Kyoto during the Heian period. Moved to its present location when Nara became the capital in 710, it comprised 175 buildings at the zenith of the Heian period. As regional conflict increased after the 1150s with the decline of the Fujiwara dynasty, Kofuku-ji raised an army of warrior monks who supported the Minamoto clan engaged by the Fujiwara to protect them against the Taira clan. The warrior monks were defeated in 1180 by a Taira army, which set the temple buildings ablaze. Having vanquished the Taira and moved the capital to Kamakura, the shogun Minamoto Yoritomo set about restoring Kofuku-ji.

A disastrous fire destroyed most of the result in 1717, but the **Northern Octagonal Hall (Hokuen-do)** and **three-story pagoda** survive intact from the Kamakura period. The **five-story pagoda** and **Eastern Golden Hall (Tokon-do)** date from the early 15th century. Reflected in nearby **Sarusawa Pond (Sarusawa-no-ike),** the pagoda is one of Nara's most photographed sights. Various halls of Kofuku-ji

The Nara deer

Schoolchildren feed greedy Nara deer.

Deer reached Japan before even the Japanese, having crossed continental land bridges during the Ice Age. Divine messengers according to Shinto, they have roamed Nara for centuries. Over generations, the herd in Nara-koen, numbering some 1,500, has perfected the doe-eyed look that guarantees maximum handouts. Stalls trade briskly in deer-feed; *shika sembei* (deer crackers) are allegedly often munched by foreigners who mistake them for local delicacies.

Deer are greedy. They have been accused of overturning trash cans—and even small people. Males can be mildly dangerous during mating season. Whatever their reputation, the deer are mainly docile and delightful. ■

contain a number of outstanding early Buddhist sculptures, as does its **Treasure Hall (Kokuho-kan)** museum.

Nara National Museum (Kokuritsu Hakubutsukan) is 550 yards (500 m) east of Kofuku-ji Temple. Built in 1895, the **West Gallery** contains an impressive collection of Buddhist art, including paintings, calligraphy, sculptures, and decorative arts from the seventh century through the Kamakura and Edo periods. In 1973 the **East Gallery** was added, and this is devoted to archaeological artifacts unearthed in the Nara region. Museum exhibits change on a regular basis; some items in the West Gallery are so precious and fragile that they are exhibited only once a year. The same applies to the treasures formerly kept in the Shoso-in Hall of Todai-ji. These include items of Chinese, Indian, and Persian origin or influence, reflecting Nara's ancient connections to the Silk Road.

Kasuga Taisha Shrine, founded by the erstwhile ruler Fujiwara-no-Michinaga (see p. 234) as a family shrine in 768, is on the southeastern edge of Nara-koen, less than a mile southeast of the National Museum. It comprises four main **Honden** halls—three dedicated to divine warriors and one to the deified ancestors of the Fujiwara line. Epitomizing the Chinese temple style in vogue between the seventh and tenth centuries, Kasuga is an architectural paradigm: Other shrines around Japan with pillars of vermilion

Crowned with moss, stone lanterns have adorned Kasuga Taisha Grand Shrine since the 11th century.

Nara National Museum

www.narahaku.go.jp

- ✉ 50 Noborioji-cho
- ☎ 0742/22-7771
- 🕒 9 a.m.–5 p.m.; open till 7 p.m. Fri. end Apr.–end Oct.; closed Mon.
- $ $$
- 🚌 Bus: Kukuritsu Hakubutsukan

Cast 1,200 years ago, the 53-foot (16 m) Buddha at Todai-ji Temple is the world's largest bronze statue.

wood and sweeping Chinese roofs are often described as being in the Kasuga style. Like most major Shinto shrines, the major buildings have been ritually demolished and identically rebuilt every 20 years. With the exception of the old **Oratory (Haiden)** and the **Function Hall (Naoraiden),** the rest of Kasuga was last reerected—for the 56th time—in 1893. The shrine approach, 875 yards (800 m) long, is bordered by some 2,000 **stone lanterns** donated by devotees since the 11th century. A thousand more, made of bronze, hang elegantly from the eaves of the buildings closer to the main precinct. Twice a year, during the Setsubun festival in early February and in August, the lighted lanterns present an enchanting spectacle enhancing the hallowed atmosphere of the shrine.

A modern building next to the parking lot near the shrine's main entrance, the **Treasure House (Homutsuden)** displays a collection of historical shrine objects including Noh masks and the trappings of Shinto ritual, ceremonies, and festivals. To the left of the shrine approach, the **Man'yo Botanical Garden (Kasuga Taisha Shin-en)** boasts all 300 plant varieties mentioned in the *Man'yoshu*, a celebrated eighth-century anthology of thousands of poems.

Beyond the road flanking Nara Park to the south is **Shin Yakushi-ji Temple.** The temple was founded in 747 by Komyo, consort of Emperor Shomu, as a means

Kasuga Taisha Shrine

- 160 Kasugano-cho
- 0742/22-7788
- Dawn to dusk
- Bus: Kasuga Taisha-Omotesando stop, then a 650-yd. (600 m) walk east

of praying for the emperor's recovery from an eye infection threatening his sight. The only surviving original structure is the **Main Hall** (formerly the dining hall), renowned for the sculptures (all National Treasures) it contains. The main object of worship is the 14-foot (2.4 m) effigy of the seated **Yakushi Nyorai,** the healing Buddha, flanked by an 11-faced Kannon (Buddhist god of mercy) and the Juni-Shinsho (12 Divine Generals). These tall, exquisitely wrought clay statues of generals in full armor actually number 11: One went AWOL centuries ago. Other notable treasures in the compound are the gilt-bronze **Ko-Yakushi** Buddha and a rare Heian-period painting of Nirvana, the Buddhist paradise.

Todai-ji Temple, on the northwestern edge of Nara-koen Park, about 1 mile (2 km) northeast of Nara station, is famous for the mighty bronze Buddha, the Daibutsu. Emperor Shomu (701–758) built the temple (completed in 752) to accommodate a colossal bronze statue of the Vairocana Buddha (the Buddha of which all others are aspects) that he had commissioned. Having renounced the world and retired as a monk, Shomu emerged from seclusion to conduct the grand dedication ceremony for the statue in 749. Like Kofuku-ji Temple, Todai-ji was torched during the conflicts ending the Heian period in 1185.

The finely sculpted octagonal **bronze lantern** in front of the main hall is an eighth-century original. The massive **Great South Gate (Nandaimon)** before the entrance also dates from the eighth century, although it was substantially restored in the 12th century after collapsing during a typhoon. The fierce guardian deities standing in niches on either side—splendid wooden carvings 26 feet (8 m) tall—are attributed to Kamakura-period sculptor Unkei and his school.

Fires and natural disasters mean that most of the precinct's buildings are 16th- and 17th-century reproductions, notably the **Hall of the Great Buddha (Daibutsuden),** rebuilt for the last time in 1708. It measures 187 feet (57 m) wide by 164 feet (50 m) deep and 157 feet (48 m) high. Although smaller than its predecessor, the hall is still one of the world's largest wooden structures; it had to be to house the **Daibutsu,** the biggest bronze statue in the world.

During the 1,200-year history of the Daibutsu, it has been damaged by multiple fires and lost its head twice during earthquakes. It

Todai-ji Temple

- 406-1 Zoshi-cho
- 0742/22-5511
- 8 a.m.–5 p.m.
- $$
- Bus: Daibutsuden

Shin Yakushi-ji Temple

- 1352 Takabatake-cho
- 0742/22-3736
- 9 a.m.–5 p.m.
- $$
- Bus: Wariishi

The solemn Omizu-tori (Water-Drawing) ceremony at Todai-ji Temple features a procession of ascetics bearing blazing torches. It can be seen nightly in early March.

was last restored in 1692. The seated colossus, weighing 550 tons and incorporating 290 pounds of gold, soars 53 feet (16 m) above its pedestal. Its sheer scale tends to undermine the artistry its Korean designer intended, but the statue still induces a sense of awe.

The main effigy is surrounded by statues of Kannon and two Heavenly Guardians, dating to the 17th and 18th centuries. A huge pillar to the right of the Daibutsu is thought to open the path of enlightenment to those able to crawl through the hole in the base—a privilege reserved for the slim.

East of the Daibutsuden, the **belfry** (12th century) contains a bell dating from 752; damaged during a typhoon, it was recast in 1239. **Nigatsu-do Hall** (Second Month Hall), rebuilt in 1669, contains effigies of Kannon that only the elite clergy have ever seen. It is celebrated for its view over the city from the veranda, as well as for the Omizu-tori (Water-Drawing) festival (March 1–14), whose grand torchlight processions attract thousands of spectators.

Sangatsu-do Hall (Third Month Hall) has stood since the eighth century and is Todai-ji's oldest structure. The marvelous period sculptures it contains are National Treasures, as are some other artworks and buildings in the precinct; they include a tall statue of Kannon attributed to Roben and 14 other major effigies. The two halls are both some 330 yards (300 m) east of the Daibutsuden. Other treasures, including those placed

there by Emperor Shomu himself, were once kept in the **Shoso-in,** north of the precinct. This long rectangular building on stilts still stands, but the treasures were moved to the Nara National Museum (see p. 239) in 1963.

BEYOND NARA

About 3 miles (5 km) west of Nara is **Toshodai-ji Temple,** headquarters of the Ritsu school of Buddhism. The temple was built in 759 by the Chinese priest Ganjin (Chien Chen) at the invitation of the emperor Shomu. Opposition from Chinese bureaucrats, five shipwrecks, and bouts of illness that finally left him blind had delayed Ganjin's arrival for ten years. Entirely Chinese in design, Toshodai-ji's main buildings survive as paradigms of Nara-period architecture. Statues inside the **Main Hall (Kondo),** among them the focal Buddha Vairocana carved by Chinese sculptors, are National Treasures. Originally the assembly hall of the Nara court, the **Lecture Hall (Kodo)** was moved here when the temple was built. Although it retains revealing details about Nara-period palace architecture (not least, front pillars that curve slightly to alter their perspective), its overall form has been lost through repairs and alterations over the centuries. The **Founder's Hall (Miei-do)** contains a famous sculpted portrait of Ganjin; more fine works of Buddhist art are exhibited in the **Shin-Hozo Treasure House,** open twice annually *(late Mar.–late May and mid-Sept.–early Nov.).*

Yakushi-ji Temple, less than a mile (800 m) south of Toshodai-ji, was founded in the seventh century. Once one of the Seven Great Temples of Nara, it is the headquarters of the Hosso sect. Yakush-ji's

(continued on p. 247)

Toshodai-ji Temple

14–46 Gojo-cho
0742/33-7900
8:30 a.m.–5 p.m.
$$
Train: Kintetsu Railway to Nishinokyo Station
Bus: Toshodaiji

Yakushi-ji Temple

457 Nishinokyo-cho
0742/33-6001
8:30 a.m.–5 p.m.
$$
Bus: 52, 97, or 98 from JR Nara Station or Kintetsu Nara Station to Yakushiji-Higaashiguchi

Hokki-ji Temple

Hokki-ji was founded in 638, allegedly according to Prince Shotoku's last wishes. The original stood at Okamoto, where the prince had a palace; moved here later, it is still sometimes known as Okamoto-dera Temple. Its greatest claim to fame is its fine three-story pagoda. Only slightly younger than the pagoda at Horyu-ji Temple but much less visited, it was built in 686 and is widely regarded as one of the finest examples of the architecture of the period. ■

Shinto

Being Shintoist is synonymous with being Japanese. Almost everyone is involved in Shinto rituals at some time: Newborn children are presented at the shrine, and most marriage ceremonies are Shinto.

The Way of the Gods

Meaning "the Way of the Gods," Shinto originated among the tribes of prehistory. It is rooted in an animist folk religion, worshiping *kami*—the gods once believed to inhabit all things under, and including, the sun. Out of many thousands of shrines, Ise-jingu in western Kansai (see p. 259) has been the most sacred for some 1,800 years. Whether inaugurating building sites or factories, or at the shrine itself, Shinto ceremonies suggest extreme antiquity. Waving leafy branches toward cardinal points to ward off evil spirits, the priest is assisted by *miko* (shrine maidens) whose stylized gyrations evoke the movements of a shaman in a trance.

Ancient Chinese influences gradually turned Shinto into an ancestor cult; it was believed that everyone, especially emperors, would become *kami* (spirit gods) after death. Different communities share the basic religion, but believe in variants; tiny hamlets boast a shrine for a protective god, and even homes contain a miniature *kamidana* (god shelf) for statues. With worshippers moved by awe and reverence rather than faith or piety, Shinto is devoid of doctrine or ethics. Its priesthood is a hereditary post serving the community by maintaining the shrine.

The shrine

A Shinto shrine is recognizable by the *torii* (gateway) at its entrance. Shrines are often decorated in white and red, the respective ritual colors of male and female. Being formless, the ancient gods go undepicted, but paired stone *komainu* (lion dogs) often stand at the entrance to guard the shrine against evil. Some shrines contain statues of animals considered divine messengers—especially the fox, the familiar (servant) of Inari, deity of the hearth and harvest. Other shrines embrace an effigy of a horse, an animal once revered for its utility; the small wooden plaques placed before it were called *ema* (horse pictures), a term now referring to votive plaques in general.

State Shinto

The name Shinto came into use only when the vague, heterogeneous beliefs were formalized in 1872 as the nationalistic state religion based on emperor worship. It was repudiated as a state religion after the war. State Shinto exalted the *Kojiki (Record of Ancient Matters)* and *Nihon Shoki (Chronicles of Japan)*. Completed in the early eighth century, both books begin with the Shinto creation myths and chronicle the reigns of emperors from to 697 B.C. to A.D. 660, the first 14 being mythical. Seen as politically expedient, the books reinforced an emperor's rule by establishing his divinity. Japan, its population, and the gods were all progeny of the female Izanami and the male Izanagi, also parents of the sun goddess Amaterasu, who was the mother of Emperor Jimmu—the first of an unbroken imperial line.

Beliefs and rituals

Many Shinto cults focus on volcanoes and mountains, and a few on phallic variants of human fertility. Above all Shinto is a farmer's religion, bound to crop cycles; the emperor's ritual duties still include the ceremonial planting and harvesting of rice on the palace grounds.

From convivial New Year bonfires in remote country shrines to spectacular annual *matsuri* (festivals) attended by hundreds of thousands, Shinto binds communities. Matsuri feature processions of ornate *mikoshi*

Opposite: Tying fortune paper to a branch for luck
Left: Purification with holy water during a sacred ceremony
Above: Kyoto's 1,500-year-old Aoi Matsuri
Below: Safety first, Shinto style: A priest blesses a new car.

(palanquins or portable shrines). Some 70 million people visit shrines at New Year to pray for the guardianship of the gods, whose assistance is invoked for a safe journey, success in exams or business, the birth of a healthy child, or protection against illness.

Shinto shuns impurity and the pollution of blood, death, and dirt. When visiting a shrine, use the cisterns standing by the shrine entrance to wash your hands and rinse your mouth before you enter (this is optional). Next, announce your presence to the god by pulling on the thick bell cord hanging before the altar; toss a few coins into the box in front of you and clap your hands twice, then put them together to pray for some 30 seconds as you bow to the altar. If few believe intrinsically today, everyone likes to play safe. Perhaps it was always so: Moved to tears of reverence before the altar at Ise-jingu, the 13th-century poet-priest Saigyo declared, "I know not at all if anything deigns to be there." ■

Five-story Pagoda (Goju-no-To)

Sutra Repository (Kyozo)

Main Hall (Kondo)

Central Gate (Chumon)

Important cultural properties

National treasures

KEY TO SITE PLAN

1 South Main Gate (Nandaimon)
2 Central Gate (Chumon)
3 Main Hall (Kondo)
4 Five-story Pagoda (Goju-no-To)
5 Great Lecture Hall (Daikodo)
6 Sutra Repository (Kyozo)
7 Bell House (Shoro)
8 Inner Sanctuary (Kami-no-Mido)
9 West Round Hall (Saiendo)
10 Hall of Prince Shotoku's Soul (Shoryoin)
11 Gallery of Temple Treasures (Daihozoden)
12 Kudara Kannon Hall (Kudara Kannon-do)
13 East Main Gate (Todaimon)
14 Hall of Visions (Yumedono)
15 Reliquary Hall (Shariden)
16 Hall of Buddhist Teachings (Denpodo)
17 Bell House (Toin Shoro)

Horyu-ji Temple

- 1-1 Horyuji Sannai, Ikuraga-cho, Ikoma-gun
- 0745/75-2555
- 8 a.m.–4 p.m.
- $$
- Train: Kansai main line from JR Nara Station to Koryuji Station
  Bus: 52, 60, 97, or 98 from JR Nara Station to Kintetsu Nara Station

(continued from p. 243)
grand buildings are long gone, but the Toto pagoda, 108 feet (33 m) high and dating from 730, is prized both for its elegance and for the unique architectural feat of making its three stories appear as six. The Main Hall (Kondo), rebuilt in 1976, houses a National Treasure—the bronze Yakushi Triad depicting the Yakushi Nyorai Buddha (associated with healing) and attendant bodhisattvas. These once-golden statues, cast in the 720s, have been smoked a glossy black through fires over the centuries. Another National Treasure is the seventh-century statue of Sho-Kannon in the Eastern Hall (Toin-do), built behind the pagoda in 1285.

Paramount among all Japan's great temples and revered for its pride of place in Japanese Buddhist culture, **Horyu-ji Temple—**diagramed at left—was founded in 607 by Prince Shotoku, architect of the first national constitution (see p. 28). The temple complex is said to have been rebuilt after a fire in 670, although some historians doubt the fire ever occurred. Either way, four of the buildings, remaining as they have been for over 1,300 years, are the oldest standing wooden structures on Earth.

Counting several buildings from the Heian and Kamakura eras, as well as additions from the 15th to 19th centuries, the complex includes a hall opened in 1998 to house the Kudara Kannon, a masterpiece of wood sculpture and the temple's most famous statue. Horyu-ji, a UNESCO World Heritage Site, holds more than 2,300 items considered of historical importance—190 of them are Important Cultural Assets or National Treasures. The temple is divided into the larger **Western Precinct (Sai-in),** lying beyond the massive 15th-century **Great South Gate (Nandaimon),** and the smaller Eastern Precinct (Toin), which embraces Chugu-ji subtemple.

The seventh-century **Main Hall (Kondo)** houses some of the era's most important bronze and wooden sculptures, visible only through wooden lattices. The hall is also dark, making it hard to see the murals depicting paradise. Badly damaged in a fire in 1949, these have been beautifully restored. To the left of the Kondo stands the magnificent seventh-century

Pagoda (Goju-no-To), the oldest in Japan; 110 feet (33 m) high, it contains an elaborate clay sculpture on the first floor, with figures illustrating various Buddhist myths. North of the main compound at the point where the surrounding cloisters meet, the **Great Lecture Hall (Daikodo)** and the statues within date from the tenth century; the original was struck by lightning.

Also replacing a damaged predecessor, the 13th-century **West Round Hall (Saiendo)** stands on a hill and contains an eighth-century Yakushi Nyorai image—the oldest dry-lacquer statue in Japan. The two long halls on either side of the central compound were formerly monks' quarters; built during the Kamakura period, the one on the east side is the **Hall of Prince Shotoku's Soul (Shoryoin)** and contains the prince's statue, wrought during the Heian period.

Passing through the ancient East Gate (Todaimon) brings you to the east precinct, with its octagonal seventh-century **Hall of Dreams (Yumedono)** pavilion. Dominating the statues it contains is a wooden portrait of the deified Prince Shotoku; his likeness retains its original gilding and is in a remarkable state of preservation. Just east of this is **Chugu-in,** a nunnery housing Japan's oldest embroidered picture—and, most notably, the exquisite seventh-century **Miroku Bosatsu,** a Buddha statue of exceptional grace and serenity.

Though many of Horyu-ji's treasures are now in Tokyo's National Museum (see pp. 95–97), about a thousand remain in the **Gallery of Temple Treasures (Daihozoden)** just east of the main precinct. Among them is the Dream-Changing Kannon sculpture, sought out for changing nightmares into auspicious dreams. A small, exquisitely decorated lacquered shrine, the Tamamushi Tabernacle belonged to Empress Suiko. The intricate metalwork on its surface once held thousands of iridescent wings of the *tamamushi* beetle. ■

Nara crafts

Ink and brushes have been manufactured in Nara for generations.

Nara craftsmen and women still fashion Kogaku-men dance-drama masks and rough-finished wooden *itto-bori* dolls. Both were used in ancient religious ceremonies.

Buddhism brought with it many arts from China, especially calligraphy and ink painting. To this day, Nara remains the center for turning out brushes and *sumi* ink tablets. Made of deer, horse, rabbit, squirrel, or badger hair, brushes come in different sizes for different functions. Sumi or *yoboku,* made from the soot of bullrushes, is combined with glue from deer horn and formed into a cake said to improve with age. Depending on the desired intensity of the ink, other ingredients may include *beni* (crimson safflower dye), powdered oyster shell, and even musk; some manufacturers' formulas are secrets handed down for generations. ■

Nara-ken

TOO OFTEN, VISITORS ARE SO TAKEN WITH NARA THE CITY that they forget about Nara the prefecture. There is much here that is worthwhile. Refreshingly rural and mountainous, the countryside boasts beautiful temples and is said to harbor the legendary heartland of the cherry tree. Indeed, the hills around the town of Yoshino are cloaked in the palest pink blossoms each spring.

According to tradition, **Muro-ji Temple** *(78 Muro, Muro-mura, tel 0745/93-2003)*, beautifully situated in a peaceful wooded valley, was founded in 681 (the exact date is not known). Rebuilt in 824 by the priest Kukai, founder of the Shingon sect, it remains an important temple of that sect.

The temple is known as the "women's Koya"; unlike the great temple Kukai founded on Koya-san (see p. 250), this one never barred female visitors. Although the buildings have undergone restorations at various times, they are noted examples of seventh-century architecture; several are National Treasures, as are the statues they contain. The five-storied **pagoda** is among the most photographed buildings in Japan.

Amid forests of tree peonies and cherry trees, **Hase-dera Temple** (Temple of Flowers, *731–1 Hase, Sakurai-shi, tel 0744-47-7001)* is a popular temple in late spring despite its remote location. Founded in 686 and enlarged by Emperor Shomu, who built the main hall, Hase-dera was once a cherished preserve of Nara-period aristocracy. Containing a celebrated 26-foot (8 m) statue of Kannon, god of mercy, the **Main Hall (Hondo)** is reached by a covered flight of stone steps.

Cherry trees originated in the town of **Yoshino,** legend has it, where they were planted in the seventh century by the priest En-no-Ozuno; he is said to have placed a curse on anyone who dared to cut them down. Whatever the truth, *yamazakura* (*Prunus cerrulata* or wild cherry)—the basis for hundreds of subsequent hybrids—is the favorite variety in Japan. Empress Jito (645–702), for one, practiced blossom viewing here. The cherries cover the hillside after mid-April, blooming higher up the mountainside as the month advances. ■

Off the beaten track, ninth-century Muro-ji Temple is cherished for its five-story pagoda and sylvan setting.

Wakayama-ken

Kii Peninsula
199 B2

Mount Koya-san
199 B2
Visitor information
By Senjuinbashi-mae bus stop
0736/56-2616
Train: Nankai Koya line from Osaka Namba Station to Gokurakubashi (1 hr. 15 min.), then cable car to Koya-san

THE KII-HANTO PENINSULA EMBRACES THE SOUTHERN TIP of Nara-ken, but the bulk of it to the southwest is in mountainous Wakayama-ken. Wooded, agricultural, and almost devoid of industry, this is Kansai's last frontier. With the Kansai International Airport only 12 miles (20 km) from Wakayama city, this may change. For now, however, even the scenic coastline is relatively unspoiled. The area is served by buses, and a local railroad line runs around the coast, but direct transportation options from major cities are limited, making it a wonderful region to explore by car. Still, you won't need a car to explore the region's principal asset: Koya-san, the mountainous and secluded home of the Shingon Buddhist sect.

Hot springs abound near **Hongu,** along the border between Nara-ken and Wakayama-ken; especially recommended are the more rustic spa villages of **Kawayu Onsen** and **Yunomine Onsen.** In the south, scenic Nachikatsuura is famous for **Nachi-no-taki Waterfall,** whose drop of 436 feet (133 m) makes it the highest cascade in Japan.

In the peninsula's northwest, hilly Koya Ryujin Quasi-National Park is the site of **Mount Koya-san,** Japan's best known Buddhist mountain retreat. At about 3,300 feet (1,005 m), Koya-san culminates in a plateau covering 5 square miles (12 sq km). It was here that Kukai (774–835), founder of the Shingon sect of Buddhism, first established a seminary in 816. The exclusive preserve of monks, the Koya-san temple city was forbidden to women until 1873. Frequent fires have left no buildings older than the 12th century; several, in fact, were reconstructed early in the 20th century. **Kongobu-ji Temple,** erected by the shogun Toyotomi Hideyoshi in 1592 and containing fine Kano school screen doors, became the focal temple—and is still the headquarters—of the Shingon sect.

Koya-san is divided into two main areas: the **Danjogoran,** just southwest of Kongobu-ji, and the **Okuno-in** to the east. In the Danjogaran complex is the **Treasure House (Reihokan),** with thousands of wonderful exhibits, many of them registered National Treasures. The latter is essentially a cemetery; more than 100,000 graves and funerary monuments have accumulated here to memorialize the great and the good for over 1,200 years of Japanese history. At the top of the Okuno-in, just south of the great **Kukai's**

Seventeenth-century painted screen doors in Kongobu-ji Temple, Mount Koya-san

The rugged coastline of Wakayama-ken

mausoleum, is the **lantern hall.** Among its 11,000 luminaries, two have burned continuously since the tenth century.

The secular part of Koya-san, with all the attributes of an ordinary small town, has no hotels. The majority of the million-odd visitors it receives annually are pilgrims; 50 of the 120 temples in the vicinity provide lodgings known as *shukubo* (see Travelwise, p. 359). Prices and sleeping arrangements are the same as in the average *ryokan* (see p. 358).

Piety is not a prerequisite for appreciating Koya-san, which is much cherished by urbanites as a stress-free retreat. An overnight stay is highly recommended, at the very least as an opportunity to touch the pulse of a unique Buddhist heartland. When the daytrippers have gone home, to stroll in the tranquil early morning or evening is a sublime experience in itself. The temples lie in tall cedar forests where the haze seems scented with incense; the lone passersby are priests and pilgrims, and the sounds of chanting and temple bells only deepen the silence. ■

Kukai (774–835)

After studying Buddhism in China, Kukai returned to Japan to found the Shingon sect. Its emphasis on esoteric Buddhism appealed to emperors and noblemen, but Kukai gained converts among the common people, too.

The life of this Buddhist saint is shrouded in myths and miracles. One concerns the rivalry between Kyoto's two main temples, the eastern To-ji Temple (of which Kukai was abbot) and the western Sai-ji Temple. After trapping the celestial rain-dragon in a huge jar, the abbot of Sai-ji apparently caused a serious drought. Kukai's prayers set it free, and rain fell once again. The seminary that Kukai built on Koya-san (see opposite) remains Japan's greatest focus of Buddhism today. ■

Osaka-jo Castle, here lit up at night, is a concrete reproduction of its colossal 16th-century predecessor.

Osaka

"*MOKARI MAKKA*?"—"MAKING ANY MONEY?" THIS IS WHAT other Japanese claim is the typical greeting between Osakans, who have a reputation as the nation's shrewdest businesspeople. Osaka's 30,000 factories produce about a quarter of Japan's industrial output. If the prefecture were a country, its GNP would make it the tenth most prosperous nation on Earth.

Osaka
199 B3
Visitor information
JR Osaka Station, 3-1 Umeda, Kita-ku
06/6345-2189

Officially, Osaka is Japan's third city. Because Tokyo and Yokohama are close enough to constitute a single megalopolis, however, most people consider Osaka to be the second. Its location on a sweeping bay prompted its use as a port during the reign of Emperor Nintoku, so Osaka has been a primary trading center since the fourth century. While samurai fortunes fell from the late 17th century on, merchants grew ever more wealthy and powerful, especially in Osaka. As the city became the national hub of trade and industry, it saw the foundation of many of today's great Japanese corporations, among them Daiwa, Marubeni, and Sumitomo.

Under the patronage of merchant princes, Osaka flourished as a center for the dramatic arts, particularly when many Kabuki exponents moved here after the

The vast Umeda Sky Building, a striking example of modern Japanese architecture, is both admired and deplored.

devas- tation of Edo in the great fire of 1657. Osaka was renowned for its Bunraku (see p. 48), and today it remains the national center for this unique form of puppetry. A prime target in World War II, the city was flattened, and all of Osaka's historic assets vanished. Osaka-jo castle survived, but it was already a concrete copy (built in 1931) of its predecessor.

Although it caters to special interests with industrial tours, Osaka is no destination for sight-seeing. Its monotony is broken by a network of canals, but it is mainly a hideous concrete agglomeration with a reputation for being driven, hectic, polluted, and crowded. This said, Osaka is a boisterous city of sybarites, with some of Japan's best nightlife—and its widest spectrum of fine food. In

Umeda Sky Building

- ✉ 1-1-88 Oyodonaka, Kita-ku
- ☎ 06/6440-3855
- 🕒 observation deck 10 a.m.–10 p.m.
- $ $$
- 🚌 underground passage from north of Osaka & Umeda stations

Marilyn beckons from a building facade in Amerika-mura, Osaka's brash and youthful America village.

The sights rival the sound and the fury of Dotomburi.

Osaka-jo Castle
www.museum.or.jp/osakajo
✉ 1-1 Osaka-jo, Chuo-ku
☎ 06/6941-3044
🕘 9 a.m.–5 p.m.;
$ keep $$; grounds free
🚉 Osaka-jo-koen Station

amusement districts and youth fashion hangouts, expect to see building facades adorned with fantastic mechanical signs and doorways surrounded by gigantic fright masks. Ugly but fun, Osaka's appeal lies in its very brashness.

With a JR loop line running around the perimeter and a subway network crisscrossing the city, Osaka is easy to get around. **Kita-ku** (northern sector) encompasses Osaka Station, surrounded by a vast warren of every imaginable kind of restaurant above and below ground. This is the main business district. Its focus is **Umeda,** an area notable for its labyrinthine shopping mall and soaring modern architecture, especially the sleek **Umeda Sky Building,** a 40-story, twin-towered titan erected in 1993. Dominating the city skyline east of center, **Osaka-jo Castle** is an impressive concrete reproduction set on its massive original walls and girded by the city's largest park. **Minami-ku** (southern sector), a veritable city of covered arcades, is Osaka's most energetic and colorful district. In its northern part, **Shin-saibashi,** you'll find the youthful fashion followers' hangout of Amerika-mura (America village), along with the upscale boutiques of Yoroppa-mura (Europe village). Lying to the south with arcades spreading down to Namba is **Dotomburi,** Osaka's famous amusement district. A rainbow array of signs and lights and a cacophony of screaming sound advertise the area's theaters, bars and pachinko parlors—as well as more risqué entertainments. Also boasting myriad restaurants catering to all budgets, Dotomburi is not surprisingly Osaka's most popular hangout. ■

School children enjoy canon at Osaka-jo Castle.

Kobe

The Port Tower and Maritime Museum sketch some striking geometry against Kobe's night sky.

THE CITY OF KOBE SITS ON THE SOUTHERN SLOPE OF Mount Rokko-san, on the west of Osaka-wan Bay. It embraces the world's sixth largest port, which handles the largest volume of cargo in Japan. A trading post from ancient times, Kobe rose to prominence when the city opened its doors to foreign traders as one of Japan's first treaty ports. In so doing, it acquired a substantial foreign population and a degree of cosmopolitanism—both of which it retains today.

Along with a mosque, a synagogue, and Christian churches, a small handful of old Western buildings still stand in the northern district of **Kita-ku.** Having been almost totally destroyed during World War II, Kobe is a modern city. It overlooks the sea and is known as a pleasant place to live, but offers few attractions to visitors.

In January 1995, about 6,000 people died when Kobe suffered Japan's worst earthquake since 1923. Some of the most severe damage occurred on the coast. Following extensive repairs, Kobe is now so much back to normal that it is hard to see where the disaster ever took place.

The artificial **Port Island** offshore is a futuristic complex with a conference center, an exhibition hall, and vast hotels. The city center, **Sannomiya,** includes the main shopping arcades and the lively **Ikuta** amusement district just to the north. East is Flower Road, well known for its foreign bars and restaurants. With its long history of foreign influence, Kobe is a good place for international cuisine, including European, Indian, and Chinese. The best Chinese restaurants are south of Motomachi shopping arcade in Kobe's Chinatown, known locally as **Nankinmachi.** Another famous gastronomic legacy of bygone days is Kobe beef—although you may feel gored by its price. ■

Kobe

199 B3

Visitor information

Inside JR Sannomiya Station; another booth on 2nd floor of JR Shin-Kobe Station

078/322-0220

Himeji

HIMEJI, A MEDIUM-SIZE CITY 34 MILES (55 KM) WEST OF Kobe, was almost obliterated by bombs during World War II, so it is nothing short of miraculous that its magnificent castle still stands. Dubbed Hakuro-jo (White Egret Castle) for its whitened woodwork and plaster walls, Himeji-jo is considered Japan's most beautiful stronghold. It is easily accessible in less than an hour on the Shinkansen line from Kyoto, Osaka, or Kobe, making Himeji a high priority for Kansai visitors.

Built on the site of a 14th-century fortress by local warlords in 1581, **Himeji-jo Castle** was restored and upgraded during the 1600s by Ikeda Terumasa, son-in-law of the shogun Tokugawa Ieyasu. Its ownership passed through various noble samurai families until the Meiji Restoration in 1868. Standing on massive unmortared walls and comprising scores of *yagura* (arrow storehouses), watch-towers, and other buildings around its magnificent main **donjon,** the castle stands today as it was finished in 1618. Complete with slits in the walls for firing arrows and guns—as well as chutes for pouring

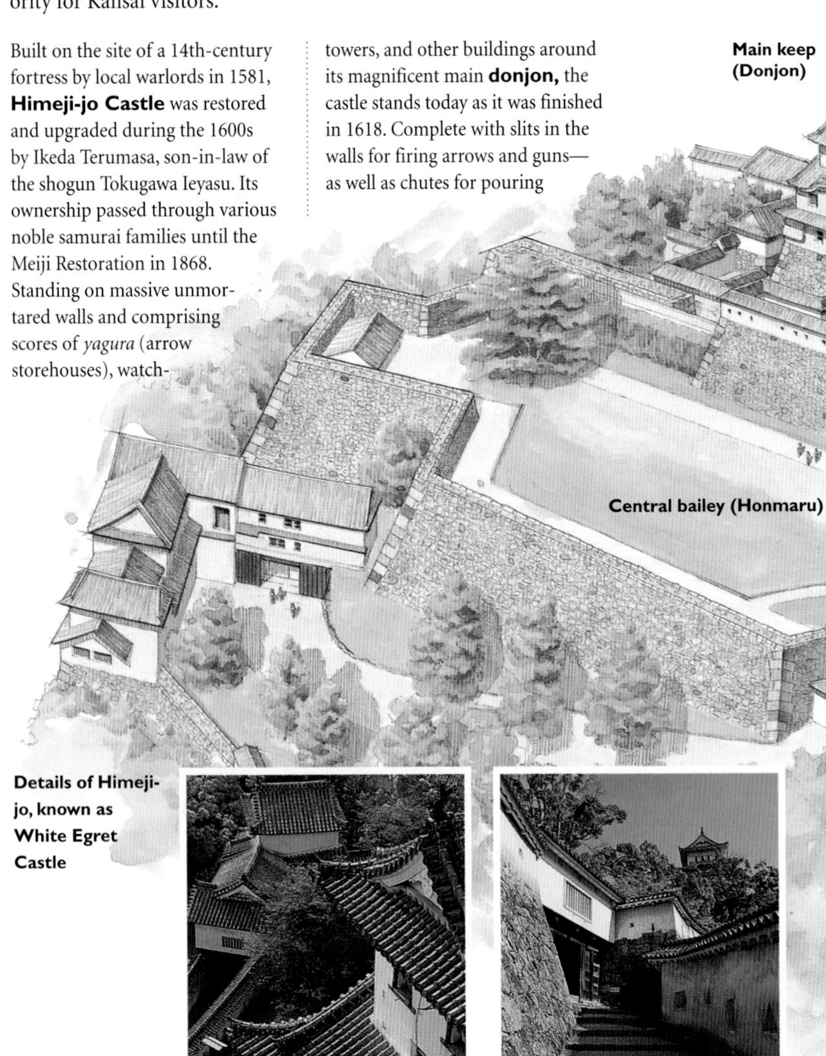

Details of Himeji-jo, known as White Egret Castle

boiling oil on invaders—this formidable fortification remains remarkably preserved because it was never attacked. Of the three moats, the outer one is now buried; it once separated the castle from the town. Parts of the central moat and all of the inner moat survive.

Between the castle buildings stretch many beautifully landscaped areas with lawns and flowering trees—a good example of the samurai way of melding an unyielding defensive structure with refined living spaces. The main donjon, while displaying the traditional five-story roof structure, actually conceals six stories—and a large cellar beneath. Perfectly echoing the balance between martial might and aesthetic sensibilities, the architectural delicacy of Himeji-jo almost belies its strategic impregnability. ■

Himeji

199 A3

Visitor information

Inside JR Himeji Station (left of central exit on north side)

0792/85-3792

Himeji-jo Castle

68 Hon-machi

0792/85-1146

9 a.m.–4 p.m. (last admission), closes at 5 p.m. in summer

$$

Rail: JR Himeji station, then 15-min. walk north

Shima-hanto

THIS SCENIC PENINSULA ON KANSAI'S EASTERN EDGE LIES within the boundaries of wooded Ise-Shima National Park. Shima-hanto's principal claim to fame is the Grand Shrine at Ise, Ise-jingu, the most sacred in all Shinto for some 1,700 years. Of the area's many resorts, the most popular is Toba, situated on a beautiful bay. The region makes a good outing from Nagoya in Central Honshu (Chubu) across the Ise-wan Bay. There is an excellent train service (JR Kintetsu line) that takes about 80 minutes.

Toba is noted for its aquarium and for **Mikimoto Pearl Island,** a museum complex that focuses on cultured pearls and features demonstrations by female pearl divers (a species saved from extinction by tourism) every half-hour. Six miles (10 km) west is Futamigaura, known for its **Husband-and-Wife Rocks (Meoto-iwa),** two curious outcrops standing in the sea. Connected by a sacred straw rope, they are symbolically wed each year during a Shinto festival on January 5.

With their many sights and recreation facilities, area resorts such as Toba and Futamiguara make a pleasant stopover for those visiting **Ise-jingu Grand Shrine,** the most ancient and holiest center of Shinto. Notoriously

Meoto-iwa (Husband-and-Wife Rocks), sacred to Shinto, are symbolically linked by a straw rope.

Water font at Ise-jingu, the shrine most sacred to Shinto

Ise

199 D2

Visitor information

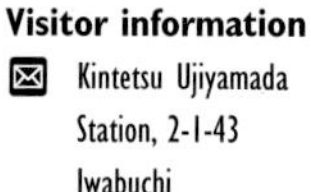

Kintetsu Ujiyamada Station, 2-1-43 Iwabuchi

0596/23-9655

Rail: Kintetsu Ise line from Nagoya (1 hr. 25 min.); Kintetsu Yamada line from Osaka or Kyoto (approx. 2 hrs.); JR from Nagoya to Ise-shi (2 hrs.)

Ise-jingu

www.isejingu.or.jp

1 Ujitachi-cho, Ise-shi

0596/24-1111

Dawn to dusk

10-min. walk from Ise-shi or Uji-Yamada Stations to Geku.

crowded, the resorts are best avoided altogether in summer.

Of Japan's thousands of Shinto shrines, Ise-jingu is paramount. The precinct comprises hundreds of subsidiary shrines consecrated to a host of deities, all set amid wooded hills and streams. The chief structures are the **Outer Shrine (Geku),** dedicated to Toyouke-Omikami (goddess of harvests, homes, and food), and the **Inner Shrine (Naiku),** dedicated to the sun goddess Amaterasu-Omikami (mythical ancestor of the emperor and the Japanese race). The two buildings stand 4 miles (6 km) apart, but they are connected by a bus that runs every 15 minutes. Made of fresh *hinoki* (cypress) wood from the Kiso mountains (see pp. 190–92), the main shrine buildings are ritually dismantled and identically reconstructed every 20 years; the process took place for the 61st time in 1993 at a cost of billions of yen.

The shrine buildings—simple, unadorned, and thatched—are architecturally akin to ancient granaries; the design features distinctive ornamental *chigi* (crossed beams protruding from the gabled ends of the roofs). The main, or inner, halls of both shrines, accessible only to high priests and the emperor, lie behind a series of enclosures fenced in various traditional styles. Although entry to the inner halls is forbidden, the structures are sufficiently visible from the outside to make a visit well worthwhile.

The outside of the main hall of the Geku is reached through three *torii* gateways and along a curving avenue through a cathedral of towering cryptomeria trees. After crossing the bridge over the Isuzu River, the approach to the Naiku is similar; almost palpably enhanced by the worship of countless millions over 1,600 years, the atmosphere is awe-inspiring. The inner sanctum of the main hall of the Naiku contains one of the great imperial treasures: the sacred bronze mirror said to have been presented to the first emperor by the sun goddess Amaterasu herself. Covered by layers of cloth placed over it repeatedly since the third century, the mirror has not been glimpsed by anyone—priests or emperors—since the day it was cast. ■

This region is divided into San-in—the northern area along the Sea of Japan—and San-yo, the more developed southern coastal region. Basking in a delightful climate, the area is also the gateway to the charming islands of the Inland Sea.

Western Honshu (Chugoku)

Introduction & map **262–63**
San-in 264–76
Hagi **265**
Hagi walk **266–67**
Tsuwano walk **268–69**
Matsue **272–74**
Izumo Taisha **274**
Daisen-Oki National Park **276**
San-yo 277–90
Okayama-ken **278–83**
Onomichi **284–85**
Hiroshima **286–87**
Miyajima **288–90**
Hotels & restaurants **375–77**

Giant wooden *torii* on the shore at Miyajima

Seto Ohashi bridge is one of the world's great feats of engineering.

Western Honshu (Chugoku)

CHUGOKU IS THE WESTERN PART of Honshu, between the island of Kyushu to the west and Hyogo-ken to the east. Coined in the distant past when only the area between Kyushu and Kanto came under any governmental administration, Chugoku literally means the "middle country." The northern coast of Chugoku is known as San-in, while the southern part—a good deal more densely populated and industrialized—is called San-yo.

The remoter **San-in** region, which covers Shimane and Tottori prefectures (the latter with miles of sand dunes) as well as northern Yamaguchi, boasts a unique combination of rural farmland, rugged coasts, and historical towns—an increasingly popular alternative for those seeking the pleasures of an older, quieter Japan.

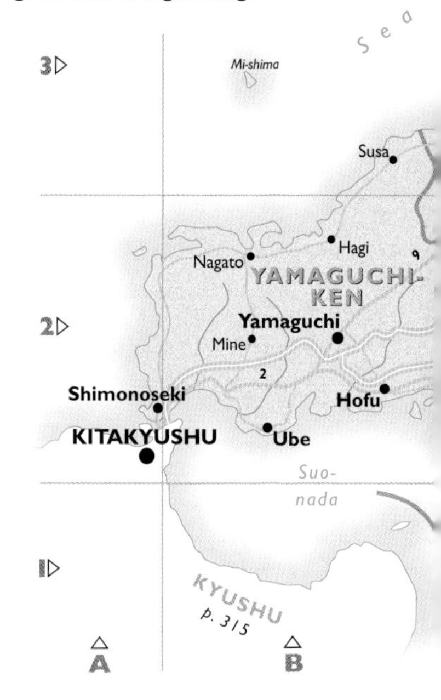

Following the paths of the great trunk roads of feudal times, the main highways and Shinkansen railroad lines from Tokyo to the island of Kyushu run through **San-yo.** This region includes the gateways to Shikoku and the islands of the Inland Sea, reached both by

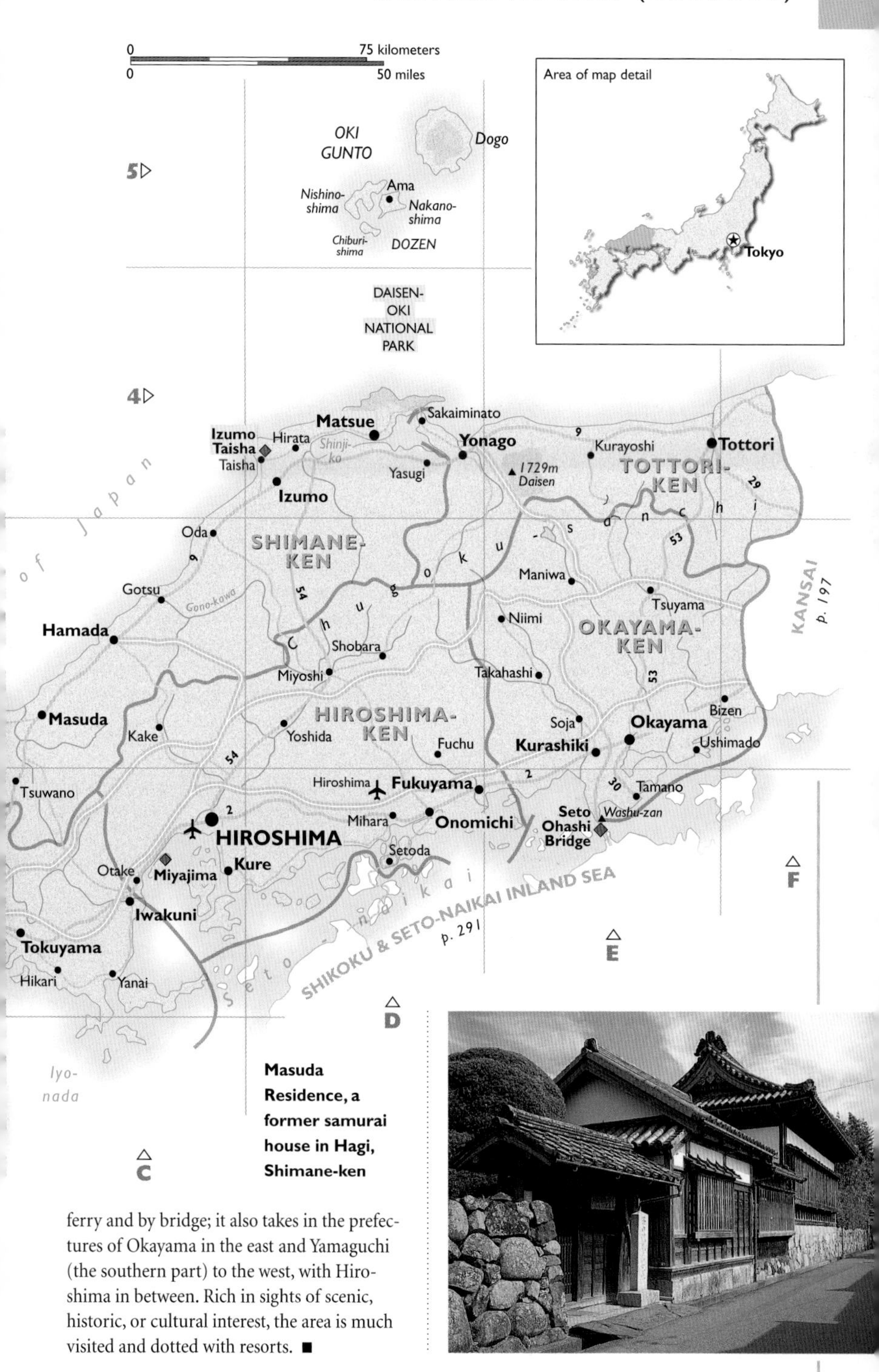

Masuda Residence, a former samurai house in Hagi, Shimane-ken

ferry and by bridge; it also takes in the prefectures of Okayama in the east and Yamaguchi (the southern part) to the west, with Hiroshima in between. Rich in sights of scenic, historic, or cultural interest, the area is much visited and dotted with resorts. ■

San-in

Despite being one of the most attractive regions in the country, the San-in coast of northern Chugoku is often omitted from travelers' itineraries. The oversight is probably due to its location on the shores of the Japan Sea, so notorious for snowy winters and abundant rainfall that people seem to forget it has a summer. Consequently, the San-in coast remains comparatively rural—and little spoiled by development.

The region has justifiably earned an off-the-beaten-track reputation. The main San-in railroad meanders along a coast largely devoted to fishing and farming, where life is more leisurely than in most of Japan. But San-in has more than excellent seascapes and mountain scenery to recommend it. The old coastal town of Hagi preserves picturesque reminders of its feudal past, as does inland Tsuwano. Matsue, adopted home of 19th-century Greek writer Lafcadio Hearn (see p. 272-74), retains a fine castle. Nearby Izumo is famed for Izumo Taisha, the second most sacred Shinto shrine in the country after Ise. Shimane-ken embraces the Oki-shoto Islands with placid scenic resorts and a rich local history. Though San-in is quieter than most places in Japan, don't let that lull you into forgetting to reserve accommodations ahead. ■

Yoshida Shoin

In 1854, Commodore Perry's visit convinced the young samurai scholar Yoshida Shoin (1830–1859) that Japan must modernize to resist colonialism. The archaic feudal government had to be overthrown and imperial power restored. Such ideas gained Shoin a following with other Choshu clansmen, among them Ito Hirobumi, who became Japan's first prime minister in 1885. The seminal architect of the 1868 Meiji Restoration, Yoshida never lived to see it; he was executed for inciting rebellion in 1859. Shoin-jinja Shrine, dedicated to him, is in eastern Hagi. ■

Samurai quarter buildings in Tsuwano

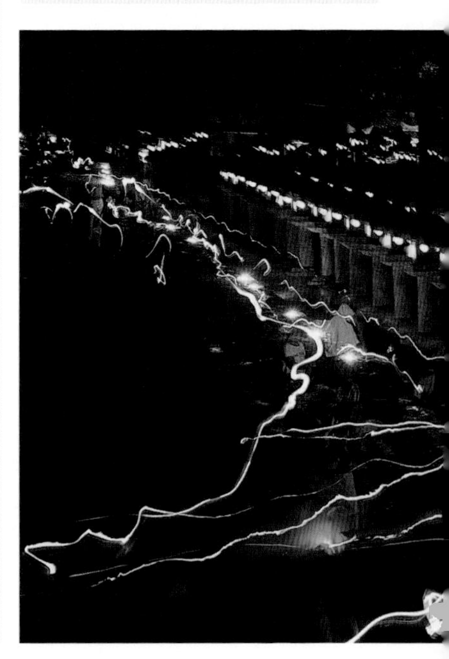

Hagi

HAGI, WITH ITS BEAUTIFULLY PRESERVED SAMURAI QUARTER, evocative castle ruins, pottery kilns, beaches, and attractive seascapes, is often regarded as the gem of the San-in coast. The town earned a spot on the map as the domain of the Choshu clan leader Mori Terumoto, who built a castle there in 1604. While Japan remained sealed to the outside world for the next 250 years, slumbering Hagi produced the Choshu clansmen most instrumental in overthrowing the old samurai regime and bringing about the Meiji Restoration of 1868. Hagi-jo Castle was destroyed by anti-feudal zealots in 1874, after which the town promptly fell back to sleep.

Hagi has long had a reputation for pottery, particularly tea ceremony vessels. The ware typically displays a deceptively rough-hewn quality. About a hundred kilns are open in the vicinity.

The main sights congregate in the west, on the delta of the Hashimoto-gawa River. The town is small enough to negotiate on foot, but there is a lot to see and a bicycle is invaluable; you can rent one at Higashi-Hagi Station as well as in hotels. Arm yourself with the excellent English-language booklet from the visitor information center, then go exploring.

On the eastern confines is the 1691 **Toko-ji Temple.** Built as a Mori family memorial temple, this is the graveyard of the first and odd-numbered members of the Mori clan; it is the counterpart to **Daisho-in,** in the southwest, which commemorates the even-numbered Mori. At the back of the Toko-ji precinct is an avenue flanked by stone lanterns. ■

Hagi
262 B2
Visitor information
Higashi-Hagi Station
0838/25-3145
Train: JR San-in line from Matsue (4 hrs.)

Toko-ji Temple
1647 Chinto
0838/26-9116
8:30 a.m.–5 p.m.
$

Daisho-in
4132 Tsubaki Oumi
0838/22-2124
8:00 a.m.–5 p.m. Apr.–Nov.; closes at 4:30 p.m. Dec.–Mar.
$

Stone lanterns light the grounds of Daisho-in l.

A hike through Hagi

If you stroll at a leisurely pace, it takes most of a day to cover all the sights mentioned in this walk. If you omit Teramachi or rent a bicycle, the time can be cut to three hours.

Start in **Jokamachi.** If you are pressed for time, take a cab from either Higashi-Hagi or Hagi Stations to **Edoya Yokocho,** the local name for the street containing the main sights. Of several houses preserved in the area, **Kikuya House (Kikuya-ke Jutaku)** ❶ is the most elaborate (*1-1 Gofuku-machi, tel 0838/25-8282, 9 a.m.–5 p.m., $$*). Representative of a wealthy Edo-period merchant's home, it was built in the mid-17th century and retains many original fixtures and furnishings. A museum in a converted *kura* (storehouse) features samurai memorabilia and antique dolls. Nearby is the **Ishii Tea Bowl Museum (Ishii Chawan Bijutsukan),** with fine displays of antique Hagi pottery.

After visiting the museum, head northwest toward Horiuchi, the inner moat district, around Hagi's former castle. On the way you will come to the old **Kuchiba House (Kuchiba-ke Jutaku)** ❷. Although the house is closed to the public, the gate in front of it, the largest in Hagi, is listed as an important National Cultural Property. A few minutes northwest is the **Mori clan tenant house (Kyu-Asa Mori-ke** ❸ *Horiuchi Shizuki-Koen, tel 0838/25-2304, 8 a.m.–6:30 p.m. Apr.–Aug., 8:30 a.m.–4:30 p.m. Nov.–Feb., 8:30 a.m.–6 p.m. Mar., $ with Hagi-jo Castle ruins),* the largest of the samurai houses open to the public. Containing rather dusty memorabilia, it gives an impression of austerity. Like

Now standing in a park, the ruins of Hagi-jo Ato Castle extend down to the shoreline.

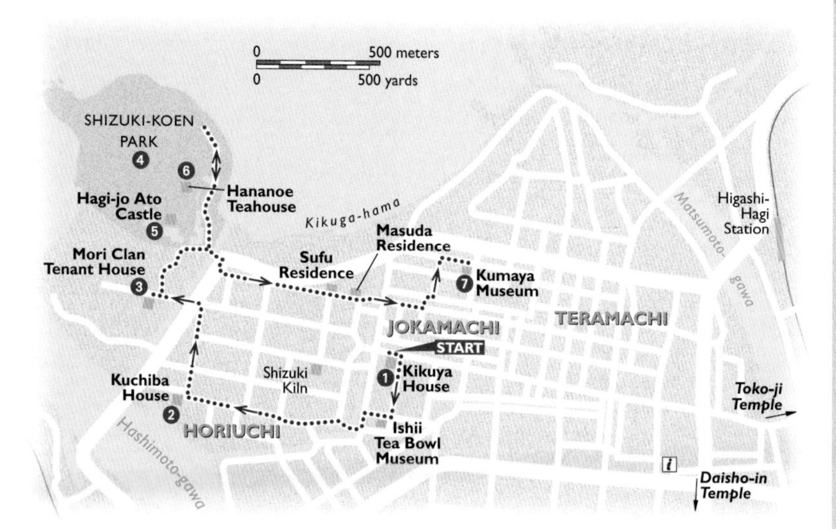

most samurai in 1868, the Mori, who were instrumental in bringing down the shogunate, were anything but rich. From here, walk about 220 yards (200 m) north to reach **Shizuki-koen Park** ❹, a spacious bit of greenery extending down to the beach and the **Ruins of Hagi-jo Castle** ❺ *(Horiuchi Shizuki-koen-nai, tel 0838/25-1826, 8 a.m.–6:30 p.m. Mar.–Oct., 8:30 a.m.–4:30 p.m. Nov.–Feb., $ with Mori House).* The castle ruins are a lovely place to wander, at the very least for the views over the sea. More than just moats, ramparts, and scattered foundation stones, these ruins include sections of collapsing outer walls and wooded areas where roof tiles litter the undergrowth. Just northwest of the ruins is the **Hananoe teahouse (Hananoe Chatei)** ❻, where you can sip green tea in a charming traditional garden. Check out the Hagi-jo Kiln on the way out of the castle's main gate.

It's a pleasant walk east around the promontory toward **Kikuga-hama Beach.** Just south of it, along the ocher-colored mud walls of the Horiuchi district, is the Mori Outer Gate and, to its east, an old **Sufu residence** featuring beautiful latticed windows. The **Masuda residence** 220 yards (200 m) eastward along the same street is not open to the public, but you can still admire it. From here walk about 440 yards (400 m) northeast to the **Kumaya Museum (Kumaya Bijutsukan)** ❼ *(47 Imauo-no-Tana-machi, tel 0838/22-7547, 9 a.m.–5 p.m., closed Mon.),* an impressive collection of Hagi memorabilia, including pottery, scrolls, and painted screens, exhibited in a converted 18th-century kura. You are now in the **Teramachi** district, home to about 20 temples. Although of relatively minor interest, some are charming enough to make this a rewarding ramble if time permits. Stretching east from the north of Shizuki-koen, Kikuga-hama Beach is scenic and pristine; cap your walk with a swim in summer. Head back toward Horiuchi; just south of it is the **Hagi Uragami Museum (Kenritsu-Hagi Bijutsukan,** *586-1 Hiyako Hagi, Yamaguchi, tel 0838/24-2400, 9 a.m.–5 p.m., closed Mon.),* which harbors an outstanding collection of *ukiyo-e* prints and historic Chinese, Korean, and local ceramics. ■

See area map pp. 262–63
Jokamachi
2.3 miles (3.6 km)
3 hours
Teramachi district

NOT TO BE MISSED

- Shizuki-koen Park
- Ruins of Hagi-jo Ato Castle
- Hananoe teahouse
- Kumaya Museum

Tsuwano walk

Tsuwano is a pleasant little town with several historical and many charming sights. Try to avoid visiting during weekends, when Tsuwano fills with visitors.

As you exit the station, the visitor information office is to your right. Pick up their excellent bilingual booklet, which exhaustively describes and maps the town. If you like,you can rent a bicycle from Kamai Shoten in front of the station.

Proceed to the intersection and turn right; walk about one third of a mile (500 m) and turn right again into a narrower road that takes you across the railroad track. Take the next right turn and walk about 200 yards (200 m), then take the left fork, which leads to **Maria Seido** ❶. This charming wooden Catholic church, set in a sylvan glade, was built in 1951 to commemorate 36 Christian martyrs who died in Tsuwano between 1868 and 1872. It stands on a site along the Otome-Toge Pass. Every May 3 during the Otome-Toge festival, a procession starting from the main Catholic church in town winds toward Maria Seido along the Jujika-no-Michi (Road of the Cross), a tree-lined path. Take this path from the southwestern side of the church, following it through the woods.

Turn left into the road as you reach it, then follow it to the next intersection. Turn right into the road leading to a small but stately temple, **Kakuozan Yomei-ji Temple** ❷ *(Ushiroda, tel 08567/2-0137)*. Built in 1420 as a contemplative retreat, it boasts fine painted interior screen doors and an attractive garden. Go right when you leave the temple compound, following the road downhill before turning right into the main road. Follow the road about half a mile (700 m) and turn sharp right into a secondary road until you see the path leading up the mountain in front of you.

From here it's a winding trek up a concrete stairway to the summit, through a tunnel formed by well over a thousand bright red *torii* gateways. At the top is **Taikodani Inari-jinja Shrine** ❸ *(Tel 08567/2-0219, 8 a.m.–4:30 p.m.)*; established in 1773, it is one of the most important shrines devoted to Inari, the deity of commerce. From the south side of the shrine, a path leads to the chairlift for the **Ruins of Tsuwano-jo Castle** ❹; following a beautifully scenic four-minute ride, this conveyance stops at a point about ten minutes' walk from the castle ruins, which in turn command a breathtaking view over the town and toward Mount Aono-san. Take the chairlift down again and rejoin a narrow road leading to a slightly wider secondary road, where you turn right. Just over 200 yards (270 m) on, turn left and then sharp left again; cross the bridge and on your right you should see the **Mori House and Memorial Museum (Mori Ogai Kyutaku)** ❺ *(Machida, tel 08567/2-3210, 9 a.m.–5 p.m. closed Mon., museum $$, residence grounds $)*. Mori was a fascinating man: A military doctor who traveled throughout Europe, he became a pioneer of realism in Japanese literature.

Maria Seido chapel, a landmark of Japanese Catholicism, is dedicated to 36 Christians martyred around 1870.

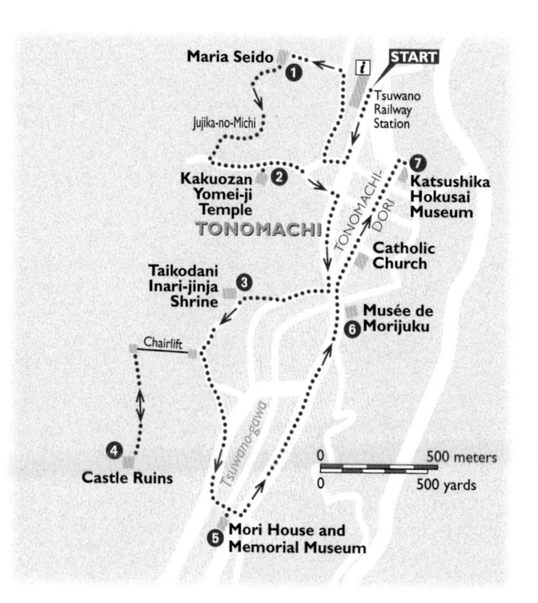

See area map page 224
Station
4 miles (6.5 km)
4 hours
Hokusai Museum

NOT TO BE MISSED

- Maria Seido chapel
- Kakuozan Yomei-ji Temple
- Taikodani Inari-jinja Shrine
- Ruins of Tsuwano-jo Castle
- Mori House and Memorial Museum

Leaving here, turn right onto Tonomachi-dori, the long street that goes through the center of town. Tsuwano's main drag, it includes Tonomachi, an avenue flanked by houses from the feudal period; their white plaster walls are characteristically patterned with panels of dark gray cross-hatching. Channels of clear water containing thousands of variegated carp run beside Tonomachi's streets—a sight particularly lovely when the irises bloom in June.

Some of the houses here are open as museums, notably the **Musée de Morijuku (Morijuku Bijutsukan)** 6 *(Mori, tel 08567/2-3200, 9 a.m.–5 p.m., $$)*, which was once a wealthy farmer's house. Endowed with a fine garden, it now exhibits the works of local contemporary artists; ask to see the camera obscura, a view of the garden projected on a wall through a pinhole aperture.

Straddling the path all the way up to Taikodani Inari-jinja Shrine, one thousand *torii* gateways form a bright red tunnel.

Just over the bridge is the Catholic Church, a delightful building dating from 1931 that reproduces Nagasaki's Oura church in candy-color pastels, with its floor covered in tatami matting. From here the avenue narrows to become Tsuwano's main street, where you will find several interesting shops selling locally made *washi* paper and *genji-maki*—a cake featuring a layer of sponge around a filling of sweet bean jam.

Keep an eye peeled for the sake brewers (look for bottles in the windows or a ball of twigs above the lintel), where you get to taste the brews for free. Finally, stroll through the **Katsushika Hokusai Museum** 7 *(Ushiroda, tel 08567/2-1850, 9:30 a.m.–5 p.m., $$)*; it harbors an extensive private collection devoted to Hokusai (1760–1849), Japan's most famous *ukiyo-e* woodblock print artist. ■

Obake—ghosts & demons

If you travel in Japan in the middle of summer, you will probably find television and theaters airing an annual crop of horror movies, Kabuki programs featuring ghost plays, and haunted rides drawing large crowds in amusement parks. Children will be glued to the comical animated adventures of Ge-Ge-Ge-no-Kitaro, the little boy who battles against ghosts and demons. The Japanese say the perfect antidote to the sultry heat is a nice cool shiver of fear, but the traditions surrounding summertime spirits go back some 1,500 years.

Comprising several species of goblin and demon, as well as the spirits of humans, animals, and even trees or umbrellas, Japan's army of demons is probably second to none in the world. These things are called *bakemono* (*obake* for short), meaning monsters or changelings. Western ghost stories are mainly for wintertime; in Japan they walk abroad mainly during O-bon, a month-long Buddhist festival for the dead starting mid-July—a highlight of the summer holidays. Like the Christian All Saints festival, O-bon is a time for remembrance. Families visit the graves of relatives and pray for them before home altars. During O-bon, the spirits of the dead return for a month-long visit. The celebrations (dancing, feasting, fireworks) are for welcoming them home, but some of the evil dead are said to jump aboard the bandwagon.

Many kinds of bakemono are unrelated to O-bon. The Setsubun festival (Feb. 3 or 4) is for driving out *oni*—horned ogres with an appetite for human flesh. The little clay figurines of froglike imps often seen in gift shops represent *kappa*. Said to inhabit lonely streams and rivers, the cute-looking kappa were nonetheless feared for sucking out the entrails of those venturing into the water—an appetite long emphasized to deter children from dangerous water play.

The winged *tengu*, inhabiting alpine forests, is a demon sometimes depicted with a stubby beak but more usually with a fierce scarlet face and an outsize nose. Originating in ancient masked drama, tengu masks often adorn the walls of Japanese-style bars and restaurants. The kindness of the tengu depends mainly upon the moral character of the beholder. Popular myth has it that the great 12th-century military hero Minamoto Yoshitsune was taught the art of swordsmanship as a child by a wise old tengu he encountered in a forest.

Animal spirits, especially foxes, figure prominently in Japanese folk beliefs. Myths about foxes are of Chinese origin, but they were adopted by the Shinto belief system and adapted. Represented as a statue around shrines dedicated to Inari, god of gain and grain, the fox is believed to be the deity's messenger or familiar. Not always benign, its supposed ability to assume human form inspired many a ghostly tale; in former times the insane were often presumed to be possessed by fox spirits. A mammal unique to Japan, the *tanuki* or raccoon dog is similarly believed to be able to change its shape. Ceramic figures of corpulent tanuki with outsize testicles, often placed in the windows of drinking haunts and sake merchants, are considered lucky.

The appearance of *Kitsune-bi* (fox fire), incandescent marsh gas or will-o-the-wisp in the countryside, is said to augur hauntings by *yurei*—ghosts. As in the West, the ghosts are thought to be transparent, but they drift away into nothing below the waist. Yurei, earthbound spirits regarded as having unfinished business (usually revenge for the wrongdoings that took their lives), were greatly feared.

Tales of ghosts and demons formed the main themes of Noh plays; the tales were compiled in storybooks and celebrated in woodblock prints by, among others, Katsushika Hokusai (1760–1849). Some are well known, as recounted by the 18th-century author Ueda Akinari, but probably the greatest writer of the genre was Lafcadio Hearn (1850–1904), still revered in Japan by his adoptive name of Koizumi Yakumo (see pp. 272–74). He retold the old tales—some hitherto handed down orally—in books such as *Kwaidan*, which have become their definitive form. Many Japanese ghost stories are as chilling as any in the West—eat your heart out, Edgar Allan Poe! ■

Demon slayers figure prominently in Japanese folktales and ghost stories. In this woodblock print by Yoshitoshi—who began to specialize in ghost pictures during the 1890s—the hero Tametomo drives away the smallpox demon.

Matsue-jo is the only authentic samurai castle on the west coast.

Matsue

Matsue

263 D4

Visitor information

Outside JR Matsue Station (in front)

0852/21-4034

Matsue-jo Castle

1-5 Tono-machi

0852/21-4030

8:30 a.m.–6:30 p.m. April–Sept.; closes earlier rest of year

$$; foreigners $

Bus: Matsue Station to Kencho-mae

SITUATED ON THE EASTERN SHORE OF LAKE SHINJI-KO, JUST inland from the coast, Matsue at first seems like another nondescript Japanese city, but its proximity to water blesses it with a number of canals and waterways. And as in many destinations in Japan, bland modern facades hide much of historical and cultural interest, especially in the north of town. You can take in the castle and samurai district in an afternoon; if you want to see other sights in the vicinity, you will need an overnight stop.

Matsue-jo Castle, completed 1611, was built by the lords of the Horio clan. The five-story main keep, which conceals a sixth floor inside, underwent renovations some 30 years later. Matsue-jo changed hands through several feudal families until it was taken from the Matsudaira family during the Meiji Restoration. Spared the destruction wrought on most feudal edifices, the keep and several buildings from the 17th century remain intact, distinguishing Matsue-jo as the only original castle standing in western Japan. Lafcadio Hearn (see p. 274) described it as brooding over the city and "fantastically

House in Matsue's Shiomi-nawate samurai quarter

grim." It no longer quite dominates the skyline as it once did, but this is a fine castle and certainly dark and grim-looking—if only because of the black wood on the facade. Inside is a collection of armor and samurai memorabilia. Just below the castle is the cultural center, **Matsue Kyodokan,** a lovely, pale gray, Western-style wooden building; the town hall in Meiji times, it now houses an excellent museum of local history.

From the castle grounds it is a delightful walk north down a wooded hill to reach the old district of **Shiomi-nawate,** a row of samurai residences beneath the castle along the north side of the moat. Among them are the Meimei-an teahouse and garden, and the **Buke-yashiki** samurai residence.

Along the way, stop at the **Jozan Inari-jinja Shrine,** an enchanting and spooky little shrine devoted to the fox deity. Hundreds of small, moss-covered, often crumbling stone fox effigies litter the precinct. The shrine was one of Hearn's favorites; he liked to stop off here each day on his way to teach at Matsue Middle School.

The **Lafcadio Hearn Residence (Koizumi Yakumo Kyukyo)** is in Shiomi-nawate. You will be handed a pamphlet at the entrance with a passage about the garden that Hearn so loved. He described it in *Glimpses of Unfamiliar Japan,* which he wrote here in 1891. It was here as well that Hearn penned his famous compilation of ghost stories, *Kwaidan* (see p. 270). The garden is somewhat threadbare, ready now for restoration rather than reverent preservation. Although you are left wondering if it ever had a kitchen or a bathroom, the rest of this small, charming house is intact. By all accounts, the Hearn/Koizumis were happy here, even though they occupied the house a scant seven months.

More poignant still is the adjacent **Lafcadio Hearn Memorial Museum (Koizumi Yakumo**

Matsue Kyodokan
- ✉ 1-59 Tono-machi
- ☎ 0852/22-3958
- 🕒 8:30 a.m.–5 p.m.
- 🚌 Bus: Matsue Station to Kencho-mae

Buke-yashiki residence
- ✉ 305 Kitahori-cho
- ☎ 0852/22-2243
- 🕒 8:30 a.m.–6:30 p.m. April–Sept.; closes at 5 p.m. rest of year
- $ $

Lafcadio Hearn Residence
- ✉ 315 Kitahori-cho
- ☎ 0852/23-0714
- 🕒 9 a.m.–4:30 p.m.
- $ $

Lafcadio Hearn's residence

Lafcadio Hearn Memorial Museum

- 322 Okudani-machi
- 0852/21-2147
- 8:30 a.m.–6:30 p.m.
- $
- Bus: From JR Matsue Station

Yakumotatsu Fudoki-no-Oka Museum

- 456 Obacho
- 0852/23-2485
- 9 a.m.–5 p.m.; closed Tues.
- $
- Bus: From Matsue

Kanden-an teahouse

- 106 Sugata-cho
- 0852/21-4288
- 10 a.m.–4 p.m.
- $$
- Bus: From JR Matsue Station

Kinenkan). On exhibit is Hearn's desk, specially made with disproportionately long legs—his only eye was so shortsighted that he had to work inches from the paper. Here too are his Japanese pipes, the suitcases he carried to Japan from America, and the phrases painted on sheets of newspaper with which he taught his children English.

Farther up in the northeast of the city is the 18th-century **Kanden-an teahouse,** set in a beautiful garden renowned for the inspired graphic effect of its stones and raked sand.

Matsue was part of the region of Izumo, which is regarded as a cradle of Japanese civilization. Six miles (10 km) south of the city is **Fudoki-no-Oka,** where archaeologists have unearthed objects dated from the first century A.D. A museum displays jewels, swords, and pottery from the many grave tumuli in the area. In the vicinity are two very old Shinto shrines; **Kamosu-jinja** with its 17th-century buildings and **Yaegaki-jinja,** whose treasure house exhibits a rare tenth-century fragment of a shrine mural depicting a beautiful mythical princess. ■

Lafcadio Hearn (1850–1904)

Lafcadio Hearn, the son of a Greek mother and an Irish father, left Greece at age six after his parents divorced. Following a lonely childhood with an aunt in England, he emigrated to the U.S. at 19, where he became a successful journalist. Posted to Japan in 1890 as a correspondent for *Harper's,* he remained there. He married Koizumi Setsu, a woman of samurai descent, and became a Japanese citizen, adopting the name Koizumi Yakumo. His compelling and charming period pieces express his enchantment with Japan. He later wrote the more penetrating *Japan—An Attempt at Interpretation,* but is best remembered for his masterly retellings of Japanese ghost stories and folktales. The frail, partially sighted Hearn died at 54 and was buried in Tokyo's Zoshigaya cemetery. Few foreigners have ever been more beloved in Japan, where Koizumi Yakumo is still revered as only a true Japanese writer could be. ■

Izumo Taisha

ABOUT FOUR MILES (6.5 KM) NORTHWEST OF IZUMO IS Taisha, site of the oldest of all Shinto shrines, Izumo Taisha Grand Shrine. Izumo figures prominently as the backdrop for Shinto creation myths laid down in the *Kojiki* and *Nihon Shoki*—chronicles of history and myth compiled in the late seventh century. One myth concerns the god Okuninushi, a son of Amaterasu, the sun goddess; he is said to have had a palace built for his retirement at Taisha, and this later became Izumo Taisha, the second most sacred Shinto shrine after Ise (see p. 259–60). The origin of Ise is thought to go back some 1,700 years; Izumo Taisha predates even that.

All Shinto shrines deter evil spirits with straw ropes festooned with paper. The one at Izumo Taisha is a colossus commensurate with the shrine's importance.

Rebuilt at intervals—though not on the regular 20-year intervals of Ise—the main shrine buildings at Izumo Taisha are quite recent, dating mainly from 1874. The precinct, surrounded by hills, is pleasantly wooded. It incorporates two long rectangular halls called *juku-sha,* which are specially provided to accommodate all eight million Shinto gods believed to visit annually in October. Legend has it that the Shinto gods take a vacation at that time; the deities pack their bags and head for Izumo, where the month of October is called Kami ari Zuki (the month when the gods are there). October in the rest of Japan , by contrast, is known as Kannazuki (the month without gods). The precinct has a **treasure house** containing historical and religious artifacts connected to the shrine.

Many worshipers come to Izumo Taisha to pray for success in marriage, this being one of the god Okuninushi's spheres of interest (along with medicine, fishing, and silkworm culture). The Izumo Grand Shrine can be comfortably visited on a day trip from Matsue. ■

Izumo Taisha Shrine

- Map: 263 D4
- Phone: 0853/53-3100
- Hours: 6 a.m.–8 p.m.
- Price: Treasure house: $
- Transport: Train & bus: from JR Matsue Station to JR Izumoshi Station, then bus to Izumo Taisha

Daisen-Oki National Park

INVOLVING SOME FOUR HOURS' TRAVEL FROM MATSUE (including the ferry crossing), the Oki-shoto Islands (Daisen-Oki National Park) are sufficiently remote to warrant the description "unspoiled." However, it may not be long before this trove of beaches, scenic coves, and fishing villages moves right onto the beaten track for summer vacations, since air service to Oki island is available.

This group of volcanic islands consists of the larger Dogo island to the east and the westward Dozen Archipelago, with its three main islands and many more islets.

Like Sado off the northwest coast of Honshu, the islands were once used as places of exile, notably for Emperor Godaigo, banished there by the shogun Ashikaga Takauji in the 14th century (see p. 33). Consequently they are rich in history as well as scenery, with several notable temples and shrines—especially on Dogo island and Ama in the Dozen group. The people of Dogo island raise cattle; in a form of bullfighting popular here, two bulls lock horns to push each other, sumo fashion, out of a ring. The Oki-shoto Islands hold many delights for the traveler who has plenty of time to explore. Inter-island ferries abound, and most local accommodations are comfortable.

If you are planning a trip to the Daisen-Oki area, arrange your itinerary with the visitor information center in Matsue. During the high season, make sure you reserve accommodations ahead. ■

Oki island coastlines tend to be delightfully unspoiled—though not always in high summer.

Oyster beds under a sunset on the San-yo coast

San-yo

The San-yo coast lies on the Seto-nakai Inland Sea; it enjoys mild winters and summers that are less humid than in most of Japan, giving it a reputation as the Far Eastern equivalent of the Mediterranean. The comparison is underscored in some places by the introduction of olive trees as a complement to peach trees, orange trees, and rice; inland the region is predominantly agricultural. Its much-touted "blue waters" are a more recent asset: Until the mid-1970s the densely populated coast suffered from over-industrialization, with severe damage to the marine ecology from chemical pollution. Since then, concerted efforts to clean up the environment have largely restored fish stocks to previous levels and improved the water quality along the beaches.

Japanese vacationers flock to resorts on islands just offshore, but beaches are not really the region's major attractions. Okayama-ken, comparatively little spoiled inland, has some beautiful scenery, while its capital, Okayama, is distinguished by one of Japan's greatest gardens, the Koraku-en. The nearby town of Kurashiki has a delightful old quarter along a canal and is a significant center for the arts.

Highly industrialized Hiroshima-ken is most visited for Hiroshima city, forever associated with the atomic bombing in 1945. But the millions of visitors to Hiroshima's commemorative Peace Memorial Park and museum often bypass the prefecture's other sights.

Just offshore and traditionally hailed as one of Japan's most scenic spots is the island of Miyajima, with the seaside shrine of Itsukushima-jinja, famed for its huge red *torii* emerging from the sea. The picturesque fishing town of Tomo-no-Ura and, above all, the temple town of Onomichiare also worth a look.

Ferry ports in Hiroshima-ken and Okayama-ken serve the islands of Seto-naikai and Shikoku, though Shikoku is now reachable via the gigantic bridges of Naruto-Ohashi (from Hyogo-ken via Awaji-shima Island) and Seto-Ohashi, south of Okayama as well as the Shimanami-Kaido bridge system south of Onomichi. ■

Borrowing nearby Okayama-jo Castle as scenery, Okayama's Koraku-en is one of Japan's most beautiful gardens.

Okayama-ken

OKAYAMA-KEN CAN BE DIVIDED INTO THE REGIONS OF northern and southern Bichu to the west, Mimasaka to the northeast, and Bizen in the southeast; Bizen includes Okayama city. Though the coastal areas sometimes suffer from urban-industrial saturation, the prefecture is rich in scenery, history, crafts, and marine assets—there is more to Okayama-ken than just the great garden and the museums of Okayama city and the townscape and art of Kurashiki. Blessed with a mild, Mediterranean-style climate, the region is important agriculturally, known for peaches and muscat grapes; the town of Ushimado has the largest olive groves in the Far East.

Takahashi

263 E3

Visitor information

Outside JR Takahashi Station

0866/22-8666

Train: Hakubi line from JR Okayama Station (1 hr.)

During the past two decades, local authorities have been concentrating increasingly on tourism, and thus undertaking conservation and restoration programs. In northern Bichu, near **Takahashi** city, you can see the fine 17th-century **Bichu Matsuyama-jo Castle,** preserved samurai houses in **Ishibiya Furusato village,** and **Raikyu-ji Temple,** noted for its landscape garden with raked sand offsetting stones and azalea bushes shaped to look like waves. In north-

ern Bichu's scenic hills is the village of **Fukiya,** which preserves merchant houses from the Edo period, when the local economy thrived on copper mining.

Although its castle is now gone, **Tsuyama** city in Mimasaka has interesting vestiges of feudal days: a samurai quarter, the Shuraku-en Garden, and the mid-19th century Tsuyama Archive, one of Japan's first centers of Western learning. Nearby there is also **Tanjo-ji Temple,** an Important Cultural Property erected at the birthplace of Honen, founder of the Jodo sect of Buddhism. Tsuyama is known for its *onsen,* but there are several more in **Maniwa,** where the pastoral scenery, complete with grazing cows, could almost be mistaken for Switzerland. In the nearby **Shoei region** is the eighth-century **Chofuku-ji Temple,** which is noted for a lovely pagoda standing in bold vermilion against a background of green hills.

Southern Bichu is best known for **Kurashiki** (see pp. 282–83), but it also has some pleasant resorts offshore, notably on the islands of Mukuchi, Shiraishi, and Manabe. The area includes **Tamashima** and its Kibi-ji Temple, renowned for its unusual Chinese garden. Looking out over the islands of Seto-naikai Inland Sea, the panorama from **Mount Washu-zan** was legendary—until the completion of the colossal 7.5-mile-long (12.3 km) **Seto Ohashi Bridge** connecting Honshu to Shikoku in 1988. If its six sections now dwarf the islands they span, the bridge is an amazing feat of engineering and a sight in its own right. Enthusiasts

Fukiya
Visitor information
☎ 0866/42-3211

Bizen city
263 F3
Visitor information
JR Imbe Station
☎ 0869/64-1100
Train: JR Ako line from Okayama to Inbe Station (40 min.)

Bichu Matsuyama-jo Castle
✉ 1 Uchiyamashita
☎ 0866/22-1487
🕘 9 a.m.–5:30 p.m. Apr.–Sep.; closes at 4:30 p.m. Oct.–Mar.
$ $

Raikyu-ji
✉ Raikyu-ji-cho
☎ 0866/22-3516
🕘 9 a.m.–5 p.m.
$ $

Tanjo-ji Temple
☎ 0867/28-2102
🕘 9 a.m.–4 p.m.
$ $

Bizen Pottery

One of the "big six" ceramic centers from medieval times, Bizen gained a reputation for unglazed stoneware prized for both looks and durability. The popularity of Bizen ware grew during the 15th century, when its rough-hewn quality was sought out by tea masters. The high iron content of the clay gives Bizen ware its typically deep red to dark brown color; it is sometimes used to make roof tiles. Varied firing techniques alter the color and produce a variety of subtle effects. The potteries of Bizen are in Imbe district. The streets around the train station abound with workshops; you can learn before buying at Bizen Ceramic Crafts Museum in Imbe Station. ■

Okayama city
262 E3
Visitor information
JR Okayama Station
086/222-2912
Train: from Tokyo San-yo Shinkansen (3 hrs. 15 min.)

Koraku-en Garden
1-5 Koraku-en
086/272-1148
7:30 a.m.–6 p.m. Apr.–Sep.; 8 a.m–5 p.m. Oct.–Mar.
$

Okayama-jo Castle
2-3-1 Marunouchi
086/225-2096
9 a.m–5 p.m.
$$

The pagoda at Chofuku-ji Temple

can get better acquainted with it at the **Seto Ohashi Memorial Bridge Museum,** or take a boat cruise around it from Kojima.

Encompassing Okayama city, the southeastern region of Bizen is famous for its pottery (see p. 279). If you are in the vicinity of **Bizen city,** take the time to see the **Shizutani School,** built in 1670 as the first public school in Japan by the Ikeda lord ruling the region. An abundance of iron made Bizen a center for sword making; at the **Bizen Osafune Museum,** which also contains local historical artifacts, you can watch swordsmiths at work. On the Bizen coast is **Ushimado,** a resort prized for its olive groves, marine views, and Mediterranean climate.

Okayama is best known for the **Koraku-en Garden.** This is one of Japan's three greatest stroll gardens, a distinction shared with the Kenroku-en in Kanazawa (see p. 180) and the Kairaku-en in Mito. The Koraku-en was commissioned by feudal lord Ikeda Tsunamasa in 1686 and completed in 1700. This masterpiece of landscaping, with ponds, watercourses, and hilly artificial islands, was carefully devised to use the castle as borrowed scenery. Here teahouses and elegant pavilions stand on lawns against backdrops of maple, cherry, and apricot trees. Streams are crossed by various kinds of bridges and enhanced in June with displays of iris. Curiously, a rice field lies on the eastern shore of the Sawa-no-ike Pond, with a tea plantation just above it.

With its carefully shaped, rotund azalea bushes providing additional splashes of color against the lawns in early summer, the Koraku-en could have inspired the sets for *The Wizard of Oz*. The walk from the garden to the castle along a leafy path on the riverbank is especially pleasant. A small riverside restaurant offers diners a great view over the castle.

Other remnants of Okayama's past were flattened with most of the city during World War II, including **Okayama-jo Castle,** which once stood at the city's heart. The castle was initially built in 1573. Painted black, it was dubbed U-jo—Crow Castle—in contrast to the famous White Egret Castle at Himeji (see pp. 256–57). The current version was built in 1966. Only the moon-viewing turret remains from the original, but the reproduction of the main donjon is realistic enough to provide a magnificent background to the Koraku-en. Inside the stronghold is a museum of samurai memorabilia, including armor, weapons, and lacquerware.

Okayama-jo Castle was reconstructed in 1966.

Okayama has several other fine museums, all located in a "cultural zone" near the Koraku-en Garden.

Okayama Prefectural Museum of Art
8-48 Tenjin-machi
086/225-4800
Closed Mon.
$

Okayama Orient Museum
31 Tenjin-machi
086/232-3636
Closed Mon.
$

Hayashibara Museum of Art
2-17-15 Marunouchi
086/223-1733
$

The Kibi Plain cycling path

Just outside the western confines of Okayama is Kibiji, a plain combining scenic beauty with historic temples and shrines. In recent years it has earned plaudits for a marvelous cycling path that takes in its main sights. From Okayama Station, four stops on the Kibi line brings you to Kibitsu, where you can rent a bicycle. Start with the Kibitsu Shrine, renowned for its architecture and long covered walkway. Pedal to Tsukuriyama burial mound (a fifth-century tumulus), then on to Bichu Kokubun-ji Temple with its beautiful five-story pagoda rising above the rice fields. Near here is Soja, birthplace of the monk Sesshu (1420–1506), the great painter and calligrapher. The 12.5 miles (20 km) of the trip to Soja will have taken you past several more temples, shrines, and burial mounds. Another 2.5 miles (4 km) north of Soja Station is Hofuku-ji Temple, where Sesshu studied as a child. After seeing it, cycle back to Soja to drop off your bike. ■

Yumeji Art Museum
- ✉ 2-1-32 Hama
- ☎ 086/271-1000
- 🕘 9 a.m–5 p.m.; closed Mon.
- $ $$

In a striking building by architect Okada Shinichi, the **Okayama Prefectural Museum of Art (Okayama-kenritsu Bijutsukan)** displays works by some of the region's greatest artists, including the ink painter Sesshu (1420–1506), the painter/writer/master swordsman Miyamoto Musashi (d. 1645), and the woodblock print master Utagawa Kuniyoshi (1797–1861).

The **Orient Museum (Oriento Bijutsukan)** contains Asian antiquities and is one of the finest museums of its kind in Japan. The **Hayashibara Museum of Art (Hayashibara Bijutsukan)** is devoted to the priceless objects and memorabilia belonging to the Ikeda clan, which ruled Okayama until 1868; its exhibits include furniture, swords, and Noh costumes, several designated National Treasures. The **Yumeji Art Museum (Yumeji Bijutsukan)** shows many works by Yumeji Takehisa, a painter and illustrator beloved in Japan; the quintessence of the early Taisho era (1912–1926), this native son of Okayama depicted willowy beauties in a style akin to European Expressionism.

Traveling 9 miles (15 km) west, you can reach **Kurashiki** by train from Okayama in roughly 15 minutes. The modern part of town near the station is unremarkable, but

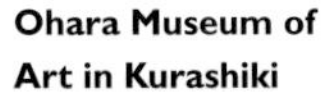

Ohara Museum of Art in Kurashiki

follow the signs for Kurashiki Bikan Chiku to discover one of Japan's most charming townscapes. Mirrored in a still canal crossed by humpbacked stone bridges and bordered by willow trees, sedate and carefully maintained old wooden merchant houses stand alongside the town's quintessential warehouses. Kurashiki means "a spread of warehouses." The warehouses came in handy again from 1889, when an important cotton textile mill was located in Kurashiki.

The warehouse buildings are typically whitewashed, with attractive black-and-white tiled features on the facades. Several have been turned into museums, reflecting Kurashiki's important role as a center for arts and culture—its assurance of preservation during the modern era.

This happy state of affairs is thanks largely to the Ohara family, owners of the Kurashiki Spinning Corporation, which prospered before World War II. A great lover of Western art, Ohara Magosaburo amassed a collection—acquired by connoisseur Kojima Torajiro on his behalf—that warranted the creation of the **Ohara Museum (Ohara Bijutsukan).**

Graced with a Grecian facade, this outstanding museum was opened in 1930; substantially enlarged since then, it is now one of the finest museums in Japan. Don't let the paradox of traveling to Japan to find a museum devoted to Western art deter you from seeing a collection that would be equally impressive in Europe. Indeed, some of the works by Western-style Japanese artists may lead you to conclude they deserve a much wider international reputation. Western art is displayed in the two-story **Main Gallery (Honkan),** featuring a substantial array of works by artists ranging from El Greco to Jasper Johns, with Gauguin, Monet, and Munch in between. The **Annex (Bunkan)** exhibits 19th-century and contemporary Japanese works in the Western tradition. Featuring rooms devoted to British ceramicist Bernard Leach and modern print master Shiko Munakata, the **Craft Gallery (Kogeikan)** also displays works by notable Japanese craftsmen of the modern era. The **Asiatic Gallery (Toyokan)** displays Kojima's remarkable collection of ancient Oriental art, including Chinese Sung and T'ang dynasty polychrome figurines.

Other notable museums include the **Kurashiki Museum of Folkcraft (Kurashiki Mingei-kan),** with some 800 household items from Japan and around the world attractively laid out in a row of storehouses, and the **Japan Rural Toy Museum (Nihon Kyodogangukan),** with a collection of around 40,000 folk toys and dolls, including many from other countries. The **Kurashiki Archaeological Museum (Kurashiki Kokokan)** displays mainly artifacts discovered in Okayama.

The far-reaching Ohara cultural legacy has prevented the indiscriminate redevelopment that has blighted all too many places in Japan; it has transformed Kurashiki into a showcase proving that conservation pays. Although tiny in area, Kurashiki's Bikan district has such a wealth of things to see that it takes up the best part of a day. You could treat yourself to a very pleasant overnight stay, especially in one of the historical *ryokans.* The Oharas' old textile factory still stands, cleverly converted into **Ivy Square,** an attractive complex of exhibition spaces, craft workshops, restaurants, cafés, stores, and a hotel. ■

Kurashiki

263 E3

Visitor information

JR Kurashiki Station

086/424-1220

Train: San-yo Honsen line or Hakubi line from JR Okayama Station (15 min.)

Ohara Museum of Art

1-1-15 Chuo

086/422-0005

$$$

Kurashiki Museum of Folkcraft

1-4-11 Chuo

086/422-1637

Closed Mon.

$$

Japan Rural Toy Museum

1-4-16 Chuo

086/422-8058

$$

Kurashiki Archaeological Museum

1-3-13 Chuo

086/422-1542

Closed Mon.

$

A spectacular view over the city and the Inland Sea unfolds from the peak of Senkoji-koen Park in Onomichi.

Onomichi

ONOMICHI IS ABOUT MIDWAY BETWEEN THE CITIES OF Okayama and Hiroshima, on a hill with a beautiful view over the islands of the Inland Sea. Established as a port during the 13th century, it prospered from trade with Ming China during the 14th. Until the end of the Edo period, it remained important as a center for shipping agents and for ferries to Shikoku.

Onomichi
263 D2
Visitor information
1F Teatro Shell-rune Bldg.
0848/20-0005
Train: Shinkansen from Okayama or Hiroshima to Shin-Onomichi Station

Today the town around the foot of the hill is largely industrial, but from higher ground the view over the Onomichi Channel, where ships cross in both directions, has all the charm of an elaborate scale model. Above all, Onomichi is a temple town and a location much favored by Japanese writers and intellectuals since the early 20th century. On the strength of a 1981 hit movie by director Obayashi Nobuhiko that was set in Onomichi, the town acquired even further acclaim.

Onomichi's temples and other sights can be covered in a walking

A cable car climbs to the top of Senkoji-koen Park.

tour, starting in **Senkoji-koen Park.** The path is steep, so it is best to take the cable car near Nagaeguchi bus stop up to the hilltop in Senkoji-koen, which is famed for its cherry trees and azaleas.

On the **Bungaku-no-Komichi** (path of literature) down through the park to **Senko-ji Temple,** commemorative stones standing in the pines are carved with the words of famous writers exalting the view, which is probably at its best from outside the temple itself. From here walk about 440 yards (400 m) eastward downhill to **Fukuzen-ji Temple,** built in 1573 and noted for its carved gates.

It is quite a climb north from here to **Saikoku-ji Temple,** but well worth the effort. Founded in the ninth century, this Buddhist temple is immediately identifiable by the gigantic *waraji* (straw sandals) at the Nio-mon gate. From here a further trek of a hundred steps takes you up to the main hall and three-story pagoda. As you walk back down, take a look at the antiquarian charm of the small **Josen-ji Temple.** Next, walk five minutes east to **Saigo-ji Temple;** built in 1543, the main hall and gate are fine examples of late Muromachi-period (1341– 1555) architecture.

Just downhill and eastward from Saigo-ji is **Jodo-ji Temple,** a lovely complex of vermilion buildings dating to 616. Onomichi is also a gateway to the **Shimanami Kaido,** a series of bridges linking Honshu with Shikoku through six islands in the Seto-naikai Inland Sea (see p. 313). The route makes a pleasant island-hopping bicycle journey (Onomichi to Imabari on Shikoku takes about eight hours), with plenty of spots to stop or overnight along the way. Bicycles can be rented by the day and dropped off at any of 14 rent-a-cycle terminals. ■

Senko-ji Temple

- ✉ 15-1 Higashi Tsuchido-cho
- ☎ 0848/23-2310
- ⏲ 9 a.m–5 p.m.

Jodo-ji Temple

- ✉ 20-28 Higashi Kubo-cho
- ☎ 0848/37-2361
- ⏲ 9 a.m–4:30 p.m.
- $ $$; treasure hall $

Shimanami Kaido Onomichi Port Rent-a-Cycle Terminal

- ✉ Higashi Gosho-cho (outside JR Onomichi)
- ☎ 0848/22-5322
- ⏲ 7 a.m–6 p.m.
- $ rental $$ per day; $$ deposit

Beneath this arch, a cenotaph contains a list of more than 200,000 A-bomb victims.

Hiroshima

"HIROSHIMA" IS A SYNONYM FOR THE HORROR OF WAR. It attracts campaigners for peace and nuclear disarmament from Japan and the rest of the world. Yet Hiroshima is also the prefectural capital of an important industrialized coastal region, a thriving new city whose optimistic inhabitants seldom mention the bomb.

Hiroshima
263 C2
Visitor information
JR Hiroshima Station
082/261-1877
Visitor information
Peace Memorial Park
082/247-6738
Train: Shinkansen from Tokyo (4 hrs.); from Kyoto (1 hr. 40 min.)

Hiroshima's **Peace Memorial Park (Heiwa Kinen-koen)** and Memorial Museum provide current and future generations with warnings from the past. The shell of a building known as the **A-Bomb Dome (Genbaku Domu)** illustrates history textbooks all over the world. Hiroshima's Industry Promotion Hall until the morning of August 6, 1945, it is now a World Heritage site, preserved much as it was after the explosion. The hypocenter—the point above which the bomb detonated—was about 110 yards (100 m) southeast of this hall. Although the dome stands northeast of the park on the opposite bank of the Motoyasu-gawa River, it is now commonly regarded as

one of the main features of the Peace Memorial Park.

Monuments commemorating the tragedy stand approximately in the park's center. The **Children's Peace Monument (Genbaku-no-Ko-no-Zo)** is festooned with garlands of thousands of colored paper cranes, a traditional "get well" symbol still made by schoolchildren all over Japan for the benefit of ailing survivors. At the center is the **Cenotaph (Genbaku Shibotsusha Ireihi).** It stands in front of the rectangular Peace Pond, where the **Flame of Peace (Heiwa-no-To)** burns: It will not be extinguished until the last nuclear weapon is destroyed. The **Hiroshima National Peace Memorial Hall for the Atomic Bomb Victims** houses photographs of those killed and testimonies of the survivors. South of the cenotaph, the **Peace Memorial Museum (Heiwa Kinen Shiryokan)** completes the picture. Exhibits include detailed "before" and "after" scale models, disturbing photographs, burned and tattered school uniforms, a twisted tricycle, and melted bottles, tiles and metal appliances.

Reminders of the prewar city are few. **Hiroshima-jo Castle,** a concrete copy of the 16th-century castle obliterated by the bomb, contains a museum. The **Shukkei-en Garden** *(2-11 Kaminobori-cho, Naka-ku),* laid out in 1620, had to be completely restored. **Fudo-in Temple** *(3-4-9 Ushita Shin-machi),* built on the Ota-gawa River in the mid-14th century, miraculously escaped damage; the main hall is a National Treasure. Crossed by broad rivers, Hiroshima is a pleasant but unremarkable city; distinctly hedonistic, it offers a wide gamut of bars and restaurants in the raucous entertainment districts of Nagarekawa and Shintenchi. ■

Peace Memorial Park
www.pcf.city.hiroshima.jp
✉ Nakajima-cho, 1-chome, Naka-ku
☎ 082/241-4004
$ Peace Memorial Museum: $
🚌 Tram: from Hiroshima Station to Genbaku-Domu-mae

Hiroshima-jo Castle
✉ 21-1 Moto-machi, Naka-ku
☎ 082/221-7512
🕒 9 a.m–6 p.m. Mar.–Nov.; closes at 5 p.m. Dec.–Feb.
$ $
🚌 Tram: 1, 2, 6 to Kamiya-cho, then 15-min. walk

The A-Bomb Dome stands as a lasting testament to the inhumanity of war.

Low tide makes the most of Miyajama's great *torii* archway.

Miyajima
263 C2
www.miyajima.or.jp

Visitor information
Inside ferry building
082/944-2011
Train: from JR Hiroshima Station to JR Miyajima-guchi station (25 min.). Tram: to Hiroden Miyajima-guchi (70 min.)
Ferry from Peace Memorial Park to Miyajima (55 min.)

Miyajima

MIYAJIMA (PROPERLY CALLED ITSUKUSHIMA) IS ONE OF Japan's three traditionally designated great scenic spots (the others are Amanohashidate in northern Kyoto-ken and Matsushima near Sendai; see pp. 161–62). Miyajima literally means "shrine island," for the spot has been sacred for around 1,500 years. Itsukushima Shrine, one of the nation's holiest Shinto shrines, complements the island's outstanding natural beauty; seeming to float above the water, its huge red *torii* gateway is as much a symbol of Japan as Fuji-san.

Just half an hour by train from Hiroshima (about an hour by tram or ferry), Miyajima can be visited quite comfortably in an afternoon. Yet there is so much to see that setting aside a whole day is a good idea. An overnight stop is a very tempting alternative, but not cheap.

Miyajima has scenic attractions year-round, from springtime cherry blossoms to autumn displays of maples in **Momijidani-koen Park,** and from beaches and seascapes to the wooded heights of Mount Misen. The perimeter of the island is almost 19 miles (30 km), making a bicycle the perfect way to get around. You can rent one next to the pier as you arrive; a battery-powered model is a good idea, as some of Miyajima's hills are quite steep. Tame deer roam the island at will, especially in the vicinity of the shrine and Momijidani-koen Park.

All the sights are concentrated on the north side of the island and up on Mount Misen. Extending along the coast between the ferry terminal and Itsukushima-jinja Shrine, Miyajima's little town is charming—if somewhat overwhelmed by souvenir stores. This is hardly surprising; Miyajima is also a center for woodcraft, both turned and carved. The most famous item is the *shakushi*, a wooden rice scoop said to have been invented here by a Buddhist priest during the Edo period and adopted all over Japan.

Itsukushima-jinja Shrine, dedicated to three sea goddesses who were daughters of the Shinto god Susano-o, is said to have been founded during the reign of Empress Suiko in 593. It reached its definitive form in 1168 under the patronage of Taira-no-Kiyomori (1118–1181), the great leader of the Heike (or Taira) clan and penultimate Heian-era ruler. The shrine, flanked by elegant covered corridors, is noted for its sweeping thatched roofs and the intense orange color of its delicate woodwork. Built on pillars right over the sea and appearing to float on the water at high tide, it is a truly outstanding example of Heian-period shrine architecture. Rows of bronze lanterns hang from the eaves; when these are lit on festive occasions along with the many stone lanterns on the shrine's coastal approach, the effect is magical. The famous **torii** is 175 yards (160 m) out from the shrine landing and stands 53 feet (16 m) high; made of camphorwood, it was rebuilt in 1875 for the eighth time.

The shrine precinct includes a nationally revered 16th-century Noh stage, used in sacred Jin-Noh performances (April 16–18). Just southwest of the shrine, the modern **treasure house** contains some 4,000 objects, 130 of which are Important Cultural Properties or National Treasures; these include fans, swords, armor, masks, and a set of famous painted sutra scrolls that once belonged to the Heike clan.

South of Itsukushima-jinja, a short climb brings you to the enchanting **Tahoto pagoda,** built in 1523. From here the view over Itsukushima-jinja and the bay is particularly beautiful. On the way you should visit **Daigan-ji Temple,** responsible for the maintenance of Itsukushima-jinja until Shinto-Buddhist unity was outlawed in 1868. Miyajima's most important temple is **Daisho-in,** higher up to the southwest, which once oversaw the shrine's administration.

Itsukushima-jinja Shrine

- 1-1 Miyajima-cho
- 0829/44-2020
- 6:30 a.m.–6 p.m. Mar.–mid-Oct.; closes at 5:30 p.m. mid-Oct.–Nov., Jan.–Feb.; closes at 5 p.m. Dec.
- $

Daigan-ji Temple

- 3 Miyajima-cho
- 0829/44-0179
- 9 a.m.–5 p.m.

Thought to have been introduced by 12th-century warrior Taira Kyomori, ancient Bugaku court dances are still performed at Itsukushima-jinja Shrine on January 2, 3, and 5.

The spectacular hilltop view over Miyajima's charming pagoda

The summit of **Mount Misen,** accessible via a cable railway or a 90-minute walk, is well worth visiting. Apart from a breathtaking panorama over the Inland Sea from the summit, this 1,740-foot (530 m) mountain is a **Monkey Park (Misen Yaen-koen).** A sighting of the monkeys is not guaranteed—they often retire to the forest—but be aware that the animals can be fractious if they do appear; they have occasionally been known to attack overly effusive visitors. The rule is twofold: Avoid eye contact, and never try to feed them. Near the summit are a number of small temples, including one said to have been frequented by the priest Kukai (774–835), founder of the Shingon sect of Buddhism.

Up a hill north of Itsukushima-jinja Shrine is evidence of the ancient melding of Shintoism and Buddhism: the main hall of the **Hokoku Shrine (Senjokaku),** famous for its library of Buddhist sutras. Senjokaku means "Hall of a Thousand Mats," though it actually contains only 450.

This impressive open-sided building, reputedly made from the wood of a single camphor tree, was commissioned by Toyotomi Hideyoshi in 1587 to honor the war dead. The original intention was to paint it red to match the magnificent early-15th-century, five-story pagoda next to it, but Hideyoshi died the following year and the building was never completed. The hall contains thousands of *shakushi*—wooden rice scoops—left as votive offerings to the gods. Originating with soldiers about to leave for the front during the Sino-Japanese War of 1894, the custom emerged from a superstitious play on words: *Meshi-toru* means "to take rice," but a homonymous verb means "to conquer." ■

Daisho-in Temple
210 Miyajima-cho
0829/44-0111
8 a.m.–5 p.m.

Hokoku Shrine
1-1 Miyajima-cho
0829/44-2020
8:30 a.m.–4:30 p.m.
$

Thousands of islets dot the Seto-naikai, or Inland Sea, which is the channel between mainland Honshu and Shikoku, the smallest of Japan's four main islands.

Shikoku & the Seto-naikai

Introduction & map **292–93**

Shikoku 294–311

Takamatsu **295–96**

Kotohira **297–98**

Tokushima-ken **299–300**

Matsuyama **301–302**

Dogo Onsen **303–304**

Uchiko **305–306**

Uwajima **307–308**

Kochi-ken **309–311**

The Seto-naikai 312–14

The islands **313–14**

Hotels & restaurants **377**

Women at the Awa-odori festival in Tokushima

Shikoku & the Seto-naikai

THE SMALLEST OF JAPAN'S MAIN ISLANDS, SHIKOKU LIES SOUTH ACROSS the Seto-naikai from Honshu. Despite a very long history of religious and political significance, it has always held the status of a poor relation. Shikoku means "four countries," referring to the feudal provinces of Sanuki, Awa, Iyo, and Tosa, now respectively the four prefectures of Kagawa (in the northeast of the island), Tokushima (south of Kagawa), Ehime (along the Inland Sea and westward), and Kochi (south and east of Ehime).

Although parts of the northern shore are heavily industrialized, Shikoku remains overwhelmingly rural and sparsely populated; the northern factories produce chemicals, but the mainstays of the island's economy are fishing and farming, especially fruits and vegetables. The respective prefectural capitals—Takamatsu, Tokushima, Matsuyama, and Kochi—are the main towns, but even these are comparatively quiet and unhurried. As the castles still standing in the last two imply, they were once the domains of feudal lords; another diminutive and charming castle remains intact in the coastal town of Uwajima in Ehime-ken. A more famous castle stands in Matsuyama, a town known, too, for its historic hot spring suburb of Dogo Onsen. Also in Ehime-ken is the town of Uchiko, unmissable for its unspoiled 19th-century buildings—many connected to a unique local candlewax industry.

Old Japan lives on in Shikoku. Traditional crafts such as ceramics, textile dyeing, weaving, and papermaking still thrive alongside colorful cultural events culminating in the frenzied Awa-odori summer festival in Tokushima (see pp. 299–300).

Between Honshu and its southerly neighbors Shikoku and Kyushu runs the Seto-naikai—literally the Sea within Channels, or Inland Sea. Of the thousands of islands, some are large enough to accommodate a population and, with towns, shrines, and temples, have a long history. Several were used as bases by the many pirates plundering ships around the Inland Sea in medieval times. Others are mere rocks capped with tufts of vegetation. Most share similar features: a rocky shoreline, a beach or two, and a pine forest on a central hill. Some of the larger islands have been inter-bridged for centuries. Nowadays the large islands—and many small ones—are spanned by huge steel bridges stretching from Shikoku. ■

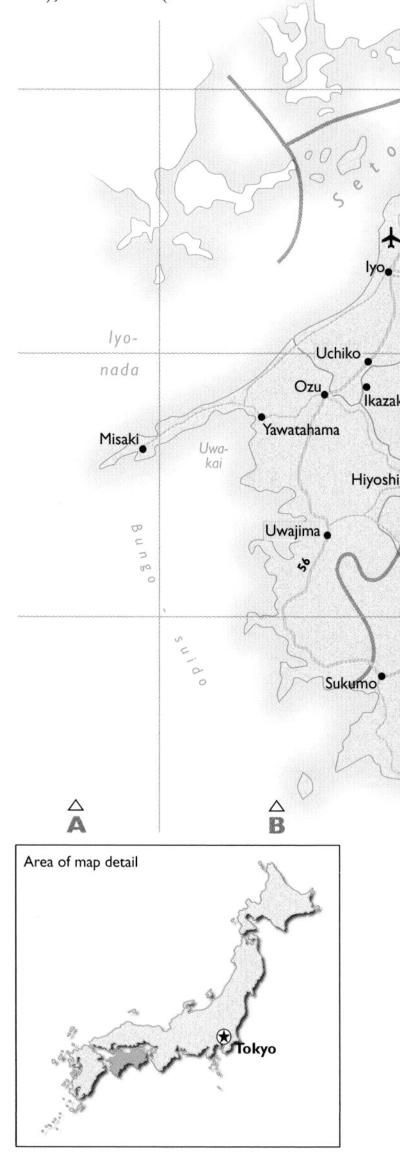

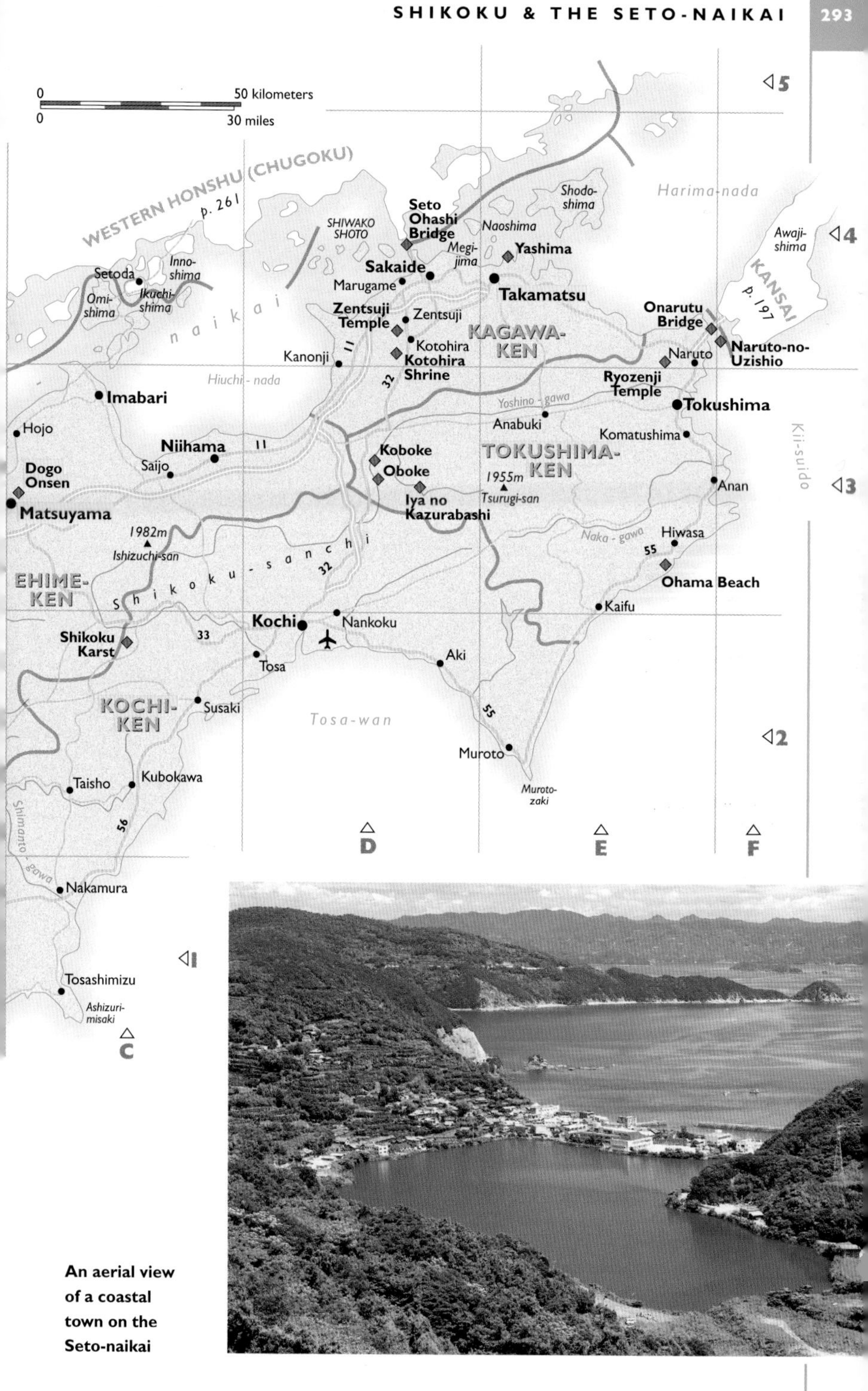

An aerial view of a coastal town on the Seto-naikai

A straggler rushes to join his pilgrim group at Reizan-ji Temple in Tokushima-ken.

Shikoku

With a fairly mountainous topography and peaks reaching nearly 6,500 feet (2,000 m) in the east and center, Shikoku's landscapes are lush and scenic. Farming villages stand against hilly backdrops, fishing villages cling to rugged coastlines, and it is still possible to find deserted beaches on the south coast. Shikoku is endlessly—and justifiably—described as off the beaten track. With new bridges linking locations on the north coast to the mainland, Honshu, and other islands, however, that is beginning to change.

Shikoku also has religious resonance. Sanuki province was the birthplace in 774 of Kukai (known posthumously as Kobo Daishi), the founder of the Shingon sect of Buddhism (see p. 226). Eighty-eight temples make up the most important pilgrimage route in Japan, a total of about 870 miles (1,400 km). The *henro*—pilgrims in Shikoku—believe that walking your way around them all is the way to rid yourself of the 88 worldly passions, thereby bringing you closer to salvation. For less pious folks with tight schedules, covering just the main sights and delights of Shikoku is feasible in about four days. ■

Beautiful Ritsurin-koen Park was laid out in the 17th century as a stroll garden for the Matsudaira feudal lords.

Takamatsu

THE ONARUTO BASHI AND SETO OHASHI BRIDGES between Shikoku and the mainland have undermined Takamatsu's status as the island's most important port, but the capital of Kagawa-ken is still the nucleus for ferries serving islands on Seto-naikai Inland Sea. One of the longest bridges in the world, the colossal Seto Ohashi linking Kagawa-ken to Honshu has itself become a tourist site (see p. 279), but the prefecture is best known for its more traditional aspects.

Takamatsu was originally the castle town that headed the feudal realm of Sanuki; **Takamatsu-jo Castle,** built in 1588, was later held by the Matsudaira clan until the 1868 Meiji Restoration. Sections of moats, ramparts, and turrets are all that remain, but **Tamamo-koen Park** (*Tel. 087/851-1521, dawn–dusk, $, 5-min. walk from JR Takamatsu Station*), containing the castle ruins, is very pleasant.

Takamatsu was badly damaged during air raids in World War II, and its surviving sights are precious few; among them, **Ritsurin-koen Park** *(1-20-16 Ritsurin-cho, tel 087/833-7411, dawn–dusk, $, 3-min. walk from JR Ritsurin-koen Kitaguchi Station),* one of Japan's most beautiful gardens, is paramount. Laid out south of the city in the 17th century, this gorgeous stroll garden was once attached to a villa built by the Matsudaira lords and destroyed after the Meiji Restoration. Ritsurin-koen took more than a century to complete and is often compared to the Koraku-en in Okayama (see pp. 280–81), one of Japan's three great gardens. Skillfully incorporating the pine-clad Mount Shiun-zan to the west, this masterpiece of landscaping is graced with ponds, curved bridges spanning meandering watercourses, artificial islands, and elegant teahouses. In one of those

Takamatsu
Map 293 E4
Visitor information
Outside JR Takamatsu Station
Tel 0878/51-2009
Train: JR Seto-Ohashi line from Okayama (1 hr.)

Above: A woman prepares *macha* (powdered green tea whisked with hot water to a froth within the bowl), the refined, bitter beverage prized for the tea ceremony.
Below: A pine tree renowned for its age, outside the Kikugetsu-tei pavilion

teahouses, **Chrysanthemum-Moon Pavilion (Kikugetsu-tei),** you can enjoy a tea ceremony as you admire the scenery. Your entry ticket to Ritsurin admits you to the Kikugetsu-tei (though tea is extra) as well as to the display of local handicrafts at the **Sanuki Folkcraft Museum (Sanuki Mingeikan).**

To the east of the city is the plateau of **Yashima,** as famous to the Japanese for its spectacular panorama over the Inland Sea as for having been the site of one of the epic battles of the 12th-century Heike Wars (see p. 31). Nearby is **Shikoku Mura** *(91 Yashima-naka-machi, tel 087/843-3111, 10-min. walk from JR Yashima Station),* an open-air museum bringing together several beautiful old farmhouses from all over the island, saved from the wrecking ball and reerected here in a spacious park.

From Takamatsu you can make a pleasant day excursion to nearby islands, notably Naoshima and Shodo-shima (see p. 314). ■

Pilgrims puff their way up the 785 stone steps to the top of Kotohira-gu Shrine.

Kotohira

SOUTHWEST OF TAKAMATSU IS THE REGION OF KOTOHIRA, wherein lies Kotohira-gu, one of Japan's most sacred Shinto shrines. Just 4 miles (6 km) north of Kotohira-gu is Zentsu-ji Temple, the birthplace of the Buddhist saint Kukai, founder of the Shingon sect. Devotees believe that Shikoku's famous 88-temple pilgrims' route was devised by Kukai himself.

The **Kotohira-gu Shrine,** better known as Kompira-san, is the most important of Shikoku's Shinto shrines and among the nation's most sacred. Located on the forested slope of Zozu-san, a 1,640-foot (500 m) hill, the shrine is dedicated to Omono-Nushi, god of seafarers and travelers. Particularly awe-inspiring to many of its visitors is the prospect of an hour's climb up 785 stone steps through the woods to get there. The ascent is not as dire as it sounds, however (except during a heatwave), for the shrine's buildings are well positioned for splitting the journey into easy stages. Climbing to Kompira-san is well worth the effort, and the spectacular views over the Sanuki Plain are a scenic lagniappe.

After passing through the imposing two-story **Main Gate (O-mon)** and along an approach lined with stone lanterns, you reach the **Treasure Hall (Homotsu-kan),** with ceramics, Noh theater masks, painted scrolls, and armor among the exhibits. The **Shoin** reception hall on the next level, which dates from 1659, contains screen doors decorated by 18th-century landscape painter Maruyama Okyo (1733–1795), the greatest of a school of naturalistic painters influenced by Western art.

A more arduous walk farther up the hill leads you on to the **Asahi-no-Yashiro** (Shrine of the Rising Sun), dating from the 1830s and famed for its ornate carvings. The next stage leads to the **Honden,**

Kotohira
Map 293 D4
Visitor information
Main street between JR Kotohira and Kotoden Kotohira stations
0877/75-3500

Kotohira-gu Shrine
892-1 Kotohira-cho, 40-min. walk from either Kotoden-Kotohira Station or JR Kotohira Station
0877/75-2121
Treasure Hall $; Shoin $

Old-fashioned *kago* palanquins are on hand if the going gets too tough up the steep steps to the Kotohira-gu Shrine.

the main hall, built on stilts on a steep incline in a fashion similar to Kiyomizu-dera temple in Kyoto (see p. 213).

On the same level is the **Emado,** a hall filled with votive offerings in maritime themes, including model ships. After another half-hour's climb you reach the final and most sacred level, **Okusha,** the inner shrine.

Near the steps leading to the entrance to the shrine compound at the bottom of the hill is the **Kanamaru-za Kabuki Theater;** the oldest Kabuki theater standing in Japan, it was built in 1835 and painstakingly restored in the 1970s. Plays are staged here during the month of April, but you can visit it any other time to see, among other things, the revolving stage from underneath.

Zentsu-ji Temple, 4 miles (6 km) to the north of Kotohira Shrine, is one of the most important temples of the Shingon sect and one of the most famous in Japan. Number 75 on the pilgrim route, it is said to have been founded by Kukai in 813 on the spot where he was born, though none of the original buildings survive. With magnificent camphor trees as old as the temple itself, the precinct has a grand five-story **pagoda** and a **Treasure Hall** containing exhibits brought back from China by Kukai himself. ■

The Sacred 88

The saint Kobo Daishi (born in 774) is popularly attributed with founding the Shikoku pilgrimage route—probably Japan's most famous. The idea is to proceed further upon the path to enlightenment and higher up the karmic cycle of reincarnation by ridding oneself of the 88 worldly passions.

Along the way there are 88 temples, one for each, running clockwise around the island and representing a distance of about 870 miles (1,400 km). Some temples, notably Ishite-ji (No. 51), sell all the proper gear—the *kasa* or conical sedge hat, a white tunic, straw sandals (which need regular replacement), Buddhist prayer beads, and a wooden staff.

The journey begins at Reizan-ji Temple in Tokushima-ken, winding up at Okubo-ji Temple in Kagawa-ken. The most arduous section is along the mountainous route linking the 16 temples in Kochi-ken (numbers 24–39 of the circuit). A few adepts really do make the trip on foot; it takes roughly two months. Even though attired to look the part, these days most pilgrims bus or drive their way around in about ten days; the majority are retirees. The route is also highly scenic—and thus a great way to discover Shikoku. ■

Zentsu-ji Temple

3-3-1 Zentsuji-cho, Zentsuji-shi, 20-min. walk from JR Zentsuji Station

0877/62-0111

Treasure Hall and Founders' Hall $$

Tokushima-ken

A spectacular natural phenomenon, the Naruto Whirlpools have been famed in Japan for centuries.

ON THE EAST OF SHIKOKU, TOKUSHIMA-KEN IS THE starting point for the 88-temple pilgrimage (see sidebar opposite). Pilgrims begin in Ryozan-ji, on the Naruto Peninsula in the north of the prefecture. The coast and mountains here have some particularly exciting natural sights.

Celebrated by Hiroshige in a woodblock print from the 1840s, the most famous seaward sight must be the **Naruto-no-Uzushio Whirlpools.** A curious natural phenomenon caused by the interaction of tidal currents in the straits between Naruto and Awaji-shima, the whirlpools occur four times daily and are best observed from the **Onaruto-bashi Bridge.** Hiwasa, a picturesque fishing town to the south, is known for a phenomenon from the animal world. Sea turtles come onshore on summer nights to lay their eggs, especially on **Ohama Beach,** alongside which is a turtle-related natural history museum. The turtle beaches are protected in summer. Tokushima's southern coast is a paradise for swimming and scuba diving. Near Shishikui you can take the Blue Marine sightseeing trip under the subtropical waters—the boat is a submarine.

Dominating the central mountain range is **Tsurugi-san** (6,414 feet/1,955 m), the second highest peak on Shikoku. Hiking options are plentiful, but cable cars run up to a point whence the summit is an easy 40-minute walk away.

In the mountains to the west of Tsurugi-san is the **Iya no Kazurabashi—**a dizzying but usable bridge (except for vertigo sufferers) made of intertwined *shirakuchi* vines, which are replaced at regular intervals. This was once the usual way to span gorges in Japan (this bridge has since been reinforced with steel safety cables); the vine bridges in Shikoku are now

The Iya no Kazurabashi vine bridge spans a dizzying drop but is reinforced with steel safety cables.

among the last. Largely because of the infrequent bus service, the bridge remains fairly remote and the surrounding area unspoiled—a spectacular experience for hikers.

Though more easily accessible, much the same applies to the **Oboke and Koboke Gorges,** where a popular 7.5-mile (12 km) boat trip from the town of Oboke takes you through some equally breathtaking scenery.

Tokushima city
293 E3
Visitor information
In front of Tokushima Station
088/622-8556
Train: Limited express from Takamatsu (1 hr. 10 min.)

The prefectural capital, **Tokushima,** was severely damaged in World War II air raids, and is probably a nicer place to live than to visit. But what it lacks in tourist sights it makes up for with its rich heritage of arts and crafts. Workshops and exhibits are devoted to *washi* papermaking, *aizome* indigo dyeing (notably for the local *shijira* textiles), and *otani yaki*—local pottery. Plain and unadorned earthenware, otani pottery is devoted mainly to kitchenware and utilitarian items—including huge jars for fermenting soybeans to make miso paste. Some jars are over 6 feet (1.8 m) tall, and potters must work in pairs to turn them.

Open to the public at various locations around the town, some of the workshops offer hands-on opportunities to try out the crafts yourself. Find out what is on offer at the **Tokushima Prefecture International Exchange Association (TOPIA,** *6th floor of JR Tokushima Building, tel 088/656-3303, www.topia.ne.jp)* or **ASTY Tokushima** *(1 Boji Higashihama, Yamashiro-cho, tel 088/624-5111),* a colossal convention center with an area devoted to exhibitions, demonstrations, and sales of local crafts. Somewhat akin to Gion Corner, the distilled culture spot in Kyoto, ASTY also stages performances of Awa Ningyo Joruri (Awa puppetry), a local equivalent of the Bunraku of Osaka (see p. 48), which originated during the 17th century and was once presented by members of farming communities. The best performances are given at the **Inugai Nosonbutai** in November; amateur groups can be seen each weekend at the puppet theater, **Awa Jurobei Yashiki** *(1-84 Honura, tel 088/665-2202).*

Above all, Tokushima is famous for the frenzied **Awa-odori festival** (August 12–15), a popular and boisterous festival. A throng of tens of thousands, most in traditional costumes from all over Japan, winds its way through the town, dancing to the hypnotic carnival music of flute and drums. "We are fools to be dancing and you are a fool to be watching," goes the chant, "So why not join in and dance?" Why not, indeed? ■

The shopping arcade in Matsuyama's Dogo Onsen district is replete with restaurants and attractive craft shops.

Matsuyama

MATSUYAMA IS THE CAPITAL OF EHIME-KEN, WHICH stretches along the northern part of Shikoku to the west coast. Presenting the traveler with a perfect balance between the rustic and the historic, this highly scenic prefecture is quintessentially Shikoku. Mount Ishizuchi-san in the south offers fine alpine panoramas, while the subtropical Uwa-kai Sea on the west, facing Kyushu, is renowned for cultured pearls and Uwakai submarine park, where you can admire gardens of coral from a glass-bottomed boat.

The city of Matsuyama is mainly modern and nondescript, except for the handful of noteworthy sights that survived World War II. Its principal attraction is the well-preserved **Matsuyama-jo Castle** *(1 Marunouchi, tel 089/921-4873, 9 a.m.–5 p.m., $$)*. Built on a hill above the city by feudal lord Kato Yoshiaki between 1602 and 1627, the castle was taken over by Gamo Tadachika when Kato was posted to Northern Honshu. The castle fell into the hands of the Matsudaira family in 1635 and was presented to the city by a descendant in 1923. Damaged by lightning in the 18th century, the main donjon was

Matsuyama

293 C3

Visitor information

JR Matsuyama Station

089/931-3914

Train: Limited express on JR Yosan line from Takamatsu (2 hrs. 20 min.)

The memorial hall for poet Shiki Masaoka

rebuilt in 1854; several turrets were damaged in arson attacks in the 1930s, and other buildings succumbed during World War II. However, the castle compound is intact overall. The harness tower, which contained military equipment and was rebuilt in 1968, is the only building to have been restored with concrete; all the others have been painstakingly put back exactly as they were, using wood and original carpentry techniques. Exhibits inside the castle include paintings, armor, and swords (none labeled in English). The castle grounds, reachable by cable car, are pleasant for strolling, especially when the cherry trees blossom in April.

Matsuyama is where Natsume Soseki (1867–1916), the most celebrated of all early modern Japanese novelists (his portrait once graced the 1,000-yen note), taught English as a young man and found inspiration for his novel *Botchan.* Soseki's boarding house has been restored as the **Gudabutsu-an,** now used for tea ceremonies and haiku poetry sessions. As the birthplace of the influential master poet Shiki Masaoka (1867–1902)—a close friend of Soseki's—Matsuyama is regarded nationally as a center for haiku. **Matsuyama Municipal Shiki Kinen Museum** (of limited interest to foreign visitors) was built to commemorate the poet, along with Matsuyama's literary past. Just southeast of Matsuyama Station is a copy of Shiki's house—the **Shiki-do,** which stands on the precinct of Shoshu-ji Temple.

Eight of the 88 temples on the pilgrim's circuit—all worth visiting for their architecture and setting—are in Matsuyama, but the most revered is **Ishite-ji Temple,** No. 51, in the northeast of the city.

In the northwestern confines of the city is the **Iyo Textile Museum (Mingei Iyo Kasuri Kaikan),** devoted to *Iyo Kasuri,* an intricate local weaving process that uses cloth dyed with natural indigo. Matsuyama is well endowed with stores selling Ehime crafts, notably objects of woven bamboo and ceramics—especially the bold yet simple blue-on-white *Tobe-yaki* ware, made today much as it was 300 years ago. ■

Matsuyama Municipal Shiki Kinen Museum
- 1-30 Dogo-koen
- 089/931-5566
- 9 a.m.–5 p.m.; closed Mon.
- $
- Tram: Dogo-onsen-eki from JR Matsuyama Station (20 min.)

Shiki-do
- 16-3 Suehiro
- 089/945-0400
- 8:30 a.m.–5 p.m.
- $

Iyo Kasuri Folk Craft Museum
- 1200 Kuman-no-dai
- 089/922-0405
- 8:10 a.m.–4:50 p.m.
- $

Dogo Onsen

Dogo Onsen's ornate main spa remains exactly as it was in the 1890s.

ABOUT 2.5 MILES (4 KM) NORTHEAST OF MATSUYAMA IS one of Japan's oldest spas. Mentioned in seventh-century historical records, Dogo Onsen is said to date back to the age of the gods. Legend has it that the curative properties of Dogo's water were first noted when a white heron miraculously mended a broken leg by dipping it into the hot jet spouting from a rock; the notion of bathing for sheer pleasure came later.

Whatever the myth, the Dogo area was the administrative and cultural capital of Iyo—now Ehime—until the end of the 16th century. Along with a number of temples and shrines and a delightful streetcar station dating to the 1900s, the area is dotted with resort hotels. These inevitably include monumental kitsch palaces, but the oldest and most famous of the baths is the **Dogo Onsen Main Building (Honkan),** an elaborate wooden structure built in Japanese castle style in 1894. Upstairs is the **Yushinden,** a special bath reserved for the Meiji imperial family, and a room said to have been used regularly by writer Natsume Soseki when the building was new. After luxuriating in the Kami-no-Yu (Water of the Gods) bathroom,

Dogo Onsen

293 C3

Visitor information

In front of Dogo Onsen Station

089/921-3708

Tram: from Matsuyama Station to Dogo Onsen

Dogo Onsen Honkan
5-6 Dogo Yunomachi
089/921-5141
Bath only $; bath with tea & sweets $$

Isaniwa-jinja Shrine
173 Sakuradani-cho
089/947-7447
5 a.m.–7 p.m.; 6 a.m.–6 p.m. in winter

Ishite-ji Temple
2-9-21 Ishite
089/977-0870
8 a.m.–5 p.m
Treasure Hall $

The Imperial Lounge at Dogo Onsen is where the Meiji imperial family would relax after bathing in the 1900s.

you are served tea in a large tatami hall—an experience with a fin-de-siècle appeal.

Just southeast of the Honkan is the imposing **Isaniwa-jinja Shrine.** Built in 1667 with a central tower in the Chinese style and adorned with intricate carvings, it is one of only three in Japan to show the distinctive architecture devoted to Hachiman, a god of war.

Another Dogo landmark, **Ishite-ji Temple** means "stone hand temple" (a local lord is said to have been born with his hand clutching a stone). Founded by Emperor Shomu in 728, this temple is No. 51 on the pilgrim's route and is said to have been rebuilt by Kukai himself (see p. 251)—though if Kukai had really built all the temples ascribed to him, he would have been an architect rather than a priest. The oldest and most noteworthy buildings date from the early 14th century: the beautiful entrance gate (a National Treasure) flanked by statues of fierce Deva kings, the **Main Hall,** and an especially fine **three-story pagoda.** All three are designated Important Cultural Properties. The **Treasure Hall** contains some 300 exhibits pertaining to the history of the temple and the pilgrimage.

Over and above the cultural and historical, Ishite-ji's main attractions reside in the weird and wonderful. With pond-side statuary on a par with garden gnomes, and a spooky "mantra cave" in which you grope through a dark tunnel toward a cavern illuminated with 1970s-style psychedelic lamps and cosmic mandalas, much of the precinct is like a Buddhist amusement park. Up the hillside are dozens more Buddhist shrines and monuments, notably serried ranks of statuettes of Jizo, the guardian deity of children, travelers, and the unborn. Near the temple entrance is a shop selling proper pilgrim garb: white robe, conical hat, staff, and straw sandals. You can't miss it; look for the 1950s-vintage mannequins modeling the gear outside. ■

Uchiko

IT WOULD BE A SHAME TO VISIT MATSUYAMA WITHOUT traveling a mere 30 miles (50 km) southwest to the lovely rural town of Uchiko. Until the end of the 1920s, Uchiko's main industry was the manufacture of candle wax extracted from the berries of local sumac trees; its output met about one-third of national demand for everything from candles to crayons. Concentrated in the district of Yokaichi-Gokoku, the former workshops and merchant houses still stand.

Homemade candles await customers at Omori Rosoku, the last candle-maker's shop in Uchiko.

Few Japanese towns can boast quite so many preserved and restored buildings as Uchiko. Painted white and cream and trimmed with black-and-white plaster work, **Yokaichi-Gokoku's** fine buildings are now part of a preservation area. Yokaichi-Gokoku is a single street 650 yards (600 m) long; along the way several buildings have been designated as Important Cultural Properties. Some of the restored buildings are still private houses, such as the **Hon Haga residence (Hon-Haga-tei),** built by the family that launched the Uchiko wax business in 1886; you can admire the house and its garden only from the street. However, the Haga family's 19th-century wax-making factory and attached private residence in the north of Yokaichi district, once the area's largest wax-making concern, is now Uchiko's star attraction, magnificently restored as the enthralling **Japan Wax Museum and Kami Haga Residence (Mokuro Shiryokan-Kami-Haga-tei).** Here you can see all the domestic furnishings and professional tools beautifully arranged in a fascinating display.

Candles have been made for generations by the same family in the workshop called **Omori**

Uchiko

Map 292 B2

Visitor information

Outside JR Uchiko Station

0893/43-1450

9 a.m.–4 p.m; closed Wed.

Train: Limited express from Matsuyama (25 min.) or Uwajima (50 min.)

Japan Wax Museum

2696 Uchiko

0893/44-2771

9 a.m.–4:30 p.m

$$

Above: The Yokaichi quarter along Uchiko's main street has barely changed since the 1880s. Below: An Uchiko craftsman fashions candles using wax made from local sumac trees.

Rosoku *(Tel 0893/43-0385, closed Mon., Fri., and every 2nd and 4th Sat.)* on Yokaichi-Gokoku, where you can watch the process. The workshop is next to the **Machiya Shiryo-kan,** a town house dating from the 1790s and restored as a period museum in 1987.

Unfortunately the government subsidizes restoration only in designated areas, so some equally remarkable houses outside the Yokaichi district are in a sorry state of repair. However, the **Uchiko-za Theater,** a Kabuki theater built in 1916 just south of the Yokaichi area, was splendidly restored in 1985. Also preserved is a former pharmacy converted into the **Business and Livelihood Museum (Akinai to Kurashi Hakubutsukan**, *1938 Uchiko, tel 0893/44-5220, 9 a.m.–4:30 p.m., $),* which uses wax mannequins to show what business was like there in the early 1920s. Exhibits in the rear building reflect the history of Uchiko crafts.

Much of Uchiko's pretty countryside is devoted to farming (rice, shiitake mushrooms, persimmons, and grapes) and forestry. The continuing exodus to large cities, as in most rural areas, is causing some economic decline. One countermeasure has been the introduction of Sightseeing Farms, where you can pick your own pears, peaches, grapes, or apples. Though often struggling, traditional industries—including candles and paper products such as lamps and umbrellas—survive in the area too. ■

Uwajima

THE MORE PLEASANT FOR SEEMING UNDERPOPULATED, Uwajima's wide boulevards and modern buildings merely enhance the lazy pace of this small port city on Shikoku's west coast. If you are taking the ferry from Uwajima to Kyushu, the city merits a peek for two noteworthy sights: its castle and Taga-jinja, a Shinto shrine with an irresistibly bizarre sex museum.

Uwajima
292 B2
Visitor information
Across from JR Uwajima Station
0895/22-3934
Train: Limited express on JR Yosan line from Matsuyama (1 hr. 30 min.)

Uwajima-jo Castle *(1 Marunouchi, tel 0895/22-2832, 9 a.m.–4 p.m., $)* was originally built in 1595, then taken over in 1616 by Masahide, son of Masamune Date, lord of Sendai. It remained in the Date family until the Meiji Restoration of 1868. Reduced from the original five stories, the three-story main keep—one of only 12 surviving feudal castles nationwide—is virtually all there is. The keep has been rebuilt several times and was restored in 1962. It is quite a trek up the hill to get there; some say that is why no one took the trouble to destroy it—the fate of most other feudal castles during the Meiji era. Just as likely, it was simply not important enough. Hardly larger than a sizable mansion—but elegantly proportioned in white and perfectly charming—the castle stands in a beautiful park with a fine view over the city.

Taga-jinja Shrine is one of

In *togyu*—sumo for bulls—the winner pushes the loser out of the ring with his horns.

Taga-jinja Shrine
✉ Fujie Niku
☎ 0895/22-3444
$ Shrine free; sex museum $$

Togyu-jo
www.tougyu.com
☎ 0895/25-3511
$ same-day $$$$$; advance $$$$

the 40-odd Shinto shrines still devoted to fertility deities. It stands in a small garden with miniature ponds and dry water pieces (stones arranged to suggest bodies of water) decked out with stone effigies of phallic gods. Already very small, the main hall is further dwarfed by the monster wooden phallus parked alongside it. To the back of it is a small building crammed with curious votive offerings, such as lengths of women's hair and broken dolls, but what really dominates the whole is the large concrete **sex museum.** Though mainly Japanese, exhibits also hail from India, Tibet, Latin America, and elsewhere; here are three floors of erotic and pornographic prints, paintings, bronze figurines, ceramics, curios, magazine clippings, and photographs.

However tempted you are, don't even think of laughing at anything in front of the high priest who mans the ticket booth. Having amassed this exhaustive and highly eccentric collection himself, he takes a dim view of those failing to take it seriously. "Even the emperor," he admonishes, "has sex."

Uwajima's other claim to fame is *togyu*—sumo for bulls. The animals, which weigh almost a ton each, lock horns; the winner is the one that drives the other out of the ring. The practice is said to have emerged from the late 17th century, when the crew of a foundering Dutch ship presented their rescuers with a pair of bulls. At **Togyu-jo,** togyu is staged only four or five times annually; call for times. ■

Kochi-ken

Summer sailors ply Kochi-ken's Shimanto-gawa River, Japan's cleanest and clearest.

EMBRACING THE CENTRAL MOUNTAINS AND THE LION'S share of the island's Pacific coast, Kochi is Shikoku's largest but emptiest prefecture, with one of the lowest population densities in Japan. Devoted to farming and forestry like Ehime-ken Prefecture, its western neighbor, it also boasts areas of genuine wilderness. In recent years its appreciable natural assets have earned it a growing reputation among lovers of the great outdoors.

Though its mild climate and fertile land (yielding two rice crops annually) have made it a choice place of habitation since prehistoric times, Kochi was sufficiently remote for mainland governments to exile renegades there during the medieval period. Kochi remained very poor until the last quarter of the 20th century. Before the Meiji period (1868–1912), it consisted of two fiefdoms, Hata and Tosa; the latter became increasingly dominant during the feudal era. Governing from Kochi-jo, the castle that still stands in the town that is now the prefectural capital (see p. 310), the Tosa lords ultimately emerged as some of the main opponents of the tottering Tokugawa shogunate in the 1860s. Among the dissenting Kochi samurai was Sakamoto

Kochi City
Map 293 D2
Visitor information
JR Kochi Station
088/882-7777
Dosan line from Takamatsu (2 hrs.)

Kochi-jo Castle
Marunouchi 1-2-1
088/824-5701
9 a.m.–4:30 p.m
$

Ryoma, one of the greatest architects and heroes of the Meiji Restoration, which he instigated by uniting the Satsuma clans (from Kyushu) and the Choshu clans (from the west coast of Chugoku). A statue commemorates Ryoma at Katsura-hama, a famous moon-viewing beach south of Kochi city. Assassinated in 1867 at only 31, he never saw the Restoration occur a year later.

Kochi is a paradise for campers, hikers, canoeists, rafting enthusiasts, swimmers, scuba divers, and even surfers (local connoisseurs have dubbed the stretches of black sand along the remote southeastern **Cape Muroto-misaki** "Little Hawaii"). The unpolluted **Shimanto-gawa River,** the only river in Japan without large-scale dams, is the nation's cleanest. The crystal-clear waters—increasingly attracting visitors, especially kayakers— extend into breathtaking mountain scenery. Farther west, near the border with Ehime-ken, is the popular and scenic **Shikoku Karst,** featuring alpine grassland with curiously formed outcroppings of limestone.

The western coast of Shikoku used to be much given to whaling, but with the decline of many species and the international ban on hunting the leviathans, **whale watching** tours have given whalers a viable alternative. The seascapes from **Susaki** southward and the landscapes crossing westward toward Uwajima are so lovely that the local train line uses open carriages in summer. Finally the coast narrows down to scenic **Cape Ashizuri-misaki,** noted as a temple stopover on the Shikoku pilgrimage—and as the birthplace of one of Japan's most extraordinary heroes, Nakahama Manjiro or John Manjiro (see below).

The center of **Kochi city,** 6 miles (10 km) from the coast and flanked by the rivers Enokuchi-gawa to the north and Kagami-gawa to the south, contains a fine feudal castle. Most other sights are farther out in the suburbs, but that makes little difference, as Kochi—although a prefectural capital—is really a small town, and sights are easily accessible on short bus or streetcar trips.

It was **Kochi-jo Castle,** on a strategic hilltop originally called Kochi-yama, that gave the prefec-

Nakahama Manjiro or John Manjiro (1827–1898)

One of Japan's most extraordinary heroes, Nakahama Manjiro was born in a poor hamlet near Ashizuri-misaki. Shipwrecked at 14 on an uninhabited island far off the coast of Honshu in 1841, he and his fellows were rescued months later by a U.S. whaling ship. For the next four years, Manjiro traveled the world with the crew. The captain recognized the lad's potential and took Manjiro back to Massachusetts, where he studied English, mathematics, and navigation as John Manjiro. He returned to Japan in 1851 and as interpreter during the negotiations between Commodore Matthew Perry and the shogunate in Edo played a key role in opening up the country. He pioneered the teaching of English at what would become Tokyo University and traveled abroad as one of Japan's first diplomats after the Meiji Restoration of 1868. ■

ture its name. Initiated by the Tosa lord Yamanouchi Kazutoyo in 1601, construction lasted a decade. The main keep suffered serious damage in a fire in 1727 and was rebuilt some 20 years later on a smaller scale; with its lovely garden setting, the castle complex became a charming aristocratic residence rather than an awe-inspiring fort.

A century later the main barracks were moved south of the castle to the bank of the Kagami-gawa River as the **Shimoyashiki Nagaya;** still standing, they are open to visitors. After feudal landowners were ousted during the early Meiji period, most of the castle buildings were destroyed, except for the main keep and the main gate. On the path between the gate and the main keep stands a statue of Itagaki Taisuke (1837–1919), a great campaigner for true democracy (as opposed to the mere substitution of authoritarian nationalism for military feudalism) during the Meiji period, and one of Tosa's greatest sons. In addition to samurai memorabilia, the **museum** inside the castle displays a Roman alphabet written by Nakahama Manjiro.

Reflecting Kochi's rural face, a picturesque market held on Sundays runs from the main gate of the castle for half a mile (1 km) along Otesuji-dori—a tradition enduring since the middle of the Edo period.

Kochi city's other main sight is the attractive hilltop **Godaisankoen Park,** which has a fine city panorama and embraces **Chikurin-ji,** a temple (No. 31 on the pilgrim circuit) founded in the eighth century and noted for its five-story pagoda.

You could also visit **Katsura-hama,** on Urado Bay about 7.5 miles (12 km) south of Kochi city, reputedly the most beautiful of the region's many beaches and a spot cherished since ancient times for moon-viewing. Because of the proliferation of "No Swimming" signs on sand that is more like grit, the appeal to foreign visitors is limited. Katsura-hama's main draws are a statue of Sakamoto Ryoma, Kochi's greatest hero, and the **Sakamoto Ryoma Memorial Museum** just west of it, housed in a striking modern building. The beach is probably better known in connection with Tosa fighting dogs. The hounds, a hybrid between a European mastiff and a bulldog, are exploited in contests where the first dog to pull down an opponent with its teeth wins. ■

Shimoyashiki Nagaya
- ✉ 1-3-35 Takajo-cho
- ☎ 088/822-6394

Chikurin-ji Temple
- ✉ Godai-san
- ☎ 088/882-3085
- 🕘 8:30 a.m.–5 p.m.
- $ Treasure house & garden: $

Sakamoto Ryoma Memorial Museum
- ✉ 830 Shiroyama, Urado
- ☎ 088/841-0001
- 🕘 9 a.m.–5 p.m.
- $ $

The powerful Tosa hound is prized for dog-fighting.

The Seto-naikai is spanned by a series of bridges that link many of the islands.

The Seto-naikai

Few views outside the Aegean equal those on the Seto-naikai—the Inland Sea. At sunset the myriad islands fade back into the horizon or seem to detach themselves against the coastline of Honshu or of Shikoku to the south.

Many of the larger islands are not only interconnected, they are also linked via the bridges and roads crossing from Honshu to Shikoku. Consequently, the islanders find themselves in an era of major change. Lesser-known islands, devoted to fishing and farming, have little to offer except seascapes and tranquillity.

If you're on your way to Shikoku and starting from the eastern end of the Seto-naikai, you can go via the Akashi Bridge near Kobe and cross over to Awaji-shima. Spanning the Inland Sea from south of Kobe to Naruto on Shikoku, Awaji-shima is the Seto-naikai's largest island. A much better gateway for exploring the Inland Sea is Takamatsu on Shikoku, which provides regular services to Shodo-shima and Oni-ga-shima.

There are many other alternatives as well. Ferries throughout the Seto-naikai start from as far east as Osaka, but the most popular routes are those in the west, notably from Hiroshima and Miyajima by sea or from Onomichi by bridge or boat. Boats on the San-yo coast also offer dozens of richly scenic one-day Seto-naikai tour options. Whatever you choose to do, seek advice first from the visitor information center in your place of departure. ■

The islands

THE MAJOR ISLANDS OF THE INLAND SEA HAVE CHANGED greatly in recent decades due to easier access, but many still retain much of their quaint charm.

Awaji-shima made headlines in 1995, when a spot just beneath the northern tip of the island was identified as the epicenter of the Kobe Earthquake. Mainly flat and scattered with pines, the island is close enough to Osaka and Kobe to have become akin to a suburban park.

The Akashi Bridge near Kobe has made Awaji-shima easily accessible from the mainland, while the Onaruto-kyo Bridge at the southern tip of the island links the island with Shikoku. Directly beneath the bridge are the spectacular Naruto whirlpools.

Ikuchi-shima, Omi-shima, and Inno-shima are all main stopping points on Seto Naikai tour-boat routes from the San-yo coast, although the Shimanami Kaido bridge system that connects them means they can also be visited by car or bus.

The focus of **Ikuchi-shima** is **Setoda,** a pleasant little town embracing all the island's main sights. You get spectacular panoramas over the Inland Sea from **Kojo-ji Temple,** built on the hilltop in 1403 and graced with a fine three-story pagoda. But the majori-

Awaji-shima

199 A2, 293 F4

Visitor information

2F Highway Oasis-kan

0799/72-0168

Bus: express from JR Sannnomiya Station (Kobe) to Awaji Interchange bus stop (35 min.)

Ikuchi-shima

293 C4

Ikuchi-shima
Visitor information
✉ 200-5 Setoda
☎ 08452/7-0051

Omi-shima
Map 293 C4
Visitor information
✉ 3260 Miyaura at the Shimanami no eki Mishima waystation
☎ 0897/82-0002

Inno-shima
Map 293 C4
Visitor information
✉ Inside ferry terminal at Habu
☎ 08452/2-3333

Naoshima
Map 293 D4
www.naoshima-is.co.jp
Visitor information
✉ Inside ferry terminal at Miyanoura
☎ 087/892-2299

Shodo-shima
Map 293 E4
Visitor information
✉ Inside Tonosho ferry terminal
☎ 0879/62-5300

Hon-jima
Map 293 D4
Visitor information
✉ Honjima Park Center
☎ 0877/27-3328
Closed Thurs.

Oyamatsumi-jinja Shrine
✉ 3327 Miyaura
☎ 0897/82-0032
8:30 a.m.–4:30 p.m.
$ $$, including Kaiji Museum

ty of the 500,000 tourists flocking to Ikuchi-shima annually are drawn down Setoda's main street to **Kosan-ji Temple** *(Tel. 08452/7-0800)*. Erected in 1936, Kosan-ji is one of Japan's greatest contributions to world kitsch. It is noted for its scaled-down reproductions of famous Japanese religious buildings; made of cheap materials such as plywood and gaudier than the originals by far, they include Nikko's Tosho-gu Shrine and Kyoto's Golden Pavilion. Learn about the island's past at the **Setoda History & Folklore Museum** *(Tel. 08452/7-18177)* on the seaward end of the main street.

The pleasant and hilly island of **Omi-shima** was the favored abode of pirates in medieval times. Its **Oyamatsumi-jinja Shrine** is as old as any Shinto shrine in Japan, including Ise, though current buildings date from 1427. The shrine is known above all for its **Treasure Hall,** which contains the finest and most extensive collection of samurai swords and armor in Japan.

Inno-shima now depends upon farming, especially flowers and fruit, but this island was once a pirate stronghold, notably for the Murakami clan. Up on a hill is **Konren-ji Temple,** which was the family temple and graveyard; next to it is their castle, known as **Innoshima Suigun-jo Pirate's Castle.** Heavily restored, the three remaining buildings are now a museum. A walk up **Shirataki-yama,** the hill dominating the island, will take you along a path flanked by more than 500 stone effigies of the Buddha and reward you with a superb view over the sea.

Easily reached by ferry, unique **Naoshima** is an art lover's delight. The underground **Chichu Art Museum** *(3449-1 Naoshima-cho, tel. 087/892-3755, closed Mon.)* was designed by Tadao Ando and features Claude Monet works lit by filtered sunshine only. Equally impressive is **Ando's Benesse House Museum** *(Gotanji Naoshima-cho, tel. 087/892-2030)* with a collection that includes Jackson Pollock, David Hockney, and Andy Warhol. The best way to get around Naoshima is by minibus, which stops at Honmura, where artists have turned traditional buildings into studios. Striking outdoor installations include a giant pumpkin sculpture by Yayoi Kusama.

The rocks used to build the ramparts of Osaka-jo Castle in the late 16th century were quarried on the larger island of **Shodo-shima;** the undelivered surpluses remain at **Omi** and **Iwagatani.** Although Shodo-shima is not short on sights, especially magnificent views, tourism increased after it was used as the setting for *24 Eyes,* a poignant 1954 movie about ordinary lives devastated by war and a teacher remembered by her pupils. The fictional teacher and her charges have been immortalized in a monument at the ferry terminal; **Tanoura's** village school, used in the movie, has become a tourist spot. The island's mountain range includes the scenic gorges of **Kanka-kei** and **Choshi-kei.** Kanka-kei has a viewing platform accessible by cable car, while Choshi-kei is near a hill where wild monkeys gather for handouts. The farming-oriented island is known for its olive groves, unusual in Japan and said to be the island'd namesake; *shodoshima* literally means "little bean island."

From the port of Marugame, to the west of Takamatsu on Shikoku, you can visit the **Shiwaku-Shoto** group, comprising about a dozen islands in all. The most notable is **Hon-jima,** where there is a street of attractive late-Edo-period houses faced with white plaster ornamented with black and white tiles. ■

The island closest to the Asian mainland, Kyushu has been a gateway to China, Korea, and the rest of the world for centuries. Kyushu is the most volcanic area in Japan—and that makes it one of the most volcanic on Earth.

Kyushu

Introduction & map **316–17**
Fukuoka **318–20**
Dazaifu **321–22**
Yanagawa **323**
Beppu **324–25**
Kumamoto-ken **326–29**
Nagasaki-ken & Nagasaki **330–37**
More places to visit on Kyushu **338–40**
Hotels & restaurants on Kyushu **377–79**

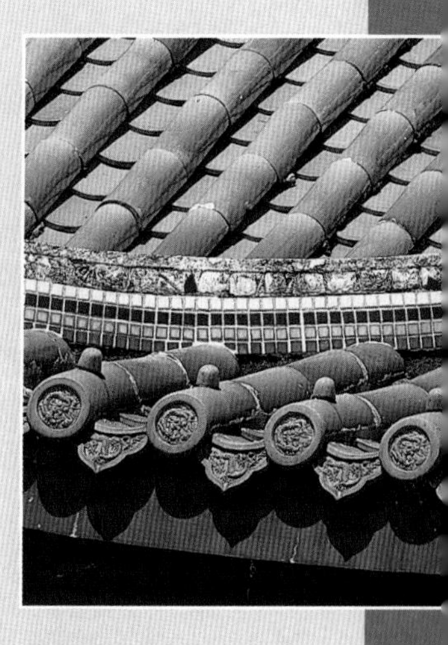

Detail from ornate Chinese temple roof in Nagasaki

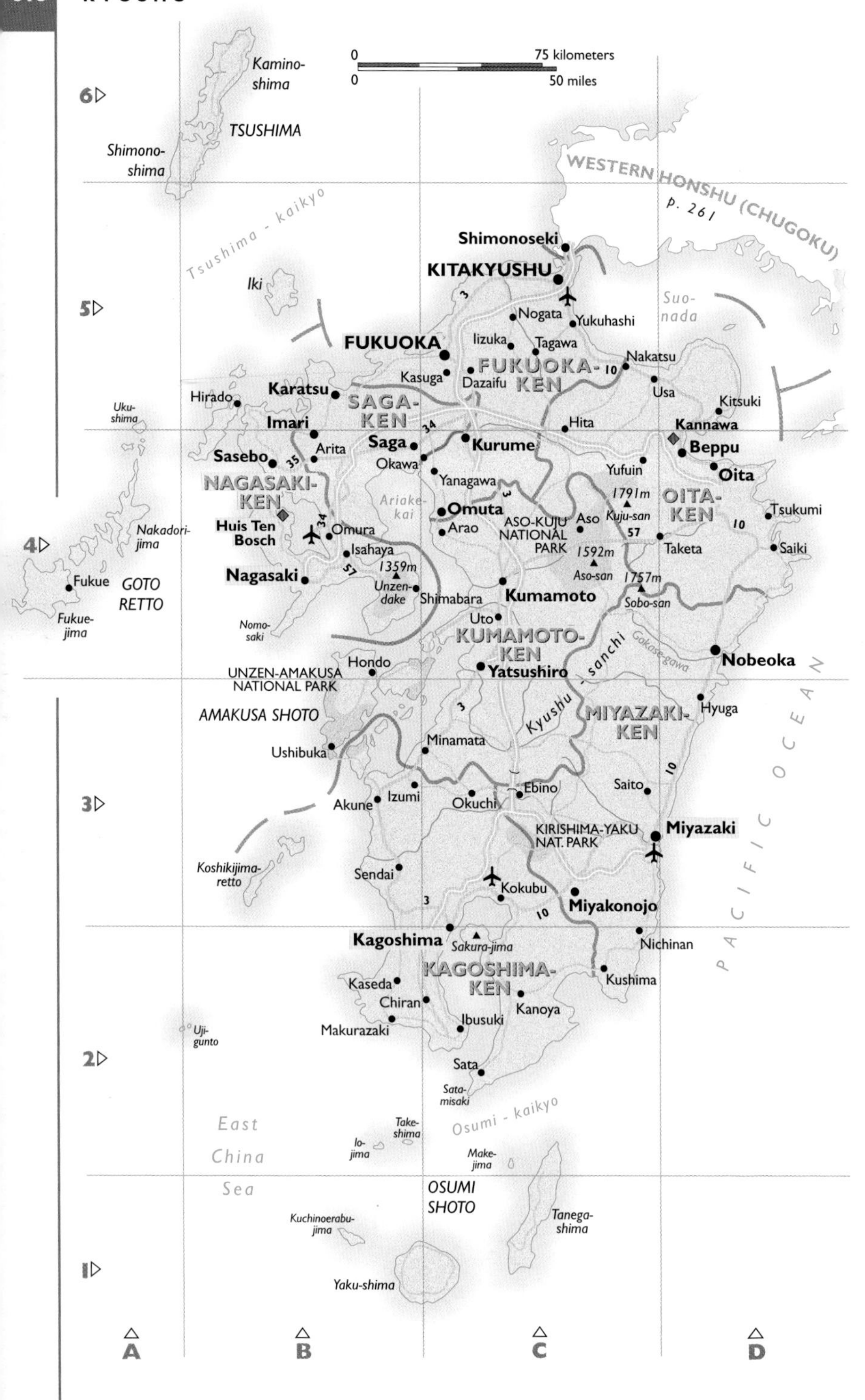

0 75 kilometers
0 50 miles
Kamino-shima
TSUSHIMA
Shimono-shima
Tsushima - kaikyo
Iki
WESTERN HONSHU (CHUGOKU)
p. 261
Shimonoseki
KITAKYUSHU
Suo-nada
Nogata
Yukuhashi
Iizuka
Tagawa
FUKUOKA
FUKUOKA-KEN
Kasuga
Dazaifu
Nakatsu
Usa
Kitsuki
Karatsu
SAGA-KEN
Hirado
Uku-shima
Imari
Hita
Kannawa
Beppu
Oita
Saga
Kurume
Arita
Sasebo
Okawa
Yufuin
Yanagawa
NAGASAKI-KEN
Ariake-kai
1791m
Kuju-san
OITA-KEN
Huis Ten Bosch
Omuta
ASO-KUJU NATIONAL PARK
Aso
Tsukumi
Omura
Arao
Nakadori-jima
Isahaya
1592m
Aso-san
Taketa
Saiki
1359m
Unzen-dake
1757m
Sobo-san
Nagasaki
Fukue
GOTO RETTO
Shimabara
Kumamoto
Fukue-jima
Uto
Nomo-saki
KUMAMOTO-KEN
Gokase-gawa
Nobeoka
Hondo
Yatsushiro
Kyushu - sanchi
UNZEN-AMAKUSA NATIONAL PARK
Hyuga
AMAKUSA SHOTO
MIYAZAKI-KEN
Minamata
Ushibuka
Saito
Ebino
Izumi
Akune
Okuchi
KIRISHIMA-YAKU NAT. PARK
Miyazaki
Koshikijima-retto
Sendai
Kokubu
Miyakonojo
PACIFIC OCEAN
Kagoshima
Sakura-jima
Nichinan
KAGOSHIMA-KEN
Kaseda
Kushima
Chiran
Kanoya
Makurazaki
Ibusuki
Uji-gunto
Sata
Sata-misaki
East China Sea
Take-shima
Osumi - kaikyo
Io-jima
Make-jima
OSUMI SHOTO
Kuchinoerabu-jima
Tanega-shima
Yaku-shima
A
B
C
D
1
2
3
4
5
6

Kyushu

THE JAPANESE ARE FOND OF COMPARING KYUSHU, WITH ITS MILD CLIMATE, vivid blue-green seas, and citrus trees, to the Mediterranean. The character of the residents is also described as Mediterranean, with traditional Japanese reserve taking a backseat to more demonstrative temperaments.

Kyushu means "nine regions," which is what it embraced in ancient times. Today it comprises seven prefectures: Fukuoka-ken, Oita-ken, Kumamoto-ken, Nagasaki-ken, and Saga-ken in the north, and Kagoshima-ken and Miyazaki-ken in the south. The most southerly of Japan's main islands and the third largest, Kyushu is linked to western Honshu by road and rail via an undersea tunnel. The island is heavily industrialized—especially the north—and wealthy: In 2003, its GDP of $430 billion equaled one percent of the world total, with most of that from Fukuoka-ken.

The first place you come to when traveling from Honshu is Kitakyushu city, really several townships engulfed in a drab urban-industrial sprawl. Vibrant and hedonistic Fukuoka, the prefectural capital and the island's largest city, offers more historical, architectural, and scenic interest. A host of islands beckons wanderers off the beaten track.

Northern Kyushu is just 125 miles (200 km) from Korea, making Nagasaki closer to Shanghai than to Tokyo. Kyushu was Japan's cradle of civilization, and its history reflects its cosmopolitanism. Archaeological sites in Saga-ken reveal the first evidence of rice farming, introduced to Japan from Korea. The world-class reputation of ceramics from Karatsu and Imari was built upon the skills of Korean craftsmen in the 16th and 17th centuries.

A cheerleader exhorts the fans at Fukuoka Dome baseball stadium.

The first Europeans to come to Japan were Portuguese sailors shipwrecked off the southern Kyushu coast in 1543. Paving the way for traders and missionaries, they introduced the Japanese to firearms and tobacco. Vestiges of bygone relations with Europe, both mercantile and religious, survive in Nagasaki city, notwithstanding the horrific destruction wrought by the atomic bomb in 1945.

Kyushu shows even more volcanic activity than the rest of Japan and has a great number of hot springs. Mount Aso-san boasts the largest caldera on Earth; its scenery makes it the most visited of Kyushu's volcanoes despite its temperamental nature. There are also several volcanoes in Miyazaki-ken, renowned for its *onsen* and beach resorts. Sakurajima, the Japanese equivalent of Vesuvius, stands smoldering just over the bay from Kagoshima, earning the city the designation "the Naples of Japan." ■

Despite its modern design, the Fukuoka City Museum houses artifacts dating back to the first century.

Fukuoka

FUKUOKA IS RAPIDLY BECOMING THE INTERNATIONAL hub of Kyushu, the nation's fourth largest economic zone. Lying on a broad bay, Fukuoka is divided into two: the northeastern sector, Hakata, which embraces the port; and Fukuoka itself, which lies on the western bank of the Naka-gawa River. Mercantile, brash, energetic, and hedonistic, the capital is Kyushu's equivalent to Osaka—and not the place to seek the prefecture's historical sights. However, what Fukuoka city lacks in historical sights is perhaps made up for by its modern architecture, some of which is strikingly innovative—especially in Tenjin, Hakata, and on the west side of the bay.

Fukuoka-Hakata

316 C5

Visitor information

JR Hakata Station

092/431-3003

Train: Shinkansen from Tokyo (4 hrs. 40 min.)

After building their castle at the outset of the Edo period, the ruling Kuroda clan gave the name Fukuoka to the samurai quarter newly dominating the plebeian and merchant harbor-town of Hakata. It was under this name that the two sections of town were administratively reunited in 1886, but local inhabitants—overwhelmingly descended from commoners rather than samurai—preferred to call it Hakata. They still do, and true native citizens like to be called

Hakatakko. If you travel to Fukuoka on the shinkansen, you might be confused: The main station is JR Hakata.

From ancient times, the port of Hakata had been the gateway for exchanges with China and Korea, though contacts with the mainland were not always peaceful. Hakata twice played a decisive role in fending off Mongol emperor Kublai Khan's attempts to invade Japan. In 1274 the Mongol invaders were strongly resisted, and after that a 12-mile (20 km) anti-Mongol wall was built along the coast. In 1281, the Mongol fleet was destroyed by a spectacular typhoon, a fortuitous intervention venerated ever since as *kamikaze*—the wind of the gods. Parts of the wall still stand at Iki-no-matsubara, Nishijin, and Imazu.

The **Fukuoka City Museum (Fukuoka-shi Hakubutsukan)** houses a gold seal unearthed in the 18th century on Shikano-shima, an island in Hakata-wan Bay. It shows just how far back Fukuoka's links with the mainland go; the seal was presented to the ruler of an erstwhile kingdom by the emperor of Han dynasty China in A.D. 57.

Hakata is the more interesting part of the city. West of the city center is the business and shopping district of Tenjin, with a futuristic underground mall and the architecturally amazing **IMS (Inter-Media Station) Building,** devoted to fashion and communications. Opened in 1999, the **Fukuoka Asian Art Museum** celebrates continental ties with displays of modern and contemporary art. Artists from 23 countries are invited to stage shows (often provocative ones) in a stylishly designed building that has great views from the seventh floor.

The city was heavily damaged during World War II air raids, so historical sights are few. Among them is **Hakozaki-gu Shrine.** Founded in 923, it is one of Japan's three great Hachiman shrines, dedicated to the eponymous Shinto god of war. The main buildings date from 1546, and the garden is famous for its peonies.

Shofuku-ji Temple, half a mile (1 km) northwest of Hakata station, is celebrated as the first Zen temple in Japan; it was reputedly built by Eisai (1141–1215), founder of the Rinzai sect, but no original structures remain. Said to have been founded in the eighth century, **Kushida-jinja Shrine,** 650 yards (600 m) west of Shofuku-ji toward Naka-gawa River, is Hakata's main shrine. It is the focus of the Hakata Gion Yamakusa festival (July 1–15), the city's great summer fete.

To the south of the shrine is

Hakozaki-gu Shrine
- 1-22-1 Hakozaki, Higashi-ku
- 092/641-7431
- Shrine free; Garden $$
- Subway: Hakozaki-Miya-mae

Shofuku-ji Temple
- 6-1 Gokusho-machi, Hakata-ku
- 092/291-0775
- Subway: Gion

Kushida-jinja Shrine
- 1-41 Kami-Kawabata-machi, Hakata-ku
- 092/291-2951
- Subway: Kawabata

Fukuoka Asian Art Museum
- 3-1 Shimokawabata-machi
- 092/263-1100
- 10 a.m.–7:30 p.m., closed Wed.
- $

Hakata Machiya Folk History
- 6-10 Reisen-machi, Hakata-ku
- 092/281-7761
- $
- Subway: Gion

Hakata Machiya Folk History (Hakata Machiya Furusato-kan), with exhibits focusing on the town and the summer festival from the Edo period to the 20th century.

The colorful old-style covered shopping arcade of **Kawabata** lies at the northern end of the shrine, currently part of a preservation-and-reconstruction package for the whole neighborhood.

Fukuoka's other attractions are more contemporary. Most of them center around **Nakasu,** the island amusement district built on what was once a sandbank in the middle of Naka-gawa. Just south of it on the east bank is the fantastic **Canal City,** a hyper-modern shopping and entertainment complex complete with bright red tiers of terraces and fanciful waterpieces providing perpetual sound-and-light shows. Wired with noise and neon, Nakasu—wall-to-wall restaurants, bars, *pachinko* parlors, strip joints, and questionable cabarets—vies with Tokyo's Shinjuku to be Japan's ultimate amusement district.

While you're there, don't miss the food stalls along the bank of Nakasu-gawa. Food vendor's carts, or *yatai,* are still trundled into amusement districts each evening. In Hakata, they are permanent—and reputed to serve the best ramen noodles in Japan. ■

Y*atai* foodstalls along the river pack 'em in with some of the finest noodles in Japan.

Dazaifu

ALMOST A SUBURB OF FUKUOKA AND JUST 40 MINUTES away by train, Dazaifu was Kyushu's seat of government from its establishment in A.D. 664 until it began to decline at the end of the 12th century. It was also important as a center for trade with China.

Opened in 2005, the **Kyushu National Museum** is a strikingly modern, expansive facility that houses such treasures as an exquisite 14th-century samurai sword and as a finely laquered Buddhist scriptures box; it also focuses on archeology, the Silk Road, and the Edo period. It boasts a high-definition theater and big playroom for kids.

The ancient government office, called the **Tofuro,** was a vermilion wooden structure with a tiled roof; all that remains are the massive foundation stones, embedded in an expanse of grassland. The same applies to vestiges of earthen walls and embankments to the west and north toward **Ono-jo fortress,** built on a hill to defend Dazaifu. This hill (then called Ono and now Shioji) holds other remnants of the distant past. Despite their rich background, the old sites are essential viewing only for those with special historical interests.

Just south of the Tofuro, you can find out more about the ancient city at **Dazaifu Exhibition Hall** *(4-6-1 Kanzeonji, Dazaifu-shi, tel 092/922-7811, closed Mon., $).* At the foot of Shioji is **Chikuzen Kokubun-ji Temple** *(4-14-1 Kokubu).* Only foundation stones remain from the huge temple precinct built by Emperor Shomu in 741, but the present temple is attractive and contains a fine eighth-century Buddha statue.

Another famous historical site is the **Kaidan-in,** an ordination hall that was one of only three in Japan during the eighth century. Next to it, to the east, is **Kanzeon-ji Temple,** once rivaling even Chikuzen Kokubun-ji in size. Although

Dazaifu Tenmangu Shrine is devoted to Sugawara-no-Michizane.

Dazaifu

316 C5

Visitor information

Nishitetsu-Dazaifu Station

092/925-1880

Train: Nishitetsu line from Fukuoka Station, change at Futsukaichi (35 min.)

Kyushu National Museum

www.kyuhaku.com

4-7-2 Ishizaka

092/918-2807

9:30 a.m.–4:30 p.m.

$

The landscape garden at Komyo-zen-ji has few rivals in Japan.

Kaidan-in
✉ 5-7-10 Kanzeonj
☎ 092/922-4559

Kanzeon-ji Temple
✉ 5-6-1 Kanzeonji
☎ 092/922-1811

Dazaifu Tenman-gu Shrine
✉ 4-7-1 Saifu
☎ 092/922-8225
🕒 6 a.m.–8 p.m. Apr.–Nov.; closes at 7 p.m. Dec.–Mar.
$ treasure house $

Komyo-zen-ji Temple
✉ 2-16-1 Saifu
☎ 092/922-4053
🕒 9 a.m.–4:30 p.m.
$ $

the old structures vanished long ago, the temple's current buildings date from the 17th century. The bell *(bonsho)*, cast around 745, is from the original temple and is reputedly Japan's oldest. Do not miss the **Treasure Hall,** which contains an outstanding collection of Buddhist statues from the 8th to 12th centuries.

The area's greatest draw is the **Dazaifu Tenman-gu Shrine,** dedicated to Sugawara-no-Michizane, a wrongfully exiled tenth-century scholar who was posthumously deified as Tenjin, the Shinto god of literature and learning. Students flock here to pay their respects. The shrine was founded in the tenth century, but the current **Main Hall,** featuring ornate carving beneath its thatched roof, was built in 1591. The precinct encompasses plum and camphor trees, as well as irises; along the approach is a watercourse spanned by a celebrated humpbacked bridge. To the right of the Main Hall is an apricot tree that, according to legend, uprooted itself from Michizane's Kyoto garden and followed him to Dazaifu. It is said to have stood on this spot for a thousand years.

Look for a craftsman painting ceramic Hakata dolls in one of the shops along the shrine approach. A Fukuoka specialty, the dolls represent traditional dancing girls; while the craftsmanship is exquisite, they tend to be aesthetically insipid.

The overwhelming majority of the hordes visiting the Tenman-gu never give a passing thought to **Komyo-zen-ji,** a Zen temple not five minutes' walk to the south. It was founded during the 13th century, though the current buildings date from the Edo period. Refined and simple, they feature expanses of tatami matting surrounded by verandas of polished wood—all intended simply for sitting and contemplating a lovely **garden.** A masterpiece of landscaping, it features white gravel "seas" beautifully raked around rocks resembling islands, and green"land" pieces consisting of mosses and trees. Try moving from one vantage point to another; the garden has been designed so that the view is perfect from any angle. ■

Yanagawa

THE PICTURESQUE LITTLE TOWN OF YANAGAWA LIES SOME 25 miles (40 km) south of Fukuoka. Like most former castle towns, Yanagawa lost its castle following the Meiji restoration; it was burned to the ground in 1873. The three moats remained, however, forming a canal network that crisscrosses the town. You get the impression that Yanagawa's citizens spent a century wondering what to do with these waterways until someone hit upon a brilliant idea: Take advantage of the town's historical sights and have boat tours shuttle visitors between them. Poled along by famously waggish boatmen past some pretty but mostly unremarkable scenery, the punts have become a major local industry. Still, it's a delightful experience.

The main focus is the **Ohana Villa,** built in 1697, but the only true survivor of the era is the villa's **Shoto-en Garden,** laid out with a pond encompassing dwarf pines and rocks to emulate Matsushima Bay in Tohoku (see p. 161). Next to it is the **Seiyokan,** a rambling Western-style mansion built by Yanagawa's feudal lords in the 1880s and currently popular as a wedding hall. The two buildings are virtually joined and contain interesting museums: In the Tachibana house are displays of Meiji-period memorabilia and utensils, while the Ohana Villa showcases a beautiful collection of Edo-period artifacts—including Noh costumes, armor, lacquerware, and miniature painted books.

The town is also pleasant to wander on foot. The north side embraces a number of quaint little temples as well as restaurants and shops. The picturesque streets by the canal have several old traditional houses, notably the birthplace of the celebrated poet Kitahara Hakushu (1885–1942), now open as the **Kitahara Hakushu Memorial Park.** ■

Yanagawa
316 C4
Visitor information
Nishitetsu-Yanagawa Station
Information & river trips: 0944/73-2145
Train: Limited express on Nishitetsu-omuta line from Fukuoka Station (45 min.)

Ohana Villa, Shoto-en Garden & Seiyokan
1 Shinhoka-machi
0944/73-2189
10 a.m.–6 p.m.
Seiyokan $$; Seiyokan & Shoto-en $$; Ohana Villa museum $

Kitahara Hakushu Memorial Park
55-1 Okinohata
0944/73-8940
9 a.m.–5 p.m.
$

The classic Yanagawa delight: a canal trip along the network of moats remaining from feudal times

Volcanic steam drifts across the cityscape of Beppu, Japan's ultimate *onsen* wonderland.

Beppu

THE TOWN OF BEPPU SITS IN AN AREA OVERFLOWING WITH volcanic hot springs. Sometimes it seems that all you have to do to make a living here is stick a pipe in the ground, turn on a faucet, and build a spa hotel around the outflow.

Beppu
316 D4
Visitor information

JR Beppu Station
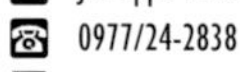
0977/24-2838
Train: from Hakata Station, Fukuoka on JR Nippon line (2 hrs. 30 min.)

The Promised Land for lovers of the long, leisurely soak, Beppu reigns supreme over all *onsen* resorts in Japan. Yet this distinction hardly qualifies it as a paragon of refinement—quite the contrary. Arriving by ferry from Shikoku, you appear to be docking in front of the Tiger Pachinko Parlor, which stands on a palm-flanked seafront boulevard aflame with garish neon signs and uninhibitedly hideous architecture. Arrive by train and you will ponder the source of the music filling the main street before finding out that it is wafting up from the storm drains.

Matched only in the realm of science fiction, Beppu is outlandish and perfectly fascinating. In this contender for the title of the world's most geothermal city, natural hot water cooks food and heats houses in winter. Onsen tourists roam the streets in cotton *yukata* (kimono-dressing gowns) emblazoned with their hotel's crest, even in the town center.

Of the eight onsen areas overall, the most important are **Beppu Onsen** in the center of town, **Kankaiji** on the hill to the north, and **Kannawa** to the northeast. The **Ekimae Koto Onsen** bathhouse in central Beppu, which is open 24 hours, goes back to the 1930s, but the most venerable is the **Takegawara** *(16-23 Moto-machi, tel 0977/23-1585)*, an imposing wooden building dating from 1879 where—apart from the usual mineral-rich hot water—the main attraction is the *suna-yu* (sand bath). Steam filtering up from the boiling water underground heats the sand, which is shoveled over you. Lying buried up to your neck, you sweat away your cares—and possibly, if you stay long enough, your skin. Suna-yu is available at **Shoningahama** beach on the eastern side of the seafront.

If you're after sheer luxury and the latest onsen technology, hilly **Kankaiji Onsen** is for you. The views over Beppu Bay are breathtaking, especially from the **Suginoi Palace** *(1 Kankaiji, tel 0977/24-1141)*, a spa and hotel complex offering an astonishing variety of aquatic attractions for families. You need not be a guest to use the facilities.

Beppu is a great city for covered malls. They are halfway down the main street from the station on your right. Festooned with colored paper lanterns and presenting a striking array of restaurants and bars, the main shopping arcades, called **Ginza** and **Yaoyoi,** offer everything from fancy souvenir shops to dingy thrift stores.

Kannawa is celebrated for its eight **Kannawa Jigoku** (Kannawa hells), where you can contemplate geysers, seething expanses of bubbling mud, and pools of steaming hot water dyed strange colors by minerals, the most famous being the red **Chi-no-Ike,** or "pond of blood." Going round them forms an extraordinary half-day excursion.

As if nature's geothermal excesses weren't weird enough, humans have sought to enhance them with grotesque statuary, crocodile farms, greenhouse banana plantations, and stalls selling eggs and vegetables cooked in the boiling pools.

Some might find things equally steamy at the **Hihokan** *(336-5 Shibuyu, tel 0977/66-8790, 9 a.m.–10 p. m., $$)*, a museum devoted to things sexual; it's just opposite the flashy Ashiya spa hotel. An outlandish cross between a castle and an Indian temple outside, it exhibits phallic statuary, erotic prints, sculptures, and amazing waxwork animations inside.

Right: In Beppu you can soak in muddy, mineral-rich hot spa water (as here) or get buried up to your neck in hot sand on the beach.

Kannawa is fascinating to wander. A constant hiss issues from the pipes, chimneys, boilers, and bizarre plumbing fixtures that feed the onsen hotels, *ryokan* (inns), and *minshuku* (small guesthouses) flanking streets and lanes of great charm.

An hour west of Beppu is the genteel resort of **Yufuin.** Featuring outdoor *rotenburo* baths, the hotels here tend to focus on a pleasant but contrived form of rusticity: The town can be toured in style by pony and trap. With annual movie and music festivals, Yufuin is one of the cultural hubs of Kyushu—in every way the antithesis of Beppu. ■

Ekimae Koto Onsen
- 13-14 Eki-mae
- 0977/21-0541
- $

Yufuin
- 316 C4

Visitor information
- JR Yufuin Station
- 0977/84-2446

Kumamoto-ken

Outstandingly well restored, Kumamoto-jo is once again one of Japan's finest castles.

ON THE WEST SIDE OF CENTRAL KYUSHU, KUMAMOTO-KEN thrives on its agricultural and marine resources and offers plenty of variety for the visitor. Off the mainland coast, some 120 islands of various sizes form the Amakusa chain, notable for its scenic beauty and historically significant as a bastion of Christianity during the 16th century. Inland is the colossal volcano of Mount Aso-san. It provides plenty of hiking opportunities and a variety of scenery, from alpine meadows and shaded gorges to the grim landscape near the menacing active crater. The prefecture hasn't earned its nickname, Hi-no-Kuni (Land of Fire), for nothing.

Although Kumamoto-ken has markedly fewer factories than Fukuoka-ken, it still suffered indiscriminate postwar industrialization. From an aesthetic viewpoint, development has proved more destructive than war in the prefectural capital, **Kumamoto.** Despite preserving precious few vestiges of the past, it's a pleasant city with a youthful atmosphere (it has two of Kyushu's most important universities) and makes a perfect base for visits to other parts of Kyushu.

Kumamoto

316 C4

Visitor information

JR Kumamoto Station

096/352-3743

Train: JR Kagoshima line from Hakata Station (1 hr. 30 min.)

Bus: From Fukuoka to Kotsu Center (2 hrs.)

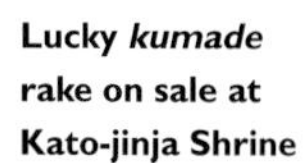

Lucky *kumade* rake on sale at Kato-jinja Shrine

Kumamoto-jo Castle

- ✉ 1-1 Honmaru
- ☎ 096/352-5900
- 🕒 8:30 a.m.–5:30 p.m. Apr.–Oct.; closes at 4:30 p.m. Nov.–Mar.
- $ $$

Suizenji-koen Park

- ✉ 8-1 Suizenji-koen
- ☎ 096/383-0074
- 🕒 7:30 a.m.–6 p.m. Mar.–Nov.; 8:30 a.m.–5 p.m. Dec.–Feb.
- $ $$

Kumamoto-jo Castle is one of the city's two major sights and, though mainly a reproduction, it is among Japan's finest castles. Completed in 1607, it was commissioned and designed by feudal lord Kato Kiyomasa. The walls of the castle form a perimeter of almost 8 miles (13 km) embracing 49 turrets; the garrison and private quarters took their water supply from 120 wells. Kato's skill as a military strategist was more than matched by his brilliance as an architect. The structural orientation ingeniously follows the topography of the land; the architectural feature of Japanese fortresses known as *musha-gaeshi* (warrior-overturn), referring to the unclimbable concave shape of the massive walls supporting the keep, is regarded as reaching perfection in Kumamoto-jo, where some call it *nezumi-gaeshi*—"mouse-overturn."

Owned by the Kato family for 44 years, the castle passed into the hands of the Hosokawas, who ruled the province until 1871. Most of the castle was burned down when samurai renegade Saigo Takamori (see p. 36) was finally routed by imperial troops during the Satsuma Rebellion in 1877. Along with the massive stone foundations, only the famous **Uto turret (Uto Yagura),** west of the main keep, survived undamaged. Beginning in 1960, restoration work has been conducted on a spectacular scale with splendid results. Seventeen original wells and 13 turrets have been resurrected. From the outside, it's hard to imagine that the new keep hides a concrete skeleton; inside is a **museum** containing fascinating exhibits devoted to the castle and both its Kato and Hosokawa rulers.

Kumamoto's other main sight is **Suizenji-koen Park,** one of Japan's most celebrated gardens. Gentaku, a noted Buddhist monk from Kyoto, came to Kumamoto in 1632 at the behest of feudal lord Hosokawa Tadatoshi to build Suizen-ji Temple, which included a magnificent garden. Upon Gentaku's demise the temple was moved elsewhere, and the Hosokawas built a teahouse on the spot. Beautifully landscaped to evoke the sights most characteristic of each of the 53 stations of the old Tokaido trunk road between Edo and Kyoto, the garden features fountains and flowering shrubs, ponds studded with rocks suggesting islands, and miniature hills (one, a cone-shape green hillock, represents Fuji-san).

Minor sights in Kumamoto include the houses of two famous 19th-century writers: Natsume Soseki, whose portrait once adorned the 1,000-yen note; and Lafcadio Hearn (see p. 274), who spent a few years here after moving from Matsue. Both houses are now museums. The **Soseki museum** is the more worthwhile; the Hearn residence hardly measures up to its counterpart in Matsue. Kumamoto has several noteworthy craft traditions. **Kumamoto Prefectural Traditional Crafts Center (Kumamoto-ken Dento Kogeikan),** just east of the castle, presents fine exhibits antique and modern; there is a sales area, and you can watch artisans at work.

Thirty miles (48 km) east of Kumamoto is **Mount Aso-san,** created when the dome of a gigantic volcano collapsed during a cataclysmic eruption some 50,000 years ago. Aso-san actually embraces five cones, of which Mount Naka-dake (5,223 ft/1,592 m) is the most active. The colossal caldera—it's the largest on Earth—is 11 miles (18 km) wide by 15 miles (24 km) long, covers an area of 98 square miles (255 sq km), and encompasses whole towns and villages with a combined population of about 80,000. The fertile volcanic soil has produced lush green meadows now used as pastureland for cattle and horses. The scenery in the vicinity is superb, even from the road up to Naka-dake from Aso Station.

Perhaps the most famous view along the way is across the lake-dotted **Kusasenri** meadow, with the intense green of **Mount Komezuka** (*komezuke* means "rice mound") rising out of it. The hill, actually a dormant volcano, gets its name from a Shinto myth about a god who scooped a chunk out of the top of a gigantic mound of rice to feed the starving population. Opposite it is the **Aso Volcanic Museum (Aso Kazan Hakubutsukan),** featuring a fascinating array of displays on the volcanology of Kyushu and other parts of the world, as well as video clips of local eruptions. You can

Boat trip on the Kuma-gawa River

Soseki Museum
- 4-22 Tsubo-machi
- 096/325-9127
- 9:30 a.m.–4:30 p.m., closed Mon.
- $

watch monitors displaying live pictures broadcast from closed-circuit television cameras mounted inside the Naka-dake crater itself.

From the **cable car station** near the top of Naka-dake, a ten-minute walk brings you to the crater edge. The shelters you see along the rim were erected there in 1960, following a sudden eruption that killed several tourists. That's the nature of Naka-dake, and as you gaze down on clouds of steam billowing up from the pallid, evil-looking, gray-green lake 320 feet (100 m) below, you start to understand it. Naka-dake was closed to visitors during eruptions in 1989 and 1990.

Several hiking trails skirt the rim and run down toward other peaks. To repeat the warning posted on ubiquitous dual-language notices: Stay clear of the crater rim, especially if you suffer from respiratory ailments. The situation is constantly monitored and the area is closed at the first signs of an eruption or poor air quality, but accidents can happen. Vents occasionally open deeper down in the crater, and the sulfurous gases they emit are highly toxic. You can assess the mood of the mountain at the visitor information center before going to Naka-dake. The center also has information on hiking trails.

About 13 miles (20 km) northeast of Naka-dake, accessible by road from Aso Station, is the lovely **Kikuchi Valley,** where the river has carved breathtaking gorges through a wooded landscape. ■

Aso-san's crater embraces an astonishing array of scenery.

Aso-san

316 C4

Visitor information

Next to JR Aso Station

0967/34-0751

Aso Volcanic Museum

Kusasenri, Aso-machi, Aso-gun

0967/34-2111

9 a.m.–5 p.m.

$$

The view across Nagasaki Harbor from Glover Garden

Nagasaki-ken & Nagasaki

OCCUPYING THE NORTHWESTERN CORNER OF KYUSHU, Nagasaki-ken contains some of Kyushu's cardinal historical and scenic sights. To make the most of both aspects in one go, you may want to begin in the east of the prefecture with a visit to the historical town of Shimabara, then hike around volcanic Unzen-Amakusa National Park.

Shimabara
316 B4
Visitor information
Shimabara ferry terminal
0957/62-3986
Express bus: from Nagasaki (2 hrs.); from Fukuoka (3 hrs.)
Ferry: from Kumamoto (1 hr.), high-speed ferry (30 min.)

The prefecture's greatest draw is its capital, with its fascinating history of contacts with Europe. The long relationship with Holland is quirkily demonstrated in Huis Ten Bosch (see p. 338). Nagasaki-ken includes Goto Retto Archipelago off the west coast, with more than 200 islands. In the east of Nagasaki-ken is the Shimabara Peninsula, noted both for the town of Shimabara on the Ariake Sea and for the scenic area around the Unzen-dake volcano.

Traversed by canals, modern **Shimabara** is a small, pleasant city popular in Japan for its historical connotations. It was here that Christians made their last stand in 1637 during the Shimabara Rebellion (1637–38). The rebels, mainly Christians, were defying harsh oppression by local rulers; 37,000 men, women, and children were massacred. Their slavery and

taxes had built the famous **Shimabara-jo Castle,** demolished during the 1870s, though the walls and impressive main gate remain. Rebuilt in 1964, the keep houses a **museum** featuring ceramics, armor, and exhibits about the rebellion and the Christians in Kyushu. Northwest of the castle is the district of **Teppo-cho,** with its picturesque thatched and whitewashed **samurai houses** (two are open to the public). The stone channels that once served as the water supply, like the town's canals, are fed by mountain springs highly prized for their purity.

Other local springs are of the hot variety—the area is volcanically hyperactive, surrounding, as it does, the ferocious **Mount Unzen-dake.** The nearby town of Unzen has such a proliferation of volcanic "hells" and springs that the streets are festooned with pipes and plumbing, feeding the spas and hissing and bubbling with steam. Popular early in the 20th century as a summer haven for Western colonials and "Shanghailanders" from China, the spa resort of Unzen possesses Japan's oldest golf course (founded in 1913) and a hotel dating to the 1930s.

The magma percolating beneath Unzen-dake bubbled upward in a major eruption in 1792, triggering violent earthquakes that killed some 15,000 people; most of them were victims of 50-foot (15 m) tidal waves that thundered in from the sea. Today the most volatile cone of Unzen-dake is **Mount Fugen-dake** (4,580 feet/1,396 m), which lies just 5 miles (8 km) southwest of central Shimabara. Fugen-dake began to erupt again in November 1990. The lava dome collapsed the following month, leading to a lava explosion in June 1991 that killed 43 people, including a group of French and American volcanologists. Intermittent eruptions continued until 1994, damaging or destroying some 2,000 buildings in the process. Some of the buried structures in the **Sembongi** district to the west of Shimabara city and along the **Mizunashi-gawa River** have been preserved as an unusual tourist attraction; only their roofs protruded from the mud and lava. As Japan's youngest mountain, the lava dome that blistered atop Fugen-dake has been called Heisei Shin-zan (Heisei new mountain). The eruption was officially declared over in 1996; depending on the volcano's activity level, however, some hiking trails around Fugen-dake may be closed. Be sure to check with the visitor information centers in Nagasaki or Unzen before heading for the hills.

Shimabara-jo Castle
- 1183-1 Jo-nai 1 chome
- 0957/62-4766
- 9 a.m.–5 p.m.
- $$

Mount Unzen-dake
- 316 B4

Visitor information
- Unzen Tourist Association (near Post Office)
- 0957/73-3434

Nagasaki Peace Park's commemorative statue

Nagasaki city

316 B4

Visitor information

JR Nagasaki Station

095/823-3631

Train: from Hakata Station, Fukuoka to JR Nagasaki Station (2 hrs.)

Urakami cathedral

095/844-1777

Mooto-machi

9 a.m.–5 p.m.; closed Mon.

Tram: Ohashi or Maruyama-machi

Hypocenter Park

Tram: Matsuyama-machi

Peace Park

Tram: Matsuyama-machi

NAGASAKI CITY

The purely practical attributes of modern Nagasaki harmonize so well with its historical and aesthetic character that it is easy to forget the city is also a vital industrial hub. On the peninsula to the west of the bay is the Mitsubishi shipyard, the world's largest corporate shipbuilding facility, although the company now mainly builds heavy machinery. Nagasaki's other great industry is fishing. Its annual catch is the largest in Japan.

As the historical point of entry for both European trade and Christianity in Japan, Nagasaki has a long and fascinating history. Many sights evoke the city's historical links with the rest of the world, despite the devastation of the atomic bombing in 1945. The northern sector, home of the Christian community, was the most extensively destroyed. Some of the old buildings farther south were spared, and others—notably the Urakami Cathedral in the north—were rebuilt. "Restoration of the city has been remarkable," declared a guidebook compiled only five years after the catastrophe, "and it appears to be almost as prosperous as before the war." Today, unless you visit the Atomic Bomb Museum and Peace Park near the hypocenter of the blast, it is hard to imagine that the bombing ever happened.

Surrounded by green, rolling hills and overlooking a deep bay, Nagasaki has recovered its reputation as one of Japan's most beautiful cities. It should be included in any visitor's itinerary in Kyushu.

Sights in the northern sector

Urakami, in the northern sector of the city, is where the atomic bomb struck the city on August 9, 1945. As a predominantly Catholic neighborhood, Urakami was the perfect site for a cathedral. Completed in 1925, the original **Urakami Cathedral (Urakami Tenshu-do)** took 30 years to build; it had a seating capacity of 6,000 and was the largest church in East Asia. The district included some 15,000 Christians before World War II, but 10,000 perished in the A-bomb explosion. Standing only 550 yards (500 m) from the hypocenter, the cathedral was vaporized by the blast; the current reproduction was completed on the site in 1959. This is Japan's most important Christian church; a special Mass conducted here by Pope John Paul II in 1981 featured the ordination of priests from around the world.

Heading north from the cathedral, you come to **Hypocenter Park,** where a simple, elegant block of black marble marks the precise spot above which the A-bomb exploded. The park also displays relics assembled from nearby, including all that remains of the original Urakami Cathedral: a section of brick wall and three blackened, eroded statues, one of them headless. To the north of the Hypocenter Park is the **Peace Park (Heiwa-koen),** locus of several memorials donated to the city of Nagasaki by various countries. The **Peace Statue (Heiwa Kinen-zo)** by prominent sculptor Kitamura Seibo dominates the park; massive and clumsily proportioned, it is not to everyone's taste.

South of the Peace Park the new **Atomic Bomb Museum (Nagasaki Genbaku Shiryokan),** which opened in 1996. Burned and twisted debris from the blast, along with horrific video presentations, make this one of the most poignant and terrifying museums anywhere. The wall clock with its hands fused at 11:02 a.m.—the exact moment of the bombing on the 9th of August, 1945—is a Nagasaki emblem.

Nagasaki is renowned for the views afforded by its hilly topography, and they don't get much better than the one from the top of 1,080-foot (330 m) **Inasa-yama,** on the other side of the Urakami-gawa River from the city. The peak is reached via cable car; the panorama over Nagasaki Harbor and the East China Sea from the observation platform is breathtaking, especially when the lights come on around the harbor. Deer and monkeys roam scenic **Inasayama-koen**

Atomic Bomb Museum

- 7-8 Hirano-machi
- 095/844-1231
- 8:30 a.m.–5 p.m.
- $
- Tram: Hamaguchi-machi

Mount Inasa Park

- Park free; cable car access $$$
- Bus: Ropeway-mae, then cable car

Grim reminder: clock with hands fused at the time the Nagasaki A-bomb detonated

The monument to the 26 Christian martyrs of Nagasaki, crucified in 1597 and canonized in 1862.

Park, where there is also an open-air concert hall.

Sights in the central and southern sectors

The city's heart and most of its sights lie in the south. Just a short distance north of Nagasaki railway station is **26 Martyrs Memorial (Nihon Niju-roku Seijin Junkyochi).** The bronze bas-relief was erected in 1962, marking the passage of one hundred years since Nagasaki's 26 Christian martyrs were canonized by Pope Pius IX.

Of particular interest is the adjacent museum, with exhibits relating to the history of Christianity in Japan. The country's "Hidden Christians" concealed items such as religious scrolls and prayer books, as well as statuettes of the Virgin Mary disguised as the Bodhisattva Kannon. The fate of the Nagasaki martyrs is thought to be connected to the *San Felipe,* a Spanish galleon wrecked on the Shikoku coast in 1596. After being rescued, its captain boasted about the might of Spain; her many overseas conquests, he claimed, had been launched by armies marching over ground prepared by Christian missionaries and their converts. When this reached the ears of the shogun Toyotomi Hideyoshi (1536–1598), who was already growing suspicious of Christian designs, he had 26 Christians—including six Jesuit friars and three children—arrested in Kansai and forcibly marched all the way to Nagasaki in midwinter. There they were crucified on Nishizaka Hill on February 5, 1597, as a warning to others.

The curious **Fukusai-ji Temple,** some 550 yards (500 m) southwest of the memorial, is one of four that were built by Chinese in the Ming dynasty style in the 1620s; the original temple burned down after the atomic bombing. Although the turtle is a symbol of longevity in Japan as much as it is in China, that hardly justifies rebuilding Fukusai-ji to look like one. This in effect is what happened in 1979; even if the incongruity of shaping a temple like a turtle escapes you, you can hardly miss the 60-foot (18 m) effigy of the Buddhist deity Kannon standing

Fukusai-ji Temple

- 2-56 Chikugo-machi, 5-min. walk from Nagasaki Station
- 095/823-2663
- 8 a.m.–4 p.m.
- $

Shofuku-ji Temple

- 3-77 Tamazono-machi
- 095/823-0282
- Tram: Sakura-machi

on its back. A bell sounds at 11:02 a.m. daily to commemorate the atomic bombing, and the interior of the temple contains a Foucault pendulum. Fukusai-ji is wildly out of tune with conventional Buddhist temple culture—and worth seeing for that very reason.

Opened in 2005, the **Nagasaki Museum of History and Culture** holds some 48,000 items detailing the city's role as Japan's sole window to the outside world. The theme here is "overseas exchange," focusing on trade with China, Korea and the Netherlands, but another highlight is a reconstruction of the Edo-period Nagasaki Magistrate's Office featuring re-enactments of trials on weekends.

Continuing east, you come to **Suwa-jinja Shrine,** originally built in 1629 by the feudal government to stem the growing influence of Christianity. Its 277 steps lead up to a grand bronze *torii* gateway in front of the shrine's main buildings, which date from the late 19th century. Nagasaki's most important and popular shrine, Suwa-jinja is the focus of the city's annual O-Kunchi festival in October. Centering on a Lion Dance, the festival parade reflects strong Chinese influence.

South of Suwa-jinja, walk alongside the picturesque canal of the Nakashima-gawa River. **Megane-bashi,** one of several bridges spanning the river, is the most famous. Built by the Chinese abbot of Kofuku-ji in 1634, it is the oldest stone-arch bridge in Japan. The name means "Spectacles Bridge" (you'll understand once you see the twin arches reflected in the water).

The street parallel to the canal on the east is Teramachi-dori. It contains a number of temples (hence the name) and is a pleasant area for strolling. The most famous of Nagasaki's four Chinese temples, **Sofuku-ji** to the southeast, was built by the Chinese monk Chonen in 1629 for the benefit of Nagasaki's large population of Chinese from Fujian. Displaying architecture of the late Ming period now rare in Southern China itself, the Main Hall and Second Gate are National Treasures. The precinct features a giant caldron used to

Stone sages seem ready to wax wise in the courtyard of ornate Koshi-byo.

Nagasaki Museum of History and Culture
www.nmhc.jp
✉ 1-1-1 Tateyama
☎ 095/818-8366
🕒 8:30 a.m.–7 p.m., closed 3rd Thurs.
$ $$
🚋 Tram: Sakura-machi

Suwa-jinja Shrine
✉ 18-15 Kaminishiyama-machi
☎ 095/824-0445
🚋 Tram: Suwajinja-mae

Sofuku-ji Temple
✉ 7-5 Kajiya-machi
☎ 095/823-2645
🕒 8 a.m.–5 p.m
$ $
🚋 Tram: Shokakuji Station

The oldest Western-style building still standing in Japan, Nagasaki's Glover Mansion was built in 1863.

Nagasaki Museum of History & Folklore
- 7-8 Hirano-machi
- 095/847-9245
- 9 a.m.–5 p.m.; closed Mon.
- Tram: Mori-machi

Glover Garden
- 8-1 Minami, Yamate-machi
- 095/822-8223
- 8 a.m.–9:30 p.m. Apr. 27–Oct. 9; closes at 6 p.m. in winter
- $$
- Tram: Oura-Tenshudo-shita

cook food for the starving during a famine in 1681. Chinese and Japanese of Chinese ancestry come here from all over Japan to celebrate Obon—the festival of the dead—on the lunar calendar from July 26 to 28.

West from Sofuku-ji toward the harbor is the one-time Dutch trading enclave of **Dejima,** a fan-shaped islet artificially fashioned from land reclaimed in Nagasaki Bay. Only a single building and various salvaged items remain at the **Nagasaki Museum of History and Folklore (Nagasaki-shi Rekishi Minzoku Shiryokan).** In the garden is a one-fifth scale model of the Dejima that was. There are main roads on either side and some new buildings, but aerial photographs reveal Dejima's fan-shaped configuration; recent excavations have unearthed whole sections of the original outer wall. The city of Nagasaki and the Japanese government have ambitious plans to restore Dejima as it was. The old trading post was accurately mapped and depicted by, among others, artist Kawahara Keiga in the early 19th century; displayed in the museum, such works will form the basis of the project, scheduled for completion in 2010.

On Minami-yamate Hill, in the south of the city and with a spectacular view over the bay, **Glover Garden (Guraba-en)—**actually a sizable park—contains the earliest wooden Western-style buildings (dating from the latter 19th century), still standing in Japan. As such, it is probably Nagasaki's most popular tourist attraction. Originally sited in other parts of the city, most of the houses were dismantled and reassembled here; among them is the **No. 2 Dock House (Kyu-Mitsubishi Dai-ni Dokku Hausu),** moved from the Mitsubishi Shipyard on the bay, and noteworthy **merchants' homes,** including the Walker, Ringer, and Alt houses. The buildings are largely of wood, with verandas and shutters in typical Far Eastern colonial style, betraying the fact that their occupants had mainly been in China before coming to Japan. **Glover Mansion (Kyu-Guraba Jutaku)** is the only one that has always stood on this spot. It was built in 1863 for Thomas Glover (1838–1911), an enterprising Scotsman who arrived in Nagasaki in 1859 and spent the rest of his life in Japan. After running a coal mine, Glover built Japan's first modern shipyard (later operated by Mitsubishi). Also an arms dealer, he supplied weapons to the Satsuma clan, which overthrew the shogunate. Glover defied the ban on travel for Japanese, helping several young men escape to study in London; among them in 1862 was Ito Hirobumi, who later became Japan's first prime minister.

The Japanese like to associate the Glover Mansion with Puccini's tragic opera, *Madam Butterfly;* a marble relief of Puccini graces the house and a statue of Japanese diva Miura Tamaki stands on the hill above it. In those days temporary marriage contracts between foreigners and locals (usually geisha) legitimized relationships far too wittingly carnal to prompt a suicide. Glover's marriage to a local woman—unlike that of Lt. Pinkerton, betrayer of the Nagasaki heroine of the opera—was permanent and produced two children.

In the same area stands **Oura Catholic Church (Oura Tenshu-do).** Built by French priest Bernard Petitjean for the foreign community in 1865, this charming church commemorates Nagasaki's 26 Christian martyrs and was the country's first in the Gothic style. It immediately attracted "Hidden Christians," who came out for the first time in 200 years—albeit with extreme caution, for Japanese were forbidden to practice the religion until 1872. The meeting between the group and Father Petitjean is captured in a bronze bas-relief in the courtyard. Designated a National Treasure, the church is much admired for its wooden architecture and fine stained-glass windows.

Charming Oura Catholic Church, built by a French priest in 1865, inspired Japan's secret Christians to emerge from centuries in hiding.

The **Confucian Shrine (Koshi-byo),** renowned for its distinctive bright yellow roof tiles and rich red walls visible from the Dutch slope, was originally built in 1893 by and for Nagasaki's Chinese community to honor the great sage Confucius. Torched in the conflagration that swept the city after the A-bomb, the shrine was rebuilt over an eight-year period and completed in 1967, then extensively refurbished in 1983. Neither this history nor the marble statues of Confucius and his 72 disciples that stand around the courtyard make this shrine unique: Built and maintained by Chinese and kept under the jurisdiction of the Chinese embassy in Tokyo, Koshi-byo is officially a little corner of China.

The adjacent **Historical Museum of China (Chugoku Rekidai Hakubutsukan)** is part of the Koshi-byo complex. It is maintained by its counterpart in Beijing and may contain up to 80 national cultural treasures from China at any given time. ■

Confucian Shrine & Historical Museum of China

- 10-36 Oura-machi
- 095/824-4022
- 8:30 a.m.–5 p.m
- $$
- Tram: Oura-Tenshudo-shita

Nagasaki's Huis Ten Bosch is a sophisticated re-creation of a classic Dutch town.

More places to visit on Kyushu

HUIS TEN BOSCH

Huis Ten Bosch (pronounced "House Ten Bosh") is probably the ultimate theme park statement in a country obsessed with theme parks. It is on Omura Bay near the town of Sasebo, some 30 miles (50 km) north of Nagasaki. The idea of a small Dutch town complete with gabled house-fronts, windmills, and canals may not sound appealing if you're chasing the Japan experience—but then a concept so outlandish and futuristic could only be Japanese. If you're traveling with kids, this could be a perfect day out. Reproducing famous buildings in Holland (including the eponymous Huis Ten Bosch royal palace and the Domtoren church tower of Utrecht) only a fraction under full size, Huis Ten Bosch is part amusement park, part residential housing.

Huis Ten Bosch is the kind of place you can imagine one day under a bubble in space. Water and sewage systems, climate control, power, even canal and harbor maintenance all derive from cutting-edge, eco-friendly technology: Built on 380 acres (152 ha) of land reclaimed for an industrial park project that was later abandoned, it features 7.5 miles (12 km) of walkways made with brick from Holland, as well as 400,000 trees and 300,000 color-coordinated tulips.

Just about every kind of quaint, picturesque, and above all Dutch-style conveyance—wheeled or floating—seems to ply Huis Ten Bosch. You can even take a trip around the bay aboard a copy of a vintage tall ship. The park has 11 museums, some devoted to antique Japanese export ceramics, antique glass, or works by Dutch artist M. C. Escher (1898–1972), a master of optical illusion. Fusing futuristic multimedia concepts, the theme park attractions include evocations of Escher's topsy-turvy world, sea travel, and a Dutch fairy tale.

316 B4 **Visitor information**
0956/27-0001 $$$$$

POTTERY TOWNS OF SAGA-KEN

Returning from ultimately futile attempts to conquer Korea in the 16th century, Toyotomi Hideyoshi's troops brought back Korean potters to work in Arita in northern Kyushu. Several, including the great Ri Sampei, later took Japanese citizenship. The Nabeshimas, feudal lords of the old province of Hizen, held their potters prisoner, which kept professional

A master potter in Arita puts the finishing touches on a delicate traditional vase.

secrets from rivals; exclusive and reclusive, the Nabeshima potteries dominated the industry until the end of the feudal era. The first Arita ceramics are said to have been created by Ri Sampei in 1616, following his discovery in the local area of kaolin—the exceptionally light clay needed to produce the hardness and whiteness of porcelain.

In 1675 the Korean potters moved from Arita to Okawachiyama, a district of the nearby coastal town of Imari. Whether made in Arita or Okawachiyama, the finished goods were exported from the port of Imari, which gave its name to this kind of pottery. The earliest variety of Imari ware was blue and white, but the Japanese ceramicist Sakaida Kakiemon introduced new polychrome glazing techniques. Applied as an overglaze enamel, the brightly colored designs of Imari were inspired by Japanese screen paintings, textile design, and lacquerware. Imari ware was exported from Dejima (Nagasaki) by the Dutch East India Company and soon caught the attention of the West for its exquisite design and quality. Influenced by Chinese pottery, Imari in turn had an impact on ceramics in Holland (Delft), England, and Germany.

Imari's popularity declined during the 19th century, when the designs became overly ornate and were applied by transfer rather than hand-painting. Kakiemon porcelain, made by Sakaida's descendants and featuring delicate enamel painting on an immaculate white background, was considered the most refined. However, potteries in Okawachiyama and Arita continued to turn out traditional Imari designs, including hand-painted ones—as indeed they still do. Declared Intangible Cultural Assets by the government, the descendants of the Kakiemon and Nabeshima pottery families are still working today.

Arita lies in a valley surrounded by the hills that yield clay. The townscape is characterized by dozens of chimneys rising from its kilns. In addition to these, Arita has a cluster of substantial museums. **Kyushu Ceramic Museum (Saga-kenritsu Kyushu Toji Bunkakan,** *Toshaku, Arita-machi, tel 0955/ 43-3681)* is highly recommended for anyone interested in the history and development of the craft over the island. Many kilns are open to the public; the most prestigious—**Kakiemon, Imaemon** (run by the descendants of the Nabeshima potters), and **Iwao Taizan—** have museums containing fine collections of old Imari ware.

In nearby **Imari,** the site of what were called the "secret kilns" in the early days is now occupied by **Nabeshima Hanyo-koen Park.** This is a kind of theme park, incorporating the ruins of the Nabeshima potteries and focusing on all there is to know about Imari pottery then and now, as well as on the working life of captive Korean potters. The center of Imari's ceramic activities, the Okawachicho area still boasts some 20 kilns. Imari has a number of museums containing not only ceramic collections but also potters working on the premises, notably the **Imari and Arita Ceramic Industry Hall** *(Okawachicho, Imari-shi, tel 0955/22-6333, closed Mon.)* and the **Imari Ware Hall** *(Shintencho, Imari-shi, tel 0955/23-8121).*

The other great Saga pottery town is **Karatsu,** 15 miles (25 km) due north of Imari. Originally based on Yi ware from Korea, Karatsu ware emerged as the tea ceremony gained popularity during the Momoyama period (1573–1603). Consisting of basic shapes and deliberately (if deceptively) rough-hewn, this type of ware was considered ideal for the tea ceremony. Still much sought after by "tea-ists," Karatsu ware displays brown- and ocher-colored glazes sometimes decorated with geometric shapes, or plants and flowers executed with bold, simple brushstrokes. Kilns are open to the public; check times with the visitor information center.

Like so many former feudal towns, Karatsu rebuilt its vanished stronghold, **Karatsu-jo Castle** *(8-15 Higashi-jonai, tel 0955/72-5697),* during the 1960s. Perched on a hill by the sea, the castle not only looks particularly fine but also contains an interesting museum devoted to local archaeology and pottery.

316 B4 **Visitor information** Imari 0955/23-3479; Karatsu 0955/72-4963

KAGOSHIMA CITY

With a pleasant climate and Mount Sakura-jima, its very own Vesuvius, smoking across the bay, vibrant Kagoshima is known as "the Naples of Japan." Of vital historical importance, Kagoshima saw the arrival of St. Francis Xavier and the Portuguese in the 16th century. It was the domain of the Satsuma—the clan instrumental in overthrowing the shogunate in 1867. The city's most famous hero is Saigo Takamori: Having successfully fought to oust the old regime, he later changed his mind and met his demise at Kumamoto-jo Castle during the Satsuma Rebellion he instigated in 1877. Badly damaged in World War II, Kagoshima has few vestiges of the past. A couple of notable Western-style buildings from the 1860s, such as Iso Foreigner's Residence, stand in the north of town, and the **Museum of the Meiji Restoration** *(ishin furusato-kan; 23-1 Kajiya-machi, Kagoshima-shi, tel 099/239-7700)* is reputed for its brilliant evocations of the period.

Kagoshima is popular for its scenic views of Sakura-jima. Ferries run at 15-minute intervals; from the ferry terminal you can board a bus to visit the volcano. If conditions near the summit are safe, Sakura-jima opens hiking trails that approach the crater, notably up to the Yunohira Observation Point.

316 B2 **Visitor information** JR Kagoshima-Chuo Station 099/253-2500

MIYAZAKI

Mountainous Miyazaki-ken, 76 percent of which is forested, is refreshingly unspoiled. Attracting Japanese holidaymakers eager for a fix of tropicana with its avenues of palm trees, however, Miyazaki city presents a rather different picture. Its huge Seagaia resort complex is famous for an enormous leisure facility incorporating golf courses, a spa and onsen, and luxury accommodation.

While **Miyazaki-jingu Shrine** is revered for its association with Shinto creation myths, the region itself shows some of the earliest signs of habitation in Japan. Dating as far back as the fourth century, the 311 burial mounds at Saitobaro constitute one of the most important archaeological sites in Japan.

Obi, near Nichinan city, is an old castle town with several old samurai houses and a castle, partially restored as a museum depicting the lifestyle of the last feudal lords.

Among Miyazaki's natural assets is Kirishima-Yaku Parkland, which includes Mount Kirishima, actually consisting of 23 peaks. Here the country's highest *onsen* resort finds adepts even in high summer. Among the prefecture's coastal resorts is Aoshima, known for its fine beaches—some of them the best suited for surfing in the country.

316 C2 **Visitor information** JR Miyazaki Station 0985/22-6469 ■

Stretching almost to Taiwan, Okinawa-ken consists of the Ryukyu-shoto—a synonym for an exotic getaway. White sands and turquoise seas grace a subtropical archipelago whose culture and atmosphere differ from those of mainland Japan.

Okinawa & the Ryukyu-shoto

Introduction & map **342–43**
Naha **344–45**
More places to visit in Okinawa & the Ryukyu-shoto **346–48**
Hotels & restaurants on Okinawa **379**

Scuba diving in the waters of the Ryukyu-shoto

Okinawa & the Ryukyu-shoto

TOO FAR AWAY TO BE ON THE ITINERARY OF MOST FOREIGNERS VISITING Japan, Okinawa-ken is a destination worthy of consideration in its own right and a firm favorite with mainland Japanese sun-worshippers, water sports enthusiasts, and outdoor fanatics. History and culture make this Japan at its most un-Japanese; to the many mainlanders who increasingly flock there, it is Japan at its most exotic.

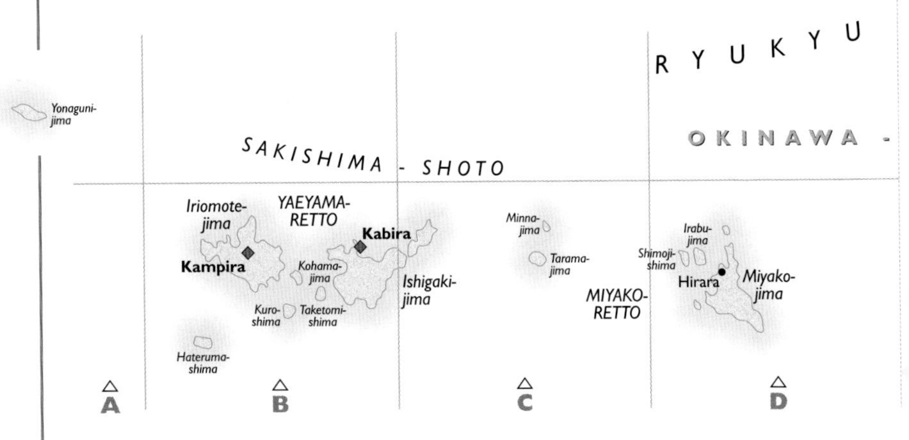

Basking in an annual mean temperature of 75°F (24°C) and lying on the same latitude as Miami and the Bahamas, Okinawa-ken is renowned for postcard-perfect coral islands, year-round hibiscus flowers, and turquoise-blue seas. Forty-seven of its 160 or so islands, known as Ryukyu-shoto, are inhabited. The largest is the main island of Okinawa Honto, or simply Okinawa, which includes the prefectural capital of Naha.

Some 200 miles (320 km) southwest, the Miyako group centers on Miyako-jima Island, known for its spectacular beaches and the picturesque old town of Hirara. More fine beaches gird adjacent islets and the Yaeyama Archipelago 60 miles (100 km) southwest. Yaeyama includes Iriomote, renowned for possessing Japan's only real jungle, and Yonaguni-jima, popular with the Japanese as the nation's westernmost island. It lies little more than 60 miles (100 km) east of Taiwan.

The Okinawans, primarily of Japanese origin, are thought to have migrated from the Japanese mainland rather than from neighboring countries. Virtually incomprehensible to other Japanese, their dialect is believed to be rooted in languages spoken in Japan more than a millennium ago. The Ryukyu islanders were seafarers and traders; an important trading bridge between Japan and Asia from the 14th century on, their kingdom reached its zenith in the 16th century.

The islands present a fascinating cultural mix, influenced by trade with China, Taiwan, and Indonesia. Traditional Okinawan textiles—the beautiful, brightly patterned *bingata* are the best known—show designs strikingly similar to the batik cloth of Java, including flowers, fish, birds, human figures, and festival scenes. The Indonesian connection is evident too in Okinawan music, which is based on a scale closer to the Javanese than the Japanese. Okinawan music spans a range of traditions, including classical, folk, and

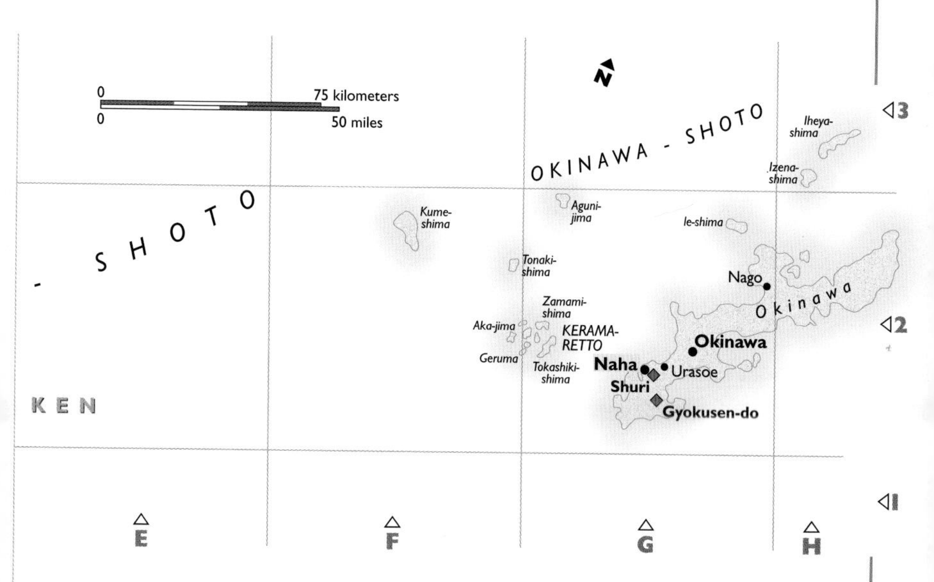

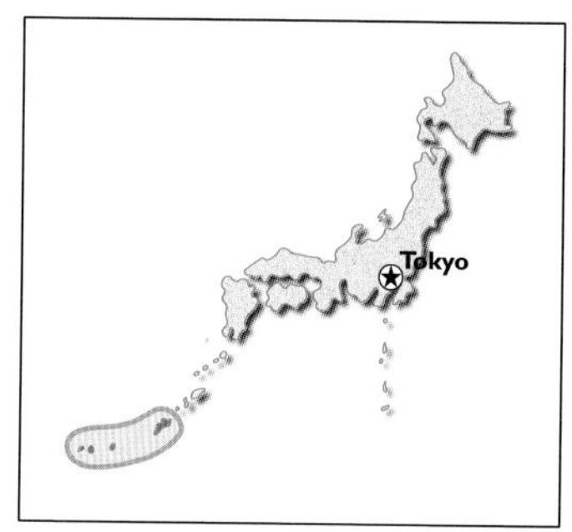

an interesting, fiercely rhythmic fusion of the latter with rock. Okinawa has several traditional dance forms; *eisa,* the most famous, is performed during the Okinawan equivalent of the Japanese O-bon festival for the dead (see p. 386).

The local architecture blends Japanese with Ming-dynasty Chinese elements. The roofs of Shuri-jo Castle in Naha and the ceramic dragons winding over them testify to this. Even private houses frequently have roofs adorned with *shi-isa,* the fierce ceramic lion-dogs once believed to drive evil spirits from the home. Like the rest of Japan, Okinawa embraces Shintoism and Buddhism, but the shi-isa is a facet of a different belief system.

With an economy based on sugarcane, pineapples, and fishing, Okinawa has always been Japan's poorest prefecture; tourism has helped the economy. Like industrialization on the mainland, however, the success of tourism has exacted a price. Large Japanese corporations went on an investment spree in Okinawa in the late 1970s, turning pineapple plantations into golf courses and dotting bays and beaches with monster concrete resorts where Muzak is piped in from speakers in the trees. That said, Okinawa is more than just a marshaling point for visiting other, less spoiled islands. It is very much the heart of a cultural heritage separating Ryukyu-shoto from the rest of Japan.

Air and ferry services run between the major islands and the mainland; all islands are interconnected by ferry and the larger islands by air. The islands are at their best from March through May. From June to October, typhoons typically occur six to eight times throughout Okinawa; although they rarely last long enough to ruin a trip, the storms may close airports. In the rainy season *(tsuyu)* from late May to June, expect heavy downpours. ■

Naha

NAHA WAS ALMOST TOTALLY DESTROYED IN 1945. THE town benefited from a layout dictated by the occupying United States Army, which ran bulldozers through the ruins to create a new main drag, Kokusai-dori. Despite subsequent jerry-building and architectural brutalism in the 1960s and 70s, the city is pleasant.

Naha's impressive Shuri-jo Castle was rebuilt using the original 18th-century plans.

Naha

343 G2

Visitor information

Naha Airport

098/857-6884

Direct flights to Naha airport from Tokyo (2 hrs. 30 min.) and other major cities

Since the mid-1980s, legislation has decreed architectural principles for new buildings; the traditional red-tiled roof is de rigueur. Running eastward from the town center, Kokusai-dori is in every way the main artery. Department stores, administrative buildings, plush fashion stores, trendy boutiques, army-surplus stores, souvenir shops (expensive and otherwise), restaurants, bars, *pachinko* parlors, and discos all seem to stand haphazardly and merrily right on or just off it. Eastward along the avenue, the shopping options become more reminiscent of an Asian bazaar as you turn right at the Mitsukoshi department store and head down the covered arcades. Called Ichiba-dori and Heiwa-dori, these lead to the colorful Dai ichi Kosetsu Ichiba—the city food market. Southeast of it is **Tsuboya,** a traditional Okinawan pottery district since the 17th century, where there are still some narrow lanes and older houses. Visit the potteries and kilns or **Tsuboya Pottery Museum.** Once purely utilitarian, Okinawan pottery consisted mainly of jars and pots; the repertoire now includes attractive sake flasks and *shi-isa* (lion figurines).

There is certainly no shortage of action after nightfall in Naha. With all the provinces of pleasure from restaurants to raunch, **Makishi** and **Maejima** districts are said to boast the greatest concentration of bars in Japan. On a more sober note, traditional performing arts are presented weekly at the **Kenritsu Kyodo Theater (Kenritsu Kyodo Gekijo),** near the Asahibashi Bridge.

Some 1.2 miles (2 km) beyond the city's eastern edge is **Shuri,** the old capital of the Ryukyu kingdom, famous for **Shuri-jo Castle,** the region's prime tourist destination. The castle was used as the Japanese Army headquarters during World War II. After the Battle of Okinawa in 1945, only the massive stone walls, including the **Kankaimon gate,** were still standing, although heavily damaged. One gate of the former shrine on the compound remains intact, but everything else was reduced to rubble. The ornate Chinese-style **Shureimon** entry gate was reconstructed in 1958 and is now a symbol of Okinawa. One of the most ambitious and successful restoration projects ever undertaken in Japan, the work was completed in 1992.

By using the surviving 18th-century plans, the restorers were able to leave the main castle buildings looking as they did in the 1700s. The main **Seiden Hall,** originally used for royal state ceremonies, is the most photographed building on Okinawa, but the whole castle compound is an enthralling sight, at the very least as a masterpiece of restoration. ■

Tsuboya Pottery Museum
- ✉ 1-9-32 Tsuboya
- ☎ 098/862-3761
- 🕒 10 a.m.–6 p.m. (last entry 5:30); closed Mon.
- $ $

Shurji-jo Castle
www.shurijo.com
- ✉ 1-2 Kinjo-cho, Shuri
- ☎ 098/886-2020
- 🕒 9 a.m.–7:30 p.m. Apr.–June, Oct.–Nov.; closes at 8:30 p.m. July–Sept.; closes at 6:30 p.m. Dec.–Mar.
- $ $$$
- 🚌 Monorail to Shurijo Station

Traditional Okinawan pottery by Kuo Takaesu

More places to visit in Okinawa & the Ryukyu-shoto

The narrow island of Okinawa is 84 miles (135 km) long. It still has fairly unspoiled areas both inland and on the coast, but most are in the north, beyond the sleepy town of Nago. Some of the best beaches around here have been taken over by plush resort hotels.

Southern Okinawa, known as **Nanbu,** is dotted with monuments and memorials to fallen soldiers and civilians; one of them, the **Konpaku-no-To** on the south coast, is dedicated to the 35,000 war dead buried in a mass grave. About 2.5 miles (4 km) southwest of Naha, the **Underground Naval Headquarters (Kyu Kaigun Shireibugo,** *236 Tomigusuku, Tomigusuku-mura, tel 098/850-4055, 8:30 a.m.–5 p.m., $, bus: 33, 46 or 101 from Naha bus station to Tomigusuku-koen-mae)* was a stronghold honeycombed with 1,640 yards (1,500 m) of tunnels; 220 yards (200 m) of these are currently open to the public, along with the rooms they connected. Some of the walls are cratered and pock-marked—a gruesome reminder of the 4,000 members of the Japanese Navy who, spurning the disgrace of defeat, committed suicide in here, mainly by hand grenade. More poignant still is **Himeyuri-no-To,** a monument commemorating the mass suicide of 200 Okinawan schoolgirls and their teachers who chose to die by remaining inside a cave in the path of a systematically bombarding U.S. tank regiment. Farther south on the coast is **Mabuni Hill (Mabuni-no-Oka),** site of the Japanese Imperial Army's last stand on June 23, 1945. In addition to the hillside's forest of monuments and memorials contributed from all over Japan, there is an interesting **Peace Memorial Museum (Heiwa Kinen Shiryokan** *(614-1 Mabuni, Itoman-shi, tel 098/997-3844, 9 a.m.–5 p.m., $, bus: from Itoman bus terminal to Heiwa-kinendo-iriguchi).*

After such grim reminders of the past, you may welcome some lighter entertainment in the form of **Gyokusendo Kingdom Village** *(Bus: 83, 54 from Naha bus terminal to Gyokusendo),* especially if you're traveling with children. This Okinawan cultural theme park has artisans demonstrating crafts such as *bingata* textile making and displays of *eisa* dancing. Underneath it all is the **Gyokusendo limestone cave,** much visited for its hundreds of thousands of stalagmites and stalactites. Nearby is the **Gyokusendo Habu-koen Park.** Be prepared here to see hapless habu vipers (an Okinawan species with a nasty but rarely fatal bite) or cobras being tossed to a voracious mongoose; such shows are one of Okinawa's more dubious tourist attractions.

Urasoe, the first capital of the Ryukyu kingdom, lies about 6 miles (10 km) north of Naha. **Joseki-koen Park** contains the ruins of the first royal castle, and a short walk beyond it is a mausoleum built for kings of the 14th century. The ruins of another feudal castle stand nearby at **Kita Naka-Gusuku,** with fine views from its hilltop site. The area's main attraction is the **Nakamura House (Nakamura-ke** *Tel 098/935-3500, 9 a.m.–5:30 p.m., $),* just over half a mile (1 km) northeast, regarded as the finest example of aristocratic rural domestic architecture still standing in Okinawa. Built during the mid-18th century, it contains many furnishings, implements, and family heirlooms showing how wealthy Okinawans lived until the early 1900s.

Okinawan textiles

Depicting flowers, fish, birds, people, festival scenes, and more in vivid colors, *bingata* textile designs rank among the finest in Japan. Bingata are hand-painted using specially prepared stencils, and demand a great deal of skill. The Ryukyus are known for textiles of other kinds, too. *Bashofu* is a lightweight fabric hand-woven out of banana fibers in the north of Okinawa island; *kasuri* is a finely woven cloth made in the south. On Miyako-jima, the specialty is lightweight, indigo-dyed *jofu.* The *minsa* fabric of Yaeyama invariably shows a centipede woven in red against a dark background. Women made these for their fiancés as a sign of betrothal; the centipede was a symbol of eternal love. ■

Former Japanese Prime Minister Junichiro Koizumi prays for war victims in front of the cenotaph at Itoman's Peace Memorial Park.

As elsewhere in Japan, development has taken its toll on many venerable buildings in Okinawa, so fine farmhouses and other buildings representative of a past way of life were dismantled in other parts of the island and reassembled in an open-air museum. **Ryukyu-mura Village** *(1130 Aza Yamada, Onna Village, tel 098/965-1234, 8:30 a.m.–6 p.m., $$)* is touristy, but it has interesting exhibits of Okinawan culture and crafts, including demonstrations on traditional performing arts, music, and textile weaving. Here again you can see regularly staged one-sided combats between mongoose and snake.

343 F1–H3 **Visitor information**
Okinawa Prefectural Tourism Federation, Naha Airport, 150 Kagamizu
098/965-1234

RYUKYU-SHOTO

You don't have to go too far from Okinawa to discover an island paradise. The spectacularly beautiful **Kerama Islands** *(Visitor information: ferry terminal on Zamami-jima, tel 098/987-2277)* are only 18 miles (30 km) offshore, placing them smack-dab on the beaten track. Of the three main islands, **Tokashiki-jima** is the largest and most crowded during the holiday season. **Zamami-jima** and **Aka-jima** are both highly prized by divers and snorkelers—the water in the Keramas remains transparent down to quite a depth. Zamami has successfully converted from whaling to whale-watching, a lucrative pursuit that draws pod-people to the island in winter. The inhabited islands are well endowed with hotels and *minshuku,* but they can get crowded; many people without a hotel reservation simply camp on the beaches of the 20 or so uninhabited islands within easy reach. Ferries run regularly between the islands, so getting around is fairly simple. From Zamami or Aka-jima you can visit the remoter island of **Geruma,** notable for the Kerama *shika*—a unique species of deer.

The **Miyako** group *(Visitor information: Miyako-jima Airport, tel 09807/2-0899),* eight islands boasting spectacular seascapes and coral reefs for diving and snorkeling, has few historical or cultural sights, except in the town of **Hirara** on the main island of **Miyako-jima.** Built low against the ground with thick surrounding walls of coral limestone, the houses here have red-tiled roofs, a style that came to replace the thatch ubiquitous over the Ryukyu-shoto only within the 20th century. Other sights include **Nakasone Toimiya—**

the ornate mausoleum of a local 15th-century military hero—and the curious **Jintoze-iseki (Tax Stone).** The stone stands 4.5 feet (1.4 m) high, and only those shorter than this were exempted from the taxes exacted by the ruling Satsuma clan of Kyushu. Taxes were sometimes paid in a lightweight, indigo cloth called *jofu* (see p. 346), still widely made today —but for the tourist rather than the taxman.

Sports are popular on Miyako-jima: Several serious scuba diving enterprises operate here, and each April the isle hosts Japan's infamous Strongman Challenge Triathlon, which involves swimming 1.8 miles (3 km), cycling 87 miles (140 km), then cooling down with a quick marathon run (26 miles/42 km).

Much less visited are Miyako's seven outlying islands, largely to the west, which are accessible by boat and possess beautiful beaches. Notable among them are **Shimoji-jima** and **Irabu-jima,** separated from each other by a narrow channel.

Continuing southwest, you come to the **Yaeyama-Shoto Islands** *(Ishigaki-jima Tourist Association, tel 09808/2-2809).* For many people, **Ishigaki-jima—**the transportation hub (both sea and air) of the Yaeyama group—is simply a stepping-stone to Taketomi-jima and Iriomote (see below). But Ishigaki boasts good beaches, diving options, and a center for black pearl culture on **Kabira-wan Bay** in the northwest. Its noteworthy sights include **Torin-ji Temple** with its 18th-century buildings, the **Yaeyama Minzoku-en village** *(967-1 Montonagura, 09808/2-8798)* devoted to the crafts (mainly textiles and pottery) of the Yaeyama group, and old cobbled streets flanked by typical low Ryukyuan buildings. Among them is the **Miyara Donchi** *(178 Okawa, tel 09808/2-2767, closed Tues.),* a fine aristocratic residence built in the early 19th century and open as a museum. At 1,726 feet (526 m), scenic Mount Omoto-dake at the center of the island is the highest point in Okinawa-ken.

Less than 15 minutes away by boat from Ishigaki-jima, **Taketomi-jima** could be accused of being flat and featureless were it not for the charm of **Taketomi village** with its low, garden-girdled houses and outstanding beaches. You can see artisans making the textiles the island is known for at **Taketomi Folk Art Center (Taketomi Mingei-kan,** *435 Taketomi, tel 09808/5-2302).* Some beaches, especially those on the west coast, are known as *hoshizunahama,* or star-sand beaches; the sand is made up of the star-shaped skeletons of tiny marine creatures.

Iriomote-jima, Japan's great tropical wilderness, has 80 miles (130 km) of coastline, mangrove swamps, and hills covered in dense, uncharted virgin forest. This island also is the home of the Iriomote wildcat, believed by some zoologists to be a living fossil. Only slightly larger than a domestic cat, the wildcat is speckled rather than striped and has slightly rounder ear tips. Experts reckon that only about 50 of the animals survive, so your chances of sighting one are slim.

Though touted as wild and unexplored, Iriomote is crisscrossed with hiking trails. The best known path traverses the island diagonally from the northwest—an exhilarating prospect if you don't mind leeches. Among spectacular scenic attractions on the island are the waterfalls at **Kampira** and **Pinaisara,** as well as some beautiful boat trips along jungle rivers that have been compared to miniature versions of the Amazon. Otherwise coastal Iriomote offers the usual options for swimming, diving, and resorts. The same goes for other small islands nearby, notably **Kohama-jima** and **Kuro-shima.**

The final stop in the Ryukyu-Shoto is **Yonaguni-jima,** an island 7 miles (11 km) long that lies just 60 miles (100 km) east of Taiwan. Short of clambering up Mount Urabu-dake (755 feet/230 m) to glimpse the distant mountains of Taiwan, there isn't a lot to see and do on Yonaguni-jima—which may explain why the island brews the strongest sake in Japan. If you sample it, don't worry about the size of the moths you might see flitting about—they would look the same if you were sober. Called *yonagunisan,* they are among the world's largest. The island's only other draw is its strange underwater rock formations. For the Japanese, Yonaguni's real attraction is its role as the last outpost. The same applies to the isle of **Hateruma-jima,** south of Iriomote. Daytrippers like to visit this tiny island's **southernmost rock (Sainantan-no-Hi),** a landmark designating the southernmost point in Japan. ■

Travelwise

Travelwise information **350–57**
Planning your trip **350–51**
How to get to Japan **351**
Getting around **351–53**
Practical advice **353–56**
Emergencies **356–57**
Language guide **357**
Hotels & restaurants **358–79**
Shopping **380–83**
Entertainment & festivals **384–88**

Festivals are a colorful part of Japanese life.

TRAVELWISE INFORMATION

PLANNING YOUR TRIP

WHEN TO GO

Japan has four distinct seasons, but spring and fall are generally the best times to visit, with the flowering cherries of spring and the autumnal reds of maple leaves constituting favorite postcard images. Rain is no stranger to either season, but fine spring weather really shows the country at its best.

Overall, the archipelago's climate ranges from Siberian (Hokkaido) to subtropical (Okinawa). There is also a mini rainy season known as *tsuyu* lasting from early June to mid-July, when hot winds from the tropical Pacific blow across Honshu, sending summer temperatures up to around 80°F (26°C), with humidity at a debilitating 80 percent plus. Summer temperatures in Kyushu and Okinawa average higher, but with less humidity the climate is more comfortable.

Despite the drawbacks of the Japanese summer, it can also be pleasant. However, peak summer travel is marred by daunting crowds and higher prices; make reservations well ahead. In Northern Honshu (Tohoku) and Hokkaido temperatures rarely go above 70°F (21°C) in late July. With the added attraction of its large wilderness, small wonder that Hokkaido is an increasingly popular summer vacation destination.

Mid-October to mid-November is the time to appreciate Japan's famous autumn colors. In early fall, from the start of September until around the end of October, the Pacific side of the country is prone to typhoons that sweep up from the tropics packing high winds and torrential rain. The oriental equivalent of the hurricane, they can occasionally cause disastrous flooding and mud slides.

Although it can get pretty cold at night, especially on high ground, winter is consistently fine and sunny on the Pacific coast. However, the area of Honshu bordering the Sea of Japan is one of the snowiest places in the world. It is also one of the rainiest: Average annual precipitation stands at 102 inches (265 cm)—about twice as much as Tokyo gets. Winter in northern Japan can be very cold indeed, with ice floes sailing past the coast in Hokkaido's far north, where the sea can freeze over for miles. Far from deterring visitors, such subarctic phenomena are what attracts them; hot springs are plentiful on Hokkaido, which also has some of the finest ski resorts in Japan.

WHAT TO TAKE

It doesn't rain as much in winter, but rainwear is sensible at any other time. Inexpensive umbrellas and plastic raincoats light enough to fold up and carry in a pocket or bag are sold everywhere.

Take account of heat and humidity when selecting summer clothing. T-shirts, light cotton shirts, or blouses usually suffice, but air-conditioning is often ferocious. The Japanese are probably the best dressed people in the world; don't wander around urban centers in beachwear, although shorts are acceptable. Coat-and-tie dress codes operate in some places, especially expensive restaurants.

You will need strong, lightweight footwear. Consider shoes that you can slip out of easily when entering temples, *ryokan,* some restaurants, or private homes. Be warned that the wooden floors of historic buildings such as castles can be bitterly cold in winter, so make sure you wear thick socks.

In summer it can get cold at higher altitudes. Take a fleece jacket or lightweight parka. Winter may be sunny and mild in many places during the daytime, but you will still need warm clothing from December through March.

If you're staying in Japanese-style accommodations or intend to visit *onsen* baths, be warned that the towels issued will be minute—the Japanese *tenugui* is hardly larger than a washcloth. If you feel you cannot get used to this, bring your own towel.

INSURANCE

Japan's medical standards are among the world's highest, but care is priced accordingly and fees are prohibitive. Make sure that medical coverage in your travel insurance is adequate. If your stay in Japan is extended, take out internationally recognized medical insurance before going.

ENTRY FORMALITIES

Passports & visas Provided they have a valid passport, U.S. and Canadian citizens may remain in Japan for 90 days without a visa. U.K. citizens are also granted 90 days at time of landing, but can apply for an extension of up to six months. Japan has a bewildering array of visa exemption agreements with different countries. If you are in doubt, call the Japanese consulate before planning your trip.

The stamp in your passport on arrival grants you temporary visitor status for the stipulated period. Whatever your allowance, you can get an extension provided that you apply ten days before its expiry date and that your total stay doesn't exceed six months. If your stay will be longer than 90 days, you must apply for an alien registration card at a town hall within your first 90 days in Japan regardless of your status. Foreigners are required by law to carry their passports (and alien registration cards, if required) at all times. Foreigners are sometimes stopped by police (usually at night) and asked to produce their papers.

A maximum of two extensions after the initial visa period is allowed if you have a good enough reason. You will probably have to provide proof that you can afford to remain. If you want to stay in Japan longer than six months and two extensions, the only way is to leave the country and re-enter. Your passport stamps will make this apparent to the immigration official, though, and you may find entry difficult. If you wish to leave Japan and come back again within the time allowed on your passport stamp, you have to apply for a re-entry visa at the immigration office.

You are forbidden to work in Japan if your status is temporary visitor or tourist. If you do want to work, you must come in on a tourist visa and find a potential employer. The employer applies for permission to engage you while you apply for a work visa at the Japanese consulate in a neighboring country.

Customs The standard allowances into Japan are 2 ounces (57 g) of perfume, gifts (duty-free items other than perfumes, spirits, and tobacco) up to a value of 200,000 yen, and three 26-ounce (760 ml) bottles of spirits; to consume, purchase, or possess alcohol in Japan you must be over age 20. The tobacco allowance is 17.5 ounces (500 g, 400 cigarettes, or 100 cigars).

Immunizations Japan requires no special immunizations, unless you arrive from an area in which diseases such as cholera or yellow fever are endemic, when you should have a World Health Organization certificate of the appropriate vaccinations.

Pets Pets may be brought to Japan provided they have health certificates. They must be examined by quarantine officers at the port of entry. Cats and dogs require certificates of vaccination against rabies. If you bring them from one of the designated rabies-free areas, the detention could be as short as 12 hours, but even with a certificate, they are usually kept in quarantine at the owner's expense for a period of at least two weeks. It can be difficult to find hotels, restaurants, (or stores) that accept pets.

HOW TO GET TO JAPAN

From the U.S. there are several flights daily to Japan both from the East Coast (average time 13 hours via the polar route) and West Coast (average time 10 hours via the Pacific route).

Bound for Tokyo, most people land at Narita airport, but there has been an increase in direct flights to other airports following airport development. The largest is the recently built Kansai International Airport, the most convenient for Osaka, Kyoto, and Kobe. The CENTRAIR (Central Japan International Airport) handles international flights for Nagoya, whose airport is now for domestic flights only. There are direct flights to Fukuoka on Kyushu from Honolulu and Guam, but not from the U.S. mainland. There are no direct flights from the U.S. or Guam to Okinawa. The nonstop route from London to Tokyo takes around 12 hours.

GETTING AROUND

FROM THE AIRPORTS

Narita airport, 41 miles (66 km) away from Tokyo, is notoriously inconvenient, but there are several options for reaching the city. A **taxi** journey costs over $200. Much cheaper, and with journeys averaging 70 minutes depending upon traffic, the **Limousine Bus** leaves for Tokyo every 10–15 minutes. You simply purchase your ticket inside the terminal building; the bus stops right outside. Most go to Tokyo City Air Terminal (TCAT), but other, less frequent services stop at major hotels in town and there's another going directly to Yokohama. At TCAT a fleet of taxis wait to take you to your hotel or if you have little luggage and know how to get there, you can take the Hanzomon subway line.

The other way into town is by **train,** though less convenient if you have a lot of luggage. Tickets for the Narita Express (NEX) are between $25 and $30; the train takes 53 minutes to Tokyo Station and 84 minutes to Shinjuku. The service also runs (less frequently) to Ikebukuro, Shinagawa, and Yokohama.

Leaving around every half hour, the Keisei Skyliner airport express train takes 60 minutes from Narita to Ueno Station in Tokyo. Trains on the Keisei line take about 20 minutes longer, but are substantially cheaper. The Sobu line runs from Narita to Tokyo Station and takes 90 minutes. The Keisei line does not accept JR Rail Passes (see p. 353).

There's a similar range of connections from Kansai International airport to either Osaka or Kyoto; the buses to the former take about an hour and to the latter 90–105 minutes. Trains take about an hour to Osaka and 70–95 minutes to Kyoto. If you have a rail pass coupon and want to take a JR train from Kansai International Airport, you can exchange it for the pass at the JR West information desk in the international arrivals lobby.

When you leave the country, both Kansai International and

Narita airports levy a departure tax; Kansai's is around $25, which is payable at the airport, and Narita's is just under $20, which is applicable at the time of ticket issue (prices may vary according to the exchange rate).

TRAVELING IN THE CITIES

Public transport in Japanese cities is fast, efficient, and relatively cheap. With the traffic jams and difficult or expensive parking, the soundest advice is to forget about driving in the city unless you're planning an extended stay.

Subways Tokyo, Fukuoka, Kobe, Kyoto, Nagoya, Osaka, Sapporo, Sendai, and Yokohama all have subway systems. As with local line trains, you generally buy tickets from a machine. Some places have English-language maps inscribed with fare tariffs; most don't. When in doubt, pay the lowest fare and then pay the difference at your destination. This is often the best policy: In Tokyo, for instance, you might change between lines owned by different companies, and the pricing can be complicated. You can always ask the ticket office staff for assistance.

Buses In many cities, public transport is provided solely by buses. Hakodate (Hokkaido), Hiroshima (Honshu), Matsuyama (Shikoku), and Nagasaki and Kumamoto (Kyushu) have streetcar systems. Not all buses or streetcars have destinations in roman letters, so it's advisable to note the *kanji* characters spelling out your destination on a piece of paper and look for it on the front of the vehicle before boarding.

In Tokyo you pay a flat fare on entering the bus, but in most other places you take a ticket out of the automatic dispenser as you enter the bus or streetcar. The number on your ticket corresponds to the stop from which you boarded. Near the ceiling on the driver's left is an electric sign showing the stop number and the amount you must pay as you leave.

Taxis In Tokyo taxis seem to be everywhere. Although prices vary slightly in different areas, they are expensive. Taking a taxi at rush hour is never a good idea, as traffic jams can be formidable; if the cab gets caught in traffic, the extra time will be charged on the meter. There is a 20 percent surcharge for cabs summoned by phone, and the same applies to all taxis after 11 p.m.

Watch for the lights on the taxi roof: Yellow means that the cab is engaged, red that it is free, and green that a surcharge is operative. Whether inside or out of the taxi, don't even think of opening or closing the door—doors are automatically controlled by the driver.

Japanese cabbies are generally polite and helpful, but a Japanese business card, or your destination written in Japanese, is advisable: Most cities are without street names, and the random numerical address system in suburban and residential areas is decipherable only to postal workers and police; your driver may have to stop and ask the way.

TRAVELING AROUND JAPAN

By rail The train is the most convenient and fastest way to travel in Japan; the standards of punctuality, comfort, and cleanliness throughout Japanese rail services are legendary. But be warned: When changing trains, it can be a long way between platforms, there may be several staircases on the way, and there is no such thing as a porter. The golden rule is to travel light. Tickets can be purchased at all train stations. The privatized **Japan Railways (JR),** comprising six companies, runs major routes throughout the country, with other links—both express and local trains—provided by regional firms. It's possible to go virtually anywhere in Japan by train.

JR's premier service is the **shinkansen,** the bullet train, inaugurated for the 1964 Olympic Games. Long the world's fastest train, it currently vies for the record with France's TGV. Tokaido (Tokyo-Osaka), Sanyo (Osaka-Hakata), and Tohoku (Tokyo-Hachinohe) are the main lines; others include the Joetsu (Omiya-Niigata) and most recently Kyushu (Yatsushiro-Kagoshima). Trains are super express, express, and limited express—respectively called *nozomi, hikari,* and *kodama* on the Tokaido and Sanyo lines. Expect impeccable service. Seat reservations are inexpensive, but book well over a month ahead for peak periods.

Discounts Children under six travel free by rail, and it's half-price for those between 6 and 11; otherwise traveling by train —and by shinkansen especially— can become very expensive. Fortunately there are several different kinds of discount options available, notably the **five-day JR Youth 18 ticket** *(seishun juhachi kippu)*, which costs around $100; it's primarily designed for students and is valid only during the college vacation periods, but you can be any age to qualify. Although substantial, savings apply to local trains only—not the shinkansen.

By far the best deal is the **JR Rail Pass,** available for 7 ($260), 14 ($410), or 21 ($520) days (prices are approximate and about one-third more in each category if you want to travel by Green Car, first class). The pass entitles you to unlimited use of transport in the JR system for the duration, including the shinkansen (except for the ultra-fast nozomi), other JR trains, JR buses, and JR ferries. If you intend to make more than one intercity journey, the rail pass is absolutely essential. Note that it must be purchased outside Japan from an authorized travel agent.

The pass must be validated within three months of the date of purchase, but the actual starting date is determined when you exchange the voucher issued by the travel agent for the actual rail pass in Japan. You can make seat reservations only once you have obtained your pass (obtainable at the JR Travel Service Center in any main line train station—the options are listed on the back of the voucher). The rules governing the passes are strict. You cannot change the date once the pass is issued, and if you lose the pass, it will not be replaced.

JR West Rail Passes or **JR Kyushu Rail Passes** also represent substantial savings; JR East Rail Pass has a discount for those aged between 12 and 25. With the exception of JR West, these passes must also be purchased outside Japan. You are eligible for JR passes only if you are entering Japan with temporary visitor status. You will need your passport bearing the relevant stamps when you exchange the voucher for the pass.

By bus Budget-conscious travelers often opt for the inter-city bus services, a cheaper (though slower) alternative to the train. Fitted with reclining seats, night buses are reasonably comfortable. Tour buses abound in every major tourist center. They can make an excellent alternative to public buses if you are in a hurry but they are costly and, unless stated otherwise, the chances are that the tour will be conducted entirely in Japanese.

By air All of Japan's prefectural capitals are connected by air; there are plenty of options for reaching smaller cities, too. The main carriers are Japan Airlines (JAL), All Nippon Airways (ANA), and Japan Air System (JAS), but since the deregulation of the air transport industry in 1986, the number of local carriers is ever increasing. Domestic flights from Tokyo leave from Haneda airport. The Limousine Bus (see p. 351) shuttles between Haneda and Narita airport.

By ferry With an increasing number of interconnecting tunnels and bridges, it's easy to forget that Japan is an island nation. But if you're fond of older, slower ways of traveling or on a tight budget, the good news is that the inter-island ferry network is extensive. It's the best way to get to Sado Island and the most attractive means of traveling the Inland Sea. An overnight ferry to Hokkaido costs less than the train. JNTO (Japan National Tourist Office) offices have information about routes, times, and costs (for JNTO centers see p. 356).

Japanese ferries are fun: Passengers simply sprawl over large carpeted (or occasionally still tatami-matted) areas on the lower decks. Having removed your shoes, you select your spot and drop—to eat and drink, play cards, read, gossip, and eventually sleep. Cabins are available at extra cost.

By car Unless you are used to driving on the left-hand side of the road and can cope with some road signs in Japanese, you would be advised not to drive in Japan. That said, the car provides an alternative way to travel if you want to venture off the beaten track. The relatively high cost of highway tolls (Tokyo to Kyoto will set you back more than $90) and the price of gas may also deter you. You need a valid international driving permit plus your own license (but if you are staying on after the international driving license expires, you will need a Japanese one). The same pattern applies to motorcycles, although you may be required to take another test in Japan, especially for bikes of 750cc and up.

Car rental operations abound in Japan, with major international firms well represented. You may be able to reserve a car in Japan through the rental firm at home (try Hertz tel 800/654-3001, or National 800/227-7368). Large rental chains often will allow you to leave a car at a different location than where you rented it for no extra cost—ask for *norisute* (drop off) options.

Japan drives on the left. The speed limits are 50 mph (80 kph) on highways, 37.5 mph (60 kph) on secondary roads, and 25 mph (40 kph) in towns. Although bilingual versions are becoming the norm, some signs may still be in Japanese only.

Cycling Bicycle theft is probably the commonest of the few crimes you'll encounter in Japan, so if you cycle, make sure you always leave your bicycle locked. Provided you have a carrying bag (*rinko baggu*—available from cycling shops) and pay a small supplement to your fare, you can take your bicycle on the train. This is a cycle-friendly country if you stay as much as possible off the main roads. Recommended areas are the foothills of the Japan Alps on Honshu, Kyushu, Shikoku, and the national park areas in Hokkaido. Many places have bicycles for rent; outlets are typically close to the train station or tourist center.

PRACTICAL ADVICE

COMMUNICATIONS

Post offices Post offices and mailboxes are identified by a sign with a red or white "T" with a bar over the top. Main city and district post offices are open 8 a.m.–7 p.m. weekdays, 8 a.m.–3 p.m. Saturdays, and 9 a.m.–

12:30 p.m. Sundays. Branch offices are open 9 a.m.–5 p.m. and closed weekends. Only larger post offices offer currency exchange and poste restante. Uncollected mail is returned to sender after ten days.

Telephones Well maintained and never vandalized, Japan's pay phones almost always work. Using both coins and prepaid telephone cards *(terehon kado)*, they are widely sold in vending machines, station kiosks, and many other outlets. The cards come in denominations of ¥500, ¥1000, ¥3000, and ¥5000.

Green phones take cards and coins, but are mainly for domestic calls. Gray phones are both international and domestic and accept both coins and cards. The same applies to orange and green phones, which additionally accept international credit cards.

Calls are 20 percent cheaper between 7 p.m. and 11 p.m. on weekdays, and from 8 p.m. on holidays and weekends. A discount of up to 40 percent operates daily between 11 p.m. and 8 a.m. You can make **operator-assisted international calls** by dialing 0051 and collect calls using 106. Calls from pay phones will be cheaper than from hotel rooms.

There are pay phones other than those mentioned above, but mainly for domestic use. Nostalgic neighborhoods might also still boast an antiquated pink, red, or turquoise phone. These only take ten-yen coins and are for local calls only.

Note that your **cell phone** from overseas will be incompatible with the Japanese system. However, cell phones can be hired from international airports, as well as in some hotels. There is also an NTT-DoCoMo Roaming-in service available. Rent a handset for ¥750 per day and you can make and receive calls from your own home number.

Japanese cell phone providers advertise on the Internet. There is a good overview at Stanford University's guide to Japan information sources: http://jguide.stanford.edu/site/cell_phone_rental_2124.html.

International calls in Japan are provided by three companies: KDDI, ISD, and IDC. Their international access numbers are 001, 0041, and 0061, respectively. Thus, to call the U.S. using KDDI, dial 001 1 before the area code and number.

English-language services (emergencies, general information, counseling) are available from Tokyo English Lifeline (TELL): 03-5774-0992 daily 9 a.m.–11 p.m., and Japan Helpline: 0120-461-997 (toll-free) or 0570-000-911 (toll-free), 24 hours.

DRINKING WATER

It is safe to drink water straight from the faucet anywhere in Japan, although it may taste chlorinated. Bottled water, imported and domestic, is very popular and widely available.

ELECTRICITY

Japan's electric current is 100v AC, running at 50 cycles in Tokyo and on the Pacific side, and at 60 cycles in western Japan.

ETIQUETTE & LOCAL CUSTOMS

There are only three absolute no-nos in Japan: soaping yourself in the bath; entering a home, temple, or shrine building without removing your shoes; and blowing your nose in public. Nose-blowing is so frowned upon that you should try to sniff and dab discreetly with a handkerchief until you can retire and blow in private.

The word for foreigner, *gaijin*, a contraction of *gaikoku jin* (outside country-person), was once used offensively, but is now neutral; strangers will politely address you as *"gaijin-san."* Either way the message is the same: If you are not Japanese, then you are an outsider. Japanese also discriminate among themselves and relationships tend to be confined to the circles defining them: mostly kinship, education, or employment.

To most foreigners, Japanese behavior will appear strikingly formal. Harmony, achieved through conformity and consensus, is of the first importance; it dictates masking private cares with public smiles along with the individual's obligation to conform with the group. Outspokenness is considered bad manners, and conversations find participants doing their utmost to agree with each other. Decisions are reached through consensus; in corporate contexts the process can take quite some time. Nodding means "I understand what you're saying," smiling is just polite, neither means "yes."

The rules of etiquette tend to focus on specific group situations and do not always apply to the street, where men often spit or, late at night, urinate against the nearest wall. The Japanese can sometimes appear churlish. You might not get an apology from someone who collides with you on the street, but, if challenged, the embarrassed offender could well be at a loss for words.

Yet if you address someone, the ice is usually broken immediately. Ask, and most people will go out of their way to help you. The Japanese do not expect foreigners to be familiar with their complex etiquette. If you abide by the universal rules of kindness and consideration, you will get along fine in Japan.

How to behave The proper greeting on meeting or parting is a bow, and its degree (i.e., how low) and repetition are determined by the amount of respect due to the recipient. For a foreigner, a slight inclination will suffice; most Japanese are used to shaking hands with foreigners. Do not embrace anyone; kissing is reserved strictly for babies and lovers.

Introductions entail an exchange of names or business cards, and it is polite to look at them before putting them away. During business meetings, cards are placed on the table. Unless you are instructed otherwise, use of the family name is preferred and carries the suffix *san* (e.g. Yamada-san: Mr. or Ms. Yamada).

In Japan, gifts are less tokens of love or friendship than repayment for favors or a response in kind. If you are entertained in a Japanese home, bring a present for your hosts, typically a bottle of wine, flowers, or fruit; a small token from your country of origin will also be appreciated. Unless among close friends, avoid anything too extravagant—the recipient may feel obliged to repay you in kind. (See also tipping, p. 356.)

Table manners As a foreigner, you will often be assumed to be incapable of using chopsticks. Use them if you can—but never stick them in the rice bowl when you have finished. Said to evoke the incense sticks burning in a bowl at a funeral, it's considered very bad manners.

Boiled rice, which is always served in its own bowl, is sacrosanct and it should remain white. Placing items into it taken from the dishes on the table is acceptable when dining on Chinese food, but sprinkling the rice with sauce is considered barbaric at any meal. The way to eat soup noodles is to raise them with your chopsticks and suck them up with a loud slurp. This cools the noodles and shows your appreciation.

Women traditionally pour drinks for men first. If your neighbor fills your glass, always return the compliment. There may be a lot of raising or clinking of glasses, invariably accompanied with the word *kampai!*—cheers!

Liquor laws

You must be over 20 years old to consume alcohol.

MEDIA

Newspapers in English are the *Japan Times* and *Daily Yomiuri;* the *Asahi-Herald Tribune* combines English-language material from the *Asahi Shimbun* with its international American counterpart.

Television Japanese television has a partly justified reputation for being terrible. Still, the game shows, samurai serials, soap operas, quiz programs, and wholly incredible commercials are worth a look for the insights they provide into the country. There are 8 TV channels in Tokyo, two of them being NHK, the national network. *NHK News* (simulcast in English) is at 7 p.m. and 9 p.m. (receivable only if the set is dual language or multiplex). Television sets in major hotels are generally multiplex or dual language, with films shown in English and Japanese. Regional TV stations abound and the number of cable, satellite, and digital TV options grows constantly, but outside private homes and premier hotels the only alternative is probably NHK.

Radio Radio is generally panned by visitors. English-language programs are largely limited to the American Forces Network (AFN) Tokyo. There are some Japanese radio stations offering programs in overseas languages, such as Inter FM (Tokyo) and Cocolo FM (Osaka), but the best option is to access Internet stations from your laptop or hotel.

Video The video system is NTSC as in the United States.

MONEY MATTERS

The Japanese currency is the yen. Bank notes come in denominations of ¥10,000, ¥5,000, ¥2,000, and ¥1,000; coins in ¥1 (white metal), ¥5 (brass, hole in center), ¥10 (copper), ¥50 (silver colored, hole in center), ¥100 (silver colored), and ¥500 (silver colored).

NATIONAL HOLIDAYS

January 1 New Year's Day—*Gantan*
January 1–3 New Year—*Oshogatsu*
January, 2nd Mon. Coming of Age Day—*Seijin-no-hi*
February 11 National Foundation Day—*Kenkoku Kinen-no-hi*
March 20 or 21 Vernal Equinox—*Shunbun-no-hi*
April 29 Greenery Day—*Midori-no-hi*
May 3 Constitution Memorial Day—*Kenpo Kinenbi*
May 4 People's Holiday—*Kokumin-no-shukujitsu*
May 5 Children's Day—*Kodomo-no-hi*
July 20 Marine Day—*Umi-no-hi*
September 15 Respect for the Aged Day—*Keiro-no-hi*
September 23 Autumn Equinox—*Shubun-no-hi*
October, 2nd Mon. Health Sports Day—*Taiiku-no-hi*
November 3 Culture Day—*Bunka-no-hi*
November 23 Labor Thanksgiving Day—*Kinro kansha-no-hi*
December 23 Emperor's Birthday—*Tenno Tanjobi*

OPENING TIMES

Banks: 9 a.m.–3 p.m. weekdays; closed weekends and holidays.
Post offices: 9 a.m.–5 p.m. (see also Communications on p. 354).
Department stores: 10 a.m.–8 p.m. (closed one day a week)
Restaurants: noon–3; 6–9 p.m (some open all day).
Private offices: 9 a.m.–5 p.m. weekdays; some are open 9 a.m.–noon on Saturdays.
Public offices: 9 a.m.–5 p.m. weekdays. Closed weekends.

SMOKING

Smokers still constitute a clear majority in Japan, although the figures are declining yearly. Smoking is prohibited throughout the subway system and on commuter train lines. It is permitted on the shinkansen and other long-distance trains, although the number of no-smoking compartments *(kin-en sha)* has recently been forced up by public opinion. Only big city restaurants with a large foreign clientele have no-smoking areas. Some international hotels have no-smoking floors or rooms.

TAXES & SURCHARGES

A 5 percent consumption tax is applicable to all goods and services; it is charged unless you purchase items tax free for export—the tax applies in restaurants and hotels. You can sometimes reduce the tax by asking hotels and *ryokan* to bill your meals and room separately. Service charges of between 10 and 20 percent are also added to your bill.

TIPPING

In a word: don't; the practice is unknown in Japan. This said, you can give a taxi driver or hotel staff member a token of your appreciation for being especially helpful. Chances are it won't be accepted, but it might if you put it into an envelope first!

TOILETS

Although the Western variety is becoming increasingly common, the most widespread is still the pan-Asian, Middle Eastern squat-toilet; the Japanese variant has a kind of hood at one end and that's the one to face. Toilet technology is a science in Japan, however, where hygiene is an obsession. The computerized Western-style Washlet toilet (increasingly common in upscale hotels) boasts a heated seat and incorporates a cleansing water jet and drier, technology to take your breath away—especially if you make a mistake over the water-temperature setting! Public toilets, especially in stations, do not have toilet paper: Either carry a pack of tissues or purchase paper from the vending machine usually located near the door.

TRAVELERS WITH DISABILITIES

For those with impaired sight, a strip of rubber indicates the edge of station platforms and musical signals give the all-clear at pedestrian crossings. Otherwise, this is not a great country for the disabled. International-class hotels have wheelchair access, but not the majority of *ryokan.* Access ramps are becoming more widespread, and staff will always offer assistance in train and subway stations, but at all costs avoid rush hour.

Before you set off, get information from the Society for the Advancement of Travel for the Handicapped, 347 5th Ave., Ste. 610, New York, NY 10016, tel 212/447-7284, fax 212/725-8253.

VISITOR INFORMATION

The Japan National Tourist Office operates TICs (Tourist Information Centers) in Tokyo (10F, Tokyo Kotsu Kaikan Bldg., 2-10-1, Yurakucho, Chiyoda-ku, tel 03/3201-3331) and nationwide. Check individual entries in the main part of the guide.

JNTO offices outside Japan

United States
1 Rockefeller Plaza, Ste, 1250, New York, NY 10020
tel 212/757-5640

515 S. Figueroa St., Suite 1470
Los Angeles, CA 90071
tel 213/623-1952

Canada
481 University Ave., Suite 306
Toronto, ON M5G 2E9
tel 416/366-7140

United Kingdom
Heathcoat House, 20 Savile Row, London W1S 3PR
tel 020-7734-9638

Websites

Japan Information Network: www.global-jin.com
Japan Travel Updates (JNTO): www.jnto.go.jp
Asahi News: www.asahi.com/english
Japan Times Online: www.japantimes.co.jp
Kansai Time Out: www.japanfile.com
Tokyo Meltdown: www.bento.com/tleisure
Metropolis: http://metropolis.co.jp

EMERGENCIES

CRIME & POLICE

Japan's streets are among the safest in the world, even at night. Most metropolitan neighborhoods have a *koban,* a police kiosk manned by up to four police officers; this system partly explains the low crime rate. Murder and crimes of violence are reassuringly rare. However, alongside a recent increase in white-collar crime, the incidence of muggings and theft committed by young people is rising. Rape is comparatively rare (though many cases are thought to go unreported). Caution and common sense are advisable around amusement districts when they empty in the wee hours. This said, honesty is one of Japan's greatest virtues, and many are the traveler's tales of lost wallets returned.

EMBASSIES & CONSULATES

United States
1-10-5 Akasaka, Minato-ku, Tokyo, tel 03/3224-5000.

Canada
7-3-38 Akasaka, Minato-ku, Tokyo, tel 03/5412-6200.

United Kingdom
1 Ichiban-cho, Chiyoda-ku, Tokyo, tel 03/5211-1100.

EMERGENCY NUMBERS

Call boxes all have an emergency red button—press this first.
Police: 110
Ambulance/Fire: 119

For credit card loss
Amex: 0120/020-120
Visa: 0120/133-173

EARTHQUAKES

Japan lies in one of the most volcanically and seismically active areas in the world. If there's an earthquake, **don't** just run out of the house (unless you're in open country)—you might be hit by falling debris, power lines, etc. **Do** immediately turn off the gas supply and all cooking and heating appliances, then hide under a table or stand in a doorway.

HEALTH

Travelers needn't be greatly concerned about contracting exotic diseases. The kind that you do have to worry about are much the same as at home. If you need to see a doctor—especially an English-speaking one—the Tokyo Medical and Surgical Clinic (32 Mori Building, 4-30 Shiba Koen 3-chome, Minato-ku, tel 03/3436-3028) is one of several options. It has a 24-hour emergency service.

Carry a sufficient supply of your own prescription drugs to cover your trip (and a letter from your physician for customs). Make sure you know not just the brand name but the generic name, for the former is likely to be wholly different in Japan. You might find some imported drugs in the American Pharmacy in Tokyo, but don't count on it elsewhere. A lot of people complain about not being able to find over-the-counter drugs that are available back home, so bring them with you. You should be able to get equivalents in Japan that give the same results. Herbal remedies (obtained from Chinese-style pharmacies) are widely available.

LANGUAGE GUIDE

airport: *kuukoo*
bank: *ginkoo*
car: *kuruma*
east: *higashi*
left: *hidari*
north: *kita*
plane: *hikoki*
post office: *yubin kyoku*
restaurant: *resutoran*
right: *migi*
south: *minami*
station: *eki*
taxi: *takushi*
temple: *tera/dera* or *-ji/-in*
ticket: *kippu* (plane ticket: *kokuuken)*
visitor (information) office: *kankoo annaisho*
train: *densha*
up: *ue*/down: *shita*
west: *nishi*

this: *kore*/that: *sore*/that (more distant, or not visible): *are*
I want to go to...:...*e ikitai desu.*
What time is it: *nanji desuka?*
hello (telephone): *moshi-moshi*
Is it near/far? *Tooi/chikai desu-ka*
no (contradiction): *ie* (usually followed with or completely replaced by *chigaimasu)*
won't do/don't do/stop it (including the "no" for women): *dame*
haven't/aren't any...:...*nai desu/...arimasen*
how much?: *ikura desuka?*
Do you speak English? *Eigo o hanasemasuka?*
I don't understand: *(Chotto) wakarimasen*
Where is (the tourist information center)?: *(Kankoo annai-shoo wa) doko desuka?*
Do you take credit cards?: *Kurejitto kaado tsukaemasu-ka?*
Do you have a room?: *O heya aitemasu-ka?*
I'd like to make a reservation for ...(two people): (*futari bun no)...yoyaku shitai no desu-ga*
Expensive: *takai*
Cheap: *yasui*
Have you anything cheaper?: *Mo chotto yasui no wa arimasen-ka?*
Please show me: *o misete kudasai*
Is there any?: *arimasu-ka?*
I want/would like: *ga hooshi no desu-ga*
Please show me: *o misete kudasai*
Big: *ooki*, little: *chiisai* (little bit: *sukoshi)*
This is too big: *chotto ooki sugimasu*
help!: *tasukete!*
danger: *abunai*
call a doctor/police: *issha/keisatsu o yonde kudasai*
I'm unwell: *chooshi ga warui desu*

(numbers/quantity of things/number of people)
one: *ichi/hitotsu/hitori*
two: *ni/futatsu/futari*
three: *san/mitsu/san nin*
four: *shi* or *yon/yotsu/yon nin*
five: *go/itsutsu/go nin*
six: *roku/muttsu/roku nin*
seven: *nana or shichi/nanatsu/ shichi nin*
eight: *hachi/yattsu/hachi nin*
nine: *kyu/kokonotsu/kyu nin*
ten: *jyu/to/ jyu nin*

HOTELS & RESTAURANTS

Although it has a broad spectrum of accommodations, Japan (and Tokyo especially) is expensive. That said, the options for tighter budgets seem to be increasing all the time.

As the recent proliferation of Japanese restaurants worldwide suggests, Japan is very much a food country. A bad meal is a rarity in Japan, where the native palate tends to be be discerning and standards of hygiene strict.

ACCOMMODATIONS

The Japan National Tourist Office (JNTO) regularly updates lists of accommodations that include the Welcome Inn Group, the Japanese Ryokan Association, the Japanese Inn Group (JIG), and youth hostels. JIG is particularly recommended. It's a great way to get acquainted with the *ryokan* (traditional inns) system. Reservations can be made over the Internet, as is also the case with many hotels of other kinds. Visit "Japan Travel Updates" on JNTO's website (www.jnto.go.jp), where you can even see what the hotel looks like.

JNTO offices overseas (see p. 356) all have the information you need to make your reservations: Try to make these at least four months ahead. Note that at New Year's (Dec. 28–Jan. 4), many family-run ryokans close for family celebrations.

If you haven't made reservations, the visitor information centers in each locality can help. Staff at visitor information desks in mainline train stations will do the same although they don't always speak English.

Western-style hotels

International chains, such as Holiday Inn, Hilton, Hyatt, and Meridien, are well represented. Japanese chains also operate Western-style hotels, including JAL (Nikko Hotels), Dai-ichi, ANA, Prince, and Tokyu. All Western-style hotels meet the highest international standards although rooms tend to be small. Many hotels also offer Japanese-style rooms, but it will be assumed that you want a Western one. If you choose Japanese style it could be more expensive. All modern hotels and some ryokan offer air-conditioning and elevators. Smaller regional hotels, ryokan, and *minshuku* (see opposite) may not have air-conditioning or elevators; you should check when making your reservations. All hotels, most ryokan, and plenty of minshuku provide TV in the rooms, and some offer English-language pay-per-view movies and cable TV. Hotels typically have a choice of bars and an array of restaurants including Japanese, Western, and Chinese; the standards of cuisine are generally high, but points scored for atmosphere are low.

Business hotels

Bijinesu hoteru are a more economical Western-style option. Targeting business travelers, they usually have small single rooms with adjoining bathroom. Don't expect room service, laundry, bellhops, or porters. You will be given towels and a *yukata* (cotton gown). There is usually a restaurant or coffee shop, but anything else, including canned drinks and beer, comes out of vending machines.

Ryokan

Some ryokan have been operating for more than a century or have been converted from large ancestral residences; others are custom built. If you want a "real Japan" experience and a glimpse of a traditional Japanese home, these are the places to stay. The average ryokan is of modest size; charged mainly on a per-person basis, the prices range from astronomical heights (¥30,000 a head is by no means unknown) to very moderate. The rate normally includes an evening meal (which is often lavish and served in your room) and breakfast—both Japanese style. Some ryokan will reserve the room without meals.

There's usually someone who speaks a little English in JIG's 80 or so ryokans. Their rooms are small, basic, and spotless and they tend to fill quickly so it is vital to make reservations in advance. Unless you speak some Japanese, do not wander into a ryokan off the street; you might be turned away.

There are certain rules to bear in mind. When you enter, step out of your shoes, leave them in the entrance hall, and don the plastic slippers provided. Use these in the corridors. You must remove them before stepping onto the tatami matting in your room as well as before entering the toilet, where you use the pairs of plastic or wooden sandals provided. Don't forget to take the sandals off again: Wandering the building in toilet slippers is bad form.

Your room contains no beds; the futon mattresses and bedding (stored in the closets) will be laid out for you by the maid. Although the mattress is placed directly on the floor, the tatami is springy enough to make this a much less spartan sleeping arrangement than it sounds. You will be given a cotton kimono that is both sleepwear and for wandering about the hotel. In winter you'll get a warm gown to wear over it.

Bathrooms tend to be communal and in many ryokan you will find thermal baths. Remember bathing etiquette (see p. 21): You must soap and rinse thoroughly before entering the communal tub.

Dinner is served early; the latest will be about 8 p.m. Smaller, family-run ryokan often impose curfews. There may be no key to lock your door.

Minshuku

Minshuku, literally "people's lodging," are family businesses usually operating in a converted private home—as are many ryokan. There is little difference in price between minshuku and the more modest ryokan, which are run along almost identical lines. Meals in the former may be served in a dining area or family kitchen rather than in the room; some serve no meals at all. Many minshuku provide no towels, though most sell the standard *tenugui* (see p. 350). Some minshuku expect you to take your own bedding from the closets, put the sheets on, and take them off again and put the bedding away in the morning. Minshuku frequently close their doors at a fixed time at night.

Dotted about mountain, *onsen,* or seaside resorts, state-owned *kokumin shukusha* are run along exactly the same lines as ryokan, but without the attentive service. Room rates on average are about $60 a head including two meals.

Pension hotels

Pronounced "pen-shon," this concept derives from the *pension* (full bed and board) formula in France. Usually frequented by young people, these are small Western-style hotels. Some are theme-conceived and specialize in sports and pastimes; many cater to a largely female clientele.

Shukubo

Temples have traditionally offered lodgings to travelers and many still do. The old concept of offering the lodging free in exchange for chores performed (e.g., sweeping, washing dishes, or gardening) sometimes still applies. You don't have to be a Buddhist to qualify. Generally Shukubo offer inexpensive accommodations, though some of the finer ones can be quite pricey. Some shukubo serve basic vegetarian food and impose a 9 p.m. curfew; others serve gourmet vegetarian cuisine and run their own bars.

Youth hostels

Membership in the International Youth Hostel Association is not essential, though most hostels offer discounts for members. They don't take children under four years, but adults of any age are welcome. Friendly, basic, and very clean, most are run like minshuku and in the Japanese style; the majority also close their doors at night. Dormitory beds cost less than $25, and single and double rooms are about $35 on average (without breakfast). Beware: Some youth hostels also maintain a teetotal-ist sing-around-the-campfire ethic guaranteed to make way-cool *gaijin* (foreigners) squirm.

Love hotels

If it stands on the fringe of an amusement district looking like Cinderella's castle while displaying garish neon signs, then it has to be a "love hotel." These accommodations are strictly for couples: Single people may be turned away. Expect rotating beds, mirrored walls or ceilings, adult videos, and vending machines containing toys devised to tickle your fancy. Rooms are often larger than hotel rooms in the same price range. Usually on a par with business hotels, prices vary according to the rooms—they are often theme-conceived. The bed might look like a 1950s Cadillac in a Chinese restaurant, or the place could be decked out like a medieval torture chamber (!).

Capsule hotels

The capsule hotel first appeared during the 1980s, and was the inebriated salaryman's dream come true: a cheap (under $40) alternative to the expense formerly incurred by missing the last suburban train. Reached by a ladder, the capsule is no larger than a ship-board berth, though extremely comfortable and endowed with all kinds of amenities, including TV. The overall design is tellingly like a beehive. Some capsule hotels also feature saunas and public baths with spa pools. The majority are for men only.

RESTAURANTS

Choosing in restaurants doesn't always require Japanese language ability. Many restaurants in big cities have English menus and where they don't, many menus have photographs of the fare served. The windows of many Japanese restaurants display disconcertingly realistic plastic models of the dishes served, so all you have to do is point. Unless you're undaunted at the prospect of a hefty check, avoid places that don't display models or menus with prices outside.

In most restaurants, a simple and often cheaper alternative to ordering à la carte is to select *teishoku*—set meals. Served on a tray, these always include a small appetizer, rice, pickles, and a bowl of piping hot *misoshiru* (soup made from miso soybean paste), the basic components of a standard Japanese meal. Low prices for set meals at lunchtime make some of the country's most expensive restaurants an affordable treat.

Sushi & sashimi

Most restaurants specialize in a certain type of cuisine. Sushi restaurants serve nothing else, except perhaps sashimi—slices of raw fish picked up with chopsticks and dipped into a sauce before eating. In sushi parlors, examples of the dishes will be in a glass case behind the counter in front of you; all you have to do is point. In larger places, fish and seafood often swim around in tanks. You can point at those too: Freshness is a golden rule in Japanese cuisine. For sushi, morsels of raw fish are placed on a bite-size bed of rice. As *norimaki,* sushi delicacies are rolled together with the rice in a sheet of dried seaweed. Like sashimi, sushi is eaten after dipping in soy spiced with *wasabi, a* fierce, bright green variety of horseradish relish.

Vegetarian food

Don't expect many Western-style vegetarian and whole food restaurants outside large cities. The majority of Japanese restaurants serve tofu (soybean curd) and some restaurants specialize in *tofu ryori*—cooking using tofu and other soybean-based products exclusively. *Shojin-ryori,* served in some temple restaurants, is a refined form of vegetarian cuisine.

Sukiyaki & kaiseki ryori

Succulent *sukiyaki* consists of choice slices of beef and vegetables cooked at the table in a sweet, soy-based stock pot. When cooked, the pieces are dipped into a sauce of soy and a raw egg before eating. *Shabu-shabu* is thin slices of beef (or pork) with vegetables cooked in bubbling broth.

Kaiseki ryori stands at the summit of Japanese cuisine. It was developed in Kyoto and derived from the delicacies served during the tea ceremony. A succession of small dishes—usually seasonable vegetables, and occasionally fish—made of the finest ingredients, kaiseki is presented with all the elegance of a fine art.

Informal eating

Options include *robatayaki* restaurants, where traditionally garbed attendants cheerfully bellow the orders out to cooks behind the counter. Food here is mainly fish and vegetables broiled over charcoal. Robatayaki are close relatives of *yakitori* restaurants, which specialize in various cuts and pieces of char-grilled vegetables and chicken on bamboo skewers. Places serving yakitori are not technically restaurants but are *nomiya*—drinking spots—easily identifiable by the one or more red paper lanterns outside. A nomiya with an extensive menu (fish, yakitori, vegetables, pot stews, and even certain Western dishes) becomes an *izakaya.* They seldom disappoint and are very good value.

Noodles

Noodles are a Japanese staple. The most common are *soba* and *udon,* a thicker variant. Probably most popular of all is *ramen,* a soup-noodle formula of Chinese origin. Fried *(yaki-soba, yaki-udon)* or in hot soup, noodles are served ubiquitously in places ranging from upscale specialists to stand-up noodle joints. Soba restaurants also serve noodles cold *(zaru-soba);* dipped in a sauce of soy with wasabi and spring onions, they make an ideal summer lunch. Noodles are often prepared *teppan-yaki* style, cooked on a hot plate on the table—usually by the customer. The same applies to cheap, delicious *okonomi-yaki.* Often described as "Japanese pizza," it consists of pieces of seafood or pork mixed with a batter consisting of egg, water, flour, and chopped cabbage, and fried like a pancake.

Okonomi-yaki, noodles, and yakitori are served by *yatai* vendors from food carts but the most common and popular dish they serve is *oden,* a variety of items—including fishcakes, seafood, and eggs—in a piping hot fish stock.

Tempura & tonkatsu

Tempura consists of shrimp, fish, and vegetables, individually deep-fried in light, crispy batter. Tempura is dipped into a small bowl of a sauce called *tsuyu* mixed with grated ginger and *daikon* (radish).

Tonkatsu consists of pork deep-fried in an egg-and-breadcrumb batter. This delicious dish finds several variants, including *ebi furai* (fried prawns) and *korokke* (potato croquettes). *Kushi-age,* originating in Osaka, is another delicious variant, consisting of a variety of skewered meat, fish, vegetables, and even cheese-based delicacies, dipped in batter and deep-fried.

International cuisine

The Japanese passion for sampling, importing, adopting, and adapting applies very much to food. Coined during the late 19th century, the term *yoshoku-ya* (Western food restaurant) still applies to places serving Euro-Japanese hybrid food. Culinary hybridization remains the order of the day, the most refined recent additions being "nouvelle Japanese" and French food served kaiseki style. The love affair with French and Italian food is a long one; many of the chefs are foreigners, but increasing numbers of Japanese spend years studying in kitchens in France and Italy before opening restaurants serving dishes on a par with the best of its country of origin. French cuisine got there first but Italian currently has the lead; even the

PRICES

HOTELS

Western-style hotels charge by the room but Japanese-style hotels charge per person. An indication of the cost is given by $ signs.

$$$$$	Over $280
$$$$	$200– $280
$$$	$120–$200
$$	$80–$120
$	Under $80

RESTAURANTS

An indication of the cost of a three-course dinner without drinks is given by $ signs.

$$$$$	Over $80
$$$$	$50–$80
$$$	$35–$50
$$	$20–$35
$	Under $20

remotest rural coffee shops often produce a *spaghetti napolitano*.

Coffee shops are always good for a Western-style snack or *moningu-setto* (morning set)—breakfast. Unlike their big city counterparts, however, coffee shops in smaller towns often don't open until mid-morning. Many will serve lunchtime meals, though be prepared for strange hybrids such as Japanese-style "wafu-pizza" with seaweed—not to mention Chinese-style ginger-pork, Italian spaghetti, noodles, tonkatsu, and potato salad—all on the same plate!

The oldest and most popular forms of non-Japanese oriental cuisine are Chinese and Korean. The past two decades have also seen a remarkable increase in authentic Indian and Thai restaurants in larger towns. Appetites for Indonesian and Malay food are escalating as well.

The hotels and restaurants listed here have been grouped first according to their region, then listed alphabetically by price category. For disabled access, it is recommended that you check with the establishment to verify the extent of their facilities.
L = lunch D = dinner

TOKYO

GINZA

GINZA CAPITAL HOTEL
$
2-1-4 TSUKIJI, CHUO-KU [MAIN] / 3-1-5 TSUKIJI, CHUO-KU [ANNEX]
TEL 03/3543-8211
FAX 03/3543-7839
www.ginza-capital.co.jp
Popular with business and leisure travelers, the Capital scores points for service, price, and convenience. Rooms are bright and comfortable. There are two buildings, but the Annex is more convenient as it's closer to the Tsukiji subway station.
576 Subway: Tsukiji, Shintomicho P Annex All major cards

THE PENINSULA TOKYO
$$$$$
1-8-1 YURAKUCHO, CHIYODA-KU
TEL 03/6270-2888
FAX 03/6270-2000
www.peninsula.com
If you want top-class luxury and service, try the Peninsula, opened in 2007. Steps from Ginza in the business district of Marunouchi, its spacious rooms have outstanding views overlooking the Imperial Palace gardens and moat.
314 Subway: Hibiya, Yurakucho; Train: Tokyo P Some rooms All major cards

SUSHIKO
$$$$$
6-3-8 GINZA
TEL 03/3571-1968
The owner-chef of this tiny sushi parlor spurns conventional displays of sectioned fish behind the counter, believing that it would impair freshness. Instead it's kept chilled out of sight, to be sliced when needed. It's widely considered to be the ultimate. Reservations recommended.
Subway: Ginza All major cards

OMATSUYA
$$$$
2F EL DORU BLD., 6-5-8 GINZA, CHUO-KU
TEL 03/3571-7053
This is about as refined as noodle cooking gets. In the evening, they grill meat, fish, and vegetables over charcoal at your table.
Subway: Ginza Closed Sun. All major cards

TEN-ICHI
$$$
6-6-5 GINZA
TEL 03/3571-1949
This flagship restaurant of a prestigious chain launched during the postwar era is one of the best places to sample tempura. The delicacy of the batter seems the product of both art and science.
Subway: Ginza All major cards

TSUKI NO SHIZUKU
$$$
GINZA 3-1, GINZA INZ B1F
TEL 03/5159-0250
Izakaya specializing in tofu and variations (*yuba, agedashi,* etc.). This Ginza favorite is known for inventive dishes to please vegetarians and carnivores. Bamboo partitions provide intimacy amid the stunning modern Japanese decor.
Subway: Ginza All major cards

AKASAKA

GRAND PRINCE HOTEL AKASAKA
$$$$
1-2 KIYOICHO, CHIYODA-KU
TEL 03/3234-1111
FAX 03/3262-5163
www.princejapan.com
This 40-story hilltop hotel designed by architect Tange Kenzo is one of Tokyo's finest. It's both minimalist and opulent, with expanses of white marble in the lobby and breathtaking cityscapes from the front rooms. Best known of its 12 restaurants is Le Trianon, serving stellar French cuisine in a 1930s building on the grounds (also the site of the popular Napoleon Bar).
761 Subway: Nagata-cho, Akasaka-mitsuke P Some rooms All major cards

IMPERIAL
$$$$$
1-1-1 UCHISAIWAICHO, CHIYODA-KU
TEL 03/3504-1111
FAX 03/3581-9146
www.imperialhotel.co.jp
Opened in 1890 and still one of the best hotels in Japan; it

was rebuilt in 1923 by Frank Lloyd Wright, and again in 1970. Rooms are luxuriously appointed with stunning views from upper stories; impeccable service and tasteful decor throughout.
1,023 Subway: Hibiya; JR: Yurakucho P Some floors All major cards

SOMETHING SPECIAL

OKURA

Often cited in international business publications as the finest hotel in Asia, the Okura has a reputation for comfort and service. The decor is understated, elegant 1950s modernism. A beautifully landscaped Japanese garden is overlooked by the finest rooms.

$$$$$
2-10-4 TORANOMON, MINATO-KU
TEL 03/3582-0111
FAX: 03/3582-3707
www.okura.com
834 Subway: Tameike-sanno, Kamiyacho, Roppongi-ichome, Toranomon P Some rooms All major cards

HILLTOP (YAMA-NO-UE)

$$$
1-1 KANDA SURUGADAI, CHIYODA-KU
TEL 03/3293-2311
FAX 03/3233-4567
www.yamanoue-hotel.co.jp
Tokyo's oldest extant Western hotel, built in the 1930s, is a firm favorite with writers and academics, matching art deco styling with old-fashioned comforts and charm.
74 Subway: Shin-Ochanomizu, Ochanomizu, Jimbocho; JR: Ochanomizu P All major cards

MERIDIEN PACIFIC TOKYO

$$$$
3-13-3 TAKANAWA, MINATO-KU
TEL 03/3445-6711
FAX 03/3445-5137
Among the Meridien's assets are a beautiful garden (once owned by the imperial family), and rooms with great views over Tokyo Bay. Panoramic lounge on 30th floor.
954 Subway/JR: Shinagawa P Some rooms All major cards

ANA INTERCONTINENTAL TOKYO

$$$$
1-12-33 AKASAKA, MINATO-KU
TEL 03/3505-1111
FAX 03/3505-1155
www.anaintercontinental-tokyo.jp
A favorite among foreign businesspeople, this stylish, recently refurbished 1980s hotel is close to Roppongi's nightlife. Highlights include a rooftop pool, the 36th-floor Manhattan Lounge, and excellent sushi and teppanyaki restaurants. However, the neighborhood is drab and congested, with an overhead expressway out front.
867 Subway: Tameike-sanno, Roppongi-ichome, Kamiyacho, Akasaka P All major cards

LA TOUR D'ARGENT

$$$$$
HOTEL NEW OTANI, 4-1 KIOI-CHO, CHIYODA-KU
TEL 03/3239-3111
The Tokyo branch of this Parisian temple of gastronomy offers superlative French cuisine in one of the city's most opulent settings. Jacket and tie. Reservations essential.
Subway: Akasaka-mitsuke Closed Mon. All major cards

INAKAYA

$$$$–$$$$$
YAMAKI BUILDING, 4-10-11 ROPPONGI, MINATO-KU
TEL 03/5775-1012
Archetypical robatayaki (see p. 360) restaurant, with cooks at charcoal braziers behind a counter laden with their raw materials (mainly fish and vegetables). It enjoys a reputation as the best and is priced accordingly.
Subway: Roppongi All major cards

ZAKURO

$$$$
TBS GARDEN BLDG, 5-1-3 AKASAKA, MINATO-KU
TEL 03/3582-6841
A great place to sample sukiyaki and shabu-shabu, though not the cheapest; you can also opt to have your meal made from Kobe beef.
Subway: Akasaka All major cards

THE SKY

$$$
HOTEL NEW OTANI, 4-1 KIOI-CHO, CHIYODA-KU
TEL 03/3238-0028
Mainly Chinese, but also Japanese—not to mention freshly baked pizza—all in a unique setting: the Hotel New Otani's revolving sky lounge.
Subway: Akasaka-mitsuke All major cards

PRICES

HOTELS

Western-style hotels charge by the room but Japanese-style hotels charge per person. An indication of the cost is given by $ signs.

$$$$$	Over $280
$$$$	$200–$280
$$$	$120–$200
$$	$80–$120
$	Under $80

RESTAURANTS

An indication of the cost of a three-course dinner without drinks is given by $ signs.

$$$$$	Over $80
$$$$	$50–$80
$$$	$35–$50
$$	$20–$35
$	Under $20

MOTI
$$–$$$
3F KIMPA BLDG, 2-14-31
AKASAKA, MINATO-KU
TEL 03/3584-6640
2F AKASAKA FLORAL PLAZA,
3-8-8 AKASAKA, MINATO-KU
TEL 03/3582-3620
This Indian restaurant is one that didn't make compromises to local taste and survived to open several branches. Great tandooris and curries.
Subway: Akasaka-mitsuke
All major cards

ROPPONGI-AZABU

IBIS
$$
7-14-4 ROPPONGI, MINATO-KU
TEL 03/3403-4411
FAX 03/3479-0609
www.ibis-hotel.com
Rooms, though very small, are well appointed and comfortable. Perfect for party animals, Ibis is within crawling distance of all the action in Roppongi.
182 Subway: Roppongi
All major cards

VILLA FONTAINE ROPPONGI ANNEX
$$
3-2-7 ROPPONGI, MINATO-KU
TEL 03/3560-5550
FAX 03/3560-5677
www.hvf.jp
This recently opened upscale business hotel with affordable luxury (and the Villa Fontaine Roppongi across the street) are very close to Roppongi with rather spacious rooms for the price. Complimentary breakfast and Internet access.
205 Subway: Roppongi-ichome
MC

AJIA KAIKAN (ASIA CENTER OF JAPAN)
$$
8-10-32 AKASAKA, MINATO-KU
TEL 03/3402-6111
FAX 03/3402-0738
www.asiacenter.or.jp
Rooms are basic and clean. Singles are minute, twins and doubles adequate. For the central location and quality, rates are outstanding, so reserve well in advance. Canteen-style restaurant.
173 Subway: Aoyama-ichome, Nogizaka
All major cards

TAKAMURA
$$$$
3-4-27 ROPPONGI, MINATO-KU
TEL 03/3585-6600
One of Tokyo's most refined kaiseki (see p. 360) restaurants. Private tatami-mat rooms in a secluded old Japanese-style house offer lovely garden views. Lunch is about half the price of dinner. Reservations essential.
Subway: Roppongi
Closed Sun. All major cards

TEMPURA FUKUSHIMA
$$$$
TANUKI BLDG B1F, 4-10-12
ROPPONGI, MINATO-KU
TEL 03/3403-5507
Founded by the chef of the centuries-old Inagiku house in Ginza, this place is a tempura paradigm (with kaiseki dishes too). Everything reflects fine traditional Japanese taste—the decor, the presentation, and, of course, the food.
Subway: Roppongi
Closed Sun. All major cards

FUKUZUSHI
$$$
5-7-8 ROPPONGI, MINATO-KU
TEL 03/3402-4116
This sushi restaurant, reputed as one of Tokyo's finest, serves exquisite fare in a minimalist modern setting.
Subway: Roppongi
Closed Sun. All major cards (evening only)

GANCHAN
$$
6-8-23 ROPPONGI, MINATO-KU
TEL 03/3478-0092
The yakitori experience at its most relaxed and delicious. Boisterous, colorful, and minute, Ganchan is a popular feeding station for the Roppongi clubbing crowd.
Subway: Roppongi All major cards

KITCHEN FIVE
$$
4-2-15 NISHI-AZABU, MINATO-KU
TEL 03/3409-8835
Everyone loves Kobayashi-san and her tiny counter restaurant, and especially her Mediterranean dishes, such as moussaka or lasagne, gleaned from her travels around Europe and Latin America. You may have to wait in line.
Subway: Roppongi
Closed Sun., Mon. All major cards

NANBANTEI
$$
NANBAN BLDG. 1F, 4-5-6
ROPPONGI, MINATO-KU
TEL 03/3402-0606
Essentially yakitori but a cut above the average—one of the specialties is meat dipped in miso sauce and grilled. The difference shows in *nanban yaki,* with succulent pieces of beef instead of chicken.
Subway: Roppongi
Closed Sun. All major cards

AOYAMA-SHIBUYA-HARAJUKU

NATIONAL CHILDREN'S CASTLE HOTEL (KODOMO NO SHIRO HOTERU)
$
5-53-1 JINGUMAE, SHIBUYA-KU
TEL 03/3797-5677
FAX 03/3406-7805
www.kodomono-shiro.or.jp
The perfect place for families, the hotel occupies the seventh and eighth floors of the Children's Castle—a kiddies' paradise featuring a rooftop playground and supervised art, music, and computer facilities. Western- and Japanese-style rooms are simple, spotless, and comfortable. Reserve well in advance.

Doors close at 11 p.m.; guests receive free tickets to Castle.
26 Subway: Omotesando; JR: Shibuya All major cards

CERULEAN TOWER TOKYU HOTEL
$$$$$
26-1 SAKURAGAOKA-CHO, SHIBUYA-KU
TEL 03/3476-3000
FAX 03/3476-3001
www.ceruleantower-hotel.com
The city panoramas are superb, the location excellent and bonuses like a Noh theater and jazz club make the Cerulean is hard to refuse. Spacious guest rooms include the Japanese type, with cypress baths. The stylish lobby has a garden view.
414 Subway: Shibuya; JR: Shibuya All major cards

SHIBUYA EXCEL HOTEL TOKYU
$$$
1-12-2 DOGENZAKA, SHIBUYA-KU
TEL 03/5457-0109
FAX 03/5457-0309
www.tokyuhotelsjapan.com
Connected to JR Shibuya Station via footbridge and underground passage, the Excel is above the busy Mark City mall. The upper floors feature superb city views, and two are reserved for women only. Rooms here aren't exactly luxurious but the location can't be beat.
408 Subway/JR: Shibuya All major cards

LE PAPILLON DE PARIS
$$$–$$$$$
HANAE MORI BLDG, 5TH FLOOR, 3-6-1 KITA-AOYAMA, MINATO-KU
TEL 03/3407-7461
Located in a beautiful building designed by Tange Kenzo, this elegant French restaurant is both gastronomically and aesthetically a haven of exquisite taste. The Sunday brunch is one of the best-known deals in town.
Subway: Omotesando
Closed Sun. D All major cards

EL CASTELLANO
$$$
2-9-12 SHIBUYA, SHIBUYA-KU
TEL 03/3407-7197
As the name suggests, this Spanish restaurant's genial owner is Castilian. Informal and high-spirited, with always authentic, delectable food. Wonderful paella and it's one of the only places in Japan serving rabbit. It can get crowded, so reserve a table.
Subway: Omotesando
Closed Sun. No credit cards

SHINJUKU

PARK HYATT TOKYO
$$$$$
3-7-1-2 NISHI-SHINJUKU
TEL 03/5322-1234
FAX 03/ 5322-1288
http://tokyo.park.hyatt.com
Located in Kenzo Tange's Park Tower Building, the Park Hyatt is the ultimate luxury hotel. Plush and beautiful, it earned world fame as the location for the movie *Lost in Translation.* Large rooms have stunning cityscapes from the windows and regal bathrooms. The four restaurants include the famed New York Grill (see below).
177 Subway: Shinjuku, Tochomae; JR: Shinjuku
Some rooms
All major cards

HOTEL CENTURY SOUTHERN TOWER
$$$
2-2-1 YOYOGI, SHIBUYA-KU
TEL 03/5354-0111
FAX 03/5354-0100
www.southerntower.co.jp
In this white skyscraper overlooking the rail tracks, the hotel starts at the 20th floor and offers one of the city's best deals for location and views. Relaxing in a stylish suite here makes the Shinjuku hubbub seem very far away; the Southern Terrace walkway outside makes for a breezy, relaxed stroll.
3751 Subway: Shinjuku, Yoyogi; JR: Shinjuku, Yoyogi All major cards

KAKIDEN
$$$$$–$$$$
3-37-11 SHINJUKU
TEL 03/3352-5121
This is the Tokyo branch of a venerable restaurant. Despite the modern building, the interior is highly traditional. Offers several set menus of refined kaiseki cuisine to suit your taste—and pocket.
Subway/JR: Shinjuku
All major cards

SOMETHING SPECIAL

NEW YORK GRILL
The Grill is one of Tokyo's prime locales for eating out in style. The food is American, including superlative steaks and seafood, in a modernist art deco setting with stunning cityscapes from the floor-to-ceiling windows. Reservations advised.
$$$$$
PARK HYATT HOTEL, 3-7-1-2 NISHI-SHINJUKU
TEL 03/5323-3458
Subway: Shinjuku All major cards

TOKAIEN
$$$
1-6-3 KABUKI-CHO, SHINJUKU-KU
TEL 03/3205-1292
A contender for the largest Korean *yakiniku* (grilled meat) restaurant in Japan, this covers nine floors offering different formulas: set meals, à la carte, all-you-can-eat, and private, sumptuous feasts.
Subway/JR: Shinjuku
Open every day till late
All major cards

TSUKIJI EDOGIN
$$$
4-5-1 TSUKIJI, CHUO-KU

TEL 03/3543-4401
The fish is virtually ocean-fresh at this venerable sushi restaurant close to Tsukiji wholesale fish market. It's packed at lunchtime.
Subway: Tsukiji
Closed alt. weekends
All major cards

UENO/ASAKUSA

ASAKUSA VIEW
$$$$
3-17-1 NISHI ASAKUSA, TAITO-KU
TEL 03/3847-1111
FAX 03/3842-2117
www.viewhotels.co.jp/asakusa/english/index.html
This 1980s tower didn't please everyone when it went up, but most concede it's a very pleasant hotel. Bright, Western-style rooms have attractive Japanese design motifs and furnishings; some overlook Senso-ji Temple.
337 Subway: Asakusa, Tawaramachi
All major cards

SOFITEL TOKYO
$$$$
2-1-48 IKENOHATA, TAITO-KU
TEL 03/5685-7111
FAX 03/5685-6171
www.sofitel.com
The outside looks like a Christmas tree made of concrete Lego bricks, but the interior is highly inspired and has superb views over Ueno Park. Beautifully appointed and close to Ueno's sights.
83 Subway: Yushima; JR: Ueno All major cards

SADACHIYO
$$-$$$
2-20-1 ASAKUSA, TAITO-KU
TEL 03/3842-6431
FAX 03 3842 6433
www.sadachiyo.co.jp
This friendly urban ryokan is a hit with adepts of the "real Japan." Rooms are beautifully designed in a modern, minimalist Japanese style with bath. Offers entertainments such as geisha-style dinners, sumo, and Sumida River boat trips. Meals are not included. Dinner in the restaurant is excellent, but expensive.
20 Subway: Asakusa, Tawaramachi All major cards

KUREMUTSU
$$$
2-2-13 ASAKUSA
TEL 03/3842-0906
This charming restaurant is in a small traditional house just below Senso-ji Temple. Dine on kaiseki set meals, sashimi, *fugu* (blowfish), or grilled fish in a country atmosphere enhanced by antique fittings.
Subway: Asakusa
Open 4–10 p.m.; Closed Mon. No credit cards

UENO SEIYOKEN GRILL
$$$
4-58 UENO-KOEN, TAITO-KU
TEL 03/3821-2181
Tokyo's oldest Western-style restaurant opened its doors in the 1870s. A nondescript building replaced the ornate original, but big windows look onto Ueno Park. The French cuisine is of a high standard.
Subway: Ueno All major cards

DAIKOKUYA
$
1-38-10 ASAKUSA
TEL 03/3844-1111
Serving tempura since the late 19th century, Daikokuya is in a traditional building painted white. What the food lacks in refinement, it makes up for with good, hearty flavor.
Subway: Asakusa No credit cards

EXCURSIONS FROM TOKYO

YOKOHAMA

Most overseas visitors come to Yokohama on a day trip from Tokyo; hotels cater to business travelers. The city's vast array of international restaurants creates the impression that Japanese cuisine takes the back seat.

SHIN-YOKOHAMA RAMEN MUSEUM
$
2-14-21-1 SHINYOKOHAMA, KOHOKU-KU
TEL 045/471-0503
Come here to learn everything about Japan's favorite noodle of Chinese origin. This food theme park's mock-up of a 1950s Shitamachi (downtown) block has nine different ramen shops chosen from throughout the archipelago.
No credit cards

HEICHINRO
$
149 YAMASHITA-CHO, NAKA-KU
TEL 045/681-3001
They do dimsum *(yamucha* in Japanese) at lunchtime here and are recommended for their Cantonese cuisine.
All major cards

KAMAKURA

RAITEI
$–$$$$
3-1 KAMAKURA-YAMA
TEL 046/732-5656
This extraordinary restaurant is a highlight of a trip to Kamakura. The location is countrified, with bamboo groves in the garden. Choose cheap and varied noodles or more expensive kaiseki sets (must reserve in advance).
All major cards

NAKAMURA-AN
$
1-7-6 KOMACHI
TEL 046/725-3500
At Kamakura's most famous noodle place, favorites include handmade soba soup noodles with tempura shrimp.
Closed Thurs. No credit cards

NIKKO

NIKKO KANAYA HOTEL
$–$$$$$
1300 KAMI-HATSUISHI, NIKKO-SHI, TOCHIGI
TEL 0288/54-0001
FAX 0288/53-2487
www.kanayahotel.co.jp/nkh

Opened by the Kanaya family in 1873; current buildings and fixtures, including a fireplace designed by Frank Lloyd Wright, reflect the Western-Japanese hybridization popular in the early 20th century. Amenities include a Japanese garden and a skating rink (winter only). The wonderful columned dining hall provides plenty of atmosphere; specialties include local rainbow trout. Reservations advisable for weekends and holidays.
71 P All major cards

TURTLE INN
$
2-16 TAKUMI-CHO, NIKKO-SHI CITY, TOCHIGI
TEL 0288/53-3168
FAX 0288/53-3883
www.turtle-nikko.com

A much-esteemed member of the Japanese Inn Group (JIG), this modern ryokan is close to the sights. The friendly, English-speaking owner will give you information about sightseeing and hiking. Both Japanese- and Western-style (with and without bath) rooms overlook the river. Be sure to order meals (which cost extra) in advance. There is a dining room, but guests can also take their meals in their rooms.
10; Hotori-an Annex 11 Taxi, bus from Nikko Station AE, V

MASUDAYA
$$
439-2 ISHIYA-MACHI, NIKKO-SHI, TOCHIGI
TEL 0288/54-2151

Built during the Taisho era (1912–1926), this venerable restaurant serves reasonably priced set meals known for incorporating *yuba* (stuffed pasta made from soybean flour), a Nikko specialty once reserved for aristocrats and priests. Reservations advisable, especially for private rooms.
Closed Thurs. No credit cards

HAKONE & FUJI FIVE LAKES

FUJI-VIEW
$$$–$$$$$
511 KATSUYAMA-MURA, MINAMI TSURU-GUN
TEL 0555/83-2211
FAX 0555/83-2128
www.fujiview.jp

A venerable hotel with a lovely lakeside (Kawaguchi-ko) location that's handy for climbing Fuji-san. Has Western and Japanese rooms (the most luxurious of the latter are in the scenic terrace garden). English-speaking staff will help plan your sightseeing.
78 P Taxi from Kawaguchi-ko Station All major cards

SOMETHING SPECIAL

FUJIYA HOTEL

One of Japan's most famous, old, and charming hotels—a paragon of Japanese-Eurasian style, architecturally, conceptually, and gastronomically. Stroll in beautiful gardens with views (and, hey, John and Yoko used to stay here for months at a time!). English spoken.

Good 1930s Japanese deco style restaurant serving a range of meals from sandwiches to opulent dinners ($–$$$$$).

$$$–$$$$$
359 MIYANOSHITA, HAKONE-MACHI, ASHIGARASHIMO-GUN
TEL 0460/82-2211
FAX 0460/82-2210
www.fujiyahotel.jp
145 JR: Miyanoshita P All major cards

ASHIWADA
$–$$$
395 NAGAHAMA, FUJI KAWAGUCHI-KO-MACHI, MINAMITSURU-GUN, YAMANASHI
TEL 0555/82-2321
FAX 0555/82-2548

This concrete structure is a bit of a blight on the lakeside, but the one place you won't see it is inside. Many of the comfortable rooms (all with bathroom) offer superb views of Kawaguchi-ko. A Japanese Inn Group (JIG) member, the hotel is convenient for sightseeing and climbing Fuji-san.
40 P All major cards

FUJI-HAKONE GUESTHOUSE
$
912 SENGOKUHARA, HAKONE-MACHI, KANAGAWA
TEL 0460/84-6577
FAX 0460/84-6578
http://hakone.syuriken.jp/hakone/

A favorite on the JIG circuit, this lies in a wooded setting with mountain views. The owners speak good English and have a reputation for being helpful; a great choice if you intend to go hiking. Communal bath only (see p. 358) with natural hot spring water; breakfast the only meal.
12 Hakone Tozan bus for Togendai from Odawara bus terminal P All major cards

HOKKAIDO

SAPPORO & OTARU

GINRINSO
$$$$$
1-1 SAKURA, OTARU-SHI, HOKKAIDO
TEL 0134/54-7010
FAX 0134/52-2011

Originally built as a herring fishermen's guild hall during the 1930s, and long a local landmark, this is now a *ryotei* (top Japanese restaurant) and one of Japan's most expensive

ryokan with beautiful rooms and exquisite service. If you want to sample Hokkaido seafood at its ultimate best, this is the place. Reserving ahead is essential.
15 P Closed Feb.–March All major cards

SAPPORO GRAND HOTEL
$–$$$$
KITA 1, NISHI 4, CHUO-KU, SAPPORO
TEL 011/261-3311
FAX 011/231-0388
www.grand1934.com
The city's longest established and most prestigious hotel (opened in 1934), ten minutes' walk south of the train station, embraces two newer buildings. Rooms are spacious and superbly appointed. Try Le Grand Chef, the hotel's plush French restaurant for wonderful local ingredients (scallops, crab, duck, salmon, lamb, etc.).
565 Subway: Odori; JR: Sapporo P All major cards

NAKAMURAYA RYOKAN
$
KITA 3, NISHI 7, CHUO-KU, SAPPORO
TEL 011/241-2111
FAX 011/241-2118
www.nakamura-ya.com
A long-established JIG ryokan now housed in a modern concrete building, this has good-size tatami rooms, all with bathroom. The cuisine, based on the local seafood, is prepared with pride.
26 Subway: Sapporo; JR: Sapporo P All major cards

HYOSETSU-NO-MON
$$–$$$$
MINAMI 5, NISHI 2, CHUO-KU, SAPPORO
TEL 011/521-3046
King crab—and only king crab—is the stuff of this famous Sapporo institution, which serves it in various formats and prices on several floors.
All major cards

SAPPORO BIER GARTEN
$$
KITA 7, HIGASHI 9, HIGASHI-KU, SAPPORO
TEL 011/742-1531
Beer is the favorite tipple in this city, and it goes best with Hokkaido's main regional dish, *Jingisukan*, or Gengis Khan lamb—thin slices of lamb, vegetables, and onion rings broiled on a cast-iron pan. The most famous place to sample it is at this cavernous beer hall and garden adjacent to the Sapporo Beer Museum.
All major cards

HAKODATE

HAKODATE KOKUSAI
$$–$$$
5-10 OTE-MACHI, HAKODATE
TEL 0138/23-5151
FAX 0138/23-0239
www.hakodate-kokusai.jp
The city's best Western-style hotel. It consists of two adjacent buildings; the sleek new building has the most expensive rooms, with great views over the harbor.
310 JR: Hakodate P All major cards

HAKODATE BEER
$$–$$$
MEIJIKAN-DORI,5-22 OTE-MACHI, HAKODATE
TEL 013/823-8000.
This popular and crowded restaurant and microbrewery is in a converted warehouse on the waterfront. You dine on Western and Japanese fare in a vast redbrick hall; copper vats behind glass produce the outstanding house brews.
All major cards

SHIKOTSU-TOYA NATIONAL PARK

DAI-ICHI TAKIMOTO-KAN
$$$–$$$$$
55 NOBORIBETSU-ONSEN-MACHI, NOBORIBETSU-SHI HOKKAIDO
TEL 0143/84-2111
FAX 0143/84-2202
www.takimotokan.co.jp
Noboribetsu Onsen is the most popular onsen resort in Hokkaido, with an exhaustive array of hot aquatic pleasures. This famous hotel is the most hideous, spectacular, and fun of the spa's many concrete monstrosities. Most rooms are Japanese-style.
399 Taxi from JR Noboribetsu P All major cards

SUN PALACE HOTEL
$–$$$$
7-1 TOYA-KO ONSEN, HOKKAIDO
TEL 0142/75-1111
FAX 0142/75-2875
The largest and most famous of the Toya-ko lakeside resort hotels boasts thermal baths and swimming pools with water slides for children. Staying at its similarly priced sister hotel, Toya Park Hotel Tensho (Tel 0142/75-4343, fax 0142/75-3918), entitles you to use the Sun Palace's bathing

PRICES

HOTELS
Western-style hotels charge by the room but Japanese-style hotels charge per person. An indication of the cost is given by $ signs.

$$$$$	Over $280
$$$$	$200– $280
$$$	$120–$200
$$	$80–$120
$	Under $80

RESTAURANTS
An indication of the cost of a three-course dinner without drinks is given by $ signs.

$$$$$	Over $80
$$$$	$50–$80
$$$	$35–$50
$$	$20–$35
$	Under $20

facilities, and vice versa.
327 P All major cards

TAKIMOTO INN
$–$$$
76 NORORIBETSU ONSEN-MACHI, NOBORIBETSU-SHI, HOKKAIDO
TEL 0143/84-2205
FAX 0143/84-2645
www.takimotoinn.co.jp
This Western-style inn is a pleasant, moderate alternative to its bigger, brasher relative, Dai-ichi Takimoto-kan. You may use the larger hotel's formidable array of spa baths and facilities for free. Rooms are fairly basic; prices include meals. Great value.
47 P All major cards

KASHOTEI HANAYA
$$–$$$$
134 NOBORIBETSU-ONSEN-MACHI, NOBORIBETSU-SHI, HOKKAIDO
TEL 0143/84-2521
FAX 0143/84-2240
www.kashoutei-hanaya.co.jp
A JIG member (mention when you book), this is a very good value. Meals are extra, served in your room. English spoken. Three Japanese rooms have bathrooms; there's a large public bathroom as well as outdoor baths—spa water, of course (see p. 358).
21 Bus from Noboribetsu Station P
All major cards

DAISETSUZAN SOUNKYO NATIONAL PARK

MOUNT VIEW
$$$-$$$$
SOUNKYO, KAMIKAWA-MACHI, KAMIKAWA-GUN
TEL 01658/5-3011
FAX 01658/5-3010
www.taisetsu-g.com
This 1980s chalet-style hotel is a welcome change from concrete-blockhouse resort hotel architecture. It lies in a valley on the village outskirts. The best (i.e., higher) rooms offer good views of the gorge. Communal hot spring bath (see p. 358). Meals included.
97 P All major cards

AKAN NATIONAL PARK

HOTEL EMERALD
$$–$$$$
AKAN-CHO ONSEN, AKAN-CHO, KUSHIRO-SHI
TEL 0154/67-2011
FAX 0154/67-2864
Considering that the lakeside Emerald's price includes meals, this is an exceptional value. The management speaks English and can set up sports programs including fishing and hunting (you need your own gun and license).
204 P All major cards

MINSHUKU KIRI
$–$$
4-3-26 AKAN-KO-ONSEN, AKAN-CHO, AKAN-GUN
TEL/FAX 0154/67-2755
Right opposite the super luxury Akan Grand Hotel is this popular, homey minshuku. Rooms are basic, clean, and Japanese style. Includes meals. Communal bathroom (see p. 358) with spa water.
7 P All major cards

NORTHERN HONSHU (TOHOKU)

AOMORI-KEN

HOTEL NEW CASTLE
$–$$$$
24-1 KAMISAYASHI-MACHI, HIROSAKI AOMORI
TEL 0172/36-1211
FAX 0172/33-4577
Hirosaki's hotels conform to all the usual conveniences, comforts, and good service predominating in Japan. An added convenience is its proximity to Hirosaki castle.
58 JR: Hirosaki P
All major cards

AOMORI GRAND HOTEL
$–$$$$
1-1-23 SHIN-MACHI, AOMORI-SHI
TEL 0177/23-1011
FAX 0177/34-0505
Though the rooms are somewhat old-fashioned, this has good standards of service and comfort. Some rooms have views over the sea.
140 JR: Aomori P
All major cards

JINTAKO
$$$$
1-6-16 YASUKATA, AOMORI-SHI
TEL 0177/22-7727
Here you can sample delicious local specialties, such as scallops broiled in the shell and warming codfish stews. Make a night of it listening to the *samisen* played live in the rousing style.
No credit cards

YAMAUTA
$$
1-2-4 O-MACHI, HIROSAKI-SHI
TEL 0172/36-1835
The fare is *izakaya* style (see p. 360) and the entertainment is provided by the owner, a famous samisen virtuoso.
Closed 1st, 3rd Mon.
No credit cards

AKITA-KEN

AKITA CASTLE
$-$$$$
1-3-5 NAKA-DORI, AKITA-SHI
TEL 018/834-1141
FAX 018/834-5588
This is a plush hotel with views of the park and moat surrounding Akita-jo's ruins.
178 JR: Akita
All major cards

KOHAMA RYOKAN
$$
6-19-6 NAKA-DORI, AKITA-SHI
TEL 018/832-5739
FAX 018/832-5845
The ndearingly eccentric owner of this popular ryokan is motherly toward guests; she claims that the parrot in the

hallway screeches for her attention exactly as her son did over 20 years ago. She takes great care with cooking (meals must be ordered in the afternoon). Rooms are well decorated; communal bath (see p. 358).
10 JR: Akita P
All major cards

SENDAI & MATSUSHIMA

METROPOLITAN SENDAI
$$-$$$$
1-1-1 CHUO, AOBA-KU, SENDAI-SHI
TEL 022/268-2525
FAX 022/268-2521
www.s-metro.stbl.co.jp

Conveniently located next to the station, this is essentially an upscale business hotel, with more amenities, space and greater comfort than usual.
298 JR: Sendai P
All major cards

HOTEL TAIKANSO
$-$$$$
10-76 INUTA, MATSUSHIMA TOWN, MIYAGI
TEL 022/354-2161
FAX 022/353-3431
www.taikanso.co.jp/eg

If you're going to stay in Matsushima, why not do as the Japanese do and treat yourself to a palatial resort hotel like this. Spectacular views, a choice of Western and Japanese rooms (the most expensive look out over the bay), tantalizing food options, and onsen baths (see p. 359). Free shuttle bus to and from the train station.
238 Loop line bus from JR Matsushimakaigan
P All major cards

DONJIKI CHAYA
$
89 AZAMACHIUCHI, MATSUSHIMA, MATSUSHIMA-CHO, MIYAGI-KEN
TEL 022/354-5855

Built in the late 1600s, this remains a charming and venerable noodle stop.
Closed weekends Dec.–March No credit cards

IWATE-KEN

METROPOLITAN MORIOKA
$-$$
2-27 MORIOKA-EKIMAE-KITA-DORI (NEW WING), 1-44 MORIOKA-EKIMAE-DORI (OLD WING), MORIOKA-SHI
TEL 019/625-1211
FAX 019/625-1210
www.metro-morioka.co.jp

The Metropolitan's new wing is slightly more expensive than the nearby old wing. Rooms in the old wing are more basic, but in both places you get comfort and service.
121 (new wing), 184 (old wing) JR: Morioka P
All major cards

AZUMAYA
$$
1-8-3 NAKA-NO-HASHI-DORI, MORIOKA-SHI
TEL 019/622-2252

This is the most famous place to eat local specialties. *Wanko soba* consists of soup noodles with fish, meat, and vegetable side dishes. The noodles are served in small bowls, and the idea is to stack up as many empty ones as you possibly can, out-eating everyone else (don't worry, competitions are by agreement). *Reimen*, more popular in summer, are thin, translucent noodles served cold with a variety of other ingredients.
No credit cards

CENTRAL HONSHU

NAGOYA

HILTON NAGOYA
$$$$
1-3-3 SAKAE, NAKA-KU, NAGOYA-SHI, AICHI-KEN
TEL 052/212-1111
FAX 052/212-1225
www.hilton.com

This well-located, 28-story hotel has large rooms with king-size beds, Japanese design motifs, and Western comforts. Great cityscapes from rooms on upper floors. Amenities include Internet connection and tennis courts. Single rooms have double beds; couples can stay at the single rate during the low season.
450 P All major cards

NAGOYA KANKO
$$$-$$$$
1-19-30 NISHIKI, NAKA-KU, NAGOYA-SHI, AICHI-KEN
TEL 052/231-7711
FAX 052/231-7719
www.nagoyakankohotel.co.jp

Nagoya's most prestigious hotel was founded in the 1930s. Though its current concrete-box architecture is unremarkable, it stands in a pleasant park, and has spacious, beautifully appointed Western-style rooms. Single rooms have double beds; couples can stay at the single rate during the low season.
375 S: Fushimi P
All major cards

ROYAL PARK INN
$$-$$$
3-27-5 MEIEKI, NAKAMURA-KU, NAGOYA-SHI, AICHI-KEN
TEL 052/581-4411
FAX 052/581-4427
www.royalparkhotels.co.jp

Built by the Daichi chain in 1997, this is typical of the best newer business hotels with stylish design, comfortable rooms, and moderate prices.
314 JR: Nagoya P
All major cards

OKURA RESTAURANT
$$$$
25F TOKYO KAIJO BLDG., 2-20-19 MARU-NO-UCHI, NAKA-KU, NAGOYA-SHI, AICHI-KEN
TEL 052/201-3201

Plush, highly reputed French restaurant popular with business executives both foreign and Japanese, serving salmon, veal, and *matsuzaka* beef according to a variety of refined recipes. Coat and tie.

Reservations essential. All major cards

RYOTEI CHIYODA
$$$$
3-15-10 MEIEKI, NAKAMURA-KU, NAGOYA
TEL 052/561-3491
Widely esteemed as *the* place to try Nagoya haute-cuisine, Chiyoda is pricey, though pretty reasonable for a ryotei. Set meals come a bit cheaper. Offers *kushiage* (kabobs), kaiseki, tempura, and more in a refined traditional decor.
All major cards

YAMAMOTOYA HONTEN
$
B1 DAI-ICHI HORIUCHI BLDG., 3-25-9 MEIEKI, NAKAMURA-KU, NAGOYA-SHI, AICHI-KEN
TEL 052/565-0278
Near Nagoya Station, this main outlet of the local noodle chain is an excellent place to try *misonikomi*. Nagoya's favorite dish is a pot stew containing udon noodles, flavored with strong-tasting red miso paste *(akamiso)*. The filling meal—always made with meat—is popular in winter. English-language menu available.
All major cards

KANAZAWA

Note that many restaurants in Kanazawa close their doors at 8 and sometimes even 7 p.m.

KANAZAWA NEW GRAND HOTEL
$$–$$$$
1-50 TAKAOKA-MACHI, KANAZAWA-SHI
TEL 076/233-1311
FAX 076/233-1591
www.newotani.co.jp
In addition to a convenient location between Kenroku-en Garden and the Nagamachi samurai district, the Grand offers great service, good views, fine cuisine in its four restaurants, and an English-speaking staff. The rooms are plush and well appointed.
101 P All major cards

HAKUCHORO HOTEL
$$–$$$
6-3 MARUNOUCHI, KANAZAWA-SHI, ISHIKAWA-KEN
TEL 076/222-1212
FAX 076/222-1120
www.hakuchoro.com
In a quiet location southeast of the station, the Hakuchoro is large, comfortable and tastefully appointed, with tradition meeting modern design, such as sashes laid across the beds. The two restaurants offer excellent regional and European cuisines; also has a spacious, Victorian-styled tea lounge.
85 Taxi from JR Kanazawa P All major cards

TSUBAJIN
$$$$$
5-1-8 TERA-MACHI, KANAZAWA-SHI. ISHIKAWA-KEN
TEL 076/241-2181
Belonging to a venerable ryokan, Tsubajin serves the very best of *kaga ryori*—the region's culinary specialty, the local equivalent of kaiseki cuisine. Dishes include crab and duck stew. Kaiseki lunches are about half the price of dinner. Reservations essential.
All major cards

KOTOBUKIYA
$$–$$$$$
2-4-13 OWARI-CHO, KANAZAWA-SHI, ISHIKAWA-KEN
TEL 076/231-6245
In this merchant house dating from the 1840s, dine in tatami rooms overlooking a garden. Mountain vegetables are cooked *kaga* style, and shojin-ryori (vegetarian cuisine) is the specialty. It's very reasonably priced at lunch; kaiseki dinners are more expensive (last orders 7 p.m.).
Closed Tues. All major cards except AE

PRICES

HOTELS
Western-style hotels charge by the room but Japanese-style hotels charge per person. An indication of the cost is given by $ signs.

$$$$$	Over $280
$$$$	$200– $280
$$$	$120–$200
$$	$80–$120
$	Under $80

RESTAURANTS
An indication of the cost of a three-course dinner without drinks is given by $ signs.

$$$$$	Over $80
$$$$	$50–$80
$$$	$35–$50
$$	$20–$35
$	Under $20

MIYOSHIAN
$$–$$$$
1-11 KENROKU-MACHI, KANAZAWA-SHI, ISHIKAWA-KEN
TEL 076/221-0127
Located on the Kenroku-en garden and over 100 years old, this delightful restaurant is the place to try kaga ryori. In winter they serve *jibuni*, duck stew; sashimi and eel on rice are on the menu in other seasons. Lunch sets (mainly *bento* boxes) are an outstanding value; a more expensive option is the kaga ryori dinner, served kaiseki style. Dinner requires a reservation for a minimum of six persons.
Closed Wed. All major cards except AE

TAKAYAMA

KAKUSHO
$$$$
2-98 BABA-CHO, TAKAYAMA-SHI, GIFU-KEN
TEL 0577/32-0174
Takayama specializes in shojin-ryori, vegetarian cuisine. Skeptical omnivores should note that the cooking and its

ingredients are varied, and come enhanced with *hoba miso,* sweet and salty soybean paste cooked on a large magnolia leaf over a tiny hibachi on the table. An old traditional building with tatami rooms looking out over a tranquil garden. One set menu. Reservation essential.
Closed Tues.–Thurs.
No credit cards

MATSUMOTO

BUENA VISTA
$$$$$
1-2-1 HONJO, MATSUMOTO-SHI
TEL 0263/37-0111
FAX 0263/37-0666
At the smartest business hotel in town, the rooms are small but comfortable. One of the hotel's five restaurants, Hanakirabe, lets you sample most kinds of Japanese cuisine at a variety of counters.
200 JR: Matsumoto
All major cards

TAIMAN
$$$–$$$$$
4-2-4 OTE, MATSUMOTO-SHI, NAGANO-KEN
TEL 0263/32-0882
The Gallic château facade and high ceilings within match this ambitious, successful under-taking in French haute cuisine. Reasonably priced for the high quality, the elaborate lunch sets are ideal if your schedule is sufficiently leisurely.
Closed Wed. Most major cards

HANATOBIRA
$$–$$$$
1-2-18 FUKASHI, MATSUMOTO-SHI, NAGANO-KEN
TEL 0263/35-7632
Kajika, a local river fish, is one of the specialties. Pleasant traditional decor with black wood on white plaster. For lunch and dinner, different price and preparation offered.
Closed Sun. All major cards

KANSAI

KYOTO

HIIRAGIYA
$$$$$
NAKAHAKUSANCHO, FUYACHO ANEKOJI-AGARU, NAKAGYO-KU
TEL 075/221-1136
FAX 075/221-1139
www.hiiragiya.co.jp
A superb traditional ryokan that has accommodated Japanese royalty. The service is attentive; the tatami rooms are beautifully appointed.
28 Subway: Karasuma-oike All major cards

WESTIN MIYAKO KYOTO
$$$$$
KEAGE, SANJO, HIGASHIYAMA-KU
TEL 075/771-7111
FAX 075/751-2490
www.westinmiyako-kyoto.com
Kyoto's most famous hotel is set on 15 acres (16 ha) of woods and manicured gardens. Opened in 1890, it's conveniently located to the sights in east Kyoto. Expect luxurious comfort and impeccable service; some rooms have wonderful views over the Higashi hills.
501 Subway: Keage
All major cards

SEIKORO
$$$$$
GOJO-SAGARU, TONYA-MACHI, HIGASHIYAMA-KU
TEL 075/561-0771
FAX 075/541-5481
www.seikoro.com
This renowned ryokan in east Kyoto was founded in 1831. Its current buildings (except a recent annex) date from late Meiji; the blend of Japanese and Western antiques is typical of the period. Prices include meals and vary based on choice of room (the best overlook the garden) and set meal. English spoken.
22 Train: Keihan-Gojo
All major cards

SOMETHING SPECIAL

TAWARAYA
Founded in the early 1700s, the Tawaraya has been patronized throughout its history by world leaders. Filled with antiques, it's an oasis of tranquillity and refinement in the center of old Kyoto, with sublime service, the most refined kaiseki cuisine, and rooms overlooking a lovely garden.
$$$$$
OIKE-SAGARU, FUYA-CHO, NAKAGYO-KU
TEL 075/211-5566
FAX 075/211-2204
18 Subway: Kyoto Shiyakusho-mae; bus or taxi from JR Kyoto All major cards

YACHIYO
$$$$
34 FUKUJI-CHO, NANZEN-JI, SAKYO-KU
TEL 075/771-4148
FAX 075/771-4140
www.ryokan-yachiyo.com
Yachiyo is very much the luxury historic ryokan. The best rooms in the oldest main building surround a delightful Japanese garden. Close to east Kyoto's Nanzen-ji Temple, it's popular with foreigners.
20 Subway: Keage
All major cards

GRANVIA KYOTO
$$$–$$$$
657 HIGASHI-SHIOKOJI-CHO, SHIOKOJI-SAGARU, KURASUMA DORI, SHIMOGYO-KU
TEL 075/344-8888
FAX 075/344-4400
www.granviakyoto.com
The hotel's location is hard to beat for convenience for rail travelers. Since all the city's routes lead to and from here, there's no shortage of buses and taxis. Rooms are stylish and there's a sky lounge with a view over the mountains.

539 JR: Kyoto Station, Karasuma Chuo-guchi, Shiokoji-sagaru, Kurasuma dori, Shimogyo-ku All major cards

KYOTO GION
$$–$$$
555 MINAMIGAWA, GION-MACHI, HIGASHIYAMA-KU
TEL 075/551-2111
FAX 075/551-2200
www.apahotel.com

In the geisha district and close to the sights of east Kyoto, this is an inexpensive option. Rooms are cramped but comfortable; ask for one with a view of the old Gion houses.
154 Train: Keihan-Shijo P All major cards

HIRAIWA INN
$
314 HAYAO-CHO, KAMINOGUCHI-AGARU, NINOMIYA-CHO-DORI, SHIMOGYO-KU
TEL 075/351-6748
FAX 075/351-6969
www2.odn.ne.jp/hiraiwa

The Hiraiwa was a founding member of the Japanese Inn Group. It's basic, clean, and very user-friendly to *gaijin* (foreigners). The main building is wooden, with a newer concrete annex. It's in a quiet neighborhood a short taxi ride from Kyoto train station.
18 Bus or taxi from JR Kyoto P AE, MC, V

KYOTO TRAVELERS INN
$–$$$
91 ENSHOJI-CHO, OKAZAKI, SAKYO-KU
TEL 075/771-0225
FAX 075/771-0226
www.k-travelersinn.com

Though small, the rooms are comfortable and clean; most have bathrooms. This business hotel is popular with travelers, as its east Kyoto location is very close to Okazaki-koen.
78 Subway: Higashiyama P All major cards

RYOKAN OHTO
$
HITOSUJIME-MINAMI-SAGARU, SHICHIJO-KAMOGAWA-HIGASHI, HIGASHIYAMA-KU
TEL 075/541-7803
FAX 075-541-7804
www.kyoto-ohto.com

This pleasant riverside ryokan in a very recent three-story concrete building is near to the Sanjosangen-do Hall. Breakfast and dinner extra.
12 Train: Keihan-Shichijo P AE, MC, V

MINOKICHI HONTEN TAKESHIGERO
$$$$$
65 TORII-CHO, AWATAGUCHI, SAKYO-KU
TEL 075/771-4185

Founded in the early 18th century, this is the main branch of a well-known kaiseki restaurant chain with branches all over Japan. It's a little slick and contrived, but the setting in east Kyoto is serene and the food is wonderful.
Subway: Higashiyama All major cards

IZUMOYA
$$$–$$$$$
SHIJO-AGARU, PONTOCHO-DORI, NAKAGYO-KU
TEL 075/211-2501

On the corner of Pontocho and Shijo-dori in central Kyoto, this multi-story restaurant offers different kinds of Japanese cuisine (tempura, shabu-shabu, sukiyaki, sashimi). It also does *kyo-kaiseki* courses—notably on a riverside veranda in summer. Reservations essential.
Train: Keihan-Shijo All major cards

JUNSEI
$$$–$$$$$
60 KUSAKAWA-CHO, NANZEN-JI, SAKYO-KU
TEL 075/761-2311

Junsei's proximity to Nanzen-ji (northeast Kyoto) makes it a bit touristy, but it's set on a pleasant garden. Some of its several buildings are over 150 years old. The excellent menu focuses on tofu, but includes shabu-shabu and sukiyaki.
Subway: Keage All major cards

SOMETHING SPECIAL

MANKAMERO

The experience in this central Kyoto institution is costly, but unique: This is your chance to find out what Japanese emperors used to eat. Mankamero has been preparing *yusoku ryori* for almost 300 years. It requires special preparation and utensils, and a qualified imperial chef in ceremonial garb. The bento lunchbox version will set you back over $50, but the real feast costs around fourfold. Emperors apparently ate pretty early; the place closes at 8. Jacket and tie; reservations essential.

$$$–$$$$$
DEMIZU-AGARU, INOKUMA-DORI, KAMIGYO-KU
TEL 075/441-5020
Subway: Marutamachi (then taxi) All major cards (bento lunch cash only)

MIKAKU
$$$–$$$$$
SHIJO-AGARU, NAWATE-DORI, HIGASHIYAMA-KU
TEL 075/525-1129

This famous old steakhouse in Gion serves meat in traditional ways, including *teppanyaki* (fried on a hot plate), sukiyaki, and a spicy version of shabu-shabu. Teppanyaki is served at a counter, dishes such as sukiyaki in tatami rooms.
Train: Keihan-Shijo
Closed Sun. All major cards

MINOKO
$$$–$$$$$
480 KIYOI-CHO, SHIMOGAWARA, GION, HIGASHIYAMA-KU
TEL 075/561-0328

Owned and managed by the same family since the early 20th century, this restaurant prepares *cha-kaiseki*—the

original kaiseki as devised for the tea ceremony. The correlation between delicate flavors and understated aesthetics doesn't get much more refined than this. Choose a *bento* lunch in a tatami room with a garden view, or a sumptuous kyo-kaiseki dinner in a private room.
Train: Keihan-Shijo All major cards

HYOTEI
$$–$$$$$
35 KUSAKAWA-CHO, NANZEN-JI, SAKYO-KU
TEL 075/771-4116
In the late 17th century, pilgrims and travelers used to stop here for refreshment on the way to Nanzen-ji. They still do today. You can have a kaiseki meal (reservations required) in one of the small garden teahouses, some of which are as old as Hyotei itself. The bento lunchboxes are cheaper, but you eat those in an ordinary (though very pleasant) dining room.
Subway: Keage Closed 2nd & 4th Tues. All major cards

NAKAMURARO
$$–$$$$$
509 MINAMIGAWA, GION-MACHI, HIGASHIYAMA-KU
TEL 075/561-0016
Near Yasaka-jinja, Nakamuraro is said to have been founded in the late 1500s, making it the oldest restaurant in Japan. It's a tiny teahouse specializing in *tofu dengaku*, soybean curd skewered, baked, and covered in miso sauce. The handsome building next door, an addition from the late 19th century, serves kaiseki ryori in tatami rooms looking over a garden.
Train: Keihan-Shijo
Usually closed Thurs.
All major cards

TEMPURA YOSHIKAWA
$$–$$$$$
OIKE-SAGARU, TOMINOKOJI-DORI, NAKAGYO-KU
TEL 075/221-5544
Small restaurant in a delightful old building in central Kyoto, serving excellent tempura and kaiseki. The price range is a bit extreme, with kyo-kaiseki dinners in the tatami rooms upstairs costing nearly ten times more than a set lunch at the counter. Last orders 8:30 p.m. English spoken.
Counter closed Sun.
All major cards

DIVO-DIVA
$$–$$$$
TAKAKURA-DORI, NAKAGYO-KU
TEL 075/256-1326
Fine food (including freshly made bread and pasta) prepared by chefs trained in Italy, reasonable prices, and trendy decor have made this central Kyoto Italian restaurant a favorite of sophisticates.
Subway: Shijo Closed Wed. All major cards except DC

IZUSEN
$$$
4 DAITOKU-JI-CHO, MURASAKINO, KITA-KU
TEL 075/491-6665
Attached to Daitoku-ji Temple (northwest Kyoto), this is ideal for a really good *shojin-ryori* (vegetarian) lunch. Beautifully presented in a lovely setting, the meal focuses on tofu cooked in a variety of ways and is served in tatami rooms, or outside in summer. Reservations recommended.
Subway: Kitaoji
Closed D & Thurs.
No credit cards

YAMATOMI
$-$$$
SHIJO-AGARU, PONTO-CHO, NAKAGYO-KU
TEL 075/221-3268
One of Kyoto's few affordable restaurants offering riverside dining on the veranda in summer. The speciality here is *Teppan-age*—you cook meat, fish, and vegetables in tempura batter at the table. Serves *oden* (hardboiled eggs, fish-cakes, and vegetables, selected from a vat of simmering fish stock) in winter.
Train: Keihan-Shijo
Closed Tues. All major cards

KERALA
$
2F LEDIC BLDG, KAWARAMACHI-DORI, SANJO-AGARU
TEL 075/251-0141
If you're tiring of Japanese food, this is a great place to sample dishes from India's Kerala region in a tastefully decorated setting. The delicious lunch set curries are a great value and will refuel you for the next few temples.
Subway: Sanjo (Keihan Line) All major cards

OKUTAN
$$
86-30 FUKUCHI-CHO, NANZEN-JI, SAKYO-KU
TEL 075/771-8709
A perennial and wonderful old standby specializing in tofu. The thatched building is on a garden (sit outside in summer) in the east of the city. They do just one set meal and you'll be surprised at how many ways tofu can be cooked (deep-fried, boiled, cut into strips like pasta...).
Subway: Keage Closed D & Thurs. No credit cards

MISOKA-AN KAWAMICHIYA
$
SANJO-AGARU, FUYA-CHO, NAKAGYO-KU
TEL 075/221-2525
They've been serving soba in this tiny building in central Kyoto forever. It even has an English menu. The specialty is *hokoro*—a satisfying soba pot stew for two containing tofu, chicken, and vegetables.
Subway: Kyoto Shiyakusho-mae Closed Thurs. All major cards

OUTLYING KYOTO

KITCHO
$$$$$
58 SUSUKI-NO-BABA-CHO, TENRYU-JI, SAGA, UKYO-KU
TEL 075/881-1101
Kitcho is often said to be the most expensive restaurant in Japan, but a meal here is generally considered the most exquisite kaiseki experience there is: Wonderful food is served on priceless antique tableware in a beautiful sylvan setting in Arashiyama.
Closed Wed. All major cards

NISHIKI
$$$
NAKANOSHIMA KANYUCHI, SAGA, UKYO-KU
TEL 075/881-8888
With a lovely setting on a river island in Arashiyama (west of Kyoto), Nishiki is famous for serving amazing seven-course kaiseki ryori at an unusually affordable price. The secret is simply that they serve it in a layered lacquered bento box. Reservations needed.
Closed Tues. All major cards

RYOAN-JI YUDOFUYA
$–$$
RYOAN-JI TEMPLE, UKYO-KU
TEL: 075/462-4742
You can't miss this lovely restaurant if you stroll through the grounds surrounding Ryoan-ji. You'll see the roofed gateway and the path beyond leading to traditional buildings alongside a pond and stream. This is where they serve their special "7 herb" *yudofu* (tofu pot stew), either on its own or as part of a reasonably priced vegetarian set meal.
Closed D No credit cards

NARA

NARA HOTEL
$$$–$$$$$
1096 TAKABATAKE-CHO
TEL 0742/26-3300
FAX 0742/23-5252
www.narahotel.co.jp
Built early last century and blending Western and Japanese architecture, the historic building is famed for its lovely dining hall. Like the high-ceilinged Japanese deco interior, the cuisine is a hybrid: The menu typically includes spaghetti and sandwiches, along with more refined meat and seafood dishes, both Western and Japanese. Dinner reservations recommended.
132 P All major cards

RYOKAN SEIKAN-SO
$
29 HIGASHI-KITSUJI-CHO
TEL 0742/22-2670
FAX 0742/22-2670
www.jpinn.com/inn/10-6.html
Many regard this 1916 ryokan in a former geisha house as the jewel in the crown of the Japanese Inn Group. Set in a lovely garden, it's centrally located near the main sights, including Todai-ji and Kofuku-ji Temples and Kasuga-jinga Shrine. Run by a friendly couple who speak English.
13 P All major cards

TSUKIHI-TEI
$$$–$$$$$
158 KASUGANO-CHO
TEL 0742/26-2021
Just behind the Kasuga Grand Shrine, this traditional restaurant offers views over the surrounding woods and some of the finest kaseiki dining in town. Nara has its own version of kaiseki cuisine and its own specialties, which include sushi wrapped in persimmon and a rather tart vegetable pickle called *Nara-zuke*. Reservations required; coat and tie.
All major cards

VAN KIO
$$
410 ROKUJO-CHO
TEL 0742/33-8942
Full marks go for both taste and originality here, where the decor comprises purchasable antiques and stone lanterns, and they serve fare steamed, using a hot ceramic plate inside a stewpot. Dishes include duck and, more expensively, Nara venison.
Closed Mon. DC, V

OSAKA

NIKKO OSAKA
$$$–$$$$$
1-3-3 NISHI-SHINSAIBASHI, CHUO-KU
TEL 06/6244-1111
FAX 06/6245-2432
www.hno.co.jp
The hotel's tapered, gleaming white tower stands out on the south side of town, near the Dotonburi amusement quarter. Typically Osakan in its rather excessive opulence, it has elegant Japanese design motifs in the Western-style rooms and an executive floor with rooms decorated by fashion designer Hanae Mori.
640 P Subway: Shinsaibashi Nearby All major cards

PRICES

HOTELS
Western-style hotels charge by the room but Japanese-style hotels charge per person. An indication of the cost is given by $ signs.

$$$$$	Over $280
$$$$	$200–$280
$$$	$120–$200
$$	$80–$120
$	Under $80

RESTAURANTS
An indication of the cost of a three-course dinner without drinks is given by $ signs.

$$$$$	Over $80
$$$$	$50–$80
$$$	$35–$50
$$	$20–$35
$	Under $20

HOTEL GRANVIA OSAKA
$$–$$$$
3-1-1 UMEDA, KITA-KU
TEL 06/6344-1235
FAX 06/6344-1130
Right over Osaka Station and with excellent city views from the upper floors, the Granvia Osaka is a cut above most upscale business hotels. Standard singles are small and dark, but the twins are bright and comfortable. The premises include a wide range of international and Japanese dining choices.
648 P All major cards

HOTEL SUNROUTE UMEDA
$–$$$
3-9-1 TOYOSAKI, KITA-KU
TEL 06/6373-1111
FAX 06/6374-0523
www.sunroute.jp
The Sunroute has stylishly designed furniture and rooms, both Western and Japanese, and with its convenient location, it's one of the best values for business hotels in town. Hankyu Umeda Station is within easy walking distance.
219 P Subway: Nakatsu All major cards

KANI DORAKU
$$$–$$$$
1-6-18 DOTONBORI, CHUO-KU
TEL 06/6211-8975
Serving crab every which way Japanese cuisine allows (raw, stewed, fried, baked, and as an ingredient in various dishes) on several floors, this is the flagship of a chain with more than 50 branches nationwide.
Subway: Namba All major cards

TAKOUME
$$
SHIN-UMEDA SHOKUDOGAI, 9-25 KAKUDA-CHO, KITA-KU
TEL 06/6311-3309
Reputedly founded during the 18th century and in a quite venerable building even now, this is considered Osaka's premier restaurant for *oden,* a savory fish stock from which you select cooked ingredients such as hardboiled eggs, fishcakes, or fried tofu. The stock is kept on the boil and the items added in; this one has reputedly been kept simmering for decades!
Subway: Namba; JR: Osaka
No credit cards

KUIDAORE
$–$$$
1-8-25 DOTONBORI, CHUO-KU
TEL 06/6211-5300
Kuidaore is an Osakan expression which means "to ruin oneself with extravagant food." A giant mechanical clown beats a drum outside this restaurant and innumerable plastic food displays fill a show window. You can sample almost any kind of Japanese food here, starting on the ground floor, where many dishes are under $10. Filling eight floors, the restaurant becomes more refined and expensive (though hardly ruinously so) as you ascend.
Subway: Namba All major cards

WESTERN HONSHU (CHUGOKU)

HAGI

HOKUMON YASHIKI
$$$$$
210 HORIUCHI, HAGI-SHI, YAMAGUCHI-KEN
TEL 0838/22-7521
FAX 0838/25-8144
Located near the castle ruins inside the Horiuchi samurai quarter, this is Hagi's most prestigious ryokan. The building is modern, a tasteful blend of Western and Japanese styles. One curious feature is an attractive English garden. Expect large, luxurious rooms and superlative kaiseki cuisine, ultrafresh seafood, and *fugu* (blowfish) delicacies in winter in the two restaurants.
44 P DC, V

HAGI GRAND HOTEL TENKU
$–$$$$
25 FURUHAGI-CHO, HAGI-SHI, YAMAGUCHI-KEN
TEL 0838/25-1211
FAX 0838/25-4422
Convenient location between Higashi Hagi Station and the sights makes this popular with foreign visitors. It's considered the town's top Western-style hotel, although nearly half the rooms are Japanese. All are comfortable, and above average size.
183 P All major cards

TOMOE RYOKAN
$$$$–$$$$$
608-53 KOBOJI, HIJIWARA, HAGI-SHI
TEL 0838/22-0150
FAX 0838/22-0152
www.tomoehagi.jp
Built of wood in 1926, it looks far older and is filled with antiques and scrolls. Beautiful rooms, some of which look out over a peaceful central garden, contain real antique features. Indeed, it's as close to the luxury traditional inn—with communal bath (see p. 358)—as you can get for its very reasonable price (which includes two meals).
25 P All major cards

TSUWANO

MEIGETSU
$–$$$$
UO-MACHI, TSUWANO-CHO, KANOASHI-GUN, SHIMANE-KEN
TEL 08567/2-0685
FAX 08567/2-0637
With dark polished wood, spacious rooms, and a delightful central garden, this is probably Tsuwano's prettiest ryokan. It also has quite a reputation for local cuisine—mountain vegetable and river fish dishes—served in a large, traditional dining room. Communal bath (see p. 358).
13 P V

KANKO HOTEL WATAYA
$$–$$$$
TAKAOKA-DORI, TSUWANO-CHO, KANOASHI-GUN
TEL 0856/72-0333
FAX 0856/72/1543
The finest accommodation in Tsuwano, the Wataya has chic Western- and Japanese-style rooms and luxurious bathing facilities, including baths that are partly outdoors. Meals are prepared with attention to detail—tofu is a specialty.
30 P All major cards

YUKI
$$$
HON-MACHI, TSUWANO-CHO, SHIMANE-KEN
TEL 08567/2-0162.
The local specialties are carp, mountain vegetables, and *konyaku* (a kind of jelly made with potato flour). The most famous place to sample them is in this traditional restaurant with a carp stream flowing through the dining room.
No credit cards

MATSUE

MINAMIKAN
$$$$$
SUETSUGU HON-MACHI, MATSUE-SHI, SHIMANE-KEN
TEL 0852/21-5131
FAX 0852/26-0351
This modern and luxurious ryokan is Matsue's most famous. Renowned for its outstanding cuisine, it's also a restaurant. It's very traditional with sublime service, natural hot spring baths, a beautiful garden, and rooms facing Lake Shinji-ko.
10 P All major cards

RYOKAN TERAZUYA
$–$$
60-3 TENJIN-MACHI, MATSUE-SHI, SHIMANE-KEN
TEL 0852/21-3480
FAX 0852/21-3422
www.mable.ne.jp/~terazuya/english/index.html
Owned by the same family for over a century, this ryokan has a good reputation for convenience, comfort, and exceptional hospitality. You can stay on a with or without meals basis—both are unbeatable value. English is spoken.
10 P No credit cards

OKAYAMA & KURASHIKI

RYOKAN KURASHIKI
$$$$–$$$$$
4-1 HON-MACHI, KURASHIKI-SHI, OKAYAMA-KEN
TEL 086/422-0730
FAX 086/422-0990
This is a 250-year-old merchant complex with a lovely inner garden right by the canal. Antiques furnish the dark, polished wood rooms. Renowned for its service and cuisine, it's open also as a restaurant and a tearoom.
19 All major cards

KURASHIKI KOKUSAI
$$$
1-1-44 CHUO, KURASHIKI-SHI, OKAYAMA-KEN
TEL 086/422-5141
FAX 086/422-5192
Comfortable and good value, this is by far the area's most respected Western-style hotel. The best rooms have great views of old Kurashiki. The rooms are tastefully decorated and the lobby exhibits 20th-century print master Munakata Shiko's largest work.
106 All major cards

OKAYAMA PLAZA
$$$
2-3-12 HAMA, OKAYAMA-SHI, OKAYAMA-KEN
TEL 086/272-1201
FAX 086/273-1557
This is an ideal hotel for both value and location close to the major sights. The comfortable rooms are larger than the norm, the best with fine views over the castle.
85 All major cards

HIROSHIMA & MIYAJIMA

IWASO RYOKAN
$$$$–$$$$$
MOMIJIDANI, MIYAJIMA-CHO, SAEKI-GUN, HIROSHIMA-KEN
TEL 0829/44-2233
FAX 0829/44-2230
www.iwaso.com
Miyajima's first, best, and most beautiful ryokan is tucked up behind Itsukushima-jinja. The best rooms are in two old, exquisite individual cottages; more economical rooms are in the modern annex. Prices include two meals and vary according to rooms and dinner menus (both must be reserved in advance).
38 P All major cards

SUNROUTE
$–$$$$$
3-3-1 OTE-MACHI, NAKA-KU
TEL 082/249-3600
FAX 082/249-3677
www.sunroutehotel.jp/hiroshima
Sunroute specializes in well-appointed business hotels, and this is one of its best. Located by the river and conveniently close to Peace Park, with some rooms overlooking it. Has a bar, and two restaurants, the Kissui (Japanese) and the Viale (Italian)—the latter with a reputation as one of the best in the city.
284 P Non-smoking rooms All major cards

KAKIBUNE KANAWA
$$–$$$$$
HEIWA-OHASHI HIGASHIZUME, OTE-MACHI 3-CHOME, NAKA-KU, HIROSHIMA-SHI, HIROSHIMA-KEN
TE: 082/241-7416
Hiroshima is famous for oysters farmed on thousands of rafts in the bay; this is *the* place to sample them. Actually a barge moored on the river at Heiwa Bridge (near Peace Park), it owes its distinguished reputation to the quality of its

seafood both cooked and raw. Jacket and tie. Reservations recommended.
All major cards

OKONOMI MURA BUILDING
$
5-13 SHINTENCHI, NAKA-KU, HIROSHIMA-SHI
TEL 082/241-2210
In this cherished Hiroshima institution, nothing goes for more than $12. This is where you eat the city's specialty, *okonomi-yaki* (or "Japanese pizza"): patties of flour and egg filled with vegetables, meat, and/or seafood, taking the place of the soba or udon noodle you get elsewhere. The building is an entire "village" *(mura)* devoted to nothing else.
No credit cards

SHIKOKU & THE SETO-NAIKAI

TAKAMATSU

TENKATSU
$$–$$$$
NISHIZUME HIROBA, HYOGO-MACHI, TAKAMATSU-SHI
TEL 087/821-5380
The restaurant is centered on a pond containing a live menu. Not surprisingly, it's renowned for its fish dishes, especially sashmi; its other specialties are *nabemono* (stews).
All major cards

TOKIWA SARYO
$$–$$$$
1-8-2 TOKIWA-CHO, TAKAMATSU-SHI
TEL 087/861-5577
Tokiwa Saryo, a palatial former luxury ryokan which is now a gastronomic landmark, boasts rooms with lacquered ceiling panels and an inner garden. Refined Japanese dining comes at very affordable prices. Reservations required for banqueting rooms.
All major cards

MATSUYAMA & UCHIKO

FUNAYA RYOKAN
$$$$$
1-33 DOGOYU-NO-MACHI, MATSUYAMA-SHI, EHIME-KEN
TEL 089/947-0278
FAX 089/943-2139
A luxurious ryokan with a history extending back to the 17th century. The buildings are mainly from the 1930s, though the latest date to 1968. Many rooms look onto an exquisite garden. With indoor and outdoor public baths, sauna, spa pool, and outstanding food and service, this is the onsen elite.
54 July–Oct. All major cards

RYOKAN MATSUNOYA
$$
1913 HON-MACHI, UCHIKO-CHO, KITA-GUN
TEL 089/344-5000
FAX 089/344-2244
The rooms are very clean and basic, but the accent here is on food. Reviewed in trendy Japanese travel magazines, this place has earned its reputation thanks to an inspired owner-chef, whose style subtly blends Japanese cuisine with Chinese and European elements. Communal bath.
10 No credit cards

ANA HOTEL MATSUYAMA
$–$$$$
3-2-1 ICHIBAN-CHO, MATSUYAMA-SHI, EHIME-KEN
TEL 089/933-5511
FAX 089/921-6053
www.ichotelsgroup.com
South of the castle and within easy reach of shops, Matsuyama's premier Western-style hotel opened in 1980. The spacious rooms are well furnished.
329 Taxi from JR Matsuyama P All major cards

MINSHUKU MIYOSHI
$
3-7-23 ISHITEI, MATSUYAMA-SHI, EHIME-KEN
TEL 089/977-2581
FAX 089/977-2581
Although the location behind a parking lot is a tad gloomy, this is an excellent value. It's just across the road from Ishitei-ji, Matsuyama's famous temple. Tatami-floored rooms are large, comfortable, and spotless, with their own toilet (communal bath; see p. 358). You can have a room with or without meals. The owners are kind to foreigners.
6 JR: Dogo P
No credit cards

KAWAMOYA
$$
1030 IKAZAKI, UCHIKO-CHO, KITA-GUN
TEL 089/344-2780
FAX 089/344-2155
This delightful hotel overlooks a river in Ikazaki, just a five-minute taxi ride from Uchiko. It has spacious, comfortable rooms, both Japanese- and Western-style. Price includes two meals (Japanese or Western); dinner must be ordered in advance.
5 P No credit cards

AJIKURA
$$–$$$
12-32 DOGOYU-NO-MACHI, MATSUYAMA-SHI, EHIME-KEN
TEL 089/934-7075
This pleasant restaurant in the shopping arcade by the Dogo tram station offers a variety of set meals, notably tempura.
Closed Tues. No credit cards

KYUSHU

FUKUOKA-DAZAIFU-YANAGAWA

DAIMARU BESSO
$$$$–$$$$$
1-20-1 YU-MACHI, CHIKUSHINO-SHI, FUKUOKA-KEN
TEL 092/924-3939
FAX 092/924-4126

First built during the 1860s and lying in an elegant garden, this is probably the most prestigious ryokan in Kyushu. All rooms have their own Japanese cypress-wood bath with spa water. Price includes two meals.
49 P All major cards

FUKUOKA GRAND HYATT
$$$$–$$$$$
1-2-82 SUMIYOSHI, HAKATA-KU, FUKUOKA-SHI
TEL 092/282-1234
FAX 092/282-2817
www.fukuoka.grand.hyatt.com
Right in the Canal City shopping-entertainment complex, which is itself an extraordinary architectural achievement, the hotel is futuristic and luxurious with beautiful rooms.
370 P All major cards

OHANA SHOTOKAN
$$$–$$$$
1 SHINHOKA-MACHI, YANAGAWA-SHI
TEL 0944/73-2189
FAX 0944/74-0872
www.ohana.co.jp
The Ohana Villa and Shoto-en Garden are the notable sights in Yanagawa. A good place to appreciate them is this luxury ryokan, which is actually part of the complex. The best rooms look over the garden. The price includes two meals.
21 P All major cards

IL PALAZZO
$$–$$$$
3-13-1 HARUYOSHI, CHUO-KU, FUKUOKA-SHI
TEL 092/716-3333
FAX 092/724-3330
Emphasizing European-style elegance, this inspired blend of traditional Milanese urban architecture was designed by Italian architect Aldo Rossi. The hotel is notable for futuristic use of light and space in its beautiful interior, as well as for its comfort, service, and restaurants.
62 Subway: Nakasu-kawabata; JR: Hakata P All major cards

CANAL CITY WASHINGTON
$–$$$
1-2-20 SUMIYOSHI, HAKATA-KU, FUKUOKA-SHI
TEL 092/282-8800
FAX 092/282-0757
This outpost of the ubiquitous business-hotel chain is well above the usual standard for comfort and amenities, and also has the advantage of a Canal City location.
423 JR: Hakata P Non-smoking floor All major cards

GOURMET CITY
$–$$$$
CENTRAZA HOTEL, 4-23 HAKATA-EKI CHUO-GAI, HAKATA-KU, FUKUOKA-SHI
TEL 092/461-0111 (HOTEL)
Several smart malls under the Hotel Centraza Hakata, just behind Hakata Station, are devoted to Chinese, Korean, Italian, French, Indian, and Thai restaurants. Look for local specialties: *fugu* (blowfish), served mainly raw in paper-thin slices, and *karashi mentai*, cod roe spiced with chili.
All major cards

BEPPU

SOMETHING SPECIAL

SUGINOI HOTEL
The spa hotels and the Japanese *onsen* enthusiast's idea of paradise (though it's mainly Western-style). It adjoins the Suginoi Palace, which provides every imaginable kind of spa bath and sauna as well as karaoke, restaurants and bars, an ice rink, golfing range, shopping malls, amusement park, bowling alley, and more. Rooms are surprisingly restrained, some with great views over the bay.
$$$–$$$$
1 KANKAIJI, BEPPU-SHI, OITA-KEN
TEL 0977/24-1141
FAX 0974/21-0010
www.suginoi-hotel.com
562 P Taxi from JR Beppu All major cards

KUMAMOTO

KUMAMOTO HOTEL CASTLE
$$$$
4-2 JOTO MACHI, KUMAMOTO-SHI
TEL 096/326-3311
FAX 096/326-3324
This comfortable, sedate hotel is close to the castle. The better rooms have fine castle views. The three restaurants include the Loire, the city's best French cuisine.
185 JR: Kami-kumamoto P All major cards

HOTEL NEW OTANI KUMAMOTO
$$–$$$
1-13-1 KASUGA, KUMAMOTO-SHI
TEL 096/326-1111
FAX 096/326-0800
www.newotani.co.jp
Everything you'd expect from the chain running one of Tokyo's largest hotels. Among the city's best accommodations, with spacious rooms featuring the latest amenities.
130 JR: Kumamoto P All major cards

SENRI
$–$$$$
7-17 SUIZENJI-KOEN, KUMAMOTO-SHI
TEL 096/384-1824
A great choice for Japanese specialties, this restaurant is located in Suizenji-koen Park; its best tatami rooms look over the famous garden. Try *karashi renkon*—lotus root stuffed with a savory mixture of miso and mustard, then sliced and deep-fried in batter.
Closed Wed. No credit cards

NAGASAKI & UNZEN

NAGASAKI PRINCE
$$$$
2-26 TAKARA-MACHI, NAGASAKI-SHI
TEL 095/821-1111
FAX 095/823-4309
www.princeresortsjapan.com

Many regard this as Nagasaki's best hotel. The ultra-modern exterior and lobby are almost belied by the old-fashioned romm comfort—where all amenities are nonetheless cutting edge.
183 JR: Nagasaki P All major cards

UNZEN KANKO
$$$–$$$$
320 UNZEN, OBAMA-CHO, UNZEN-CITY
TEL 0957/73-3263
FAX 0957/73-3419

Most accommodations in Unzen are modern, but for something reflecting the golden age of Asian travel, try this famous hotel. It was built on spacious grounds early in the 1930s as a hot spa resort hotel for foreigners and retains period fixtures.
48 P All major cards

HOLIDAY INN
$$–$$$
6-24 DOZA-MACHI, NAGASAKI-SHI
TEL 095/828-1234
FAX 095/828-0178
www.ichotelsgroup.com

In the center of town, this is Nagasaki's best in the middle price range. Rooms present a full range of American-style amenities; tasteful overall Euro-Japanese decor evoking old Nagasaki is a bonus.
87 P All major cards

KAGETSU
$$$–$$$$$
2-1 MARUYAMA-CHO, NAGASAKI-SHI
TEL 095/822-0191

Set in a former geisha house, this is the best place for *shippoku*—a kind of *kaiseki*, (served to two or more diners) that presents delicacies of Japanese, Chinese, and even Portuguese origin. Although dinner prices are almost prohibitive, lunch is merely expensive. Reservations advisable.
Closed Tues. All major cards

SHIKAIRO
$$–$$$$
4-5 MATSUGAE-CHO, NAGASAKI-SHI
TEL 095/822-1296

Nagasaki's noodle specialties are *champon*, a hearty Chinese-style noodle soup with vegetables and meat or seafood, and *sara udon*, udon noodles stir-fried with similar ingredients. This restaurant is said to have invented these dishes when it opened back in 1899. Sadly it moved into four floors of a concrete building during the 1970s, but there's a wealth of Chinese dishes on an English menu.
Most major cards

KAGOSHIMA

KAGOSHIMA TOKYU
$–$$$$$
22-1 KAMOIKE-SHIN-MACHI, KAGOSHIMA-SHI
TEL 099/257-2411
FAX 099/253-3323
www.tokyuhotelsjapan.com

The relatively upscale Tokyu business hotel chain surpasses itself with this branch, near the botanical gardens in the Kamoike waterfront area. Many of the luxurious rooms have great volcano views.
206 P All major cards

SHIROYAMA KANKO HOTEL
$$$$
41-1 SHINSHOIN-CHO, KAGOSHIMA-SHI
TEL 099/224-2211
FAX 099/224-2222

Atop a wooded 350-foot-high (105 m) hill, Kagoshima's finest hotel has well-appointed, comfortable rooms, some with superb views of the city and Mount Sakurajima. The hotel is famous for the views from the top-floor sky lounge.
365 Taxi from JR Kagoshima-chuo P All major cards

KUMASOTEI
$$$–$$$$$
6-10 HIGASHI SENGOKU-CHO, KAGOSHIMA-SHI
TEL 099/222-6356

This restaurant is the best place to sample Kagoshima's regional cuisine, *Satsuma ryori* (the province's former name was Satsuma), renowned by Japanese gourmets.
All major cards

OKINAWA & THE RYUKYU-SHOTO

NAHA

NIKKO NAHA GRAND CASTLE
$$$$
1-132-1 SHURI YAMAKAWA-CHO, NAHA-SHI, OKINAWA-KEN
TEL 098/886-5454
FAX 098/887-0070

Located on the hill at Shuri, near the castle, this towering white hotel meets all the standards you would expect from JAL's Nikko chain.
340 Monorail: Kibo Station P All major cards

HOTEL SUN PALACE KYOYU
$–$$$$
2-5-1 KUMOJI, NAHA-SHI, OKINAWA-KEN
TEL 098/863-4181
FAX 098/861-1313

Behind an inspired facade featuring tiers of balconies festooned with tropical plants, this provides bright, breezy rooms with a full range of amenities down to fax machines. Great value.
75 P All major cards

HOTELS & RESTAURANTS

SHOPPING

The average Japanese city has a shopping precinct *(shoten gai)*, an arcade *(aakeedo)*—usually simply a street covered with a glass roof—a covered food market, and an underground mall, all around the main train station. In larger cities such as Tokyo this pattern may be repeated in several different districts. Both underground malls *(chikagai)* and shopping arcades are great for bargains, particularly photographic equipment, electronics, leather goods, and clothing. In many cities you'll find some interesting junk shops and used clothing stores in arcades, but don't expect any great finds by way of vintage kimono and obi sashes; in recent years prices have gone through the roof even in rural areas.

Some stores offer goods tax free; however, this option applies only to electronic and computer goods, photographic equipment, and jewelry (if it contains precious metals and gems). Many cheap-jack souvenir stores are emblazoned with the term "tax free," when in fact you will be paying regular prices for goods to which the concession doesn't apply. When purchasing tax free, you will need your passport; the store will give you a form to be given to customs when leaving the country.

Antiques

Ceramics and *tansu* chests generally command high prices; although attractive and ubiquitous, *ukiyo-e* prints frequently sell more cheaply overseas. The number of flea markets is growing, although in most cases their prices are only slightly less than in stores. However, they often present a variety of very attractive items made between the 1890s and 1930s that won't break your budget.

Clothing

If you are tall, you may have difficulty with clothing sizes in Japan. Always try on shoes or clothing before purchasing. Some garments carry the "F" (free size) label, but for Americans this is not always the one-size-fits-all guarantee it is for the Japanese.

The less expensive silk kimono you find in large tourist outlets are probably made in China. The real thing, which ranges from seriously expensive to astronomical, can be made to measure in specialty stores. However, they are heavy and impractical and the large *obi* sash is restrictive. It's preferable to go for the more affordable cotton *yukata;* used either as sleepwear or in high summer, they come ready-made or made-to-order in a range of attractive designs.

Department stores

Wonderful places to buy quality Japanese goods, including ceramics and lacquerware. Many of them have food halls in the basement with a fascinating selection of homegrown and imported goods. Stores such as Seibu, Isetan, Marui, and Matsuya operate on a chain basis, often with branches in major cities. The twice yearly sales in these stores offer exceptional discounts. Lasting a week each, sales are held generally from the second Friday in January and July. Prices on designer clothing, for instance, plummet by 50 percent on average.

Discount stores

These appeared around Japan during the 1990s. Every town now has a *hyaku-en kinitsu* (¥100-only) outlet, with an astonishing array of goods (mainly made in China) including stationery, household goods, and novelties each costing exactly ¥100.

Electronics, electrical goods, & computer stores

Goods are at discounted prices. But beware: U.S. and Japanese computer systems are usually incompatible. When it comes to audio and video, always make sure that the specifications and current match those back home.

Souvenirs

Most of the goods for sale at gift shops and souvenir stalls will be kitsch: hideous calendars, garish sake drinking sets, fluorescent paintings on velvet, key chains, cheap novelties, and so on. The most plentiful souvenirs are the edible kind; every region has its own specialties. In the cake and candy line, there are *sembei* (rice crackers) and *mochi* (a chewy sweet made with rice flour).

Traditional arts & crafts

These make by far the best buys in Japan. They include ceramics, textiles, paper and paperware (umbrellas, fans, hand-painted kites, stationery, etc.), dolls, wood and bamboo products, woodblock prints (antique and modern), cloisonné, and lacquerware. The crafts vary regionally, but craft shops, specialty stores, and department stores in large cities usually offer a range of goods from different parts of the country.

TOKYO

Tokyo has a reputation as a paradise for shopaholics, with something for everyone from platinum card holders to backpackers. The main shopping districts vary because of local consumer trends—Ginza is conservative and upscale, Shibuya a favorite with the young—or by specializing in certain kinds of goods. Akihabara is known for electronics, Harajuku for teen fashion, Kappabashi for catering supplies (including the incredible food models you see in restaurant windows), Jimbocho for books, and Kotto-dori in Aoyama for antiques. Aoyama also has its famous "Killer-dori," named for the prices in its designer outlets.

Markets
The space underneath elevated train tracks has been used for covered markets or filled in with a miscellany of stores since World War II.

Ameyoko Ameya-yoko-cho, Ueno. Tokyo's most exciting street market (see p. 93) is less touristy than the International Arcade.
International Arcade 1-7-23 Uchisaiwai-cho, Chiyoda-ku, tel 03/3591-2764. A huge array of goods and tax-free discounts.

GINZA

Ginza is Tokyo's Fifth Avenue, with a great variety of shops and upscale department stores. More department stores are to be located just west of Ginza in Yurakucho.

Antique Mall Ginza 1-20-15 Ginza, Chuo-ku, tel 03/3535-2115, closed Wed. A fantastic emporium with around 300 stalls selling antiques both Japanese and from around the world. There's certainly something here to cherish and (if very lucky) even a bargain.
Bunkado 5-14-1 Ginza, Chuo-ku, tel 03/3541-8325, closed Sun. Renowned for handicrafts from around Japan, including ceramics and lacquerware.
Kyukyodo 5-7-4 Ginza, Chuo-ku, tel 03/3571-4429. Sells incense, handmade paper, traditional stationery, brushes, and calligraphy requisites. Also stocks a marvelous selection of papercraft, including boxes and miniature chests of drawers.
Mikimoto 4-5-5 Ginza, Chuo-ku, tel 03/3535-4611, closed Wed. Owned by the descendants of Mikimoto Kokichi, who invented the cultured pearl technique, this shop has branches nationwide.
Mitsukoshi 4-6-16 Ginza, Chuo-ku, tel 03/3562-1111. An elegant department store stocking the finest goods both Japanese and imported, with prices to match.
Nihonshu Center 1-1-21 Nishi Shimbashi, Minato-ku, tel 03/3519-2091, closed Sat.–Sun. *Nihonshu* is the proper word for sake. You can sample some of 6,000 variations for a nominal fee
Sakai Kokodo Gallery 1-2-14 Yurakucho, Chiyoda-ku, tel 03/3591-4678. Long-established dealer in woodblock prints, the range here goes from vintage rarities to high-quality modern reproductions.
Seibu 2-5-1 Yurakucho, Chiyoda-ku, tel 03/3286-0111. The local branch of the department store.
Sony Showroom Sony Bldg., 5-3-1 Ginza, Chuo-ku, tel 03/3573-2371. This corner building at the main intersection is a Ginza landmark; all the latest audio-visual gadgetry and games technology are there for you to try out, as well as a multitude of audio, visual, and digital gizmos.

ROPPONGI

Aoyama Book Center 6-1-20 Roppongi, Minato-ku, tel 03/3479-0479. Book and magazine store emphasizing art, photography, and design, with a decent-size selection of books in English.
Axis Building 5-17-1 Roppongi, Minato-ku, tel 03/3587-2781. With stores variously devoted to furnishing and crafts (e.g. ceramics and textiles), this sleek building is the ideal place for an overview of the best of contem-porary Japanese interior design.
Nuno Tokyo B1F Axis Bldg. (see above), tel 03/3582-7997. "Nuno" is Japanese for "textile" and also the name of a firm run by elite textile designer Reiko Sudo and colleagues and founded in 1983. Nuno fabrics meld the ancestral with the futuristic, the artisanal with the digital,The shop also sells clothes.

SHIBUYA

Daiso 100 yen plaza Udagawacho 27-4, Shibuya-ku, tel 03/5459-3601. Spawned by recession and still thriving, gaudy ¥100 (hyaku-en) stores are omnipresent in Tokyo and nation-wide. Five floors of ¥100 kitchen and bathroom ware, accessories, toys, souvenirs, and gadgets you never knew you needed.
Hysteric Glamour 6-23-2 Jingumae, Shibuya-ku, tel 03/3409-7227. Flagship store of a chain famed for ultrahip, grunge, and manga-inspired fashion. There are also two branches in LaForet (1-11-6 Jingumae, Shibuya-ku, tel 03/3475- 0411), a sleek Harajuku landmark containing over 100 boutiques.
Issey Miyake 3-18-11 Minami Aoyama, Minato-ku, tel 03/3423-1407. Issey changed the face of world fashion in the 1980s with his revolutionary use of tailoring, fabrics, pleats, and plastics. Affordable or not, it's well worth a look.
Kiddyland 6-1-9 Jingu-mae, Shibuya-ku, tel 03/3409-3431. It's the ultimate store for toys, gadgets, gimmicks, models, etc.
Loft 21-1 Udagawa-cho, Shibuya-ku, tel 03/3462-3807. This "creative store" (a Seibu offshoot), featuring furnishings, fabrics, and endless supplies and materials for hobbies, arts, and crafts, places great emphasis on style.
Mujirushi Ryohin 2-12-28 Kita Aoyama, Minato-ku, tel 03/3478-5800. Sells high-quality generic goods—everything from noodles to bicycles, with clothes and household items in between.
Oriental Bazaar 5-9-13 Jingumae, Shibuya-ku, tel 03/3400-3933, closed Thurs. Though touristy, the best place for souvenirs: prints, ceramics, lacquerware, paperware, and lamps, as well as affordable antiques and vintage kimono.
Parco 15-1 Udagawa-cho, Shibuya-ku, tel 03/3464-5111. Originally an offshoot of Seibu, this store launched the concept of the "fashion building"—several floors devoted solely to clothing, containing boutiques and sections operated by all the world's major designer brands.
Seibu 21-1 Udagawa-cho, Shibuya-ku, tel 03/3462-0111.

The store had a seminal influence on fashion in Japan and remains outstanding for clothing, household goods, and gifts. Basement food hall.
Tokyu Hands 12-18 Udagawa-cho, Shibuya-ku, tel 03/5489-5111. A great home handyman store, with several floors of tools, materials, and accessories required for arts, crafts, and hobbies.

SHINJUKU & IKEBUKURO

Shopping of all kinds at all prices—department stores, high-fashion outlets, general discount stores, and, most famously, discount camera stores west of Shinjuku Station.

Camera Sakuraya 3-17-2 Shinjuku, Shinjuku-ku, tel 03/3354-3636. This photographic shop is esteemed for new and used equipment and noted for its discounts.
Kinokuniya Bookstore 3-17-7 Shinjuku, tel 03/3354-0131. This is still one of the city's best places for foreign books, magazines, and paperbacks.
Marui 3-30-16 Shinjuku, tel 03/3354-0101. A comprehensive and trendy department store in four sections. All you need to know is that *kan* means building, then choose between Young Kan, Fashion Kan, Men's Kan, and Interior Kan.
Seibu 1-28-1 Minami Ikebukuro, Toshima-ku, tel 03/3981-0111. The original flagship store, and still Seibu's largest branch. (See Shibuya, p. 381)
Sunshine City 3-1-3 Higashi Ikebukuro, Toshima-ku, tel 03/3989-3331. One of Tokyo's tallest and largest buildings contains a branch of Mitsukoshi department store and a gargantuan shopping mall.
The Japan Traditional Craft Center 1-11-1 Nishi-Ikebukuro, 1F Metropolitan Plaza Building, tel 03/5954-6066. The cream of Japanese traditional craftsmanship (ceramics, lacquerware, et al) is not only exhibited here, but also for sale.
Tobu Metropolitan Plaza, 1-1-25 Nishi Ikebukuro, Toshima-ku, tel 03/3981-2211. The rival store to Seibu expanded during the mid-1990s, and here includes not only the colossal store itself, but also the Tobu Museum of Art.
Yodobashi Camera Nishiguchi Honten, 1-11-1 Nishi Shinjuku, Shinjuku-ku, tel 03/3346-1010. Several floors of video, discount cameras and accessories, and general photographic items. There are often great bargains, but don't buy any digital or electronic goods without first checking on system compatibility.

UENO-ASAKUSUA

Great for handmade traditional goods, including hardware and carpenter's tools, kimono and accessories, fans, wooden combs, and paper lanterns.

Adachi-ya 2-22-12 Asakusa, Taito-ku, tel 03/3841-4915, closed Tues. Traditional working clothes, notably the blue denim *hanten* (or *happi* coat), the Edo-period townsman's garb still worn at festivals.
Hanato 2-25-6 Asakusa, Taito-ku, tel 03/3841-6411, closed Tues. An old-fashioned fireman's lantern bearing your name in *hiragana* characters? No problem: Hanato makes any kind of paper lantern *(chochin)* to order.
Kurodaya 1-2-11 Asakusa, Taito-ku, tel 03/3844-7511, closed Mon. Premier outlet for *washi* paper and papercraft, including kites and festival masks.
Matsuya 1-4-1 Hanakawado, Taito-ku, tel 03/3842-1111. There are often excellent craft exhibitions here, promoting ceramics, woodcraft, and lacquerware, with demonstrations by craftspeople from around Japan.
Sukeroku 2-3-1 Asakusa, Taito-ku, tel 03/3844-0577. This is the last store on the right as you walk up Nakamise to Senso-ji. It sells exquisite miniatures representing period people, houses, and shops, as well as other delightful statuettes.
Yonoya 1-37-10 Asakusa, tel 03/3844-1755, closed Wed. A specialist in handcrafted wooden combs and hair ornaments for the past 150 years; beautiful goods in a beautiful little shop.

AKIHABARA-KANDA

Akihabara's Denki Gai (Electric Town) is famous for sheer spectacle (see p. 98–99). Good for electronic and electrical goods and bargains (though rare) do turn up for those who really know what they're looking for.

Laox Computer-kan 1-7-6 Soto Kanda, Chiyoda-ku, tel 03/5256-3111. A computer superstore six stories high. If it isn't here, you probably won't find it in Japan.
Oya Shobo 1-1 Kanda Jimbocho, Chiyoda-ku, tel 03/3291-0062. One of the most famous dealers in the used book district, this specialist in period maps and antique books (the illustrated ones are highly attractive) also has a good selection of *ukiyo-e* prints.
Yodobashi Akiba 1-1 Kanda Hanaokacho, Chiyoda-ku, tel 03/5209-1010. Located on the east side of JR Akihabara Station, this is the neighborhood's latest electronics superstore. It's great for cameras, appliances, PCs, toys and plastic models.

CENTRAL HONSHU

NAGOYA

There are several department stores here starting with **Meitetsu** at the train station, beneath which is a large underground shopping arcade. If you like junk-shops and antiques, you should explore the Osu Arcade and vicinity. There's a weekend flea market at intervals at Osu Kannon Temple; check with the visitor information office or the International Forum Building (see p. 69) for schedules.

Noritake has been famous for Western-style ceramics and chinaware for over a century; you can visit the factory, the **Noritake Craft Center** (Tel 052/561-7114), but an advance reservation is essential.

KANAZAWA

Kanazawa has been a center for ceramics since feudal times, and is known for *Ohi* and *Kutani* pottery. Devised for the tea ceremony, Ohi ware has beautiful warm-colored glazes; Kutani ware has ornate decoration in glowing colors.
In the southwest of town is **Kutani Kosengama** (Kosen Kutani Pottery Kiln, 5-3-3 Nomachi, tel 076/241-0902), which has a large sale room.

A major producer of gold leaf since ancient times, Kanazawa is also renowned for Kaga lacquerware *(Kaga maki-e)*, featuring intricate designs highlighted with gold and silver dust. The Japanese know the area most of all for *kaga yuzen*—a distinctive dyeing and stenciling technique for silk kimono fabrics. Just north of the Kenroku-en Garden, the **Ishikawa Bussankan** (Ishikawa Prefectural Products Shop, tel 076/222-7788) has all the specialties of the prefecture—arts, crafts, and edibles; it also includes a restaurant. Other specialty craft workshops in Kanazawa can be visited by arrangement through the visitor information center.

TAKAYAMA

There is plenty of local color in Takayama's morning street markets *(asa-ichi)*, which trade daily in produce and flowers grown by local farmers, as well as handicrafts. Both are open from 7 a.m. to noon, one at Jinya-mae near the historic government building and the other on the eastern bank of the Miya-gawa River, across from Kajibashi bridge.

The old town center of Sanmachi Suji holds an antique market on the 7th of each month from May through October. Good pieces won't come cheap, but will still be priced much lower than in Kyoto or Tokyo.

KANSAI

KYOTO

Kyoto's shopping is concentrated in the center of town, especially along Shijo-dori up to the intersection with Kawaramachi-dori. Shopping arcades sprawl from beneath the station and there's also a range of shops in the city's covered arcades: Shinkyogoku and Teramachi.

Kyoto's department stores have large selections of traditional local products and gifts. Among them are **Hankyu** (68 Shin-cho, Shijo-dori, Shimogyu-ku, tel 075/223-2288), **Kintetsu** (Karasuma-dori, Shimogyo-ku, tel 075/361-1111, closed Thurs.), and **Daimaru** (Shijo-dori, Shimogyo-ku, tel 075/211-8111).
Kagoshin 4-7 Sanjo-dori, Ohashi Higashi, Higashiyama-ku, tel 075/771-0209, closed Sun. In business since the 1860s, this shop specializes in high-quality objects made of bamboo, including ikebana items, woven baskets, and bamboo lacquerware.
Kasagen 284 Kitagawa, Gion-machi, Higashiyama-ku, tel 075/561-2832, closed Wed. Has sold oiled paper umbrellas for well over a century.
Kyoto Handicraft Center 21 Shogoin, Entomi-cho, Sakyo-ku, tel 075/761-5080. Artisans and craftspeople not only work on the spot, but also let the public try some of the techniques.
Kyoto Tojiki Kaikan (Kyoto Ceramics Center) 570-3 Shiraito-cho, Gojo-dori, Higashiyama-ku, tel 075/541-1102. Two floors of works by members of the local potters' cooperative.
Miyawaki Baisen-an Rokkaku-dori, Tominokoji Nishi-iru, Nakagyo-ku, tel 075/221-0181. This famous shop first started selling fans to geisha, actors, and the general public about 180 years ago and maintains its reputation for the handmade, genuine article today.
Nishijin Orimono Textile Center Imadegawa, Horikawa-dori, Kamigyo-ku, tel 075/451-9231. You can watch designers, dyers, and weavers at work on kimono silk of the highest quality; there's a sales area—though the price for a good piece large enough for a garment could well cost more than your entire trip to Japan.
Tachikichi Shijo-Tominokoji, Shimogyo-ku, tel 075/255-3507, closed Wed. One of the best places for ceramics, with a huge selection of both modern and traditional styles on four floors.
Takashimaya 52 Shin-cho, Shijo-dori, Shimogyo-ku, tel 075/221-8811. Department store reputed to have the best selection of traditional gifts. Some staff at the information counters speak English.
Tanakaya Shijo-dori, Yanaginobanba-higashi, Shimogyo-ku, tel 075/221-1959, closed Wed. A specialist in Japanese dolls, especially the local *kyo-ningyo*. Upstairs is a gallery of their antique counterparts.
Union Kyoto Craft Center 275 Kitagawa, Gion-machi, Higashiyama-ku, tel 075/561-9660. Here you can see all local arts and crafts in one place.
Yamato Mingei-ten Takoyaku-shi-agaru, Kawaramachi-dori, Nakagyo-ku, tel 075/221-2641, closed Wed. Folk craft shop selling a miscellany of quality handmade items both local and from all over Japan.

ENTERTAINMENT & FESTIVALS

Easy to find for being concentrated in amusement districts, the array of entertainments in large Japanese cities is exhaustive. Even smaller towns have a district with bars, restaurants, discos, movie theaters—and more louche entertainments.

Many visitors to Japan are attracted by the festivals taking place all over the country. You will find information about the different festivals, both countrywide and regional, here.

You'll find English-language listings in magazines such as *Tokyo Journal* and *Kansai Time Out,* as well as on the Internet (e.g. Tokyo Meltdown, see p. 356). You can also check Tokyo and Kansai (Kyoto and Osaka) movie and theater programs in the English-language newspapers (see p. 355). In other areas, you should pick up the newsletters in visitor information centers, which list special events, fairs, exhibitions, and festivals.

Going to the movies is an easy option—more than two-thirds are imports (overwhelmingly from the U.S.) and, with the exception of animated features, are always subtitled and screened in the original language.

Entertainment districts also present a substantial selection of live music venues. Watch the listings: rock, rap, hip-hop, garage, house, techno, thrash, heavy metal, blues, jazz—you name it, someone somewhere is playing it. Discos often bar men unaccompanied by women. Most places charge women lower rates; some have dress codes.

Tokyo, Kyoto, and other large cities feature traditional theater forms including Kabuki and Noh. Elsewhere they are rare; you're more likely to see Western-style performing arts, notably world-class classical music.

TOKYO

When it comes to going out on the town, choose between the entertainment districts of Shinjuku, Roppongi, and Shibuya, with plenty more alternatives in the Aoyama, Ebisu, and Nishi-Azabu neighborhoods.

BARS & CLUBS

The *Tokyo Journal* listings are excellent for bars and clubs. Fashions come and go at an alarming rate in Japan, so be aware that suggestions here may have lost favor or vanished by the time this book goes to press.

Acaraje Tropicana B1 Edge Blvd., 1-1-1 Nishi Azabu, Minato-ku, tel 03/3479-4690. Hippest and most authentic Brazilian dive in town, great samba, lambada, and food. Nearby is **Acaraje,** its smaller parent (Tel 03/3401-0973).

A971 9-7-2 Akasaka, Minato-ku, tel 03/5413-3210. Taking its name from the address, A971 is a hipster bar nestled in the new Tokyo Midtown complex that attracts plenty of party people on Saturday nights.

Blue Note 5-13-3 Minami Aoyama, Minato-ku, tel 03/5485-0088, closed Sun. Like its New York counterpart, this is the place to catch the greatest names in jazz. Two sets nightly at 7 and 9:30.

Gas Panic Togensha Bldg., 2, & 3F, 3-14-13 Roppongi, Minato-ku, tel 03/3405-0633. Actually two bars and a dance club in one, this is cheap, hip, always crowded, and remains popular despite a reputation for occasional brawls.

Hanezawa Garden 3-12-15 Hiro, Shibuya-ku, tel 03 3400 2013, closed Oct.–March. A beer garden that's actually in a real (Japanese) garden. You can dine on barbecued food beneath trees festooned with colored lanterns. Delightful—despite dreadful canned Hawaiian music.

Kento's 6F Takiyamacho Bldg., 6-7-12 Ginza, Chuo-ku, tel 03/3572-9161. Another nostalgia fest, with 1950s and '60s hits played by bands sporting box jackets and ducktails. Also at B1 Dai-ni Renu Bldg., 5-3-1 Roppongi, tel 03/3401-5755.

Lexington Queen 3-13-14 Roppongi, Minato-ku, tel 03/3401-1661. Established in 1980, the Lex is where international screen, stage, and rock celebrities visiting Tokyo wind up until the wee small hours—hosted by genial manager Bill Hersey.

The Crocodile B1 New Sekiguchi Bldg., 6-18-8 Jingumae, Shibuya-ku, tel 03/3499-5205. Thirty years on, the Croc is still cool, still hip—depending on the night and the band. An attractive bar and premier Tokyo "live house" popular with a mixed crowd of all ages.

Heartland 6-10-1 Roppongi, Minato-ku, tel 03/5772-7600. Tucked under the Roppongi Hills complex, Heartland is a stylish bar popular with the expat financial industry crowd. It's a great spot to down 500 yen bottles of Heartland beer on Friday and Saturday nights.

FOR CHILDREN

Tokyo Disneyland
1-1 Maihama, Urayasu-shi, Chiba-ken, tel 045/683-3777, www.tokyodisneyresort.co.jp. This is useful if you're traveling with youngsters underwhelmed by museums and temples. A successful clone of its California parent and only a 15-minute train ride to Urayasu (from JR Tokyo Station on the JR Keiyo line to Maihama Station; the park is outside the station). Hours and prices vary seasonally.

To reserve tickets for shows, telephone (or get someone to do it for you) the main booking agencies: **Ticket Pia** (Tel 0570/02-9999), and the largest, **CN Playguide** (Tel 03/5802-9999). Agencies also sell tickets for sports events.

SUMO

The nation's most important sumo tournaments take place at the **Kokugikan** (National Sumo Hall, 1-3-28 Yokoami, Sumida-ku, Tokyo, tel 03/3623-5111) from the 1st or 2nd Sunday to the 3rd or 4th Sunday in January and May and from the 2nd to 4th Sunday in September.

THEATER

Tokyo has the largest number of playhouses staging traditional theater such as Kabuki and Noh (see pp. 46–49). Programs are seasonal and irregular; check for details in the English-language press or with the Japan National Tourist Office.

Kabuki-za 4-12-15 Ginza, Chuo-ku, tel 03/3541-3131. Two Kabuki programs daily.
Shinbashi Embujo 6-18-2 Ginza, Chuo-ku, tel 03/3541-2600. Mainly traditional fare, including Kabuki and seasonal dance presentations by the dwindling *shimabashi* geisha.
Kokuritsu Gekijo (National Theater) 4-1 Hayabusa-cho, Chiyoda-ku, tel 03/3265-7411. Sometimes presents Bunraku puppet theater; at other times, anything from Kabuki to works by contemporary composers.
Takarazuka Theater 1-1-3 Yurakucho, Chiyoda-ku, tel 03/5251-2001. Tokyo branch of the all-female opera company: lavish revues, operettas, and musicals. Reserve ahead for a good seat.

HOKKAIDO

SAPPORO

The action in Sapporo is concentrated in Susukino, where side streets present a seemingly unending array of bars and clubs. Depending on the season, you can grab a beer from a vending machine and join in what seems like a party watching a ball game up on the giant TV screen over the area's main intersection.

Gaijin Bar 2F M's Space, Minami 2, Nishi 7, tel 011/272-1033, closed Sun. This is one of the city's top expat hangouts.
King Xmhu Minami 7, Nishi 4, tel 011/531-1388. Pronounced "mu," the hottest dance spot features a colossal Aztec-style effigy of the king dominating the facade with glowing red eyes; a cadaverous interior matches it with glowing laser-eyed demon masks and trendy decor.
500 Bar Minami 4, Nishi 2, Chuo-ku, tel 011/562-2556. As the name suggests, all drinks at this chic chain are 500 yen. The menu has everything from cured ham to honey on toast.

CENTRAL HONSHU

NAGOYA

Has a Noh theater and the Misono-za Kabuki theater, but programs are irregular. Check local listings available from the visitor information center.

There is a concentration of bars and night spots in an energetic amusement district around Sakae 3-Chome.

Sumo is one of the highlights of the summer. Tournaments are held from the 1st to 3rd Sunday in July at the **Aichi-ken Taiikukan** (Aichi Prefectural Gymnasium, 1-1 Ninomaru, Naka-ku, Nagoya, tel 052/971-2516).

KANAZAWA

A leading center for Noh drama for centuries. The place to see it is the **Ishikawa Prefectural Noh Theater** (Tel 076/264-2598). Programs run every week during summer but less regularly at other times. Check the visitor information center for schedules.

KANSAI

KYOTO

BARS & CLUBS

Metro Keihan Marutamachi station, tel 075/752-4765. This is Kyoto's most happenin' place. It features star foreign bands and DJs, art exhibits, fringe theater, and/or weird and wacky theme nights. It's fairly small and gets very crowded on weekends.
Pig & Whistle 2F Shobi Bldg., 115 Ohashi-cho, Sanjo Ohashi, tel 075/761-6022. Lively British-style pub, offering such delights as darts and fish and chips.

THEATER

Noh and Kabuki both originated in Kyoto. The same applies to geisha dance spectaculars; in addition to those mentioned below, others are also presented in the fall. Check for programs at the visitor information center.

Gion Corner 570-2 Minamigawa, Gion-machi, Higashiyama-ku, tel 075/561-1119. A small theater offering an eclectic digest of traditional entertainments from Bunraku puppet drama excerpts to the tea ceremony. It's tacky and touristy, but fun.
Minami-za Kawabata-dori, tel 075/561-1155. This famous Kyoto landmark on the southern bank of the Kamo River is Japan's oldest Kabuki theater.
Gion Kobu Kaburenjo 570-2 Minamigawa, Gion-machi, Higashiyama-ku, tel 075/541-3391. The theater where *maiko* (trainee geisha) have been presenting glittering *Miayko Odori* (cherry dance) spectaculars each April for almost 150 years.
Ponto-cho Kaburenjo Theater Ponto-cho, Sanjo Sagaru, Nakagyo-ku, tel 075/221-2025. Ponto-cho maiko and geisha present *Kamo-gawa odori* (Kamo River dance) spectaculars here twice a year—in May and mid-October to mid-November.

OSAKA

Osaka rivals Tokyo as the nation's most hedonistic city; its entertainment district is Dotonburi, just south of the center between Shinsaibashi and Namba subway stations.

Many expat-friendly dives lie north of Dotonburi in hot and hip **Amerika Mura** (America Village), named from its many U.S.-style fashion outlets. Packing R&B, reggae, hip-hop, and salsa, **SAM & DAVE 05** (B1F, 1-21-19, Nagahoribashi, Chuo-ku, Osaka, tel 06/6251-5333) really rocks. It's the greatest of an expanding club chain (No. 2 is nearby at Shinsaibashi). A popular hangout for locals and expats, **The Pig & Whistle** (IS Bldg., 2F, 1-32 Shinsaibashi-suji, 2-chome, tel 06/6213-6911) proffers a British pub experience —down to the fish and chips.

SUMO

Sumo tournaments are held in Osaka from the 2nd Sunday to 4th Sunday in March at the **Osaka Furitsu Taiiku Kaikan** (3-4-36 Namba-Naka, Naniwa-ku, Osaka, tel 06/6631-0121), near Namba subway station.

THEATER

Check schedules either at the visitor information center or in publications such as *Kansai Time Out* magazine and *Meet Osaka.*

National Bunraku Theater of Japan 1-12-10 Nipponbashi, Chuo-ku, tel 06/6212-2531. Bunraku, the puppet theater form originated in Osaka. It is worth going to see; performances have three-week runs in January, March, April, June to August, and November.

KYUSHU

FUKUOKA

Nakasu amusement district, comprising restaurants, bars, nightclubs, theaters, and discos, is considered one of Japan's best; it is said to rival Tokyo's Shinjuku for raunch. Tenjin, northwest of Nakasu, also has nightspots.

Check the schedule at the **Fukuoka Blue Note** (2-7-6 Tenjin, Chuo-ku, Fukuoka City, tel 092/715-6666), opening late 2000, which hosts international jazz giants when they tour Japan. Fukuoka is also a sumo city, hosting major tournaments from the 2nd to the 4th Sunday in November at the **Fukuoka Kokusai Center** (2-2 Chikko-Hon-machi, Hakata-ku, Fukuoka-shi, tel 092/272-1111).

FESTIVALS

The *matsuri* (festival) is where the Japanese go to find the "real Japan." Rituals and customs, food and drink, clothing and trappings, music and dance are all redolent of a cultural identity predating Western influence by centuries. A matsuri gives enough local color to constitute the highlight of a trip to Japan. Shinto festival parades always include *mikoshi*, the ornately decorated, gilded palanquins supported on long, thick wooden poles and carried around the streets by scores of chanting bearers. Each mikoshi (some weighing several tons) was thought to be the means of conveyance for a deity; the object of the festival was to show the gods a good time.

Some matsuri are nostalgic pageants with parades of geisha or samurai warriors; others, especially Buddhist festivals such as O-bon, commemorate the dead (which doesn't mean doom and gloom in Japan). Many festivals include markets selling food and sweets, good luck charms, plants, and cheap toys. If you plan to attend a major festival, bear in mind that hotels in the area will be packed solid. There are many hundreds of festivals; those below are merely a few of the more important ones; Confirm actual festival dates at local visitor centers.

COUNTRYWIDE

JANUARY

Seijin-no-hi—Coming of Age Day (2nd Mon.). This national holiday targets all who will reach 20 years of age within the year. Young people often go sightseeing (at shrines and temples) in formal attire.

FEBRUARY

Setsubun—Parting of the Seasons (Feb. 3 or 4). Marks the last day of winter. Many shrines and temples host traditional celebrations, often followed by performances with costumed demons and deities.

MARCH

Hina Matsuri—Doll's Festival or Peach Blossom Festival (Feb. 1–4). A girls' festival: Dolls representing an imperial couple of ancient times, with attendant court, are displayed on specially erected shelves in homes.

APRIL

Hanami—Flower Viewing. Colleagues, friends, and families indulge in bibulous picnics beneath flowering cherry trees. **Hana Matsuri**—Flower Festival (April 8). Celebrates Buddha's birthday in temples nationwide.

AUGUST

O-Bon—Festival of the Dead or Lantern Festival (mid Aug.). Opens a season coinciding with the summer vacation. Different events and festivals are held in different places, notably *Bon odori* dancing, spectacular firework displays, and the charming custom of floating candles (each representing a soul) along rivers aboard little paper boats.

NOVEMBER

Shichi-go-san (Nov. 15). Children aged 7 *(shichi)*, 5 *(go)*, and 3 *(san)* don traditional finery and go to Shinto shrines nationwide for ritual blessing.

TOKYO

JANUARY

Dezome-shiki —New Year Firemen's Parade (Jan. 6). Attired in period garb, firemen parade along Harumi dori on Tokyo Bay, and perform stunning acrobatic feats atop high bamboo ladders.

MAY

Sanja Matsuri (close to May 17). Crowds of people, many in period costume, throng the streets of Asakusa.

JUNE

Sanno Matsuri (June 10–16 annually). Held at Hie-jinja Shrine. Mounted priests lead a lively parade along Akasaka's main avenue every other year.

JULY

Fireworks (last Sat. in July). Held in Asakusa over Sumida-gawa River, this is Japan's greatest fireworks display.

NOVEMBER

Tori-no-Ichi—Rooster Fair (early to mid-Nov., depending on the year). Night markets at Otori-jinja in Asakusa and Hanazono-jinja in Shinjuku. Ornately decorated *kumade* (rakes) are sold (to encourage the gods to help businesses rake in plenty of cash). A marvelous all-night street party, with stalls selling sake, noodles, and yakitori (broiled, skewered chicken).

DECEMBER

Hagoita Ichi (Dec. 17–19). A festive all-night market at Senso-ji Temple. *Hagoita* (battledores), faced with elaborate cloth bas-reliefs inspired from woodblock prints, are still sold here.

EXCURSIONS FROM TOKYO

APRIL

Kamakura Matsuri (2nd to 3rd Sun. in April). Focuses on the Tsurugaoka Hachiman-gu Shrine, and features dances and a parade of historical samurai figures. A *yabusame* (archery on horseback) contest in samurai regalia is an exciting highlight.

MAY

Sennin Gyoretsu (May 17–18). The festival at Tosho-gu Shrine in Nikko culminates with breath-taking pageantry, including a thousand men in samurai armor.

SEPTEMBER

Yabusame (Sept. 16). Tsurugaoka Hachiman-gu Shrine, Kamakura. The most exciting demonstration of yabusame (archery on horseback).

OCTOBER

Toshogu Matsuri (Oct. 17). Autumn Festival at Tosho-gu Shrine, Nikko, featuring a parade of mounted priests and samurai.

NOVEMBER

Daimyo Gyoretsu (Nov. 3). This costumed pageant evokes 17th-century processions of *daimyo* along the Tokaido road in Hakone-Yumoto.

HOKKAIDO

FEBRUARY

Yuki Matsuri—Snow Festival (early Feb.). World-famous Sapporo festival in which intricate and ornate snow sculptures decorate the center of the city.

NORTHERN HONSHU (TOHOKU)

FEBRUARY

Kamakura Matsuri (Feb. 15–16). This children's festival happens in several places, the most famous at Yokote, Akita-ken. It's named after the snow houses *(kamakura)* built for the event; children sit snugly in their candlelit igloos around a brazier for boiling sweet sake, which they offer around.

JUNE

Chaguchagu Umakko— Horse Festival (June 15). In Morioka, dealers and breeders parade their gaily decorated horses to be blessed at the Sozen Shrine.

AUGUST

Nebuta and **Neputa** (Aug. 1–7). These festivals, held at the same time in Aomori and Hirosaki, feature a spectacular parade of huge, beautifully painted, and ornate lanterns.

Kanto Matsuri (Aug. 4–7). Akita City. As the highlight of a rousing parade, men hold huge poles festooned with lanterns, balancing them on their hands, shoulders, chins, and foreheads.

DECEMBER

Namahage (Dec. 31). Held on the Oga-hanto Peninsula in Akita-ken. Groups of bachelors don demon costumes and go from house to house bellowing "Are there any rascals in here?" Residents entertain these *Namahage* with rice cakes and sake.

CENTRAL HONSHU

MARCH

Tagata Honen Matsuri—Bumper Harvest Festival (March 15). One of Japan's 40-odd remaining phallic shrines, Tagata-jinja, near Inuyama, is renowned for this rousing festival, with a street parade of huge wooden phalli.

APRIL

Takayama Matsuri (April 14–15). This festival centers on Takayama's Hie Shrine. A splendid parade with 12 ornate *yatai*—wheeled juggernauts with performing *karakuri* automatons.

MAY

Cormorant fishing (season opens May 11). This fascinating (if these days purely touristic) activity can be seen on the Nagara River, Gifu-ken, almost nightly until Oct. 15. Birds have been trained to catch fish drawn to the surface by the light of braziers hanging from the boats.

OCTOBER

Takayama Hachimangu Matsuri (Oct. 9–10). Centered on Hachiman-gu Shrine, Takayama, this lively festival dating from the 15th century is renowned for its beautiful floats and *mikoshi*.

KANSAI

JANUARY

Toka Ebisu (Jan. 9–11). At Imamiya Ebisu Shrine in Osaka, thousands pay their respects to Ebisu, a god of plenty, and patron of business workers and fishermen. A parade of women in sumptuous kimono is carried aboard ornate palanquins.
Wakakasuyama-yaki (Jan. 15). The grass on Wakakasu-yama Hill (in Nara-koen Park) is burned to commemorate the ending of rivalry between two temples in the 10th century. Rousing celebrations and a spectacular fireworks display.

FEBRUARY

Mantoro—Lantern Lighting Ceremony (Feb. 3 or 4). This magical event takes place in Nara to usher in the spring. All 3,000 bronze and stone lanterns at Kasuga Taisha Shrine are lit.

MARCH

Omizutori—Water-drawing Ceremony (March 1–14). Performed annually at Todai-ji Temple in Nara, since the ninth century. The most exciting day is the 12th, when the water is drawn from the Wakasa Well as bearers swing huge torches producing showers of sparks, while priests blow conch shells.

MAY

Aoi Matsuri—Hollyhock Festival (May 15). Held at Shimogamo and Kami-gamo Shrines, Kyoto. With lavish costumes and rich pageantry commemorating visits by courtiers and priests.
Mifune Matsuri (3rd Sun. in May). Poets, musicians, and dancers in period costume perform aboard boats on the Oi River, at Arashiyama.

JUNE

Takigi Noh (June 1 & 2). A torch lit Noh performance, featuring some of the foremost protagonists of the art, in the open air at the Heian Shrine.
Rice Planting Ceremony (June 14). Sumiyoshi Shrine celebrates a rice planting ceremony led by 12 beauties.

JULY

Gion Matsuri (throughout July—parade July17). This famous festival commemorates the sudden end to a ninth-century plague and centers on the Yasaka Shrine in Kyoto. The climax is a costumed parade.

AUGUST

Daimonji (Aug. 16). To the accompaniment of festivities and fireworks, the huge character *dai* (meaning "big") is etched in fire on the slope of Nyoiga-dake over the city of Kyoto.

OCTOBER

Jidai Matsuri—Eras Festival (Oct. 22). Heian Shrine, Kyoto. The highlight is a pageant celebrating the foundation of the city in 794, with costumes evoking that and later eras.

DECEMBER

Okera Mairi (Dec. 31). A huge bonfire is lit at midnight in Yasaka-jinja Shrine compound in Kyoto; everyone tries to take home kindling to start the first fire of the new year. Similar festivities are held at the same time at shrines throughout Japan.

WESTERN HONSHU (CHUGOKU)

FEBRUARY

Eyo (3rd Sat. in Feb.). The most famous of the *hadaka matsuri* (naked festivals) held at several locations in Japan. In this one, at Saidai-ji Temple, Saidaiji, Okayama-ken, hundreds of youths wearing only loincloths compete within the confined space of a temple tower to catch two wands which, believed to guarantee a lifetime's good luck, are thrown down into the throng by priests. This is not open to the casual participant.

JUNE

Kangensai Music Festival (June 17—lunar calender, so the date changes annually). Displays of ancient court dances and music aboard ornate boats at Itsukushima Shrine, Miyajima.

AUGUST

Peace Ceremony (Aug. 6). Held in Hiroshima. Prayers for the souls of the A-bomb victims.

OCTOBER

Kenka Matsuri—Fighting Festival (Oct. 14–15). At Matsubara-jinja, Himeji, groups of bearers compete to lead the parade and be first at the shrine, each trying to push over their rivals' huge *mikoshi;* fun, but can be dangerous.

SHIKOKU & THE SETO-NAIKAI

JULY

Warei Natsu Matsuri (July 23, 24). Firework displays, torchlit parades, and bullfights on Uwajima.

AUGUST

Awa-odori (Aug. 12–15). Costumed and carousing citizens of Tokushima are joined by thousands of visitors, to become the "dancing fools" partying in the city streets for four days.

KYUSHU

MAY

Hakata Dontaku (May 3–4) A colorful street parade in Fukuoka with costumed revelers attired as gods and demons, some on horseback.

JULY

Hakata Gion Yamakasa (July 1–15). The climax on the last day consists of teams racing huge floats representing castles, dolls, etc., through Fukuoka's streets.

OCTOBER

O-Kunchi (Oct. 7–9). Focused on Suwa-jinja Shrine, Nagasaki. Highlights show strong Chinese influence (dragon dances), and some floats evoke historical contacts with Europe.

INDEX

Bold page numbers indicate illustrations

A

A-Bomb Dome, Hiroshima 286–87
Abashiri 130, 146
Abashiri Prison Museum (Hakubutsukan Abashiri Kangoku)146
Hokkaido Museum of Northern Peoples (Hoppo Minzoku Hakubutsukan) 146
Mount Tento-zan 146
Agematsu 192
Agriculture 26
Aichi-ken 174–77
Inuyama 176–77
Nagoya 174–76
Aikawa 196
Aikawa Museum 196
Ainu 136, **136,** 137, 152, 157
Ainu Museum 133
Aka-jima 347
Akan Kohan 148–49
Akan National Park 148–50
Akan Kohan 148–49
Io-zan 150
Kawayu Onsen 150
Lake Akan-ko 148
Lake Kussharo-ko 150
Lake Mashu-ko 150, **150**
Lake Onneto-ko 149
Me-Akan-dake 149
O-Akan-dake 149
Sunayu hot springs 150
Akihabara 98-99
Akita city 157, 158
Kanto festival 158, **159**
Senshu-koen Park 158
Akita-ken 157–60
Akita city 157, 158
Hachimantai Plateau 157
Hinokinai-gawa River 158
Kakunodate 157, 158
Lake Tazawa-ko 157, **157,** 158
Lake Towada-ko 157
Mount Komaga-take 158
Nyutu Onsen 158
Oga-hanto Peninsula 157
Akiu Otaki Waterfall 161
Allied Occupation 40–41
Ameyoko market 91
Ani-jima 106
Aoba-jo Castle 161
Aomori 154
Munakata Memorial Museum 154
Nebuta festival 154, 156
Aomori-ken 154–56
Aomori city 154
Lake Towada-ko 156
Nambu 156
Oirase Keiryu Gorge 156
Sannai Maruyama Iseki 154
Shimokita-hanto Peninsula 155
Tsugaru 156
Aoshima 340
Aoyagi-ke 160
Aoyama-Harajuku-Shibuya 78–85
Arashiyama 229–31
Daikaku-ji Temple 220, 230
Gio-ji Temple 230
Jojakko-ji Temple 230
Katsura Imperial Villa 231
Nembutsu-ji Temple 230
Nison-in 230
Okochi Sanso Villa 230
Osawa-no-ike Pond 230
Saiho-ji Temple **221,** 230–31
Takikuchi-dera Temple 230
Tenryu-ji Temple 229
Architecture 42, 44, 66–67, 76, 343
Arita 339–40
Arita Ceramic Fair 340
Arita Ceramic Museum 339
Arita Museum of History and Archaeological Pottery 339
Kyushu Ceramic Art Museum 339
Asahikawa 143
Asakura Chosokan 96
Asakusa 100, 102–104
Asama onsen 188
Aso Volcanic Museum (Aso Kazan Hakubutsukan) 329
Asuka period 28
Atami 128
MOA Museum of Art 128
Atom Bomb Museum (Genbaku Shiryokan), Nagasaki 333, **333**
Atsuta-jingu Shrine 175
Awa Puppet Theater (Awa Jurobei Yashiki) 300
Awa-odori Festival 300
Awaja-shima 312, 313
Azuchi–Momoyama period 34

B

Bamboo 57–58
Bars 74–75
Basho, Matsuo 45, 152, 161, 163, 165, 169
Bears 26, 147, 149
Beers, wines and spirits 25–26
Benten-do Temple 96
Beppu 324–35, **324**
Beppu Onsen 325, **325**
Kankaiji Onsen 325
Takegawara 325
Bichu 278–79
Bichu Matsuyama-jo Castle 278
Kokubun-ji Temple 281
Bizen 280
Bizen Osafune Museum 280
Shizutani School 280
Bizen pottery 279
Black pearl culture 348
Bridgestone Museum of Art (Burijisuton Bijutsukan) 70
Buddhism 22, 23, 30, 31, 226–27
Bullfighting 276, **307,** 308
Bumper Harvest festival 176–77
Business and Livelihood Museum) Akinai to Kurashi Hakubutsukan 306
Byodo-in Temple 234, **234**

C

Cape Ashizuri-misaki 310
Cape Esan-misaki 139
Cape Gongen 156
Cape Muroto-zaki 310
Cape Soya-misaki 144
Cenotaph 287
Central Honshu 171–96
Aichi-ken 174–77
Hokuriku 172, 178–81
hotels and restaurants 369–70
Kamikochi Valley 189, **189**
Kanazawa 172, 178–81,**178, 179, 180, 181**
Kiso Valley (Kisoji) 190–92, **190**
map 172–73
Matsumoto 188, **188**
Nagano-ken 186–87,
Sado-ga-shima Island 172, 193–96,
Takayama 172, 182–85
Tokai 172
Century Tower 66
Ceramics 55–56, 181, 264, 279, 338–40, 345
Chi-no-Ike 325
Chichi-jima 106
Chido Museum 170
Chikurin-ji 311
Chikuzen Kokubun-ji Temple 321
Children's Peace Monument 287
Chinese Memorial Hall (Chuka Kai-kan), Hakodate 140
Chinese Museum of History 337
Chion-in Temple 216, 218–19
Chofuku-ji Temple 279
Chosho-ji Temple 156
Choshikei 314
Christianity 22, 23, 33–34, 334, 337
Chrysanthemum-Moon Pavilion 295–96
Chubu *see* Central Honshu
Chugoku *see* Western Honshu
Chugu-in 248
Chuson-ji Temple 166, **166**
Cinema industry 53–54
Climate and seasons 350
Clock Tower, Sapporo 133
Coffee shops 361
Colonial expansion 37
Confucian Shrine 337
Confucianism 22–23
Cormorant fishing **176,** 234
Crafts 54–55, 154, **158, 248**
Culture and the arts 42–58

D

Daibutsu, Kamakura 111, **111,** 112
Daibutsu, Nara **240–241,** 241–42
Daigan-ji Temple 289
Daigo-ji Temple 232
Daihozoden 248
Daikaku-ji Temple 220, 230
Daimyo Clock Museum 98
Dairyu-ji Temple 185
Daisen-in **222,** 223
Daisen-Oki National Park 276
Daisetsuzan National Park 143
Soun-kyo Gorge 143
Tennin-kyo 143
Daisho-in, Hagi 265
Daisho-in, Miyajima 289
Daitoku-ji Temple 222
Dance 48–50, 196, **289,** 343
Dazaifu 321–22
Chikuzen Kokubun-ji Temple 321
Dazaifu Tenman-gu Shrine **321,** 322
Kaidan-in 321
Kanzeon-ji Temple 321–22
Komyo-zen-ji 322, **322**
Ono fortress 321
Tofuro 321
Dejima 336
Dembo-in Garden 103–104
Denshokan Museum 160
Dewa Sanzan 170
Dogo Island 276
Dogo Onsen 303–304
Isaniwa-jinja Shrine 304
Ishite-ji Temple 304
Dolls 58
Dozen Archipelago 276
Driving 353

E

Earthquakes and volcanoes 137, **137,** 331, 357
Edo period 34–36

Edo-Tokyo Museum (Edo-Tokyo Hakubutsukan) 104
Eikan-do Temple 211–12
Emergencies 356–57
Ena-jinja Shrine 185
Energy sources 26
Engaku-ji Temple 112–13
Entry formalities 350–51
Eniwa-dake 135
Enryaku-ji Temple 235
Entertainment 384–86
Entsu-ji Temple 155
Entsu-in 163

F

Festivals 386–88
Flame of Peace 287
Flamme d'Or building 66, **67**, 104
Floating Poetry Festival (Gokusui-no-en) 167
Floating World 35–36, 74
Flora and fauna 26
Flower arrangement 42
Food and drink 24–26
Foreigners' Cemetery, Hakodate 140
Forestry 26
Fudoki-no-Oka 274
Fuji Five Lakes (Fuji-go-ko) 128
Fuji-Hakone-Izu 108–109, 121–28,
  Fuji-Hakone-Izu National Park 121
  Fuji-san 121, 124–28, **121, 122, 124–25**
  Hakone 121, 122–23
  Izu-Hanto 128
  Lake Ashi-ko 121
Fukiya 279
Fukuoka 317, 318–20, **318–19, 320**
  Canal City 320
  Fukuoka City Museum (Fukuoka Hakubutsukan) 319
  Hakata 319
  Hakata Museum of Local History (Hakata Machiya Furusato-kan) 319–20
  Hakozaki-jinja Shrine 319
  IMS (Inter-Media Station) Building 319
  Kawabata 320
  Kushida-jinja Shrine 319
  Nakasu **318–19**, 320
  Shofuku-ji Temple 319
Fukusai-ji Temple, Nagasaki 334–35
Fukuura-jima 162
Fukuzen-ji Temple, Onomichi 285
Funodomari 145
Furano 130, 143
Fushimi Inari Taisha Shrine **199**, 231–32
Futaarasan-jinja Shrine, Nikko 119
Futamiguara 259

G

Gaikoujin Bochi 140
Gallery of Temple Treasures, Horyu-ji Temple 248
Gannen-ji Temple, Kanazawa, Tosho-gu Shrine, Nikko 181
Gardens 42, 220–21, **220–21**
Gas-san 170
Gate of Sunlight, Tosho-gu Shrine, Nikko 118
Geibikei Gorge 167
Geisha 206–207, **206, 207**, 218
Genbaku Domu, Hiroshima 286–87
Genbikei Gorge 167
Genji Scroll 175
Geruma 347
Ghosts and demons 270–71, **271**
Gifu-ken 178
Ginkaku-ji Temple 212–13
Ginza-Hibiya-Yurakucho 68–70
Gio-ji Temple, Kyoto 230
Gion Kobu Kaburenjo Theater 218
Glover Garden 336
Glover Mansion **336**, 336–37
Godai-san-koen Park, Kochi 311
Godai-do 162
Goryokaku, Hakodate 138
Goryokaku Tower 139
Goryokaku-koen Park, Hakodate 138
Goto Retto Archipelago 330
Great Buddha, Kamakura 111, **111**, 112
Great Buddha, Nara **240**, 241–42
Gudabutsu Hermitage, Matsuyama 302
Gyokusendo Habu-koen Park, Okinawa 346
Gyokusendo Kingdom Village, Okinawa 346
Gyokusendo limestone cave, Okinawa 346

H

Hachimantai Plateau 157
Hagi 264, 265–67
  Daisho-in **264–5**, 265
  Hagi-jo Ato Castle **266**, 267
  Hananoe Teahouse 267
  Ishii Tea Bowl Museum 266
  Kikuga-hama Beach 267
  Kikuya House 266
  Kuchiba House 266
  Kumaya Museum 267
  Masuda Residence 267
  Mori Clan Tenant House 266–67
  Shizuki-koen Park 267
  Sufu residence 267
  Teramachi 267
  Toko-ji Temple 265
Hagi pottery 264, 265
Haguro-san 170
Haha-jima 106
Haikara-kan, Kakunodate 160
Haiku 45, 165, 169
Hakkoda-san 156
Hakodate 138–41, **138**
  Cape Esan-misaki 139
  Chinese Memorial Hall (Chuka Kai-kan) 140
  Foreigners' Cemetery (Gaikoujin Bochi) 140
  Goryokaku 138
  Goryokaku Tower 139
  Goryokaku-koen Park 138
  Hakodate Episcopal Church (Sei Yohane Kyokai) 141
  map 141
  Motomachi 139
  Motomachi-koen Park 141
  Mount Hakodate-yama 139
  Mount Hakodate-yama cable car 141
  Old Branch Office of the Hokkaido Government (Kyu-Hokkaido-cho Hakodate-shicho-chosha) 141
  Old British Consulate (Kyu Igirisu Ryoji-kan) 140
  Old Hakodate Post Office (Kyu-Hakodate Yubinkyoku) 141
  Old Public Hall 141
  Old Russian Consulate (Kyu Roshia Ryoji-kan) 140
  Roman Catholic Church (Katorikku Motomachi Kyokai) 141
  Russian Orthodox Church (Hakodate Harisutosu-sei Kyokai) 141
  Soma Company Building 140
  walk 140–41
  waterfront 141
  Yunokawa Onsen 139
Hakone 121, 122–23
  Hakone Art Museum (Hakone Bijutsukan) 122
  Hakone Gongen Shrine **122**, 123
  Hakone Open-air Museum (Chokoku-no-Mori Bijutsukan) 122
  Hakone Barrier (Hakone Sekishoato) 123
  Lake Ashino-ko 123
  Natural Science Museum (Owakudani Shizen Kagakukan) 123
  Owakudani 122–23, **123**
Hakozaki-jinja Shrine, Fukuoka 319
Hamarikyu-teien Garden, Tokyo 73
Hanae Mori Building 66, 83
Hanami (cherry blossom viewing) 91, 156, 249
Hananoe Teahouse (Hananoe chaya), Hagi 267
Hanazono-jinja Shrine, Tokyo 87
Hase-dera Temple, Kamakura 112
Hase-dera Temple, Nara-ken 249
Hateruma-jima 348
Hayashibara Museum of Art (Hayashibara Bijutsukan), Okayama 282
Hearn, Lafcadio 270, 273–74, **274**, 328
Heian period 30–31
Heian-jingu Shrine 209–10, **209, 210**
Heisei era 41
Heiwa Kinen-koen, Hiroshima 286
Hell Valley (Jigokudani), Hokkaido 137
Hida Folk Village (Hida Minzoku Mura), Takayama **184**, 185
Hida Kokubun-ji Temple, Takayama 182, 184
Hidari Jingoro Museum, Takamatsu 296
Hie-jinja Shrine, Tokyo 77
Hikone 236, **236**
Himeji 256–57
  Himeji-jo Castle 256–57, **256, 256–57**
Himenuma Pond 144
Himeyuri-no-To, Okinawao 346
Hinokan, Kannawa 325
Hinokinai-gawa River 158
Hiraizumi 152, 164, 165–67,
  Chuson-ji Temple 166, **166**
  Floating Poetry Festival 167
  Motsu-ji Temple 166–67, 220
Hirasawa 191
Hirohito, Emperor 37, 38, 40
Hirosaki 152, 156
  Choshi-ji Temple 156

Hirosaki-jo Castle 156
Zenrin-gai 156
Hirosaki Cherry Blossom Festival 156
Hiroshima 286–87
A-Bomb Dome (Genbaku Domu) 286–87, **287**
Cenotaph 287, **286–87**
Children's Peace Monument 287
Flame of Peace 287
Fudo-in Temple 287
Hiroshima-jo Castle 287
Peace Memorial Museum 287
Peace Memorial Park (Heiwa Kinen-koen) 286
Shukkei-en Garden 287
Hiroshima-ken 277
Historical Village of Hokkaido (Hokkaido Kaitaku-no-Mura) 134
History of Japan 28–41
Hiwatari festival 106, **106**
Hokkaido 129–50
Abashiri and Shiretoko National Park 146–47
Akan and Kushiro Shitsugen National Parks 148–50
central Hokkaido 143
Daisetsuzan National Park 143
Hakodate 138–41
hotels and restaurants 366–68
map 130–31
Onuma Quasi-National Park 142
Rishiri-Rebun-Sarubetsu National Park 144–45
Sapporo 130, 132–34
Shikotsu-Toya National Park 130, 135–37
Hokkaido Museum of Northern Peoples 146
Hokki-ji Temple 243
Hokuriku 172, 178–81
Hon Haga Residence 305
Hon-jima 314
Honen-in Temple 212
Hongu 250
Horikiri Shobuen Iris Garden 106
Horyu-ji Temple 247–48, **247–48**
Hoshun-in, Kyoto 223
Hostess bars 74
Hot springs 120, 128, 130, 137, 147, 150, **155,**158, 250, 303–304, 324–25, **325,** 331
Hotels and restaurants 258–379
Hotoke-ga-ura 155
Huis Ten Bosch 338, **338**
Husband and Wife Rocks (Meoto-iwa) 259, **258–59**
Hypocenter Park 333

I

Idemitsu Museum of Arts (Idemitsu Bijutsukan) 69
Ieyasu, Tokugawa 32, 34, 115, 174–75, 204, 205
Ikebana 42
Ikebukuro 86, 89
Ikuchi-jima 313
Imari 339, 340
Imari Ware Exhibition Center 340
Imari-Arita Traditional Crafts Center 340
Nabeshima Hanyo-koen Park 340
Imperial Palace, Kyoto 205
Imperial Palace, Tokyo 63–64
IMS (Inter-Media Station) Building 319
Inasa-yama 333
Inasayama-koen Park 334
Incense 214
Inno-shima 314
Innoshima Suigun-jo Pirate's Castle 314
Konren-ji Temple 314
International Forum Building **44,** 66, 69
Inuyama 176–77
Bumper Harvest Festival 176–77
Inuyama-jo Castle 176
Japan Monkey Park 176
Jo-an 176
Meiji-mura Village 177
Oagata-jinja Shrine 177
Tagata-jinja Shrine 176–77
Uraku-en Garden 176
Io-zan, Akan National Park 150
Io-zan, Shiretoko National Park 147
Irabu-jima 348
Iriomote-jima 342, 348
Isaniwa-jinja Shrine, Dogo Onsen 304
Ise-jingu Grand Shrine 259–60
Ishibiya Furusato village 278
Ishigaki-jima 348
Miyara Donchi 348
Torin-ji Temple 348
Yaeyama Minzoku-en Village 348
Ishii Tea Bowl Museum (Ishii Chawan Bijutsukan) 266
Ishikawa Museum of Traditional Products and Crafts 181
Ishikawa Prefectural Museum of Arts 181
Ishikawa-ken 178
Ishite-ji Temple 302, 304
Itsukushima *see* Miyajima
Itsukushima-jinja Shrine 277, 288, 289, **289**
Iwate-ken 164–67
Geibikei Gorge 167
Genbikei Gorge 167
Hiraizumi 152, 164, 165–67
Kurikoma Quasi-National Park 165
Morioka 164
Rikuchu Coast National Park 164–65
Takkaku-no-Iwaya 167
Towada Hachimantai National Park 165
Iwayasan Temple, Sado-ga-shima 196
Iwo-jima 106
Iya no Kazurabashi 299–300, **300**
Iyo Textile Museum (Iyo Kasuri Kaikan) 302
Izu-Hanto 128
Izumo 264
Izumo Taisha 264, 275

J

Jakko-in 233
Japan
agriculture 26
architecture 66–67, 76, 343
culture and the arts 42–58
economy 10, 12–13
education system 18–19
employment 13–15
energy sources 26
family life 17–18
flora and fauna 26
food and drink 24–26
history 28–41
homes 19–21
language 19
manners and behavior 23–24
men and women 16–18
religion 22–23, 226–27, 244–45
work ethic 13–14
writing systems 19
Japan Monkey Park 176
Japan Toy Museum (Nihon Kyodogangukan), Kurashiki 283
Japan Wax Museum and Kami Haga Residence 305
Japanese Crane Reserve 150
Jidai Matsuri festival 210
Jikko-in 233
Jimbocho 105
Jintoze-iseki, Miyako-jima 347
Jo-an teahouse 176
Jodo Shinshu sect 203
Jodo-ji Temple, Onomichi 285
Jojako-ji Temple, Arashiyama 230
Jomon people 28
Joseki-koen Park, Okinawa 346
Josen-ji Temple, Onomichi 285
Jyozan Inari-jinja Shrine, Matsue 273

K

Kabuki 47–48
Kabukicho 87
Kabuki-za Theater 70, **70**
Kafuka 145
Kagoshima 340
Meji Museum 340
Kaidan-in, Dazaifu 321
Kaikaro teahouse 181
Kaiko-ji Temple 170
Kairyu-ji Temple, Onomichi 285
Kakunodate 157, 158, 160
Aoyagi-ke 160
Buke-yashiki 160
Denshokan Museum 160
Haikara-kan 160
Kawarada house 160
Kamakura 108, 111–13
Engaku-ji Temple 112–13
Great Buddha 111, **111,** 112
Hase-dera Temple 112
Kencho-ji Temple 113
Kotoku-in Temple 112
Matsugaoka Treasure House 113
National Treasure Museum (Kokuhokan) 112
Toke-ji Temple 113
Tsurugaoka Hachiman-gu Shrine 112, **112–13**
Kamakura period 32–33
Kamikochi Valley 178, 189, **189**
Kappabashi 189, **189**
Myojin pond 189
Taisho-ike 189
Kamosu-jinja Shrine, Matsue 274
Kamuiwakka-no-taki, Hokkaido 147
Kanamazu-za Theater, Kotohira 298
Kanazawa 172, 178–81
Higashi 181
Ishikawa Museum of Traditional Products and Crafts 181
Ishikawa Prefectural Museum of Arts 181
Ishikawa-mon Gate 180, **180**
Kaikaro 181
Kanazawa Shinise 181
Kenroku-en Garden **178–79,** 180, **221**
Kosen Kutani Pottery Kiln 181
Myoryu-ji Temple 181
Nomura House 180–81

INDEX

Saihitsu-an 181
Seisonkaku Villa 180
Shimajaya 181
Teramachi 181
Kanden-an teahouse 274
Kanei-ji Kyomizu Kannon-do Temple, Tokyo 96
Kanei-ji Pagoda, Tokyo 96
Kankakei gorge, Shodo-shima 314
Kannawa 325
Chi-no-Ike 325
Hinokan 325
Kannawa Jigoku 325
Kanran-tei, Matsushima 162
Kansai 197–260
Himeji 256–57
hotels and restaurants 371–75
Kobe 198, 255
Kyoto 198, 200–33
Lake Biwa-ko and Hikone 236
map 199
Mount Hiei-zan 235
Nara 198, 237–43
Nara-ken 249
Osaka 198, 252–54
Shiga-ken 199
Shima-hanto Peninsula 258–60
Uji 234
Wakayama-ken 199, 250–51
Kanto festival 158
Kanzeon-ji Temple, Dazaifu 321–22
Kappabashi 189, **189**
Karatsu 340
Karatsu-jo Castle 340
Nakazato Taroemon 340
Kasuga Taisha Grand Shrine 239–40, **239**
Katsura Imperial Villa 231
Katsura-hama 311
Sakamoto Ryoma Memorial Museum 311
Katsushika Hokusai Museum, Tsuwano 269
Kawabata Yasunari 45, **45**
Kawagoe 106
dozozukuri (merchants' houses) 106
Kita-in Temple 106
Kawarada house 160
Kawayu Onsen, Hokkaido 150
Kawayu Onsen, Wakayama-ken 250
Kegon-no-taki Waterfall 120, **120**
Kencho-ji Temple, Kamakura 113
Kenritsu Kyodo Theater, Naha 345
Kenroku-en Garden, Kanazawa **178–79,** 180
Keramas 347
Kibiji 281
Bitchu Kokubun-ji Temple 281
Hofuku-ji Temple 281
Kibitsu Shrine 281
Soja 281
Tsukuriyama burial mound 281
Kibune 233
Kikuchi Valley 329
Kikuga-hama Beach, Hagi 267
Kikugetsu-tei, Takamatsu 295–96
Kikuya House 266
Kinkaku-ji Temple 223, **223**
Kiso Fukushima 191–92
Kiso Valley 178–79, 190–92
Kisoji 190–92
Agematsu 192
Hirasawa 191
Kiso Fukushima 191–92
Magome 192
Mount On-take 191
Narai 191, **191**
Niekawa 191
Tsumago **190,** 192, **192**
Kita Naka-Gsuku, Okinawa 346
Kitakyushu city 317
Kitanomaru-koen Park, Tokyo 64
Kiyomizu-dera 213–14, **212–13, 214,** 216
Kobe 198, 255, **255**
Kochi city 310–11
Chikurin-ji 311
Godai-san-koen Park 311
Kochi-jo Castle 311
Shimoyashiki Nagaya 311
Kochi-ken 309–11
Cape Ashizuri-misaki 310
Cape Muroto-zaki 310
Katsura-hama 311
Kochi city 310–11
Shikoku Karst 310
Shimanto-gawa River 310
whale watching 310
Kodai-ji Temple 214, 217
Kodo drummers 194, 195
Kodo (the way of incense) 214
Kofuku-ji Temple 238–39, **238**
Kofun period 28
Kohama-jima 348
Koho-an, Kyoto 223
Koizumi Yagumo Kyukyo, Matsue 273, **274**
Kojo-ji Temple 313–14
Kokyo 63–64
Komyo-zen-ji, Dazaifu 322
Konchi-in, Kyoto 211
Kongobu-ji Temple, Koya-san 250, **250**
Konpaku-no-To, Okinawa 346
Konren-ji Temple, Inno-shima 314
Koraku-en Garden 277, **278–79,** 280–81
Koryu-ji Temple, Uzumasa 228
Kosan-ji Temple, Setodo 314
Koto-in, Kyoto 223
Kotohira 297–98
Kanamazu-za Theater 298
Kotohira-gu Shrine 297–98, **297, 298**
Zentsu-ji Temple 298
Koya-san 198–99, 250–51
Kukai 250, 251
Kumamato-ken 326–29
Aso Volcanic Museum 329
Kikuchi Valley 329
Kumamoto 327–28
Mount Aso-san 328–29, **328–29**
Mount Komezuka 329
Kumamoto 327–28
Kumamoto-jo Castle 327, **326–27**
Kumoto Prefecture Traditional Crafts Center 328
Soseki Museum 328
Suizenji-koen Park 328
Kumaya Museum (Kumaya Bijutsukan) 267
Kumoto Prefecture Traditional Crafts Center (Kumoto-ken Dento kogeikan) 328
Kurashiki 277, 282–83
Ivy Square 283
Japan Toy Museum 283
Kurashiki Museum of Archaeology 283
Kurashiki Museum of Folkcraft 283
Ohara Museum 282–83
Kurikoma Quasi-National Park 165
Kuro-shima 348
Kusakabe Folk Museum (Kusakabe Mingei Kan), Takayama 184
Kushida-jinja Shrine, Fukuoka 319
Kushiro Shitsugen National Park 150
Japanese Crane Reserve 150
Kushiro Marsh 150
Kutsugata, Hokkaido 145
Kyoto 198, 200–33
Arashiyama 229–31
central Kyoto 202–208
Chion-in Temple 217, 218–19
Daigo-ji Temple 232
Daisen-in **222,** 223
Daitoku-ji Temple 222
eastern Kyoto 209–19
Eikan-do Temple 211–12
Fushimi Inari Taisha Shrine 231–32
Ginkaku-ji Temple 212–13
Gion 209, 218–19
Gion Corner 218
Gion Kobu Kaburenjo Theater 218
Heian-jingu Shrine 209–10, **209**
Higashiyama 216–17, **216–17**
Honen-in Temple 212
Hoshun-in 223
Kaifuku-in 224
Kawaramachi 208
Kinkaku-ji Temple 223, **223**
Kiyomizu-dera Temple **212–13,** 213–14, **214,** 216
Kiyomizu-zaka 216
Kodai-ji Temple 214, 217
Koho-an 223
Konchi-in 211
Koryu-ji Temple 228
Koto-in 223
Kyoto Imperial Palace 205
Kyoto National Museum 215
Manpuku-ji Temple 232
maps 200–201, 217
Maruyama-koen Park 209, 217, 218
Minamiza Theater 218, **219**
Miroku-Bosatsu 228
Myoshin-ji Temple 224
Nanzen-in 211
Nanzen-ji Temple 210–11
Nijo-jo Castle **203,** 204–205, **204**
Ninna-ji Temple 224–25
Nishi Hongan-ji Temple 202–203
Otowa Waterfall 213
outlying Kyoto 228–33
Path of Philosophy 209
Poets Hermitage 233
Pontocho 208
Pontocho Kaburenjo Theater 208
Reiho-kan Treasure House 224
Reiun-in 224
Rin-untei teahouse 233
Ryoan-ji Temple 223–24
Ryugen-in 223
Sanjusangen-do Temple 215, **215**
Shinsen-en Garden 205
Shoren-in Temple 217, 219
Shugakuin Imperial Villa 232–33
Tenju-an 211
To-ji Temple **202,** 204
Toei Movie Land 228–29
Tofuku-ji Temple 231
walk 216–17
western Kyoto 222–25

Yasaka Pagoda 216–17
Yasaka-jinja Shrine 217, 218
Kyoto Gosho 205
Kyushu 315–40
Beppu and the spas of Oita-ken 324–25
Dazaifu 321–22
Fukuoka 317, 318–20, **318–19, 320**
hotels and restaurants 377–79
Huis Ten Bosch 338, **338**
Kagoshima City 340
Kitakyushu 317
Kumamato-ken 326–29
map 316
Miyazaki 340
Nagasaki-ken 330–37
Saga pottery towns 338–40
Yanagawa 323

L

Lacquerware 56–57, 190, 191
Lafcadio Hearn Memorial Museum 273–74
Lafcadio Hearn Residence 273, **274**
Lake Akan-ko 148
Lake Ashi-ko 121
Lake Ashino-ko 123
Lake Biwa-ko 236
Lake Chuzenji-ko 120
Lake Kawaguchi-ko 128
Lake Konuma-ko 142
Lake Kussharo-ko 150
Lake Mashu-ko **148,** 150
Lake Onneto-ko 149
Lake Tazawa-ko 157, **157,** 158
Lake Towada-ko 156, 157
Lake Toya-ko 136
Lake Yamanaka-ko 128
Landmark Tower 110
L:anguage guide 357
Literature 44–45

M

Magome 192
Manabe 279
Maniwa 279
Manjiro, Nakahama (John Mung) 310, **310**
Mano 193
Mano Goryo 193
Manpuku-ji Temple 232
Man'yo Botanical Garden 240
Maria Sei-do 268, **268**
Martial arts 58
26 Martyrs Memorial 334, **334**
Maruyama-koen Park 209, 217, 218
Matsue 264, 272–74
Buke-yashiki 273
Fudoki-no-Oka 274
Jyozan Inari-jinja Shrine 273
Kamosu-jinja 274
Kanden-an teahouse 274
Lafcadio Hearn Memorial Museum 273–74
Lafcadio Hearn Residence (Koizumi Yagumo Kyukyo) 273, **274**
Matsue Cultural Center (Matsue Kyodokan) 273
Matsue-jo Castle 272–73
Shiomi-nawate 273, **273**
Yaegaki-jinja 274
Matsugaoka Treasure House 113
Matsumae 142
Matsumoto 188
Asama Onsen 188
Matsumoto-jo Castle 188, **188**
Nihon Minzoku Shiryokan Museum 188
Nihon Ukiyo-e Hakubutsukan Museum 188
Utsukushigahara Heights 188
Utsukushigahara Onsen 188
Matsuri festivals 22
Matsushima Bay 152, **160–61,** 161–62
Entsuin 163
Fukuura-jima 162
Godaido 162, **162–63**
hermitages 163
Kanrantei 162
Seiryuden Treasure Museum 163
Zuigan-ji Temple 162–63
Matsuyama 301–302
Gudabutsu Hermitage 302
Ishite-ji Temple 302
Iyo Textile Museum 302
Matsuyama-jo Castle 301–302
Shiki Memorial Hall 302, **302**
Shikido 302
Me-Akan-dake 149
Megane-bashi, Nagasaki 335
Meiji period 36–37
Meiji-jingu Inner Gardens 80, 85, **85–86**
Meiji-jingu Shrine 80, 83–85, **84, 85**
Meiji-jingu Treasure House 85
Meiji-mura Village 177
Meji Museum 340
Memorial Hall, Sendai 161
Mikimoto Pearl Island 259
Minamiza Theater 218, **219**
Misen-san 290
Miyajima 277, 288–90, **288**
Daigan-ji Temple289
Daisho-in 289
Itsukushima-jinja Shrine 277, 288, 289, **289**
Misen-san 290
Momijidani-koen Park 288
monkey reserve 290
Tahoto pagoda 289
Miyako islands 347–48
Miyako-jima 347
Miyara Donchi, Ishigaki-jima 348
Miyazaki 340
Kirishima-Yaku Parkland 340
Miyazaki-jingu Shrine 340
Ocean Dome 340
Mizu shobai (water trade) 74–75
Mizunashi Valley 331
MOA Museum of Art (MOA Bijutsukan), Atami 128
Mogami Gorge 168
Momijidani-koen Park, Miyajima 288
Monbetsu-dake 135
Mongol Wars 32–33
Monkey reserve 290
Mori Clan Tenant House, Hagi 266–67
Mori House and Memorial Museum (Mori Ogai Kyutaku), Tsuwano 268
Morioka 164
Motsu-ji Temple, Hiraizumi 166–67, 220
Mount Aso-san 328–29, **328–29**
Mount Fugen-dake 331–32
Mount Fuji-san 121, **121, 124–25,** 124–28
Mount Hakodate-yama 139, 141
Mount Hiei-zan 235
Enryaku-ji Temple 235, **235**
Yase-Yuen cable car 235
Mount Komaga-take 158
Mount Komezuka 328
Mount Koya-san 250–51
Kongobu-ji Temple 250, **250**
Mount On-take 191
Mount Osore-zan 155
Mount Sakurajima 340
Mount Takao-san 106, **106**
Mount Tento-zan 146
Mount Tsurugi-san 299
Mount Unzen-dake 331
Mount Usu-zan 137
Mount Washu-zan 279
Mount Zao-san 169
Mukuchi 279
Munakata Memorial Museum (Munakata Shiko Kinekan) 154
Muro-ji Temple, Nara-ken 249, **249**
Muromachi–Ashikaga shogunate 33–34
Musée de Morijuku, Tsuwano 269
Music 46, 50–51, 195, 342–43
Myojin pond, Kamikochi Valley 189
Myoryu-ji Temple, Kanazawa 181

N

Nabeshima Hanyo-koen Park, Imari 340
Nachi-no-taki Waterfall 250
Nagano-ken 178–79, 186–87
Nagasaki 332–37
Atom Bomb Museum 333, **333**
Chinese Museum of History 337
Confucian Shrine **335,** 337
Dejima 336
Fukusai-ji Temple 334–35
Glover Garden **330–31,** 336
Glover Mansion **336,** 337
Hypocenter Park 333
Inasa-yama 334
Insayama-koen Park 334
26 Martyrs Memorial (Nihon Niju-roku seijin junkyochi) 334, **334**
Megane-bashi 335
merchants' homes 336
Nagasaki Museum of History and Folklore 336
No. 2 Dock Building 336
Oura Catholic Church 337, **337**
Peace Park 333
Shofuku-ji Temple 335
Suwa-jinja Shrine 335
Urakami Cathedral 333
Nagasaki-ken 330–7
Mizunashi Valley 331
Mount Fugen-dake 331–32
Mount Unzen-dake 331
Shimabara 330–31
Nagoya 174–76
Atsuta-jingu Shrine 175
Nagoya-jo Castle **174,** 175
Ninomaru Garden 175
Osu 176
Osu Kannon Temple 176, **176**
Tokugawa Museum of Art (Tokugawa Bijutsukan) 175
Naha 344–45, **344**
Kenritsu Kyodo Theater 345
Shuri 345
Shuri-jo Castle 345
Tsuboya 344
Tsuboya Pottery Association 345

Nakamura House, Urasoe 346
Nambu 156
Nanzen-in 211
Nanzen-ji Temple 210–11
Nara 30, 198, 237–43
Daibutsu **240–41,** 241–42
Hokki-ji Temple 243
Horyu-ji Temple **246–47,** 247–48
Kasuga Taisha Grand Shrine 239–40, **239**
Kofuku-ji Temple 238–39, **238**
Man'yo Botanical Garden 240
Nara National Museum (Kokuritsu Hakubutsukan) 239
Nara-koen Park 237
Shin Yakushi-ji Temple 240–41
Todai-ji Temple 241–43
Toshodai-ji Temple 243
Yakushi-ji Temple 243, 246–47
Nara deer 238, **238**
Nara-ken 249
Hase-dera Temple 249
Muro-ji Temple 249, **249**
Yoshino 249
Nara-koen Park, Nara 237
Narai 191, **191**
Naruko 161
Naruto-no-Uzushio Whirlpools 299, **299**
National holidays 355
National Museum of Modern Art (Kokuritsu Kindai Bijutsukan), Tokyo 65
National Museum of Western Art (Kokuritsu Seiyo Bijutsukan), Tokyo 92
National Science Museum (Kokuritsu Kagaku Hakubutsukan), Tokyo 92
National Treasures 166, 188, 202, 228, 247, 279, 336
Natsume Soseki 45, 302, 303
Natural Science Museum, Owakudani 123
Nebuta Festival 154, 156, **156**
Nembutsu-ji, Kyoto 230
Nezu Institute of Fine Art (Nezu Bijutsukan), Tokyo 81
Nezu-jinja Shrine, Tokyo 96
Niekawa 191
Nippon Budokan, Tokyo 64
Nihon Minzoku Shiryokan Museum, Matsumoto 188
Nihon Ukiyo-e Hakubutsukan Museum, Matsumoto 188
Niigata 179
Niigata-ken 178, 179
Nijo-jo Castle **203,** 204–205, **204**
Nikko 109, 114–20
Futaarasan-jinja Shrine 119
Rinno-ji Temple 114–15
Shin-kyo 114
Taiyuin 119–20
Tosho-gu Shrine 115–19, **115, 116–17, 117, 118**
Tosho-gu Shrine Treasure House 119
Yomeimon 118
Nikko Edo Village 120, **120**
Nikko National Park 120
Kegon-no-taki Waterfall 120, **120**
Lake Chuzenji-ko 120
Nikko Edo Village 120
Yumoto Onsen 120
Ningyocho, Tokyo 105
Ninna-ji Temple, Kyoto 224–25
Ninomaru Garden, Nagoya 175
Nippon Budokan 64
Nishi Hongan-ji Temple, Kyoto 202–203
Nison-in, Arashiyama 230
Noboribetsu Onsen 130, 137
Noh theater 46–47, 179, 270
Nomura House (Nomura Buke Zashiki) 180–81
Northern Honshu (Tohoku) 151–70
Akita-ken 157–60
Aomori-ken 154–56
hotels and restaurants 368–69
Iwate-ken 164–67
map 153
Sendai and Matsushima 161–63
Yamagata-ken 168–70
Noto-hanto Peninsula 178
Nyutu Onsen, Akita-ken 158

O

O-Akan-dake, Hokkaido 149
Oagata-jinja Shrine, Aichi-ken 177
Obake (ghosts and demons) 270–71, **271**
Oboke & Koboke Gorges, Tokushima-ken 300
Odori-koen Park 132, **132–33**
Oga-hanto Peninsula 157
Ogasawara-shoto Islands 106
Ogi, Sado-ga-shima 194–95, **194**
Ohama Beach, Shikoku 299
Ohana Villa, Yanagawa 323
Ohara 233
Jakko-in Temple 233
Jikko-in 233
Sanzen-in Temple 233
Shoren-in Temple 233
Ohara Museum (Ohara Bijutsukan), Kurashiki 282–83
Oirase Keiryu Gorge, Aomori-ken 156
Okayama city 280–82
Hayashibara Museum of Art (Hayashibara Bijutsukan) 282
Koraku-en Garden 277, **278–79,** 280–81
Okayama Prefectural Museum of Art (Okayama-kenritsu Bijutsukan) 282
Okayama-jo Castle 281
Orient Museum (Oriento Bijutsukan) 282
Yumeji Art Museum (Yumeji Bijutsukan) 282
Okayama-jo Castle 281
Okayama-ken 277, 278–83
Bichu 278–79
Bichu Matsuyama-jo Castle 278
Bizen 280
Fukiya 279
Ishibiya Furusato 278
Kibiji 281
Koraku-en 277, 280–81
Kurashiki 282–83
Maniwa 279
Mount Washu-zan 279
Okayama city 280–81
Raikyu-ji Temple 278–79
Seto Ohashi Bridge 279–80
Shoei 279
Takahashi 278
Tamashima 279
Tsuyama 279
Ushimado 280
Okhotsk Ryuhyo Museum 146
Oki-shoto Islands 264, 276
Okinawa 342, 344–47
Gyokusendo Habu-koen Park 346
Gyokusendo Kingdom Village 346
Gyokusendo limestone cave 346
Konpaku-no-To 346
Mabuni Hill 346
Naha 344–45
Peace Memorial Museum 346
Ryuku mura Village 346–47
Tower of Lilies 346
Underground Naval Headquarters 346
Urasoe 346
Okinawa-ken 341–8
hotels and restaurants 379
map 342–43
Okinawa 346–47
Ryuku-shoto Islands 342
Okochi Sanso Villa, Kyoto 230
Omi-shima 314
Oyamazumi-jinja Shrine 314
Omikuji (fortune papers) 87, 245
Omori Rosoku, Uchiko 306
Omotesando, Tokyo 79
Onaruto-bashi Bridge. Shikoku 299
Oniga-shima 314
Ono fortress, Dazaifu 321
Onomichi 277, 284–85, **284–85**
Fukuzen-ji Temple 285
Jodo-ji Temple 285
Josen-ji Temple 285
Kairyu-ji Temple 285
Path of Literature 285
Saigo-ji Temple 285
Saikoku-ji Temple 285
Senko-ji Temple 285
Senkoji-koen Park 285, **285**
Ontake-kyo 191
Onuma Quasi-National Park, Hokkaido 142
Orient Museum, Okayama 282
Osaka 198, 252–54
Dotombori 254, **254**
Kita-ku 254
Minami-ku 254
Osaka Station 254
Osako-jo Castle **252,** 254
Shinsaibashi 254
Umeda 254
Umeda Sky Building **253,** 254
Osaki-Hachiman-jinja Shrine, Sendai 161
Osawa-no-ike Pond, Kyoto 230
Oshidomari, Hokkaido 145
Osu Kannon Temple 176, **176**
Ota Memorial Museum of Art (Ota Kinen Bijutsukan) 80–81
Otaru, Hokkaido 134
Otaru Canal Walk 134
Otaru Museum (Otaru-shi Hakubutsukan) 134
Otowa Waterfall, Kyoto 213
Otsu 236
Oura Catholic Church (Oura Tenshu-do), 337 **337**

Owakudani 122–23
Oyamazumi-jinja Shrine, Omi-shima 314

P

Pachinko 88, **88**
Painting 51–52
Paper making 56
Peace Memorial Museum, Hiroshima 287
Peace Memorial Museum, Okinawa 346
Peace Memorial Park, Hiroshima 286
Peace Park, Nagasaki 333
Perry, Commodore Matthew 36, 128, 141, 310
Phallic shrines 176–77
Piano bars 74
Poets Hermitage (Shisendo), Kyoto 233
Pontocho Kaburenjo Theater, Kyoto 208
Poroto Kotan 137
Port Island, Kobe 255
Public transport 352–53
Puppet theater 48, 300, 313

R

Raikyu-ji Temple, Takahashi 278–79
Rausu, Hokkaido 146
Rausu-dake 147
Rebun-dake 145
Rebun-to 145
  Funodomari 145
  Kafuka 145
  Rebun-dake 145
  Reizan-ji Temple, Tokushima **294**
Religion 22–23, 226–27, 244–45
Rice and noodles 24
Rikuchu Kaigan National Park 164–65
Rin'un-tei teahouse, Kyoto 233
Rinno-ji Temple, Nikko 114–15
Rishiri-Rebun-Sarobetsu National Park 144–45
  Rebun-to 145
  Rishiri-to 144–45
  Sarobetsu Plain 144, 145
Rishiri-to 144–45
  Himenuma Pond 144
  Kutsugata 145
  Oshidomari 145
Rishiri-zan 144
Risshaku-ji (Yama-dera Temple), Yamagata 169
Ritsurin-koen Park, Takamatsu 295, **295**
Roppongi-Shiba-koen Park 76–77
Ryoan-ji Temple 223–24
Ryotei restaurants 76
Ryotsu, Sago-ga-shima 194
Ryotsu Kaikan Hall 194
Ryugen-in, Kyoto 223
Ryuku mura Village, Okinawa 346–47
Ryukyu-shoto Islands, The 342, 347–48

S

Sacred 88 (pilgrimage route) 294, 298
Sado Kinzan Mine 193, 196
Sado okesa (Sado dancing) 196
Sado-ga-shima Island 172, 193–96
  Aikawa 196
  Aikawa Museum (Aikawa Kyodo Hakubutsukan) 196
  Iwayasan Temple 196
  Mano 193
  Mano Goryo 193
  Ogi 194–95
  Ryotsu 194
  Ryotsu Kaikan Hall 194
  Sado Kinzan Mine 193, 196
  Sadokoku Ogi Minzoku Hakubutsukan Folk Museum 196
  Sawata 193
  Senkaku-wan 194
  Shiawase-jizo Temple 196
  Shukunegi Village 196
  Sadokoku Folk Museum (Ogi Minzoku Hakubutsukan) 196
Saga pottery towns 338–40
Saigo-ji Temple, Onomichi 285
Saihitsu-an, Kanazawa 181
Saiho-ji Temple, Kyoto **221,** 230–31
Saikoku-ji Temple, Onomichi 285
Sakamoto Ryoma Memorial Museum, Katsura-hama 311
Sakata 169
  Honma-ke Kyu-hontei 169
  Kaiko-ji Temple 170
Sake 25
Salarymen 13–14
Samurai 31–32, 34
Samurai houses 160, 169, **264,** 266–67, 273, **273,** 278, 331
San-in 262, 264–76
  Hagi 264, 265–67
  Izumo Taisha 264, 275
  Matsue 264, 272–74
  Oki Islands 264, 276
  Tsuwano 264, 268–69
San-yo 263, 277–90
  Hiroshima 286–87
  Miyajima 277, 288–90
  Okayama-ken 277, 278–83
  Onomichi 277, 284–85
Sanjusangen-do Temple, Kyoto 215
Sankei-en Garden, Yokohama 110
Sannai Maruyama Iseki, Aomori-ken 154
Sanshin Gosaiden Shrine 170
Sanuki Folkcraft Museum, Takamatsu 296
Sanzen-in Temple, Kyoto 233
Sapporo 130, 132–34
  Ainu Museum 133
  Clock Tower 133
  Historical Village of Hokkaido 134
  Museum of Natural History 133
  Odori-koen Park 130, 132
  Old Hokkaido Government Building 133
  Ramen Alley 134, **134**
  Sapporo Beer Garden and Museum 133
  Sapporo Factory 133
  Shokubutsu-en Botanical Gardens 133
  Susukino amusement quarter 133–34
Sapporo Ginza Lion beer hall 69
Sarobetsu Plain 144, 145
Sawata, Sado-ga-shima 193
Science Museum (Kagaku Bijutsukan), Tokyo 64–65
Sculpture 52
Seiryuden Treasure Museum, Matsushima 163
Seisonkaku Villa, Kanazawa 180
Sen-no-Rikyu 225
Sendai 152, 161–62
  Aoba-jo Castle 161
  Memorial Hall 161
  Osaki-Hachiman-jinja Shrine 161
Senkaku-wan Bay 194
Senko-ji Temple, Onomichi 285
Senkoji-koen Park, Onomichi 285
Senshu-koen Park, Akita 158
Senso-ji Temple, Tokyo 103, **103**
Seto Ohashi Bridge 279–80, 295
Seto Ohashi Memorial Bridge Museum 280
Seto-naikai, The 279, 312, **312–13**
  islands 313–14
Setoda 313–14
  Kojo-ji Temple 313
  Kosan-ji Temple 313–14
  Setoda History and Folklore Museum 314
Sex museums 308, 325
Shiawase-jizo Temple, Sado-ga-shima 196
Shiga-ken 199
Shikido, Matsuyama 302
Shikoku 292, **293,** 294
Shikoku Karst 310
Shikoku mura 296
Shikoku and the Seto-naikai 291–314
  Dogo Onsen 303–304
  hotels and restaurants 376–77
  Kochi-ken 309–11
  Kotohira 297–98
  map 292–93
  Matsuyama 301–302
  Shikoku 292, 294
  Takamatsu 295–96
  Seto-naikai 292
  Tokushima-ken 299–300
  Uchiko 305–306
  Uwajima 307–308
Shikotsu-ko 135
Shikotsu-Toya National Park 130, 135–37
  Eniwa-dake 135
  Hell Valley 137
  Lake Toya-ko **135,** 136
  Monbetsu-dake 135
  Mount Usu-zan 137
  Noboribetsu Onsen 130, 137
  Poroto Kotan 137
  Shikotsu Kohan 135
  Shikotsu-ko 135
  Shiraoi 137
  Showa Shinzan New Mountain 137
  Tarumae-zan 135–36
Shima-hanto Peninsula 258–60
  Futamiguara 259
  Husband and Wife Rocks **258–59,** 259
  Ise-jingu Grand Shrine 259–60
  Mikimoto Pearl Island 259
  Toba 259
Shimabara 330–31
  samurai houses 331
  Shimabara-jo Castle 331
Shimabara Peninsula 330
Shimanto-gawa River 310
Shimo-jima 348
Shimokita-hanto Peninsula 155
  Entsu-ji Temple 155
  Hotoke-ga-ura 155
  Mount Osore-zan 155
Shin Yakushi-ji Temple, Nara 240–41
Shin-kyo (Sacred Bridge) 114, **114**
Shinjuku 86, 87–89
  Shinjuku National Garden, Tokyo 87
Shinobazu Pond, Tokyo 96

Shinsen-en Garden, Kyoto 205
Shinto 22, 244–45
Shinto shrines 244
Shirakami Mountains 156
Shiraoi, Hokkaido 137
Shiretoko National Park 146–47
  Io-zan 147
  Kamuiwakka-no-taki 147
  Rausu 146
  Rausu-dake 147
  Shiretoko Five Lakes 147
  Shiretoko Iwaobetsu Youth Hostel 147
  Utoro 146
Shiroyama-koen Park, Takayama 184–85
Shitamachi History Museum (Shitamachi Fuzoku Shiryokan), Tokyo 93
Shizuki-koen Park, Hagi 267
Shodo-shima 314
  Choshikei 314
  Kankakei 314
  Tanoura 314
Shoei 279
  Chofuku-ji Temple 279
Shofuki-ji Temple, Nagasaki 335
Shofuku-ji Temple, Fukuoka 319
Shokubutsu-en Botanical Gardens, Sapporo 133
Shopping 280–83
Shoren-in, Kyoto 217, 233
Shoren-ji Temple, Takayama 184–85
Shoto-en Garden, Yanagawa 323
Shotoku Taishi, Prince 229, 248
Showa period 38–40
Showa Shinzan New Mountain 137
Shrine and temple architecture 42
Shrine and temple merchandise 87
Shugakuin Imperial Villa 232–33
Shugaku-in Rikyu, Kyoto 232–33
Shukkei-en Garden, Hiroshima 287
Shukunegi Village, Sado-ga-shima 196
Shuri, Naha 345
  Shuri-jo Castle 345
  Sonohyanu Shrine 345
Silk Museum (Shiruku Hakubutsukan), Yokohama 110
Snakes 346
Sofuku-ji, Nagasaki 335–36
Sogetsu Art Center (Sogetsu Kaikan), Tokyo 77
Sonohyanu-jinja Shrine, Naha, Okinawa 345
Soseki Museum, Kumamoto 328
Soun-kyo Gorge 143
Sports 49
Suizenji-koen Park 327–28
Sumida-koen Park, Tokyo 104
Sumo Museum (Sumo Hakubutsukan) 104
Sumo Stadium 104, **104**
Sunayu Onsen 150
Sunshine 60 Building 89
Suntory Museum of Art (Santori Bijutsukan) 77
Suwa-jinja Shrine, Nagasaki 335
Suwa-jinja Shrine, Tokyo 97

T

Tachibana House, Yanagawa 323
Taga-jinja Shrine, Uwajima 307–308
Tagata-jinja Shrine, Inuyama 176–77
Tahoto pagoda, Miyajima 289
Taikodani Inari-jinja Shrine, Tsuwano 268
Taisho period 37–38
Taisho-ike 189
Taiyuin, Nikko 119–20
Takahashi 278
Takamatsu 295–96
  Chrysanthemum-Moon Pavilion (Kikugetsu-tei) 295–96, **296**
  Hidari Jingoro Museum 296
  Ritsurin-koen Park 295, **295**
  Sanuki Folkcraft Museum 296
  Shikoku mura 296
  Tamamo-jo Castle 295
  Tamamo-jo-koen Park 295
  Yashima 296
Takayama 172, 178, 182–85
  Dairyu-ji Temple 185
  Ena-jinja Shrine 185
  Hida Folk Village (Hida Minzoku Mura) **184,** 185
  Hida Kokubun-ji Temple 182, 184
  Kusakabe Folk Museum (Kusakabe Mingei Kan) **183,** 184
  markets 185
  Sanmachi Suji 182
  Shiroyama-koen Park 184–85
  Shoren-ji Temple 184–85
  Takayama Festival Floats Museum (Takayama Yatai Kaikan) 182
  Teramachi 185
  Yoshijima-ke House 184
Taketomi-jima 348
Takikuchi-dera, Kyoto 230
Tamashima 279
  Kibi-ji Temple 279
Tanjo-ji Temple, Tsuyama 279
Tanoura 314
Taraibune (fishing boats) **194,** 195
Tarama 348
Tarumae-zan 135–36
Tea ceremony 42, 225
Tenju-an, Kyoto 211
Tenkyu-in, Kyoto 225
Tenryu-ji Temple, Arishiyama 229
Textiles 58, 342, 346
Theater 46–48
Three Dewa Mountains (Dewa Sanzan) 169–70
To-ji Temple, Kyoto **202,** 204
Toba 259
Tobishima 169
Todai-ji Temple, Nara **240–41,** 241–43, **242–43**
Toei Movie Land 228–29
Tofuku-ji Temple, Kyoto 231
Tohoku *see* Northern Honshu
Toilets 20–21, 356
Tokashiki-jima 347
Toke-ji Temple, Kamakura 113
Toko-ji Temple, Hagi 265
Tokugawa Museum of Art (Tokugawa Bijutsukan), Nagoya 175
Tokushima city 300
  Awa Puppet Theater 300
  Awa-odori Festival 300
Tokushima-ken 299–300
  Iya no Kazurabashi 299–300, **300**
  Mount Tsurugi-san 299
  Naruto-no-Uzushio Whirlpools 299
  Oboke and Koboke Gorges 300
  Ohama Beach 299
  Onaruto-bashi Bridge 299
  Tokushima city 300
Tokyo 59–106
  Akasaka Fudo-san Temple 77
  Akasaka-Nagatacho 76–77
  Akihabara 105
  Ameyoko market 91
  Aoyama-Harajuku-Shibuya 80–87
  Asakusa 100, 102–104
  Benten-do Temple **94,** 96
  Bridgestone Museum of Art 69–70
  central Tokyo 62–65
  Dembo-in Garden 103–104
  Denki Gai 105, **105**
  Edo-Tokyo Museum 104
  excursions from 107–28
  Flamme d'Or building 66, **66,** 104
  Ginza-Hibiya-Yurakucho 68–70
  Hamarikyu-teien Garden 73, **73**
  Hanae Mori building 66, 83
  Hanazono-jinja Shrine 87, **87**
  Hie Jinja Shrine 77
  Horikiri Shobuen Iris Garden 106
  hotels and restaurants 361–65
  Idemitsu Museum of Arts 69
  Ikebukuro 86, 89
  Imperial Palace 63–64
  International Forum Building **44,** 66, 69
  Jimbocho 105
  Kabukicho **86,** 87
  Kabuki-za Theater 70, **70**
  Kanei-ji Kyomizu Kannon-do Temple 96
  Kanei-ji Pagoda 96
  Kappabashi wholesale market 104
  Kawagoe 106
  Kitanomaru-koen Park 64
  maps 60–61, 81, 97
  Meiji-jingu Inner Gardens 80, **84–85,** 85
  Meiji-jingu Shrine 80, 83–85, **84, 85**
  Meiji-jingu Treasure House 85
  Mount Takao san 106, **106**
  National Museum of Modern Art 65
  National Museum of Western Art 92
  National Science Museum 92
  Nezu Institute of Fine Art 81
  Nezu-jinja Shrine 96
  Ningyocho 105
  Nippon Budokan 64
  Ogasawara-shoto Islands 106
  Omotesando 79, **79**
  Ota Memorial Museum of Art 80–81
  Roppongi-Shiba-koen Park 76–77
  Sapporo Ginza Lion beer hall 69
  Science Museum 64–65
  Senso-ji Temple 103, **103**
  Shinjuku 66, 86, **86–87,** 87–89, **88**

Shinjuku National Garden 87
Shinobazu Pond 96
Shitamachi History Museum 93
Sumida-koen Park 104
Sumo Museum 104
Sumo Stadium 104, **104**
Sunshine 60 Building 89
Suwa-jinja Shrine 97
Tokyo Metropolitan Art Space 89
Tokyo Metropolitan Government Office 66, 86, 88–89, **89**
Tokyo Metropolitan Wholesale Market 72, **72–73**
Tokyo National Museum 93–95, **94–95, 95**
Tokyo Stock Exchange 69
Tokyo Tower 77
Tosho-gu Shrine 93, **93,** 96
Tsukiji Hongan-ji Temple 72–73
Tsukudajima 71–73
Ueno 90–97
Ueno Zoo 93
Ueno-koen Park 90, **90,** 92–95, 96
walks 80–81, 96–97
Yanaka Hill 92
Yasukuni-jinja Shrine 65
Yoshiwara 102
Yoyogi-koen Park 79, 83
Yushima-tenjin Shrine 91
Yushukan 65
Zojo-ji Temple 77, **77**
Tokyo, excursions from 107–28
Fuji-Hakone-Izu 121–8
hotels and restaurants 365–66
Kamakura 111–13
map 109
Nikko 114–20
Yokohama 110
Tokyo Metropolitan Art Space 89
Tokyo Metropolitan Central Wholesale Market (Chuo Oroshi-uri shijo) 72, **72**
Tokyo Metropolitan Government Office 66, 86, 88–89, **89**
Tokyo Metropolitan Gymnasium 66
Tokyo National Museum (Tokyo Kokuritsu Hakubutsukan) 93–95, **94–95, 95**
Tokyo Stock Exchange 69
Tokyo Tower 77
Torin-ji Temple, Ishigaki-jima 348
Tosa fighting dogs 311
Tosho-gu Shrine, Nikko 115–19, **115, 116–17. 117, 118**
Tosho-gu Shrine, Tokyo 93, **93,** 96
Toshodai-ji Temple, Nara-ken 243
Toson, Shimozaki 192
Towada Hachimantai National Park 165
Trains 352–53
Tsugaru, Aomori-ken 156
Cape Gongen 156
Hakkoda-san 156
Hirosaki 156
Shirakami Mountains 156
Tsukiji Hongan-ji Temple 72–73
Tsukudajima 71–73
Tsumago 192
Tsunami 128
Tsurugaoka Hachiman-gu Shrine 112
Tsuruoka 170
Chido Museum 170
Tsuwano 264, **264,** 268–69
Katsushika Hokusai Museum 269
Maria Sei-do 268, **268**
Mori House and Memorial Museum 268
Musée de Morijuku 269
Taikodani Inari-jinja Shrine 268, **269**
Tsuwano-jo Castle 268
Yomei-ji Temple 268
Tsuyama 279
Tanjo-ji Temple 279
Turtle beaches 299

U

Uchiko 305–306
Business and Livelihood Museum (Akinai to Kurashi Hakubutsukan) 306
Hon Haga Residence 305
Japan Wax Museum and Kami Haga Residence 305
Machiya Shiryo-kan 306
Omori Rosoku **305,** 306,
Soko Kan 305–306
Uchiko-za Theater 306
Yokaichi-Gokoku 305, **306**
Uchiko-za Theater 306
Ueno 90–97
Ueno Zoo, Tokyo 93
Ueno-koen Park 90, **90,** 92–95, 96
Uji 234
Byodo-in Temple 234, **234**
Umeda Sky Building **253,** 254
Underground Naval Headquarters, Okinawa 346
Urakami Cathedral, Nagasaki 333
Uraku-en garden, Inuyama 176
Urasoe, Okinawa 346
Joseki-koen Park 346
Kita Naka-Gsuku 346
Nakamura House 346
Ushimado, Okayama-ken 280
Utoro, Hokkaido 146
Utsukushigahara Heights, Matsumoto 188
Utsukushigahara Onsen, Matsumoto 188
Uwajima 307–308
sex museum 308
Taga-jinja Shrine 307–308
Uwajima-jo Castle 307

V

Visitor information 356
Visual arts 51–58
Volcanoes and earthquakes 128, 357

W

Wakayama-ken 199, 250–51, **251**
Hongu 250
Kawayu Onsen 250
Mount Koya-san 250–51
Nachi-no-taki Waterfall 250
Yunomine Onsen 250
Wakkanai, Hokkaido 144
Western Honshu (Chugoku) 261–90
Daisen-Oki National Park 276
Hagi 265–67
Hiroshima 286–87
hotels and restaurants 375–77
Izumo Taisha 275
map 262–63
Matsue 272–74
Miyajima 288–90
Okayama-ken 277, 278–83
Onomichi 284–85
San-in 262, 264–76
San-yo 263, 277–90
Tsuwano 268–69
Whale watching 310, 347
Woodcraft 57, 158
World wars 37, 38, 39–40

Y

Yaegaki-jinja, Matsue 274
Yaeyama Archipelago 342
Yaeyama Minzoku-en village, Ishigaki-jima 348
Yaeyama-Shoto Islands 348
Yakuo-in, Mount Takao-san 106
Yakushi-ji Temple, Nara-ken 243, 246–47
Yamabushi sect 170
Yama-dera Temple **168,** 169, **169**
Yamagata 169
Yama-dera Temple **168,** 169, **169**
Yamagata-ken 168–70
Mogami Gorge 168
Mount Zao-san 169
Sakata 169
Three Dewa Mountains (Dewa Sanzan) 169–70
Tobishima 169
Tsuruoka 169
Yamagata 169
Yanagawa 323, **323**
Ohana Villa 323
Shoto-en Garden 323
Tachibana House 323
Yanagawa Municipal Folk Museum 323
Yanaka Hill, Tokyo 92
Yasaka Pagoda, Kyoto 216–17
Yasaka-jinja Shrine, Kyoto 217, 218
Yashima, Takamatsu 296
Yasukuni-jinja Shrine, Tokyo 65
Yayoi period 28
Yokohama 108, 110, **110**
Landmark Tower 110
Sankei-en Garden 110
Silk Museum (Shiruku Hakubutsukan) 110
Yokohama Maritime Museum 110
Yomei-ji Temple, Tsuwano 268
Yomeimon, Nikko 118
Yonaguni-jima 342, 348
Yoritomo 31, 32, 165
Yoshijima-ke House, Takayama 184
Yoshino, Nara-ken 249
Yoshitsune 31–32, 165
Yoshiwara 102
Yoyogi-koen Park, Tokyo 79, 83
Yudono-san 170
Yumoto Onsen 120
Yunokawa Onsen 139
Yunomine Onsen 250
Yushima-tenjin Shrine, Tokyo 91
Yushukan, Tokyo 65

Z

Zamami-jima 347
Zen Buddhism 23, 32, 42, 220, 227
Zenko-ji Temple, Nagano 186–87, 187
Zentsu-ji Temple, Kotohira 298
Zojo-ji Temple 77, **77**
Zuigan-ji Temple, Matsushima 162–63

ILLUSTRATIONS CREDITS

Abbreviations for terms appearing below: (t) top; (b) bottom; (l) left; (r) right; (c) center.

Cover: (l), Powerstock/Zefa. (c), Corbis UK Ltd. (r) DAJ/Getty Images.

1, Ken Straiton. 2/3, Images Colour Library. 4, Iconotec/Alamy Ltd. 9, Asian Art & Archaeology, Inc./Corbis UK Ltd. 11, Justin Guariglia/Corbis. 12/13, Gavin Hellier/Getty Images. 14/15, Jose Fuste Raga/Corbis. 16/17, Richard T. Nowitz/Corbis. 17, Bon Color Photo Agency. 18, Harry Gruyaert/Magnum Photos. 19 Jeremy Sutton-Hibbert/Alamy Ltd. 20/21, Images Colour Library. 22, Karen Kasmauski/National Geographic Society. 23, Peter Essick/National Geographic Society. 24, Bill Bachman/Alamy Ltd. 24/25, Dave Bartruff/Danita Delimont Agency/drr.net. 27, Bon Color Photo Agency. 29, Bon Color Photo Agency. 30/31, Michael S. Yamashita/ Corbis UK Ltd. 33, Werner Forman Archive. 34/35, Bon Color Photo Agency. 37, Corbis UK Ltd. 38, Corbis UK Ltd. 39, David Samuel Robbins/Corbis UK Ltd. 40, National Geographic Society. 41, National Geographic Society. 43, Bon Color Photo Agency. 44, Ken Straiton. 45, Corbis UK Ltd. 46/47, Michael S. Yamashita/Corbis UK Ltd. 48/49, Farl & Nazima Kowall/Corbis UK Ltd. 50, Koichi Kamoshida/Getty Images. 51, Bon Color Photo Agency. 52(l), Christie's Images/Corbis. 52(r), Ken Straiton. 53, Corbis UK Ltd. 54/55, Sissie Brimberg/National Geographic Society. 56, Bon Color Photo Agency. 56/57, Michael S. Yamashita/ Corbis UK Ltd. 59, Michael S. Yamashita/Corbis UK Ltd. 62/63, Travel Pix Collection/age fotostock. 64, Ken Straiton. 64/65, Bon Color Photo Agency. 67(t), Bon Color Photo Agency. 67(bl), Orion Press. 67(br), Ken Straiton. 68/69, Jose Fuste Raga/ age fotostock. 69, Ken Straiton. 70(t), Orion Press. 70(b), Ken Straiton. 71, Peter M. Wilson/Corbis. 72/73, James Stanfield/National Geographic Society. 73, Steven Vidler/Eurasia Press/ Corbis. 75(tl), Robert Holmes/Corbis UK Ltd. 75(tr), M. Glover/Impact Photos. 75(b), M. Henley/Impact Photos. 76/77, Luc Novovitch/offiwent.com/drr.net. 77, Wolfgang Kaehler/Corbis UK Ltd. 78/79, Justin Guariglia. 79, Sylvain Grandadam/age fotostock. 82, Ken Straiton. 83, Ken Straiton. 84, Ken Straiton. 84/85, Bon Color Photo Agency. 85, Ken Straiton. 86/87, P. Narayan/age fotostock. 87, Ken Straiton. 88(t), Michael S. Yamashita/Corbis. 88(b), Hiro Nogami/Q Photo International Inc. 89, Ken Straiton. 90, Jim Holmes/Axiom. 91, Jack Fields/Corbis UK Ltd. 92, Bon Color Photo Agency. 93, Ken Straiton. 95, Sakamoto Photo Research Laboratory/Corbis. 98/99, Iain Masterton/ Alamy Ltd. 100, Ken Straiton. 101(t), John Dakers/Life File. 101(bl), Ken Straiton. 101(br), Ken Straiton. 102/103, Ken Straiton. 103, Ken Straiton. 104, Ken Straiton. 105, Orion Press. 106, Bon Color Photo Agency. 107, Ken Straiton. 108, Orion Press. 110, P. Narayan/age fotostock. 111, Bon Color Photo Agency. 112/113, Ken Straiton. 114/115, Bon Color Photo Agency. 115, Dave Bartruff/ Corbis UK Ltd. 116/117, Bon Color Photo Agency. 117, Orion Press. 118, James Davis Travel Photography. 119, Bon Color Photo Agency. 120(t), Bon Color Photo Agency. 120(b), Richard T. Nowitz/Corbis UK Ltd. 121, Gettyone/Stone. 122, Bon Color Photo Agency. 123, Orion Press. 124/125, Karen Kasmauski/National Geographic Society. 126/127, Bruce Osborn. 129, Bon Color Photo Agency. 131, Orion Press. 132/133, Bon Color Photo Agency. 133, Orion Press. 134, Bon Color Photo Agency. 135, Bon Color Photo Agency. 136, Bon Color Photo Agency. 136/137, Bon Color Photo Agency. 138/139, Bon Color Photo Agency. 139, Bon Color Photo Agency. 140, Bon Color Photo Agency. 142/143, Orion Press. 142, Art Wolfe/ Gettyone/Stone. 143, Bon Color Photo Agency. 144/145, Bon Color Photo Agency. 146, Michael S. Yamashita/ Corbis UK Ltd. 146/147, Ryuzo Toytaka/Q Photo International Inc. 148/149, Bon Color Photo Agency. 149, Bon Color Photo Agency. 150, James Nelson/Gettyone/Stone. 151, Image Bank. 152, Bon Color Photo Agency. 155, Ken Straiton. 156, Orion Press. 157, Bon Color Photo Agency. 159, Orion Press. 160/161, Orion Press. 162/163, Orion Press. 164/165, Timothy G. Laman/National Geographic/Getty Images. 166, Bon Color Photo Agency. 166/167, Michael S. Yamashita/Corbis UK Ltd. 168, Orion Press. 169, Orion Press. 171, Ken Straiton. 172, Mitchell Coster/ Axiom. 174, Ken Straiton. 175, Ken Straiton. 176, Bon Color Photo Agency. 177, Ken Straiton. 178, Bon Color Photo Agency. 178/179, Bon Color Photo Agency. 180, Orion Press. 181, Ken Straiton. 182, Orion Press. 183, Bon Color Photo Agency. 184(t), Ken Straiton. 184(b), Ken Straiton. 185, Ken Straiton. 186/187, B.S.P.I./Corbis. 187, Ken Straiton. 188, AA Photo Library/Douglas Corrance. 189, Bon Color Photo Agency. 190, Orion Press. 191(t), Ken Straiton. 191(b), Ken Straiton. 192, Ken Straiton. 193, Bon Color Photo Agency. 194, Bon Color Photo Agency. 194/195, Orion Press. 196, Bon Color Photo Agency. 197, Bon Color Photo Agency. 198, Bon Color Photo Agency. 199, Getty Images. 202/203, Nigel Hicks. 203, Bon Color Photo Agency. 204(l), Robert Holmes/Corbis UK Ltd. 204(r), Francesco Venturi; Kea Publishing Services Ltd./Corbis UK Ltd. 206, Images Colour Library. 207, Gettyone/Stone. 208, Jim Holmes/ Axiom. 209, Orion Press. 210/211, Bon Color Photo Agency. 211, Orion Press. 212, Orion Press. 212/213, Orion Press. 214, Ken Straiton. 214/215, Ken Straiton. 216/217, Gavin Hellier/JAI/Corbis. 218, Ken Straiton. 219, Orion Press. 220, Bob Krist/CORBIS. 221(tl), Michael S. Yamashita/ Corbis UK Ltd. 221(tr), Bon Color Photo Agency. 221(b), Bon Color Photo Agency. 222, Ken Straiton. 222/223, Ken Straiton. 224, Ken Straiton. 226/227, Michael Freeman/ Corbis UK Ltd. 228, Jon Hicks/Corbis. 230, Orion Press. 232, Ken Straiton. 233, Bon Color Photo Agency. 234/235, Orion Press. 235, Bon Color Photo Agency. 236, Bon Color Photo Agency. 237, Ken Straiton. 238(t), Paul A. Berry/Corbis UK Ltd. 238(b), Nik Wheeler/Corbis UK Ltd. 239, Orion Press. 240/241, Ken Straiton. 242/243, Bon Color Photo Agency. 244, Jim Holmes/Axiom. 245(tl), Nicholas DeVore/Gettyone/Stone. 245(tr), Bon Color Photo Agency. 245(b), Photo Japan/Alamy Ltd. 248, Jed & Kaoru Share/Corbis. 249, Orion Press. 250, Ken Straiton. 251, Bon Color Photo Agency. 252/253, Bon Color Photo Agency. 253(t), Orion Press. 253(b), Michael S. Yamashita/Corbis UK Ltd. 254(t), Bon Color Photo Agency. 254(b), J. Marshall – Tribaleye Images/ Alamy Ltd. 255, Ken Straiton. 256(l), Ken Straiton. 256(r), Ken Straiton. 258/259, Bon Color Photo Agency. 260, Pacific Press Service. 261, Bon Color Photo Agency. 262, Bon Color Photo Agency. 263, Bon Color Photo Agency. 264, Orion Press. 264/265, Bon Color Photo Agency. 266, Bon Color Photo Agency. 268, Bon Color Photo Agency. 269, Bon Color Photo Agency. 271, Steiner & Co./Graphic Communication Ltd. 272/273, Orion Press. 273, Orion Press. 274(t), Bon Color Photo Agency. 274(b), AA Photo Library/ Douglas Corrance. 275, Bon Color Photo Agency. 276, Bon Color Photo Agency. 277, Michael S. Yamashita/ Corbis UK Ltd. 278/279, Bon Color Photo Agency. 280, Bon Color Photo Agency. 281, Bon Color Photo Agency. 282, Orion Press. 284/285, Bon Color Photo Agency. 285, Orion Press. 286/287, Bon Color Photo Agency. 287, Orion Press. 288, Bon Color Photo Agency. 289, Jack Fields/Corbis UK Ltd. 290, Orion Press. 291, Chad Elhers/Gettyone/ Stone. 293, Bon Color Photo Agency. 294, Bon Color Photo Agency. 295, Orion Press. 296(t), Michael S. Yamashita/Corbis UK Ltd. 296(b), Bon Color Photo Agency. 297, The Purcell Team/Corbis UK Ltd. 298, Bon Color Photo Agency. 299, Orion Press. 300, Orion Press. 301, Bruce Osborn/ Ozone Inc. 302, Bon Color Photo

Agency. 303, Bon Color Photo Agency. 304, AA Photo Library/Jim Holmes. 305, Ken Straiton. 306(t), Bon Color Photo Agency. 306(b), Ken Straiton. 307, Michael S. Yamashita/Corbis UK Ltd. 308/309 Orion Press. 310, Bon Color Photo Agency. 311, Yann Arthus-Bertrand/Corbis UK Ltd. 312/313, Bon Color Photo Agency. 315, Bon Color Photo Agency. 317, Michael S. Yamashita/National Geographic Society. 318/319, JTB/drr.net. 320, Bon Color Photo Agency. 321, Orion Press. 322, Bon Color Photo Agency. 323, Orion Press. 324/325, Michael S. Yamashita/National Geographic Society. 325, Bruce Osborn/Ozone Inc. 326/327, Q Photo International Inc. 327, AA Photo Library/Jim Holmes. 328/329, Orion Press. 328, Bon Color Photo Agency. 330/331, Bon Color Photo Agency. 332, Getty Images. 333, Paul Chesley/Gettyone/Stone. 334, Orion Press. 335, Bon Color Photo Agency. 336, Bon Color Photo Agency. 337, Orion Press. 338, Michael S. Yamashita/Corbis UK Ltd. 339, Bon Color Photo Agency. 341, Orion Press. 344, Pacific Press Service. 345, Ken Straiton. 347, AFP/AFP/Getty Images. 349, Bon Color Photo Agency.

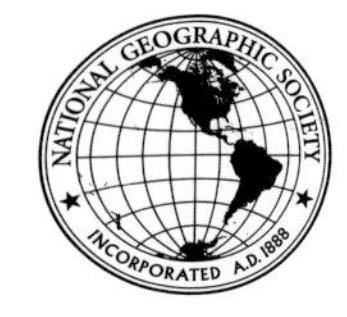

Founded in 1888, the National Geographic Society is one of the largest nonprofit scientific and educational organizations in the world. It reaches more than 285 million people worldwide each month through its official journal, NATIONAL GEOGRAPHIC, and its four other magazines; the National Geographic Channel; television documentaries; radio programs; films; books; videos and DVDs; maps; and interactive media. National Geographic has funded more than 8,000 scientific research projects and supports an education program combating geographic illiteracy.

For more information, please call 1-800-NGS LINE (647-5463) or write to the following address:

National Geographic Society,1145 17th Street N.W.,Washington, D.C. 20036-4688 U.S.A.

Visit us online at: www.national geographic.com/books

For information about special discounts for bulk purchases, please contact National Geographic Books Special Sales: ngspecsales@ngs.org

Printed in Toledo, Spain

Published by the National Geographic Society

John M. Fahey, Jr., *President and Chief Executive Officer*
Gilbert M. Grosvenor, *Chairman of the Board*
Nina D. Hoffman, *Executive Vice President; President, Book Publishing Group*
Kevin Mulroy, *Senior Vice President and Publisher*
Marianne Koszorus, *Design Director*
Elizabeth L. Newhouse, *Director of Travel Publishing*
Barbara A. Noe, *Senior Editor and Series Editor*
Cinda Rose, *Art Director*
Carl Mehler, *Director of Maps*
Gary Colbert, *Production Director*
Jennifer A. Thornton, *Managing Editor*
Richard S. Wain, *Production Project Manager*
Kay Kobor Hankins, *Contributor*

Staff for 2008 edition

Caroline Hickey, *Project Manager*
Timothy N. Hornyak, *Editorial Consultant*
Paula Kelly, Michael McNey, Carol Stroud, Timothy Stoutzenberger, Jane Sunderland, Ruth Thompson, Meredith Wilcox, *Contributors*

First edition: Edited and designed by AA Publishing (a trading name of Automobile Association Developments Limited, whose registered office is Norfolk House, Priestley Road, Basingstoke, Hampshire, England RG24 9NY. Registered number: 1878835).
Rachel Alder, *Project Manager*
David Austin, *Senior Art Editor*
Marilynne Lanng, *Senior Editor*
Phil Barfoot, *Designer*
Inna Nogeste, *Senior Cartographic Editor*
Richard Firth, *Production Director*
Steve Gilchrist, *Prepress Production Controller*
Cartography by AA Cartographic Production
Picture research by Zooid Pictures Ltd.
Cutaway illustrations drawn by Maltings Partnership, Derby, England

***National Geographic Traveler: Japan.* Third edition 2008**
ISBN: 978-1-4262-0234-6

The Library of Congress has cataloged the first edition as follows:

Library of Congress Cataloging-in- Publication Data
Bornoff Nicholas.
National Geographic Traveler: Japan / Nicholas Bornoff
p cm
Includes index.
ISBN 0-7922-7563-2 (alk. paper)
1. Japan—Guidebooks. 1. Title
DC16.N37 1999
914.404'839—dc21 98-54974

CIP

The information in this book has been carefully checked and to the best of our knowledge is accurate. However, details are subject to change, and the National Geographic Society cannot be responsible for such changes, or for errors or omissions. Assessments of sites, hotels, and restaurants are basedon the author's subjective opinions, which do not necessarily reflect the publisher's opinion. The publisher cannot be responsible for any consequences arising from the use of this book.